A VEDIC GRAMMAR FOR STUDENTS

A VEDIC GRAMMAR FOR STUDENTS

BY

ARTHUR ANTHONY MACDONELL

GYAN

Published by

GYAN

Gyan Publishing House
5, Ansari Road
Daryaganj, New Delhi-110002
Phone: 011-47034999, 9811692060
E-mail: books@gyanbooks.com

Distribution Network
gyanbooks.com
India, USA, Canada, UK, Australia

ISBN: 978-93-6280-453-2 (HB)
First Published, 1916

2nd Impression 2024

Printed at: Gyan Press, Delhi.

A VEDIC GRAMMAR FOR STUDENTS
Author: ARTHUR ANTHONY MACDONELL

A VEDIC GRAMMAR FOR STUDENTS

BY

ARTHUR ANTHONY MACDONELL

M.A., PH.D.

BODEN PROFESSOR OF SANSKRIT IN THE
UNIVERSITY OF OXFORD
FELLOW OF BALLIOL COLLEGE; FELLOW OF THE BRITISH ACADEMY;
FELLOW OF THE ROYAL DANISH ACADEMY

INCLUDING A CHAPTER ON SYNTAX AND THREE
APPENDIXES: LIST OF VERBS, METRE, ACCENT

OXFORD
AT THE CLARENDON PRESS
1916

PREFACE

A practical Vedic grammar has long been a desideratum. It is one of the chief aids to the study of the hymns of the Veda called for forty-three years ago in the preface to his edition of the Rigveda by Max Müller, who adds, 'I doubt not that the time will come when no one in India will call himself a Sanskrit scholar who cannot construe the hymns of the ancient Rishis of his country'. It is mainly due to the lack of such a work that the study of Vedic literature, despite its great linguistic and religious importance, has never taken its proper place by the side of the study of Classical Sanskrit either in England or India. Whitney's excellent *Sanskrit Grammar*, indeed, treats the earlier language in its historical connexion with the later, but for this very reason students are, as I have often been assured, unable to acquire from it a clear knowledge of either the one or the other, because beginners cannot keep the two dialects apart in the process of learning. Till the publication of my large *Vedic Grammar* in 1910, no single work comprehensively presented the early language by itself. That work is, however, too extensive and detailed for the needs of the student, being intended rather as a book of reference for the scholar. Hence I have often been urged to bring out a short practical grammar which would do for the Vedic language what my *Sanskrit Grammar for Beginners* does for the Classical language. In the second edition (1911) of the latter work I therefore pledged myself to meet this demand as soon as I could. The present volume redeems that pledge.

When planning the book I resolved, after much reflection, to make it correspond paragraph by paragraph to the *Sanskrit Grammar*; this being the best way to enable students to compare and contrast every phenomenon of the earlier and the later language. To this extent the present book presupposes the other; but it can quite well be used independently. The experience of many years' teaching, however, leads me to dissuade beginners from starting the study of Sanskrit by means of the present grammar. Students should, in my opinion, always commence with classical Sanskrit, which is more regular and definite, as well as much more restricted in the number of its inflexional forms. A good working knowledge of the later language should therefore be acquired before taking up Vedic grammar, which can then be rapidly learned.

In carrying out the parallelism of this grammar with the other I have experienced a good deal of difficulty in numbering the corresponding paragraphs satisfactorily, because certain groups of matter are found exclusively in the Vedic language, as the numerous subjunctive forms, or much more fully, as the dozen types of infinitive compared with only one in Sanskrit; while some Sanskrit formations, as the periphrastic future, are non-existent in the earlier language. Nevertheless, I have, I think, succeeded in arranging the figures in such a way that the corresponding paragraphs of the two grammars can always be easily compared. The only exception is the first chapter, consisting of fifteen paragraphs, which in the *Sanskrit Grammar* deals with the Nāgarī alphabet. As the present work throughout uses transliteration only, it seemed superfluous to repeat the description of the letters given in the earlier work. I have accordingly substituted a general phonetic survey of Vedic sounds as enabling the student to understand clearly the linguistic history of Sanskrit. The employment of transliteration has been necessary because by this means alone could analysis by hyphens and accentuation be adequately indicated. Duplication with Nāgarī characters, as in the *Sanskrit Grammar*, would have increased the size and the cost of the book without any compensating advantage. An account of the accent, as of vital importance in Vedic grammar, would naturally have found a place in the body of the book, but owing to the entire absence of this subject in the *Sanskrit Grammar* and to the fulness which its treatment requires, its introduction there was impossible. The accent is accordingly dealt with in Appendix III as a substitute for the 'Chief Peculiarities of Vedic Grammar' appearing at the end of the *Sanskrit Grammar*.

The term Vedic is here used to comprehend not only the metrical language of the hymns, but also the prose of the Brāhmaṇas and of the Brāhmaṇa-like portions of the Atharvaveda and of various recensions of the Yajurveda. The grammatical material from the later period is mainly given in small type, and is in any case regularly indicated by the addition of the letter B (for Brāhmaṇa). Otherwise the phase of the earlier language presented is that of the Rigveda, as being both the oldest and furnishing the most abundant material. But forms from the other Vedas are often also supplied without any distinguishing mark as long as they conform to the standard of the Rigveda. If, however, such forms are in any way abnormal, or if it seemed advisable to point out that they do not come from the Rigveda, this is indicated by an added abbreviation in brackets, as '(AV.)' for '(Atharvaveda).' On the other hand '(RV.)' is sometimes added in order to indicate, for some reason or other, that a form is restricted to the Rigveda. It is, of course, impossible to go much into detail thus in a practical work; but the exact source of any particular form can always be ascertained by reference to the large *Vedic Grammar.* The grammatical usage of the other Vedas, when it differs from that of the Rigveda, is regularly explained. The reference is given with precise figures when syntactical examples are taken from the Rigveda, but with abbreviations only (as TS. for Taittirīya Saṃhitā or ŚB. for Śatapatha Brāhmaṇa) when they come from elsewhere. Syntactical citations are not always metrically intact because words that are unnecessary to illustrate the usage in question are often omitted. The accent in verbal forms that happen to occur in Vedic texts without it, is nevertheless given if its position is undoubted, but when there is any uncertainty it is left out. In the list of verbs (Appendix I) the third person singular is often given as the typical form even when only other persons actually occur. Otherwise only forms that have been positively noted are enumerated.

I ought to mention that in inflected words final **s**, **r**, and **d** of endings are given in their historical form, not according to the law of allowable finals (§ 27); e.g. **dūtás**, not **dūtáḥ**; **tásmād**, not **tásmāt**; **pitúr**, not **pitúḥ**; but when used syntactically they appear in accordance with the rules of Sandhi; e.g. **devā́nām dūtáḥ**; **vṛtrásya vadhā́t.**

The present book is to a great extent based on my large *Vedic Grammar.* It is, however, by no means simply an abridgement of that work. For besides being differently arranged, so as to agree with the scheme of the *Sanskrit Grammar*, it contains much matter excluded from the *Vedic Grammar* by the limitations imposed on the latter work as one of the volumes of Bühler's *Encyclopaedia of Indo-Aryan Research.* Thus it adds a full treatment of Vedic Syntax and an account of the Vedic metres. Appendix I, moreover, contains a list of Vedic verbs (similar to that in the *Sanskrit Grammar*), which though all their forms appear in their appropriate place within the body of the *Vedic Grammar*, are not again presented there in the form of an alphabetical list, as is done here for the benefit of the learner. Having subjected all the verbal forms to a revision, I have classified some doubtful or ambiguous ones more satisfactorily, and added some others which were inadvertently omitted in the large work. Moreover, a full alphabetical list of conjunctive and adverbial particles embracing forty pages and describing the syntactical uses of these words has been added in order to correspond to § 180 of the *Sanskrit Grammar*. The present work therefore constitutes a supplement to, as well as an abridgement of, the *Vedic Grammar*, thus in reality setting forth the subject with more completeness as a whole, though in a comparatively brief form, than the larger work. I may add that this grammar is shortly to be followed by a *Vedic Reader* consisting of selected hymns of the Rigveda and supplying microscopic explanations of every point on which the elementary learner requires information. These two books will, I hope, enable him in a short time to become an independent student of the sacred literature of ancient India.

For the purposes of this book I have chiefly exploited my own *Vedic Grammar* (1910), but I have also utilized Delbrück's *Altindische Syntax* (1888) for syntactical material, and Whitney's *Roots* (1885) for the verbal forms of the Brāhmaṇa literature. In describing the metres (Appendix II) I have found Oldenberg's *Die Hymnen des Ṛigveda* (1888), and Arnold's *Vedic Metre* (1905) very useful.

I am indebted to Dr. James Morison and to my former pupil, Professor A. B. Keith, for reading all the first proofs with great care, and thus saving me from many misprints that would have escaped my own notice. Professor Keith has also suggested important modifications of some of my grammatical statements. Lastly, I must congratulate

Mr. J. C. Pembrey, Hon. M.A., Oriental Reader at the Clarendon Press, on having completed the task of reading the final proofs of this grammar, now all but seventy years after correcting Professor H. H. Wilson's *Sanskrit Grammar* in 1847. This is a record in the history of Oriental, and most probably of any, professional proof reading for the press.

A. A. MACDONELL.

6 Chadlington Road, Oxford.
March 30, 1916.

CONTENTS

CHAPTER V: INDECLINABLE WORDS

CHAPTER VI: NOMINAL STEM FORMATION AND COMPOUNDS

CHAPTER VII: SYNTAX

LIST OF ABBREVIATIONS

A. = accusative case.
Ā. = Ātmanepada, middle voice.
AA. = Aitareya Āraṇyaka.
AB. = Aitareya Brāhmaṇa.
Ab. = ablative case.
act. = active voice.
AV. = Atharvaveda.
Av. = Avesta.
B. = Brāhmaṇa.
C. = Classical Sanskrit.
D. = dative case.
du. = dual number.
f. = feminine.
G. = genitive case.
Gk. = Greek.
I. = instrumental case.
IE. = Indo-European.
I-Ir. = Indo-Iranian.
ind. = indicative mood.
K. = Kāṭhaka Saṃhitā.
KB. = Kauṣītaki Brāhmaṇa.
L. = locative case.
Lat. = Latin.
m. = masculine.
mid. = middle voice.
MS. = Maitrāyaṇī Saṃhitā.
N. = nominative case.
P. = Parasmaipada, active voice.
PB. = Pañcaviṃśa (= Tāṇḍya) Brāhmaṇa.
pl. = plural number.
RV. = Rigveda.
ŚB. = Śatapatha Brāhmaṇa.
s. = singular number.
SV. = Sāmaveda.
TA. = Taittirīya Āraṇyaka.
TB. = Taittirīya Brāhmaṇa.
TS. = Taittirīya Saṃhitā.
V. = Vedic (in the narrow sense as opposed to B. = Brāhmaṇa).
VS. = Vājasaneyi Saṃhitā.
YV. = Yajurveda.

N.B.—Other abbreviations will be found at the beginning of Appendix I and of the Vedic Index.

CORRECTIONS

P. 25, line 24, for **amī́ iti** read **amī́ íti**.
P. 27, line 29, last word, read **á-srat**.
P. 133, line 5, for **bíbhṛmáhe** read **bibhṛmáhe**.
P. 144, line 31, for *stride* read *strike*.
P. 156, lines 6 and 10, for **ci-ket-a-t** and **ci-ket-a-thas** read **cí-ket-a-t** and **cí-ket-a-thas**.
P. 158, line 21, for (**vaś** *desire*) read (**vāś** *bellow*).
P. 174, lines 30 and 31, delete **cucyuvīmáhi** and **cucyavīráta** (cp. p. 382 under **cyu**).
P. 188, footnote, for 'gerundive' read 'gerund'.
P. 200, line 6, for 'f **yaj**' read 'of **yaj**'.
P. 215, line 32, for **tā́vām̐̆** read **tā́vām̐**; similarly, pp. 220, line 15, 221, line 4, 222, line 4, 238, line 9, 242, line 30, for n̐̆ read m̐.
P. 273, footnote, last line but one, for 'hciefly' read 'chiefly'.
P. 286, line 15, for 'follows' read 'precedes'.
P. 340, line 17, for **tā́ni** read **tyā́ni**.
P. 347, at the end of line 10, add (i. 81[5]).
,, ,, line 17, for **vā** read **vā́**.
,, ,, line 21, for **duścarmā** read **duścármā**.
P. 348, line 28, for **vettu** read **véttu**.
P. 350, line 20, after *wisdom* add (i. 42[7]).
P. 351, line 28, for **abhi** read **abhí**.
· 352, line 31, for **vā́yum** read **vāyúm**.
,, ,, line 34, for (v. 69[1]) read (vi. 59[1]).

CHAPTER I

PHONETIC INTRODUCTION

1. Vedic, or the language of the literature of the Vedas, is represented by two main linguistic strata, in each of which, again, earlier and later phases may be distinguished. The older period is that of the Mantras, the hymns and spells addressed to the gods, which are contained in the various Saṃhitās. Of these the Rigveda, which is the most important, represents the earliest stage. The later period is that of the prose theological treatises called Brāhmaṇas. Linguistically even the oldest of them are posterior to most of the latest parts of the Saṃhitās, approximating to the stage of Classical Sanskrit. But they still retain the use of the subjunctive and employ many different types of the infinitive, while Sanskrit has lost the former and preserves only one single type of the latter. The prose of these works, however, to some extent represents better than the language of the Mantras the normal features of Vedic syntax, which in the latter is somewhat interfered with by the exigences of metre.

The language of the works forming appendices to the Brāhmaṇas, that is, of the Āraṇyakas and Upaniṣads, forms a transition to that of the Sūtras, which is practically identical with Classical Sanskrit.

The linguistic material of the Rigveda, being more ancient, extensive, and authentic than that of the other Saṃhitās, all of which borrow largely from it, is taken as the basis of this grammar. It is, however, considerably supplemented from the other Saṃhitās. The grammatical forms of the Brāhmaṇas, where they differ from those of Classical Sanskrit, have been indicated in notes, while their syntax is fully dealt with, because it illustrates the construction of sentences better than the metrical hymns of the Vedas.

2. The hymns of the Vedas were composed many centuries before the introduction of writing into India, which can hardly have taken place much earlier than 600 B.C. They were handed down till probably long after that event by oral tradition, which has lasted down to the present day. Apart from such tradition, the text of the Saṃhitās has been preserved in manuscripts, the earliest of which, owing to the adverse climatic conditions of India, are scarcely five centuries old. How soon they were first committed to writing, and whether the hymns of the Rigveda were edited in the form of the Saṃhitā and Pada texts with the aid of writing, there seems insufficient evidence to decide; but it is almost inconceivable that voluminous prose works such as the Brāhmaṇas, in particular the Śatapatha Brāhmaṇa, could have been composed and preserved without such aid.[1]

3. The sounds of the Vedic language. There are altogether fifty-two sounds, thirteen of which are vocalic and thirty-nine consonantal. They are the following:—

a. Nine simple vowels: **a ā i ī u ū ṛ ṝ ḷ**; four diphthongs: **e o ai au.**

b. Twenty-two mutes divided into five classes, each of which has its nasal, making a group of twenty-seven:

(*α*) five gutturals (velars): **k kh g gh ṅ**;

(*β*) five palatals: **c ch j jh**[2] **ñ**;

---

[1] The text of the Vedas, with the exception of Aufrecht's and Weber's transliterated editions of the RV. and the TS., is always printed in the Devanāgarī character. The latter having been fully described in my *Sanskrit Grammar for Beginners* (§§ 4–14), it is unnecessary to repeat what is there stated. It will suffice here to give a summary account of all the sounds of the Vedic language.

[2] This sound is very rare, occurring only once in the RV. and not at all in the AV.

(γ) seven cerebrals[1]: ṭ ṭh, ḍ and ḷ,[2] ḍh and ḷh,[2] ṇ;

(δ) five dentals: t th d dh n;

(ε) five labials: p ph b bh m;

c. Four semivowels: y (palatal), r (cerebral), l (dental), v (labial);

d. Three sibilants: ś (palatal), ṣ (cerebral), s (dental);

e. One aspiration: h;

f. One pure nasal: ṃ (ṁ) called Anusvāra (*after-sound*).

g. Three voiceless spirants: ḥ (Visarjanīya), ẖ (Jihvāmūlīya), ḫ (Upadhmānīya).

4. *a.* **The simple vowels:**

ă ordinarily represents an original short vowel (IE. ă ĕ ŏ); but it also often replaces an original sonant nasal, representing the reduced form of the unaccented syllables **an** and **am**, as **sat-á** beside **sánt-am** *being*; **ga-tá** *gone* beside **á-gam-at** *has gone*.

ā represents both a simple long vowel (IE. ā ē ō) and a contraction; e. g. **mātár** (Lat. *māter*) *mother*; **ā́sam** = **á-as-am** *I was*. It frequently also represents the unaccented syllable **an**; e. g. **khā-tá** *dug* from **khan** *dig*.

i is ordinarily an original vowel; e. g. **div-í** (Gk. δῐϝί) *in heaven*. It is also frequently the low grade of **e** and **ya**; e. g. **vid-má** (ἴδμεν) *we know* beside **véd-a** (οἶδα) *I know*; **náv-iṣṭha** *newest* beside **náv-yas** *newer*. It also represents the low grade of radical ā; e. g. **śiṣ-ṭá** *taught* beside **śā́s-ti** *teaches*.

ī is an original vowel; e. g. **jīv-á** *living*. But it also often represents the low grade of **yā**; e. g. **aś-ī-máhi** *we would attain* beside **aś-yā́m** *I would attain*; or a contraction; e. g. **īṣúr** *they have sped* (= **i-iṣ-úr** 3. pl. pf. of **iṣ**); **matī́** *by thought* (= **matíā**).

---

[1] This is much the rarest class of mutes, being scarcely half as common as even the palatals.

[2] These two sounds take the place of ḍ ḍh respectively between vowels in the RV. texts; e. g. **ī́ḷe** (but **ī́ḍya**), **mīḷhúṣe** (but **mīḍhvā́n**).

u is an original vowel; e.g. **mádhu** (Gk. μέθυ) *honey*. It is also the low grade of **o** and **va**; e.g. **yug-á** n. *yoke* beside **yóg-a** m. *yoking*; **sup-tá** *asleep* beside **sváp-na** m. *sleep*.

ū is an original vowel; e.g. **bhrū́** (ὀ-φρύ-ς) f. *brow*. It is also the low grade of **au** and **vā**; e.g. **dhū-tá** *shaken* beside **dhau-tárī** f. *shaking*; **sūd** *sweeten* beside **svād** *enjoy*; and often represents a contraction; e.g. **ūc-úr** = **u-uc-úr** *they have spoken* (3. pl. pf. of **vac**); **bāhū́** *the two arms* = **bāhú-ā**.

ṛ is a vocalic **r**, being the low grade of **ar** and **ra**; e.g. **kṛ-tá** *done* beside **ca-kár-a** *I have done*; **gṛbh-ī-tá** *seized* beside **grábh-a** m. *seizure*.

ṝ occurs only in the acc. and gen. pl. m. and f. of **ar** stems (in which it is the lengthened low grade); e.g. **pitṝ́n**, **mātṝḥ**; **pitṝṇā́m**, **svásṝṇām**.

ḷ is a vocalic **l**, being the low grade of **al**, occurring only in a few forms or derivatives of the verb **kḷp** (**kalp**) *be in order*: **cākḷpré** 3. pl. pf.; **cīkḷpāti** 3. s. aor. subj.; **kḷ́pti** (VS.) f. *arrangement* beside **kalpasva** 2. s. impv. mid., **kálp-a** m. *pious work*.

b. **The diphthongs.**

ē and **ō** stand for the original genuine diphthongs **ăi ău**. They represent (1) the high grade corresponding to the weak grade vowels **i** and **u**; e.g. **séc-ati** *pours* beside **sik-tá** *poured*; **bhój-am** beside **bhúj-am** aor. of **bhuj** *enjoy*; (2) the result of the coalescence of **ă** with **ĭ** and **ŭ** in external and internal Sandhi; e.g. **éndra** = **á indra**; **ó cit** = **á u cit**; **padé** = **padá ī** du. n. *two steps*; **bháveta** = **bháva īta** 3. s. opt. *might be*; **maghón** (= **maghá un**) weak stem of **maghávan** *bountiful*; (3) **e** = **az** in a few words before **d, dh, h**; e.g. **e-dhí** *be* 2. s. impv. of **as** beside **ás-ti**; **o** = **az** before **bh** of case-endings, and before **y** and **v** of secondary suffixes; e.g. **dvéṣo-bhis** inst. pl. of **dvéṣas** n. *hatred*;

duvo-yú *wishing to give* (beside **duvas-yú**); **sáho-van** *mighty* beside **sáhas-vant.**

ai and **au** etymologically represent **āi** and **āu**, as is indicated by the fact that they become **āy** and **āv** in Sandhi; e.g. **gā́v-as** *cows* beside **gáu-s**; and that the Sandhi of **a** with **e** (= ăi) and **o** (= ău) is **ai** and **au** respectively.

5. Vowel gradation. Simple vowels are found to interchange in derivation as well as in verbal and nominal inflexion with fuller syllables, or if short also with long vowels. This change is dependent on shift of accent: the fuller or long syllable remains unchanged while it bears the accent, but is reduced to a simple or short vowel when left by the accent. This interchange is termed vowel gradation. Five different series of such gradation may be distinguished.

a. **The Guṇa series.** Here the accented high grade syllables **e, o, ar, al**, constituting the fundamental stage and called Guṇa (cp. 17 *a*) by the native grammarians, interchange with the unaccented low grade syllables **i, u, ṛ, ḷ** respectively. Beside the Guṇa syllables appear, but much less frequently, the syllables **ai, au, ār** (**āl** does not occur), which are called Vṛddhi by the same authorities and may be regarded as a lengthened variety of the Guṇa syllables. Examples are: **didéś-a** *has pointed out*: **diṣ-ṭá** *pointed out*; **é-mi** *I go*: **i-más** *we go*; **āp-nó-mi** *I obtain*: **āp-nu-más** *we obtain*; **várdhāya** *to further*: **vṛdhā́ya**, id.

a. The low grade of both Guṇa and Vṛddhi may be **ī, ū, ĭr, ŭr**; as **bibháy-a** *I have feared* and **bibhā́y-a** *has feared*: **bhī-tá** *frightened*; **juhā́v-a** *has invoked*: **hū-tá** *invoked*; **tatā́r-a** *has crossed*: **tir-áte** *crosses* and **tīr-ṇá** *crossed*.

b. **The Samprasāraṇa series.** Here the accented high grade syllables **ya, va, ra** (corresponding to the Guṇa stage **e, o, ar**) interchange with the unaccented low grade vowels **i, u, ṛ**; e.g. **i-yáj-a** *I have sacrificed*: **iṣ-ṭá** *sacrificed*; **váṣ-ṭi** *desires*: **uś-mási** *we desire*; **ja-gráh-a** *I have seized*: **ja-gṛh-úr** *they have seized*.

a. Similarly the long syllables **yā**, **vā**, **rā** are reduced to **ī**, **ū**, **ĭr**; e. g. **jyā́** f. *might*: **jī-yá-te** *is overcome*; **brū-yā́-t** *would say*: **bruv-ī-tá** id.; **svād-ú** *sweet*: **sūd-áya-ti** *sweetens*; **drā́gh-īyas** *longer*: **dīrgh-á** *long*.

c. **The ă series.**

1. In its low grade stage **a** would normally disappear, but as a rule it remains because its loss would in most cases lead to unpronounceable or obscure forms; e. g. **ás-ti** *is*: **s-ánti** *they are*; **ja-gám-a** *I have gone*: **ja-gm-úr** *they have gone*; **pád-ya-te** *goes*: **pi-bd-aná** *standing firm*; **hán-ti** *slays*: **ghn-ánti** *they slay*.

2. The low grade of the Vṛddhi vowel **ā** is either **a** or total loss; e. g. **pā́d** m. *foot*: **pad-ā́** *with the foot*; **dadhā́-ti** *puts*: **dadh-mási** *we put*; **pu-nā́-ti** *purifies*: **pu-n-ánti** *they purify*; **da-dā́-ti** *gives*: **devá-t-ta** *given by the gods*.

3. When **ā** represents the Guṇa stage its low grade is normally **i**; e. g. **sthā́-s** *thou hast stood*: **sthi-tá** *stood*.

a. Sometimes it is **ī** owing to analogy; e. g. **pu-nā́-ti** *purifies*: **pu-nī-hí** *purify*. Sometimes, especially when the low grade syllable has a secondary accent, it is **a**; e. g. **gā́h-ate** *plunges*: **gáh-ana** n. *depth*.

d. **The ai and au series.**

The low grade of **ai** (which appears as **āy** before vowels and **ā** before consonants) is **ī**; e. g. **gā́y-ati** *sings*, **gā-thá** m. *song*: **gī-tá** *sung*.

The low grade of **au** (which is parallel to **vā**: 5 *b a*) is **ū**; e. g. **dhā́v-ati** *washes*: **dhū-tá** *washed*; **dhau-tárī** f. *shaking*: **dhū́-ti** m. *shaker*, **dhū-má** m. *smoke*.

e. **Secondary shortening of ī, ū, ṝ.** The low grade syllables **ī**, **ū**, **ĭr** and **ŭr** (= **ṝ**) are further reduced to **i**, **u**, **ṛ**, owing to shift of accent from its normal position in a word to its beginning, in compounds, reduplicated forms, and vocatives; e. g. **ā́-huti** f. *invocation*: **-hūti** *call*; **dī́di-vi** *shining*: **dī-páya** *kindle*; **cár-kṛ-ṣe** *thou commemoratest*: **kīr-tí** f. *praise* (from root **kṝ**); **pi-pṛ-tā́m** 3. du.: **pūr-tá** *full* (root **pṝ**); **dévi** voc.: **devī́** nom. *goddess*; **śváśru** voc.: **śva-śrū́-s** nom. *mother-in-law*.

The Consonants.

6. The **guttural** mutes represent the Indo-European velars (that is, q-sounds). In the combination **k-ṣ** the guttural is the regular phonetic modification of a palatal before **s**; e.g. **dṛś** *see*: aor. **ádṛk-ṣata**; **vac** *speak*: fut. **vak-ṣyáti**.

7. The **palatals** form two series, the earlier and the later.

a. **Original palatals** are represented by **ch** and **ś**, and to some extent by **j** and **h**.

1. The aspirate **ch** is derived from an IE. double sound, s + aspirated palatal mute; e. g. **chid** *cut off* = Gk. σχιδ. But in the inchoative suffix **cha** it seems to represent s + unaspirated palatal mute; e. g. **gáchā-mi** = Gk. βάσκω.

2. The sibilant **ś** represents an IE. palatal (which seems to have been pronounced dialectically either as a spirant or a mute); e. g. **śatám** 100 = Lat. *centum*, Gk. ἑ-κατόν.

3. The old palatal j (originally the media of ś = I-Ir. *ź*, French j) is recognizable by appearing as a cerebral when final or before mutes; e. g. **yáj-ati** *sacrifices* beside aor. **á-yāṭ** *has sacrificed*, **yáṣ-ṭṛ** *sacrificer*, **iṣ-ṭá** *sacrificed*.

4. The breathing **h** represents the old palatal aspirate I-Ir. **źh**. It is recognizable as an old palatal when, either as final or before t, it is replaced by a cerebral; e. g. **váh-ati** *carries* beside **á-vāṭ** *has carried*.

b. The **new palatals** are c and to some extent j and h. They are derived from gutturals (velars), being interchangeable, in most roots and formatives, with gutturals; e. g. **śóc-ati** *shines* beside **śók-a** m. *flame*, **śúk-van** *flaming*, **śuk-rá** *brilliant*; **yuj-e** *I yoke* beside **yug-á** n. *yoke*, **yóg-a** m. *yoking*, **yuk-tá** *yoked*, **-yúg-van** *yoking*; **du-dróh-a** *has injured* beside **drógh-a** *injurious*.

a. The original gutturals were changed to palatals by the palatal sounds i, ī, y immediately following; e. g. **cit-tá** *noticed* beside **két-a** m. *will* from **cit** *perceive*; **ój-īyas** *stronger* beside **ug-rá** *strong*; **druh-yú**, a proper name, beside **drógh-a** *injurious*.

8. The **cerebrals** are entirely secondary, being a specifically Indian product and unknown in the Indo-Iranian period. They are probably due to aboriginal, especially Dravidian, influence. They are still rare in the RV., where they never occur initially, but only medially and finally. They have as a rule arisen from dentals immediately following the cerebral **ṣ** (= original **s, ś, j, h**) or r-sounds (**r, ṛ, ṝ**); e. g. **duṣ-ṭára** (= **dus-tára**) *invincible*; **váṣ-ṭi** (= **váś-ti**) *wishes*; **mṛṣ-ṭá** (= **mṛj-tá**) *cleansed*; **nīḍá** (= **niẓdá**)[1] *nest*; **dū-ḍhí** (= **duẓ-dhí**) *ill-disposed*; **dṛḍhá**[2] (= **dṛh-tá**) *firm*; **nṛ-ṇā́m** (= **nṛ-nā́m**) *of men*.

Final cerebral mutes represent the old palatals **j, ś, h**; e. g. **rā́ṭ** (= **rā́j**) m. *ruler* nom. s.; **vípāṭ** (= **ví-pāś**) f. a river; **ṣā́ṭ** (= **sā́h**) *overcoming*; **á-vāṭ** (= **á-vāh-t**) *has conveyed* (3. s. aor. of **vah**).

9. *a.* The **dentals** are original sounds, representing the corresponding IE. dentals. The mutes **t** and **d**, however, sometimes take the place of original **s** before **s** and **bh** respectively; e. g. **á-vāt-sīs** (AV.) aor. of **vas** *dwell*; **mād-bhís** inst. pl. of **mā́s** *month*.

b. The **labials** as a rule represent the corresponding IE. sounds. But **b** is very rarely inherited; the number of words containing this sound has, however, been greatly increased in various ways. Thus it often replaces **p** or **bh** in Sandhi and **bh** in reduplication; e. g. **pi-bd-aná** *firm* beside **pad-á** n. *place*; **rab-dhá** *taken* beside **rábhante** *they take*; **ba-bhū́va** *has been* from **bhū** *be*. There are also many words containing **b** which seem to have a foreign origin.

10. The **nasals**. Of the five nasals belonging to the corresponding five classes of mutes, only the dental **n** and the labial **m** appear independently and in any part of a word,

---

[1] **ẓ** (= **s** or old palatal **źh**), the soft form of **ṣ**, has always disappeared after cerebralizing **d** or **dh** and lengthening the preceding vowel.

[2] Though written as a short vowel the **ṛ** is prosodically long.

initially, medially, and finally; e. g. **mātṛ́** f. *mother*, **nā́man** n. *name*. The remaining three are always dependent on a contiguous sound. The guttural **ṅ**, the palatal **ñ**, and the cerebral **ṇ** are never initial, and the last two are never final. The guttural **ṅ** appears finally only when a following **k** or **g** has been dropped, as in stems ending in **ñc** or **ñj** and in those compounded with **dṛ́ś**; e. g. **pratyáṅ** nom. s. of **pratyáñc** *facing*; **kī-dṛ́ṅ** nom. s. of **kī-dṛ́ś** *of what kind?*

a. Medially **ṅ** appears regularly only before gutturals; e. g. **aṅká** m. *hook*; **aṅkháya** *embrace*; **áṅga** n. *limb*; **jáṅghā** f. *leg*. Before other consonants it appears only when **k** or **g** has been dropped; e. g. **yuṅ-dhi** for **yuṅg-dhi** (= **yuñj-dhi**) 2. s. impv. of **yuj** *join*.

b. The palatal nasal occurs only before or after **c** or **j**, and before **ch**; e. g. **páñca** *five*; **yaj-ñá** m. *sacrifice*; **vā́ñchantu** *let them desire*.

c. The cerebral **ṇ** appears within a word only, either before cerebral mutes or replacing dental **n** after **ṛ**, **r**, or **ṣ** (either immediately preceding or separated from it by certain intervening letters); e. g. **daṇḍá** m. *staff*; **nṛ-ṇā́m** *of men*; **várṇa** m. *colour*; **uṣṇá** *hot*; **krámaṇa** n. *step*.

d. The dental **n** is the commonest of the nasals; it is more frequent than **m**, and about three times as frequent as the other three taken together. As a rule it represents IE. **n**; but it also appears in place of the dental **d** or **t**, and of labial **m** before certain suffixes. It is substituted for **d** before the suffix **-na**; and for **d** or **t** before the **m** of secondary suffixes; e. g. **án-na** n. *food* (from **ad** *eat*); **vidyún-mant** *gleaming* (**vidyút** f. *lightning*); **mṛ́n-maya** *earthen* (**mṛ́d** f. *earth*). It is substituted for **m** before **t**; before suffixal **m** or **v**; and before suffixal **s** or **t** that have been dropped as final; e. g. **yan-trá** n. *rein* (**yam** *restrain*); **á-gan-ma, gán-vahi** (aor. of **gam** *go*); **á-gan** (= **á-gam-s, á-gam-t**) 2. 3. s. aor. of **gam** *go*; **á-yān** (= **á-yam-s-t**) 3. s. aor. of **yam** *restrain*; **dán** gen. of **dám** *house* (= **dam-s**).

e. The labial **m** as a rule represents IE. m; e. g. **nā́man**, Lat. *nomen*. It is by far the commonest labial sound, being more frequent than the four labial mutes taken together.

f. **The pure nasal.** Distinct from the five class nasals is the pure nasal, variously called Anusvāra and Anunāsika, which always follows a vowel and is formed by the breath passing through the nose unmodified by the influence of any consonant. The former is usually written with a dot before consonants, the latter as ◡ before vowels. The proper use of Anusvāra is not before mutes, but before sibilants and **h** (which have no class nasal). When final, Anusvāra usually represents **m**, sometimes **n** (66 A 2). Medially Anusvāra regularly appears before sibilants and **h**; e. g. **vaṃśá** m. *reed*; **havíṃṣi** *offerings*; **māṃsá** n. *flesh*; **siṃhá** m. *lion*. It usually appears before **s**, where it always represents **m** or **n**; e. g. **máṃsate** 3. s. subj. aor. of **man** *think*; **piṃṣanti** beside **pináṣṭi** from **piṣ** *crush*; **kraṃsyáte** fut. of **kram** *stride*. When Anusvāra appears before **ś** or **h** (= IE. guttural or palatal) it represents the corresponding class nasal.

11. The semivowels. The semivowels **y**, **r**, **l**, **v** are peculiar in having each a vowel corresponding to it, viz. **i**, **ṛ**, **ḷ**, **u** respectively. They are called **anta(ḥ)sthā** in the Prātiśākhyas, or 'intermediate', as standing midway between vowels and consonants.

a. The semivowel **y** is constantly written for **i** before other vowels within the Veda itself. It also sometimes appears without etymological justification, especially after roots in **-ā**, before vowel suffixes; e. g. **dā́-y-i** 3. s. aor. pass. of **dā** *give*. Otherwise it is based either on IE. i̭ (= Gk. spiritus asper) or voiced palatal spirant **y** (= Gk. ζ); e. g. **yá-s** *who* (Gk. ὅ-ς), **yaj** *sacrifice* (Gk. ἅγ-ιος); but **yas** *boil* (Gk. ζέω), **yuj** *yoke* (Gk. ζυγ-). It is probably due to this difference of origin that **yas** *boil* and **yam** *restrain* reduplicate with **ya** in the perfect, but **yaj** *sacrifice* with **i**.

b. The semivowel **v** is constantly written for **u** before other vowels within the Veda itself. Otherwise it seems always to be based on IE. **u̯**, that is, on a **v** interchangeable with **u**, but never on an IE. spirant **v** not interchangeable with **u**.

c. The semivowel **r** generally corresponds to IE. **r**, but also often to IE. **l**. As Old Iranian invariably has **r** for both, it seems as if there had been a tendency to rhotacism in the Indo-Iranian period. In order to account for the Vedic relation of **r** to **l**, it appears necessary to assume a mixture of three dialects: one in which the IE. **r** and **l** were kept apart; another in which IE. **l** became **r** (the Vedic dialect); and a third in which IE. **r** became **l** throughout (the later **Māgadhī**).

r is secondary when it takes the place of phonetic **ḍ** (= **ẓ**) as the final of stems in **is** and **us** before endings beginning with **bh**; e. g. **havír-bhis** and **vápur-bhis**. This substitution is due to the influence of external Sandhi, where **is** and **us** would become **ir** and **ur**.

a. Metathesis of **r** takes place when **ă̆r** would be followed by **ṣ** or **h** + consonant. It appears in forms of **dṛś** *see* and **sṛj** *send forth*; e. g. **dráṣṭum** *to see*, **sáṃsraṣṭṛ** *one who engages in battle*; also in **brahmán** m. *priest*, **bráhman** n. *devotion* beside **barhís** n. *sacrificial litter* (from **bṛh** or **barh** *make big*); and in a few other words.

d. The semivowel **l** represents IE. **l** and in a few instances IE. **r**. It is rarer than in any cognate language except Old Iranian, in which it does not occur at all. It is much rarer than **r**, which is seven times as frequent. A gradual increase of **l** is apparent in the RV.; thus in the tenth book are found the verbs **mluc** and **labh**, and the nouns **lóman**, **lohitá**, which in the earlier books appear as **mruc** *sink*, **rabh** *seize*, **róman** n. *hair*, **rohitá** *red*. This letter occurs eight times as often in the latest parts of the RV. as in the oldest; and it is seven times as common in the AV. as in the RV. It seems likely that the recorded Vedic dialect was descended from an Indo-Iranian one in which rhotacism had removed every l; but that there must have been another Vedic dialect in which IE. r and l were kept distinct, and a third in which IE. r became l throughout; from the latter two l must have found its way into the literary language to an increasing extent. In the oldest parts of the RV. there are no verbal forms preserving IE. l, and only a few nouns: (u)**loká** m. *free space*, **śloka** m. *call*, and **-miśla** *mixed.*

a. In the later Saṃhitās l occasionally occurs both medially and finally for ḍ; e. g. **íle** (VS. Kaṇva) = **íḍe** (RV. **íḷe**); **bál íti** (AV.), cf. RV. **báḷ itthá.** In a good many words l is probably of foreign origin.

12. The sibilants are all voiceless, but there are various traces of the earlier existence of voiced sibilants (cp. 7 *a* 3; 8; 15, 2 *k*). There is a considerable interchange between the sibilants, chiefly as a result of assimilation.

a. The **palatal sibilant ś** represents an IE. palatal (mute or spirant). Besides being the regular substitute for dental s in external Sandhi before voiceless palatals (e. g. **índraś ca**), it occasionally represents that sibilant within words by assimilation; e. g. **śváśura** (Lat. *socer*) *father-in-law*; **śaśá** (IE. *kasó*) m. *hare.* Sometimes this substitution takes place, without assimilation, under the influence of allied words, as in **kéśa** m. *hair* beside **késara** (Lat. *caesaries*). It is also to some extent confused with the other two sibilants in the Saṃhitās, but here it interchanges much oftener with s than with ṣ. Before s the palatal ś becomes k, regularly when medial, sometimes when final; e. g. **dṛ́k-ṣ-a-se** 2. s. aor. subj. mid., and **-dṛ́k**[s] nom. s. from **dṛś** *see.*

b. The **cerebral ṣ** is, like the cerebral mutes, altogether secondary, always representing either an original palatal or an original dental sibilant. Medially it represents the palatals ś (= I-Ir. ś) and j (= I-Ir. ź) and the combination kṣ before the cerebral tenues ṭ ṭh (themselves produced from dental tenues by this ṣ); e. g. **naṣ-ṭá** from **naś** *be lost*; **mṛṣ-ṭa** 3. s. impf., from **mṛj** *wipe*; **taṣ-ṭá** from **takṣ** *hew.*

Medially it is regularly, and initially very frequently, substituted for dental **s** after vowels other than **ă** and after the consonants **k**, **r**, **ṣ**; e. g. **tiṣṭhati** from **sthā** *stand*; **su-ṣup-ur** 3. pl. pf. from **svap** *sleep*; **ṛṣabhá** m. *bull*; **ukṣán** m. *ox*; **varṣá** n. *rain*; **havíṣ-ṣu** *in oblations*; **ánu ṣṭuvanti** *they praise*; **go-ṣáṇi** *winning cattle*; **diví ṣán** *being in heaven*.

Occasionally **ṣ** represents dental **s** as a result of assimilation; e. g. **ṣáṣ** *six* (Lat. *sex*); **ṣā́ṭ** *victorious* nom. s. from **sáh** *overcoming*.

c. The dental **s** as a rule represents IE. **s**; e. g. **áśva-s** *horse*, Lat. *equo-s*; **ás-ti**, Gk. ἔσ-τι. In Sandhi it is often replaced by the palatal **ś** and still oftener by the cerebral **ṣ**.

13. The **breathing h** is a secondary sound representing as a rule the second half of an original guttural or palatal aspirate, but occasionally of the dental **dh** and the labial **bh**. It usually stands for palatalized **gh**, this origin being recognizable by the appearance of the guttural in cognate forms; e. g. **hán-ti** *strikes* beside **ghn-ánti**, **jaghā́na**; **dudróha** *has injured* beside **drógha** *injurious*. It sometimes represents an old palatal aspirate (= I-Ir. **źh**), as is recognizable by its being replaced as final or before **t** by a cerebral; e. g. **váh-ati** *carries* beside **á-vāṭ** *has carried*, **ūḍhá** (= **uẓ-ḍhá**) for **vah-tá**. It stands for **dh** e. g. in **gā́h-ate** *plunges* beside **gādhá** n. *ford*; **hi-tá** *placed* beside **dhi-tá** from **dhā** *put*. It represents **bh** in the verb **grah** *seize* beside **grabh**. The various origins of **h** led to a certain amount of confusion in the groups of forms from roots containing that sound. Thus beside **mugdhá**, the phonetic past participle of **muh** *be confused*, appears **mūḍhá** (AV.) *bewildered*.

14. Voiceless spirants. There are three such representing original final **s** or **r**. **Visarjanīya** has its proper place in pausā. **Jihvāmūlīya** (*formed at the root of the tongue*) is the guttural spirant and is appropriate before initial voiceless gutturals (**k, kh**). Upadhmānīya (*on-breathing*) is the bi-labial spirant f and appears before voiceless labials (**p, ph**). Visarjanīya may take the place of the latter two, and always does so in the printed texts of the Saṃhitās.

15. Ancient pronunciation. As regards the pronunciation prevailing about 500 B.C. we have a sufficiently exact knowledge derived from the transcription of Sanskrit words in foreign languages, especially Greek ; from the information contained in the old grammarians, Pāṇini and his school ; and especially from the detailed statements of the Prātiśākhyas, the ancient phonetic works dealing with the Saṃhitās. The internal evidence supplied by the phonetic changes occurring in the language of the texts themselves and the external evidence of comparative philology justify us in concluding that the pronunciation in the period of the Saṃhitās was practically the same as in Pāṇini's time. The only possible exceptions are a very few doubtful points. The following few remarks will therefore suffice on the subject of pronunciation :

1. *a*. **The vowels.** The simple vowels ĭ, ŭ and ā were pronounced as in Italian. But ă in the time of the Prātiśākhyas was already sounded as a very short close neutral vowel like the u in English *but*. It is, however, probable from the fact that the metre hardly ever admits of ă being elided after **e** and **o** in the RV., though the written text drops it in about 75 per cent. of the occurrences, that at the time when the hymns were composed the pronunciation of ă was still open, but that, at the time when the Saṃhitā text was constituted, the close pronunciation was already becoming general.

The vowel ṛ, now usually sounded as ri (an early pronunciation as shown by the confusion of ṛ and ri in ancient inscriptions and MSS.), was in the Saṃhitās pronounced as a vocalic r, somewhat like the sound in the final syllable of the French *chambre*. It is described in the RV. Prātiśākhya as containing an r in the middle. This agrees with ere, the equivalent of ṛ in Old Iranian.

The very rare vowel ḷ, now usually pronounced as lri, was in the Saṃhitās a vocalic l, described in the RV. Prātiśākhya as corresponding to l representing an original r.

b. The diphthongs e and o were already pronounced as the simple long vowels ē and ō in the time of the Prātiśākhyas; and that this was even the case in the Saṃhitās is shown by the fact that their Sandhi before a was no longer ay and av, and that the a was beginning to be elided after e and o. But that they represent the original genuine diphthongs ăi and ău is shown by the fact that they are produced in Sandhi by the coalescence of a with i and u.

The diphthongs ai and au are at the present day pronounced as ăi and ău, and were so pronounced even at the time of the Prātiśākhyas. But that they etymologically represent āi and āu is shown by their Sandhi.

c. **Lengthened vowels.** The vowels i and u were often pronounced long before suffixal y; e. g. sū-yá-te *is pressed* (√su); janī-yánt *desiring a wife* (jáni); also before r when a consonant follows; e.g. gīr-bhís (but gír-as); a, i, u often become long before v; e. g. ā́-vidh-yat *he wounded* (a is augment); ji-gī-vā́ṃs *having conquered* (√ji); ṛtā́-van *observing order* (ṛtá); yā́-vant *how great*; as compensation for the loss of a following consonant; e. g. gū-ḍhá for guh-tá (15, 2 *k*); they are also often pronounced long for metrical reasons; e. g. śrudhī hávam *hear our prayer.*

d. **Svarabhakti.**[1] When a consonant is in conjunction with r or a nasal, the metre shows that a very short vowel[2] must often be pronounced between them; e. g. índra = índ^{a}ra; yajñá = yaj^{a}ná *sacrifice*; gnā́ = g^{a}nā́ *woman.*

---

[1] A term used in the Prātiśākhyas and meaning 'vowel-part'.

[2] Described by the Prātiśākhyas as equal to $\frac{1}{8}$, $\frac{1}{4}$, or $\frac{1}{2}$ *mora* in length and generally as equivalent to a in sound.

e. **Loss of vowels.** With very few exceptions the only vowel lost is initial **a** which, in one per cent. of its occurrences in the RV. and about 20 per cent. in the AV. and the metrical portions of the YV., is dropped in Sandhi after **e** and **o.** In a few words the disappearance of initial **a** is prehistoric; e. g. **ví** *bird* (Lat. *avi-s*); **sánti** *they are* (Lat. *sunt*).

f. **Hiatus.** In the written text of the Saṃhitās hiatus, though as a rule tolerated in diphthongs only, appears in Sandhi when a final **s, y, v** has been dropped before a following vowel; when final **ī, ū, e** of dual endings are followed by vowels; and when **a** remains after final **e** and **o.**

Though not written, hiatus is common elsewhere also in the Saṃhitās: **y** and **v** must often be pronounced as **i** and **u**, and a long vowel or diphthong as two vowels, the original vowels of contractions having often to be restored both within a word and in Sandhi; e.g. **jyéṣṭha** *mightiest* as **jyá-iṣṭha** (= **jyā́-iṣṭha** from **jyā** *be mighty*).

2. **Consonants.** *a.* The aspirates were double sounds, consisting of mutes followed by a breathing; thus **k-h** is pronounced as in 'ink-horn'; **t-h** as in 'pot-house'; **p-h** as in 'top-heavy'; **g-h** as in 'log-house'; **d-h** as in 'mad-house'; **b-h** as in 'Hob-house'.

b. The **gutturals** were no doubt velars or sounds produced by the back of the tongue against the soft palate. They are described by the Prātiśākhyas as formed at the 'root of the tongue' and at the 'root of the jaw'.

c. The palatals **c, j, ch** are pronounced like **ch** in 'church', **j** in 'join', and **ch** in the second part of 'Churchill'.

d. The cerebrals were pronounced somewhat like the so-called dentals **t, d, n** in English, but with the tip of the tongue turned farther back against the roof of the mouth. They include the cerebral **ḷ** and **ḷh** which in Rigvedic texts take the place of **ḍ** and **ḍh** between vowels. The latter occurs medially only; the former finally also.

Examples are: íḷā *refreshment*; turā-ṣáḷ abhi-bhūtyójāḥ; á-ṣāḷha *invincible*.

e. The **dentals** in the time of the Prātiśākhyas were post-dentals, being produced by the tongue, according to their description, at the 'root of the teeth' (danta-mūla).

f. The class **nasals** are produced with organs of speech in the same position as for the formation of the corresponding mutes while the breath passes through the nose. The **pure nasal**, when called Anunāsika, combines with the preceding vowel to form a single sound, a nasalized vowel, as in the French 'bon'; when called Anusvāra (*after-sound*), it forms in combination with the preceding vowel two successive sounds, a pure vowel immediately followed by the pure nasal, though seeming to form a single sound, as in the English 'ba-ng' (where, however, the nasal is guttural, not pure).

g. The **semivowel** y is the voiced palatal spirant produced in the same place as the palatal vowel i. The semivowel v is described by the Prātiśākhyas as a voiced labio-dental spirant. It is like the English v or the German w. The semivowel r must originally have been a cerebral, as is shown by its phonetic effect on a following dental n. By the time of the Prātiśākhyas it was pronounced in other positions also. Thus the RV. Prātiśākhya speaks of it as either post-dental or produced farther back (but not as cerebral).

The semivowel l is described in the Prātiśākhyas as pronounced in the same position as the dentals, which means that it was a post-dental.

h. The **sibilants** are all voiceless. The dental s sounds like s in 'sin'; the cerebral ṣ like sh in 'shun' (but with the tip of the tongue farther back); while the palatal is produced midway between the two, being the sibilant pronounced in the same place as the spirant in the German *ich*. Though the voiced sibilants z, ź (palatal = French j),

ẓ, ẓh (cerebral) have entirely disappeared, they have generally left traces of their former existence in the phonetic changes they have produced.

i. The sound **h** was undoubtedly pronounced as a voiced breathing in the Saṃhitās. The Prātiśākhyas describe it as voiced and as identical with the second element of voiced aspirates (**g-h, d-h, b-h**). This is corroborated by the spelling ळ्ह **ḷ-h** (= **ḍh**) beside ळ **ḷ** (= **ḍ**).

j. There are three **voiceless spirants** appearing only as finals. The usual one, called Visarjanīya in the Prātiśākhyas, is according to the Taittirīya Prātiśākhya articulated in the same place as the end of the preceding vowels. Its place may be taken by Jihvāmūlīya before the voiceless initial gutturals **k, kh**; and by Upadhmānīya before the voiceless initial labials **p, ph**. These two are regarded by the RV. Prātiśākhya as forming the second half of the voiceless aspirates **kh** and **ph** respectively (just as **h** forms the second half of **gh, bh,** &c.). They are therefore the guttural spirant (Greek) χ and the bilabial spirant **f** respectively.

k. **Loss of consonants.** This is almost entirely confined to groups of consonants. When the group is final, all but the first element, as a rule, is dropped in pausā and in Sandhi (28). In initial consonant groups a sibilant is often lost before a mute; e. g. **candrá** *shining* beside **ścandrá**; **stanayitnú** m. beside **tanayitnú** *thunder*; **tāyú** m. beside **stāyú** *thief*; **tṛ́** beside **stṛ́** m. *star*; **páśyati** *sees* beside **spáś** m. *spy*, **-spaṣ-ṭa** *seen*. In a medial group the sibilants **s** and **ṣ** regularly disappear between mutes; e. g. **á-bhak-ta**, 3. s. aor. for **á-bhak-ṣ-ṭa** beside **á-bhak-ṣ-i**. A mute may disappear between a nasal and a mute; e. g. **yuṅ-dhí** for **yuṅg-dhí**.

a. Medially, voiced sibilants, the dental **z**, the cerebral **ẓ**, and the palatal **ź**, have disappeared before the voiced dentals **d, dh,** and **h**, but nearly always leaving a trace of their former existence. Only in the two roots containing **ā**,

ās *sit*, **śās** *order*, the sibilant has disappeared without a trace: **á-dhvam, śa-śā-dhi.** But when **a** preceded the **z** the loss of the sibilant is indicated by **e** taking the place of **az**; e. g. **e-dhí** (for **az-dhí**) from **as** *be*; **sed**, perfect stem of **sad** *sit* for **sazd**; similarly in **de-hí** *give* (for **daz-dhí**) beside **dad-dhí.** When other vowels than **ă** preceded, the **z** was cerebralized and disappeared after cerebralizing the following dental and lengthening the preceding vowel; thus **á-sto-ḍhvam** (= **á-stoẓ-ḍhvam** for **á-sto-s-dhvam**) 2. pl. aor. beside **á-sto-ṣ-ṭa**; similarly **mīḍhá** n. *reward* (Gk. μισθό-ς). Similarly the old voiced palatal **ź** disappeared after cerebralizing a following **d** or **dh** and lengthening the preceding vowel; e. g. **tā-ḍhi** for **taź-ḍhi** (= **tak̑-ṣ-dhi**) from **takṣ** *fashion*; **ṣo-ḍhā́** for **ṣaṣ-dhā́** (= **sak̑-ṣ-dhā́**) beside **ṣaṣ-ṭhá** *sixth*. Still commoner is the loss of the old aspirated palatal **źh** represented by **h**, which was dropped after cerebralizing and aspirating a following **t** and lengthening the preceding vowel; e. g. **sā́-ḍhṛ** for **sáh-tṛ** *conqueror* from **sah**; **gūḍhá** *concealed* for **guh-tá** (from **guźh-tá**).

l. **Haplology.** When two identical or similar syllables are in juxtaposition, one of them is sometimes dropped; e. g. **tuvī-rá[va]-vān** *roaring mightily* beside **tuvī-ráva**; **ir[adh]ádhyai** inf. of **iradh** *seek to win*; **ma-dúgha** m. a plant yielding honey, beside **madhu-dúgha** *shedding sweetness*; **śīrṣa-[sa]ktí** f. *headache.*

CHAPTER II

RULES OF SANDHI OR EUPHONIC COMBINATION OF SOUNDS

16. Though the sentence is naturally the unit of speech, which forms an unbroken chain of syllables euphonically combined, it is strictly so only in the prose portions of the AV. and the YV. But as the great bulk of the Vedas is metrical, the editors of the Saṃhitā text treat the hemistich (generally consisting of two Pādas or verses) as the euphonic unit, being specially strict in applying the rules of Sandhi between the verses forming the hemistich. But the evidence of metre supported by that of accent shows that the Pāda is the true euphonic unit. The form which the final of a word shows varies according as it appears in pausā at the end of a Pāda, or in combination with a following word within the Pāda. With the former is concerned the law of finals in pausā, with the latter the rules of Sandhi. **Avoidance of hiatus** and **assimilation** are the leading principles on which the rules of Sandhi are based.

Though both are in general founded on the same phonetic laws, it is necessary, owing to certain differences, to distinguish **external Sandhi**, which determines the changes of final and initial letters of words, from **internal Sandhi**, which applies to the final letters of verbal roots and nominal stems when followed by certain suffixes and terminations.

a. The rules of external Sandhi apply with few exceptions (which are survivals from an earlier stage of external Sandhi) to words forming compounds, and to final letters of nominal stems before the case-endings beginning with consonants (**-bhyām -bhis, -bhyas, -su**) or before secondary (182, 2) suffixes beginning with any consonant except **y**.

A. External Sandhi.

Classification of Vowels.

17. Vowels are divided into

A. 1. Simple vowels: **a ā; i ī; u ū; ṛ ṝ; ḷ.**

2. Guṇa vowels: **a ā; e o ar al.**

3. Vṛddhi vowels: **ā ; ai ; au ; ār.**[1]

a. Guṇa (*secondary quality*) has the appearance of being the simple vowel strengthened by combination with a preceding **a** according to the rule (19*a*) of external Sandhi (except that **a** itself remains unchanged); Vṛddhi (*increase*), of being the Guṇa vowel strengthened by combination with another **a**.[2]

B. 1. Vowels liable to be changed into semivowels: **i, ī; u, ū; ṛ**[3] and the diphthongs **e, ai, o, au** (the latter half of which is i or u): consonantal vowels.

2. Vowels not liable to be changed into semivowels (and only capable of coalescence): **a, ā**: unconsonantal vowels.

Combination of Final and Initial Vowels.

18. If the same simple vowel (short or long) occurs at the end of one word and the beginning of the next, contraction resulting in the long vowel[4] is the rule in the written text of the Saṃhitās. Thus **ihā́sti = ihá asti; índrā́ = índra ā́; tvā̄gne = tvā agne; vī̀dám = ví idám; sūktám = su uktám.**

---

[1] The Vṛddhi form of ḷ (which would be āl) does not occur.

[2] In this vowel gradation, as Comparative Philology shows, the Guṇa vowel represents the normal stage, from which the simple vowel was reduced by loss of accent, while Vṛddhi is a lengthened variety of Guṇa (5 *a*). The reduction of the syllables **ya, va, ra** (which are parallel with the Guṇa stage) to the corresponding vowels **i, u, ṛ** (5 *b*) is termed Samprasāraṇa (*distraction*).

[3] ṝ never appears under conditions rendering it liable to be changed into r (cp. 4 *a*, p. 4).

[4] ṝ does not occur because ṛ ṛ never meet in the Saṃhitās, and final ṛ does not even occur in the RV.

a. The contraction of ā + a and of ŭ + ŭ occasionally does not take place, even in the written text of the RV., both between the Pādas of a hemistich and within a Pāda; thus **manīṣā́ | agníḥ**; **manīṣā́ abhí**; **vīḷū́ utá**; **sú ūrdhváḥ**; and in a compound, **su-ūtáyaḥ**.

b. On the other hand, the metre requires the contracted vowels of the written text to be restored in pronunciation. In such cases the restored initial is long by nature or position, while the preceding final, if long, must be shortened.[1] Thus **cāsā́t** is pronounced as **ca āsā́t**; **cārcata** as **ca arcata**; **mā́péḥ** as **mā́ āpéḥ** (for **mā́ āpéḥ**); **mṛḷatīdṛ́śe** as **mṛḷati īdṛ́śe**; **yántī́ndavaḥ** as **yánti índavaḥ**; **bhavantūkṣáṇaḥ** as **bhavantu ukṣáṇaḥ**. When the first word is a monosyllable (especially **ví** or **hí**), the written contractions ī and ū are usually to be pronounced with hiatus; thus **hī́ndra** as **hí índra**.

19. a and ā

a. coalesce with the simple vowels ĭ[2] and ŭ to the Guṇa vowels e and o[3] respectively; e.g. **ihéha** = **ihá iha**; **pitéva** = **pitā́ iva**; **ém** = **ā́ īm**; **óbhā́** = **ā́ ubhā́**.[4] They are never contracted to ar in the written text of the RV. or VS.;[5] but the metre shows that the combination is sometimes to be pronounced as ar, for instance in the compound **sapta-ṛṣáyaḥ** *the seven seers* = **saptarṣáyaḥ**.

---

[1] Because of the prosodical rule that a long vowel is always shortened before another vowel. Cf. note 5.

[2] Occasionally ā + i remain uncontracted in the written text of the RV., as **jyā́ iyám**, **pibā imám**, **raṇayā ihá**.

[3] This contraction is a survival because ē and ō are simple long vowels, but they were originally = āi, āu.

[4] But in many instances where the contraction is written, the original simple vowels must be restored with hiatus; thus **subhágoṣā́ḥ** = **subhágā uṣā́ḥ**.

[5] ā is always shortened or nasalized before ṛ in the written text; e.g. **tátha ṛtúḥ** (for **táthā**); **vipanyā́m̐ ṛtásya** (for **vipanyā́**).

b. coalesce with Guṇa vowels to Vṛddhi; e. g. **áibhiḥ** = **á ebhiḥ.**[1]

c. are absorbed by Vṛddhi vowels; e. g. **sómasyauśijáḥ** = **sómasya auśijáḥ.**

20. The simple consonantal vowels ĭ and ŭ before dissimilar vowels or before diphthongs are regularly changed to the semivowels **y** and **v** respectively in the written text of the Saṃhitās; e. g. **práty āyam** = **práti āyam**; **jánitry ajījanat** = **jánitrī ajījanat**; **á tv étā** = **á tú étā.** But the evidence of the metre shows that this **y** or **v** nearly always has the syllabic value of ĭ or ŭ.[2] Thus **vy ùṣáḥ** must be read as **ví uṣáḥ**; **vidátheṣv añján** as **vidátheṣu añján.**

a. Final **ṛ** (which does not occur in the RV.) becomes **r** before a dissimilar vowel; an example is **vijñātr ètát** = **vijñātṛ́ etát** (ŚB.).

21. The Guṇa vowels **e** and **o**

a. remain unchanged before **a**,[3] which is generally[4] elided in the written text of the Saṃhitās, but according to the evidence of the metre, must almost invariably in the RV., and generally in the AV. and YV., be pronounced,[5] whether written or not.[6] In **deváso aptúraḥ** (i. 3⁸) the **a** is both

---

[1] ă instead of contracting with **e** is sometimes nasalized before it: **aminantam̐ évaiḥ** (for **a e**); **upásthām̐ éká** (for **ā e**). Again ă is sometimes elided before **e** and **o**; as **úp'eṣatu** (for **a e**), **yáth'ohiṣe** (for **ā o**).

[2] Because ī and ū are prosodically shortened before a following vowel (p. 22, note 1).

[3] The exceptional treatment of **e** in **stótava ambyàm** for **stótave ambyàm** is a survival showing that the Sandhi of **e** and **o** before **a** was originally the same as before other vowels.

[4] In the RV. it is elided in about 75 per cent., in the AV. in about 66 per cent. of its occurrences.

[5] In the RV. it must be pronounced in 99 per cent., in the AV. and the metrical parts of the YV. in about 80 per cent. of its occurrences.

[6] The frequent elision of the **a** in the written text compared with its almost invariable retention in the original text of the RV., indicates a period of transition between the latter and the total elision of the post-Vedic period.

written and pronounced; in **sūnávé 'gne** (i. 1[9]) it must be restored as **sūnáve | ágne**.

b. before every other vowel (or diphthong) would naturally[1] become **ay** and **av** (the form they assume within a word), but the former drops the semivowel throughout, while the latter does so only before **ŭ**; e. g. **agna ihá** (for **agnay**); **vā́ya ukthébhiḥ** (for **vā́yav**); but **vā́yav ā́ yāhi.**

22. The Vṛddhi vowels **ai** and **au** are treated before every vowel (including **a**) or diphthong exactly in the same way as **e** and **o** before vowels other than **a**. Thus **ai** becomes **ā** (through **āy**) throughout, but **au** only before **ŭ**[2] (through **āv**); e. g. **tásmā akṣí** (for **tásmāy**), **tásmā índrāya**; **sujihvā́ úpa** (for **sujihvā́v**), but **tā́v ā́, tā́v indrāgnī.**

a. The (secondary) hiatus caused by the dropping of **y** and **v** in the above cases (21 *b* and 22) as a rule remains. But further contraction is sometimes actually written in the Saṃhitās; e. g. **sártavā́jáu** for **sártavā́ ājáu** (through **sártavā́y** for **sártavái**); **vā́sáu** for **vā́ asáu** (through **vā́y** for **vái**). Sometimes, again, the contraction, though not written, is required by the metre. Thus **ta indra** must be pronounced as **tendra**, and **goṣṭhá úpa** (AV.) for **goṣṭhé úpa** (through **goṣṭháy**) as **goṣṭhópa.**

Irregular Vowel Sandhi.

23. **Vṛddhi** instead of Guṇa results from the contraction of

a. the preposition **ā́** (in the AV. and VS.) with initial **ṛ** in **ā́rti** = **ā́ ṛti** and in **ā́rchatu** = **ā́ ṛchatu.** In the case of the latter verb, the TS. extends this contraction to prepositions ending in **a**: **úpārchati** = **úpa ṛchati** and **avārcháti** = **ava ṛcháti.**

---

[1] Because **e** and **o** were originally = **ăi** and **ău.**

[2] This is also the Sandhi of the AB. and KB.

b. The preposition **prá** (in the RV.) with initial i in **práiṣayúr** = **prá iṣayúr**.

c. The augment **a** with the initial vowels i, u, r ;[1] e. g. **áichas** 2. s. impf. of **iṣ** *wish* ; **áunat** 3. s. impf. of **ud** *wet* ; **ā́rta** 3. s. aor. of **ṛ** *go*.

Absence of Vowel Sandhi.

24. The particle **u** is unchangeable[2] in pronunciation before vowels, though as a rule written as **v** after a consonant ;[3] e. g. **bhā́ u aṃśáve**, but **ávéd v índra**. When it combines with the final **ă** of a particle to **o**, in **ó** = **ā́ u**, **átho** = **átha u**, **utó** = **utá u**, **mó** = **mā́ u**, it remains unchanged even in the written text ; e. g. **átho índrāya**.

25. *a.* The ī and ū of the dual (nom. acc.) never change to **y** and **v**. This dual ī is never to be pronounced short, but the ū sometimes is ; e. g. **hárī** (◡ –) **ṛtásya**, but **sādhū́** (– ◡) **asmai**. This ī may remain before i, as in **hárī iva**, but in several instances the contraction is written, as in **ródasīmé** = **ródasī imé**, while in several others, though not written, it must be pronounced.

b. The rare locatives singular in ī and ū are also regularly written unchanged in the RV.,[4] but they seem always to be treated as prosodically short.

c. The ī of the nom. *plur.* m. (of the pronoun **asáu**) **amī́** is always given as unchangeable in the Pada text (**amī́ iti**), but it never happens to occur before a vowel in the RV.

---

[1] This is perhaps a survival of a prehistoric contraction of ā (the original form of the augment) with i, u, r to āi, āu, ār.

[2] The term applied by the native phoneticians to unchangeable vowels is **pragṛhya** *separated*. Such vowels are indicated in the Pada text by an appended iti. u is always there written in its lengthened and nasalized form as ūm̐ iti.

[3] It is occasionally written unchanged in its lengthened form even after a consonant, as **tám ū akṛṇvan**.

[4] Except **védy asyā́m**, to be pronounced **védī asyā́m**.

a. The ī of the nom. s. in **pṛthivī́**, **pṛthu-jráyī**, **samrā́jñī** rarely, of the instr. **suśámī** once, and of the instr. **ūtī́** often, remains unchanged before vowels;[1] e.g. **samrā́jñī ádhi**, **suśámī abhūvan**.

26. The diphthong **e** is unchangeable in various nominal and verbal forms.

a. The **e** of the nom. acc. dual (= **a** + **ī**), fem. and neut. of **a** stems, is not liable to Sandhi;[2] e.g. **ródasī ubhé ṛghāyámāṇam**.

b. The verbal dual **e**[3] of the 2. 3. pres. and perf. mid. never combines, though it is nearly always prosodically shortened; e.g. **parimamnā́thĕ asmā́n**.

c. The **e** of the locative of the pronominal forms **tvé** *in thee*, **asmé**[4] *in us*, **yuṣmé** *in you* are unchangeable;[5] e.g. **tvé ít**; **asmé ā́yuḥ**; **yuṣmé itthā́**.

Combination of Final and Initial Consonants.

27. The external Sandhi of consonants is primarily and almost exclusively concerned with the assimilation of a final to a following initial sound. Since the Sandhi of final consonants generally speaking starts from the form they assume in pausā,[6] it is necessary to state the law of allowable finals at the outset. That law may be formulated as follows: only unaspirated hard mutes, nasals, and Visarjanīya are tolerated, and palatals are excluded, as finals. By this law the thirty-nine consonants classified in § 3 are reduced to

---

[1] The unchangeableness of the vowel here being only occasional is not indicated with **iti** in the Pada text.

[2] Except **dhíṣṇyemé** for **dhíṣṇye imé**, as it is also probably to be pronounced.

[3] Under the influence of the nominal dual **e**; for there was originally no difference between this dual **e** and any other **e** in middle forms, such as the dual **vahe**, sing. **te**, and the plur. **ante**.

[4] Also used as dat. in the RV.

[5] They are always written with **iti** in the Pada text.

[6] Final **n** and **r** are, however, to a considerable extent treated not on the basis of their pausal form, but of etymology.

the following eight as permissible in pausā :—**k**, **ṅ** ; **ṭ** ; **t**, **n** ; **p**, **m** ; Visarjanīya.

The aspirate and soft mutes (3 *b*) are eliminated, leaving only hard unaspirated mutes to represent them. The palatals (3 *b* *β*), including **ś** (3 *d*), and **h** (3 *e*), are replaced by **k** or **ṭ** (**ñ** by **ṅ**).

ṣ (3 *d*) is replaced by **ṭ**, **s** (3 *d*) and **r** (3 *c*) by Visarjanīya.

The nasal **ṇ** (3 *b* *γ*) and the three semivowels **y**, **l**, **v** (3 *c*) do not occur.

28. The rule is that only a **single consonant** may be final. Hence all but the first of a group of consonants must be dropped; e. g. **ábhavan** 3. pl. impf. *were* (for **ábhavant**); **tā́n** acc. pl. *those* (for **tā́ns**); **tudán** *striking* (for **tudánts**); **prā́ṅ** *forward* (through **prā́ṅk** for **prā́ñc-s**); **áchān** 3. s. aor. *has pleased* (for **áchantst**).

a. **k**, **ṭ**, or **t**, when they follow an **r** and belong to the root, are allowed to remain;[1] e. g. **várk** 3. s. aor. of **vṛj** *bend* (for **várk-t**); **ū́rk** nom. s. of **ū́rj** *strength*; **á-mārṭ** 3. s. impf. of **mṛj** *wipe*; **ā́-vart** 3. s. aor. of **vṛt** *turn*; **su-hā́rt** nom. s. of **suhā́rd** *friend*.

a. There are seven instances in the Saṃhitās in which a suffixal **s** or **t** is retained instead of the preceding radical consonant. (1) **s** thus appears in the following four nominatives sing.: **sadha-mā́s** beside **sadha-mā́t** (for **sadha-mā́d-s**) *companion of the feast*; **ava-yā́s** (for **ava-yā́j-s**) f. *sacrificial share*; **ā́vayās** (for **ā́vayāj-s**) m. a kind of priest; **puro-ḍā́s** *sacrificial cake* (for **puro-ḍā́ś-s**).[2] (2) **s** or **t** similarly appears in the following four singular verbal preterite forms: **á-yā-s** (for **á-yaj-s**) beside **a-yāṭ** 2 s. aor. of **yaj** *sacrifice*; **á-srās** (for **á-sraj-s**) 2. s. aor. of **sṛj** *emit*; **á-bhanas** (for **á-bhanak-s**) 2. s. impf. of **bhañj** *break*; and **á-srat** (for **a-sras-t**)[3] 3. s. aor. of **sras** *fall*.

---

[1] The only instance of a suffix remaining after **r** is in **dar-t** 3. s. aor. of **dṛ** *cleave* beside **á-dar** 2. s. (for **á-dar-s**).

[2] The **s** is probably due to the analogy of nominatives, like **mā́s** *moon*, **draviṇo-dā́-s** *wealth-giver*, &c.

[3] The appearance of **s** or **t** here is due to the beginnings of the

Classification of Consonants.

29. The assimilation, of which the application of the rules of consonant Sandhi consists, is of two kinds. It is concerned either with a shift of the phonetic position in which a consonant is articulated, or with a change of the quality of the consonant. Hence it is necessary to understand fully the classification of consonants from these two aspects. In § 3 *b c d* (cp. 15, 2*b*–*h*) an arrangement according to the place of articulation is given of all the consonants except four, the breathing h and the three voiceless spirants, which are phonetically described in § 15, 2 *i j*.

a. Contact of the tongue with the throat produces the gutturals, with the palate the palatals, with the roof of the mouth the cerebrals, with the teeth the dentals, while contact between the lips produces the labials.

b. In forming the **nasals** of the five classes, the breath partially passes through the nose while the tongue or the lips are in the position for articulating the corresponding tenuis. The real Anusvāra is formed in the nose only, while the tongue is in the position for forming the particular vowel which the Anusvāra accompanies.

c. The **semivowels** **y**, **r**, l, v are palatal, cerebral, dental, and labial respectively, pronounced in the same position as the corresponding vowels i, ṛ, ḷ, u, the tongue being in partial contact with the place of articulation in the first three, and the lips in partial contact in the fourth.

d. The three **sibilants** are hard spirants produced by partial contact of the tongue with the palate, roof, and teeth respectively. There are no corresponding soft sibilants (English z, French j), but their prehistoric existence may be inferred from various phenomena of Sandhi (cp. 15, 2 *k a*).

---

tendency to normalize the terminations so as to have s in the 2. s. and t in the 3. s. Some half-dozen examples of this have been found in the Brāhmaṇas; e. g. á-ves 2. s. impf. (= á-ved-s) from vid *know*.

e. **h** and **ḥ** are respectively soft and hard spirants produced without any contact, and articulated in the position of the vowel that precedes or follows. **h** occurs only before soft letters, **ḥ** only after vowels and before certain hard letters.

30. Quality of consonants.

Consonants are

1. either **hard** (surd, voiceless): **k kh, c ch, ṭ ṭh, t th, p ph**; **ś ṣ s**; **ḥ ẖ ḫ** (3);

or **soft** (sonant, voiced): all the rest (3) (besides all the vowels and diphthongs).

2. either **aspirated**: **kh gh, ch jh, ṭh ḍh ḻh, th dh, ph bh, h ḥ ẖ ḫ, ś ṣ s**;

or **unaspirated**: all the rest.

Hence the change of **c** to **k** is a change of the position of articulation (palatal to guttural), and that of **c** to **j** is a change of quality (hard to soft); while the change of **c** to **g** (hard palatal to soft guttural) or of **t** to **j** (hard dental to soft palatal) is one of both position and quality.

31. It is essential to remember that consonant Sandhi cannot be applied till finals have been reduced to one of the eight allowable sounds (27). The latter are then modified without reference to their etymological value (except partially in the case of **n** and Visarjanīya). Only six of these allowable finals occur at all frequently, viz. **k, t, n, p, m,** and Visarjanīya, while the cerebral **ṭ** and the guttural **ṅ** are rare.

I. Changes of Quality.

32. A final consonant (that is, a mute or Visarjanīya) is assimilated in quality to the following initial, becoming soft before soft initials, and remaining hard before hard initials (consonants).

Hence final **k, ṭ, t, p** before vowels and soft consonants become **g, ḍ, d, b** respectively; e.g. **arvā́g rā́dhaḥ** (through **arvā́k** for **arvā́c**); **havyavā́ḍ juhvā̀syaḥ** (through **-vā́ṭ** for **-vā́h**); **ṣā́ḻ urvī́ḥ** (through **ṣā́ṭ** for **ṣā́ṣ**: cp. 3 *b* γ); **gámad**

vā́jebhiḥ (for **gámat**); **agníd ṛtāyatáḥ** (through **agnít** for **agnídh**); **triṣṭúb gāyatrī́** (through **triṣṭúp** for **triṣṭúbh**); **abjā́** (for **ap-jā́**).

33. Final **k, ṭ, t, p** before **n** or **m** may, and in practice regularly do, become the nasal of their own class; e.g. **prā́ṇaṅ mártyasya** (through **prā́ṇag** for **prā́ṇak**); **virā́ṇ mitrā́váruṇayoḥ** (through **virā́ḍ** for **virā́ṭ**); **ṣáṇ-ṇavati** (TS.) (through **ṣáṭ-**) for **ṣáṣ-navati**; **ā́sīn nó** (through **ā́sīd** for **ā́sīt**); **tán mitrásya** (for **tád**); **trikakúm nivártat** (through **trikakúb** for **trikakúp** from **trikakúbh**).

34. Final **t** becomes **l** through **d**; e.g. **áṅgāl lómnaḥ** (for **áṅgāt**).

35. Since the nasals have no corresponding hard sounds, they remain unchanged in quality before initial hard sounds. The guttural **ṅ**,[1] which is rare, remains otherwise unmodified also (cp. 52); but it may before sibilants insert a transitional **k**, e.g. **pratyáṅk sá** beside **pratyáṅ sá**. Final **m** is liable to change of position before all consonants (42). Final dental **n** is liable to change before vowels (42, 52), palatals, dentals, the semivowel **l**, and sometimes **p** (40).

36. The dental nasal **n** remains unchanged before (1) the gutturals **k, kh, g, gh**; (2) the labials **p**,[2] **ph, b, bh, m**; (3) the soft dentals **d, dh, n**; generally also before **t** (40, 2); (4) the semivowels **y, r, v**, and the breathing **h**; (5) the cerebral and the dental sibilants **ṣ** and **s**.

a. Before **ṣ** and **s** a transitional **t** may be inserted, e.g. **áhan-t sáhasā**; **tā́n-t sám**.

II. Changes of Position.

37. The only four final consonants (27) liable to change of position are the **dental t** and **n**, the **labial m**, and **Visarjanīya**.

---

[1] The palatal and cerebral nasals, as has already been stated, do not occur as finals.

[2] Before **p** it sometimes becomes **ṃḥ**; cp. 40, 5.

a. The two dentals become palatal before palatals.[1]

b. Visarjanīya and m adapt themselves to the phonetic position of the following consonant.

1. Final t.

38. Final t before palatals (c, j, ch, ś) is changed to a palatal (c or j); e.g. **tác cákṣuḥ** for **tát cákṣuḥ**; **yātayáj-jana** for **yātayát-jana**; **rohíc chyāvā́** for **rohít śyāvā́**.[2]

2. Final n.

39. Final n before vowels is changed, after a long vowel, to Anusvāra: if the preceding vowel is ā, to m̐, if it is ī, ū, ṝ, to m̐r;[3] e.g. **sárgām̐ íva** for **sárgān**; **vidvā́m̐ agne** for **vidvā́n**; **paridhī́m̐r áti** for **paridhī́n**; **abhī́śūm̐r iva** for **abhī́śūn**; **nṝ́m̐r**[4] **abhí** for **nṝ́n**.

40. 1. Final n before all palatals that occur becomes palatal ñ; e.g. **ūrdhvā́ñ caráthāya** for **ūrdhvā́n**; **tā́ñ juṣethām** for **tā́n**; **vajriñ śnathihi** for **vajrin**; but since before ś a transitional t may be inserted, **vajrnt śnathihi** may (through **vajriñc**[5] **śnathihi**) become **vajṛñ chnathihi**.[6]

a. Before c the palatal sibilant is sometimes inserted[7] in the RV., the preceding n then becoming Anusvāra. This

---

[1] Final dentals never come into contact with initial cerebrals in the Saṃhitās. No initial cerebral mutes occur in the RV., and even the cerebral sibilant ṣ occurs only in **ṣáṣ** *six* and its compounds, and once in **ṣáṭ** for **ṣáṭ** from **ṣáh**.

[2] On the change of ś to ch after c see 53.

[3] Both m̐ and m̐r here represent original ns through m̐ḥ, the Sandhi of ḥ being here the same as that of āḥ īḥ ūḥ ṝḥ before vowels. ān īn ūn remain unchanged at the end of a Pāda (as being in pausā) before a vowel; e. g. **devayā́nān**ǀ**átandraḥ** (i. 72[7]).

[4] **ṝm̐r** occurs only once, otherwise remaining unchanged as ṝn, because two r sounds are avoided in the same syllable (cf. *Vedic Grammar*, § 79).

[5] That is, t before ś becomes c (38).

[6] That is, after c initial ś may become ch (53).

[7] There are no examples of the inserted sibilant before ch in the Saṃhitās.

insertion takes place, only when the sibilant is etymologically justified,[1] almost exclusively (though not without exception even here[2]) before **ca** and **cid**; e.g. **anuyājáṃś ca, amenā́ṃś cit**. In the later Saṃhitās the inserted sibilant becomes commoner, occurring even where not etymologically justified.[3]

2. Final n usually remains unchanged before dental t,[4] e.g. **tvā́vān tmánā**; but the dental sibilant is sometimes inserted in the RV., the preceding n then becoming Anusvāra. This insertion takes place, only when the sibilant is historically justified;[1] e.g. **āvádaṃs tvám** (for **āvádan**). In the later Saṃhitās the inserted sibilant becomes commoner, occurring even where not etymologically justified.[3]

3. Final n before initial l always becomes nazalized l̐; e.g. **jigīvā́l̐ lakṣám**.

4. Though final n generally remains unchanged before y, r, v, h (36, 4), **ān, īn, ūn** sometimes become **ām̐, īm̐r, ūm̐r** as before vowels (39); e.g. **devā́n havāmahe**; but **svávām̐ yātu** (for **svávān**); **dadvā́m̐ vā** (for **dadvā́n**); **pī́vo-annām̐ rayivṛ́dhaḥ** (for **annān**); **paṇī́m̐r hatam** (for **paṇī́n**); **dásyūm̐r yónau** (for **dásyūn**).

5. Final n when etymologically representing ns sometimes becomes **ṃḥ** before p (36, 2); thus **nṝ́ṃḥ pāhi** (for **nṝ́n**); **nṝ́ṃḥ pā́tram**; **svátavāṃḥ pāyúḥ** (for **svátavān**).

3. Final m.

41. Final m remains unchanged before vowels; e.g. **agním īḷe** *I praise Agni.*

---

[1] That is, in the nom. s. and acc. pl. m., which originally ended in ns.

[2] E.g. **paśū́ñ ca sthātṝ́ñ carátham** (i. 72[6]).

[3] As in the 3. pl. impf., e.g. **ábhavan** (originally **ábhavan-t**) and the voc. and loc. of n stems, e.g. **rā́jan** (which never ended in s).

[4] No initial th occurs in the RV.

a. In a very few instances the **m** is dropped and the vowels thereupon contract. This Sandhi is mostly indicated by the metre only: thus **rāṣṭrám ihá** must be pronounced **rāṣṭréhá**. It is very rarely written, as in **durgáhaitát** for **durgáham etát**. The Pada text, however, neither here (**durgáhā etát**) nor elsewhere analyses a contraction in this way.

42. Final **m** before consonants is changed

1. before the semivowel **r**, the three sibilants **ś, ṣ, s** and the breathing **h** to Anusvāra; e.g. **hótāraṃ ratnadhā́tamam** (for **hótāram**); **várdhamānaṃ své** (for **várdhamānam**); **mitrā́ṃ huve** (for **mitrám**).[1]

2. before **y, l, v** it becomes nasalized **y̐, l̐, v̐**; but the printed texts regularly use Anusvāra[2] instead; e.g. **sáṃ yudhí**; **yajñáṃ vaṣṭu.**[3]

3. before mutes it becomes the class nasal,[4] and **n** before **n**[5]; e.g. **bhadráṅ kariṣyási**; **tyáñ camasám**; **návan tváṣṭuḥ**; **bhadrán naḥ**. Most MSS. and the printed texts, however, represent this assimilated **m** by Anusvāra[6]; e.g. **bhadráṃ kariṣyási**; **tyáṃ camasám**; **návaṃ tváṣṭuḥ**; **bhadráṃ naḥ.**

a. This Sandhi is identical with that of **n** before the palatals **c, j, ch** (40) and the soft dentals **d, dh, n** (36, 3), and of **t** before **n** (33).

---

[1] Anusvāra seems to have been used originally before the sibilants and **h** only. Compounds like **sam-rā́j** show that **m** originally remained unchanged before **r** (49 *b*).

[2] The Taittirīya Prātiśākhya allows the optional use of Anusvāra before these semivowels.

[3] Forms with internal **m** like **yam-yámāna** and **ápa-mlukta** show that **m** originally remained unchanged in external Sandhi before **y** and **l**; and forms like **jagan-vā́n** (from **gam** *go*) point to its having at one time become **n** before **v** in Sandhi.

[4] Before labials it of course remains.

[5] This assimilation before **n** being identical with that of **d**, led to ambiguity in some instances and consequent wrong analysis by the Padapāṭha.

[6] Max Müller in his editions prints Anusvāra throughout, even before labials; Aufrecht has Anusvāra except before labials, where he retains **m**.

4. Final Visarjanīya.

43. Visarjanīya is the spirant to which the hard **s** and the corresponding soft **r** are reduced in pausā. If followed by a hard sound,

1. a palatal (**c, ch**) or a dental (**t**) mute, it becomes the corresponding sibilant; e. g. **devā́ś cakṛmá** (through **devā́ḥ** for **devā́s**); **pū́ś ca** (through **pū́ḥ ca** for **pū́r ca**);[1] **yás te** (for **yáḥ**); **áṇvībhis tánā** (for **-bhiḥ**).

a. Visarjanīya, if preceded by ĭ and ŭ, before dental **t** often becomes cerebral **ṣ**, which cerebralizes the following initial **t** to **ṭ**. In the RV. this occurs chiefly, and in the later Vedas only, before pronouns; e. g. **agníṣ ṭe**; **krátuṣ ṭám**; also **nákiṣ ṭanū́ṣu**. In compounds this change takes place in all the Saṃhitās; e. g. **dúṣ-ṭara** *hard to pass.*[2]

2. a guttural (**k, kh**) or labial (**p, ph**) mute, it either remains or becomes Jihvāmūlīya (ḫ) before the gutturals and Upadhmānīya (ḫ) before the labials; e. g. **víṣṇoḥ kármāṇi** (for **víṣṇos**); **índraḥ páñca** (for **índras**); **púnaḥ-punaḥ** (for **púnar**); **dyáuḥ pṛthivī́**.

a. After ă it often, in the RV., becomes **s**, and **ṣ** after ĭ, ŭ, ṝ;[3] e. g. **divás pári**; **pátnīvatas kṛdhi**; **dyáuṣ pitā́**. In compounds this change takes place regularly in all the Saṃhitās; e. g. **paras-pā́** *far-protecting*; **haviṣ-pā́** *drinking the offering*; **duṣ-kṛ́t** *evil-doing*, **duṣ-pád** *evil-footed.*

3. a simple sibilant, it either remains or is assimilated; e. g. **vaḥ śivátamaḥ** or **vaś śivátamaḥ**; **dévīḥ ṣáṭ** or **dévīṣ ṣáṭ**; **naḥ sapátnāḥ** or **nas sapátnāḥ**; **púnaḥ sám** or **púnas sám.**[4] Assimilation is undoubtedly the original Sandhi;

---

[1] This combination (in which Visarjanīya represents original **r**) is contrary to etymology, but is universal in sentence Sandhi and is subject to only two exceptions in compounds: **svàr-cakṣas** and **svàr-canas.**

[2] The only exception in the RV. is **cátus-triṃśat** *thirty-four.*

[3] This treatment before gutturals and labials corresponds to that before **t** (1 *a*), and was doubtless the original one in sentence Sandhi.

[4] This combination (in which Visarjanīya represents original **r**), though contrary to etymology, is universal in external Sandhi; but

but the MSS. usually employ Visarjanīya and European editions regularly do so.

a. Before a sibilant immediately followed by a hard mute, a final Visarjanīya is dropped; e.g. **mandíbhi stómebhiḥ** (through **mandíbhiḥ** for **mandíbhis**); **du-ṣṭutí** f. *ill-praise* (for **duṣ-ṣṭutí**). The dropping is prescribed by the Prātiśākhyas of the RV., the VS., and the TS., and is applied by Aufrecht in his edition of the RV.

b. Before a sibilant immediately followed by a nasal or semivowel, a final Visarjanīya is optionally dropped; e.g. **kṛta śrávaḥ** (for **kṛtaḥ**); **ni-svarám** (through **niḥ-** for **nis-**).

44. Visarjanīya (except after **a** or **ā**) before a **soft sound** (vowel or consonant) is changed to **r**; e.g. **ṛ́ṣibhir ī́ḍyaḥ** (through **ṛ́ṣibhiḥ** for **ṛ́ṣibhis**); **agnír hótā** (through **agníḥ** for **agnís**); **paribhū́r ási** (through **-bhū́ḥ** for **-bhū́s**).

45. 1. The final syllable **āḥ** (= **ās**) drops its Visarjanīya before vowels or soft consonants; e.g. **sutā́ imé** (through **sutā́ḥ** for **sutā́s**); **víśvā ví** (through **víśvāḥ** for **víśvās**).

2. The **final** syllable **aḥ** (= **as**)

a. drops its Visarjanīya before vowels except **a**; e.g. **khya ā́** (through **khyaḥ** for **khyas**).

b. before soft consonants and before **a**, is changed to **o**, after which **a** may be elided (21 *a*); e.g. **índavo vām** (through **índavaḥ** for **índavas**); **no áti** (through **naḥ** for **nas**) or **nó 'ti**.

46. The final syllables **aḥ** (= **ar**) and **āḥ** (= **ār**), in the comparatively few instances[1] in which the Visarjanīya represents an etymological **r**, do not form an exception (45) to the general rule (44); e.g. **prātár agníḥ**; **púnar naḥ**; **svàr druháḥ**; **vā́r avāyatī́**.

---

in compounds the original **r** frequently remains; e.g. **vanar-ṣád**, **dhūr-ṣád**, &c. This survival shows that **r** originally remained before sibilants in sentence Sandhi.

[1] **r** is original in **dvā́r** *door*, **vā́r** *protector*, **vā́r** *water*; **áhar** *day*, **uṣár** *dawn*, **ū́dhar** *udder*, **vádhar** *weapon*, **vánar** *wood*, **svàr** *light*; **antár** *within*, **avár** *down*, **púnar** *again*, **prātár** *early*; the voc. of **ṛ** stems, e.g. **bhrā́tar**; the 2. 3. s. of past tenses from roots in **ṛ**, e.g. **āvar**, from **vṛ** *cover*.

47. r followed by r is always dropped, a preceding short vowel being lengthened; e.g. **púnā rūpáṇi** for **púnar.**[1]

48. The three pronouns (nom. m. s.) **sáḥ** *that*, **syáḥ** *that*, **eṣáḥ** *this*, drop the Visarjanīya before all consonants;[2] e.g. **sá vánāni, syá dūtáḥ, eṣá tám.** The Visarjanīya is here otherwise treated regularly;[3] at the end of a Pāda, e.g. **padīṣṭá sáḥ । cakra eṣáḥ ।**, and before vowels, e.g. **só apáḥ, eṣó asura, eṣó 'mandan** (for **amandan**); **sá óṣadhīḥ, eṣá índraḥ.**

a. **sá,** however, generally combines in the RV. with a following vowel; e.g. **sásmai** for **sá asmai**; **séd** for **sá íd**; **sáuṣadhīḥ** for **sá óṣadhīḥ.**

Sandhi in Compounds.

49. The euphonic combination at the junction of the members of compounds is on the whole subject to the rules prevailing in external Sandhi. Thus the evidence of metre shows that contracted vowels are often to be pronounced with hiatus when the initial vowel of the second member is prosodically long (cp. 18 *b*); e.g. **yuktá-aśva** (for **yuktáśva**) *having yoked horses*, **devá-iddha** *kindled by the gods* (for **devéddha**), **ácha-ukti** (for **áchokti**) *invitation*.

Compounds have, however, preserved many archaisms of Sandhi which have disappeared from Sandhi in the sentence.

a. In **viś-páti** *lord of the house* and **viś-pátnī** *mistress of the house* **ś** remains instead of the **ṭ**[4] required by external Sandhi.

b. In **sam-ráj** *sovereign ruler* **m** appears instead of the Anusvāra required before **r** (42, 1), as in **saṃ-rájantam.**

---

[1] In a few instances **o** appears instead of **ā** (= **ar**) under the influence of **aḥ** as the pausal form of neuters in **as**; e. g. **ū́dho romaśám** (for **ū́dhā** = **ū́dhar**); also in the compound **aho-rātrá** for **ahā-**.

[2] **sáḥ,** however, twice retains it in the RV.; **sáḥ pálikníḥ** (v. 2[4]) and **sás táva** (viii. 33[16]) for **sáḥ.**

[3] **syáḥ** never occurs in the RV. before a vowel or at the end of a Pāda.

[4] **viś-páti** has in post-Vedic Sanskrit become **viṭpati.**

c. A group of compounds formed with **dus** *ill* as first member combine that adverb with a following **d** and **n** to **dū-ḍ** (= **duṣ-d**) and **dū-ṇ** (= **duṣ-n**) instead of **dur-d** and **dur-ṇ**:[1] **dū-ḍábha** (for **dus-dábha**) *hard to deceive*, **dū-ḍáś** *not worshipping* (for **dus-dáś**), **dū-ḍhí** *malevolent* (for **dus-dhí**); **dū-ṇáśa** *hard to attain* (for **dur-náśa**), **dū-ṇáśa** (for **dus-náśa**) *hard to attain* and *hard to destroy*.

d. Final (etymological) **r** in the first member is preserved in the RV. before hard sounds where the rules of external Sandhi require Visarjanīya or a sibilant (43): **vār-kāryá** *producing water*; **svàr-cakṣas** *brilliant as light*; **pū́r-pati** *lord of the stronghold*, **svàr-pati** *lord of heaven*; **vanar-ṣád** and **vanar-ṣád** *sitting in the wood*, **dhūr-ṣád** *being on the yoke*; **svar-ṣā́** *winning light*; **svàr-ṣāti** *acquisition of light*.[2] The VS. also has **ahar-páti** *lord of day*, and **dhūr-ṣā́h** *bearing the yoke*.[3]

e. Radical stems in **ir**, **ur** mostly lengthen their vowel before consonants (as they do within the simple word);[2] e.g. **dhūr-ṣád** *being on the yoke*, **pūr-yā́ṇa** *leading to the fort*.[4]

50. Compounds further often contain archaisms which though still existing in external Sandhi are obsolescent and disappear entirely in later periods of the language.

a. In six compounds **ścandrá** *bright* retains its old initial sibilant in the second member; e.g. **áśva-ścandra** *brilliant with horses*, **puru-ścandrá** *very brilliant*. As an independent word it is, excepting three occurrences in the RV., invariably **candrá**.[5]

b. A final **s** of the first member or an initial **s** of the second member is cerebralized; e.g. **duṣ-ṭára** *hard to cross*, **duḥ-ṣáha** *hard to resist*.[6]

---

[1] But **dur-** the form required by the later external Sandhi is already commoner in the RV.; e.g. **dur-dṛ́śīka**, **dur-ṇā́man**.

[2] Nouns ending in radical **r** retain the **r** before the ending **su** of the loc. pl.; **gīr-ṣú**, **dhūr-ṣú**, **pūr-ṣú**.

[3] External Sandhi gradually encroaches here in the later Saṃhitās; e.g. **svàḥ-pati** in the SV.

[4] But **gir** retains its short vowel in **gír-vaṇas** *fond of praise* and **gír-vāhas** *praised in song*.

[5] How nearly extinct **ścandrá** is as an independent word is indicated by the fact that in the analysis of its six compounds it always appears as **candrá** in the Padapāṭha.

[6] In post-Vedic Sanskrit only **dustara**, **duḥsaha**.

c. A dental **n** in the second member is cerebralized after **ṛ, r, ṣ** in the first member:

a. almost invariably, whether initial, medial, or final in a root, when a verbal derivative is compounded with a preposition that contains **r**; e. g. **nir-ṇíj** f. *bright garment*, **pári-hṇuta** *denied*, **prāṇ-á** m. *breath*; and even in suffixes, as **pra-yā́ṇa** n. *advance* (from **yā** *go*).

β. predominantly in other compounds when the second member is a verbal noun; e. g. **grāma-ṇī́** *chief of a village*, **dur-gā́ṇi** *dangers*, **pitṛ-yā́ṇa** *trodden by the fathers*, **rakṣo-hā́ṇ** *demon-slaying*; but **puro-yā́van** beside **prātar-yā́vaṇ** *going out early*. Cerebralization never takes place in **-ghn** the weak form of **-han** *killing*; nor in **akṣā-náh** *tied to the axle*, **kravya-vā́hana** *conveying corpses*, **carma-mná** *tanner*, **yuṣmā́-nīta** *led by you*.

γ. less regularly when the second member is an ordinary (non-verbal) noun; e. g. **urū-ṇasá** *broad-nosed*, **prá-ṇapāt** *great-grandson*; but **candrá-nirṇij** *having a brilliant garment*, **púnar-nava** *again renewed*.

d. The final vowel of the first member is often lengthened, especially before **v**; e. g. **annā́-vṛdh** *prospering by food*. This is often due to an old rhythmical tendency (also appearing in the sentence) to lengthen a vowel before a single consonant between two short syllables; e. g. **rathā-sáh** *able to draw the car*.

e. Final **ā** or **ī** of the first member is often shortened before a group of consonants or a long syllable; e. g. **ū́rṇa-mradas** *soft as wool* (**ū́rṇā**); **pṛthivi-ṣṭhā́** *standing on the earth* (**pṛthivī́**); **amīva-cā́tana** *driving away disease* (**ámīvā**).

Doubling of Consonants.

51. The palatal **ch** etymologically represents a double sound and metrically lengthens a preceding short vowel. For the latter reason the RV. Prātiśākhya prescribes the doubling of **ch** (in the form of **cch**) after a short vowel, and, as regards long vowels, after **ā́** only, when a vowel follows.[1] This rule is followed by Max Müller in his editions of the RV.; e. g. **utá cchadíḥ**, **ā-cchád-vidhāna**, but **me chantsat**.

---

[1] The Vedic MSS. almost invariably write the simple **ch**, and this practice is followed by Aufrecht in his edition of the Rigveda and L. v. Schroeder in his edition of the MS. It is also followed in the present work.

52. Before vowels final **ṅ** and **n**, if preceded by a short vowel, are doubled; e.g. **kīdṛ́ṅṅ índraḥ; áhann índraḥ.** Though the nasal is always written double, the metre shows that this rule is only partially applied as regards pronunciation in the RV.

a. The compound **vṛṣaṇ-aśvá** *with stallions as steeds* (**ṇ** = **n**) is an exception.

Initial Aspiration.

53. After a final **c**, initial **ś** regularly becomes **ch**; e.g. **yác chaknávāma** for **yád śaknávāma.**

a. The same change occasionally takes place after **ṭ**; thus **vípāṭ chutudrī́** (for **śutudrī́**); **turāṣā́ṭ chuṣmī́** (for **śuṣmī́**).

54. Initial **h**, after softening a preceding **k, ṭ, t, p,** is changed to the soft aspirate of that mute; e.g. **sadhryàg ghitā́** for **hitā́**; **ávāḍ ḍhavyā́ni** for **ávāṭ havyā́ni**; **sī́dad dhótā** for **sī́dat hótā.**

55. If **gh, dh, bh,** or **h** are at the end of a (radical) syllable beginning with **g, d,** or **b,** and lose their aspiration as final or otherwise, the initial consonants are aspirated by way of compensation;[1] e.g. from **dagh** *reach* the 3. s. injunctive is **dhak** (for **dagh-t**); **-búdh** *waking* becomes **-bhút**; **dúh** *milking* becomes **dhúk.**

B. Internal Sandhi.

56. The rules of internal Sandhi apply to the finals of roots and nominal and verbal stems before all endings of declension (except those beginning with consonants of the middle stem: 73 *a*) and conjugation, before primary suffixes (182, 1) and before secondary suffixes (182, 2) beginning with a vowel or **y**. Many of these rules agree with those of external Sandhi. The most important of those which differ from external Sandhi are the following:

---

[1] This is not really compensation but the survival of the original initial aspiration of such roots, which was lost owing to the avoidance of an aspirate at the beginning and end of the same syllable. Hence when the final aspirate disappeared, the initial returned.

Final Vowels.

57. In many cases before a vowel ī is changed to **iy**; u and ū to **uv**; e.g. **dhī + e = dhiy-é** dat. s. *for thought*; **bhū + i = bhuv-í** *on earth*; **yu-yuv-é** *has joined* (√**yu**).

58. Final ṛ before **y** becomes **ri** (154, 3); e.g. **kṛ** *make*: **kri-yáte** 3. s. pres. pass. *is done*. Final ṝ before consonant terminations is changed to **īr**, after labials to **ūr**; e.g. **gṝ** *swallow*: **gīr-yáte** *is swallowed*, **gīr-ṇá** *swallowed*; **pṝ** *fill*: **pūr-yáte** *is filled*, **pūr-ṇá** *filled*.

59. **e, ai, o, au** are changed before suffixes beginning with vowels or **y** to **ay, āy, av, āv** respectively; e.g. **śe + u = śay-ú** *lying*; **rai + e = rāy-é** *for wealth*; **go + e = gáv-e** *for a cow*; **nau + i = nāv-í** *in a boat*; **go + ya = gáv-ya** *relating to cows*.

Final Consonants.

60. The most notable divergence from external Sandhi is the unchangeableness of the final consonants (cp. 32) of roots and verbal or nominal stems before suffixes and terminations beginning with vowels, semivowels and nasals (while before other letters they usually follow the rules of external Sandhi); e.g. **vắc-ya** *to be spoken*, **duras-yú** *worshipping*, **yáśas-vat** *glorious*; **vác-mi** *I speak* (but **vákti** *speaks*); **voc-am** *I will speak*, **papṛc-yāt** *would mix*; **prắñc-aḥ** nom. pl. *forward*.

a. Before the primary suffix **na**, **d** is assimilated; e.g. **án-na** n. *food* (for **ad-na**), **chin-ná** *cut off* (for **chid-na**); and before the secondary suffixes **mant** and **maya**, **t** and **d**; e.g. **vidyún-mant** *accompanied by lightning* (**vidyút**) and **mṛn-máya** *consisting of clay* (**mṛ́d**). In the nominal case-form **ṣaṇ-ṇắm** (for **ṣaṭ-nắm**) *of six* (**ṣáṣ**) the final **ṭ** is assimilated.

61. Nominal or verbal stems ending in consonants and followed by terminations consisting of a single consonant, drop the termination altogether, two consonants not being tolerated at the end of a word (28). The final consonant that remains is then treated according to the rules of external

Sandhi. Thus **prāñc + s** nom. s. *forward* becomes **práṅ** (the **s** being first dropped, the palatals being changed to gutturals by 27, and the **k** being then dropped by 28); similarly **a-doh + t = á-dhok** *he milked* (55).

62. Aspirates followed by any sounds except vowels, semivowels or nasals (60) lose their aspiration; e. g. **randh + dhí = rand-dhí**[1] 2. s. aor. impv. *subject*; **labh + sya-te = lap-syate** (B.) 3. s. fut. *will take*; but **yudh-í** *in battle*; **ā-rábh-ya** *seizing*.

a. A lost soft aspirate is, if possible, thrown back before **dhv, bh, s** (55); e. g. **ind-dhvam** 2. pl. impv. of **indh** *kindle*; **bhud-bhís** inst. pl., **bhut-sú** loc. pl. But before **s** this rule applies only partially; thus from **dabh** *harm*: des. **díp-sa-ti** *desires to injure*, **dip-sú** *intending to hurt*; **bhas** *chew*: **báps-a-ti** *chews*; **guh** *hide*: des. **ju-guk-ṣa-tas** beside **aghukṣat**; **dah** *burn*: part. **dákṣat** beside **dhákṣant**; **duh** *milk*: aor. **á-dukṣat** beside **á-dhukṣat**.

b. But it is thrown forward on a following **t** and **th**,[2] which are softened; e. g. **rabh + ta = rab-dhá** *seized*; **ruṇádh + ti = ruṇád-dhi**; **rundh + tām = rund-dhām** 3. s. impv. *let him obstruct*.

63. Palatals. *a.* While **c** regularly becomes guttural before consonants (cf. 61; 27; 7 *b*), **j** in some cases (the majority) becomes guttural (**k, g**),[3] in others cerebral (**ṭ, ḍ, ṣ**);

---

[1] For the Vedic language tolerates two aspirates neither at the beginning and the end of the same syllable, nor at the end of one and the beginning of the next. On the other hand, there is no loss of aspiration in the root if an aspirate (after a vowel) which belongs to a suffix or a second member of a compound follows; e. g. **vibhú-bhis** *with the Vibhus*; **garbha-dhí** m. *breeding-place*. (The two imperatives **bo-dhí** *be* for **bho-dhí**, and **ja-hí** *strike* for **jha-hí**, follow the general rule.)

[2] Except in the case of the root **dhā** *place*, the weak stem of which **dadh** (following the analogy of 62 *a*) becomes **dhat** before **t** and **th** (cf. 134 B *b*).

[3] **j** always becomes **k** before a conjugational **s** (cp. 144, 4); e. g. **mṛk-ṣva** 2. s. impv. of **mṛj** *wipe*.

e. g. **uk-tá** *spoken* (√**vac**); **yuk-tá** *joined* (√**yuj**); **rug-ṇá** *broken* (√**ruj**: cp. 65); but **rā́ṭ** nom. s. *king* (for **rāj + s**); **mṛḍ-ḍhi** 2. s. impv. *wipe* (for **mṛj-dhi**); **rāṣ-ṭrá** *kingdom* (for **rāj-tra**: cp. 64).

b. The palatal **ś** before **bh** (73 *a*) normally becomes **ḍ**;[1] **k** before **s**;[2] always **ṣ** before **t** and **th** (cp. 64); e. g. **paḍ-bhís** *with looks* (**páś**), **viḍ-bhís** *with tribes* (**víś**); **vek-ṣyási** fut. of **viś** *enter*; **vik-ṣú** loc. pl. (**víś**); **dík** nom. s. of **díś** *direction*; **nák** nom. s. of **náś** *night*; **viṣ-ṭá** *entered* (√**viś**).

c. **c** and **j** (not **ś**) palatalize a following **n**; e. g. **yaj + na** = **yaj-ñá** *sacrifice*, but **praś-ná** *question*.

d. The **ch** of the root **prach** *ask* is treated like **ś**: **á-prāk-ṣīt** 3. s. **iṣ**- aor., **á-prāṭ** 3. s. **s**- aor. (= **á-prach-s-t**); **pṛṣ-ṭá** *asked*, **práṣ-ṭum** inf. *to ask*.

64. Cerebrals change following dentals to cerebrals (39); e. g. **iṣ + tá** = **iṣ-ṭá**; **av-iṣ + dhi** = **aviḍ-ḍhí** 2. s. impv. **iṣ**- aor. of **av**; **ṣaṇ + nām** (for **ṣaṭ-nām**) = **ṣaṇ-ṇā́m** (cp. 33, 60 *a*).

a. While the cerebral sibilant **ṣ** seems always[3] to become a cerebral mute (**ṭ** or **ḍ**) in declension and becomes **ḍ** in conjugation, it regularly becomes **k** before **s** in conjugation (cp. 63 *b* and 67); e. g. **dviṣ + s** = **dvíṭ** nom. s. *hating*, **vi-prúṣ + s** = **vi-prúṭ** *drop*, **vi-prúḍ-bhis** inst. pl.; **av-iṣ + dhi** = **aviḍ-ḍhí** 2. s. impv. **iṣ**- aor. of **av** *favour*; **dviṣ + sa-t** = **dvik-ṣat** 3. s. inj. **sa**- aor. of **dviṣ** *hate*.

65. Change of dental n to cerebral ṇ.

A preceding cerebral **ṛ**, **ṝ**, **r**, **ṣ** (even though vowels, guttural or labial mutes or nasals, **y**, **v**, or **h** intervene) changes a dental **n** (followed by a vowel or **n**, **m**, **y**, **v**) to cerebral **ṇ**; e. g. **nṛ + nām** = **nṛṇā́m** *of men*; **pitṝ + nām** = **pitṝṇā́m** *of fathers*; **var + na** = **várṇa** m. *colour*; **uṣ + na** = **uṣṇá** *hot*;

---

[1] **g** in cases of **díś** and **dṛ́ś**: **dig-bhyás**, **dṛg-bhís**.

[2] But in the nom. **víṭ** (**víś**), **ví-pāṭ** (**ví-pāś**) and **spáṭ** *spy* (**spáś**) the cerebral has taken the place of the phonetic **k** owing to the influence of other forms in which the cerebral is phonetic.

[3] No example occurs of this sound before the **su** of the loc. plur.

krámaṇa n. *step* (vowels and labial nasal intervene), **arkéṇa** (guttural and vowel); **gṛbhṇā́ti** *seizes* (labial mute); **brahmaṇyā́** *devotion* (vowel, h, labial nasal, vowel; n followed by y).[1]

This rule is followed throughout within a word even when a ṣ which it contains is produced by Sandhi; e.g. **u ṣuvāṇáḥ** (for **u suvānáḥ**).

a. The cerebralization of n takes place almost as regularly in verbs compounded with the prepositions **prá** *before*, **párā** *away*, **pári** *round*, **nír** (for **nís**) *out*, as well as in nominal derivatives of these combinations; e.g. **parā-ṇúde** (**nud** *thrust*), **pra-ṇetṛ́** *guide* (**nī** *lead*); **pári-hṇuta** *denied*; **prā́ṇiti** *breathes* (√**an**); **nír haṇyāt** (**han** *strike*), but not in forms with **ghn** (e.g. **abhi-pra-ghnánti**); **prá hiṇomi**, but **pari-hinómi** (**hi** *impel*).

b. In nominal compounds n is usually cerebralized when it is the initial of the second member in the RV.; e.g. **dur-ṇā́man** *ill-named*, **prá-ṇapāt** *great-grandson*; but **tri-nāká** n. *third heaven*. It is less frequent medially; e.g. **pūrvāhṇá** *forenoon*, **vṛ́ṣa-maṇas** *manly-spirited*, but **ṛ́ṣi-manas** *of far-seeing mind*; **nṛ-pā́ṇa** *giving drink to men*, but **pari-pā́na** n. *drink* (cp. 50 *c β*).

c. Cerebralization is even extended to external Sandhi in a closely connected following word, most often initially in the enclitic **nas** *us*, rarely in other monosyllables such as **nú** *now*, **ná** *like*, occasionally in other words also;[2] e.g. **sahó ṣú ṇaḥ**; **pári ṇetā́ . . . viśat.** It sometimes occurs medially, oftenest in the enclitic pronoun **ena** *this*; e.g. **índra eṇam.** It occasionally appears in accented words also after final r; e.g. **gór óheṇa.**

Table showing when n changes to ṇ.

ṛ ṝ r ṣ	in spite of intervening vowels, gutturals (including h), labials (including v), and y	change n to ṇ	if followed by vowels, n, m, y, v.

[1] There are two exceptions to this rule in the RV., the gen. plur. **úṣṭrānām** and **rāṣṭrā́nām**.

[2] After the final cerebral ṭ of **ṣáṭ** (for **ṣáṣ** *six*), assimilated to the following n (33), initial dental n is cerebralized in **ṣáṇ-ṇavati** *ninety-six* (TS.) and in **ṣaṇ ṇiramimīta** (B.).

66 A. **The dental n**

1. remains unchanged before **y** and **v**; e.g. **han-yáte** *is slain*; **tan-v-āná** *stretching*, **índhan-van** *possessed of fuel* (**indhana**), **āsan-vánt** *having a mouth*.

2. as final of a root becomes Anusvāra before **s**; e.g. **jí-ghāṃ-sa-ti** *wishes to kill* (√**han**); also when it is inserted before final **s** or **ṣ** in the neuter plural (71 *c*; 83); e.g. **énāṃs-i** n. pl. of **énas** *sin*; **havíṃṣ-i** n. pl. of **havís** *oblation* (83).

B. **The dental s**

1. **becomes** dental **t** as the final of roots or nominal stems

a. before the **s** of verbal suffixes (future, aorist, desiderative) in the three verbs **vas** *dwell*, **vas** *shine*, and **ghas** *eat*; thus **a-vāt-sīs** *thou hast dwelt*; **vát-syati** *will shine*; **ji-ghat-sati** *wishes to eat* (171, 5) and **jighat-sú** *hungry*.[1]

b. before case-endings with initial **bh** in the reduplicated perf. participle and in four other words: thus **jāgṛvád-bhis** inst. pl. *having awakened*; **uṣád-bhis** from **uṣás** f. *dawn*; **mād-bhís, mād-bhyás** from **mā́s** m. *month*; **svátavad-bhyas** from **svá-tavas** *self-strong*. This change was extended without phonetic justification[2] to the nom. acc. s. n. in the RV., as **tatan-vát** *extending far*.

2. **disappears**

a. between mutes; e.g. **á-bhak-ta** 3. s. s- aor., for **á-bhak-s-ta** beside **á-bhak-ṣ-i**, of **bhaj** *share*; **caṣ-ṭe** for **cakṣ-ṭe** (= original **caś-s-te**) 3. s. pres. of **cakṣ** *speak*; **a-gdha** *uneaten* for **a-ghs-ta** from **ghas** *eat*.

A similar loss occurs in verbal compounds formed with

---

[1] The change of **s** to **t** before the **t** of the 3. s. of a past tense, as in **vy-àvāt** *has shone forth* from **vi-vas**, is probably not a phonetic change, but is rather due to the influence of the 3. s. of other preterites with **t**; ***á-vās-t** having thus become **á-vāt** instead of ***ávās**.

[2] There having been no case-ending **s** here. No example occurs in the RV. and AV. of a loc. pl. in **vat-su**.

the preposition **ud** and the roots **sthā** *stand* and **stambh** *support*; e. g. **út-thita** and **út-tabhita** *raised up*.

b. before **dh**; e. g. **śā-dhi** for **śās-dhi** 2. s. impv. of **śās** *order*; **ā-dhvam** 2 pl. mid. impv. of **ās** *sit*; also after becoming **ṣ** and cerebralizing the following dental; e. g. **á-sto-ḍhvam** (for **á-sto-ṣ-dhvam**) 2. pl. aor. of **stu** *praise*.

67. Change of dental s to cerebral ṣ.

A preceding vowel except **ă** (even though Anusvāra[1] intervenes) as well as **k, r, ṣ** change dental **s** (followed by a vowel, **s, t, th, n, m, y, v**) to cerebral **ṣ**;[2] e. g. from **havís** *oblation*: **havíṣ-ā** inst. s., **havíṃṣ-i** nom. pl.; **cákṣus** n. *eye*: **cákṣuṣ-ā** inst. s., **cákṣūṃṣ-i** nom. pl.; **havíṣ-ṣu** loc. pl.; **sráj** f. *wreath*: **srak-ṣú** loc. pl.; **gír** f. *song*: **gīr-ṣú** loc. pl.; **tí-ṣṭhati** *stands* from **sthā** *stand*; **cákṣuṣ-mant** *possessing eyes*; **bhavi-ṣyáti** *will be* from **bhū** *be*; **su-ṣvápa** *has slept* from **svap** *sleep*. But **sarpíḥ** (final); **mánas-ā** (**a** precedes); **us-rá**[3] *matutinal*.

a. The cerebralization of **s** regularly takes place in the RV. initially in verbal compounds after prepositions ending in **i** and **u**, as well as in nominal derivatives from such compound verbs; also after the preposition **nís** *out*; e. g. **ní ṣīda** *sit down*, **ánu ṣṭuvanti** *they praise*; **niḥ-ṣáhamāṇaḥ** *conquering*.[4]

b. In nominal compounds, **s** is more usually cerebralized than not, when the initial **s** of the second member is preceded by vowels other than **ă**; e. g. **su-ṣóma** *having abundant Soma*. But **s** is often retained in the RV., not only when **ṛ** or **r** follows, as in **hṛdi-spṛ́ś** *touching the heart*, **ṛṣi-svará** *sung by seers*, but also when there is no such cause to prevent

---

[1] The **s**, however, remains in forms of **hiṃs** *injure*, **niṃs** *kiss*, and **puṃs** *man*, probably under the influence of the strong forms **hinásti**, **púmāṃsam**, &c.

[2] Words in which **s** otherwise follows **r** or any vowel but **ă** must be of foreign origin, as **bṛ́saya** a demon, **bísa** n. *root fibre*, **busá** n. *vapour*.

[3] **s** remains when immediately followed by **r** or **ṛ**, e. g. **tisrás**, **tisṛ́bhis**, **tisṛṇā́m** f. of **tri** *three*; **usrás** gen., **usrí** and **usrā́m** loc., beside **uṣar** voc. *dawn*.

[4] The **s** remains unchanged when followed by **ṛ** (even when **t** intervenes) or **r** (even though **a** intervenes, with additional **m** or **v** in **smar** *remember* and **svar** *sound*).

the change; e. g. **gó-sakhi** beside **gó-ṣakhi** *possessing cattle.* After **r** the **s** becomes **ṣ** in **svar-ṣā́** *light winning*, **svàr-ṣāti** f. *obtainment of light.*

c. Cerebralization is even extended to external Sandhi in initial **s** after a final **i** and **u** in the RV. when the two words are syntactically closely connected. This change chiefly takes place in monosyllabic pronouns and particles, such as **sá**, **syá**, **sīm**, **sma**, **svid**, and particularly **sú**; e.g. **ū ṣú**. It also occurs in numerous verbal forms and participles; e.g. **yūyáṃ hí ṣṭhā́** *for ye are*, **diví ṣán** *being in heaven.* In other words the change is rare; e.g. **trí ṣadhásthā.**[1] In the later Saṃhitās this form of external Sandhi is very rare except in the combination **ŭ ṣú.**

Table showing when **s** changes to **ṣ**.

Vowels except ă (in spite of intervening Anusvāra), k, r, ṣ	change s to ṣ	if followed by vowels, t, th, n, m, y, v.

68. The labial **m** remains unchanged before **y**, **r**, **l** (cp. 60 and 42 B 1); e. g. **yam-yámāna** *being guided*, **vam-rá** m. *ant*, **ápa-mlukta** *concealed.* But before suffixes beginning with **v** it becomes **n**; e.g. **jagan-vā́n** *having gone* (from **gam** *go*).

69. *a.* The breathing **h** becomes **k** in all roots before **s**; e.g. **dhák-ṣi** 2. s. pres. from **dah** *burn*; **sak-ṣi** 2. s. pres. from **sah** *prevail.*

b. In roots beginning with **d** it is treated like **gh** before **t**, **th**, **dh**; e.g. **dah + tá = dag-dhá** *burnt* (62 *b*), **duh + tām = dug-dhām** 3. du. pres. Similarly treated is the oldest form of the perf. pass. participle of the root **muh**: **mug-dhá** *bewildered.*

c. **h** in all other roots is treated like an aspirate cerebral, which after changing a following **t**, **th**, **dh** to **ḍh** and

[1] In the RV. occurs the Sandhi **yájuḥ ṣkannám** (for **skannám**) without cerebralization of the **nn** (cp. 65).

lengthening a preceding short vowel, is dropped; e. g. sah + ta = sā-ḍhá[1] *overcome*; rih + ta = rī-ḍhá *licked*; muh + ta = mū-ḍhá (AV.) *bewildered*; vah + ta = ū-ḍhá;[2] vah + dhvám = vo-ḍhvám (VS.).[3]

d. An exception to *c* is the root nah *bind*, in which h is treated as dh: nad-dhá *bound*. An exception to both *b* and *c* is the root dṛh: dṛ-ḍhá *firm* (begins with d and has a short vowel).[4]

CHAPTER III

DECLENSION

70. Declension, or the inflexion of nominal stems by means of endings that express the various syntactical relations represented by the cases, is most conveniently treated, owing to characteristic difference of form, meaning, and use, under (1) nouns (including adjectives); (2) numerals; (3) pronouns.

In Vedic there are

a. **three genders**: masculine, feminine, and neuter;

b. **three numbers**: singular, dual, and plural;

c. **eight cases**: nominative, vocative, accusative, instrumental, dative, ablative, genitive, locative.[5]

---

[1] In all these past participles the ḍh is in the RV. written as ḷh.

[2] With Samprasāraṇa.

[3] Through vaẓh-dhvam: aẓh here becoming o just as original as (through az) becomes o (cp. 45 *b*).

[4] Before this ḍh the vowel ṛ never appears lengthened, but it is prosodically long (cp. 8, note 2).

[5] This is the order of the cases in the Hindu Sanskrit grammarians, excepting the vocative, which is not regarded by them as a case. It is convenient as the only arrangement by which such cases as are identical in form, either in the singular, the dual, or the plural, may be grouped together.

71. The normal **case-endings** added to the stem are the following:—

	Singular. M. F.	Singular. N.	Dual. M. F.	Dual. N.	Plural. M. F.	Plural. N.
N.	s	—[b]				
V.	—[a]	—	au	ī	as	i[c]
A.	am	—				
I.	ā				bhis	
D.	e		bhyām		bhyas	
Ab.	as					
G.			os		ām	
L.	i				su	

a. The vocative is the same (apart from the accent) as the nominative in all numbers except the *masc. and fem. sing.* of vowel stems generally and the *masc. sing.* of consonant stems in **-an, -man, -van; -mant, -vant; -in; -as; -yāṃs, -vāṃs; -tar.**

b. The nom. acc. sing. has the bare stem excepting the words in **-a,** which add **m.**

c. The nom. voc. acc. plur. neut. before the ending i insert n after a vowel stem and before a single final mute or sibilant of a consonant stem (modifying the n according to the character of the consonant: cp. 66 A 2).

72. An important distinction in declension is that between the **strong** and the **weak** stem. It is fully developed only in derivative consonant stems formed with the suffixes **-añc, -an, -man, -van; -ant, -mant, -vant; -tar; -yāṃs, -vāṃs.** In the first four and in the last the weak stem is further reduced before vowel endings. The stem here has three forms, which may be distinguished as **strong, middle,** and **weakest.**

a. Shift of accent was the cause of the distinction. The stem, having been accented in the strong cases, here naturally preserved its full form; but it was shortened in the weak cases by the accent falling on the endings. For a similar reason the last vowel of the strong stem, if long, is regularly shortened in the vocative, because the accent always shifts to the first syllable in that case.

73. The strong stem appears in the following cases:

Nom. voc. acc. sing.
Nom. voc. acc. dual } of masc. nouns.[1]
Nom. voc. (not acc.) plur.
Nom voc. acc. plural only of neuters.

a. When the stem has three forms, the middle stem appears before terminations beginning with a consonant[2] (**bhyām, bhis, bhyas, su**); the weakest before terminations beginning with a vowel in the remaining weak cases; e.g. **pratyáñc-au** nom. du.; **pratyág-bhis** inst. pl.; **pratīc-ós** gen. du. (93).

b. In neuters with three stems, the nom. voc. acc. sing. are middle, the nom. voc. acc. du. weakest; e.g. **pratyák** sing.; **pratīc-í** du.; **pratyáñc-i** pl. (93). The other cases are as in the masc.

NOUNS.

74. Nominal stems are, owing to divergences of inflexion, best classified under the main divisions of consonant and vowel declension.

I. Stems ending in consonants[3] may be subdivided into A. unchangeable; B. changeable.

II. Stems ending in vowels into those in A. a and ā; B. i and u; C. ī and ū.

---

[1] Excepting names of relationship in -**tar** (101), nearly all nouns with changeable stems form their feminine with the suffix -ī (100).

[2] Changeable stems are named in this grammar in their strong and original form, though the middle form would be more practical, inasmuch as that is the form in which changeable stems appear as prior member in compounds.

[3] Some Sanskrit grammars begin with the vowel declension in a (II. A) since this contains the majority of all the declined stems in the language. But it appears preferable to begin with the consonant declension which adds the normal endings (71) without modification.

I. A. Unchangeable Stems.

75. These stems are for the most part primary or radical, but also include some secondary or derivative words. They end in consonants of all classes except gutturals (these having always become palatals, which however revert to the original sound in certain cases). They are liable to such changes only as are required by the rules of Sandhi before the consonant terminations (cp. 16 *a*). Masculines and feminines ending in the same consonant are inflected exactly alike; and the neuters differ only in the acc. s. and nom. voc. acc. du. and pl.

76. The final consonants of the stem retain their original sound before vowel terminations (71); but when there is no ending (i.e. in the nom. sing., in which the **s** of the m. and f. is dropped), and before the ending **su** of the loc. pl., they must be reduced to one of the letters **k, ṭ, t, p** or Visarjanīya (27) which respectively become **g, ḍ, d, b** or **r** before the terminations beginning with **bh**.

a. The voc. sing. m. f. is the same as the nom. except in stems in (derivative) **as** (83).

b. Forms of the nom. voc. acc. pl. n. seem not to occur in the Saṃhitās[1] except in the derivative **as, is, us** stems, where they are common; e.g. **ápāṃsī, arcíṃṣi, cákṣūṃṣi.**

Stems in Dentals.

77. Paradigm **tri-vṛ́t** m. f. n. *threefold.*

Sing.		Dual.		Plur.	
N. m. f. **trivṛ́t**	n. **trivṛ́t**	N.A. m.f.	**trivṛ́t-ā,**	N. m. f.	**trivṛ́t-as**
A. m. f. **trivṛ́t-am**	n. **trivṛ́t**		**trivṛ́t-au**	A. m. f.	**trivṛ́t-as**
I.	**trivṛ́t-ā**	I. D. Ab.	[**trivṛd-bhyām**]	I.	**-bhiṣ**
D.	**trivṛ́t-e**			D.Ab.	[**-bhyas**]
Ab. G.	**trivṛ́t-as**	G.	[**trivṛ́t-os**]	G.	**trivṛ́t-ām**
L.	**trivṛ́t-i**	L.	**trivṛ́t-os**	L.	**trivṛ́t-su**
				m. f. V.	**trívṛt-as.**

[1] But in the Brāhmaṇas are found from **-bhṛt** *bearing*, **-vṛt** *turning*, **-hu-t** *sacrificing* the N. pl. n. forms **-bhṛ́nti, -vṛnti, -hunti.**

1. Of the **stems** in **t** most are radical, nearly thirty of them being formed with a determinative **t** added to roots ending in the short vowels **i, u, ṛ**; e.g. **jí-t** *conquering*, **śrú-t** *hearing*, **kṛ́-t** *making*. Nearly all of them, however, appear as the last member of compounds, except **cít** f. *thought*; **dyú-t** f. *brilliance*; **nṛ́t** f. *dancing*; **vṛ́-t** f. *host*. From **sarva-hu-t** *offering completely* occurs in N. pl. n. the form **sarva-hunti** in the AB. There are also a few derivative stems formed with the suffixes **-vat, -tāt, -it, -ut,** and secondary **-t**; e.g. **pra-vát** f. *height*, **devá-tāt** f. *divine service*; **sar-ít** f. *stream*; **mar-út** m. *storm-god*; **yákṛ-t** n. *liver*, **śákṛ-t** n. *excrement*.

2. There are only three stems in **th**: **káprth**, n. *penis*, **páth** m. *path*, **abhi-śnáth** adj. *piercing*.

3. *a*. About 100 stems end in radical **d**, all but a few being roots used as the final member of compounds; e. g. nom. **adri-bhíd** *mountain-cleaving*. Only eight occur as monosyllabic substantives: **níd** f. *contempt*, **bhíd** f. *destroyer*, **víd** f. *knowledge*, **úd** f. *wave*, **múd** f. *joy*, **mṛ́d** f. *clay*, **hṛ́d** n. *heart* (used in weak cases only); and **pád** m. *foot*. The latter lengthens its vowel in the strong cases:

Sing. N. **pā́t**. A. **pā́d-am**. I. **pad-ā́**. D. **pad-é**. Ab.G. **pad-ás**. L. **pad-í**.
Du. N.A. **pā́d-ā**. I. Ab. **pad-bhyā́m**. G.L. **pad-ós**.
Pl. N. **pā́d-as**. A. **pad-ás**. I. **pad-bhís**. D. **pad-bhyás**. G. **pad-ā́m**. L. **pat-sú**.

b. There are also six stems formed with derivative **d** (suffixal **-ad -ud**), seemingly all feminine: **dṛṣ-ád** and **dhṛṣ-ád** *nether millstone*, **bhas-ád** *hind quarters*, **van-ád** *longing*, **śar-ád** *autumn*, **kak-úd** *summit*, **kāk-úd** *palate*.

4. There are about fifty radical stems in **dh**, simple or compound. They are almost restricted to m. and f., no distinctively n. forms (N. A. du. pl.) occurring and only four forms being used as n. in the G. L. s. Seven stems appear

as monosyllabic nouns: **vṛ́dh** *strengthening* as a masc. adj., the rest as fem. substantives: **nádh** *bond*; **srídh** *foe*; **kṣúdh** *hunger*; **yúdh** *fight*; **mṛ́dh** *conflict*; **vṛ́dh** *prosperity*; **spṛ́dh** *battle*.

5. Radical stems in **n** are formed from half a dozen roots. Four of these are monosyllabic substantives: **tán** f. *succession*; **rán** m. *joy*; **ván** m. *wood*; **svár** adj. *sounding*.[1] There are also the compound adjectives **tuvi-ṣván** *roaring aloud* and **go-ṣán** *winning cows*. **Han** *slaying* occurs as the final member of at least thirty-five compounds, but as it follows for the most part the analogy of the **an** stems, it will be treated under these (92).

Stems in Labials.

78. These stems, which end in **p**, **bh**, and **m** only, are not numerous. No neuters occur in the first two and only one or two in the last.

1. All the monosyllabic stems in **p** are fem. substantives. They are: **áp** *water*, **kṛ́p** *beauty*, **kṣáp** *night*, **kṣíp** *finger*, **ríp** *deceit*, **rúp** *earth*, **víp** *rod*. There are also about a dozen compounds, all adjectives except **vi-ṣṭáp** f. *summit*. Three of the adjectives occur as f., the rest as m.; e. g. **paśu-tṛ́p** m. *delighting in cattle*.

a. **áp** lengthens the stem in the N.V. pl. **ā́p-as**, a form sometimes used for the A. also. The forms occurring are: Sing. I. **ap-ā́**. Ab.G. **ap-ás**. Du.N. **ā́p-ā**. Pl.N.V. **ā́p-as**. A. **ap-ás**. I. **ad-bhís**. D.Ab. **ad-bhyás**. G. **ap-ā́m**. L. **ap-sú**.

2. The six uncompounded stems in **bh** are all f. substantives: **kṣúbh** *push*, **gṛ́bh** *seizing*, **nábh** *destroyer*, **śúbh** *splendour*, **stúbh** *praise* (also adj. *praising*), and **kakúbh** *peak*. There are also more than a dozen compounds: the substantives are all f., the rest being m. or f. adjectives; there are

---

[1] The accent of these stems is irregular in remaining on the radical syllable (App. III. 11, 1), except **tanā́** (beside **tánā**) and **vanā́m**.

no neuters. The cases of **tri-ṣṭúbh** f. *triple praise* (a metre) are: Sing. N. **triṣṭúp.** A. **triṣṭúbh-am.** I. **triṣṭúbh-ā.** D. **triṣṭúbh-e.** Ab. **triṣṭúbh-as.** L. **triṣṭúbh-i**; Pl. A. **triṣṭúbh-as.**

a. **nábh** lengthens its vowel in the N. pl. **nā́bh-as.** A. **nábh-as.**

3. There are five or six monosyllabic stems in **m**, and one compound: **śám** n. *happiness*, **dám** n. (?) *house*, **kṣám, gám, jám** f. *earth*, **hím** m. (?) *cold*; **saṃ-nám** f. *favour*.

a. **Gám** and **jám** syncopate in the s. I.Ab.G.: **gm-ā́, jm-ā́; gm-ás, jm-ás; kṣám** syncopates in the Ab. G. s. and lengthens its vowel in N. du. pl.: **kṣm-ás; kṣā́m-ā; kṣā́m-as. Dám** has the G. s. **dán** (for **dám-s**) in the expressions **pátir dán** and **pátī dán** = **dám-patis** and **dám-patī** *lord of the house* and *lord and lady of the house*.

Stems in Palatals.

79. The palatals (**c, j, ś**) undergo a change of organ when final and before consonant terminations (cp. 63). **c** always becomes guttural (**k** or **g**), **j** and **ś** nearly always become guttural, but sometimes cerebral (**ṭ** or **ḍ**).

1. The unchangeable stems in **c**[1] when uncompounded are monosyllabic and almost exclusively f. substantives. **Tvác** *skin*, however, twice occurs as a m., and **krúñc** *curlew* is m. Compounds, as adjectives, are often m., but only one form occurs as a n., in the adv. **ā-pṛ́k** *in a mixed manner*. **Vā́c** *speech* would be declined as follows:

Sing. N.V. **vā́k.** A. **vā́c-am** (Lat. *voc-em*). I. **vāc-ā́.** D. **vāc-é.** Ab.G. **vāc-ás.** L. **vāc-í.**
Dual. N.A.V. **vā́c-ā, vā́c-au.** I. **vā́g-bhyā́m.**
Plur. N.V. **vā́c-as.** A. **vā́c-as** (rarely **vāc-ás**). I. **vāg-bhís.** D.Ab. **vāg-bhyás.** G. **vāc-ā́m.**

---

[1] Stems in derivative **añc** are changeable (93).

Similarly declined are :—**tvác** *skin*[1]; **síc** *hem*; **rúc** *lustre*, **śúc** *flame*, **srúc** *ladle*; **ṛ́c** *stanza*, **mṛ́c** *injury*; **ni-mrúc** *sunset* and other compounds. **Krúñc** forms its N. s. **krúṅ**, du. **krúñcau**.

2. There is only one stem in ch, formed from the root **pṛch** *ask*: N. du. m. **bandhu-pṛ́ch-ā** *asking after kinsmen*; also the D. and A. infinitive forms **pṛch-é** *to ask*, **sam-pṛ́ch-e** *to greet*; **vi-pṛ́ch-am** and **sam-pṛ́ch-am** *to ask*.

3. *a*. Uncompounded radical stems in j are mostly f. substantives; but **áj** *driver*, **víj** *stake at play* are m., and **yúj**,[2] **rā́j**, **bhrā́j** are m. as well as f. Neut. forms occur in compound adjectives, but never the distinctively n. endings of the N.A.V. du. and pl.[3]

When the j is derived from a guttural, it becomes a guttural in the N. s. and before consonant endings; when derived from an old palatal, it becomes a cerebral in the N. s.[4] and before consonants, but **k** before the **su** of the L. pl.

Thus in the N. **ū́rk** (**ū́rj**) *vigour*; **nir-ṇík** (**nir-ṇíj**) *bright garment*; but **bhrā́ṭ** m. *shining* (**bhrā́j**), **rā́ṭ** m. *king*, f. *mistress*; L. pl. **srak-ṣú** *garlands* (**sráj**), **pra-yák-ṣu** *offerings* (**pra-yáj**).

a. The N. of **ava-yā́j** f. *share of the sacrificial oblation* and of **ā́vayāj** m. *priest who offers the oblation* is anomalous in dropping the j and adding the s of the nom.: **ava-yā́s**, **ā́vayās** (cp. 28 *a*).

b. There are seven m. and f. adj. or subst. formed with the suffixes **-aj** and **-ij**: **á-svapn-aj** *sleepless*, **tṛṣṇ-áj** *thirsty*,

---

[1] From **vyac** *extend* occurs the strong form **uru-vyáñcam** *far extending*, and from **sac** *accompany* only the strong forms A. **-sā́c-am**, and N. pl. **-sā́c-as**.

[2] This word meaning *companion* also has a nasalized form in N.A. s. du.: **yúṅ** (for **yúṅk**), **yúñj-am**, **yúñj-ā**.

[3] But in a Brāhmaṇa **-bhāj** *sharing* forms the N. pl. n. form **-bhāñji**.

[4] Except in **ṛtv-ík** from **ṛtu-íj** m. *sacrificing in due season, priest* (from **yaj** *sacrifice*).

dhṛṣ-áj *bold*, **san-áj** *old*; **uś-íj** *desiring*, **bhur-íj** f. *arm*, **vaṇ-íj** m. *trader*. There is also the n. **ásṛj**[1] *blood*.

uśíj m.f. would be declined as follows:

Sing. N. **uśík**. A. **uśíj-am**. I. **uśíj-ā**. D. **uśíj-e**. G. **uśíj-as**.

Du. N. **uśíj-ā**. G.L. **uśíj-os**.

Pl. N. **uśíj-as**. A. **uśíj-as**. I. **uśíg-bhis**. D. **uśíg-bhyas**. G. **uśíj-ām**.

4. There are about sixty monosyllabic and compound stems in **ś** formed from about a dozen roots. Nine monosyllabic stems are f.: **dáś** *worship*, **díś** *direction*, **dṛ́ś** *look*, **náś** *night*, **páś** *sight*, **píś** *ornament*, **práś** *dispute*, **víś** *settlement*, **vríś** *finger*. Two are m.: **íś** *lord* and **spáś** *spy*. All the rest are compounds (about twenty of them formed from **-dṛ́ś**). Some half-dozen cases of the latter are used as neuter, but no distinctively n. forms (N.A. du. pl.) occur.

The **ś**, as it represents an old palatal, normally becomes cerebral **ḍ** before **bh**, but in **díś** and **dṛ́ś** a guttural. Before the **su** of the L. pl. it phonetically and regularly becomes **k**. It usually also becomes **k** in the N. s. (which originally ended in s), as **dík**, **nák**; but cerebral **ṭ** in **spáś** and **vi-spáś** *spy*, **víś** and **ví-pāś** a river.

The normal forms, if made from **víś** *settlement*, would be:

N.V. **víṭ**. A. **víś-am**. I. **viś-ā́**. D. **viś-é**. Ab.G. **viś-ás**. L. **viś-í**.

Du. N.A. **víś-ā**, **víś-au**.

Pl. N.A. **víś-as**. I. **viḍ-bhís**. D. **viḍ-bhyás**. G. **viś-ā́m**. L. **vik-ṣú**.

a. The N. of some compounds of **dṛ́ś** is nasalized, as **kī-dṛ́ṅ** (for **kī-dṛ́ṅk**) *of what kind?*, but **tā-dṛ́k** *such*.

The N. s irregularly represents the final palatal (28 *a*) in **puroḍā́ś** m. *sacrificial cake*: N. **puroḍā́s**, A. **puroḍā́śam**.

---

[1] This word is of obscure origin, but the j probably represents a reduced suffix.

Stems in Cerebrals.

80. The only cerebral stems that occur end in **ḍ** and **ṣ**. Of the former there are only two: **íḍ** f. *praise* (only found in s. I. **īḍ-ā́**) and **íḍ** f. *refreshment* (only in s. I. **iḍ-ā́** and G. **iḍ-ás**).

There are a number of stems from about a dozen roots ending in **ṣ** preceded by **i**, **u**, **ṛ**, or **k**. Seven of these are uncompounded: **íṣ** f. *refreshment*, **tvíṣ** f. *excitement*, **dvíṣ** f. *hatred*, **ríṣ** f. *injury*; **úṣ** f. *dawn*; **pṛ́kṣ** f. *satiation*; **dadhṛ́ṣ** *bold*. The rest are compounds of the above or of **miṣ** *wink*, **sriṣ** *lean*, **ukṣ** *sprinkle*, **muṣ** *steal*, **pruṣ** *drip*, **dhṛṣ** *dare*, **vṛṣ** *rain*; **ákṣ** *eye*. The **ṣ** becomes **ṭ** in the N., and **ḍ** before **bh**, but is of course dropped when **k** precedes; e.g. N. **dvíṭ**, **vi-prúṭ** f. *drop*, **an-ák** *eyeless, blind*; I. pl. **vi-prúḍ-bhis**.

a. The final becomes **k** in the adverbial neuter form **dadhṛ́k** *boldly*.

Stems in h.

81. There are some eighty stems formed from about a dozen roots. All three genders are found in their inflexion, but the neuter is rare, occurring in two stems only, and never in the plural. Of monosyllabic stems **níh** *destroyer*, **míh** *mist*, **gúh** *hiding-place*, **rúh** *sprout* are f., **drúh** *fiend* is m. or f., **sáh** *conqueror* is m., **máh** *great*, m. and n. All the rest are compounds, more than fifty being formed from the three roots **druh** *hate*, **vah** *carry*, **sah** *overcome*; over thirty of them from the last.[1] The two stems **uṣṇíh** f. a metre, and **saráh** *bee* are obscure in origin.

a. As **h** represents both the old guttural **gh** and the old palatal **jh** it should phonetically become **g** or **ḍ** before **bh**, but the cerebral represents both in the only two forms that occur with a **bh** ending. In the only L. pl. that occurs,

---

[1] **upā-náh** f. *shoe* occurs only in the L. s. **upā-náh-i**. Judging by the inflexion of the word in classical Sanskrit the **h** would become a dental in the N. s. and before consonant endings.

anaḍút-su (from **anaḍ-váh**), the **h** unphonetically became **ṭ**, which has been dissimilated to **t**. In the N. the phonetic **k** appears in the six forms **-dhak**, **-dhuk**, **-dhruk**, **-ruk**, **-spṛk**, **uṣṇík**, and the unphonetic **ṭ** in the three forms **-vāṭ**, **ṣā́ṭ**, **saráṭ**.

b. Stems formed from **vah**[1] and **sah** lengthen the radical vowel in the strong cases, the former always, the latter generally.

The forms actually occurring if made from **sáh** *victorious* would be:

Sing. N.V. m. f. **ṣā́ṭ**.[2] A. m. f. **sā́h-am**. I. **sah-ā́**. D. **sah-é**. Ab.G. **sah-ás**. L. **sah-í**.

Du. N.A.V. m. f. **sā́h-ā** and **sā́h-au**. N.A. n. **sah-ī́**.

Pl. N.A.V. m. f. **sā́h-as**. A. m. **sáh-as** and **sah-ás**; f. **sáh-as**. D. **ṣaḍ-bhyás**. G. m. **sah-ā́m**. L. m. **ṣaṭ-sú**.

Stems in r.[3]

82. There are over fifty stems in radical **r**.[4] The preceding vowel is nearly always **i** or **u**, only two stems containing **ā** and three **a**. Twelve stems are monosyllabic (seven f.,[5] three m.,[6] two n.[7]), the rest being compounds. The **r** remains before the **su** of the L. pl., and the radical vowel

[1] **anaḍ-váh** being a changeable stem with three forms is treated under the irregular changeable stems (96).

[2] When **h** becomes **ṭ** the initial **s** is cerebralized.

[3] There are no stems in **l**; while the five which may be regarded as ending in the semivowels **y** or **v** are treated below (102) as **ai**, **o**, or **au** stems.

[4] The stems in which the **r** is derivative (and preceded by **a**), in the suffixes **-ar** and **-tar**, are treated below (101) as **ṛ** stems.

[5] **gír** *praise*, **dvā́r** *door*, **dhúr** *burden*, **púr** *stronghold*, **tár** *star*, **psúr** *victuals*, **stár** *star*.

[6] **gír** *praising*, **vā́r** *protector*, **múr** *destroyer*.

[7] **vā́r** *water*, **svàr** *light*.

is lengthened in the N. s. and before consonant endings. The forms occurring, if made from **púr**, would be:

Sing. N. **pū́r**. A. **púr-am**. D. **pur-é**. Ab.G. **pur-ás**. L. **pur-í**.

Du. N.A. **púr-ā**, **púr-au**.

Pl. N.V. **púr-as**. A. **púr-as**. I. **pūr-bhís**. D. **pūr-bhyás**. G. **pur-ā́m**. L. **pūr-ṣú**.

a. **dvā́r** has the weakened A. pl. form **dúras** (also once **durás** and once **dvā́ras**), the only weak case occurring.

b. **tár** occurs in one (strong) form only, N. pl. **tā́r-as**, and **stár** in one (weak) form only, I. pl. **stṛ́bhis**.[1]

c. **svàr** n. *light* has the two contracted forms D. **sūr-é**, G. **sū́r-as**.[2] It drops the case-ending in the L. s.[3] **súar**.

Stems in s.

83. 1. The radical **s** stems number about forty. A dozen are monosyllabic, five being m.: **jñā́s** *relative*, **mā́s** *month*, **vás**[4] *abode*, **puṃs** *male*,[5] **śā́s** *ruler*; two f.: **kā́s** *cough*, **nā́s** *nose*; five n.: **ā́s** *face*, **bhā́s** *light*, **mā́s** *flesh*, **dós** *arm*, **yós** *welfare*. The rest are compounds, e.g. **su-dā́s** *giving well, liberal*.

a. Before **bh** the **s** becomes **d** in the two forms I. **mād-bhís** and D. **mād-bhyás**, and **r** in the only other one that occurs: **dor-bhyā́m**.

b. The A. pl. has the accentuation of weak cases in **mās-ás** and **jñās-ás**.

2. The derivative stems in **s** are formed with the suffixes **-as**, **-is**, **-us**, and are, with few exceptions, neuter substantives. All of them lengthen their final vowel in the N.V.A. pl. n., e.g. **mánāṃsi**, **jyótīṃṣi**, **cákṣūṃṣi**. The m. and f. are mostly compounds with these stems as their final member.

a. The **as** stems consist almost entirely of neuters, which

---

[1] With irregular accent. [2] With the accent of a disyllabic.

[3] Like the an stems (90, 2). [4] This word might be a feminine.

[5] This word will be treated later (96, 3) as an irregular changeable stem.

are accented on the root, as **mán-as** *mind*, but these as final members of adjective compounds may be inflected in all three genders. There are also a few primary masculines, which are accented on the suffix, being either substantives, as **rakṣ-ás** m. *demon*, or adjectives (some of which occur also in the f. as well as n.), as **ap-ás** *active*; and one primary f., **uṣ-ás** *dawn*.

The N. s. m. f. lengthens the vowel of the suffix: e. g. **áṅgirās** m., **uṣā́s**[1] f., **su-mánās** m. f. In about a dozen compounds the long vowel appears (owing to the influence of the m.) in the n. also; e. g. **ū́rṇa-mradās** *soft as wool*.

Before endings with initial **bh** the suffix **as** becomes **o** (45 *b*). The forms actually occurring, if made from **áp-as**, n. (Lat. *ŏpus*) *work* and **ap-ás** m. f. *active* would be as follows:

Sing. N. **ápas**; **apā́s**. A. **ápas**; **apás-am**. I. **ápas-ā**; **apás-ā**. D. **ápas-e**; **apás-e**. Ab. **ápas-as**; **apás-as**. L. **ápas-i**; **apás-i**. V. **ápas**.

Du. N.A.V. **ápas-ī**; **apás-ā**, **apás-au**.[2] D. **apó-bhyām**. G. **ápas-os**.

Pl. **ápāṃs-i**; **apás-as**. I. **ápo-bhis**; **apó-bhis**. D. **ápo-bhyas**; **apó-bhyas**. G. **ápas-ām**; **apás-ām**. L. **ápas-su**; **apás-su**.

Similarly N. n. **yáśas** *glory*, m. f. **yaśā́s** *glorious*; f. **apsarā́s** *nymph*.

a. A number of forms have the appearance of being contractions in the A. s. and N.A. pl. m. f.: **ām** = **asam** and **ās** = **asas**; thus **mahā́m** *great*, **vedhā́m** *ordainer*, **uṣā́m** *dawn*, **jarā́m** *old age*, **medhā́m** *wisdom*, **vayā́m** *vigour*, **án-āgām** *sinless*, **apsarā́m**. Pl. N. m. **áṅgirās**, **án-āgās**, **ná-vedās** *cognisant*, **sa-jóṣās** *united*; f. **medhā́s**, **á-joṣās** *insatiable*, **ná-vedās**, **su-rā́dhās** *bountiful*. A. m. **án-āgās**, **su-medhā́s** (?) *intelligent*; f. **uṣā́s**.

---

[1] The vowel of this word is optionally lengthened in the A. s., N. A. du., N. V. pl.: **uṣā́s-am** beside **uṣás-am**, &c.

[2] The ending **au** is here very rare and occurs chiefly in the later Saṃhitās.

b. The is stems, numbering about a dozen, consist primarily of neuters only. When they form final members of compounds, they are secondarily inflected as m.; only one single such form, N. s. **svá-śocis** *self-radiant*, occurs as a f.

The final s becomes ṣ before vowel-endings and the L. pl. **su**, and r before **bh**. The inflexion of the n. differs from that of the m. in the A. s., N.A. du. and pl. The actual forms occurring, if made from **śocís** *glow* in the n. and from **-śocis** m. (when it differs from the n.), would be:

Sing. N. **śocís**; A. **śocís**; m. **-śociṣ-am.** I. **śocíṣ-ā.** D. **śocíṣ-e.** Ab.G. **śocíṣ-as.** L. **śocíṣ-i.** V. **śócis.**
Pl. N.A. **śocíṃṣ-i**, m. **-śociṣ-as.** I. **śocír-bhis.** D. **śocír-bhyas.** G. **śocíṣ-ām.** L. **śocíṣ-ṣu** (67).

a. **āśís** f. *prayer*, which is not really an is stem, being derived from **ā+śis** (the reduced form of the root **śās**), is inflected thus: N. **āśís.** A. **āśíṣ-am.** I. **āśíṣ-ā.** Pl. N. A. **āśíṣ-as.**

c. The **us** stems, numbering at least sixteen exclusive of compounds, comprise several primary masculines as well as neuters; three of the latter when compounded are also inflected as f. Eleven of the **us** stems are n. substantives, all but one (**janús** *birth*) accented on the radical syllable; four of these (**árus, cákṣus, tápus, vápus**) are also used as m. adjectives. Three of the exclusively m. **us** stems are adjectives accented on the suffix, while two (**náhus, mánus**) are substantives accented on the root.

The final **s** becomes **ṣ** before vowel endings, and **r** before **bh**. The inflexion of the n. is the same as that of the m. except in the A. s. and N.A. du. pl. The only f. forms (about half a dozen) occur in the N. and A.: e. g. N. **cákṣus** *seeing*, A. du. **tápuṣ-ā** *hot*.

The actual forms occurring, if made from **cákṣus** *eye* as n. and *seeing* as m. would be:

Sing. N. **cákṣus.** A. **cákṣus**; m. **cákṣuṣ-am.** I. **cákṣuṣ-ā.** D. **cákṣuṣ-e.** Ab.G. **cákṣuṣ-as.** L. **cákṣuṣ-i.**
Du. N.A. **cákṣuṣ-ī**; m. **cákṣuṣ-ā.** D. **cákṣur-bhyām.**
Pl. N.A. **cákṣūṃṣ-i**; m. **cákṣuṣ-as.** I. **cákṣur-bhis.** D. **cákṣur-bhyas.** G. **cákṣuṣ-ām.**

I. B. Changeable Stems.

84. Regular changeable stems are found only among derivative nouns formed with suffixes ending in the dentals **t**, **n**, **s**, or the palatal **c**. Those in **t** are formed with the suffixes **-ant**, **-mant**, **-vant**; those in **n** with **-an**, **-man**, **-van**, and **-in**, **-min**, **-vin**; those in **s** with **-yāṃs** and **-vāṃs**; those in **c** with **-añc** (properly a root meaning *to bend*). The stems in **-ant** (85–86), **-in** (87), **-yāms** (88) have two forms, strong and weak; those in **-an** (90–92), **-vāṁs** (89), and **-añc** (93) have three, strong, middle, and weakest (73).

Nouns with Two Stems.

85. Stems in **-ant** comprise present,[1] future, and aorist participles (156) active (m. and n.).[2] The strong stem is in **-ant**, the weak in **-at**[3]; e. g. **ad-ánt** and **ad-at** *eating* from **ad** *eat*. These participles are inflected in the m. and n. only, the f. having a special stem in ī.[2] The n. inflexion differs from the m. in the N.V.A. s. du. pl. only. The accent, if resting on the suffix, shifts in weak cases to the endings that begin with vowels.

---

[1] Excepting those of the reduplicating verbs and a few others that follow their analogy (85 *b*).

[2] On the formation of the f. stems see 95.

[3] In Latin and Greek the distinction was lost by normalization: G. *edentis*, ἔδοντος.

MASCULINE.

	SINGULAR.		DUAL.		PLURAL.
N.	adán[1] (Gk. ἔδων)		adánt-ā -au		adánt-as (Gk. ἔδοντες)
V.	ádan		ádant-ā -au		ádantas
A.	adánt-am (Lat. *edentem*)		adánt-ā -au		adat-ás
I.	adat-ā́			I.	adád-bhis
D.	adat-é	D.	adád-bhyām	D.Ab.	adád-bhyas
Ab.G.	adat-ás	G.	adat-ós	G.	adat-ā́m
L.	adat-í			L.	adát-su

NEUTER.

	SINGULAR	DUAL	PLURAL
N.A.	adát	adat-ī́	adánt-i

Other examples are: **árc-ant** *singing*, **sī́d-ant** (**sad** *sit*), **ghn-ánt** (**han** *slay*), **y-ant** (**i** *go*), **s-ánt** (**as** *be*); **páśy-ant** *seeing*; **ich-ánt** *wishing*; **kṛṇv-ánt** *doing*; **sunv-ánt** *pressing*; **bhañj-ánt** *breaking*; **jān-ánt** *knowing*; **janáy-ant** *begetting*; **yúyuts-ant** *wishing to fight*; fut. **kariṣy-ánt** *about to do*; aor. **sákṣ-ant** (**sah** *overcome*).

a. The analogy of these participles is followed by a few adjectives that have lost their old participial meaning: **ṛhánt** *weak*, **pṛ́ṣant** *spotted*, **bṛhánt** *great*, **rúśant** *brilliant*; also the substantive **dánt**[2] *tooth*. The adj. **mahánt** *great*, also originally a participle,[3] deviates from the participial declension in lengthening the vowel of the suffix in the strong forms:

Sing. N. m. **mahā́n**; n. **mahát**. A. **mahā́nt-am**. I. **mahat-ā́**.
Du. N.A. **mahā́nt-ā, -au**. D. **mahád-bhyām**.
Pl. N. **mahā́nt-as**. A. **mahat-ás**. I. **mahád-bhis**. L. **mahát-su**.

---

[1] For original **adánt-s**, cp. Lat. *edens*.

[2] Probably an old participle of **ad** *eat* with prehistoric loss of the initial **a** like **s-ánt** *being* from **as** *be*.

[3] From the root **mah** (originally **magh**). Cp. Lat. *mag-nu-s*.

b. The participles of verbs with a reduplicating present base, i. e. those of the third class (127, 2) and intensives (172), do not distinguish a strong stem,[1] in other words, have **at** throughout; e. g. **bíbhyat** *fearing*, **ghánighn-at** *repeatedly killing* (√**han**). The analogy of these participles is followed by a few others formed from unreduplicated bases: **dáś-at** *worshipping*, **śás-at** *instructing*; also **dákṣ-at** and **dhákṣ-at** aor. part. of **dah** *burn*. A few others, again, originally participles, have come to be used as substantives with a shift of accent to the suffix. Three of these are f. and two m.: **vahát**,[2] **sravát**[3] f. *stream*; **vehát**[4] f. *barren cow*; **vāghát** m. *sacrificer*; **saścát**[5] m. *pursuer*. Besides the first three substantives just mentioned there are no feminines except the adjective **a-saścát** *unequalled*[6] when used as a f. Hardly any n. forms occur except from the old reduplicated participle **jág-at** *going*, *living* (from **gā** *go*), used chiefly as a substantive meaning *the animate world*. The inflexion of these reduplicated stems in **at** is like that of the compounded radical **t** stems (77), the accent never shifting to the endings.

The forms occurring if made from **dádat** *giving* (√**dā**) would be:

Sing. N. m. n. **dádat**. A. m. **dádat-am**. I. **dádat-ā**. D. **dádat-e**. G. **dádat-as**. L. **dádat-i**.

Plur. N.A. **dádat-as**. I. **dádad-bhis**. G. **dádat-ām**.

86. The **adjective stems** formed with the suffixes **-mant** and **-vant**, which both mean *possessing*, are inflected exactly alike and differ from the stems in **-ant** solely in lengthening the vowel of the suffix in the N. s. m.[7] The V. of these stems

---

[1] Which has been weakened because here the accent is regularly on the reduplicative syllable.

[2] But **váh-ant** *carrying* as a participle.

[3] But **sráv-ant** *flowing*. [4] The derivation of this word is uncertain.

[5] But **sáśc-at** as a participle (from **sac** *accompany*).

[6] Lit. *having no equal*; but **á-saścant-ī** as the f. of the participle **sáścat**.

[7] The f. is formed with **ī** from the weak stem: **mat-ī**, **vat-ī** (95).

is regularly[1] formed with **mas** and **vas**[2]; e.g. **háviṣ-mas** from **haviṣ-mant**; **bhága-vas** from **bhága-vant**.

From **gó-mant** *possessed of cows* would be formed:

Sing. N. m. **gómān**; n. **gómat**. A. m. **gómant-am**. L. **gó-mat-i**. V. m. **gómas**.

Pl. N. m. **gómant-as**; n. **gómānt-i**.[3] A. m. **gómat-as**. L. **gómat-su**.

87. Adjective stems are formed with the suffixes **-in**, **-min**, **-vin**, which mean *possessing*. Those in **-in** are very common, those in **-vin** number nearly twenty, but there is only one in **-min**: **ṛg-mín** *praising*. They are declined in the m. and n. only;[4] but the n. forms are very rare, occurring in the s. N. I. G. only. These stems sometimes come to be used as m. substantives; e.g. **gāth-ín** *singer*. As in all derivative stems ending in **n**, the vowel of the suffix is lengthened in the N. s. m., and the **n** disappears in that case (in the n. also) and before consonant endings.

The forms actually occurring, if made from **hast-ín** *having hands*, would be as follows:

Sing. m. N. **hastī́**. A. **hastín-am**. I. **hastín-ā**. D. **hastín-e**. Ab.G. **hastín-as**. L. **hastín-i**. V. **hástin**.

Du. m. N.A. **hastín-ā, -au**. I.D. **hastí-bhyām**. G.L. **hastín-os**.

Pl. m. N. **hastín-as**. I. **hastí-bhis**. D. **hastí-bhyas**. G. **hastín-ām**. L. **hastí-ṣu**.

Sing. n. N. **hastí**. I. **hastín-ā**. G. **hastín-as**.

---

[1] There are sixteen in the **RV**. in **vas** and only three in the later **van** (of which there are eight more in the **AV**.). There are six vocatives in **mas** in the RV., but no example of the form in **man**.

[2] There are also vocatives in **vas** from stems in **van** and **vāṃs** (cp. the V. in **yas** from stems in **yāṃs**).

[3] The only two forms that occur are **ghṛtávānti** and **paśumánti**. The Padapāṭha reads **vanti** and **manti** in these forms, and the lengthening of the vowel seems metrical.

[4] The f. stem is formed with **ī**: **aśvín** *possessing horses*; f. **aśvín-ī**.

88. 3. **Comparative** stems are formed with the suffix **yāṃs**, which is nearly always added with the connecting vowel **ī** to the accented root. Only two stems are formed with **yāṃs** exclusively: **jyā́-yāṃs** *greater* and **sán-yāṃs** *older*; six others are formed with **yāṃs** as well as **ī-yāṃs**; e.g. **bhū́-yāṃs** and **bháv-īyāṃs** *more*. The strong stem is reduced in the weak cases, by dropping the nasal and shortening the vowel, to **yas**. These stems are declined in the m. and n. only.[1] No forms of the du. occur, and in the pl. only the N. A. G. are found. The V. s. ends in **yas**.[2] The forms actually occurring, if made from **kán-īyāṃs** *younger*, would be as follows:

MASCULINE.

	SINGULAR.	PLURAL.
N.	**kánīyān**	**kánīyāṃsas**
A.	**kánīyāṃs-am**	**kánīyas-as**
I.	**kánīyas-ā**	
D.	**kánīyas-e**	
Ab. G.	**kánīyas-as**	G. **kánīyas-ām**
L.	**kánīyas-i**	
V.	**kánīyas**	

NEUTER.

N.A.	**kánīyas**	**kánīyāṃs-i**

The I.D.Ab.G. sing. n., identical with the m., also occur.

Nouns with Three Stems.

89. 1. The stem of the **perf. part.** active is formed with the suffix **vāṃs**. This is reduced in the weak cases in two ways: before consonant terminations (by dropping the nasal

[1] The f. is formed by adding ī to the weak stem, e.g. **préyas-ī** *dearer*.

[2] Cp. the **mant, vant** (86), and the **vāṃs** (89) stems.

and shortening the vowel) to **vas** which becomes **vat**[1]; and before vowel terminations (by loss of the nasal accompanied by Samprasāraṇa) to **us** which becomes **uṣ**. There are thus three stems: **vāṃs, vat,** and **uṣ**. The accent always rests on the suffix in uncompounded forms. The inflexion is restricted to the m. and n.[2] The only specifically n. form occurring is the A. s. The V. s. is regularly formed with **vas**.[3] The forms actually occurring, if made from **cakṛvā́ṃs** *having done*, would be as follows:

MASCULINE.

	SINGULAR.	DUAL.	PLURAL.
N.	**cakṛvā́n**	**cakṛvā́ṃs-ā**	**cakṛvā́ṃs-as**
A.	**cakṛvā́ṃs-am**	**cakṛvā́ṃs-ā**	**cakrúṣ-as**
I.	**cakrúṣ-ā**		**cakṛvád-bhis**
D.	**cakrúṣ-e**		
Ab.G.	**cakrúṣ-as**		G. **cakrúṣ-ām**
V.	**cákṛ-vas**		

NEUTER.

N.A.	**cakṛ-vát**	—	—

a. In about a dozen of these participles the suffix **vāṃs** is preceded by **i** (either as a reduced form of final radical **ā** or as a connecting vowel):

jajñi-vā́n (from **jñā** *know*), **tasthi-vā́n** (**sthā** *stand*), **papi-vā́n** (**pā** *drink*), **yayi-vā́n** (**yā** *go*), **rari-vā́n** (**rā** *give*); **īy-i-vā́n** (**i** *go*), **jagm-i-vā́n** (beside **jagan-vā́n**[4]: **gam** *go*), **papt-i-vā́n** (**pat** *fly*), **proṣ-i-vā́n** (**pra + vas** *dwell*), **viviś-i-vā́n** (**viś** *enter*);

[1] On the change of **s** to **t** cp. 66 B 1 *b*.

[2] The f. is formed with **ī** from the weakest stem: e. g. **cakrúṣ-ī**.

[3] Cp. the **mant, vant** (86), and the **yāṃs** stems (88).

[4] On the change of **m** to **n** see 68.

ok-i-vấn[1] (uc *be wont*). This i is dropped before **uṣ**; e. g. **tasth-úṣ-ā, īy-úṣ-as, jagm-úṣ-e.**

90. 2. **Nouns in an, man, van** include a large number of words, those in van being by far the commonest, those in **an** the least frequent. These stems are almost restricted to m. and n.;[2] but some forms of adjective stems serve as f., and there is one specifically f. stem **yóṣ-an** *woman*.

In the strong cases the **a** of the suffix is usually lengthened, e. g. **ádhvān-am**; but in half a dozen **an** and **man** stems it remains unchanged, e. g. **arya-máṇ-am.** In the weak cases the **a** is often syncopated before vowel endings, though never when **man** and **van** are preceded by a consonant, e. g. I. s. **grấvṇā** from **grấvan** *pressing stone* (but **áś-man-ā** *stone*), while before consonant endings the final **n** disappears,[3] e. g. **rấja-bhis.** In the RV. syncopation never takes place in the N.A. du. n., nor with one exception (**śata-dấvni**) in the L. s.

As in all other **n** stems, the nasal is dropped in the N. s., e. g. m. **ádhvā**, n. **kárma.** But there are two peculiarities of inflexion which, being common to these three groups, do not appear elsewhere in the consonant declension. The ending of the L. s. is in the RV. dropped more often than not; e. g. **mūrdhán** beside **mūrdhán-i** *on the head.* In the N.A. pl. n. both the final **n** of the stem and the termination i are, in the RV., dropped in nineteen stems, e. g. **kárma**;[4] while they are retained in eighteen, e. g. **kármāṇi.**

1. The **an** stems, which are both m. and n.,[5] besides the

---

[1] With reversion to guttural, lack of reduplication, and strengthened radical vowel.

[2] The stems in an and man form their f. with ī added to their weakest form; those in van substitute varī.

[3] That is, the a represents an original sonant nasal.

[4] Seven of these appear with ā in the Saṃhitā text, but with ă, like the rest, in the Pada text. The evidence of the Avesta indicates that the ā form of the Saṃhitā is the older.

[5] Six or seven adjectival forms are used as f.

F 2

one f. **yóṣan**, are not numerous. In the strong forms **ṛbhu-kṣán** *chief of the Ṛbhus*, **pūṣ-án**, a god, and **yóṣ-an** *woman* retain short **a**; **ukṣ-án** *ox* and **vṛ́ṣ-an** *bull* fluctuate between **a** and **ā**. In the inflexion of these stems (unlike those in **man** and **van**) the concurrence of three consonants is not avoided; e. g. **śīrṣṇ-ā́**, I. of **śīrṣ-án**.

a. Six stems belong etymologically to this group though seeming to belong to one of the other two. They are: **yú-v-an**[1] m. *youth*, **śv-án**[1] m. *dog*, **ṛjí-śvan**[2] m. a man, **mātarí-śvan**[2] m. a demi-god, **ví-bhv-an**[3] *far-reaching*, **pári-jm-an**[4] *going round*. **śīrṣ-án** n. is an extended form of **śíras** *head* = **śir(a)s-án**.

The normal forms, if made from **rā́jan** *king*, would be:

SINGULAR.	DUAL.	PLURAL.
N. **rā́jā**	N.A. **rā́jān-ā, -au**	N. **rā́jān-as**
A. **rā́jān-am**		A. **rā́jñ-as**
V. **rā́jan**[5]		
I. **rā́jñ-ā**	I.D. **rā́ja-bhyām**	I. **rā́ja-bhis**
D. **rā́jñ-e**		D. **rā́ja-bhyas**
Ab.G. **rā́jñ-as**	G. **rā́jñ-os**	G. **rā́jñ-ām**
L. **rā́jan-i**, **rā́jan**		L. **rā́ja-su**

The n. differs in the N.A. only. No example of the s. N.A. occurs (p. 70, n. 1). But the du. of **áhan** *day* is **áhan-ī**, pl. **áhān-i**.

2. The stems in **man** are about equally divided between m. and n., the former being mostly agent nouns, the latter verbal abstracts. About a dozen forms from these stems as final members of compounds are used as feminines.[6] In

---

[1] See below, 91. 3, 4.

[2] Probably from **śū** *grow*.

[3] From **bhū** *be*.

[4] From **gam** *go*.

[5] The V. of **mātarí-śvan** is **mā́tari-śvas** as if from a stem in **van**.

[6] No certain examples of f. formed with **ī** from **man** stems are found in the RV., though the AV. has five such at the end of compounds.

the strong forms **arya-mán** m. a god, **t-mán** m. *self*, **jé-man** *victorious* retain the short vowel in the suffix. In the weak forms, even when the suffix is preceded by a vowel, about a dozen forms do not syncopate the **a**, e.g. **bhū́-man-ā**, **dā́-man-e**. In the I. s. seven stems not only syncopate, but drop either the **m** or the **n** as well: **prathi-n-ā́**, **pre-ṇ-ā́**, **bhū-n-ā́**, **mahi-n-ā́**, **vari-ṇ-ā́**; **drāghm-ā́**, **raśm-ā́**.

The normal forms, if made from **áś-man** (Gk. ἄκμων) m. *stone*, would be:—

Sing. N. **áśmā**. A. **áśmān-am**. I. **áśman-ā**.[1] D. **áśman-e**.[1] Ab.G. **áśman-as**. L. **áśman-i** and **áśman**. V. **áśman**.

Du. N.A.V. **áśmān-ā**. L. **áśman-os**.

Plur. N.V. **áśmān-as**. A. **áśman-as**. I. **áśma-bhis**. D. **áśma-bhyas**. G. **áśman-ām**. L. **áśma-su**.

The n. differs in the N.A. only. These cases from **kárman** *act* are:

Sing. **kárma**. Du. **kármaṇ-ī**. Pl. **kármāṇ-i**, **kármā**, **kárma**.

3. The stems in **van** are chiefly verbal adjectives and are almost exclusively declined in the m. Hardly a dozen of them make n. forms, and only five or six forms are used as f.[2] In the strong cases there is only one example of the **a** remaining short: **anarváṇ-am**. In the weak cases, when the suffix is preceded by a vowel, the **a** is always syncopated in the Saṃhitā text except in the forms **dā-ván-e**, **vasu-ván-e**, and **ṛtā́-van-i**. The V. is usually formed in **van**, but there are four in **vas**: **ṛtā-vas**, **eva-yā-vas**, **prātar-it-vas**, **vi-bhā-vas**.[3]

---

[1] When the suffix is preceded by a vowel, the **a** is generally syncopated, as **mahi-mn-ā́**, also **mahi-n-ā́**, &c.

[2] The f. of these stems is otherwise formed with **ī**, which is, however, never added to **van**, but regularly to a collateral suffix **vara**. Twenty-five such stems in **varī** are found in the RV.

[3] Cp. the **mant**, **vant**, **yāṃs**, **vāṃs** stems.

The normal forms occurring, if made from **grā́-van** m. *pressing-stone*, would be:

Sing. N. **grā́vā**. A. **grā́vāṇ-am**. I. **grā́vṇ-ā**. D. **grā́vṇ-e**. Ab.G. **grā́vṇ-as**. L. **grā́vaṇ-i** and **grā́van**. V. **grā́van**.
Du. N.A.V. **grā́vāṇ-ā, -au**. I. **grā́va-bhyām**. G. **grā́vṇ-os**.
Pl. N.V. **grā́vāṇ-as**. A. **grā́vṇ-as**. I. **grā́va-bhis**. D. **grā́va-bhyas**. G. **grā́vṇ-ām**. L. **grā́va-su**.

The n. differs in the N.A. only. These cases (the du. does not occur) formed from **dhánvan** *bow* are: Sing. **dhánva**. Pl. **dhánvāni, dhánvā, dhánva.**

Irregular Stems in an.

91. 1. **Pánth-an** m. *path*, forming the strong stem **pánthān**, is best treated under the irregular stems in radical ā (97 A. 2 *a*).

2. **áh-an** n. *day*, otherwise regular, supplements the N. s. with **áh-ar**.[1]

3. **śv-án** m. *dog*, otherwise inflected like **rā́jan**, takes Samprasāraṇa in its weakest stem **śún**,[2] which, as representing an originally disyllabic stem,[3] retains the accent:

SINGULAR.	DUAL.	PLURAL.
N. **śvā́** (κύων)	**śvā́n-ā, -au**	**śvā́n-as**
A. **śvā́n-am**	**śvā́n-ā, -au**	**śún-as**
I. **śún-ā**		I. **śvá-bhis**
G. **śún-as** (κυνός)		D. **śvá-bhyas**
		G. **śún-ām**

---

[1] The normal N. in a appears to have been avoided in an stems, collateral stems always being substituted in this case, as **ákṣi** for **akṣán** *eye*, &c.

[2] So also in Greek: κυνός = **śún-as**.

[3] Cp. Greek κύων.

4. **yú-v-an**, m. *youth*, otherwise regular, forms its weakest stem, **yū́n**, by Samprasāraṇa and contraction[1] (**yú-un**):

SINGULAR.	DUAL.	PLURAL.
N. **yúvā**	N.A. **yúvān-ā**	N.V. **yúvān-as**
V. **yúvan**		
A. **yúvān-am**		A. **yū́n-as**
D. **yū́n-e**[2]		I. **yúva-bhis**
G. **yū́n-as**		D. **yúva-bhyas**

5. **maghá-van**[3] *bountiful*, an epithet of Indra, also forms its weakest stem, **maghón**, by Samprasāraṇa and contraction (**maghá-un**):

SINGULAR.	DUAL.	PLURAL.
N. **maghá-vā**	**maghá-vān-ā**	**maghá-vān-as**
V. **mágha-van**		
A. **maghá-vān-am**		**maghón-as**
G. **maghón-as**	**maghón-os**	**maghón-ām**

6. **ū́dhan** n. *udder* supplements the N. s. with **ū́dhar** and **ū́dhas**; before consonant endings, the latter stem also occurs: pl. L. **ū́dhas-su**.

92. The root **han**, which forms the final member of thirty-five compounds in the RV., follows, for the most part, the analogy of derivative stems in **an**. The strong stem is

---

[1] Cp. Lat. *juven-is* and *jūn-ior*.

[2] The stem retains the accent because it represents a disyllable; cp. **śván**.

[3] The supplementary stem **maghá-vant** is also used in the following cases: N. **maghávān**. Pl. I. **maghávad-bhis**. D. **maghávad-bhyas**. L. **maghávat-su**.

-**han** (with a long vowel in the N. s. only), the middle is -**há**, and the weakest -**ghn**.[1] The cases that occur would in the compound **vṛtra-hán** *Vṛtra-slaying* be:

SINGULAR.	DUAL.	PLURAL.
N. **vṛtra-hā́**	N.A. **vṛtra-háṇ-ā, -au**	N. **vṛtra-háṇ-as**
V. **vṛ́tra-han**		
A. **vṛtra-háṇam**		A. **vṛtra-ghn-ás**
I. **vṛtra-ghn-ā́**		I. **vṛtra-há-bhis**
D. **vṛtra-ghn-é**		
G. **vṛtra-ghn-ás**		
L. **vṛtra-ghn-í**		

3. Adjectives in añc.

93. These words, the suffix[2] of which generally expresses the meaning of *-ward*, form the strong stem in **añc**, the middle in **īc** or **ūc**[3] (according as **ac** is preceded by **y** or **v**). About fourteen stems have a weakest form in **īc**, and about six in **ūc**, which, if they are the contractions of accented syllables, shift the accent to the endings.[4] They are inflected in the m. and n. only, the f. being formed with **ī** from the weakest stem. The only cases occurring in the pl. are the N.A. and in the du. N.A.L.

The forms actually found, if made from **praty-áñc** *turned towards*, would be:

---

[1] Here the **h** reverts to the original guttural aspirate; the **n** in this combination is never cerebralized.

[2] Properly the root **añc** *bend*, which has, however, practically acquired the character of a suffix.

[3] Here **ya** and **va** irregularly contract to **ī** and **ū**, instead of **i** and **u**.

[4] This is the general rule of the RV., but not of the AV. Thus A. pl. **pratīc-ás** RV., **pratī́c-as** AV.

MASCULINE.

SINGULAR.	DUAL.	PLURAL.
N. pratyáṅ (61)	N.A. pratyáñc-ā, -au	N. pratyáñc-as
A. pratyáñc-am		A. pratīc-ás
I. pratīc-ā́		
D. pratīc-é		
Ab.G. pratīc-ás		
L. pratīc-í	L. pratīc-ós	

NEUTER.

N.A. pratyák	pratīc-ī́

a. Other words similarly declined are:

STRONG STEM.	MIDDLE STEM.	WEAKEST STEM.
ny-áñc *downward*	ny-ák	nīc[1]
sam-y-áñc[2] *united*	sam-y-ák	sam-īc
tir-y-áñc[3] *transverse*	tir-y-ák	tiráś-c
úd-añc *upward*	úd-ak	úd-īc[4]
anv-áñc *following*	anv-ák	anūc
víṣv-añc *all-pervading*	víṣv-ak	víṣūc

b. About a dozen stems, in which the **añc** is preceded by a word ending in **a**, have no weakest form. Such are **ápāñc** *backward*, **arvā́ñc** *hitherward*, **ávāñc** *downward*, **devā́ñc** *godward*, **párāñc** *turned away*, **prā́ñc** *forward*. The only

[1] The stem nīc seems to have retained the accent; for the f. is nī́c-ī (not nīc-ī́), and the I. nīcā́ being used adverbially probably has an adverbial shift of accent. devadryáñc *godward* also retains the accent on the suffix: I. devadrī́cā.

[2] The y is here inserted by analogy.

[3] Here tiri takes the place of tirás *across*, from which the weakest stem tiraśc (= tirás + ac) is formed.

[4] ī, though no y precedes the a of the suffix, by analogy.

cases occurring in the du. and pl. are the N.A. m. The inflexion of these words may be illustrated by **ápāñc**:

Sing. m. N. **ápāṅ** (61). A. **ápāñc-am.** I. **ápāc-ā.** L. **ápāc-i.**

Du. N.A. **ápāñc-ā, ápāñc-au.**

Pl. N. **ápāñc-as.** A. **ápāc-as.**

The only distinctively n. form is N.A. s. **prā́k.**[1] The f. is formed from the weak stem with **ī**: **prā́c-ī.**

94. The points to be noted about changeable stems are:

1. The vowel of the suffix is lengthened in the N. s. m. except in **ant** and **añc** stems: **gó-mān, agni-vā́n; kánīyān; cakṛ-vā́n; rā́jā; áśmā, grā́vā, yúv-ā; hastī́, ṛg-mī́, taras-vī́;** but **ad-án, pratyáṅ.**

2. The N. sing. ends in a nasal in all changeable stems except those in **n**, which drop it.

3. All changeable stems that lengthen the vowel in the N. s. m. shorten it in the V. Those that drop the **n** in the N., retain it in the V., while those that have **n** (after **ā**) in the N. drop it in the V., and add **s**:

thus **rā́jan** (N. **rā́jā**),[2] **áśman** (N. **áśmā**), **grā́van** (N. **grā́vā**), **yúvan** (N. **yúvā**);[3] **hástin** (N. **hastī́**); **háviṣmas** (N. **havíṣmān**), **márutvas**[4] (N. **marútvān**); **kánīyas** (N. **kánīyān**); **cákṛvas** (N. **cákṛvān**).

a. The only changeable stems in which the V. does not differ in form (though it does in accent) from the N. are the **ant** and **añc** stems: **ádan** (N. **adán**); **prátyaṅ** (N. **pratyáṅ**).

95. The feminines of nouns with changeable stems are

---

[1] In B. some half-dozen N.A. plur. n. forms occur: **prā́ñci, pratyáñci, arvā́ñci, samyáñci, sadhryañci, anvañci.**

[2] One **an** stem has a V. in **as**: **mātari-śv-as** (p. 68, n. 5).

[3] Four **van** stems form their V. in **vas**: **ṛtā-vas, eva-yā-vas, prātar-it-vas, vi-bhā-vas.**

[4] The RV. has three vocatives in **van**: **arvan, śatāvan, śavasāvan.** The AV. has five others, but none in **vas**.

formed by adding ī to the weak stem (when there are two stems) or the weakest (when there are three); e. g. **adat-ī́** (m. **adánt**); **dhenumát-ī** (m. **dhenumánt**), **ámavat-ī** (m. **ámavant**); **arkín-ī** (m. **arkín**); **návyas-ī** (m. **návīyāṃs**); **jagmúṣ-ī** (m. **jagm-i-vā́ṃs**); **sam-rā́jñ-ī** (m. **rā́jan**), **maghón-ī** (m. **maghávan**), **-ghn-ī** (m. **-hán**); **pratīc-ī́** (m. **pratyáñc**); **avitr-ī́** (m. **avitā́r**).

a. The f. of the present participle active of the first conjugation (125) is made from the strong m. stem in **ant** (cp. 156); that of the second conjugation from the weak stem in **at**; e. g. **bhávant-ī** *being*, **uchánt-ī**[1] *shining*, **púṣyant-ī** *obtaining abundantly*, **codáyant-ī** *urging*; but **ghnat-ī́** (m. **ghnánt**) *slaying*, **píprat-ī** *furthering* (m. **píprat**), **kṛṇvat-ī́** (m. **kṛṇvánt**), **yuñjat-ī́** (m. **yuñjánt**) *yoking*, **punat-ī́** (m. **punánt**) *purifying*.

b. The f. of the simple future participle is formed like the present participle of the first conjugation: **sū́-ṣyant-ī** *about to bring forth*, **san-iṣyánt-ī** *going to obtain*.

c. Adjectives in **van** form their f. in **var-ī**; e. g. **pī́-van** (πίων) *fat*, f. **pī́-var-ī** (πίειρα = πίϝερια). The f. of the irregular **yú-v-an** *young* (91. 4) is **yuva-tí**.

Irregular Nouns with Changeable Stems.

96. 1. **ap** f. *water* lengthens its vowel in the strong cases du. and pl. and substitutes **t** for **p** before **bh**. The forms occurring are:

Sing. I. **ap-ā́**. Ab.G. **ap-ás**. Du. N. **ā́pā**.[2] Pl. N.V. **ā́p-as**. A. **ap-ás**. I. **ad-bhís**. D. **ad-bhyás**. G. **ap-ā́m**. L. **ap-sú**.

2. **anaḍ-váh** m. *ox* (lit. *cart-drawer*, from **ánas** + **vah**) has three stems: the last syllable is lengthened in the strong stem **anaḍ-vā́h**; and shortened by Samprasāraṇa in the weakest **anaḍ-úh** and in the middle **anaḍ-úd** (dissimilated

---

[1] The weak stem appears once in **siñc-at-ī́** *sprinkling* beside the regular **siñc-ánt-ī**.

[2] In a compound.

for anaḍ-úḍ). The N. is irregularly formed as if from a stem in vant. The forms occurring are:

SINGULAR.	DUAL.	PLURAL.
N. anaḍ-vā́n	N. anaḍ-vā́h-au	N. anaḍ-vā́h-as
A. anaḍ-vā́h-am	A. anaḍ-vā́h-au	A. anaḍ-úh-as
G. anaḍ-úh-as		D. anaḍ-úd-bhis
L. anaḍ-úh-i		L. anaḍ-út-su

3. pú-maṃs[1] m. *man* has three forms: its a is lengthened in the strong stem, and syncopated in the weakest to puṃs, in the middle to pum.[2] The forms occurring are:

SINGULAR.	PLURAL.
N. púmān (89. 1)	púmāṃs-as
V. púmas	
A. púmāṃs-am	puṃs-ás
Ab.G. puṃs-ás	G. puṃs-ā́m
L. puṃs-í	L. puṃ-sú

II. Stems ending in Vowels.

97. A. 1. The stems in derivative a (m. n.)[3] and ā (f.)[4] constitute the most important declensions because the former embraces more than one half of all nominal stems, and the latter includes more feminines than any other declension.

---

1 Probably an old compound, with the second part of which the Lat. *mās* 'male' may be allied.

2 With necessary loss of the s between consonants: cp. 28 and 16 *a*.

3 N. -as, -am = Gk. -ος, -ον; Lat. -*us*, -*um*.

4 -ā = Gk. -α, -η; Lat. -*a*.

These two declensions[1] are also the most irregular since the endings diverge from the normal ones here more than elsewhere. The a declension is the only one in which the N.A. n. has an ending in the singular, and in which the Ab. s. is distinguished from the G. The inflexion of the n. differs from that of the m. in the N.A.V. s. du., and pl. only. The forms actually occurring, if made from **priyá** *dear*, would be:

	SINGULAR.			PLURAL.	
	MASC.	FEM.		MASC.	FEM.
N.	priyá-s	priyā́	N.	priyā́s priyā́sas[7]	priyā́s priyā́sas[12]
A.	priyá-m	priyā́-m	A.	priyā́n[8]	priyā́s
I.	priyéṇa[2] priyā́[3]	priyáyā[2] priyā́	I.	priyáis[9] priyébhis	priyā́bhis
D.	priyā́ya	priyā́-yai[5]	D.Ab.	priyébhyas	priyā́bhyas
Ab.	priyā́t[4]	priyā́-yās[5] (Ab. G.)			
G.	priyásya[2]		G.	priyā́-ṇ-ām[10]	priyā́-ṇ-ām
L.	priyé	priyā́-yām[5]	L.	priyéṣu[11]	priyā́su[11]
V.	príya	príye[6]	V.	príyās príyāsas	príyās

Dual. N.A. m. **priyā́**,[13] **priyáu**; f. **priyé**.
I.D.Ab. m. f. n. **priyā́bhyām**.
G.L. m.f.n. **priyá-y-os**.

---

[1] Certain adjectives in -as -a -am follow the pronominal declension (110).

[2] These terminations originally came from the pronominal declension (110). The final of ena is often lengthened (enā).

[3] This form, made with the normal I. ending ā, is rare.

[4] This ending is preserved in the Lat. *o* for *od* (e.g. *Gnaivod* in inscriptions) and in the Greek (Cretic) adverb *τῶ-δε hence*.

[5] The terminations yai (=yā-e), yās (= yā-as), yām are due to the influence of the feminines in ī (originally yā), e.g. devyái, devyā́s, devyā́m (cp. 100).

(For notes 6–13 see next page.)

a. The N.A. neuter forms are: Sing. **priyá-m.** Du. **priyé.** Pl. **priyā́**[14] and **priyā́-ṇ-i.**[15]

a. In the Brāhmaṇas and Sūtras the D. s. f. ending **ai** is used instead of the Ab.G. ending **ās** both in this declension and elsewhere (98. 3 *a*); e. g. **jīrṇāyai tvacaḥ** *of dead skin.*

2. Radical **ā** stems, m. and f.,[16] are common in the RV., being formed from about thirty roots. Most of them appear only as the final member of compounds, but four are used as monosyllables in the m.: **jā́** *child,* **trā́** *protector,* **dā́** *giver,* **sthā́** *standing*; and seven in the f.: **kṣā́** *abode,* **khā́** *well,* **gnā́** *divine woman,* **jā́** *child,* **jyā́** *bowstring,* **mā́** *measure,* **vrā́** *troop.*[17] The forms occurring in the oblique cases are so

---

6 The form **amba**, occurring thrice in the RV., may have a V. meaning, *O mother!* The VS. and TS. have the V. **ámbe** as from a stem **ámbā** *mother.*

7 This form seems to consist of a double ending: **as-as**. The form in **as** is about twice in the RV. and twenty-four times in the AV. as frequent as that in **asas**.

8 That the ending was originally **-ns** is shown by the Sandhi (40. 2); cp. Gothic *-ans*, Gk. inscr. *-ονς*.

9 This ending is preserved in such Greek datives as ἵπποις. It is slightly commoner in the RV. than **priyébhis**, but in the AV. it is five times as common. It is almost always used in the Brāhmaṇas.

10 The **n** seems to have been due to the influence of the **n** stems.

11 The **u** of **su** is almost invariably to be read with hiatus, even before **u**.

12 This form is rare in the RV., being probably due to the influence of the many masculines.

13 The du. in **ā** is more than seven times as common as that in **au** in the RV.

14 The form in **ā** is commoner in the RV. than that in **āni** in the proportion of three to two. In the AV. the proportion is reversed.

15 This form is due to the influence of the **an** stems, which form their n. pl. in both **ā** and **āni**, e. g. **nā́mā** and **nā́māni**.

16 There are no distinctively n. forms, as the radical vowel in that gender is always shortened to **a**, and the stem is then inflected according to the derivative declension.

17 These stems become less common in the later Saṃhitās, where they often shorten the final vowel to **a**, and are then inflected like derivative **a** stems.

rare that some endings, such as those of the L. s., the G.L. du., and the G. pl. are not represented at all. The m. always takes s in the N. s., but the f. often drops it, doubtless owing to the influence of the derivative ā stems. The radical vowel is dropped before the endings e[1] and as of the D. and G. s. The forms actually occurring, if made from jā́ *child* m. f., would be:

Sing. N. jā́-s, f. also jā́. A. jā́m. I. jā́. D. j-é. G. j-ás. V. jā́-s.

Dual. N.A.V. jā́ and jáu. I. jā́-bhyām.[2]

Plur. N. jā́s. A. jā́s. I. jā́-bhis. D. jā́-bhyas. Ab. jā́-bhyas. L. jā́-su.

a. Five anomalously formed m. derivative stems in ā follow the analogy of the radical ā stems.

The strong stem of pathí m. *path* is in the RV. pánthā only: Sing. N. pánthā-s. A. pánthā-m. Pl. N. pánthās. The AV. has besides the stem pánthān: Sing. N. pánthā. A. pánthānam. Pl. N. pánthān-as.

From the adverb táthā *thus* is formed the sing. N. á-tathā-s *not saying 'yes'*.

uśánā m., a seer, has a N. like a f.: uśánā. A. uśánā-m. D. uśán-e.

mánthā *churning stick* and mahā́ *great* form the A. mánthā-m and mahā́-m.

3. Radical a stems, m. n., numbering about twenty, consist almost entirely of stems in radical ā that has been shortened to a. Excepting kha n. *aperture* they appear as final members of compounds only; e. g. prathama-já *first-born*. -ha *slaying* is a reduced form of han; e. g. śatru-há *slaying enemies*.

98. B. Stems in i and u (m.f.n.).

Both declensions embrace a large number of nouns of all genders. But the i declension contains comparatively few n. stems, and, excepting the N.A. s. and pl., n. forms are

---

[1] Not, however, in most of the dative infinitives; e. g. parā-dái *to give up*, pra-khyái *to see*, prati-mái *imitate* (cp. 167).

[2] Contrary to the rule generally applicable to monosyllabic stems, the accent remains on the radical syllable throughout.

rare in it, not occurring at all in several cases. In the u declension the masculines greatly preponderate, being about four times as numerous as the f. and n. stems taken together, while the neuters here greatly outnumber the feminines. The inflexion, which is closely parallel in both groups, is practically the same in all genders except that the N.A. s. and pl. n. differ from the m. and f., and the A. pl. m. and f. differ from each other. The final vowel of the stem shows Guṇa in three of the weak cases of the s. (D.Ab.G.), as well as in the V. s. and the N. pl. m. f., while it is abnormally strengthened in the L. s. The normal ending **as** of the Ab.G. s. is reduced to **s**, while that of the L. s. is always dropped in the i declension and usually in the **u** declension. The inflexion of the **n** stems has influenced the i declension in the I. s. only, but the u declension in the G.Ab. and L. also. Oxytone stems, when i and u are changed to **y** and **v**, throw the accent on a following vowel, not as Svarita, but as Udātta, and even on the **nām** of the G. pl., though the stem vowel in that case does not lose its syllabic value.

The adjectives **śúc-i** *bright* and **mádh-u** *sweet* may be used to illustrate the forms actually occurring:

SINGULAR.

	m.	f.	n.	m.	f.	n.
N.	**śúci-s**	**śúci-s**	**śúci**	**mádhu-s**	**mádhu-s**	**mádhu**
A.	**śúci-m**	**śúci-m**	**śúci**	**mádhu-m**	**mádhu-m**	**mádhu**
I.	**śúcy-ā**[1] **śúci-n-ā**	**śúcy-ā**[2] **śúcī** **śúci**	**śúci-n-ā**	**mádhv-ā**[3] **mádhu-n-ā**	**mádhv-ā**	**mádhu-n-ā**

---

1 Five stems in the RV. form their I. like **śúcyā**, but twenty-five (under the influence of the n declension) like **śúcinā**.

2 This is the normal formation, but the contracted form in ī is more than twice as common in the RV. The latter is in the RV. further shortened to i in about a dozen words.

3 The normally formed I. in ā is made in the m. by only four stems, but that with **nā** by thirty in the RV.; in the n. the **nā** form is used almost exclusively.

	m.	f.	n.	m.	f.	n.
D.	**śúcay-e**	**śúcay-e**[4]	**śúcaye**	**mádhav-e**[7]	**mádhav-e**	**mádhav-e**[10] **mádhu-n-e**
Ab.	**śúce-s**[1]	**śúce-s**	[**śúce-s**]	**mádho-s**	**mádho-s**	**mádho-s**[11] **mádhu-n-as**
G.	**śúce-s**	**śúce-s**[5]	**śúce-s**	**mádho-s**[8] **mádhv-as**	**mádho-s**	**mádho-s**[12] **mádhu-n-as**
L.	**śúcā** **śúcau**[2]	**śúcā**[6] **śúcau**	**śúcā** **śúcau**	**mádhav-i**[9] **mádhau**	**mádhau**	**mádhav-i**[13] **mádhau** **mádhu-n-i**
V.	**śúce**	**śúce**	[**śúci**]	**mádho**	**mádho**	**mádhu**

DUAL.

	m.	f.	n.	m.	f.	n.
A.V.	**śúcī**[3]	**śúcī**	**śúcī**	**mádhū**[3]	**mádhū**	**mádhv-ī**[14]
D.Ab.		**śúci-bhyām**				
L.		**śúcy-os**		**mádhv-os**	**mádhv-os**	**mádhu-n-os**[15]

---

[1] **arí** m.f. *devout* and **ávi** m. *sheep* have **ary-ás** and **ávy-as**.

[2] The form in **au** is more than twice as common as that in **ā** in m. and f.

[3] The derivative **i**, **u** and **ī** stems are the only ones that do not take **ā** or **au** in the dual.

[4] **ūtí** *with aid* is often used as a D. The RV. has seven datives in **ai**, e.g. **bhṛty-ái** *for sustenance*, following the analogy of the **ī** declension.

[5] The RV. has six forms according to the **ī** declension, e.g. **yuvaty-ás**.

[6] The form **védī** *on the altar*, occurring twice, is the only L. from an **i** stem with the normal ending **i** (= **védi-i**).

[7] This type occurs from over sixty stems, the normal formation (**mádhv-e**) from only three stems in the RV.

[8] The normally formed type **mádhv-as** is followed by six stems, the prevailing type **mádho-s** by over seventy in the RV.

[9] Seven stems follow this type, while nineteen follow **mádhau** in the RV.

[10] From one stem also **mádhv-e**.

[11] Once also **mádhv-as**.

[12] Also **mádhv-as**, **vásv-as**.

[13] Only in the form **sánav-i**.

[14] The only example in RV. is **urv-í** *the two earths*. The VS. has **jánu-n-ī** *two knees*.

[15] The only example is **jánu-n-os** (AV.).

PLURAL.

	m.	f.	n.	m.	f.	n.
N.V.	śúcay-as[1]	śúcay-as[3]	śúcī[4] śúci	mádhav-as[5]	mádhav-as[6]	mádhū[7] mádhu
A.	śúcī-n[2]	śúcī-s	śúcī-n-i	mádhū-n[2]	mádhū-s	mádhū-n
I.	śúci-bhis			mádhu-bhis		
D.Ab.	śúci-bhyas			mádhu-bhyas		
G.	śúcī-n-ām			mádhū-n-ām		
L.	śúci-ṣu			mádhu-ṣu		

a. Twenty-seven i stems in the RV. show forms according to the derivative ī declension in the D.Ab.G.L. s. f.: e. g. bhṛtí f. *sustenance*: D. bhṛty-ái; bhū́mi f. *earth*: Ab.G. bhū́my-ās, L. bhū́my-ām. Such forms in ai, ās, ām are much commoner in the AV. In B. ai is regularly used instead of ās (cp. 97 *a* α). Besides the numerous I. s. forms in nā the RV. has half a dozen i stems showing the influence of the n declension in the incipient use of the endings nī in the N.A.V. du. n. and ni in the N.A. pl. n.

In the u declension the RV. has only three forms following the analogy of the derivative i declension: íṣu f. *arrow*: D. íṣv-ai, G. íṣv-ās, su-vā́stv-ās *of the (river) Suvāstu* (all in late passages).[8] There are

---

[1] The only stem not taking Guṇa is arí *devout* which has the N. pl. ary-ás m. f.

[2] The original ending ns is in both śúcīn and mádhūn preserved in the Sandhi forms of ṃs or ṃr (39, 40).

[3] About ten stems in i in the RV. have N. pl. forms according to the derivative ī declension; e. g. avánīs *streams* beside avánayas.

[4] The normal type śúcī (= śúci-i) is of about the same frequency as its shortened form śúci, both together occurring about fifty times in the RV. The secondary type śúcīni occurs about fourteen times.

[5] There is only one example of the N. pl. m. without Guṇa: mádhv-as itself occurring four times.

[6] There are two examples of the N. pl. f. without Guṇa: mádhv-as and śatá-kratv-as *having a hundred powers*.

[7] The type without ending is made from twelve stems, the form with shortened vowel being nearly twice as common as that with ū. The secondary type mádhūni is more frequent than mádhū̆.

[8] In B. the D. s. f. ending ai is here regularly used instead of the Ab.G. ās.

also some forms following the analogy of the ū declension: A. á-bhīrv-am from á-bhīru *fearless* **and N. du. and pl. in yuv-ā and yuv-as from several stems derived with the suffix yu. Besides the numerous I. singulars m. and n., there are many alternative n. forms, in the remaining cases of the s. and N. A. pl., following the n declension: D. mádhu-ne, kaśípu-ne; Ab. mádhu-nas, sā́nu-nas; G. cā́ru-ṇas, dā́ru-ṇas, drú-ṇas, mádhu-nas, vásu-nas; L. ā́yu-ni, sā́nu-ni; dā́ru-ṇi; N.A. pl. dā́rū-ṇi, &c.**

b. **There is no example of a V. s. n. from an i stem, and the only one from an u stem is gúggulu (AV.). This seems to indicate that the V. s. in these stems was identical with the N.**

c. **Adjectives in u often use this stem for the f. also; e. g. cā́ru** *dear*; **otherwise they form the f. in ū, as tanú m., tanū́ f.** *thin* **(Lat.** *tenu-is*); **or in ī, as urú m., urv-ī́ f.** *wide.*

d. **There are about a dozen stems in which final i seems to be radical in a secondary sense as representing a reduced form of roots ending in a. They are mostly m. compounds formed with -dhi; e.g. ni-dhí** *treasury.* **There are also about eight stems formed from roots in u, all of which except dyú** *day* **are final members of compounds; e. g. raghu-drú** *running swiftly*; **besides some twelve stems in which u is radical in a secondary sense, as representing the shortened form of the vowel of three roots in ū; e.g. su-pū́** *clarifying well* **(from pū** *purify*), **pari-bhū́** *surrounding* **(from bhū** *be*).

The inflexion of these radical i and u stems is exactly the same as that of the derivative i and u stems given above.

Irregularities.

99. 1. **páti** (Gk. πόσι-ς) m. *husband* is irregular in the D.G.L. s.: **páty-e, páty-ur,**[1] **páty-au**; while the I. in this sense has the normal form **páty-ā**. When it means *lord*, either as a simple word or as final member of a compound, it is regular: D. **pátay-e, bṛ́has-pátay-e**, G. **páte-s, prajā́-pate-s**, L. **gó-patau**; while the I. in this sense is formed with **nā: páti-nā, bṛ́has-pátinā.** The f. is **pátnī** (Gk. πότνια) *wife* and *lady*.

---

[1] **The anomalous ending appears to be due to the influence of the Ab.G. in the names of relationship (101) in ṛ like pitúr, G. of pitṛ́** *father.*

a. The f. jáni *wife* takes the anomalous ending ur in the G.: jány-ur.[1] It has the further anomaly of forming its N. jánī like the derivative ī declension.

2. **sákh-i** m. *friend*, besides having irregularities like **páti** in the weak cases of the s., has a strong stem formed with Vṛddhi: N. **sákhā**, A. **sákhāy-am**, I. **sákhy-ā**, D. **sákhy-e**, Ab.G. **sákhy-ur**,[1] V. **sákhe**.[2] Du. **sákhāy-ā** and **sákhāy-au**; Pl. N. **sákhāy-as**, A. **sákhī-n**, I. **sákhi-bhis**, D. **sákhi-bhyas**, G. **sákhī-n-ām**.

a. In the RV. sákhi occurs as the final member of eight compounds in which it is inflected in the same way and is also used as a f.; e.g. marút-sakhā N. m. f. *having the Maruts as friends.*

3. **arí** *devout* is irregular in forming several cases like the radical ī stems (except in accentuation): sing. A. **ary-ám** (beside **arí-m**) m., G. **ary-ás** m.; pl. N. **ary-ás** m. f., A. **ary-ás** m. f.

a. The VS. has also the N. s. arī́-s, beside the regular arí-s of the RV. ávi *sheep* (Lat. *ovi-s*) also takes the normal ending as in the G. s.: ávy-as. ví m. *bird* has in the RV. the N. s. vé-s beside ví-s.

4. The neuters **ákṣi** *eye*, **ásthi** *bone*, **dádhi** *curds*, **sákthi** *thigh*, form their weakest cases from stems in **án**; e. g. I. **dadhn-ā́**, **sakthn-ā́**; G. **akṣṇ-ás**, **asthn-ás**, **dadhn-ás**. Du. N. **ákṣi-ṇī** (AV.), I. **sákthi-bhyām**, G. **akṣṇ-ós**, but **sákthy-os** (VS.). In the pl. the **an** stems are used in the N.A. also: **akṣā́ṇ-i** (beside **ákṣī-ṇi**, AV.), **asthā́n-i** (beside **ásthī-ni**, AV.), **sakthā́n-i**; I. **akṣá-bhis**, **asthá-bhis**; D. **asthá-bhyas**.

5. **dyú** m. f. *sky* (originally **di̯u̯**, weak grade of **dyo**, 102, 3) retains this stem before consonant terminations (taking Vṛddhi in the N.V. s.), but changes it to **div** before vowels:

[1] Influenced, like pátyur, by the names of relationship in ṛ (101).
[2] Formed regularly like śúce from śúci.

Sing. N. dyáu-s (Ζεύς = Δjεύς). A. dív-am.[1] I. div-ā́. D. div-é. Ab.G. div-ás (ΔιϜός). L. div-í (ΔιϜί). V. dyàu-s[2] (Ζεῦ).
Pl.N. dív-as.[1] A. m. dyū́n,[3] f. dív-as. I. dyú-bhis.[3]

100. C. Stems in ī and ū are mostly f. when substantives, but a great many as final members of compounds are adjectives used in the m. as well as f.

I. The ī stems are very differently inflected according as they are radical (*a*) or derivative (*b*). The analogy of the primary radical group (1) is closely followed both in inflexion and accentuation by a secondary group (2) of about eighty polysyllabic stems which, though formed with derivative ī, are for the sake of clearness best treated as a division of the radical group.

a. The normal endings as they appear in the inflexion of consonant stems are taken throughout this declension. The G. pl., however, preserves the normal ending ām in one single form only (dhiy-ā́m), nām being otherwise always added. The N. s. always adds s. Accentuation on the final syllable of the stem is characteristic of this declension, and, except in monosyllabic stems, the acute remains on that syllable throughout. Before vowel endings the ī is split to iy in monosyllabic nouns, even when they are final members of compounds,[4] as A. dhíy-am, pl. N. nā́nā-dhiy-as *having diverse intentions*; but in roots as final members of

---

[1] The stem dív, the Samprasāraṇa form of dyáv, has made its way into the strong cases, A. s. and N. pl., owing to the very frequent weak cases div-ás, &c., which taken together occur more than 350 times in the RV.

[2] i.e. díau-s to be pronounced as a disyllable. The s of the N. is retained in this form.

[3] These two forms, which occur only in the RV. or passages borrowed from it, always mean *days*.

[4] Except accented -dhī́, as ā-dhíam (but su-dhī́ follows the general rule, as su-dhíy-as).

compounds only when two consonants precede,[1] as **yajña-príy-am** *sacrifice-loving*, but **yajña-nyàm** (= **yajña-níam**) *leading the sacrifice*. Otherwise ī is always written as **y**, but is invariably to be pronounced as i, as **nady-àm** pronounced **nadíam**[2] *stream*.

The monosyllabic stems belonging to the radical class are the feminines dhī́ *thought*, bhī́ *fear*, śrī́ *glory*, and the m. vī́ *receiver* (occurring only once in the N. s.). The compounds of the first three, being mostly Bahuvrīhis (189), and the compounds formed from the roots **krī** *buy*, **nī** *lead*, **prī** *love*, **mī** *diminish*, **vī** *move*, **śī** *lie*, **śrī** *mix*, being mostly accusative Tatpuruṣas (187), are both m. and f.

The secondary group consists of more than eighty polysyllabic stems accented on the final syllable and probably for this reason following the analogy of the radical compounds. Excepting about half a dozen they are substantives, nearly all f. The masculines are **ahī́** *serpent*, **rathī́** *charioteer*, and about eight compounds.

b. The declension in derivative ī embraces a large number of stems formed by means of the suffix ī (originally **yā**) largely to supply a f. to m. words, and not normally accenting the suffix.[3] It also includes a large number of miscellaneous f. stems of an independent character having no corresponding m., as **śác-ī** *might*. It includes seven m. stems, five of

---

[1] In the secondary radical group (*a* 2, p. 87) the ī is split only in samudrī́ and partly in cakrī́.

[2] The resolved forms given below are spelt with i (not iy as they may have been pronounced) so as to avoid confusion with the written forms of the Saṃhitā text that are spelt with iy. Again the resolved vowel is given as ĭ (not ī) because long vowels are regularly shortened in pronunciation before vowels (p. 22, notes 1 and 5).

[3] The exceptions are mostly stems in which the preceding syllable, having been reduced, throws the accent forward, e. g. urú, f. urv-ī́, *wide*; or in which, as proper names, the accent has shifted to indicate a change of meaning, e. g. asiknī́ a river, but ásiknī *black*.

which are proper names: **Tiraścī́, Nā́mī, Pṛ́thī, Mā́talī, Sóbharī,** besides **rā́ṣṭrī** *ruler*, **sirī́** *weaver*.

The inflexion of these stems[1] differs from that of the radical ī stems in three respects:—(1) no s is added in the N. s. m. or f.; (2) the endings diverge considerably from the normal ones, the s. A. taking **m**, the D. **ai**, the Ab.G. **ās**, the L. **ām**, the pl. N.V.A. **s**; (3) stems accented on the final vowel shift the acute to the ending in the weak cases of the s., in the G.L. du., and in the G. pl.

a. Radical Stems.			*b.* Derivative Stems.	
1. **dhī́** f. *thought.*		2. **rathī́** m. f. *charioteer.*		**devī́** f. *goddess.*

Singular.

N.	**dhī́-s**	**rathī́-s**		**devī́**
A.	**dhíy-am**	**rathí-am**		**devī́-m**
I.	**dhiy-ā́**	**rathí-ā**		**devy-ā́**
D.	**dhiy-é**	**rathí-e**		**devy-ā́i**
G.	**dhiy-ás**	**rathí-as**	Ab.G.	**devy-ā́s**
			L.	**devy-ā́m**
V.		**ráthi**	V.	**dévi**

Dual.

N.A.	**dhíy-ā, -au**	**rathí-ā**	N.A.	**devī́**
			V.	**dévī**
I.	**dhī-bhyā́m**	**rathī́-bhyām**	D.Ab.	**devī́-bhyām**
G.L.	**dhiy-ós**	**rathí-os**		**devy-ós**

[1] In the later language the derivative group (*b*) absorbs the secondary radical group (*a* 2), while borrowing from the latter the N.A.V. du. and the N.V. pl. forms.

PLURAL.

N. dhíy-as		rathí-as		deví-s
A. dhíy-as		rathí-as		deví-s
I. dhī-bhís		rathī́-bhis		devī́-bhis
	D.	rathī́-bhyas		devī́-bhyas
G. dhī-n-ā́m[1]	G.	rathī́-n-ām		devī́-n-ām
L. dhī-ṣú	L.	rathī́-ṣu		devī́-ṣu
			V.	dévī-s

a. Other words belonging to the secondary radical class (*a* 2) are: **kumārī́** *girl* (A. **kumāríam**), **tandrī́** *weariness* (N. **tandrī́s**), **dūtī́** *messenger* (N. **dūtī́s**), **nadī́** *stream* (A. **nadíam**), **lakṣmī́** *mark* (N. **lakṣmī́s**, A. **lakṣmíam**), **siṃhī́** *lioness* (N. **siṃhī́s**, A. **siṃhíam**).

β. **strī́** *woman*, originally a disyllable, is inflected as a radical monosyllabic stem in the sing. A. and pl. N.A.I.: **stríy-am**; **stríy-as**, **strī-bhís** (accent); but retains traces of its derivative origin in the s. N. **strī́** (no s), D. **striy-ái**[2] (AV.), G. **striy-ā́s**, L. **striy-ā́m** (AV.).

II. The ū declension, which comprises both radical and derivative stems, is much more homogeneous than the ī declension. The inflexion of these two classes corresponds exactly to that of the two divisions of the radical ī declension. Practically all the stems in this declension are oxytones (including both the compound radical and the derivative stems).

a. In the radical class there are seven monosyllabic stems, five of which are f.: **dū́** *gift*, **bhū́** *earth*, **brū́** *brow*, **syū́** *thread*, **srū́** *stream*; one m. and f.: **sū́** *begetter* and *mother*; one m.: **jū́** *speeding, steed*. There are further two reduplicated f. substantives and one adjective: **juhū́** *tongue*, **juhū́** *sacrificial spoon*; **jógū** *singing aloud*. Finally, there are about sixty compounds, almost exclusively formed from about eleven roots, e. g. **pari-bhū́** *surrounding*.

---

[1] **dhī-n-ā́m** occurs seven times in the RV., **dhiy-ā́m** only once, the latter being the only example of the normal ending.

[2] In B. this form is used for the G.; e.g. **striyai payaḥ** *woman's milk*.

b. The derivative class comprises two divisions: the one consists of about eighteen oxytone f. substantives, several of which correspond to m. or n. stems in **u** accented on the first syllable, e.g. **a-grū́** (m. **á-gru**) *maid*; the other and more numerous division consists of oxytone f. adjectives corresponding to m. oxytones, e.g. **babhrū́** (m. **babhrú**) *brown.*

a. The normal endings as they appear in the inflexion of consonant stems are taken throughout this declension (radical and derivative).[1] The G. pl., however, takes the normal **ām** in uncompounded radical stems only,[2] but **nām** in all others. The N. s. always adds **s**. Before vowel endings the **ū** is split into **uv** in monosyllabic nouns and generally in compounds with roots as final member (even when preceded by a single consonant). In the minority of such compounds (some nine in the RV.) and in all derivative stems,[3] it is written as **v**, but pronounced as **u**.[4] Thus A. **bhúv-am**, **ā-bhúv-am** *present*; but **vi-bhú-am** *eminent*, **tanú-am**.

The forms occurring if made from **bhū́** *earth* and **tanū́** *body* would be the following:

SINGULAR.

	RADICAL.		DERIVATIVE.
N.	**bhū́-s**		**tanū́-s**
A.	**bhúv-am**		**tanú-am**
I.	**bhuv-ā́**		**tanú-ā**
		D.	**tanú-e**
Ab.G.	**bhuv-ás**	Ab.G.	**tanú-as**
L.	**bhuv-í**	L.	**tanú-i** / **tanū́**
		V.	**tánu**

---

[1] The derivative stems show an incipient tendency to be influenced by the inflexion of the derivative ī declension. The RV. has only one such form: **śvaśruā́m**; the AV. has at least ten such; the VS. has A. **puṃścalū́-m** *courtesan*, D. **tanv-ā́i**, G. **tanv-ā́s**. In B. the D. s. f. ending **ai** is used for **ās**; e.g. **dhenvā́i rétaḥ** *the seed of the cow.*

[2] Judging by the only two forms that occur, **bhuvā́m** and **jóguvām**.

[3] It is, however, split in the derivative stems **a-grū́**, **kadrū́** *Soma vessel*, in adjectives when **ū** is preceded by **y**, and in **bībhatsū́** *loathing.*

[4] Hence in such forms it is given below as **u** (short because a vowel is shortened before another in pronunciation; cp. p. 22, note 1).

DUAL.

N.A.	bhúv-ā	N.A.	tanú-ā
I.	bhū-bhyā́m	D.	tanū́-bhyām
L.	bhuv-ós	L.	tanú-os

PLURAL.

N.	bhúv-as	N.	tanú-as
A.	bhúv-as	A.	tanú-as
		I.	tanū́-bhis
G.	bhuv-ā́m	D.	tanū́-bhyas
		G.	tanū́-n-ām

101. D. Stems in **ṛ** (m. and f.), which in origin are consonant stems in derivative **ar** or **tar**, closely resemble **an** stems (90) in their declension. Derivative stems in **ṛ** consist of two groups, the one formed with the original suffix **ar**, the other with **tar**. The former is a small group of only eight stems, the latter a very large one of more than 150. Both groups agree in distinguishing **strong** and **weak** cases. The strong stem ends in **ar** or **ār**, which in the weak forms is reduced to **r** before vowels and **ṛ** before consonants. Both groups further agree in dropping the final of the stem in the N. s. m. f., which case always ends in **ā**. They resemble the vowel declension in adding the ending **n** in the A. pl. m. and **s** in the A. pl. f.,[1] and in inserting **n** before the **ām** of the G. pl.[2] They have the peculiar ending **ur** in the G. s.[3]

1. The stems in **ar** are: m. **dev-ṛ́** *husband's brother*, **nṛ́**[4] *man*; f. **us-ṛ́** *dawn*, **nánāndṛ** *husband's sister*, **svásṛ**[5] *sister*; n. **áh-ar** *day*, **ū́dh-ar** *udder*, **vádh-ar** *weapon*, which

[1] Except **usr-ás**.

[2] Except **svásr-ām** and **nár-ām**.

[3] Except **nár-as** and **usr-ás**.

[4] This word is probably derived with the suffix **ar**.

[5] In this word the **ṛ** is probably radical: **svá-sar**.

occur in the N.A. s. only.[1] The forms that occur of the first five stems are:

a. Sing. A. **devár-am.** Pl. N. **devár-as.** L. **devṛ́-ṣu.**

b. Sing. A. **nár-am** (*ἀ-νέρ-α*). D. **nár-e.** G. **nár-as.** L. **nár-i** (Ep. Gk. *ἀ-νέρ-ι*). Du. N.A. **nár-ā.** V. **nár-ā** and **nár-au.** Pl. N.V. **nár-as** (Ep. Gk. *ἀ-νέρ-ες*). A. **nṝ́-n.** I. **nṛ́-bhis.** D.A. **nṛ́-bhyas.** G. **nar-ā́m** and **nṛ-ṇ-ā́m.**[2] L. **nṛ́-ṣu.**

c. Sing. G. **usr-ás.** L. **usr-í** and **usr-ā́m.**[3] V. **úṣar.** Pl. A. **usr-ás.**

d. Sing. G. **nánāndur.** L. **nánāndari.**

e. Sing. N. **svásā.** A. **svásār-am.** I. **svásr-ā.** D. **svásr-e.** Ab.G. **svás-ur.** Du. **svásār-ā, -au.** L. **svásr-os.** Pl. N. **svásār-as.** A. **svásṝ-s.** I. **svásṛ-bhis.** G. **svásr-ām**[4] and **svásṝ-ṇ-ām.**

2. This group includes two subdivisions, the one forming its strong stem in **tar**, the other in **tār** (Gk. *-τηρ*, *-τωρ*, Lat. *-tor*). The former consists of a small class of five names of relationship: three m., **pi-tár** *father*, **bhrā́-tar** *brother*, **náp-tar** *grandson*, and two f., **duh-i-tár** *daughter* and **mā-tár** *mother*, together with the m. and f. compounds formed from them. The second division consists of more than 150 stems (including compounds) which are either agent nouns accented chiefly on the suffix, or participles accented chiefly on the root. These stems are never f., and only four are n.

In the **tṛ** declension three stems are to be distinguished: the strong, **tar** or **tār**; the middle, **tṛ**; and the weakest, **tr.** The names of relationship take the Guṇa form,[5] agent nouns the Vṛddhi form of the

---

[1] **áh-ar** and **ū́dh-ar** form their other cases from the **an** stems **áh-an** and **ū́dh-an.** Cp. 91. 6. [2] Often to be pronounced **nṝṇā́m.**

[3] Following the analogy of the derivative ī declension.

[4] **svásr-ām** and **nar-ā́m** are the only two forms of the **ṛ** declension in which **ām** is added direct to the stem.

[5] The strong stem **náp-tar** does not occur in the RV., **nápāt** taking its place.

strong stem. The inflexion of the m. and f. differs in the A. pl. only. The sing. G. is formed in ur, the L. in ari, the V. in ar ; the pl. A. m. in tṝn, f. tṝs, G. in tṝṇām.

The inflexion of the three stems **dā-tṛ́** m. *giver* (δω-τήρ, *da-tor*), **pi-tṛ́** m. *father* (πᾰ-τήρ, *pă-ter*), **mā-tṛ́** f. *mother* (μή-τηρ, *mā-ter*) is as follows:

Singular.

N.	**dātā́**	**pitā́**	**mātā́**
A.	**dātā́r-am**	**pitár-am**	**mātár-am**
I.	**dātr-ā́**	**pitr-ā́**	**mātr-ā́**
D.	**dātr-é**	**pitr-é**	**mātr-é**
Ab.G.	**dātúr**	**pitúr**	**mātúr**
L.	**dātár-i**	**pitár-i** (πατέρ-ι)	**mātár-i**
V.	**dā́tar** (δῶτερ)	**pítar** (*Ju-piter*)	**mā́tar** (μῆτερ)

Dual.

N.A.	**dātā́r-ā, -au**	**pitár-ā, -au**	**mātár-ā, -au**
I.D.	**dātṛ́-bhyām**	**pitṛ́-bhyām**	**mātṛ́-bhyām**
G.L.	**dātr-ós**	**pitr-ós**	**mātr-ós**

Plural.

N.	**dātā́r-as**	**pitár-as**	**mātár-as**
A.	**dātṝ́n**	**pitṝ́n**	**mātṝ́-s**
I.	**dātṛ́-bhis**	**pitṛ́-bhis**	**mātṛ́-bhis**
D.Ab.	**dātṛ́-bhyas**	**pitṛ́-bhyas**	**mātṛ́-bhyas**
G.	**dātṝ-ṇ-ā́m**	**pitṝ-ṇ-ā́m**	**mātṝ-ṇ-ā́m**
L.	**dātṛ́-ṣu**	**pitṛ́-ṣu**	**mātṛ́-ṣu**
V.	**dā́tār-as**	**pítar-as**	**mā́tar-as**

a. **náp-tṛ** in the RV. occurs in the weak stem only: Sing. I. **náptr-ā**, D. **náptr-e**, G. **nápt-ur**. Pl. I. **náptṛ-bhis**. It is supplemented in the strong forms by **nápāt** (Lat. *nepōt-*): Sing. N.V. **nápāt**. A. **nápāt-am**.—Du. N.A. **nápāt-ā**.—Pl. N.V. **nápāt-as**. In the TS. occurs **náptār-am** (like **svásār-am** among the **ṛ** stems).

b. The only n. stems occurring are **dhar-tṛ́** *prop*, **dhmā-tṛ́** *smithy*, **sthā-tṛ́** *stationary*, **vi-dhar-tṛ́** *meting out*, and of these only about half a dozen forms occur. The only oblique cases met with are the G. **sthātúr** and the L. **dhmātári**. The N.A. s. owing to its rarity seems never to have acquired fixity in the Veda, but **sthātár** represents the normal form. In B. the N.A. form in **ṛ** begins to be used in an adjectival sense: **bhartṛ́** *supporting*, **janayitṛ́** *creative*.

c. The f. of agent nouns in **tṛ** is formed with **ī** from the weak stem of the m., e. g. **jánitr-ī** *mother* (inflected like **deví**).

102. E. Stems in **ai, o, au**. The only stems in diphthongs are: **rái** m. and (rarely) f. *wealth*, **gó** m. *bull*, f. *cow*, **dyó** m. f. *sky*, **náu** f. *ship*, **gláu** m. f. *lump*. They form a transition from the consonant to the vowel declension; for while they take the normal endings like the ordinary consonant declension, they add **s** in the N. s. m. f. and have a vowel before the endings with initial consonant. There are no neuter forms.

1. **rái** appears as **rāy** before vowels and **rā** before consonants. The forms occurring are: Sing. A. **rā́-m** (Lat. *re-m*). I. **rāy-ā́**. D. **rāy-é** (Lat. *rē-ī*). Ab.G. **rāy-ás**.—Pl. N. **rā́y-as**. A. **rāy-ás**.[1] G. **rāy-ā́m**.

2. **go** has as its strong form **gau** which appears as **gā** in the A. s. and pl. The Ab.G. are irregular in adding **s** only instead of **as**.[2] The forms occurring are: Sing. N. **gáu-s** (*βoῦ-ς*). A. **gā́-m** (*βῶ-ν*). I. **gáv-ā**. D. **gáv-e**. Ab.G. **gó-s**. L. **gáv-i**.—Du. **gā́v-ā, -au**.—Pl. N. **gā́v-as**. A. **gā́-s**. I. **gó-bhis**. D. **gó-bhyas**. G. **gáv-ām** and **gó-n-ām**.[3] L. **gó-ṣu**. V. **gā́v-as**.

---

[1] Rarely **rā́y-as**; once **rā́-s** (SV.).

[2] As regards accentuation this word is not treated as a monosyllabic stem, never shifting the accent to the endings.

[3] This form, which follows the vowel declension and is much less common than **gáv-ām**, occurs at the end of a Pāda only.

3. **dyó** m. f. *sky* (cp. 99. 5) is declined like **gó**. The forms occurring are: Sing. N. **dyáu-s**[1] (Ζεύς). A. **dyā́m** (Lat. *diem*). Ab.G. **dyó-s**. L. **dyáv-i**. V. **dyáu-s** and **dyàu-s**[2] (Ζεῦ).—Du. N.A. **dyā́v-ā**.—Pl. N.V. **dyā́v-as**.

4. **náu** is inflected quite regularly as far as can be judged by the few forms occurring: Sing. N. **náu-s** (ναῦ-ς). N. **nā́v-am** (νῆϝα). I. **nāv-ā́**. G. **nāv-ás** (νηϝ-ός). L. **nāv-í** (νηϝ-ί).—Pl. N. **nā́v-as** (νῆϝ-ες, *nāv-es*). A. **nā́v-as** (νῆϝ-ας). I. **náu-bhis** (ναῦ-φι).

5. **gláu** occurs in two forms only: Sing. N. **gláu-s** and Pl. I. **glau-bhís**.[3]

Degrees of Comparison.

103. 1. The secondary suffixes of the comparative **tara**[4] (Gk. -τερο) and the superlative **tama** (Lat. *-timo*) are regularly added to nominal stems (both simple and compound), substantives as well as adjectives, generally to the weak or middle stem; e.g. **priyá-tara** *dearer*, **tavás-tara** *stronger*, **vápuṣ-ṭara** *more wonderful*, **bhágavat-tara** *more bounteous*; **vṛtra-tára** *a worse Vṛtra*; **bhūri-dā́vat-tara** *giving more abundantly*; **śaśvat-tamá** *most constant*; **ratna-dhā́-tama** *best bestower of treasure*; **híraṇya-vāśī-mat-tama** *best wielder of the golden axe*; **rathī́-tama** *best charioteer*.

a. The final **n** of the stem is retained before these suffixes; e.g. **madín-tara** *more gladdening*, **vṛṣán-tama** *most manly*. An **n** is sometimes even inserted; e.g. **surabhí-n-tara** *more fragrant*; **rayín-tama** *very rich*.

---

[1] The same as the N. of **dyu** (99. 5).

[2] That is, **díau-s** with the proper V. accent, but with anomalous retention of the N. **s**.

[3] The N. pl. **glāv-as** also occurs in the AB.

[4] These secondary comparatives and superlatives are commoner than the primary in the proportion of three to two.

b. In a few instances the strong stem of a present participle is used; e.g. **vṛ́dhan-tama** *being most mighty*, **sáhan-tama** *most victorious*; and the weakest stem of a perfect participle: **vidúṣ-ṭara** *wiser*; **mīḷhúṣ-ṭama** *most gracious*.

c. These secondary suffixes are occasionally found added to the primary comparatives and superlatives, e.g. **śréṣṭha-tama** *most beautiful*.

d. They also form a comparative and superlative from the preposition **úd** *up*: **út-tara** *higher*, **ut-tamá**[1] *highest*.

e. These suffixes[2] form their f. in **ā**; e.g. **mātṛ́-tamā** *most motherly*.

2. The primary suffix of the comparative **īyāṃs** (Gk. *-ιων*, Lat. *-ior*) and that of the superlative **iṣṭha** (Gk. *-ιστο*) are added directly to the root, which is regularly accented[3] and gunates ĭ and ŭ, but leaves a unchanged apart from nasalization in a few instances. Final radical ā combines with the initial of the suffix to e, which is, however, usually to be read as two syllables. Examples are: **téj-īyāṃs** *sharper*, **téj-iṣṭha** *very sharp* (**tij** *be sharp*); **jáv-īyāṃs** *quicker*, **jáv-iṣṭha** *quickest* (**jū** *be swift*); **yáj-īyāṃs** *sacrificing better*, **yáj-iṣṭha** *sacrificing best*; **máṃh-iṣṭha** *most liberal* (**mah** *bestow abundantly*); **jyéṣṭha** *greatest* and **jyeṣṭhá** *eldest* (**jyā** *overcome*).

a. In many instances these superlatives attach themselves in meaning to derivative adjectives, being formed from the root which the latter contain; e.g. **áṇ-īyāṃs** *smaller*, **áṇ-iṣṭha** *smallest* beside **áṇ-u** *minute*; **dáv-īyāṃs** *farther* beside **dū-rá** *far*; **drā́gh-īyāṃs** *longer*, **drā́gh-iṣṭha** *longest* beside **dīrgh-á** *long*; **lágh-īyāṃs** *lighter* beside **lagh-ú** *light*; **vár-īyāṃs** *wider*, **vár-iṣṭha** *widest* beside **ur-ú** *wide*; **śáś-īyāṃs** *more frequent* beside **śáś-vant** *constant*; **óṣ-iṣṭha** *very quick* beside **óṣ-am** *quickly*; **bárh-iṣṭha** *very lofty* beside **bṛh-ánt** *great*; **yáv-iṣṭha** *youngest* beside **yúv-an** *youth*; **vár-iṣṭha** *most excellent* beside **vár-a** *choice*; **sā́dh-iṣṭha** *straightest* beside **sādh-ú** *straight*.

---

[1] With the accent of the ordinal suffix **tamá**.

[2] When used as an ordinal suffix **tama** forms its f. in accented **ī** (cp. 107).

[3] Except **jyeṣṭhá** meaning *eldest* and **kaniṣṭhá** meaning *youngest*.

β. In a few examples the suffix is added to the derivative form of the root which appears in the adjective; thus **áś-iṣṭha** (*ὤκ-ιστο-ς*) beside **áś-u** (*ὠκ-ύ-ς*) *swift* (from **aś** *reach*); **tī́kṣṇ-īyāṃs** *sharper* beside **tīkṣṇá** *sharp* (from **tij** *be sharp*); **náv-īyāṃs** *newer*, **náv-iṣṭha** *newest* beside **náva** *new*; **svā́d-īyāṃs** (*ἡδίων*, *suāv-ior*) *sweeter*, **svā́d-iṣṭha** (*ἥδ-ιστο-ς*) beside **svād-ú** (*ἡδ-ύ-ς*, *suāv-i-s*) *sweet* (from **svad** *be sweet*).[1]

a. Beside the usual forms in **īyāṃs** there occur about half a dozen alternative comparatives made with the shorter form of the suffix, **yāṃs**: **táv-yāṃs** (**táv-īyāṃs**) *stronger*; **náv-yāṃs** (**náv-īyāṃ-s**) *newer*; **pán-yāṃs** (**pán-īyāṃs**) *more wonderful*, **bhū́-yāṃs**[2] (**bháv-īyāṃs**) *becoming more, greater*; **rábh-yāṃs** (**rábh-īyāṃs**) *more violent*; **sáh-yāṃs** (**sáh-īyāṃs**) *stronger*. Some half-dozen more have no alternative form beside them: **jyā́-yāṃs** *greater, older*; **pré-yāṃs** *dearer*, **pré-ṣṭha** *dearest* (**priyá** *dear*); **vás-yāṃs** *better*, **vás-iṣṭha** *best* (**vásu** *good*); **śré-yāṃs** (*κρείων*) *better*, **śré-ṣṭha** *best* (**śrī** *be bright*), **sán-yāṃs** (Lat. *sen-ior*) *older* (**sána** *old*), **sthé-yāṃs** *most steadfast* (**sthi-rá** *firm*).

b. Some comparatives and superlatives belong to their positives in sense only; e.g. **kán-īyāṃs**[3] *lesser, younger*, **kán-iṣṭha** *smallest*[4] and **kan-iṣṭhá** *youngest* (**álpa** *small*); **néd-īyāṃs** (Av. *nazd-yah*) *nearer*, **néd-iṣṭha** (Av. *nazd-iṣta*) *nearest* (**antiká** *near*), **várṣ-īyāṃs** *higher*, **várṣ-iṣṭha**[5] *highest* (**vṛddhá** *grown up*).

---

[1] From the adj. **pāpá** *bad*, the radical element of which is uncertain, is formed direct the comparative **pā́p-īyāṃs** in the TS.

[2] Here the vowel remains unchanged. This is also the case in the corresponding superlative **bhū́-y-iṣṭha**, which moreover adds the suffix with an intervening **y**.

[3] Cp. **kan-yā̀** *girl* (= **kaníā**), Gk. *καινό-ς* (= *καν̯ιό-ς*).

[4] Appears in this sense in the TS.

[5] Cp. **várṣ-man** n., **varṣ-mán** m. *height*.

NUMERALS.

104. Cardinals.

1. **é-ka.**
2. **dvá** (δύο, Lat. *duo*).
3. **trí** (τρί, Lat. *tri*).
4. **catúr** (Lat. *quatuor*).
5. **páñca** (πέντε).
6. **ṣáṣ** (ἕξ, Lat. *sex*).
7. **saptá** (ἑπτά).
8. **aṣṭā́**[1] (ὀκτώ, Lat. *octō*, Gothic *ahtau*).
9. **náva** (Lat. *novem*).
10. **dáśa**[2] (δέκα).
11. **ékā-daśa.**[3]
12. **dvā́-daśa**[4] (δώ-δεκα).
13. **tráyo-daśa.**[5]
14. **cátur-daśa.**[6]
15. **páñca-daśa.**
16. **ṣó-ḍaśa.**[7]
17. **saptá-daśa.**
18. **aṣṭā́-daśa.**[1]
19. **náva-daśa.**
20. **viṃśatí**[8] (Lat. *viginti*).
30. **triṃ-śát.**
40. **catvāriṃ-śát.**[9]
50. **pañcā-śát** (πεν-τή-κοντα).
60. **ṣaṣ-ṭí.**[10]
70. **sapta-tí.**
80. **aśī-tí.**[11]
90. **nava-tí.**
100. **śatám** (ἑ-κατόν, Lat. *centum*).
1,000. **sahásra n.**
10,000. **a-yúta n.**
100,000. **ni-yúta n.**
1,000,000. **pra-yúta n.**
10,000,000. **árbuda n.**
100,000,000. **nyàrbuda n.**

---

[1] **aṣṭā́** is an old dual form.

[2] The cardinals between 10 and 20 are Dvandva compounds formed by prefixing the accented unit to **daśa** *ten*.

[3] Here **ékā** stands for **éka** under the influence of **dvā́-daśa.**

[4] Here the N. du. is retained instead of the stem form **dva.**

[5] **tráyo**, for **tráyas** (45. 2), is the N. pl. (105).

[6] **catúr** as first member of a compound is regularly accented **cátur-.**

[7] For **ṣaṣ-daśa** through **ṣaẓ-daśa** (cp. 69 *c*, note 3).

[8] This and the remaining cardinals are substantives. Those from *twenty* to *ninety* are either old compounds (adj. and substantive: *two decades*, &c.) or derivatives formed with **-ti.**

[9] **catvārim** for **catvāri**, n. pl. (105), like **viṃśatí** and **triṃśát.**

[10] *Sixty* to *ninety* are abstract f. nouns derived from the simple cardinals (except **aśī-tí**) meaning *hexad of tens*, &c.

[11] **aśī-** is radically cognate to **aṣ-ṭā.**

a. The numbers intermediate between the decades 20–100 are Dvandva compounds formed by prefixing the accented unit to the decade; e. g. **aṣṭā́-viṃśati** 28; **éka-triṃśat** 31; **tráyas-triṃśat** 33; **náva-catvāriṃśat** 49; **náva-ṣaṣṭi** 69; **návāśīti** 89; **páñca-navati** 95, **ṣáṇ-ṇavati** 96, **aṣṭā́-navati** 98; **éka-śatam** 101, **cátuḥ-śatam** 104, **triṃśác-chatam** 130.

a. Intermediate numbers may also be expressed by adding together unit and decade with or without **ca**; e.g. **náva ca navatíṃ ca** *ninety and nine*, **navatiṃ náva** *ninety-nine*.

β. In the TS. the number preceding a decade is also expressed by **ékān ná** *by one not* = *minus one*; thus **ékān ná viṃśatí** *twenty less one* = 19; **ékān ná catvāriṃśát** 39; **ékān ná ṣaṣṭí** 59; **ékān nā́śīti** 79; **ékān ná śatám** 99.

b. There are two ways of forming multiples. The larger number in the du. or pl. may be multiplied by the smaller used as an adjective; e. g. **dvé śaté** 200; **ṣaṣṭíṃ sahásrā** 60,000; **tríṇi śatā́ trī́ sahásrāṇi triṃśác ca náva ca** 3,339. Otherwise the multiplier prefixed to the larger number forms with it a possessive (adjective) compound accented on the last syllable; e. g. **tráyastriṃśat tri-śatā́ḥ ṣaṭ-sahasrā́ḥ** 6,333.

a. Multiples of numbers below 100 are sometimes formed in these two ways; e.g. **navatī́r náva** *nine nineties* = 810; **tri-saptá** 21, **tri-ṇavá** 27.

Declension of Cardinals.

105. Only the first four cardinals, like other adjectives, distinguish the genders. **éka** *one*, while inflected chiefly in the s., forms a pl.[1] also in the sense of *some*; **dvá** *two* is of course inflected in the dual only.

1. **éka** is declined like the pronominal adjectives **víśva**

---

[1] A N. f. du. form of **éka** in the sense of *a certain* appears in **éke yuvatī́** (AV.) *a certain pair of maidens*.

and **sárva**[1] (120 *b*). The forms occurring in the Saṃhitās are:

m. s. N. **ékas**. A. **ékam**. I. **ékena**. G. **ékasya**. L. **ékasmin**. Pl. N. **éke**. D. **ékebhyas**.

f. s. N. **ékā**. A. **ékām**. I. **ékayā**. G. **ékasyās**. Pl. N. **ékās**.

n. s. N. **ékam**. Pl. N. **ékā**.

2. **dvá** *two* is declined quite regularly as a dual, like **priyá** (97 A. 1). The forms occurring are:

m. N. **dvā́**,[2] **dváu**. I. **dvā́bhyām**. G. **dváyos**. L. **dváyos**.

f. N. **dvé**. I. **dvā́bhyām**.

n. N. **dvé**. L. **dváyos**.

3. **trí** *three* is declined in the m. n. pl. quite regularly, like **śúci** (98 B). The f. stem is **tisṛ́**,[3] the inflexion of which differs in the N.A. from other ṛ stems[4] by adding the normal ending as to the unmodified stem. The forms occurring are:

m. Pl. **tráyas**. A. **trī́n**. I. **tribhís**. D. **tribhyás**. G. **trīṇā́m**. L. **triṣú**.

f. N. **tisrás**. A. **tisrás**. I. **tisṛ́bhis**. D. **tisṛ́bhyas**. G. **tisṝṇā́m**.[5]

n. N.A. **trī́**, **trī́ṇi**.

4. **catúr** *four* in the m. n. has the strong stem **catvā́r** (cp. Lat. *quatuor*). In the G. pl., though the stem ends in

---

[1] The only form of the Ab. s. occurring, **ékāt**, follows the nominal declension; it is used in forming compound numerals, **ékān ná triṃśát** 29, &c. (TS.); **ékasmāt**, used in the same way, occurs in a B. passage of the TS.

[2] The dual form is retained in the numeral compound **dvā́-daśa** 12. Otherwise **dvi** is used as the stem in compounds, as **dvi-pád** *biped*, and in derivation, as **dví-dhā** *in two ways*, &c.

[3] Probably for **tri-sṛ́**, formed like **svá-sṛ** (101. 1, note 5).

[4] Except **nar-ás** (101. 1 *c*).

[5] Once written **tisṛṇā́m**, though the ṛ is actually long metrically.

a consonant, n is inserted before the case-ending.[1] The f. stem is **cátasṛ**, which is inflected exactly like **tisṛ́** and shifts its accent like **páñca**. The forms occurring are:

m. N. **catvā́r-as**. A. **catúr-as**. I. **catúr-bhis**. D. **catúr-bhyas**. G. **catur-ṇā́m**.[2]

f. N. A. **cátasr-as**. I. **catasṛ́-bhis**. D. **catasṛ́-bhyas**. G. **catasṛṇā́m**.

n. N.A. **catvā́r-i**.

106. The cardinals from *five* to *nineteen*, though used adjectivally, do not distinguish gender and take no ending in the N.A.[3] They also have in common the peculiarity of accenting **a** before the consonant terminations[4] and the final syllable in the G.

a. The forms of **ṣáṣ** *six* occurring in the Saṃhitās are:

N.A. **ṣáṭ** (27). I. **ṣaḍ-bhís**. D. **ṣaḍ-bhyás**. L. **ṣaṭ-sú**.

b. The forms of **aṣṭā́** *eight* indicate that it was an old dual.[5] The forms that occur are:

N.A. **aṣṭā́**,[6] **aṣṭáu**. I. **aṣṭā-bhís**. D. **aṣṭā-bhyás**. L. **aṣṭā-sú**.

c. **páñca** *five* as well as **saptá** *seven* and the cardinals from *nine* to *nineteen* are declined like neuters in **an** (90. 2) except in the G., which follows **priyá** (97). The forms occurring are:

N.A. **páñca**. I. **pañcá-bhis**. D. **pañcá-bhyas**. G. **pañ-cānā́m**. L. **pañcá-su**.

---

[1] Like **ṣaṇ-ṇā́m**, the G. of **ṣáṣ**, which, however, does not seem to occur in any of the Saṃhitās.

[2] With accent on the final syllable like the G. of **páñca**, &c.

[3] Except **aṣṭā́** and **aṣṭáu** which are N. A. dual forms.

[4] Except **aṣṭā́**, which accents the terminations.

[5] Meaning probably *the two tetrads* (perhaps with reference to the fingers of the two hands).

[6] **aṣṭā** is the stem used as the first member of compounds in the RV., but **aṣṭa** begins to be used in the AV.

N.A. saptá. I. saptá-bhis. D.Ab. saptá-bhyas. G. saptānā́m.

N.A. náva. I. navá-bhis. D. navá-bhyas. G. navānā́m.

N.A. dáśa. I. daśá-bhis. D. daśá-bhyas. G. daśānā́m. L. daśá-su.

N.A. ékādaśa. D. ekādaśá-bhyas. N. dvā́daśa. D. dvādaśá-bhyas. N. tráyodaśa. I. trayodaśá-bhis. D. trayodaśá-bhyas. N. páñcadaśa. D. pañcadaśá-bhyas. N. ṣóḍaśa. D. ṣoḍaśá-bhyas. N. saptádaśa. D. saptadaśá-bhyas. N. aṣṭā́daśa. D. aṣṭādaśá-bhyas. N. návadaśa. I. navadaśá-bhis. D. ékān ná viṃśatyái (TS.).

d. The cardinals for the decades from *twenty* to *ninety* with their compounds are f. substantives, nearly always inflected in the sing. and according to the declension of the stem final; e. g. **N. viṃśatí-s. A. viṃśatí-m. I. viṃśaty-ā́. N. triṃśát. A. triṃśát-am. I. triṃśát-ā. L. triṃśát-i.** If the sense requires it these numerals may be used in the pl.; e. g. **náva navatī́s** *nine nineties*; **navānā́ṃ navatīnā́m** *of nine nineties.*

śatá *hundred* and **sahásra** *thousand* are neuters, which may be declined in all numbers; e. g. **dvé śaté** *two hundred*; **saptá śatā́ni** *seven hundred*; **trī́ sahásrāṇi** *three thousand.*

a. In the group *five* to *nineteen* the bare stem may be used in the oblique cases agreeing with substantives; e. g. **saptá hótṛbhiḥ** *with seven priests* (cp. 194 B *a*).

Ordinals.

107. The ordinals, being all adjectives ending in **a**, are declined in the m. and n. like **priyá**. The f. is formed with **ī** (declined like **devī́**) except in the first four, which take **ā**.

The ordinals from *first* to *tenth* are formed with various suffixes, viz. **(t)ī́ya, tha, thama, ma.** The formation of the first four is somewhat irregular. The stems of the ordinals from *eleventh* to *nineteenth* differ from those of the corresponding cardinals only in being accented on the final syllable; their inflexion differs from that of the latter in following **priyá**. Thus **ekādaśá** *eleventh* forms the cases: m. s. A. **ekādaśá-m**. Pl. N. **ekādaśā́sas**. A. **ekādaśā́n**. I. **ekādaśáis**.

The ordinals from *twentieth* to *ninetieth* (including their compounds), which also end in accented **á**, seem to be abbreviated forms of the corresponding cardinals; e. g. **catvāriṃśá** *fortieth.*[1]

The ordinals for *hundredth* and *thousandth* are formed with the superlative suffix **tama** accented on the final syllable: **śata-tamá, sahasra-tamá.**[2]

1st **pra-thamá**,[3] f. **ā́**.[4]
2nd **dvi-t-ī́ya**,[5] f. **ā**.
3rd **tṛt-ī́ya**,[6] f. **ā** (Lat. *tert-iu-s*).
4th { **tur-ī́ya**,[7] f. **ā** (for **catur-ī́ya** through **k-tur-ī́ya**). **catur-thá**, f. **ī́** (*τέταρ-το-ς*, Lat. *quartu-s*). }
5th **pañca-má**, f. **ī́**.
6th **ṣaṣ-ṭhá** (Lat. *sex-tu-s*).
7th { **saptá-tha**. **sapta-má** (Lat. *septi-mu-s*). }
8th **aṣṭa-má**.
9th **nava-má**.
10th **daśa-má** (Lat. *deci-mu-s*).

---

[1] Only about three examples of this formation have been noted in the Saṃhitās, and four in the Brāhmaṇas.

[2] **Sahasra-tamá** has been noted in B. only.

[3] Probably for **pra-tamá** *foremost*, the **th** being due to the influence of **catur-thá**, &c.

[4] Both **prathamā́** and **tṛtī́yā** have one case-form each according to the pronominal declension in the AV.: G. **prathamásyās** and L. **tṛtī́yasyām**.

[5] From an older **dvi-tá** *second*.

[6] From an older **tṛ-tá** *third*.

[7] When used in the fractional sense of *one-fourth* accented on the first syllable: **túrīya** (AV.); similarly in B. **cáturtha** *one-fourth*, **tṛ́tīya** *one-third*.

11th	**ekā-daśá.**	52nd	**dvā-pañcāśá** (B.).
21st	**eka-viṃśá.**	61st	**eka-ṣaṣ-ṭá** (B.).
34th	**catus-triṃśá** (B.).	100th	**śata-tamá.**
40th	**catvāriṃśá.**	1000th	**sahasra-tamá** (B.).
48th	**aṣṭā-catvāriṃśá.**		

Numeral Derivatives.

108. A number of derivatives, chiefly adverbs, are formed from the cardinals.

a. **Multiplicative adverbs**: **sa-kṛ́t** *once* (lit. *one making*); **dví-s** *twice* (Gk. *δί-ς*, Lat. *bi-s*); **trí-s** *thrice* (Gk. *τρί-ς*, Lat. *tri-s*); **catús** *four times* (for **catúr-s**). Others are expressed by the cardinal and the form **kṛ́tv-as** *times* (probably *makings* A. pl. of **kṛ́tu**) which is used as a separate word except in **aṣṭa-kṛ́tvas** (AV.) *eight times*; e. g. **dáśa kṛ́tvas** (AV.) *ten times*, **bhū́ri kṛ́tvas** *many times*.

b. **Adverbs of manner** formed with the suffix **dhā**: **dví-dhā** *in two ways or parts*, **trí-dhā** and **tre-dhā́**, **catur-dhā́**, **pañca-dhā́**, **ṣo-ḍhā́**, **sapta-dhā́**, **aṣṭa-dhā́**, **nava-dhā́**, **sahasra-dhā́**.

c. A few **multiplicative adjectives** derived with the suffixes **a**, **taya**, **vaya** meaning *-fold*: **tray-á** *threefold*, **dvay-á** *twofold*; **dáśa-taya** *tenfold*; **cátur-vaya** *fourfold*.

PRONOUNS

109. Pronouns differ from nouns both in origin and declension. They are derived from a small class of roots with a demonstrative sense, and they have several distinct peculiarities of inflexion. These peculiarities have in varying degrees been extended to several groups of adjectives.

A. Personal Pronouns.

This class displays the greatest number of peculiarities: they are for each person derived from several roots or combinations of roots; they are specially irregular in inflexion; they do not distinguish gender, nor to some extent even number. Some resemble neuters in form; a few have no apparent case-ending; in two of them the A. pl. m. does duty as f. also.

	SINGULAR.		PLURAL.	
N.	ah-ám *I*	tv-ám *thou*	vay-ám *we*	yū-y-ám[7] *ye*
A.	mā́m *me*	tv-ā́m *thee*	asmā́n[3] *us*	yuṣmā́n[3] *you*
I.	má-y-ā *by me*	tvā́ / tvá-y-ā *by thee*	asmā́-bhis *by us*	
D.	má-hyam[1] / má-hya *to me*	tú-bhyam[1] *to thee*	asmá-bhyam *for us*	yuṣmá-bhyam *for you*
Ab.	mád *from me*	tvád *from thee*	asmád *from us*	yuṣmád *from you*
G.	má-ma *of me*	táva *of thee*	asmā́ka-m[4] *of us*	yuṣmā́ka-m[4] *of you*
L.	má-y-i *in me*	tvé[2] / tvá-y-i *in thee*	asmā́-su[5] / asmé[6] *in us*	yuṣmé *in you*

---

[1] Cp. Lat. *mihi* and *tibi*.

[2] Only this, the normal form (= tvá-i), is found in the RV. The irregular tváyi appears in the later Saṃhitās.

[3] asmā́n and yuṣmā́n are new formations according to the nominal declension. The stems are compounds of the pronominal elements a + sma and yu + sma. The VS. twice has the distinctly f. new formation yuṣmā́s.

[4] asmā́kam and yuṣmā́kam are properly the A. n. s. of the possessives asmā́ka *our*, yuṣmā́ka *your*.

[5] asmā́su is a new formation following the analogy of asmā́bhis.

[6] asmé is also used as D.

[7] Changed from original yūṣ-ám by the influence of vay-ám.

Dual. N. **vā́m** [1] and **āvám** (ŚB.) *we two.* A. **āvā́m** [2] (ŚB.) *us two.* Ab. **āvā-bhyām** (K.) and **āvád** (TS.) *from us two.* G. **āváy-os** (ŚB.) *of us two.*

N. **yuvám** *ye two.* A. **yuvā́m** *you two.* I. **yuvá-bhyām** and **yuvā́-bhyām** *by you two.* Ab. **yuvád** *from you two.* G. **yuv-ós** [3] and **yuváy-os** *of you two.*

a. The following unaccented forms, inadmissible at the beginning of a sentence, are also used: Sing. A. **mā, tvā.** D.G. **me** [4] (Gk. μοι), **te** [4] (Gk. τοι). Du. A.D.G. **nau** (Gk. νῶι), **vām.** Pl. A.D.G. **nas** (Lat. *nōs*), **vas** (Lat. *vōs*).

b. The usual stems of these pronouns used in derivation or as first member of compounds are: **ma, asma; tva, yuva, yuṣma;** thus **asma-drúh** *hating us*; **tvá-yata** *presented by thee*; **yuva-yú** *desiring you two*; **yuṣma-yánt** *desiring you.* But the forms **mad, asmad, tvad** occur a few times as first member of compounds; thus **mát-kṛta** *done by me*; **asmát-sakhi** *having us as companions*; **tvád-yoni** *derived from thee.*

B. Demonstrative Pronouns.

110. The inflexion of these pronouns, as compared with the nominal **a** declension, has the following peculiarities: 1. in the sing. **d** is added instead of **m** in the N.A. n.; the element **sma** appears between the root and the ending in the D.Ab.L. m. n., and **syā** in the D.Ab.G.L. f.; **in** (instead of **i**) is the ending in the L. m. n. 2. in the pl. the N. m. ends in **e** instead of **ās**; the G. has **s** instead of **n** before the ending **ām.**

The stem **tá** *that* (also *he, she, it*) may be taken as the type for the inflexion of adjectival pronouns:

---

[1] **vā́m** (probably abbreviated for **āvā́m**), occurring once in the RV., seems to be the only N. du. form found in the Saṃhitās.

[2] The N. **āvám** (ŚB.) and A. **āvā́m** (K. ŚB.) seem to have been the normal forms judging by **yuvám** and **yuvā́m.**

[3] **yuv-ós** occurs in the RV., **yuváy-os** in the TS.

[4] **me** and **te**, originally L., have come to be used as D. and G.

	Singular.			Plural.		
	MASC.	NEUT.	FEM.	MASC.	NEUT.	FEM.
N.	sá-s[1]	tá-d	sā́	té (τοί)	tā́ and	tā́-s
A.	tá-m[2]	tá-d	tā́-m	tā́n	tā́ni	tā́-s
I.	téna[3]		tá-y-ā	té-bhis, táis (τοῖς)		tā́-bhis
D.	tá-smai[4]		tá-syai[4]	té-bhyas		tā́-bhyas
Ab.	tá-smād[5]		tá-syās			
G.	tá-sya[6]		tá-syās	té-ṣ-ām[8]		tā́-s-ām[9]
L.	tá-smin, sá-smin[7]		tá-syām	té-ṣu		tā́-su

Dual.

N.A. m. tā́, táu, f. té, n. té. I.Ab. m. f. tā́-bhyām. G.L. m. n. táy-os.

a. The stem tá is frequently used in derivation, especially that of adverbs, as tá-thā *thus*; the n. form tád often appears as first member of a compound; e. g. tád-apas *accustomed to that work.*

a. There are three other demonstratives derived from tá:

1. e-tá[10] *this here* is inflected exactly like tá. The forms that occur are:

---

[1] On the Sandhi of sás cp. 48; sá, sā́, tá-d = Gk. ὁ, ἡ, τό; Gothic *sa*, *sō*, *that-a* (Eng. *that*, Lat. *is-tud*).

[2] tá-m, tā́-m, tá-d = Gk. τό-ν, τή-ν, τό.

[3] Sometimes ténā.

[4] These forms have the normal ending e: = tásma-e, tásyā-e. In B. tásyai is substituted for the G. tásyās.

[5] The Chāndogya Upaniṣad once has sasmād.

[6] Homeric Gk. τοῖο (for *tósi̯o*).

[7] sásmin occurs nine times in the RV., tásmin twenty-two times.

[8] Cp. Lat. *is-tōrum.*

[9] Gk. τάων (for τάσων), cp. Lat. *is-tārum.*

[10] The stem used in derivation and composition is eta; e. g. etā́-vant *so great*, etā-dṛ́ś *such*. In B. etad is sometimes thus used: etad-dā́ *giving this*, etan-máya *consisting of this*.

m. Sing. N. **eṣá-s** (67, 48). A. **etám**. I. **eténa**. D. **etásmai**. Ab. **etásmād**. G. **etásya**.—Du. N. **etā́**, **etáu**.—Pl. N. **eté**. A. **etā́n**. I. **etébhis**, **etáis**. D. **etébhyas**.
f. Sing. N. **eṣā́**. A. **etā́m**. I. **etáyā**. L. **etásyām**.—Du. N. **eté**. Pl. **etā́s**. A. **etā́s**. I. **etā́bhis**. L. **etā́su**.
n. Sing. N. **etád**. Pl. N. **etā́**, **etā́ni**.

2. **tyá** is derived from **tá** with the suffix **ya** and means *that*. It is common in the RV., but rare in the later Saṃhitās.[1] Unlike **tá** it is used adjectivally only, hardly ever occurring without its substantive. It never begins a sentence except when followed by the particles **u**, **cid**, **nú**, or **sú**.

The forms occurring are:

m. Sing. N. **syá**.[2] A. **tyám**. G. **tyásya**.—Du. N. **tyā́**.—Pl. N. **tyé**. A. **tyā́n**. I. **tyébhis**.
f. Sing. N. **syā́**. A. **tyā́m**. I. **tyā́**. G. **tyásyās**.—Du. N. **tyé**.—Pl. N. **tyā́s**. A. **tyā́s**.
n. Sing. **tyád**. Pl. **tyā́**, **tyā́ni**.

3. A very rare derivative is **ta-ká** *this little*, which occurs only twice in the RV. in the two A. sing. forms m. **taká-m**, n. **taká-d**.

a. **simá** seems to have the sense of an emphatic demonstrative.[3] The forms occurring are: Sing. N. **simás**. V. **síma**. D. **simásmai** (n.). Ab. **simásmād**. Pl. **simé**.

111. In the inflexion of the demonstrative which in the N. s. m. appears as **ayám** *this here* the two pronominal

---

[1] It is also found a few times in B.
[2] See 48, note 3.
[3] It is generally given the meaning of *every*, *all*, but the above is the more probable sense.

roots i (which nearly always has a double ending) and a[1] are employed, the former in the N. (except the m. s.) and A., the latter in all the other cases. The A. s. m. f. starts from i-m (the A. of i), which appears in the du. and pl. also, so that all these cases have the appearance of being formed from a stem imá.[2]

	SINGULAR.			PLURAL.		
	MASC.	NEUT.	FEM.	MASC.	NEUT.	FEM.
N.	a-y-ám	i-d-ám	i-y-ám	i-m-é	i-m-ā́	i-m-ā́s
A.	im-ám[3]	i-d-ám	i-m-ā́m	i-m-ā́n	i-m-ā́ni	i-m-ā́s
I.	e-nā́[4]		a-y-ā́[7]	e-bhís		ā-bhís
D.	a-smái		a-syái	e-bhyás		ā-bhyás
Ab.	a-smā́d[5]		a-syā́s			
G.	a-syá[6]		a-syā́s	e-ṣ-ā́m		ā-s-ā́m
L.	a-smín		a-syā́m	e-ṣú		ā-sú

DUAL.

N.A. m. im-ā́, -áu. f. im-é. n. im-é. m. D.Ab. ā-bhyā́m. m. G.L. a-y-ós.

---

[1] These two roots are frequently used in derivation; e.g. á-tra *here*, á-tha *then*; i-dā́ *now*, i-há *here*, í-tara *other*.

[2] From this stem is formed the adverb imá-thā *thus*.

[3] Here i-m is the A. of i, from which is also formed the A. f. ī-m and the n. í-d, both used as particles.

[4] Also twice ena. enā́ and the remaining oblique cases, when used as nouns and unemphatic, may lose their accent.

[5] The Ab., according to the nominal declension, ā́d is used as a conjunction.

[6] Both asya and asmai may be accented ásya and ásmai when emphatic at the beginning of a Pāda. The form imásya occurs once in the RV. instead of asyá; and imasmai in the AA. for asmai.

[7] Instead of ayā́ the form anáyā occurs twice in the RV.: it is the only form from ana found in the Saṃhitās.

112. The demonstrative corresponding to **ayám** employed to express remoteness in the sense of *that there, you,* and having in the N. s. the curious forms m. f. **a-s-áu**, n. **a-d-ás**, uses throughout its inflexion the root **a**, but always in an extended form. The fundamental stem used in every case (except the N. s.) is **a-m** A. m. of **a**. This is extended by the addition of the particle **u** to **amu**,[1] which appears throughout the sing. (with **ū** in A. f.) except the N. In the pl. **amū́** is the f. and **amī́** the m. stem (except the A.).

The forms occurring are:

m. Sing. N. **a-sáu.**[2] A. **a-m-ú-m.** I. **amú-n-ā.** D. **amú-ṣmai.** Ab. **amú-ṣmād.** G. **amú-ṣya.**[3] L. **amú-ṣmin.**—Pl. **amī́.** A. **amū́n.** D. **amī́-bhyas.** G. **amī́-ṣām.**

f. Sing. N. **a-sáu.**[2] A. **a-m-ū́-m.** I. **amu-y-ā́.**[4] D. **amú-ṣyai.** G. **amú-ṣyās.**—Du. N. **amū́.**—Pl. N. **amū́-s.** A. **amū́-s.**

n. Sing. N. **a-d-ás.**[5] Pl. N. **amū́.**

a. The unaccented defective pronoun of the third person **e-na**[6] (*he, she, it*) is declined in the A. of all numbers, besides the I. s. and the G. du.

A. sing. m. **ena-m**, f. **enā-m**, n. **ena-d.**—Du. m. **enau**, f. **ene.**—Pl. m. **enān**, f. **enā-s.**

I. sing. **enena.** G. du. **en-os** (RV.), **enay-os** (AV.).

a. Another unaccented demonstrative pronoun restricted to the RV. (excepting one form in the AV. and the TS.) is **tva** meaning *one, many*

---

[1] This stem is used in derivation; e.g. **amú-tas** *thence*, **amú-tra** *there*, **amú-thā** *thus* (B.).

[2] Here the pronominal root **a** seems to be compounded with **sa** extended by the particle **u**: **a-sá-u** and **a-sā́-u**.

[3] This is the only example of **sya** being added to any but an **a** stem.

[4] Used adverbially, with shifted accent.

[5] Here the neuter **a-d** of the pronominal root **a** is extended with the suffix **as**.

[6] Here we have the same **e** (L. of **a**) as in **é-ka** *one*, **e-vá** *thus*.

a one, generally repeated in the sense of *one another*. The n. **tvad** meaning *partly* is also found in B. The forms occurring are:

Sing. N. m. **tvas**, f. **tvā**, n. **tvad**. A. m. **tvam**. I. m. **tvena**. D. m. **tvasmai**, f. **tvasyai**.—Pl. m. **tve**.

β. The pronoun **avá** *this* occurs only in the G. du. form **avós** in combination with **vām** meaning *of you two being such* (used like **sa** in **sá tvám** *thou as such*).

γ. The pronoun **áma**[1] *this* occurs only once in the AV. (also in the AB.) in the formula **ámo 'hám asmi** *this am I*.

C. Interrogative Pronoun.

113. The interrogative **ká** *who? which? what?* used as both substantive and adjective, is inflected exactly like **tá**, excepting the alternative neuter form **kí-m**,[2] which instead of the pronominal **d** has the nominal **m** (never elsewhere attached to a stem in **i**). The forms occurring are:

m. Sing. **ká-s**. A. **ká-m**. I. **kéna**. D. **ká-smai**. Ab. **ká-smād**. G. **ká-sya**. L. **ká-smin**.—Du. N. **káu**.—Pl. **ké**. I. **ké-bhis**. L. **ké-ṣu**.

f. Sing. N. **kā́**. A. **kā́-m**. I. **ká-y-ā**. G. **ká-syās**.—Pl. N. **kā́-s**. A. **kā́-s**. L. **kā́-su**.

n. Sing. N.A. **ká-d** and **kí-m**.[3]—Pl. N. **kā́** and **kā́ni**.

a. In derivation the stems **ki** and **ku** as well as **ka** are used; e.g. **kí-y-ant** *how great?* **kú-ha** *where?* **ká-ti** *how many?*

As first member of a compound **kad** occurs twice: **kat-payá** *greatly swelling*, **kád-artha** *having what purpose?* **kim** is similarly used a few times in the later Saṃhitās and the Brāhmaṇas; e.g. **kiṃ-kará** *servant*.

b. **ká-ya**, an extended form of **ká**, occurring in the G. only, is found in combination with **cid**: **káyasya cid** *of whomsoever*.

---

[1] From this pronoun are derived the I. and Ab. adverbs (with shifted accent) **amā́** *at home* and **amā́d** *from near*.

[2] The N. s. m. is preserved as a petrified form in **ná-ki-s** and **mā́-ki-s** *no one, nothing*.

[3] The relative frequency of **ká-d** and **kí-m** is in the RV. as two to three.

D. Relative Pronoun.

114. The relative pronoun **yá** *who, which, what* is declined exactly like **tá.** The forms occurring are:

m. Sing. N. **yá-s.** A. **yá-m.** I. **yénā** [1] and **yéna.** D. **yá-smai.** Ab. **yá-smād.** [2] G. **yá-sya.** L. **yá-smin.**

Du. N. **yā́, yáu.** D. **yā́-bhyām.** G. **yá-y-os.** L. **yá-y-os** and **y-ós.** [3]

Pl. N. **yé.** A. **yā́n.** I. **yé-bhis** and **yáis.** D. **yé-bhyas.** G. **yé-ṣ-ām.** L. **yé-ṣu.**

f. Sing. N. **yā́.** A. **yā́-m.** I. **yá-y-ā.** G. **yá-syās.** L. **yá-syām.**

Du. N. **yé.** G.L. **yá-y-os.**

Pl. N. **yā́-s.** A. **yā́-s.** I. **yā́-bhis.** D. **yā́-bhyas.** G. **yā́-s-ām.** L. **yā́-su.**

n. N.A. Sing. **yá-d.** Du. **yé.** Pl. **yā́, yā́ni.**

a. The stem of **yá** is used to form derivatives; e. g. **yá-thā** *as.* It also appears as first member of a compound in **yā-dṛ́ś** *which like.* The neuter **yád** is also once used thus in the RV.: **yát-kāma** *desiring what*; and a few times later, as **yad-devatyà** *having what deity* (K.), **yat-kārín** *doing what* (ŚB.).

b. A form of the relative extended with the diminutive suffix **ka, ya-ká** *who*, occurs only in the sing. N. m. **ya-ká-s,** f. **ya-kā́,** and the pl. N. m. **ya-ké.**

E. Reflexive Pronouns.

115. *a.* The reflexive indeclinable substantive **sva-y-ám** [4] *self* is properly used as a N. referring to all three persons. Sometimes, however, its N. nature being forgotten, it is

---

[1] **yénā** is twice as common in the RV. as **yéna,** but the Pada text always reads **yéna.**

[2] The Ab., formed according to the nominal declension, **yád** is used as a conjunction.

[3] **y-ós** for **yá-y-os** like **yuv-ós** for **yuvá-y-os** (p. 105, note 3).

[4] Derived from **svá** with suffix **am** and interposed **y** (like **a-y-ám** from **a**).

used as an A.; e.g. **áyuji svayáṃ dhurí** *I have yoked myself to the pole*; or as agreeing in sense with another case. It occasionally means *spontaneously*.

b. **tanū́** *body* is used in the RV. to express *self* in other cases than the N. and in all numbers. The reflexive pronoun **svá** and a possessive G. may be added; e.g. **yájasva tanvàm** *worship thyself* and **yájasva tanvàṃ táva svā́m** *worship thine own self*. The reflexive sense of **tanū** has disappeared in B.

a. There are one or two instances in the RV. of the incipient use of **ātmán** *soul* in a reflexive sense; e.g. **bálaṃ dádhāna ātmáni** *putting force into himself*. The A. **ātmā́nam** is frequently thus used in the later Saṃhitās (though never in the RV.) and in B.

c. **svá** *own* is a reflexive adjective referring to all three persons and numbers. It is inflected like an ordinary adjective (**priyá**) in the RV. (except the two isolated pronominal forms **svásmin** and **svásyās**). The forms occurring are:

m. Sing. N. **svás** (Lat. *suus*). A. **svám**. I. **svéna** and **svénā**. D. **svā́ya**. Ab. **svā́d**. G. **svásya**. L. **své** and **svásmin** (RV.).

Pl. N. **svā́s**. A. **svā́n**. I. **svébhis** and **sváis**. D. **svébhyas**. G. **svā́nām**. L. **svéṣu**.

f. Sing. N. **svā́** (Lat. *sua*). A. **svā́m**. I. **sváyā**. D. **svā́yai**. Ab. **svā́yās**. G. **svásyās** (RV.). L. **svā́yām**.

Pl. N. **svā́s**. A. **svā́s**. I. **svā́bhis**. L. **svā́su**.

n. Sing. N.A. **svám** (Lat. *suum*). Pl. A. **svā́** (Lat. *sua*).

a. As first member of compounds **svá** several times appears in the substantive (as well as the adj.) sense; e.g. **svá-yukta** *self-yoked*. **svayám** is similarly used in the Saṃhitās; e.g. **svayaṃ-jā́** *self-born*.

F. Possessive Pronouns.

116. Possessive pronouns are rare because the G. of the personal pronoun is generally used to express the sense which they convey.

a. The possessives of the first person are **máma-ka** and **māma-ká**[1] *my* and **asmá-ka** *our.* The forms occurring are:

Sing. D. **mámakāya.** G. **mámakasya.**

Sing. N. m. **māmaká-s.** n. **māmaká-m.** Pl. G. **māmakā́nām.**

Sing. N.A. n. **asmā́ka-m.**[2] I. **asmā́kena.** Pl. N. m. **asmā́kāsas.** I. **asmā́ke-bhis.**

The n. s. **asmā́kam**, by far the commonest of these forms, is used as the G. pl. of the personal pronoun = *of us* (109).

b. The possessives of the second person are **tāva-ká**[3] *thy* (only D. pl. **tāvakébhyas**), **tvá** *thy* (only I. pl. f. **tvā́-bhis**), and **yuṣmā́-ka** *your.* Of the latter, three forms occur: I. s. m. **yuṣmā́kena**, pl. f. **yuṣmā́kā-bhis**, and the N.A. n. **yuṣmā́kam** used as the G. pl. of the second personal pronoun = *of you.*

c. Besides being used reflexively **svá** is fairly often employed as a simple possessive, generally of the third person (like Lat. *suus*), *his, her, their,* but also of the second, *thy, your,* and of the first, *my, our.* The inflexion (115 *c*) is the same in both senses.

G. Pronominal Compounds and Derivatives.

117. With **-dṛ́ś**[4] in the RV. and other Saṃhitās, and with **-dṛkṣa** in the VS. are formed the following pronominal compounds: **ī-dṛ́ś, tā-dṛ́ś, etā-dṛ́ś** *such,* **kī-dṛ́ś**[5] *what like?* **yā-dṛ́ś**[6] *what like*; **ī-dṛ́kṣa, etā-dṛ́kṣa** *such.*

---

[1] Both formed from the G. of the personal pronoun **máma.** There also occurs once in the RV. the derivative **mā́-k-īna** *my.*

[2] The VS. has once the N. s. **āsmāká-s** *our* formed like **māmaká** beside **mámaka.**

[3] Formed from the G. **táva.**

[4] In the Brāhmaṇas (SB.) **-dṛśa** begins to appear: **ī-dṛ́śa, tā-dṛ́śa, yā-dṛ́śa.**

[5] N. s. m. **kī-dṛ́ṅ.**

[6] With the very anomalous L. s. **yādṛ́śmin.**

a. With the suffix **-ka**, conveying a diminutive or contemptuous meaning, very rarely used derivatives are formed from the pronouns **tá, yá, sá,** and **asáu**: **ta-ká** *that little* (110. 3), **yá-ka** *who, which* (114 *b*), **sa-ká** (only N. s. f. **sa-ká̄**), **asakáu** N. s. f. *that little* (VS.).

b. With the comparative suffix **-tara** derivatives are formed from **i, ká, yá,** and with the superlative suffix **-tama** from the latter two (cp. 120): **í-tara** *other*, **ka-tará** *which of two?* **ya-tará** *who or which of two*; **ka-tamá** *who or which of many?* **ya-tamá** *who or which of many.*

118. *a.* With **ti** derivatives with a numerical sense are formed from **ká, tá,** and **yá**: **ká-ti** *how many?* (Lat. *quot*); **tá-ti** *so many* (Lat. *toti-dem*); **yá-ti** *as many.* No inflected forms of these words occur. They appear in the sense of the N.A. pl. only.

b. With **yant** expressing the quantitative meaning of *much* derivatives are formed from **i** and **ki**: **í-yant** *so much*: n. s. N. **íyat**, pl. **íyānti**; f. s. D. **íyatyai**; **kí-yant** *how much?*: sing. N. n. **kíyat**; f. **kíyatī.** D. m. **kíyate.** L. **kíyāti** (for **kíyati**).

c. With **vant** are formed derivatives from personal pronouns with the sense of *like, attached to*; and from others in the quantitative sense of *great*; thus **tvā́-vant** *like thee*, **mā́-vant** *like me*, **yuvā́-vant** *devoted to you two* (only D. **yuvā́vate**); **yuṣmā́-vant** *belonging to you* (only L. pl. **yuṣmā́vatsu**); **etā́-vant** and **tā́-vant** *so great*; **yā́-vant** *as great*; **ī́-vant** *so great* (s. N. n. **ī́vat.** D. m. n. **ī́vate.** G. **ī́vatas**; pl. A. m. **ī́vatas**); **kī́-vant** *how far?* (G. s. **kī́vatas**).

Indefinite Pronouns.

119. *a.* The only simple pronoun which has an undoubtedly indefinite sense is **sama** (unaccented) *any, every.* The six forms that occur are: m. s. A. **samam.** D. **samasmai.** Ab. **samasmād.** G. **samasya.** L. **samasmin.** Pl. N. **same.**

b. Compound indefinite pronouns are formed by combining the particles **ca**, **cana**, or **cid** with the interrogative **ká**; thus **káś ca** *any, any one*; **káś caná** *any one soever, every*; **káś cid** *any, some*; *any one, some one.*

Pronominal Adjectives.

120. Several adjectives derived from or allied in meaning to pronouns, follow the pronominal declension (110) altogether or in part.

a. The adjectives that strictly adhere to the **pronominal** type of inflexion are **anyá** *other* and the derivatives formed with **tara** and **tama** from **ká** and **yá**. The specifically pronominal cases of the latter that have been met with are: Sing. N. n. **katará-d, yatará-d; katamá-d, yatamá-d.** D. **katamá-smai.** G. f. **katamá-syās.** L. f. **yatamá-syām.** Pl. N. m. **katamé, yatamé, yataré** (K.). From **ítara** occur in the Kāṭhaka Saṃhitā m. D. s. **itarasmai** and N. pl. **itare.** The forms of **anyá** that occur are:

m. Sing. N. **anyá-s.** A. **anyá-m.** I. **anyéna.** D. **anyá-smai.** G. **anyá-sya.** L. **anyá-smin.**—Pl. N. **anyé.** A. **anyā́n.** I. **anyé-bhis** and **anyáis.** D. **anyé-bhyas.** G. **anyé-ṣām.** L. **anyé-ṣu.**

f. Sing. N. **anyā́.** A. **anyā́m.** I. **anyá-y-ā.** D. **anyá-syai.** G. **anyá-syās.** L. **anyá-syām.**—Du. N. **anyé.**—Pl. N. **anyā́-s.** A. **anyā́-s.** I. **anyā́-bhis.** G. **anyā́-sām.** L. **anyā́-su.**

n. Sing. N. **anyá-d.**—Du. I. **anyā́-bhyām.**—Pl. N. **anyā́.**

b. **víśva** *all*, **sárva** *whole*, **éka** *one* are **partially pronominal**, differing only in taking **m** instead of **d** in the N.A. s. n. Thus:

Sing. D. **víśvasmai.**[1] Ab. **víśvasmād.**[1] L. **víśvasmin.**[1]

---

[1] The RV. has the nominal forms D. **víśvāya**, Ab. **víśvāt**, L. **víśve**, once each.

Pl. N. **víśve**. G. m. **víśveṣām**. f. **víśvāsām**; but sing. N. n. **víśvam**.

Sing. D. m. **sárvasmai**. f. **sárvasyai**. Ab. m. **sárvasmād**. Pl. m. N. **sárve**. G. **sárveṣām**. f. **sárvāsām**; but sing. N. n. **sárvam**.

Sing. G. f. **ékasyās**. L. m. **ékasmin**.[1] Pl. N. m. **éke**; but sing. N. n. **ékam**.

c. More than a dozen other adjectives, having pronominal affinities in form or meaning, **occasionally** have **pronominal** case-forms (but always **m** instead of **d** in the N.A. s. n.):

1. Eight adjectives formed with the comparative suffixes **-tara** and **-ra**, and the superlative suffix **-ma**: **út-tara** *higher, later*:

Sing. Ab. L. **úttarasmād** and **úttarasmin** beside **úttarād** and **úttare**. L. f. **úttarasyām**. Pl. N. **úttare**. G. **úttareṣām** (K.).

ápa-ra, áva-ra, úpa-ra *lower*: sing. L. **aparasmin** (K.). Pl. N. m. **ápare, ávare, úpare** beside **áparāsas, ávarāsas, úparāsas** and **úparās**.

ava-má *lowest*: L. s. f. **avamásyām**.

upa-má *highest*: L. s. f. **upamásyām**.

para-má *farthest*: sing. f. G. **paramásyās**. L. **paramásyām**. Pl. m. N. **paramé** (K.).

madhya-má *middlemost*: sing. f. L. **madhyamásyām**.

2. Five other adjectives with a comparative or pronominal sense:

pára *ulterior*: sing. D. m. **párasmai**. Ab. m. **párasmād**. L. m. **párasmin** beside **páre**. G. f. **párasyās**. Pl. m. N. **páre** beside **párāsas**. G. **páreṣām**.

pū́rva *prior*: sing. D. **pū́rvasmai**. Ab. **pū́rvasmād**. L. **pū́rvasmin** (K.), f. **pū́rvasyām**. Pl. N. m. **pū́rve** (very common) beside **pū́rvāsas** (very rare). G. m. **pū́rveṣām**, f. **pū́rvāsām**.

---

[1] The AV. once has **éke** as L. sing.

néma[1] *other*: sing. L. m. **némasmin**. Pl. N. m. **néme**, but G. **nemānām** (unaccented).

svá *own* (116 c), otherwise following the nominal declension, has once sing. G. f. **svásyās** and once L. n. **svásmin**.

samāná *similar, common* has once sing. Ab. n. **samānásmād** beside **samānā́d**.

3. Four adjectives, numerical in form or meaning, have occasional pronominal endings: **prathamá** *first* has the sing. G. f. **prathamásyās**;[2] **tṛtī́ya** *third* has sing. L. f. **tṛtī́yasyām**;[2] **úbhaya** *of both kinds* has pl. m. G. **úbhayeṣām** and N. **úbhaye** beside **úbhayāsas** and **úbhayās**;[3] **kévala** *exclusive* has once pl. N. m. **kévale**.

CHAPTER IV

CONJUGATION

121. Vedic verbs are inflected in two voices, active and middle. The middle forms may be employed in a passive sense, except in the present system, which has a special passive stem inflected with the middle endings. Some verbs are conjugated in both active and middle, e. g. **kṛṇó-ti** and **kṛṇu-té** *makes*; others in one voice only, e. g. **ás-ti** *is*; others partly in one, partly in the other; e. g. **várta-te** *turns*, but perfect **va-várt-a** *has turned*.

a. The Vedic verb has in each tense and mood three **numbers**, Singular, Dual, and Plural, all in regular use,

---

[1] Perhaps from **ná + ima** *not this*.

[2] Cp. 107, note 4.

[3] **ubhá** *both* is declined in the Du. only: N.A. m. **ubhā́**, f. **ubhé**. I. **ubhā́bhyām**. G. **ubháyos**.

with three persons in each (except the imperative in which the first persons are wanting).

122. There are **five tenses** in ordinary use, the present, the imperfect, the perfect, the aorist, and the future. The terms imperfect, perfect, aorist are here used in a purely formal sense, that is, as corresponding in formation to the Greek tenses bearing those names. No Vedic tense has an imperfect meaning, while the perfect sense is generally expressed by the aorist.

a. Besides the indicative there are **four moods**, the subjunctive, the injunctive, the optative, and the imperative, all of which are formed from the stems of the present, the perfect, and the aorist. The imperfect has no moods; and the only modal form occurring in the future is the unique subjunctive **kariṣyás** from **kṛ** *make*.

a. The subjunctive, very common in the RV. and the AV., is three or four times as frequent as the optative; the latter, comparatively rare in the Saṃhitās, occurs far oftener than the former in the Brāhmaṇas. Both form stems with a special modal affix.

The subj. adds **a** to the indicative stem: when the latter distinguishes a strong and a weak stem, the **a** is attached to the former, while it coalesces to **ā** with the final of **a** stems. Thus the pr. subj. stem of **duh** *milk* is **dóh-a**, of **yuj** *join* **yunáj-a**, but of **bhū** *be* **bhávā**.

The opt. adds **yā** or **ī**, which when strong and weak stems are distinguished are attached to the latter. Stems in **a** take **ī** throughout; others take **ī** in the mid., **yā** in the act.; thus the pr. opt. stem of **bhū** is **bháve** (= **bháva-ī**); of **duh** and **yuj**, act. **duh-yá́**, **yuñj-yá́**, mid. **duh-ī**, **yuñj-ī**.

The inj. is identical in form with an unaugmented past tense (impf., aor., plup.). It is very common in the RV., but has almost disappeared from the Brāhmaṇas, except when used with the prohibitive particle **má́**.

The impv. has no modal affix, adding its endings direct to the tense stem; e. g. 2. s. pr. **vid-dhí** *know*, pf. **mumug-dhí** *release*, aor. **śru-dhí** *hear*. In the 2. 3. du. and 2. pl. act. and mid. (ending in **tam**, **tām**; **āthām**, **ātām**; **ta**; **dhvam**) it is identical with the inj.

b. **Participles**, active and middle, are formed from the tense stem of the present, future, aorist, and perfect. There are also passive participles, present, perfect, and future; the first being formed from the passive stem in **ya**, the other two from the root.

c. There are also **gerunds**, which are stereotyped cases (chiefly instrumentals) of verbal nouns and having the value of indeclinable active participles with a prevailingly past sense; e. g. **gatví** and **gatvā́ya** *having gone.*

d. There are about a dozen differently formed types of **infinitives**, which are cases of verbal nouns made directly or with a suffix from the root, and hardly ever connected with a tense stem; e. g. **ídh-am** *to kindle*; **gán-tavái** *to go.*

The Present System.

123. While the perfect, aorist, and future tenses add the endings directly (or after inserting a sibilant) to the root, the present group (that is, the present with its moods and participles, and the imperfect) forms a special stem, which is made in eight different ways by primary verbs.

The Eight Classes.

124. These eight classes are divided into **two conjugations**. In the first, which comprises the first, fourth, and sixth classes, the present stem ends in **a** and remains unchanged throughout (like the **a** declension). The secondary conjugations in **a** (desideratives, intensives, causatives, denominatives) as well as the future follow this conjugation in their inflexion. The second or **graded conjugation** is characterized by shift of accent between stem and ending, accompanied by vowel gradation. It comprises the remaining five classes, in which the terminations are added directly to the final of the root or to the (graded) suffixes **no** or **nā**, and the stem is **changeable**, being either **strong** or **weak**.

A. First Conjugation.

125. 1. The **first** or **Bhū** class adds **a** to the last letter of the root, which being accented takes Guṇa of a final vowel (short or long) and of a short medial vowel followed by one consonant; e. g. **ji** *conquer*: **jáy-a**; **bhū** *be*: **bháv-a**; **budh** *awake*: **bódh-a.**

2. The **sixth** or **Tud** class adds an accented **á** to the root, which being unaccented has no Guṇa. Before this **a** final **ṝ** is changed to **ir.**

3. The **fourth** or **Div** class adds **ya** to the last letter of the root, which is accented;[1] e. g. **nah** *bind*: **náh-ya**; **div** *play*: **dī́v-ya** (cp. 15, 1 *c*).

B. Second Conjugation.

126. The strong forms are:

1. The singular present and imperfect active;
2. The whole subjunctive;
3. The third person singular imperative active.

In these forms the vowel of the root or of the affix, being accented, is strengthened; while in the weak forms it is reduced because the terminations are accented.

a. In the ninth class the accented form of the affix is **nā́**, the unaccented **nī** or **n**; in the seventh they are respectively **ná** and **n.**

127. 1. The **second** or **root** class adds the terminations directly to the root (in the subjunctive and optative with the intervening modal suffix). The radical vowel in the strong forms is accented[2] and takes Guṇa if possible (125, 1);

---

[1] The weak form in some instances assumed by the root points to the **ya** having originally been accented (cp. 133 B 1).

[2] Except in the augmented (128 *c*) imperfect singular because the augment is invariably accented.

e. g. from **i** *go*: sing. 1. **é-mi, é-ṣi, é-ti**; **dviṣ** *hate*: **dvéṣ-mi, dvék-ṣi, dvéṣ-ṭi.**

2. The **third** or **reduplicating** class adds the terminations directly to the reduplicated root, which in the strong forms takes Guṇa if possible. Contrary to analogy, the accent is not, in the majority of verbs belonging to this class, on the root in the strong forms, but on the reduplicative syllable (which is also accented in the 3. pl. act. and mid.).[1] Thus **hu** *sacrifice*: Sing. 1. **ju-hó-mi**, pl. 1. **ju-hu-más**; **bhṛ** *bear*: Sing. 1. **bí-bhar-mi**, pl. 1. **bibhṛ-más**, 3. **bí-bhr-ati.**[2]

3. The **seventh** or **infixing** nasal class adds the terminations directly to the final consonant, before which **ná** is inserted in the strong and **n** in the weak forms; e. g. **yuj** *join*: **yu-ná-j-mi, yuñj-más.**

4. The **fifth** or **nu** class adds in the strong forms the accented syllable **nó**, which in the weak forms is reduced to **nu**; e. g. **kṛ** *make*: **kṛ-ṇó-mi, kṛṇ-más.**[3]

a. Four roots ending in **n** have the appearance of being formed with a suffix **u**, but this is probably due to the **an** of the root being reduced to the sonant nasal; thus from **tan** *stretch* **ta-nu** (for **tn̥-nu**). In the tenth Maṇḍala of the RV. the anomalous weak stem **kur-u** appears three times (beside the normal **kṛ-ṇu**) and the strong stem **karo** in the AV. These stems gave rise to the eighth or **u** class of Sanskrit grammar.

5. The **ninth** or **nā** class adds to the root in the strong forms the accented syllable **nā́**, which in the weak forms is reduced to **nī** before consonants and **n** before vowels. The root shows a tendency to be weakened. Thus **grabh** *seize*: **gṛbh-ṇā́-mi**, pl. 1. **gṛbh-ṇī-mási** and **gṛbh-ṇī-más**, 3. **gṛbh-ṇ-ánti.**

---

[1] It is doubtless as a result of this accentuation that these verbs lose the **n** of the endings in these two forms: **bíbhr-ati, bíbhr-ate.**

[2] The intensives conjugated in the active (172) follow this class.

[3] The **u** is dropped before the **m** of the 1. pl. ind. act. and mid.

The Augment.

128. The imperfect, pluperfect, aorist, and conditional generally prefix to the stem the accented syllable a which gives to those forms the sense of past time.

a. This augment sometimes appears lengthened before the n, y, r, v of seven or eight roots: aor. **ā́-naṭ** (**naś** *attain*); impf. **ā́-yunak**, aor. **ā́-yukta**, **ā́-yukṣātām** (**yuj** *join*); impf. **ā́-riṇak** and aor. **ā́-raik** (**ric** *leave*); aor. **ā́-var** (**vṛ** *cover*); impf. **ā́-vṛṇi** (**vṛ** *choose*); impf. **ā́-vṛṇak** (**vṛj** *turn*), impf. **ā́-vidhyat** (**vyadh** *wound*).

b. The augment contracts with the initial vowels **i**, **u**, **ṛ** to the Vṛddhi vowels **ai**, **au**, **ār**; e.g. **áichat** impf. of **iṣ** *wish*; **áunat** impf. of **ud** *wet*; **ā́r-ta** (Gk. ὦρ-το) 3. s. aor. mid. of **ṛ** *go*.

c. The augment is very often dropped: this is doubtless a survival from the time when it was an independent particle that could be dispensed with if the past sense was clear from the context. In the RV. the unaugmented forms of past tenses are much more than half as numerous as the augmented ones. In sense the forms that drop the augment are either indicative or injunctive, these being about equal in number in the RV. About one-third of the injunctives in the RV. are used with the prohibitive particle **mā́** (Gk. μή). In the AV. nearly all the unaugmented forms are injunctives, of which four-fifths are used with **mā́**.

Reduplication.

129. Five verbal formations take reduplication: the present stem of the third conjugational class, the perfect (with the pluperfect), one kind of aorist, the desiderative, and the intensive. Each of these has certain peculiarities, which must be treated separately under the special rules of reduplication (130, 135, 149, 170, 173). Common to all are the following:

General Rules of Reduplication.

1. The first syllable of a root (i. e. that portion of it which ends with a vowel)[1] is reduplicated; e. g. **budh** *perceive*: **bu-budh.**

2. Aspirated letters are represented by the corresponding unaspirated;[2] e. g. **bhī** *fear*: **bi-bhī**; **dhā** *put*: **da-dhā.**

3. Gutturals are represented by the corresponding palatals,[2] h by j; e. g. **gam** *go*: **ja-gam**; **khan** *dig*: **ca-khan**; **han** *smite*: **ja-ghan.**

4. If the root begins with more than one consonant, the first only is reduplicated; e. g. **kram** *stride*: **ca-kram.**

5. If a root begins with a sibilant followed by a hard consonant, the latter is reduplicated; e. g. **sthā** *stand*: **ta-sthā**; **skand** *leap*: **ca-skand.** But **svaj** *embrace*: **sa-svaj** (v is soft); **smi** *smile*: **si-ṣmi** (m is soft).

6. If the radical vowel, whether final or medial, is long, it is shortened in the reduplicative syllable;[3] e. g. **dā** *give*: **da-dā**; **rādh** *succeed*: **ra-rādh.**

Special Rule of Reduplication for the Third Class.

130. ṛ and ṝ are represented in reduplication by **i**; e. g. **bhṛ** *bear*: **bí-bhar-ti**; **pṝ** *fill*: **pí-par-ti.** The root **vṛt** *turn* is the only exception: **va-várt(t)-i.**

a. Thirteen roots also reduplicate ă with i,[4] while nine do so with a.

---

[1] This is not always the case in the reduplication of intensives (173 *b*).

[2] There are some exceptions to this rule in the reduplication of intensives (173, 3).

[3] This rule does not apply to intensives (173), nor for the most part to the reduplicated aorist (149, 2), and in the reduplicated perfect it is subject to numerous exceptions (139, 9).

[4] Three of these, **pā** *drink*, **sthā** *stand*, **han** *slay*, have permanently gone over to the a conjugation, while **ghrā** *smell* is beginning to do so.

Terminations.

131. The following table gives the terminations, which are on the whole the same for all verbs, of the present system. The chief difference is in the optative which is characterized by e[1] in the first, and yā́ and ī[2] in the second conjugation. The present indicative has the primary (mi, si, ti, &c.), and the imperfect, the optative, and (with some modifications) the imperative have the secondary terminations (m, s, t, &c.), while the subjunctive fluctuates between the two. Of the other tenses the future takes the primary, and the pluperfect and the aorist, with the benedictive and the conditional, take the secondary terminations; while the perfect has in the active (with many variations) the secondary, and in the middle the primary endings.

The following distinctions between the two conjugations should be noted. In the first or a conjugation (as in the a declension) the accent is never on the terminations, but always on the same syllable of the stem (the root in the first and fourth, the affix in the sixth class), which therefore remains unchanged. On the other hand, in the second conjugation (as in the declension of changeable stems) the accent falls on the strong stem, which is reduced in the weak forms by the shifting of the accent to the endings. In the second conjugation therefore the endings are accented except in the strong forms (126). The same applies to the unaugmented imperfect (128).

---

[1] That is, ī coalescing with the final a of the stem; e. g. bháv-e = bháva-ī.

[2] That is, the modal affix shows vowel gradation (5 *b*).

ACTIVE.

	PRESENT.	IMPERFECT.	OPTATIVE.		SUBJ.	IMPV.
			1st conj.	2nd conj.		
1.	mi[1]	(a)-m[5]	īyam[8]	yā́m	āni, ā	—
2.	si	s	īs	yā́s	a-si, a-s	—, tāt[9] dhi, hi
3.	ti	t	īt	yā́t	a-ti, a-t	tu
1.	vas[1]	va[1]	īva	yā́va	ā-va	—
2.	thas	tam	ītam	yā́tam	a-thas	tam
3.	tas	tām	ītām	yā́tām	a-tas	tām
1.	masi,[2] mas[1]	ma[1]	īma	yā́ma	ā-ma	—
2.	tha, thana[3]	ta, tana[6]	īta	yā́ta	a-tha	ta, tana[10]
3.	(a)-nti[4]	(a)-n, ur[7]	īyur	yúr	a-n	(a)-ntu[4]

[1] The final a of the stem in the first conjugation is lengthened before m or v: **bhávā-mi, bhávā-vas.**

[2] In the RV. **masi** is more than five times as common as **mas**, but in the AV. **mas** is rather commoner than **masi.**

[3] The only example of the ending **thana** in the **a** conjugation is **váda-thana.**

[4] Reduplicated verbs and others treated as such drop the n in the 3. pl. ind. pr. and impv. act. In the whole second conj. the n is dropped in the 3. pl. pres. impf. impv. mid.

[5] m in the first (**á-bhava-m**), **am** in the second (**á-dveṣ-am**).

[6] There are no examples of this ending in the **a** conjugation.

[7] The ending **ur** is taken by nearly all the verbs of the reduplicating class and by several of the root class.

[8] These endings coalesce with the final **a** of the stem to **eyam, es, et,** &c.

[9] Verbs of the **a** conjugation have normally no ending in the 2. s. impv.; but they not infrequently add **tāt**, which occurs in B. also. In the graded conjugation **dhi, hi, tāt** are added to the weak stem, and **āna** in some verbs of the ninth class: e.g. **ad-dhí, śṛṇu-dhi; śṛṇu-hi, punī-hi; aś-āna; vit-tāt, kṛṇu-tāt.**

[10] Only two examples occur in the **a** conjugation: **bhája-tana** and **náhya-tana.**

MIDDLE.

	PRESENT.	IMPF.	OPTATIVE.	SUBJUNCTIVE.	IMPERATIVE.
1.	e	i[2]	īya[4]	ai	—
2.	se	thās	ī-thās	a-se, a-sai[5]	sva
3.	te	ta	ī-ta	a-te, a-tai[6]	tām, ām
1.	vahe[1]	vahi[1]	ī-vahi	ā-vahai	—
2.	ethe[3] (1), áthe (2)	ethām[3] (1), āthām (2)	ī-y-āthām	aithe	ethām[3] (1) āthām (2)
3.	ete[3] (1), áte (2)	etām[3] (1), ātām (2)	ī-y-ātām	aite	etām[3] (1) ātām (2)
1.	mahe[1]	mahi[1]	ī-mahi	ā-mahai, ā-mahe	—
2.	dhve	dhvam	ī-dhvam	a-dhvai	dhvam
3.	nte (1), áte (2)	nta (1), ata (2)	ī-r-an	a-ntai[7], a-nta[8]	ntām (1) atām (2)

[1] The final a of the first conjugation is lengthened before m and v.

[2] This i combines with the final a of the first conjugation to e: bháve.

[3] In these forms e takes the place of the final a of the a conjugation.

[4] This modal ī combines with the final a of the first conjugation to e: bháveya, &c.

[5] The RV. has a-se only, the AV. and the Brāhmaṇas a-sai only.

[6] The form a-te is almost exclusively used in the RV., while a-tai is the prevailing one in the AV., and the only one later.

[7] The ending a-ntai occurs in B. only.

[8] The form in a-nta in the a conjugation, where it is very common, e.g. bhava-nta, is an injunctive; but in the graded conjugation a subj., e.g. kṛṇav-a-nta (inj. kṛṇvata).

Paradigms.

132. Since the three classes of the first conjugation, as well as all the secondary verbs the stems of which end in a, are inflected exactly alike,[1] one paradigm will suffice for all of them. The injunctive is not given here because its forms are identical with the unaugmented imperfect. Forms of which no examples are found in the Saṃhitās are added in square brackets.

[1] All other conjugational stems ending in a, the passive (154), the a future (151), the a (141 *a*), the sa (147), and the reduplicated (149) aor. are similarly inflected.

FIRST CONJUGATION.

First Class: bhū *be*:

Present.

ACTIVE.

	SINGULAR.	DUAL.	PLURAL.
1.	bhávā-mi	bhávā-vas	bhávā-masi bhávā-mas
2.	bháva-si	bháva-thas	bháva-tha
3.	bháva-ti	bháva-tas	bháva-nti

Imperfect.

1.	á-bhava-m	[á-bhavā-va]	á-bhavā-ma
2.	á-bhava-s	á-bhava-tam	á-bhava-ta
3.	á-bhava-t	á-bhava-tām	á-bhava-n

Imperative.

2.	bháva bháva-tāt	bháva-tam	bháva-ta
3.	bháva-tu	bháva-tām	bháva-ntu

Subjunctive.

1.	bhávā-ni bhávā	bhávā-va	bhávā-ma
2.	bhávā-si bhávā-s	bhávā-thas	bhávā-tha
3.	bhávā-ti bhávā-t	bhávā-tas	bhávā-n

Optative.

1.	bháv-eyam	[bháv-eva]	bháv-ema
2.	bháv-es	[bháv-etam]	[bháv-eta]
3.	bháv-et	bháv-etām	bháv-eyur

Participle.

bháv-ant, f. -ī

FIRST CONJUGATION.

Present stem **bháv-a.**

MIDDLE.

Present.

SINGULAR.	DUAL.	PLURAL.
bháv-e	**bhávā-vahe**	**bhávā-mahe**
bháva-se	[**bháv-ethe**]	**bháva-dhve**
bháva-te	**bháv-ete**	**bháva-nte**

Imperfect.

á-bhav-e	[**á-bhavā-vahi**]	[**á-bhavā-mahi**]
á-bhava-thās	**á-bhav-ethām**	[**á-bhava-dhvam**]
á-bhava-ta	**á-bhav-etām**	**á-bhava-nta**

Imperative.

bháva-sva	**bháv-ethām**	**bháva-dhvam**
bháva-tām	**bháv-etām**	**bháva-ntām**

Subjunctive.

bháv-ai	**bhávā-vahai**	**bhávā-mahai**
{ **bhávā-se** **bhávā-sai** (AV.)	**bháv-aithe**	[**bhávā-dhve**]
{ **bhávā-te** **bhávā-tai**	**bháv-aite**	[**bhávā-nte**]

Optative.

bháv-eya	**bháv-evahi**	**bháv-emahi**
[**bháv-ethās**]	[**bháv-eyāthām**]	[**bháv-edhvam**]
bháv-eta	[**bháv-eyātām**]	[**bháv-eran**]

Participle.

bháva-māna, f. **ā**

SECOND CONJUGATION.

Second Class: i *go*: Present stem **é, i.**

ACTIVE.

Present.

	SINGULAR.	DUAL.	PLURAL.
1.	é-mi	[i-vás]	i-mási i-más
2.	é-ṣi	i-thás	i-thá i-thána
3.	é-ti	i-tás	y-ánti

Imperfect.

1.	ā́y-am	[ái-va]	ái-ma
2.	ái-s	ái-tam	ái-ta ái-tana
3.	ái-t	ái-tām	ā́y-an

Imperative.

2.	i-hí, i-tā́t	i-tám	i-tá i-tána
3.	é-tu	i-tā́m	y-ántu

Subjunctive.

1.	áy-āni áy-ā	áy-ā-va	áy-ā-ma
2.	áy-a-si áy-a-s	áy-a-thas	áy-a-tha
3.	áy-a-ti áy-a-t	áy-a-tas	áy-a-n

Optative.

1.	i-yā́m	i-yā́-va	i-yā́-ma
2.	i-yā́-s	i-yā́-tām	i-yā́-ta
3.	i-yā́-t	i-yā́-tām	i-yúr

Participle.

y-ánt, f. y-at-ī́

SECOND CONJUGATION.

brū *speak*: Present stem **bráv, brū.**

MIDDLE.

Present.

SINGULAR.	DUAL.	PLURAL.
bruv-é	[brū-váhe]	brū-máhe
brū-ṣé	bruv-ā́the	brū-dhvé
brū-té / bruv-é	bruv-ā́te	bruv-áte

Imperfect.

SINGULAR.	DUAL.	PLURAL.
[á-bruv-i]	[á-brū-vahi]	[á-brū-mahi]
á-brū-thās	[á-bruv-āthām]	á-brū-dhvam
á-brū-ta	[á-bruv-ātām]	á-bruv-ata

Imperative.

SINGULAR.	DUAL.	PLURAL.
brū-ṣvá	[bruv-ā́thām]	brū-dhvám
brū-tā́m	[bruv-ā́tām]	bruv-átām

Subjunctive.

SINGULAR.	DUAL.	PLURAL.
bráv-ai	bráv-ā-vahai	bráv-ā-mahai
bráv-a-se	bráv-aithe	[bráv-a-dhve]
bráv-a-te	bráv-aite	bráv-a-nta

Optative.

SINGULAR.	DUAL.	PLURAL.
bruv-ī-yá	[bruv-ī-váhi]	bruv-ī-máhi
[bruv-ī-thā́s]	[bruv-ī-yā́thām]	[bruv-ī-dhvám]
bruv-ī-tá	[bruv-ī-yā́tām]	[bruv-ī-rán]

Participle.

bruv-āṇá, f. ā́

Third Class: bhṛ *bear*:

ACTIVE.

Present.

	SINGULAR.	DUAL.	PLURAL.
1.	bíbhar-mi	[bibhṛ-vás]	bibhṛ-mási bibhṛ-más
2.	bíbhar-ṣi	bibhṛ-thás	bibhṛ-thá
3.	bíbhar-ti	bibhṛ-tás	bíbhr-ati

Imperfect.

1.	á-bibhar-am	[á-bibhṛ-va]	á-bibhṛ-ma
2.	á-bibhar (28)	á-bibhṛ-tam	á-bibhṛ-ta á-bibhṛ-tana
3.	á-bibhar (28)	á-bibhṛ-tām	á-bibhr-an á-bibhar-ur

Imperative.

2.	bibhṛ-hí bibhṛ-tā́t	bibhṛ-tám	bibhṛ-tá bibhṛ-tána
3.	bíbhar-tu	bibhṛ-tā́m	bíbhr-atu

Subjunctive.

1.	bíbhar-āṇi	[bíbhar-ā-va]	bíbhar-ā-ma
2.	bíbhar-a-s	bíbhar-a-thas	[bíbhar-a-tha]
3.	bíbhar-a-t	[bíbhar-a-tas]	bíbhar-a-n

Optative.

1.	bibhṛ-yā́m	[bibhṛ-yā́-va]	bibhṛ-yā́-ma
2.	bibhṛ-yā́-s	[bibhṛ-yā́-tam]	[bibhṛ-yā́-ta]
3.	bibhṛ-yā́-t	bibhṛ-yā́-tām	bibhṛ-yúr

Participle.

bíbhr-at, f. bíbhr-at-ī

Present stem **bíbhar, bibhṛ.**

MIDDLE.

Present.

SINGULAR.	DUAL.	PLURAL.
bíbhr-e	**bibhṛ-váhe**	**bíbhṛ-máhe**
bibhṛ-ṣé	**bíbhr-āthe**	**bibhṛ-dhvé**
bibhṛ-té	**bíbhr-āte**	**bíbhr-ate**

Imperfect.

[á-bibhr-i]	**á-bibhṛ-vahi**]	[á-bibhṛ-mahi]
á-bibhṛ-thās	[á-bibhr-āthām]	[á-bibhṛ-dhvam]
á-bibhṛ-ta	[á-bibhr-ātām]	**á-bibhr-ata**

Imperative.

bibhṛ-ṣvá	**bíbhr-āthām**	**bibhṛ-dhvám**
bibhṛ-tā́m	[bíbhr-ātām]	**bíbhr-atām**

Subjunctive.

[bíbhar-ai]	**bíbhar-ā-vahai**	**bíbhar-ā-mahai**
bíbhar-a-se	[bíbhar-aithe]	[bíbhar-a-dhve]
bíbhar-a-te	[bíbhar-aite]	**bíbhar-a-nta**

Optative.

bíbhr-īya	[bíbhr-ī-vahi]	**bíbhr-ī-mahi**
[bíbhr-ī-thās]	[bíbhr-ī-yāthām]	[bíbhr-ī-dhvam]
bíbhr-ī-ta	[bíbhr-ī-yātām]	**bíbhr-ī-ran**

Participle.

bíbhr-āṇa, f. ā

Fifth Class: kṛ *make*:

ACTIVE.

Present.

	SINGULAR.	DUAL.	PLURAL.
1.	kṛ-ṇó-mi	[kṛṇ-vás]	kṛṇ-mási kṛṇ-más
2.	kṛ-ṇó-ṣi	kṛṇu-thás	kṛṇu-thá
3.	kṛ-ṇó-ti	kṛṇu-tás	kṛṇv-ánti

Imperfect.

1.	á-kṛṇav-am	[á-kṛṇ-va]	[á-kṛṇ-ma]
2.	á-kṛṇo-s	á-kṛṇu-tam	á-kṛṇu-ta
3.	á-kṛṇo-t	á-kṛṇu-tām	á-kṛṇv-an

Imperative.

2.	kṛṇu-hí kṛṇú kṛṇu-tā́t	kṛṇu-tám	kṛṇu-tá kṛṇó-ta kṛṇó-tana
3.	[kṛṇó-tu]	kṛṇu-tā́m	kṛṇv-ántu

Subjunctive.

1.	kṛṇáv-ā kṛṇáv-āni	kṛṇáv-ā-va	kṛṇáv-ā-ma
2.	kṛṇáv-a-s	[kṛṇáv-a-thas]	kṛṇáv-a-tha
3.	kṛṇáv-a-t	[kṛṇáv-a-tas]	kṛṇáv-a-n

Optative.

1.	kṛṇu-yā́m	[kṛṇu-yā́-va]	kṛṇu-yā́-ma
2.	[kṛṇu-yā́-s]	[kṛṇu-yā́-tam]	[kṛṇu-yā́-ta]
3.	kṛṇu-yā́-t	[kṛṇu-yā́-tām]	[kṛṇu-yúr]

Participle.

kṛṇv-ánt, f. kṛṇv-at-ī́

Present stem **kṛ-ṇó, kṛ-ṇu.**

MIDDLE.

Present.

SINGULAR.	DUAL.	PLURAL.
kṛṇv-é	**[kṛṇ-váhe]**	**kṛṇ-máhe**
kṛṇu-ṣé	**kṛṇv-ā́the**	**[kṛṇu-dhvé]**
{kṛṇu-té / kṛṇv-é}	**[kṛṇv-ā́te]**	**kṛṇv-áte**

Imperfect.

[á-kṛṇv-i]	**[á-kṛṇ-vahi]**	**[á-kṛṇ-mahi]**
á-kṛṇu-thās	**[á-kṛṇv-āthām]**	**á-kṛṇu-dhvam**
á-kṛṇu-ta	**[á-kṛṇv-ātām]**	**á-kṛṇv-ata**

Imperative.

kṛṇu-ṣvá	**kṛṇv-ā́thām**	**kṛṇu-dhvám**
kṛṇu-tā́m	**[kṛṇv-ā́tām]**	**kṛṇv-átām**

Subjunctive.

kṛṇáv-ai	**kṛṇáv-ā-vahai**	**kṛṇáv-ā-mahai**
kṛṇáv-a-se	**kṛṇáv-aithe**	**[kṛṇáv-a-dhve]**
kṛṇáv-a-te	**kṛṇáv-aite**	**kṛṇáv-a-nta**

Optative.

[kṛṇv-īyá]	**[kṛṇv-ī-váhi]**	**[kṛṇv-ī-máhi]**
[kṛṇv-ī-thā́s]	**[kṛṇv-ī-yā́thām]**	**[kṛṇv-ī-dhvám]**
kṛṇv-ī-tá	**[kṛṇv-ī-yā́tām]**	**[kṛṇv-ī-rán]**

Participle.

kṛṇv-āná, f. ā́

Seventh Class: yuj *join*:

ACTIVE.

Present.

	SINGULAR.	DUAL.	PLURAL.
1.	yu-ná-j-mi	[yuñj-vás]	yuñj-más
2.	yu-ná-k-ṣi (63, 67)	[yuṅk-thás]	[yuṅk-thá]
3.	yu-ná-k-ti (63)	[yuṅk-tás]	yuñj-ánti

Imperfect.

1.	[á-yunaj-am]	[á-yuñj-va]	[á-yuñj-ma]
2.	á-yunak (63, 61)	á-yuṅk-tam	[á-yuṅk-ta]
3.	á-yunak (63, 61)	[á-yuṅk-tām]	á-yuñj-an

Imperative.

2.	yuṅ-dhí (10 *a*)	yuṅ-tám (10 *a*)	yuṅ-tá / yunák-ta, -tana
3.	yunák-tu	yuṅ-tā́m	yuñj-ántu

Subjunctive.

1.	[yunáj-āni]	yunáj-ā-va	yunáj-ā-ma
2.	yunáj-a-s	[yunáj-a-thas]	[yunáj-a-tha]
3.	yunáj-a-t	yunáj-a-tas	yunáj-a-n

Optative.

1.	[yuñj-yā́m]	[yuñj-yā́-va]	[yuñj-yā́-ma]
2.	[yuñj-yā́-s]	[yuñj-yā́-tam]	[yuñj-yā́-ta]
3.	yuñj-yā́-t	[yuñj-yā́-tām]	[yuñj-yúr]

Participle.

yuñj-ánt, f. yuñj-at-ī́

Present stem: **yu-ná-j, yu-ñ-j.**

MIDDLE.

Present.

SINGULAR.	DUAL.	PLURAL.
yuñj-é	**[yuñj-váhe]**	**[yuñj-máhe]**
yuṅk-ṣé	**yuñj-ā́the**	**yuṅg-dhvé**
yuṅk-té	**yuñj-ā́te**	**yuñj-áte**

Imperfect.

[á-yuñj-i]	**[á-yuñj-vahi]**	**[á-yuñj-mahi]**
[á-yuṅk-thās]	**[á-yuñj-āthām]**	**[á-yuṅg-dhvam]**
[á-yuṅk-ta]	**[á-yuñj-ātām]**	**á-yuñj-ata**

Imperative.

yuṅk-ṣvá (63, 67)	**yuñj-ā́thām**	**yuṅg-dhvám**
yuṅ-tā́m	**[yuñj-ā́tām]**	**yuñj-átām**

Subjunctive.

[yunáj-ai]	**[yunáj-ā-vahai]**	**yunáj-ā-mahai**
[yunáj-a-se]	**[yunáj-aithe]**	**[yunáj-a-dhve]**
yunáj-a-te	**[yunáj-aite]**	**[yunáj-a-nta]**

Optative.

[yuñj-īyá]	**[yuñj-ī-vahi]**	**[yuñj-ī-máhi]**
[yuñj-ī-thā́s]	**[yuñj-ī-yā́thām]**	**[yuñj-ī-dhvám]**
yuñj-ī-tá	**[yuñj-ī-yā́tām]**	**[yuñj-ī-rán]**

Participle.

yuñj-āná, f. **ā́**

Ninth Class : grabh ***seize*****:**

ACTIVE.

Present.

	SINGULAR.	DUAL.	PLURAL.
1.	gṛbh-ṇā́-mi	[gṛbh-ṇī-vás]	gṛbh-ṇī-mási gṛbh-ṇī-más
2.	gṛbh-ṇā́-si	gṛbh-ṇī-thás	gṛbh-ṇī-thá gṛbh-ṇī-thána
3.	gṛbh-ṇā́-ti	gṛbh-ṇī-tás	gṛbh-ṇ-ánti

Imperfect.

1.	á-gṛbh-ṇā-m	[á-gṛbh-ṇī-va]	[á-gṛbh-ṇī-ma]
2.	á-gṛbh-ṇā-s	á-gṛbh-ṇī-tam	á-gṛbh-ṇī-ta
3.	á-gṛbh-ṇā-t	[á-gṛbh-ṇī-tām]	á-gṛbh-ṇ-an

Imperative.

2.	gṛbh-ṇī-hí gṛbh-ṇī-tā́t gṛbh-āṇá	gṛbh-ṇī-tám	gṛbh-ṇī-tá gṛbh-ṇī-tána
3.	gṛbh-ṇā́-tu	gṛbh-ṇī-tā́m	gṛbh-ṇ-ántu

Subjunctive.

1.	gṛbh-ṇ-ā́ni	[gṛbh-ṇā́-va]	gṛbh-ṇā́-ma
2.	gṛbh-ṇā́-s	[gṛbh-ṇā́-thas]	gṛbh-ṇā́-tha
3.	gṛbh-ṇā́-t gṛbh-ṇā́-ti	[gṛbh-ṇā́-tas]	gṛbh-ṇā́-n

Optative.

1.	gṛbh-ṇī-yā́m	[gṛbh-ṇī-yā́-va]	[gṛbh-ṇī-yā́-ma]
2.	gṛbh-ṇī-yā́-s	[gṛbh-ṇī-yā́-tam]	[gṛbh-ṇī-yā́-ta]
3.	gṛbh-ṇī-yā́-t	[gṛbh-ṇī-yā́-tām]	[gṛbh-ṇī-yúr]

Participle.

gṛbh-ṇ-ánt, f. gṛbh-ṇ-at-ī́.

Present stem **gṛbh-ṇā́, gṛbh-ṇī, gṛbh-ṇ.**

Middle.

Present.

SINGULAR.	DUAL.	PLURAL.
gṛbh-ṇ-é	[**gṛbh-ṇī-váhe**]	**gṛbh-ṇī-máhe**
gṛbh-ṇī-ṣé	[**gṛbh-ṇ-ā́the**]	[**gṛbh-ṇī-dhvé**]
gṛbh-ṇī-té	[**gṛbh-ṇ-ā́te**]	**gṛbh-ṇ-áte**

Imperfect.

á-gṛbh-ṇ-i	[**á-gṛbh-ṇī-vahi**]	**á-gṛbh-ṇī-mahi**
[**á-gṛbh-ṇī-thās**]	[**á-gṛbh-ṇ-āthām**]	[**á-gṛbh-ṇī-dhvam**]
á-gṛbh-ṇī-ta	[**á-gṛbh-ṇ-ātām**]	**á-gṛbh-ṇ-ata**

Imperative.

gṛbh-ṇī-ṣvá	[**gṛbh-ṇ-ā́thām**]	**gṛbh-ṇī-dhvám**
gṛbh-ṇī-tā́m	[**gṛbh-ṇ-ā́tām**]	**gṛbh-ṇ-átām**

Subjunctive.

[**gṛbh-ṇ-ái**]	**gṛbh-ṇā́-vahai**	**gṛbh-ṇā́-mahai**
[**gṛbh-ṇā́-se**]	[**gṛbh-ṇ-áithe**]	[**gṛbh-ṇā́-dhve**]
[**gṛbh-ṇā́-te**]	[**gṛbh-ṇ-áite**]	[**gṛbh-ṇā́-nta**]

Optative.

[**gṛbh-ṇ-īyá**]	[**gṛbh-ṇ-ī-váhi**]	[**gṛbh-ṇ-ī-máhi**]
[**gṛbh-ṇ-īthā́s**]	[**gṛbh-ṇ-ī-yā́thām**]	[**gṛbh-ṇ-ī-dhvám**]
gṛbh-ṇ-ītá	**gṛbh-ṇ-ī-yā́tām**]	[**gṛbh-ṇ-ī-rán**]

Participle.

gṛbh-ṇ-āná, f. ā́

Irregularities of the Present Stem.

First Conjugation.

133. A. **First or Bhū Class.** 1. The radical vowel is lengthened in **guh** *hide* and in **kram** *stride* (in the act. only): **gū́ha,**[1] **krā́ma-ti** (but mid. **krā́ma-te**); **ūh** *consider* takes Guṇa: **óh-a**;[2] **kṛp** *lament* does not take Guṇa: **kṛ́p-a.**[3]

2. **gam** *go*, **yam** *restrain*, **yu** *separate* form their present stems with **cha** (Gk. σκ): **gá-cha** (Gk. *βά-σκω*), **yá-cha, yú-cha.**

3. *a.* The four roots **pā** *drink*, **sthā** *stand*, **sac** *accompany*, **sad** *sit* form present stems that originally belonged to the reduplicating class: **píba** (Lat. *bibo*); **tíṣṭha** (*ἵστη-μι*, Lat. *sisto*); **sáśca**[4] (for **sá-s(a)c-a**); **sī́da** (for **sí-s(a)d-a**; Lat. *sīdo*).

b. Four stems are transfers from the fifth or **nu** class, being either used beside or having entirely superseded the simpler original stems: **í-nv-a-ti** (from i *send*) beside **i-nó-ti**; **jí-nv-a-ti** (from **ji** *quicken*) beside **ji-nó-ṣi**; **hí-nv-a-ti** (from **hi** *impel*) beside **hi-nó-ti**; **pí-nv-a** *fatten*, doubtless originally **pí-nu** (√**pī̆**).

4. **daṃś** *bite* and **sañj** *hang* lose their nasal: **dáś-a, sáj-a.**

5. The ending **tāt** (besides being regularly used in the 2. s. impv. by twelve verbs) is exceptionally used for the 3. s. in **gácha-tāt** and **smára-tāt.** Only one example occurs, in this class, of the 2. pl. impv. act. ending **tana**: **bhája-tana**; and one of **dhva** (for **dhvam**) in the 2. pl. mid.: **yája-dhva.**

---

[1] Instead of taking Guṇa.

[2] But **ūh** *remove* remains unchanged (125, 1).

[3] Against 125, 1.

[4] A reminiscence of the reduplicative origin of this stem is the loss of the nasal in the 3. pl. pres. **sáśc-ati** and 3. pl. inj. mid. **saśc-ata.**

B. **Fourth or Ya Class.** 1. The radical syllable is reduced in seven verbs: **spaś** *see* loses its initial: **páś-ya**; **vyadh** *pierce* takes Samprasāraṇa: **vídh-ya**; **ā** is shortened in **dhā** *suck*: **dhá-ya**; **mā** *exchange*: **má-ya**; **vā** *weave*: **vá-ya**; **vyā** *envelope*: **vyá-ya**; **hvā** *call*: **hvá-ya.**

2. Final **r̥̄** sometimes becomes both **īr** and **ūr**: **jr̥̄** *waste away*: **jū́r-ya** and **jī́r-ya** (AV.); **tr̥̄** *cross*: **tū́r-ya** and **tī́r-ya**; **pr̥̄** *fill* becomes **pū́r-ya** only (because of its initial labial).

3. **śram** *be weary* lengthens its vowel: **śrā́m-ya**; in B. **tam** *faint* and **mad** *be exhilarated* do the same: **tā́m-ya, mā́d-ya.**

C. **Sixth Class.** 1. The radical vowel is nasalized in eight verbs: **kr̥t** *cut*: **kr̥nt-á**; **tr̥p** *be pleased*: **tr̥mp-á**; **piś** *adorn*: **piṃś-á**; **muc** *release*: **muñc-á**; **lip** *smear*: **limp-á**; **lup** *break*: **lump-á**; **vid** *find*: **vind-á**; **sic** *sprinkle*: **siñc-á.** Three other roots, **tud** *thrust*, **dr̥h** *make firm*, **śubh** *shine* have occasional nasalized forms.

2. Four roots form their present stem with the suffix **cha** (cp. A 2): **iṣ** *wish*: **i-chá**; **r̥** *go*: **r̥-chá**; **praś** *ask*: **pr̥-chá**;[1] **vas** *shine*: **u-chá.** The root **vraśc** *cut*, which seems to be formed with **c**,[2] takes Samprasāraṇa: **vr̥śc-á.**

3. Three roots in **r̥̄**, **kr̥̄** *scatter*, **gr̥̄** *swallow*, **tr̥̄** *cross*, form the present stems **kir-á, gir-á, tir-á** (beside **tár-a**).

a. Beside the normal use of the imperative suffix **tāt** for the 2. s. in **mr̥ḍá-tāt, viśá-tāt, vr̥há-tāt, suvá-tāt,** it also appears for the 3. s. in **viśá-tāt.**

134. A. Second or Root Class.

1. The root is irregularly **strengthened** in the following verbs:

a. **kṣṇu** *whet*, **yu** *unite*, **nu** and **stu** *praise* take Vr̥ddhi instead of Guṇa in the strong forms before terminations

---

[1] With Samprasāraṇa and loss of **ś**. Cp. Lat. *prec-or* and *po(rc)-sco*, and Old German *frag-en* 'ask' and *for-scon* (*forschen*).

[2] Cp. **-vras-ka** *cutting*, past participle **vr̥k-ṇá** *cut*, and **vŕ̥k-a** *wolf*.

beginning with consonants;[1] e.g. **stáu-mi, á-stau-t,** but **á-stav-am.**

b. **mṛj** *wipe* takes Vṛddhi in the strong forms: **mā́rj-mi, mā́rṣ-ṭi,** but **mṛj-más, mṛj-ánti.**

c. **śī** *lie* mid. takes Guṇa and accents the radical syllable throughout its weak forms: e.g. s. 1. 3. **śáy-e,** 2. **śé-ṣe** (*κεῖ-σαι*). It has the additional irregularity of inserting **r** before the endings in the 3. pl. pr., impv., impf.: **śé-r-ate, śé-r-atām, á-śe-r-an.**

a. **i** *go*, **brū** *speak*, **stu** *praise*, **han** *slay* before the ending of the 2. pl. impv. act. have the alternative forms **é-ta** and **é-tana, brávī-tana, stó-ta, hán-tana.** **Brū** has the same irregularity in the 2. pl. impf. **ábravī-ta** and **ábravī-tana.**

2. The **root** is irregularly **weakened** in the following verbs:

a. **vaś** *desire* takes Samprasāraṇa in the weak forms: 1. pl. **uś-mási,** part. **uś-āná,** but 1. s. **váś-mi.**

b. **as** *be* drops its initial **a** in the optative and all the weak forms of the pr. and impv.; e.g. opt. **s-yā́t** *would be*; pr. **s-más** *we are*, **s-ánti** (Lat. *sunt*) *they are*; impv. du. 2. **s-tám,** pl. 2. **s-tá,** 3. **s-ántu.** The 2. s. impv. preserves the vowel (in an altered form) in **e-dhí** (for **az-dhí,** Av. *zdī*). In the impf. it inserts **ī** before the endings of the 2. 3. s.: **ā́s-ī-s, ā́s-ī-t** (beside **ā́s** = **ā́s-t**).

c. **han** *slay* in weak forms loses its **n** before terminations beginning with consonants (except **m, y, v**), as **ha-thá,** but **hán-ti.** In the 3. pl. pr., impv., impf., and part., the **a** is syncopated and **h** reverts to the original guttural **gh**: **ghn-ánti, ghn-ántu, á-ghn-an; ghn-ánt.** The 2. s. impv. is **ja-hí** (for **jha-hí**), with palatalized initial instead of **gha-hí.**

---

[1] In B. **ru** *cry*, **su** *impel*, **sku** *tear*, **snu** *distil* have the same peculiarity: **rau-ti, sau-ti, skau-ti, snau-ti.**

3. A vowel or semivowel is irregularly inserted in the following verbs:

a. The roots **an** *breathe*, **rud** *weep*, **vam** *vomit*, **śvas** *blow*, **svap** *sleep* insert **i** before all terminations beginning with a consonant, except in the 2. 3. s. impf., where they insert **ī**; e.g. **án-i-ti, ā́n-ī-t; a-vam-ī-t; śvas-i-ti.**

b. The roots **īḍ** *praise* and **īś** *rule* add **i** in some forms of the 2. s. and pl. mid.: **ī́ḍ-i-ṣva; ī́ś-i-ṣe** (beside **ī́k-ṣe**), **īśi-dhve.** Occasional forms (2. s. impv.) with connecting **i** from other roots also occur: **jan-i-ṣva** *be born*, **vas-i-ṣva** *clothe*, **śnath-i-hi** *pierce*, **stan-i-hi** *thunder*.

c. The root **brū** *speak* inserts **ī** in the strong forms before terminations beginning with consonants: **bráv-ī-mi, á-brav-ī-t;** **am** *injure* inserts **ī** before consonants; thus **am-ī-ti, am-ī-ṣva, ām-ī-t** (TS.).

4. With regard to the endings:

a. The root **śās** *order* loses the **n** in the 3. pl. act. and mid., and in the part.: **śās-ate, śās-atu, śā́s-at.**

b. The root **duh** *milk* is very anomalous in its endings. The irregular forms are the following: act. impf. 3. s. **á-duh-a-t** beside **á-dhok**, 3. pl. **á-duh-ran** beside **á-duh-an** and **duh-úr**; opt. 3. s. **duh-īyát** (for **duh-yā́t**), 3. pl. **duh-ī-yán** (for **duh-yúr**). Mid. pr. ind. 3. pl. **duh-ré** and **duh-rate** beside the regular **duh-até**;[1] impv. 3. s. **duh-ā́m**,[2] 3. pl. **duh-rā́m** and **duh-rátām**; part. **dúgh-āna.**

c. Roots ending in **ā** take **ur** instead of **an** in the 3. pl. impf. act.; e.g. **pā** *protect*: **á-p-ur.** A few roots ending in consonants show the same irregularity; e.g. **tviṣ** *be stirred*: **á-tviṣ-ur.**

a. The verbs **īś** *rule*, **duh** *milk*, **vid** *find*, **śī** *lie* frequently, and **cit** *observe*, **brū** *speak* rarely, take **e** instead of **te**[3] in the 3. s. pr. mid.: **ī́ś-e, duh-é, vid-é, śáy-e; cit-é, bruv-é.**

β. In the AV. and B. subj. forms with **ā** instead of **a** are not uncommon; e.g. **áy-ā-s, ás-ā-t,**[4] **bráv-ā-thas, hán-ā-tha, ád-ā-n.**

---

[1] But with irregular accent, as also **rih-até** *they lick*.

[2] In the AV. the 3. s. impv. mid. is similarly formed in **śáy-ām.**

[3] This irregularity occurs in B. also.

[4] In B. subj. forms with primary endings are very rare.

B. **Third or Reduplicating Class.**

1. Roots ending in ā drop the radical vowel before terminations beginning with vowels; e. g. **mā** *measure*: 1. s. **mím-e**, 3. pl. **mím-ate.**

a. The ā of **mā** *measure*, **mā** *bellow*, **rā** *give*, **śā** *sharpen*, **hā** *go away* is in weak forms usually changed to ī before consonants (cp. 5 *c*): **mímī-te**; **rarī-thā́s**;[1] **śiśī-mási**; **jíhī-te.**

b. **dā** *give*, **dhā** *place*, the two commonest verbs in this class, use **dad** and **dadh** as their stems in all weak forms: **dád-mahe, dadh-mási.** When the aspiration of **dadh** is lost before **t, th, s** it is thrown back on the initial: **dhat-té, dhat-thá, dhat-svá.** The 2. s. impv. act. is **de-hí** (for **daz-dhí**) beside **dad-dhí** and **dat-tā́t**; and **dhe-hí** (for **dhaz-dhí**) beside **dhat-tā́t.**

2. The root **vyac** takes Samprasāraṇa, e. g. 3. du. pr. **vivik-tás**; **hvar** *be crooked* makes some forms with Samprasāraṇa and then reduplicates with **u**: e.g. **ju-hūr-thās**, 2. s. inj. mid.

3. **bhas** *chew*, **sac** *accompany*, **has** *laugh* syncopate the radical vowel in weak forms; thus **bá-ps-ati** 3 pl. ind. pr. (but **ba-bhas-a-t** 3. s. subj.); **sá-śc-ati** 3. pl. ind. pr., **sá-śc-ata** 3. pl. inj.; **já-kṣ-at** (for **ja-gh(a)s-at**) pr. part.

a. The roots **ṛ** *go*, **dā** *give*, **dhā** *put*, **pṛ** *cross*, **yu** *separate*, **śā** *sharpen*, **hu** *sacrifice* have several forms with a strong vowel in the 2. impv. act. s. **yu-yo-dhí, śi-śā-dhí** (beside **śi-śī-hí**); du. **yu-yó-tam** (beside **yu-yu-tám**); pl. **í-y-ar-ta, dá-dā-ta** and **dá-dā-tana, dá-dhā-ta** and **dá-dhā-tana, pí-par-tana, yu-yó-ta** and **yu-yó-tana, ju-hó-ta** and **ju-hó-tana. dā, dhā, hā** *leave*, have similar strong forms in the 2. pl. impf.: **á-da-dā-ta, á-dadhā-ta, á-jahā-tana.**

β. There are numerous transfers from this to other classes. The roots **pā** *drink*, **sthā** *stand*, **han** *stride* form such stems according to the a conjugation exclusively, **píba, tíṣṭha, jíghna** (cp. 133 A. 3 *a*); while **ghrā** *smell*, **bhas** *chew*, **mā** *bellow*, **rā** *give*, **sac** *accompany* occasionally use the a stems **jíghra, bápsa, míma, rára, sáśca.** The roots **dā** *give* and **dhā** *put* also make some forms from their weak stems according to the

---

[1] But 2. s. impv. act. **rarā-sva** (AV.).

a conjugation, as 3. s. pr. mid. **dád-a-te**, 3. pl. act. **dádh-a-nti**, 3. pl. impv. **dádh-a-ntu**. The former, dad, has even an incipient tendency to become a root; thus it forms the past part. pass. **dat-tá** *given*.

C. Fifth or Nu Class. 1. The u of the suffix is dropped before the m of the 1. pl. ind. act. and mid., as **kṛṇ-más**, **kṛṇ-máhe**.

2. When **nu** is preceded by a consonant its u becomes **uv** before vowel endings; e.g. 3. pl. pr. **aś-nuv-ánti** (but **su-nv-ánti**).

3. **śru** *hear* forms (by dissimilation) the stem **śṛ-ṇu**, and **vṛ** *cover* (with interchange of vowel and semivowel) **ūr-ṇu** beside the regular **vṛ-ṇu**.

4. Beside the regular and very frequent present stem **kṛ-ṇu**[1] (from **kṛ** *make*) there begins to appear in the tenth Maṇḍala of the RV. the very anomalous **kuru.**[2] The strong form of this stem, **karó**, which has the further anomaly of Guṇa in the root, first appears in the AV.[3]

a. The four roots ending in n, tan *stretch*, man *think*, van *win*, san *gain*, have the appearance of forming their stem with the suffix u, as tan-u. These (with three later roots) form a separate (eighth) class according to the Hindu grammarians. But the a of these present stems in reality probably represents the sonant nasal, = tn̥-nu. This group was joined by kur-u, the late and anomalous present stem of kṛ *make* (cp. C 4).

β. Five stems of this class, i-nu, ṛ-ṇu, ji-nu, pi-nu, hi-nu, have come to be used frequently as secondary roots forming present stems according to the a conjugation : ínv-a, ṛ́ṇv-a, jínv-a, pínv-a, hínv-a.

γ. In the 3. pl. pr. mid. six verbs of this class take the ending re[4] with connecting vowel i : inv-i-ré, ṛṇv-i-ré, pinv-i-ré, śṛṇv-i-ré, sunv-i-ré, hinv-i-ré.

---

[1] After the preposition pari *around* this stem prefixes an unoriginal s : pari-ṣ-kṛṇv-ánti *they adorn*.

[2] Twice in the 2. s. impv. kuru and once in the 1. pl. pr. ind. kur-mas.

[3] But the forms made from kṛṇu are still six times as common in the AV. as those from karó, kuru, which are the only stems used in B.

[4] Like duh-re in the root class.

δ. In the impv. the 2. s. act. has the ending **hi**, as **śṛṇu-hí**, three times as often in the RV. as the form without ending, as **śṛṇu**; in the AV. it occurs only about one-sixth as often as the latter; in B. it has almost disappeared. In the RV. the ending **dhi** also occurs in **śṛṇu-dhí**. The ending **tāt** occurs in **kṛṇu-tāt, hinu-tat, kuru-tāt**. In the 2. du. are found the strong forms **kṛṇo-tam, hino-tam**; and in the 2. pl. **kṛṇó-ta** and **kṛṇó-tana, śṛṇó-ta** and **śṛṇó-tana, sunó-ta** and **sunó-tana, hinó-ta** and **hinó-tana**; **tanó-ta** and **karó-ta**.

D. Infixing Nasal Class. 1. **añj** *anoint*, **bhañj** *break*, **hiṃs** *injure* drop their nasal before inserting **na**: as **a-ná-k-ti, bha-ná-k-ti, hi-ná-s-ti.**

2. **tṛh** *crush* infixes **né** in the strong forms; e.g. **tṛ-ṇé-ḍhi** (69 *c*).

E. Ninth or Nā Class. 1. The three roots **jī** *overpower*, **jū** *hasten*, **pū** *purify* shorten their vowel before the affix: **ji-nā́-mi, ju-nā́-si, pu-nā́-ti.**

2. **grabh** *seize* and its later form **grah** take Samprasāraṇa: **gṛbh-ṇā́-mi, gṛh-ṇā́-mi** (AV.).

3. **jñā** *know* and the four roots which in forms outside the present system appear with a nasal, **bandh** *bind*, **manth** *shake*, **skambh** *make firm*, **stambh** *prop*, drop their nasal: **jā-nā́-ti, badh-nā́-ti, math-nā́-ti, skabh-nā́-ti, stabh-nā́-ti.**

4. Four roots ending in consonants, **aś** *eat*, **grah** *seize*, **bandh** *bind*, **stambh** *prop*, have the peculiar ending **āna** in the 2. s. impv. act.: **aś-āná, gṛh-āṇá, badh-āná, stabh-āná.**

a. **pṛ** *fill* and **mṛ** *crush* make, beside the regular stems **pṛṇá** and **mṛṇá**, the transfer stems, according to the **a** conjugation, **pṛṇá** and **mṛṇá**, from which several forms occur.

The Perfect Tense.

135. This tense is formed by reduplication. Like the present, it has, besides an indicative, the subjunctive, injunctive, optative, and imperative moods, as well as participles, and an augmented form, the pluperfect. It is very common, being formed by nearly 300 verbs in the Saṃhitās.

Special Rules of Reduplication.

1. **ṛ** and **ṝ** (= **ar**) and **ḷ** (= **al**) always reduplicate with **ă** (cp. 139, 9); e. g. **kṛ** *do*: **ca-kṛ**; **tṝ** *cross*: **ta-tṛ**; **kḷp** *be adapted*: **cā-kḷp**; **ṛ** *go*: **ār** (= **a-ar**).

2. Initial **a** or **ā** becomes **ā**; e. g. **an** *breathe*: **ān**; **āp** *obtain*: **āp**. The long vowels **ī** and **ū** remain unchanged (= **i-ī** and **u-ū**); e. g. **īṣ** *move*: 1. s. **īṣ-é**; **ūh** *consider*: 3. s. **ūh-é**.

3. Roots beginning with **i** and **u** contract **i+i** to **ī** and **u+u** to **ū** except in the sing. act., where the reduplicative syllable is separated from the strong radical syllable by its own semivowel: e. g. **i** *go*: 2. s. **i-y-é-tha**; **uc** *be pleased*: 2. s. mid. **ūc-i-ṣé**, but 3. s. act. **u-v-óc-a**.

4. Roots containing **ya** or **va** and liable to Samprasāraṇa in other forms (such as the past part. pass.) reduplicate with **i** and **u** respectively. There are four such with **ya**: **tyaj** *forsake*, **yaj** *sacrifice*, **vyac** *extend*, **syand** *move on*: **ti-tyaj, i-yaj, vi-vyac, si-ṣyand**; and five with **va**: **vac**[1] *speak*, **vad** *speak*, **vap** *strew*, **vah** *carry*, **svap** *sleep*: **u-vac, u-vad, u-vap, u-vah, su-ṣvap.** On the other hand the three roots **yam** *stretch*, **van** *win*, **vas** *wear* have the full reduplication **ya** or **va** throughout: **ya-yam, va-van, va-vas.**

136. The singular perfect active is strong (like the sing. pr. and impf. act.), the root being accented; the remaining forms are weak, the terminations being accented. The endings are the following:

	Active.			Middle.		
	SING.	DUAL	PLUR.	SING.	DUAL	PLUR.
1.	**a**	[**vá**]	**má**	**é**	[**váhe**]	**máhe**
2.	**tha**	**áthur**	**á**	**sé**	**ā́the**	**dhvé**
3.	**a**	**átur**	**úr**	**é**	**ā́te**	**ré**

[1] **vac** has two forms with the full reduplication: 3. s. act. **va-vắc-a** and 2. s. mid. **va-vak-ṣé**.

a. Terminations beginning with initial consonants are as a rule added directly to the stem; **mahe** is invariably so added. The endings **tha, ma, se, re** are nearly always added direct to stems ending in vowels; thus from **dā** *give*: **dadā́-tha**; **ji** *conquer*: **ji-gé-tha**; **nī** *lead*: **niné-tha**; **su** *press*: **suṣu-má**; **hū** *call*: **juhū-ré**; **kṛ** *make*: **cakár-tha, cakṛ-má, cakṛ-ṣé,** but **cakr-i-ré.**[1] The same endings **tha, ma, se, re** are added directly to roots ending in consonants, if the final syllable of the stem is prosodically short, but with connecting **i**[2] if it is long;[3] e. g. **tatán-tha**; **jagan-má, jagṛbh-má, yuyuj-má**; **vivit-sé**; **cā-kḷp-ré, tatas-ré, yuyuj-ré, vivid-ré**; but **uvóc-i-tha, ūc-i-má, papt-i-má**; **īj-i-ré.**

b. Before terminations beginning with vowels (cp. 137, 1 *a*)

1. ĭ preceded by one consonant become **y**, if preceded by more than one, **iy**; e. g. **bhī** *fear*: **bibhy-átur**; **śri** *resort*: **śiśriy-é.**

2. ŭ ordinarily become **uv**; e. g. **yu** *join*: **yuyuv-é**; **śru** *hear*: **śuśruv-é**; **śū** *swell*: **śūśuv-é.**[4]

3. **ṛ** becomes **r**, **ṝ** becomes **ir**; e. g. **kṛ** *make*: **cakr-é, cakr-á**; **tṝ** *cross*: **titir-úr**; **stṝ** *strew*: **tistir-é.**

The Strong Stem.

1. Short vowels followed by a single consonant take Guṇa throughout the singular active; e. g. **diś** *point*: **di-déś-a**; **uc** *be wont*: **uv-óc-a**; **kṛt** *cut*: **ca-kárt-a**; but **jinv** *quicken*: **ji-jinv-áthur.**

---

[1] Roots in ṛ always add re with connecting i.

[2] The final radical vowel ā in weak forms is reduced to i, e. g. from dhā *put*, dadhi-dhve. This reduced vowel in the very common verbs dā and dhā was probably the starting-point for the use of i as a connecting vowel in other verbs.

[3] This is due to the rhythmic rule that the stem may not have two prosodically short vowels in successive syllables. Cp. p. 155, note 2.

[4] But hū *call*: juhv-é; bhū *be*: babhū́v-a; sū *bring forth*: sa-sū́v-a.

2. Final vowels take Vṛddhi in the 3. s.;[1] e.g. nī *lead*: **ni-nā́y-a**; **śru** *hear*: **śu-śrā́v-a**; **kṛ** *make*: **ca-kā́r-a**.

3. Medial **a** followed by a single consonant takes Vṛddhi in the 3. s.;[1] e.g. **han** *strike*: **ja-ghā́n-a**, but **takṣ** *fashion* **ta-tákṣ-a**.

4. Roots ending in ā take the anomalous ending **au** in the 1. and 3. s. act.; e.g. **dhā** *put*: **da-dháu**. The only exception is the root **prā** *fill*, which once forms the 3. s. **pa-prā́** beside the regular **pa-práu**.

The Weak Stem.

137. 1. In roots containing the vowels ĭ, ŭ, ṛ the **radical syllable** remains **unchanged** except by Sandhi; e.g. **yuj** *join*: **yu-yuj-má**; vid *find*: **vi-vid-é**; **kṛ** *make*: **ca-kṛ-má**.

a. Before terminations beginning with vowels, ĭ and ṛ, if preceded by one consonant become **y** and **r**, if by more than one, **iy** and **ar**; while ŭ and ṝ regularly become **uv** and **ir**; e.g. ji *conquer*: **ji-gy-úr**; **bhī** *fear*: **bi-bhy-úr**; **kṛ** *make*: **cakr-úr**; **śri** *resort*: **śi-śriy-é**; **yu** *join*: **yu-yuv-é**; **śru** *hear*: **śu-śruv-é**; **śū** *swell*: **śū-śuv-é**; **tṝ** *cross*: **ti-tir-úr**; **stṝ** *strew*: **ti-stir-é**.

2. In roots containing a medial **a** or final ā the **radical syllable is weakened.**

a. About a dozen roots in which **a** is preceded and followed by a single consonant (e. g. **pat**) and which reduplicate the initial consonant unchanged (this excludes roots beginning with aspirates, gutturals, and for the most part v) contract the two syllables to one containing the diphthong **e** (cp. Lat. *fac-io, fēc-i*).[2] They are the following:

---

[1] The 1. sing. never takes Vṛddhi in the RV. and AV. In an Upaniṣad and a Sūtra **cakāra** occurs as 1. sing. and in a Sūtra **jigāya** (√ji) also.

[2] This vowel spread from contracted forms like **sa-zd** (Av. *hazd*) weak perfect stem of **sad** *sit* (az becoming **e**; cp. 134, 2 *b* and 133 A 1).

tap *heat*, **dabh** *harm*, **nam** *bend*, **pac** *cook*, **pat** *fly*, **yat**[1] *stretch*, **yam**[1] *extend*, **rabh** *grasp*, **labh** *take*, **śak** *be able*, **śap** *curse*, **sap** *serve*. Examples are: **pat** : **pet-átur**; **śak** : **śek-úr**.

The two roots **tan** *stretch* and **sac** *follow* join this class in the AV.

b. Four roots with medial **a** but initial guttural, syncopate their vowel: **khan** *dig*: **ca-khn**; **gam** *go*: **ja-gm**; **ghas** *eat*: **ja-kṣ**; **han** *smite*: **ja-ghn**.

Six other roots, though conforming to the conditions described above (2 *a*), syncopate the **a** instead of contracting: **jan** *beget*: **ja-jñ**; **tan** *stretch*: **ta-tn**; **pan** *admire*: **pa-pn**; **man** *think*: **ma-mn**; **van** *win*: **va-vn**; **sac** *follow*: **sa-śc**.

a. **pat** *fly* both contracts and syncopates in the RV.: **pet** and **pa-pt**.

c. Eight roots containing the syllables **ya, va, ra** take Samprasāraṇa: **yaj**[2] *sacrifice*, **vac** and **vad** *speak*, **vap** *strew*, **vas** *dwell*, **vah** *carry*, **svap** *sleep*, **grabh** and **grah** *seize*; e.g. **su-ṣup, ja-gṛbh** and **ja-gṛh**. In the first six, as they reduplicate with i or u, the result is a contraction to ī and ū. Thus **yaj**: **īj** (= i-ij); **vac**: **ūc** (= u-uc).

d. A few roots with medial **a** and penultimate nasal, drop the latter: **krand** *cry out*: **ca-krad**; **taṃs** *shake*: **ta-tas**; **skambh** *prop*: **ca-skabh** (AV.); **stambh** *prop*: **ta-stabh**.

e. Roots ending in **ā** reduce it to **i** before consonants and drop it before vowels; e.g. **dhā** *place*: **dadhi-má**; **dadh-úr**.

---

[1] In the wk. perfect of **yat** and **yam** the contraction is based on the combination of the full reduplicative syllable and the radical syllable with Samprasāraṇa: **yet** = **ya-it**, **yem** = **ya-im**.

[2] From **yaj** occurs one form according to the contracting class (2 *a*): **yej-é**.

Paradigms of the Reduplicated Perfect.

138. 1. tud *strike*: strong stem **tu-tód**; weak **tu-tud.**

ACTIVE.

	SINGULAR.	DUAL.	PLURAL.
1.	**tu-tód-a**	[**tu-tud-vá**]	**tu-tud-má**
2.	**tu-tód-i-tha**	**tu-tud-áthur**	**tu-tud-á**
3.	**tu-tód-a**	**tu-tud-átur**	**tu-tud-úr**

MIDDLE.

1.	**tu-tud-é**[1]	[**tu-tud-váhe**]	**tu-tud-máhe**
2.	**tu-tut-sé**	**tu-tud-ā́the**	[**tu-tud-dhvé**][2]
3.	**tu-tud-é**	**tu-tud-ā́te**	**tu-tud-ré**

2. kṛ *do*: strong stem **ca-kár, ca-kā́r**; weak **cakṛ, cakr.**

ACTIVE.

1.	**ca-kár-a**	[**ca-kṛ-vá**]	**ca-kṛ-má**
2.	**ca-kár-tha**	**ca-kr-áthur**	**ca-kr-á**
3.	**ca-kā́r-a**	**ca-kr-átur**	**ca-kr-úr**

MIDDLE.

1.	**ca-kr-é**	[**ca-kṛ-váhe**]	**ca-kṛ-máhe**
2.	**cá-kṛ-ṣé**	**ca-kr-ā́the**	**ca-kṛ-dhvé**
3.	**ca-kr-é**	**ca-kr-ā́te**	**ca-kr-i-ré**

3. dhā *place*: strong stem **da-dhā́**; weak **da-dh, da-dhi.**

ACTIVE.

1.	[**da-dháu**]	[**da-dhi-vá**]	**da-dhi-má**
2.	**da-dhā́-tha**	**da-dh-áthur**	**da-dh-á**
3.	**da-dháu**	**da-dh-átur**	**da-dh-úr**

MIDDLE.

1.	**da-dh-é**	[**da-dhi-váhe**]	**da-dhi-máhe**
2.	**da-dhi-ṣé**	**da-dh-ā́the**	**da-dhi-dhvé**
3.	**da-dh-é**	**da-dh-ā́te**	**da-dhi-ré**

[1] Lat. *tu-tud-ī.* [2] The only example of this form is **dadhi-dhvé.**

4. **nī** *lead*: strong stem **ni-né, ni-nái**; weak **ni-nī.**

ACTIVE.

	SINGULAR.	DUAL.	PLURAL.
1.	**ni-náy-a**	**[ni-nī-vá]**	**ni-nī-má**
2.	**ni-né-tha**	**ni-ny-áthur**	**ni-ny-á**
3.	**ni-nấy-a**	**ni-ny-átur**	**ni-ny-úr**

MIDDLE.

1.	**ni-ny-é**	**[ni-nī-váhe]**	**ni-nī-máhe**
2.	**ni-nī-ṣé**	**ni-ny-ấthe**	**ni-nī-dhvé**
3.	**ni-ny-é**	**ni-ny-ấte**	**ni-nī-ré**

5. **stu** *praise*: strong stem **tu-ṣṭó, tu-ṣṭáu**; weak **tu-ṣṭu.**

ACTIVE.

1.	**tu-ṣṭáv-a**	**[tu-ṣṭu-vá]**	**tu-ṣṭu-má**
2.	**tu-ṣṭó-tha**	**tu-ṣṭuv-áthur**	**tu-ṣṭuv-á**
3.	**tu-ṣṭấv-a**	**tu-ṣṭuv-átur**	**tu-ṣṭuv-úr**

MIDDLE.

1.	**tu-ṣṭuv-é**	**[tu-ṣṭu-váhe]**	**tu-ṣṭu-máhe**
2.	**tu-ṣṭu-ṣé**	**tu-ṣṭuv-ấthe**	**tu-ṣṭu-dhvé**
3.	**tu-ṣṭuv-é**	**tu-ṣṭuv-ấte**	**tu-ṣṭuv-i-ré**

6. **tap** *heat*: strong stem **ta-táp, ta-tấp**; weak **tep.**

ACTIVE.

1.	**ta-táp-a**	**[tep-i-vá]**	**tep-i-má**
2.	**ta-táp-tha**	**tep-áthur**	**tep-á**
3.	**ta-tấp-a**	**tep-átur**	**tep-úr**

MIDDLE.

1.	**tep-é**	**[tep-i-váhe]**	**[tep-i-máhe]**
2.	**tep-i-ṣé**	**tep-ấthe**	**[tep-i-dhvé]**
3.	**tep-é**	**tep-ấte**	**tep-i-ré**

7. **gam** *go*: strong stem **ja-gám, ja-gā́m**; weak **ja-gm.**

ACTIVE.

	SINGULAR.	DUAL.	PLURAL.
1.	**ja-gám-a**	**[ja-gan-vá]**	**ja-gan-má**
2.	**ja-gán-tha**	**ja-gm-áthur**	**ja-gm-á**
3.	**ja-gā́ma**	**ja-gm-átur**	**ja-gm-úr**

MIDDLE.

1.	**ja-gm-é**	**[ja-gan-váhe]**	**ja-gan-máhe**
2.	**ja-gm-i-ṣé**	**ja-gm-ā́the**	**ja-gm-i-dhvé**
3.	**ja-gm-é**	**ja-gm-ā́te**	**ja-gm-i-ré**

8. **vac** *speak*: strong stem **u-vác, u-vā́c**; weak **ūc.**

ACTIVE.

1.	**u-vác-a**	**[ūc-i-vá]**	**ūc-i-má**
2.	**u-vák-tha**	**ūc-áthur**	**ūc-á**
3.	**u-vā́c-a**	**ūc-átur**	**ūc-úr**

MIDDLE.

1.	**ūc-é**	**[ūc-i-váhe]**	**[ūc-i-máhe]**
2.	**ūc-i-ṣé**	**ūc-ā́the**	**[ūc-i-dhvé]**
3.	**ūc-é**	**[ūc-ā́te]**	**ūc-i-ré**

Irregularities.

139. 1. **bhaj** *share*, though beginning with an aspirate, follows the analogy of the contracting perfects with **e** (137, 2 *a*); e. g. **ba-bhā́j-a**: **bhej-é.** **bandh** *bind*, after dropping its nasal, does the same; e. g. **ba-bándh-a**: **bedh-úr** (AV.).

2. **yam** *guide*, **van** *win*, **vas** *wear* have the full reduplication throughout (135, 4); **yam** takes Samprasāraṇa of the radical syllable: **ya-yā́ma**: **yem-é** (= **ya-im-e**); **van** syncopates its **a**: **va-vā́n-a, va-vn-é**; **vas** retains its radical syllable unweakened throughout: **vā-vas-e** (cp. 139, 9).

3. **vid** *know* forms an unreduplicated perfect with present meaning: 1. **véd-a** *I know* (*οἶδα*, German *weiss*), 2. **vét-tha** (*οἶσ-θα*; *weiss-t*), 3. **véd-a** (*οἶδε*; *weiss*); pl. 1. **vid-má** (*ἴδ-μεν*; *wissen*), 2. **vid-á**, 3. **vid-úr**.

a. A few isolated unreduplicated forms from about six other roots occur: **takṣ-áthur**; **skambh-áthur** and **skambh-úr**; **cet-átur**; **yam-átur** and **yam-úr**; **nind-i-má**; **arh-i-ré**.

4. The initial of **ci** *gather*, **ci** *observe*, **cit** *perceive*, **ji** *conquer*, **han** *kill* reverts to the original guttural in the radical syllable: 3. s. act. **ci-káy-a**, **ci-két-a**, **ji-gáy-a**, **ja-ghán-a**. **bhṛ** *bear* almost invariably reduplicates with **j** in the RV.: **ja-bhár-tha**, **ja-bhára**, **ja-bhr-úr**; **ja-bhr-é**, **ja-bhr-i-ṣé**, **ja-bhr-i-ré**; but only once with **b**: **ba-bhr-é**.

5. **ah** *say* is defective, forming only the 3. s. and pl.: **áh-a** and **āh-úr**. The two additional forms 2. s. **át-tha**, 3. du. **āh-átur** occur in the Brāhmaṇas.

6. Five roots beginning with a prosodically long **a** reduplicate with **ān**: **aṃś** *attain*, **añj** *anoint*, **ardh** *thrive*, **arc** *praise*, **arh** *deserve*. Only the first two make several forms. Here the radical nasal is repeated with the initial vowel: s. 3. **ān-áṃś-a** (Gk. *ἤν-εγκ-α*); pl. 1. **ān-áś-má**, 2. **ān-aś-á**, 3. **ān-aś-úr**; mid. s. 3. **ān-aś-é**;[1] s. 3. **ān-áñja**, mid. s. 1. **ān-aj-é**, pl. 3. **ān-aj-ré**. The analogy spread from these to the roots which have no nasal: pl. 3. **ān-ṛc-úr**, **ān-ṛdh-úr**, **ān-ṛh-úr**; mid. s. 3. **ān-ṛc-é**, **ān-ṛdh-é**.

7. **bhū** *be* has the double irregularity of reduplicating with **a** and retaining its **ū** throughout (cp. Gk. *πε-φύ-āσι*): sing. 1. **ba-bhū́-v-a** (Gk. *πέ-φυ-κα*). 2. **ba-bhū́-tha** and **ba-bhū́-v-i-tha**. 3. **ba-bhū́-v-a**. Du. 2. **ba-bhū-v-áthur**. 3. **ba-bhū-v-átur**. Pl. 1. **ba-bhū-v-i-má**. 2. **ba-bhū-v-á**. 3. **ba-bhū-v-úr**.

---

[1] In a Sūtra occurs the 2. pl. mid. **ān-aś-a-dhve**.

sū *bring forth* has the same peculiarities[1] in **sa-sū-v-a**, the only perfect form of this root occurring.

8. **cyu** *stir* reduplicates **ci-cyu** (beside **cu-cyu**) and **dyut** *shine* similarly **di-dyut**. This was due to the vocalic pronunciation of the **y**: **ci̯u, di̯ut**.

9. The reduplicative vowel is lengthened in more than thirty perfect stems; e.g. **kan** *be pleased*: **cā-kan**; **gṛ** *wake*: **jā-gṛ**; **kḷp** *be adapted*: **cā-kḷp**; **dhī** *think*: **dī-dhī**; **tu** *be strong*: **tū-tu**; **śū** *swell*: **śū-śu**.[2]

a. In the Mantra portion of the Saṃhitās there once occurs a periphrastic perfect form with the reduplicated perfect of **kṛ** *make* governing the acc. of a fem. substantive in **ā** derived from a secondary (causative) verbal stem. This form is **gamayā́m cakāra** (AV.) *he caused to go* (lit. *made a causing to go*). In the Brāhmaṇa parts of the later Saṃhitās (TS., MS., K.) such periphrastic forms are occasionally met with, and they become more frequent in the regular Brāhmaṇas.

Moods of the Perfect.

140. Modal forms of the perfect are of rare occurrence in the Saṃhitās except the RV.

1. The **subjunctive** is normally formed by adding **a** to the strong perfect stem accented on the radical syllable. In the active the secondary endings are the more usual; when the primary endings are used the reduplicative syllable is in several forms accented.[3] In about a dozen forms the weak stem is used. Middle forms, of which only seven or

---

[1] The root **śī** *lie* also reduplicates with **a** in the part. **śa-śay-āná**. These three, **bhū, sū, śī**, are the only roots with an **i** or **u** vowel that reduplicate with **a**.

[2] Here the radical vowel itself is shortened. The quantitative form of the stem is subject to the rule that it may not contain two prosodically short vowels (except in the 1. s. act.). Hence **sah** reduplicates either as **sā-sah** or **sa-sāh** (in a weak form).

[3] Cp. the accentuation of the reduplicating class in the present system.

eight occur, are almost restricted to the 3. sing. Examples are:

Act. s. 1. **an-aj-ā**[1] (**añj** *anoint*); 2. **ta-tán-a-s** (**tan** *stretch*), **bu-bódh-a-s** (**budh** *wake*), **pi-práy-a-s** (**prī** *please*); **jú-joṣ-a-si** (**juṣ** *enjoy*); **ci-kit-a-s** (**cit** *observe*), **mu-muc-a-s** (**muc** *release*). 3. **ci-ket-a-t, ja-ghán-a-t** (**han** *smite*), **ta-tán-a-t, tu-ṣṭáv-a-t** (√**stu** *praise*), **pi-práy-a-t**; **dí-deś-a-ti** (**diś** *point*), **bú-bodh-a-ti, mú-moc-a-ti**; **mu-muc-a-t, vi-vid-a-t** (**vid** *find*).

Du. 2. **ci-ket-a-thas, jú-joṣ-a-thas.** Pl. 1. **ta-tán-ā-ma.** 2. **ju-joṣ-a-tha.** 3. **ta-tán-a-n.**

Mid. s. 3. **ta-táp-a-te, jú-joṣ-a-te.** Pl. 1. **an-áś-ā-mahai.**[1]

2. The **injunctive**[2] occurs in hardly a dozen forms, a few in the sing. act., the rest in the 3. pl. mid.; e.g. s. 2. **śa-śās** (= **śa-śās-s**: **śās** *order*). 3. **dū-dho-t** (**dhū** *shake*), **su-sro-t** (**sru** *flow*); mid. pl. 3. **ta-tán-a-nta** (cp. 140, 6).

3. The **optative** is formed by adding the accented modal suffix combined with the endings to the weak perfect stem. The active forms are much commoner than the middle. Examples are:

Act. s. 1. **ān-aś-yā́m,**[3] **ja-gam-yā́m, ri-ric-yā́m, va-vṛt-yā́m.** 2. **ba-bhū-yā́s, va-vṛt-yā́s.** 3. **an-aj-yā́t,**[1] **ja-gam-yā́t, va-vṛt-yā́t, ba-bhū-yā́t.**

Du. 2. **ja-gam-yā́tam.** Pl. 1. **va-vṛt-yā́-ma.** 3. **ja-gam-yúr, va-vṛt-yúr.**

Mid. s. 1. **va-vṛt-īyá.** 2. **vā-vṛdh-ī-thā́s.** 3. **va-vṛt-ī-tá.** Pl. 1. **va-vṛt-ī-máhi.**

a. There also occurs one mid. precative form **sā-sah-ī-ṣ-ṭhā́s** (**sah** *overcome*).

---

[1] In these three forms the **ā** of the reduplicative syllable **ān** is shortened as if the indicative contained an augment.

[2] Identical in form with the unaugmented pluperfect (140, 6).

[3] From **aṃś** *attain*, with the long reduplicative vowel retained. Cp. 139, 6.

4. The **imperative** perfect is formed like that of the present reduplicating class, the radical syllable being weak except in the 3. s. act., where it is strong. Nearly all the forms occurring, which number about twenty, are active. Examples are:

Act. s. 2. **ci-kid-dhí** (√**cit**), **di-diḍ-ḍhí** (√**diś**), **mu-mug-dhí** (√**muc**), **śa-śā-dhí** (√**śās**).[1] 3. **ba-bhū́-tu,**[2] **mu-mók-tu.**

Du. 2. **mu-muk-tam, va-vṛk-tam** (**vṛj** *twist*). Pl. 2. **di-diṣ-ṭana** (√**diś**), **va-vṛt-tana.**

Mid. s. 2. **va-vṛt-svá.** Pl. 2. **va-vṛd-dhvám.**

Participle.

5. Both active and middle forms of the perfect participle are common. It is formed from the weak perfect stem, with the accent on the suffix, as **cakṛ-vā́ṃs, cakr-āṇá.** If, in the active form, the stem is reduced to a monosyllable, the suffix is nearly always added with the connecting vowel **i**, but not when the stem is unreduplicated; e.g. **papt-i-vā́ṃs** (Gk. πεπτ-ώς), but **vid-vā́ṃs** (Gk. εἰδ-ώς). Examples are:

Act. ja-gan-vā́ṃs (√**gam**), **ja-gṛbh-vā́ṃs** (√**grabh**), **ji-gī-vā́ṃs** (√**ji**), **jū-ju-vā́ṃs**[3] (√**jū**), **ta-sthi-vā́ṃs** (√**sthā**), **ba-bhū-vā́ṃs** (Gk. πε-φυ-ώς), **ri-rik-vā́ṃs** (√**ric**), **va-vṛt-vā́ṃs, vā-vṛdh-vā́ṃs,**[3] **sā-sah-vā́ṃs,**[3] **su-ṣup-vā́ṃs** (√**svap**); **īy-i-vā́ṃs** (√**i**), **ūṣ-i-vā́ṃs** (**vas** *dwell*); **dāś-vā́ṃs** (**dāś** *worship*), **sāh-vā́ṃs** (√**sah**).

Mid. ān-aj-āná (√**añj**), **ān-aś-āná** (√**aṃś**), **īj-āná** (√**yaj**), **ūc-āná** (√**vac**), **ja-gm-āná** (√**gam**), **ti-stir-āṇá** (√**stṝ**), **tep-āná** (√**tap**), **pa-spaś-āná** (√**spaś**), **bhej-āná** (√**bhaj**),

---

[1] Cp. Gk. κέ-κλυ-θι, 2. pl. κέ-κλυ-τε (κλυ = **śru** *hear*).

[2] With ū unchanged as in strong forms elsewhere (139, 7).

[3] With long reduplicative vowel.

yem-āná (√**yam**), **vā-vṛdh-āná**, **śa-śay-āná** (√**śī**), **śi-śriy-āṇá** (√**śri**), **si-ṣmiy-āṇá** (√**smi**), **su-ṣup-āṇá** (√**svap**), **seh-āná** (√**sah**).

Pluperfect.

6. Corresponding to the imperfect there is an augmented form of the perfect called the pluperfect. The strong stem is used in the singular active, the weak elsewhere. The secondary endings only are used; in the 3. pl. **ur** always appears in the active and **iran**[1] in the middle. The **s** and **t** of the 2. and 3. s. are in some forms preserved by an interposed **ī**. There are also several forms made with thematic **a** in this tense. The augment is often dropped, as in other past tenses. The total number of pluperfect forms occurring is about sixty. Examples are:

Act. s. 1. **á-cacakṣ-am**, **á-jagrabh-am**, **á-tuṣṭav-am**; **cakar-am**, **ciket-am** (√**cit**). 2. **ā-jagan** (= **á-jagam-s**); **na-nam-a-s**; **á-viveś-ī-s** (√**viś**). 3. **á-jagan** (= **á-jagam-t**), **a-ciket** (√**cit**); **rā-ran** (= **rāran-t**: **ran** *rejoice*); **á-jagrabh-ī-t**; **á-cikit-a-t** and **á-ciket-a-t**; **tastambh-a-t**.

Du. 2. **á-mu-muk-tam**; **mu-muk-tam**. 3. **á-vāvaś-ī-tām** (**vaś** *desire*).

Pl. 2. **á-jagan-ta**; **á-cucyav-ī-tana**. 3. **á-cucyav-ur**.

Mid. s. 1. **á-śuśrav-i**. 3. **didiṣ-ṭa** (√**diś**). Pl. 3. **á-cakr-iran**, **á-jagm-iran**, **á-pec-iran**; **á-vavṛt-ran**, **á-sasṛg-ram** (√**sṛj**).[2] There are also several transfer forms as from **a** stems; e.g. **á-titviṣ-a-nta**, **cakṛp-á-nta**, **dá-dhṛṣ-a-nta**.

Aorist.

141. This tense is of very common occurrence in the Vedas, being formed from more that 450 roots. It is an

---

[1] Two forms take **ran** only instead of **iran**. There are also several transfer forms in **anta**.

[2] With reversion of the palatal to original guttural, and ending **ram** for **ran**.

augmented tense, taking the secondary endings and forming moods and participles. It is distinguished from the imperfect by having no corresponding present and by difference of meaning. There are two types of aorist. The first or sigmatic aorist is formed by inserting **s**, with or without an added **a**, between the root and the endings. It is taken by more than 200 roots. The second aorist adds the endings to the simple or the reduplicated root either directly or with the connecting vowel **a**. It is taken by over 250 roots. There are four forms of the first Aorist, and three of the second. Upwards of 50 roots take more than one form. One verb, **budh** *wake*, has forms from five varieties of this tense.

First Aorist.

a. The stem of the **first form** is made by adding to the augmented root the suffix **sa**. It is inflected like an imperfect of the sixth or **á** class of the first conjugation, the **sá** being accented in unaugmented forms. It is taken in the Saṃhitās by only ten roots[1] containing one of the vowels **i, u, ṛ**, and ending in one of the consonants **j, ś, ṣ**, or **h**, all of which phonetically become **k** before **s**.[2] These roots are: **mṛj** *wipe*, **yaj** *sacrifice*, **vṛj** *twist*; **kruś** *cry out*, **mṛś** and **spṛś** *touch*; **dviṣ** *hate*; **guh** *hide*, **duh** *milk*, **ruh** *ascend*. In the indicative no dual forms are found; and in the mid. only the 3. s. and pl. are met with. The only moods occurring are the injunctive and the imperative, with altogether fewer than a dozen forms. This form of the aorist corresponds to the Greek First Aorist (e.g. ἔ-δειξε, Lat. *dixi-t*). The augment, as in other past tenses, is sometimes dropped.

---

[1] In B. nine additional roots take the sa aorist: **kṛṣ** *drag*, **diś** *point*, **dih** *smear*, **dṛś** *see*, **druh** *be hostile*, **piṣ** *crush*, **mih** *mingere*, **viś** *enter*, **vṛh** *tear*; and in S. **lih** *lick*.

[2] The stem of this aorist therefore always ends in **kṣa**.

Indicative. Act. s. 1. **ávṛkṣam.** 2. **ádrukṣas** (B.), **ádhukṣas.** 3. **ákrukṣat, ághukṣat, ádukṣat**[1] and **ádhukṣat, ámṛkṣat** (√mṛś), **árukṣat, áspṛkṣat.** Pl. 1. **ámṛkṣāma** (√mṛj), **árukṣāma.** 3. **ádhukṣan; dukṣan**[1] and **dhukṣan.**

Mid. s. 3. **ádhukṣata; dukṣata**[1] and **dhukṣata.** Pl. 3. **ámṛkṣanta** (√mṛj).

In the **injunctive** only the following forms occur:

Act. s. 2. **dukṣás,**[1] **mṛkṣás** (√mṛś). 3. **dvikṣát.** Pl. 2. **mṛkṣata** (√mṛś).

Mid. s. 3. **dukṣáta**[1] and **dhukṣáta, dvikṣáta.** Pl. 3. **dhukṣánta.**

In the **imperative** only three forms occur:

Act. du. 2. **mṛkṣátam** (√mṛj). 3. **yakṣátām.**

Mid. s. 2. **dhukṣásva.**

142. The other three forms of the First Aorist are made by adding to the augmented root the suffixes **s, iṣ, s-iṣ** respectively. They are inflected like imperfects of the second or graded conjugation. The **siṣ** form is used in the act. only (excepting three optative forms) and is taken by not more than six roots. The other two are very common, being formed from nearly 300 roots in V. and B. taken together.

Second or s form.

143. This form of the aorist is taken by at least 135 roots in V. and B. In addition to the indicative it forms all the moods and a participle.

Indicative.

1. The radical vowel as a rule takes **Vṛddhi** (**a** being lengthened) **in the active.** In the middle, excepting final ĭ and u (which take Guṇa) the radical vowel remains un-

[1] On these forms without initial aspiration cp. 62 *a*.

changed. The only point in which the inflexion differs from that of the imperfect of the graded conjugation is that the 3. pl. act. invariably ends in ur. In the active, the endings s and t of the 2. 3. s. disappear and the tense sign also, unless the root ends in a vowel; e.g. **á-hār** = **á-hār-s-t**, but **á-hā-s** = **á-hā-s-t**. The AV. and TS., however, less often than not, insert a connecting ī before these endings,[1] thus preserving both the latter and the s of the tense stem; e.g. **á-naik-ṣ-ī-t** (**nij** *wash*). The forms of the indicative actually occurring would, if made from **bhṛ** *bear* in the active, and from **budh** *wake* in the middle, be as follows:

ACTIVE.

	SINGULAR.	DUAL.	PLURAL.
1.	**á-bhār-ṣ-am**	[**á-bhārṣ-va**]	**á-bhārṣ-ma**
2.	**á-bhār**	**á-bhārṣ-ṭam**	**á-bhārṣ-ṭa**
3.	**á-bhār**	**á-bhārṣ-ṭām**	**á-bhār-ṣ-ur**

MIDDLE.

	SINGULAR.	DUAL.	PLURAL.
1.	**á-bhut-s-i** (62 *a*)	[**á-bhut-s-vahi**]	**á-bhut-s-mahi**
2.	**á-bud-dhās** (62 *b*)	**á-bhut-s-āthām**	**á-bhud-dhvam** (62 *a*)
3.	**á-bud-dha** (62 *b*)	**á-bhut-s-ātām**	**á-bhut-s-ata**

The middle voice, as exemplified by a root ending in u, **stu** *praise*, is inflected as follows:

Sing. 1. **á-sto-ṣ-i**. 2. **á-sto-ṣ-ṭhās**. 3. **á-sto-ṣ-ṭa**. Du. 1. [**á-sto-ṣ-vahi**]. 2. [**á-sto-ṣ-āthām**]. 3. **á-sto-ṣ-ātām**. Pl. 1. **á-sto-ṣ-mahi**. 2. **á-sto-ḍhvam** (66 B 2 *b*). 3. **á-sto-ṣ-ata**.

---

[1] The RV. and K. have no forms with the inserted ī; while in B. the chief forms without it are **adrāk** (**dṛś** *see*) and **ayāṭ** (**yaj** *sacrifice*); also **bhais** (√**bhī**) = **bhais-s**, which while losing the s ending preserves the appearance of a 2. sing.

2. The **subjunctive** is common in the RV.[1] in active forms, but not in the middle. The root regularly takes Guṇa throughout (active and middle). The primary endings are frequent. The forms occurring, if made from **stu** *praise*, would be:

Act. sing. 1. **stó-ṣ-āṇi**. 2. **stó-ṣ-a-si, stó-ṣ-a-s**. 3. **stó-ṣ-a-ti, stó-ṣ-a-t**. Du. 2. **stó-ṣ-a-thas**. 3. **stó-ṣ-a-tas**. Pl. 1. **stó-ṣ-ā-ma**. 2. **stó-ṣ-a-tha**. 3. **stó-ṣ-a-n**.

Mid. sing. 1. **stó-ṣ-ai**. 2. **stó-ṣ-a-se**. 3. **stó-ṣ-a-te**. Du. 2. **stó-ṣ-āthe** (for **stó-ṣ-aithe**). Pl. 3. **stó-ṣ-a-nte**.

3. **Injunctive** forms are fairly common. When normal they are of course identical with the unaugmented indicative. But the sing. 1. act. is irregular in never taking Vṛddhi: all the forms of it that occur either have Guṇa, as **sto-ṣ-am, je-ṣ-am** (√ji); or lengthen the radical vowel, as **yū-ṣ-am** (yu *separate*); or substitute e for ā in roots ending in ā, as **ye-ṣ-am** (yā *go*), **ge-ṣ-am** (gā *go*), **sthe-ṣ-am** (sthā *stand*). The latter irregularity also appears in pl. 1: **je-ṣ-ma, ge-ṣ-ma, de-ṣ-ma** (dā *give*), beside the normal **yau-ṣ-ma** (yu *separate*).

4. The **optative** occurs in the middle only, the 2. 3. s. always having the precative s (with one exception). The forms actually occurring are:

Sing. 1. **di-ṣ-īyá**[2] (dā *cut*), **bhak-ṣ-īyá** (bhaj *divide*), **ma-s-īyá**[3] (man *think*), **muk-ṣ-īyá** (muc *release*), **rā-s-īyá** (rā *give*), **sāk-ṣ-īyá**[4] (AV.), **stṛ-ṣ-īyá** (stṝ *strew*). 2. **maṃ-s-ī-ṣ-ṭhā́s**[5] (man *think*). 3. **dar-ṣ-ī-ṣ-ṭa** (dṛ *tear*), **bhak-ṣ-īta**[6] (SV.), **maṃ-s-ī-ṣ-ṭa, mṛk-ṣ-ī-ṣ-ṭa** (mṛc *injure*). Du. 2.

---

[1] Subjunctives of this aor. are very rare in B. except **yakṣ-a-t** (√**yaj**) and **vakṣ-a-t** (√**vah**).

[2] With radical ā reduced to i: cp. 5 *c*. Similarly **dhi-ṣ-īya** (√**dhā**) in B.

[3] With an reduced to a (= sonant nasal).

[4] From **sah** *overcome*, with radical vowel lengthened.

[5] Anusvāra for n (66 A 2).

[6] Without the precative s.

trá-s-ī-thām[1] (**trā** *protect*). Pl. 1. **bhak-ṣ-ī-máhi, maṃ-s-ī-máhi,**[2] **vaṃ-s-ī-máhi** and **va-s-ī-máhi**[3] (**van** *win*), **sak-ṣ-ī-máhi** (**sac** *follow*), **dhuk-ṣ-ī-máhi** (**duh** *milk*). 3. **maṃ-s-īrata.**

5. Only six imperative forms occur, and four of these are transfers (with thematic **a**). They are: Act. s. 2. **ne-ṣ-a** (**nī** *lead*) and **par-ṣ-a** (**pṛ** *take across*). Mid. s. 2. **sák-ṣva** (√**sah**). 3. **rā-s-a-tām.** Du. 2. **rā-s-āthām.** Pl. 3. **rā-s-a-ntām.**

6. Only two or three forms of the active participle occur: **dák-ṣ-at**[4] and **dhák-ṣ-at** (**dah** *burn*), **sák-ṣ-at** (√**sah**).

About a dozen stems, irregularly formed by adding **s** to the root with an intermediate **a** and taking the regular ending **āna**, may be accounted middle **s** aorist participles; e. g. **mand-a-s-āná** *rejoicing*, **yam-a-s-āná** *being driven.*

Irregularities of the s form.

144. 1. Before the suffix **s**, (*a*) final radical **n** (as well as **m**) becomes Anusvāra (66 A 2), as **á-maṃ-s-ata** (√**man**), **vaṃ-s-ī-máhi** (√**van**); (*b*) **s** becomes **t** in the verb **vas** *dwell* and possibly also in **vas** *shine*: **á-vāt-s-ī-s**[5] (AV.) *thou hast dwelt* and **á-vāt** (= **á-vas-s-t**) *has shone* (AV.).

2. The RV. has one example of an incipient tendency to preserve the **s** and **t** of the 2. 3. s. in 2. s. **á-yā-s** (=**a-yaj-s-s**) beside the phonetically regular form of the 3. s. **á-yāṭ** (= **á-yaj-s-t**). The AV. has three or four examples of this: s. 2. **srā-s** (= **sraj-s-s**: √**sṛj**); 3. **á-śrai-t** (= **á-śrai-s-t**:

---

[1] For **trā-s-īyāthām.**

[2] With Anusvāra for **n** (66 A 2).

[3] With **an** reduced to **a** (= sonant nasal).

[4] Without initial aspiration: cp. 62 *a* and 156 *a*.

[5] See 66 B 1. In an Upaniṣad the 2. du. appears as **á-vās-tam**, the aor. suffix **s** having been lost without affecting the radical **s**.

√**śri**); **á-hai-t** (= **á-hai-s-t**: √**hi**); **á-vā-t**[1] (= **a-vas-s-t**: **vas** *shine*). The later Saṃhitās here frequently preserve these endings by inserting ī before them: s. 2. **á-rāt-s-ī-s** (√**rādh**), **á-vāt-s-ī-s** (**vas** *dwell*); 3. **á-tāṃ-s-ī-t** (√**tan**), **á-naik-ṣ-ī-t** (√**nij**), **tāp-s-ī-t** (√**tap**), **bhai-ṣ-ī-t** (√**bhī**), **vāk-ṣ-ī-t** (√**vah**), **hā-s-ī-t**, **hvār-ṣ-ī-t** (√**hvar**).

a. The ending **dhvam** (before which the **s** of the aor. is lost) becomes **ḍhvam** when the **s** would have been cerebralized (66 B 2): **á-sto-ḍhvam** (= **á-sto-ẓ-ḍhvam**) is the only example.

3. The roots **dā** *give* and **dā** *cut* reduce the radical vowel to i in **á-di-ṣ-i**, **di-ṣ-īyá**; **gam**, **man**, **van** lose their nasal in **á-ga-smahi**, **ma-s-īyá**, **va-s-ī-máhi** (beside **vaṃ-s-ī-máhi**); while **sah** lengthens its vowel in **á-sāk-ṣ-i**, **sāk-ṣ-i**; **sāk-ṣ-āma**; **sāk-ṣ-īya**; **sā́k-ṣva**.

4. The roots **sṛj** *emit* and **pṛc** *mix* take metathesis in the act.: s. 2. **srā-s** (= **srāk**). 3. **á-srāk**; **á-prāk**. Du. 2. **á-srāṣ-ṭam**.

5. The following are the forms occurring in the 3. s. ind. act. in which (*a*) the ending **t** is lost: **á-jai-s** (√**ji**), **á-prā-s**, **á-hā-s**; (*b*) both the tense-sign **s** and the ending **t** are lost:[2] **á-krān** (**krand** *cry out*), **á-kṣār** (**kṣar** *flow*), **á-cait** (**cit** *perceive*), **á-chān** (**chand** *seem*), **á-tān** (**tan** *stretch*), **á-tsār** (**tsar** *approach stealthily*), **á-dyaut** (**dyut** *shine*), **á-dhāk** (**dah** *burn*), **á-prāk** (**pṛc** *mix*), **á-prāṭ** (**prach** *ask*), **á-bhār** (**bhṛ**), **á-yāṭ** (**yaj** *sacrifice*), **á-yān** (**yam** *guide*), **á-raut** (**rudh** *obstruct*), **á-vāṭ** (**vah** *convey*), **á-vāt**[1] (**vas** *shine*), **á-śvait** (**śvit** *be bright*), **á-syān** (**syand** *move on*), **á-srāk** (**sṛj** *emit*), **á-svār** (**svar** *sound*), **á-hār** (**hṛ** *take*), **ā́-raik** (**ric** *leave*).

6. After a consonant other than **n**, **m**, **r** the tense sign **s** is dropped before **t**, **th**, and **dh**; e.g. **á-bhak-ta** (beside **á-bhak-ṣ-i**); **á-muk-thās** (beside **á-muk-ṣ-i**).

---

[1] But the **t** may in this instance represent the changed final radical **s**: 144, 1 (*b*). There are a few additional examples in B.: **ajait** (beside **ajais** and **ajaiṣīt**: √**ji**); **acait** (√**ci**); **nait** (√**nī**).

[2] And even the final consonant of the root when there are two (28).

Third or iṣ form.

145. About 145 roots take this aorist in V. and B. It differs from the **s** aorist merely in adding the **s** with the connecting vowel **i**, which changes it to **ṣ** (67).

Indicative.

1. The radical vowel as a rule takes **Guṇa throughout**; but in the active a final vowel takes Vṛddhi and a medial vowel is sometimes lengthened. The endings are the same as those of the **s** aorist except that the 2. 3. s. end in **īs** (= **iṣ-s**) and **īt** (= **iṣ-t**). This aorist has all the moods, but no participle. Middle forms are not common and very few occur except in the 2. 3. sing.

The normal forms occurring, if made from **kram** *stride*, would be:

Act. sing. 1. **á-kram-iṣ-am.** 2. **á-kram-īs.** 3. **á-kram-īt.** Du. 3. **á-kram-iṣ-ṭam.** Pl. 1. **á-kram-iṣ-ma.** 3. **á-kram-iṣ-ur.**

Mid. sing. 1. **á-kram-iṣ-i.** 2. **á-kram-iṣ-ṭhās.** 3. **á-kram-iṣ-ṭa.** Du. 3. **á-kram-iṣ-ātām.** Pl. 3. **á-kram-iṣ-ata.**

2. **Subjunctive** forms are rare except in the 2. 3. s. act. Examples are:

Act. sing. 1. **dáv-iṣ-āṇi.** 2. **áv-iṣ-a-s, kā́n-iṣ-a-s.** 3. **kā́r-iṣ-a-t, bódh-iṣ-a-t.** Pl. 3. **sán-iṣ-a-n.**

Mid. pl. 1. **yā́c-iṣ-ā-mahe.** 3. **sán-iṣ-a-nta.**

3. **Injunctive** are commonor than subjunctive forms. They occur most frequently in the 2. 3. s. and plur. Examples are:

Act. sing. 1. **śáṃs-iṣ-am** (**śaṃs** *praise*). 2. **áv-īs** (**av** *favour*), **tā́r-īs** (**tṝ** *cross*), **yódh-īs** (**yudh** *fight*), **sā́v-īs** (**sū** *generate*). 3. **áś-īt** (**aś** *eat*), **tā́r-īt.** Du. 2. **tā́riṣ-ṭam, márdh-iṣ-ṭam** (**mṛdh** *neglect*). Pl. 1. **śrám-iṣ-ma.** 2. **vádh-iṣ-ṭa** and **vádh-iṣ-ṭana.** 3. **jār-iṣ-ur** (**jṝ** *waste away*).

Mid. sing. 1. **rā́dh-iṣ-i** (**rādh** *succeed*). 2. **márṣ-iṣ-ṭhās**

(**mṛṣ** *not heed*). 3. **páv-iṣ-ṭa** (**pū** *purify*). Pl. 1. **vyáth-iṣ-mahi** (**vyath** *waver*).

4. **Optative** forms are rare, occurring in the middle only. The 2. 3. s. take the precative **s**. Examples are:

Sing. 1. **edh-iṣ-īyá** (**edh** *thrive*). 2. **mod-iṣ-ī-ṣ-ṭhā́s** (**mud** *rejoice*). 3. **jan-iṣ-ī-ṣ-ṭá**. Du. 1. **sah-iṣ-ī-váhi**. Pl. **tār-iṣ-ī-máhi**.

5. **Imperative** forms are rare, occurring in the active only. Sing. 2. **av-iḍ-ḍhí**. 3. **av-iṣ-ṭu**. Du. 2. **av-iṣ-ṭám**. 3. **av-iṣ-ṭā́m**. Pl. 2. **av-iṣ-ṭána**.

a. The radical medial **a** is lengthened in **kan** *enjoy*, **car** *move*, **das** *waste*, **mad** *exhilarate*, **stan** *thunder*, **svan** *sound*, and optionally in **vad** *speak*, **ran** *rejoice*, **san** *gain*, **sah** *prevail*; while the radical syllable appears in a reduced or unstrengthened form in the opt. s. 1. mid. of **gam** and **ruc** *shine*: **gm-iṣ-īyá** and **ruc-iṣ-īyá**.

b. The root **grabh** *seize* takes the connecting vowel **ī** (as it does in other verbal forms) instead of **i**, as **á-grabh-īṣ-ma**.

c. In s. 1. ind. act. the ending **īm** appears instead of **iṣ-am** in the three forms **á-kram-īm**, **á-grabh-īm**, and **vadh-īm**, doubtless owing to the analogy of the 2. 3. s. in **īs**, **īt**. In B. is also found **a-grah-aiṣ-am** (√**grah**).

Fourth or siṣ form.

146. This form differs from the preceding one simply in prefixing an additional **s** to the suffix. Only seven verbs ending in **ā**, **n**, or **m**, **gā** *sing*, **jñā** *know*,[1] **pyā** *fill up*, **yā** *go*, **hā** *leave*, **van** *win*, **ram** *rejoice*, take this aorist. The total number of forms occurring is under twenty; and middle forms are found in the optative only. The forms occurring are:

1. **Indicative**. Sing. 1. **á-yā-siṣ-am**. Du. 3. **á-yā-siṣ-ṭām**. Pl. 2. **á-yā-siṣ-ṭa**. 3. **á-gā-siṣ-ur**, **á-yā-siṣ-ur**.

2. **Subjunctive**. Sing. 3. **gā́-siṣ-a-t**, **yā́-siṣ-a-t**.

---

[1] In B. also occurs **dhyā** *think*, besides forms in **s-īt** from **drā** *sleep*, **vā** *blow*, **hvā** *call*.

3. **Optative.** Sing. 1. **vaṃ-siṣ-īyá.** 2. **yā-siṣ-ī-ṣ-ṭhā́s,**[1] Pl. 1. **pyā-siṣ-ī-mahi.**

4. **Injunctive.** Sing. 1. **raṃ-siṣ-am.** Du. 2. **hā-siṣ-ṭam.** 3. **hā-siṣ-ṭām.** Pl. 2. **hā-siṣ-ṭa.** 3. **hā-siṣ-ur.**

5. **Imperative.** Du. 2. **yā-siṣ-ṭám.** Pl. 2. **yā-sīṣ-ṭá.**[2]

Second Aorist.

147. This aorist resembles an imperfect formed directly from the root, the terminations being added with or without the connecting vowel **a**.

The **first form** is like an imperfect of the accented **á** class (125, 2), the stem being formed by adding **a** to the unmodified root.[3] It corresponds to the second aorist of the first conjugation in Greek. It is taken, in V. and B. together, by nearly eighty roots, chiefly with a medial vowel. Middle forms are rare.

1. **Indicative.** The forms actually occurring would, if made from **vid** *find*, be as follows:

Act. sing. 1. **ávidam.** 2. **ávidas.** 3. **ávidat.** Du. 1. **ávidāva.** Pl. 1. **ávidāma.** 2. **ávidata.** 3. **ávidan.**

Mid. sing. 1. **ávide.** 2. **ávidathās.** 3. **ávidata.** Du. 1. **ávidāvahi.** 3. **ávidetām.** Pl. 1. **ávidāmahi.** 3. **ávidanta.**

2. The **subjunctive** forms from the same root would be:

Act. sing. 2. **vidā́si, vidā́s.** 3. **vidā́ti, vidā́t.** Du. 1. **vidā́va.** 2. **vidā́thas.** 3. **vidā́tas.** Pl. 1. **vidā́ma.** 2. **vidā́tha, vidā́thana.**

Mid. sing. 3. **vidā́te.** Pl. 1. **vidā́mahe.**

3. The **injunctive** forms from **vid** would be:

Act. sing. 1. **vidám.** 2. **vidás.** 3. **vidát.** Pl. 3. **vidán.**

Mid. sing. 3. **vidáta.** Pl. 1. **vidā́mahi.** 3. **vidánta.**

4. The **optative** is rare in V., but not infrequent in B.

---

[1] With precative **s**.

[2] With **ī** for **i**.

[3] Three roots with **ṛ**, however, show forms with Guṇa (147 *a* 2 and *c*).

It is almost restricted to the active. The forms from **vid** would be:

Act. sing. 1. **vidéyam.** 2. **vidés.** 3. **vidét.** Pl. 1. **vidéma.**

Mid. sing. 1. **vidéya.** Pl. 1. **vidémahi.** There also occurs one precative form, s. 3. **vidéṣṭa** (AV.).

5. **Imperative** forms are rare and almost restricted to the active. Those made by **sad** *sit* are:

Sing. 2. **sadá.** 3. **sadátu.** Du. 2. **sadátam.** 3. **sadátām.** Pl. 2. **sadáta, sadátana.** 3. **sadántu.**

Mid. pl. 2. **sadadhvam.** 3. **sadantām.**

6. **Rather** more than a dozen examples of the **participle,** taking active and middle together, occur: e. g. **tṛp-ánt, śucánt; guhámāna, śucámāna.**

Irregularities.

a. Several roots form transfer stems according to this instead of the root form, chiefly by reducing the radical syllable.

1. **khyā** *see*, **vyā** *envelope*, **hvā** *call* shorten their **ā** to **a**: **á-khya-t, á-vya-t, á-hva-t**; **dā** *give*, **dhā** *put*, **sthā** *stand* occasionally do the same, in the forms **ā́-da-t**; **á-dha-t** (SV.) and **dha-t**; **ā́-stha-t** (AV.); **śās** *order* shortens ā to i; e. g. 3. s. inj. **śíṣat**, part. **śiṣánt.**

2. **kṛ** *make* and **gam** *go* form a few transfers from the root class in the AV., retaining the strong radical vowel: **á-kar-a-t, á-gam-a-t, á-gam-a-n.**

b. The root is reduced by the loss of its nasal in **krand** *cry out*, **taṃs** *shake*, **dhvaṃs** *scatter*, **bhraṃś** *fall*, **randh** *make subject*, **sraṃs** *fall*; e. g. 3. sing. **átasat**; pl. **dhvasán**; subj. pl. 1. **radhāma**; inj. sing. 1. **radham**; 2. **kradas**; 3. **bhraśat.**

c. The root takes Guṇa in **ṛ** *go*, **dṛś** *see*, **sṛ** *flow*; e. g. **ár-anta** (unaugmented 3. pl. ind. mid.); **dárś-am** (s. 1. inj., but pl. 3. inj. **dṛśán**, opt. 1. s. **dṛśéyam**, pl. **dṛśéma**); **sárat** (unaugmented 3. s.).

Second Form: Root Aorist.

148. This form of the simple aorist is taken by about 100 roots in V., and about 25 others in B., the commonest being those with medial **a** (about 30). It corresponds to the second aorist of the second conjugation in Greek. It is inflected in both active and middle.

Indicative.

1. The root is strong in the sing. act., but weak elsewhere. Roots ending in vowels, however, tend to retain the strong vowel throughout the active except the 3. pl. Those ending in **ā** regularly retain that vowel throughout the ind. act. except in 3. pl. where it is dropped before **ur**, which is always the ending in these verbs. In the 3. pl. mid. the ending **ran** is more than twice as common as **ata**; **ram** as well as **ran** is taken by three roots.

a. The forms occurring from roots ending in **ā**, if made from **sthā**, would be:

Act. sing. 1. **á-sthā-m** (ἔ-στη-ν). 2. **á-sthā-s.** 3. **á-sthā-t** (ἔ-στη). Du. 2. **á-sthā-tam.** 3. **á-sthā-tām.** Pl. 1. **á-sthā-ma** (ἔ-στη-μεν). 2. **á-sthā-ta.** 3. **á-sth-ur.**

Mid. sing. 2. **á-sthi-thās** (ἐ-στά-θης). 3. **á-sthi-ta.** Pl. 1. **á-sthi-mahi.** 3. **á-sthi-ran.**

b. Roots in **ṛ** take Guṇa throughout the ind. act. except the 3. pl. The forms from **kṛ** would be:

Act. sing. 1. **á-kar-am.** 2. **á-kar.** 3. **á-kar.** Du. 2. **á-kar-tam.** 3. **á-kar-tām.** Pl. 1. **á-kar-ma.** 2. **á-kar-ta.** 3. **á-kr-an.**

Mid. sing. 1. **á-kr-i.** 2. **á-kṛ-thās.** 3. **á-kṛ-ta.** Du. 1. **á-kṛ-vahi.** 3. **á-kṛ-tām.** Pl. 1. **á-kṛ-mahi.** 2. **á-kṛ-dhvam.** 3. **á-kr-ata.**

c. **bhū** *be* retains its **ū** throughout (as in the perfect), interposing **v** between it and a following **a**:

Act. 1. **á-bhuv-am.**[1] 2. **á-bhū-s.** 3. **á-bhū-t** (ἔ-φῡ). Du. 2. **á-bhū-tam.** 3. **á-bhū-tām.** Pl. 1. **á-bhū-ma** (ἔ-φυ-μεν). 2. **á-bhū-ta** and **á-bhū-tana.** 3. **á-bhū-v-an.**

d. The following are forms of the 2. 3. s. act. in which

---

[1] With split ū; in the later language **a-bhūv-am.**

the endings s and t are lost: 2. **á-kar**, **á-gan** (= **á-gam-s**), **á-ghas**, **á-var** (**vṛ** *cover*), **á-spar** (**spṛ** *win*); with lengthened augment: **ā́-naṭ**[1] (**naś** *attain*), **ā́-var** (**vṛ** *cover*), **ā́-vas**[2] (**vas** *shine*). 3. **á-kar**, **á-kran**[3] (**kram** *stride*), **á-gan**,[3] **á-ghas**, **á-cet** (**cit** *observe*), **á-tan**, **á-dar** (**dṛ** *pierce*), **á-bhet** (**bhid** *pierce*), **á-bhrāṭ** (**bhrāj** *shine*), **á-mok** (**muc** *release*), **á-myak** (**myakṣ** *be situated*), **á-vart** (**vṛt** *turn*), **á-star**; with lengthened augment: **ā́-naṭ**,[4] **ā́-var** (**vṛ** *cover*), **ā́-vas**[2] (**vas** *shine*); without augment: **vark**[5] (**vṛj** *twist*), **skan**[6] (**skand** *leap*).

e. In the 3. pl. act. and mid. roots with medial **a** are syncopated: **á-kṣ-an** (=**á-ghas-an**), **á-gm-an** (=**á-gam-an**); **á-gm-ata** (= **á-gam-ata**), **á-tn-ata** (= **á-tan-ata**); but in the 2. 3. s. mid. they lose their nasal: **á-ga-thās**, **á-ga-ta**, **á-ma-ta** (but 1. du. **gan-vahi**, pl. **á-gan-mahi**).

f. Final **ā** is in the mid. ind. reduced to **i**, and before **m** also to **ī**; e.g. 2. **á-di-thās**, **á-sthi-thās**. 3. **á-dhi-ta** (ἔ-θε-το). Pl. 1. **á-dhi-mahi** (TS.) and **á-dī-mahi** (VS.), **á-dhī-mahi**.

g. In the 3. s. ind. **ghas** is reduced to **g**: **gdha** (=**ghas-ta**)[7]; while **ṛ** *go* takes Guṇa: **ár-ta** (unaugmented) and **ā́r-ta** (ὦρ-το), 3. pl. **ā́r-ata**.

h. The forms taking **ran** in 3. pl. mid. are: **á-kṛp-ran**, **á-gṛbh-ran**, **á-jus-ran**, **á-dṛś-ran**, **á-pad-ran**, **á-budh-ran**, **á-yuj-ran**, **á-vas-ran** (**vas** *shine*), **á-viś-ran**, **á-vṛt-ran**, **á-sṛg-ran**,[8] **á-sthi-ran**, **á-spṛdh-ran**; with **ram**: **á-dṛś-ram**, **á-budh-ram**, **á-sṛg-ram**.[8]

---

1 For **á-naś-s**, the phonetic result of which should have been **ā́-nak** (63 *b*).

2 For **ā́-vas-s**, **ā-vas-t**. These forms have by an oversight been omitted in § 499 of my *Vedic Grammar*.

3 For **á-kram-t**, **á-gam-t**.

4 For **ā́-naś-t**.

5 For **varj-t**.

6 For **skand-t**.

7 By syncopation **gh-s-ta**; loss of **s** between consonants (66 B 2 *a*) **gh-ta**, and loss of aspiration, which is thrown forward on the **t** and renders it sonant (62 *b*).

8 With reversion to the original guttural.

2. The subjunctive is common, nearly 100 forms being met with. The forms occurring, if made from **kṛ**, would be:

Act. sing. 1. **kárā** and **kár-āṇi**. 2. **kár-a-si** and **kár-a-s**. 3. **kár-a-ti** and **kár-a-t**.[1] Du. 2. **kár-a-thas**. 3. **kár-a-tas**. Pl. 1. **kár-ā-ma**. 3. **kár-anti**, **kár-a-n**.

Mid. sing. 2. **kár-a-se**. 3. **kár-a-te**.[2] Pl. 1. **kár-ā-mahe** and **kár-ā-mahai**. 3. **kár-anta**.

3. The injunctive is fairly frequent, nearly sixty forms of it being met with. Examples are:

Act. sing. 1. **kar-am**, **darś-am**,[3] **bhuv-am**, **bhoj-am**. 2. **je-s**, **bhū-s**, **bhé-s** (**bhī** *fear*), **dhak**[4] (**dagh** *reach*), **bhet** (**bhid** *split*), **rok** (**ruj** *break*). 3. **bhū-t**, **śre-t** (√**śri**), **nak** and **naṭ** (**naś** *attain*). Pl. 1. **dagh-ma**, **bhū-ma**; **ched-ma**,[5] **ho-ma**[5] (**hū** *call*). 3. **bhūv-an**, **vr-an** (**vṛ** *cover*); **kram-ur**, **dur** (**dā** *give*), **dh-úr** (**dhā** *put*).

Mid. sing. 1. **naṃś-i** (**naṃś** = **naś** *attain*). 2. **nut-thās** (**nud** *push*), **mṛ-thā́s** (**mṛ** *die*), **mṛṣ-ṭhās** (**mṛṣ** *neglect*), **rik-thās** (**ric** *leave*). 3. **ar-ta** (**ṛ** *go*), **aṣ-ṭa** (**aś** *attain*), **vik-ta** (**vij** *tremble*), **vṛ-ta** (**vṛ** *choose*). Pl. 1. **dhī-mahi** (**dhā** *put*).

4. More than forty optative forms are met with. Examples are:

Act. sing. 1. **aś-yā́m** (**aś** *obtain*), **vṛj-yā́m**, **de-yā́m** (**dā** *give*). 2. **aś-yā́s**, **ṛdh-yā́s**, **gam-yā́s**, **jñe-yā́s**, **bhū-yā́s**. 3. **bhū-yā́t**[6] (AV.). Pl. 1. **aś-yā́ma**, **ṛdh-yā́ma**, **kri-yā́ma**, **bhū-yā́ma**, **sthe-yā́ma**. 3. **aś-yúr** (**aś** *attain*), **dhe-yúr**.

Mid. sing. 1. **aś-īyá**. 3. **ar-ī-tá** (**ṛ** *go*). Pl. 1. **aś-ī-máhi**, **idh-ī-máhi** (**idh** *kindle*), **naś-ī-máhi** (**naś** *reach*).

---

[1] The root is weak in the isolated forms **ṛ́dh-a-t**, **bhúv-a-t**, **śrúv-a-t**.

[2] The weak root appears once in the form **idh-a-té**. The weak root also appears once in the 2. du. form **ṛdh-āthe**.

[3] This may, however, be an irregular a aorist: cp. 147 *c*.

[4] For **dagh-s**.

[5] With strong radical vowel.

[6] The RV. has no forms of the 3. s. in **yāt**, but only precatives in **yās** (= **yās-t**).

a. There are also about thirty precative forms (made from about twenty roots in the Saṃhitās), all of which except two are active. Examples are:

Act. sing. 1. **bhū-yā́sam.** 3. **aś-yā́s** (= **aś-yā́s-t**), **gam-yā́s**, **dagh-yā́s**, **pe-yā́s** (pā *drink*), **bhū-yā́s.** Du. 2. **bhū-yā́stam.** Pl. 1. **kri-yā́sma.** 2. **bhū-yā́sta.**

Mid. s. 3. **pad-ī-ṣ-ṭa, muc-ī-ṣ-ṭa.**

5. Over ninety forms of the imperative occur, all but about twelve being active. Several forms in the 2. persons act. have a strong root, which is then usually accented. Examples are:

Act. s. 2. **kṛ-dhí, ga-dhí** (gam), **pūr-dhí** (pṝ *fill*), **bo-dhí,**[1] **yó-dhi**[2] (yudh *fight*), **śag-dhí** (śak *be able*); **ga-hí** (gam *go*), **mā-hi** (mā *measure*), **sā-hi** (sā *bind*). 3. **gán-tu** (gam *go*), **dhā́-tu, bhū́-tu, śró-tu.**

Du. 2. **kṛ-tám** and **kar-tam** (AV.), **ga-tám** and **gan-tám, dā-tam, dhak-tam** (dagh *reach*), **bhū-tám, var-tam** (vṛ *cover*), **vo-ḷhám** (vah *carry*), **śru-tám.** 3. **gan-tām, pā-tām, vo-ḷhā́m.** Pl. 2. **kṛ-ta** and **kár-ta, ga-ta** and **gán-ta, bhū-tá, yán-ta, śru-ta** and **śró-ta; kár-tana, gán-tana, dhā-tana, bhū-tana.** 3. **gám-antu, dhāntu, śruv-antu.**

Mid. s. 2. **kṛ-ṣvá, dhi-ṣvá** (dhā *put*), **yuk-ṣvá** (yuj *join*); accented on the root: **mát-sva, yák-ṣva** (yaj *sacrifice*), **rā́-sva, vám̐-sva** (van *win*), **sák-ṣva** (sac *follow*). Pl. 2. **kṛ-dhvam, vo-ḍhvam.**

6. Of the participle only seven or eight examples occur in the active, but nearly forty in the middle. Examples are:

Act. **ṛdh-ánt, kr-ánt, gm-ánt, sthā́nt.**

Mid. **ar-āṇá, idh-āná, kr-āṇá, dṛ́ś-āna** and **dṛś-āná, budh-āná, bhiy-āná, vr-āṇá** (vṛ *cover*), **śubh-āná** and **śum-bhāná, suv-āná** (always to be pronounced **svāná**) and **sv-āná** (SV.).

---

[1] Formed from both bhū *be* (for **bhū-dhí**) and budh *awake* (for **bód-dhi** instead of **bud-dhí**).

[2] For **yud-dhí** (through **yód-dhi**).

Third or Reduplicated Form.

149. This aorist is formed from nearly ninety verbs in the Saṃhitās and from nearly thirty more in the Brāhmaṇas. Though (with a few slight exceptions) unconnected in form with the causative, it has come to be connected with the causative in sense, having a causative meaning when the corresponding verb in **aya** has that meaning. The characteristic feature of this aorist is the almost invariable quantitative sequence of a long reduplicative and a short radical vowel (– ◡). In order to bring about this rhythm, the reduplicative vowel (unless it becomes long by position) is lengthened, if the radical vowel is (or is made) prosodically short. With this view the radical vowel is shortened in **vāś** *bellow*, **sādh** *succeed*, **hīḍ** *be hostile* and, by dropping the nasal, in **krand** *cry out*, **jambh** *crush*, **randh** *subject*, **syand** *flow*, **sraṃs** *fall*. The stem of the great majority of forms is made with a thematic **a**. But about a dozen roots ending in vowels (**ā**, **i**, **ŭ**, **ṛ**) and **svap** *sleep* make occasional forms from stems without thematic **a**, the inflexion then being like that of an imperfect of the reduplicating class (127, 2). A medial radical vowel remains unchanged or is weakened, but a final vowel takes Guṇa. All the moods occur, but no participle.

Special Rules of Reduplication.

a. The vowels **ă**, **ṝ̆**, **ḷ** are represented in the reduplicative syllable by **i**.

b. The vowel of the reduplicative syllable, unless already long by position, is lengthened.

1. The forms of the **indicative** actually occurring would, if made from **jan** *beget*, be as follows:

Act. s. 1. **ájījanam**. 2. **ájījanas**. 3. **ájījanat**. Du. 2. **ájījanatam**. Pl. 1. **ájījanāma**. 2. **ájījanata**. 3. **ájījanan**.

Mid. s. 3. **ájījanata**. Pl. 2. **ájījanadhvam**. 3. **ájījananta**.

The following are examples:

Act. s. 1. **ánīnaśam** (**naś** *be lost*), **ácīkṛṣam** (**kṛṣ** *drag*), **ápiplavam** (B.), **ápīparam** (**pṛ** *pass*). 2. **áci-krad-as**, **ábūbhuvas**; **siṣvapas**; without thematic **a**: **á-jīgar** (**gṛ** *swallow* and **gṛ** *waken*); **síṣvap**. 3. **ácīkḷpat**, **ácucyavat** (K.), **ájīhiḍat** (√**hīḍ**), **ádidyutat**, **ábūbudhat**, **ávīvaśat** (√**vāś**), **ávī-vṛdhat**, **ásiṣyadat** (√**syand**); **bībhayat**, **śiśnathat** (**śnath** *pierce*); without thematic **a**: **á-śiśre-t** (√**śri**), **á-śiśnat**. Pl. 3. **ávīvaśan** (√**vāś**), **ásisrasan** (√**sraṃs**), **ásīṣadan** (√**sad**); **ábībhajur** (B.).

Mid. s. 3. **ávīvarata** (**vṛ** *cover*). Pl. 2. **ávīvṛdhadhvam**. 3. **ábībhayanta**, **ávīvaśanta** (√**vāś**), **ásiṣyadanta**.

2. The **subjunctive** is rare, only about a dozen forms occurring, all active except one. Examples are:

Act. s. 1. **rāradhā**. 2. **tītapāsi**. 3. **cīkḷpāti**, **pispṛśati**,[1] **sīṣadhāti** (√**sādh**). Pl. 1. **rīramāma**, **sīṣadhāma**.

3. **Injunctive** forms are fairly common, more than fifty occurring in the active, but only five in the middle. Examples are:

Act. s. 1. **cukrudham**, **dīdharam** (**dhṛ** *hold*). 2. **cikṣipas**, **pispṛśas**, **rīradhas**, **sīṣadhas**. 3. **cucyavat**, **dīdharat**, **mīmayat** (**mā** *bellow*), **siṣvadat** (**svad** *sweeten*).

Du. 2. **jihvaratam**. Pl. 2. **rīradhata**. 3. **rīraman**, **śūśucan** (**śuc** *shine*). 3. **sīṣapanta** (**sap** *serve*).

4. The **optative** forms number hardly a dozen, being made from only three roots, mostly from **vac** *speak*, the rest from **cyu** *stir* and **riṣ** *hurt*. They are:

Act. s. 1. **vocéyam**. 2. **rīriṣes**, **vocés**. 3. **vocét**.

Du. 2. **vocétam**. Pl. 1. **vocéma**. 3. **vocéyur**.

Mid. s. 1. **vocéya**. Pl. 1. **cucyuv-ī-mahi**,[1] **vocémahi**. 3. **cucyav-ī-rata**.[1] There is also the 3. s. mid. precative form **rīriṣ-ī-ṣ-ṭa**.

---

[1] Without thematic **a**.

5. Hardly more than a dozen imperative forms occur, all of them active. These are:

Sing. 2. vocatāt. 3. vocatu.

Du. 2. jigṛtám[1] (gṛ *waken*), didhṛtám,[1] vocatam. Pl. 2. jigṛ-tá,[1] didhṛtá,[1] paptata, vocata, suṣūdáta (AV.). 3. pūpurantu (pṛ *fill*), śiśrathantu.

Irregularities.

a. 1. The reduplicative syllable of dyut *shine* has i[2]: á-didyutat; that of am *injure* repeats the whole root[3]: ám-am-at (= á-am-am-at); while it is left short in jigṛtám, jigṛtá (beside á-jīgar), didhṛtám, didhṛtá (beside á-dīdharat), and in the isolated inj. didīpas for dīdīpas (dīp *shine*).

2. The radical syllable suffers contraction or syncopation (as in the weak forms of the perfect) in the three verbs naś *be lost*, vac *speak*, and pat *fall*; thus á-neś-at (= á-nanaś-at), á-voc-at (= á-va-uc-at: cp. Gk. ἔ-ειπ-ο-ν) and á-papt-at. Having all had the reduplicative vowel of the perfect (while the regular aorist reduplicative ī appears in the alternative forms á-nīnaś-at and á-pīpat-at), they were probably pluperfects in origin. But they have come to be aorists as is shown by their meaning and by the occurrence of modal forms (as vocatu, &c., and paptata).

3. The initial of the suffix is retained from the causative stems jñā-paya, sthā-paya, hā-paya, bhī-ṣaya, ar-paya, jā-paya (√ji). The radical vowel is reduced to i in the first four, while the reduplicative vowel comes after instead of before the radical vowel in the fifth: thus á-ji-jñip-at; á-ti-ṣṭhip-at; jī-hip-as; bī-bhiṣ-as, bī-bhiṣ-athās; arp-ip-am[4]; á-jī-jap-a-ta[5] (VS.).

Benedictive or Precative.

150. This is a form of the optative which adds an s after the modal suffix and which is made almost exclusively from aorist stems. In the RV. it occurs in the 1. 3. s. and

---

[1] Without thematic a.

[2] Cp. its perfect reduplication: 139, 8.

[3] Cp. the perfect reduplication of roots with a + nasal (139, 6).

[4] Here the p of the suffix is not only retained, but reduplicated.

[5] The causative of ji *conquer* from which this aor. is formed, would normally have been jāy-aya. In B. also occurs the form á-jī-jip-ata.

1. pl. active, and in the 2. 3. s. mid. The endings together with the modal suffix are:

Act. s. 1. **yā-s-am.** 3. **yā-s** (= **yās-s**); pl. 1. **yā-s-ma.**

Mid. s. 2. **ī-ṣ-ṭhās.** 3. **ī-ṣ-ṭa.**

a. The only perfect precative occurring is the 2. s. mid.: **sā-sah-ī-ṣ-ṭhā́s.**

b. Of the root aorist nearly thirty precatives are met with in the Saṃhitās. They occur in the act. 1. 3. s., 2. du., 1. 2. pl.; mid. 3. s. (see 148, 4 *a*). The **a** aorist and the reduplicated aor. have one precative form each in the 3. s. mid. (147, 4 and 149, 4). In the **s** aorist four precative forms occur in the 2. and 3. s. mid. (see 143, 4).

Simple Future.

151. The stem is formed by adding the suffix **syá** or (rather less frequently with connecting i) **i-ṣyá** to the root. As the future sense is often expressed by the subjunctive and sometimes also by the indicative, the future tense is not common in the RV., being formed from only sixteen roots, while the AV. makes it from about thirty-two others, and the TS. forms it from over sixty roots. In V. and B. taken together over one hundred form the future in **sya** and over eighty that in **iṣya.** The only derivative verbs that form the future (always with **iṣya**) are causatives, of which four stems appear, two in the RV. and two in the AV. Roots ending in **ṛ** always take **iṣya,** whereas those ending in other vowels generally take **sya.**

a. Final vowels and prosodically short medial vowels take Guṇa, final **ā** and medial **a** remaining unchanged; e. g. ji *conquer*: **je-ṣyá**; nī *lead*: **ne-ṣyá**; **dā** *give*: **dā-syá**; mih *shed water*: **mek-ṣyá**; yuj *join*: **yok-ṣyá**; **kṛt** *cut*: **kart-syá**; dah *burn*: **dhak-ṣyá**; **bandh** *bind*: **bhant-syá**; **bhū** *be*: **bhav-iṣyá**; sṛ *flow*: **sar-iṣyá**; vṛt *turn*: **vart-iṣyá.**

a. Causatives, which always take **iṣya**, retain the present stem, dropping only the final **a**; thus **dhāray-iṣyá** (**dhṛ** *support*); **vāsay-iṣyá** (**vas** *wear*); **dūṣ-ay-iṣyá** (**duṣ** *spoil*); **vāray-iṣyá** (**vṛ** *cover*).

b. The inflexion of the future is like that of the present of the first conjugation (**bhávāmi**). Middle forms occur in the sing. only. The forms met with, if made from **kṛ** *do*, would be:

Act. s. 1. **kar-iṣyā́mi**. 2. **kar-iṣyási**. 3. **kar-iṣyáti**.

Du. 2. **kar-iṣyáthas**. 3. **kar-iṣyátas**. Pl. 1. **kar-iṣyā́-mas, -masi**. 2. **kar-iṣyátha**. 3. **kar-iṣyánti**.

Mid. s. 1. **kar-iṣyé**. 2. **kar-iṣyáse**. 3. **kar-iṣyáte**.

1. Only one subjunctive, the 2. s. act. **kar-iṣyā́s**, has been met with in V., and one other, 1. du. mid., **not-syāva-hai** (**nud** *push*) in B.

2. More than twenty participles occur, of which only four are mid. Examples are:

Act. **kar-iṣy-ánt**, **dhak-ṣy-ánt** (√**dah**); mid. **yak-ṣyá-māṇa** (√**yaj**), **staviṣyá-māṇa** (√**stu**).

Irregularities.

c. In **sū** *bring forth* the future stem is formed with unchanged final vowel, which is moreover accented: **sū́-ṣya**; while the medial **a** of **sah** is lengthened: **sāk-ṣyá**.

Periphrastic Future.

152. There is no certain example of this form of the future in the Saṃhitās. But such a phrase as **anv-āgantā́ yajñápatir vo átra** (TS., VS.) *the sacrificer is following after you here* may be an example of its incipient use.[1]

In B. this future is taken by nearly thirty roots. It is made by using the N. s. of an agent noun in **tṛ** (180), to which the present of the verb **as** *be* is added in the 1. 2. persons, while in the 3. persons du. and pl. the N. du. and pl. appear. The use of this tense-form is

---

[1] The forerunners in V. of this new tense-formation in B. are the agent nouns in **tṛ** which, generally accented on the root, are used participially governing an acc. and may be employed predicatively with or without the copula; e. g. **dā́tā yó vánitā maghám** (iii. 13[3]) *who gives and wins bounty*.

almost limited to the active, only a few isolated examples being found in the middle. Forms occurring, if made from bhū *be*, **would be: Act. sing. 1. bhavitā́smi; 3. bhavitā́. Pl. 1. bhavitā́smas; 3. bhavitā́ras. Mid. sing. 1. 2. bhavitā́se. Pl. 1. bhavitā́smahe.**

Conditional.

153. This is a past tense of the future meaning *would have.* Only one example occurs in the Saṃhitās: **á-bhar-iṣya-t** (RV. ii. 30[2]) *was going to bear off.* This form is very rare in B. also, except in the ŚB. where it is found more than fifty times.

Passive.

154. The passive, which takes the terminations of the middle, differs from the latter only in the forms made from the present stem and in the 3. s. aor. From the middle of verbs of the fourth class it differs in accent only: **náh-ya-te** *binds*: **nah-yá-te** *is bound.*

The stem is formed by adding accented **yá** to the root, which appears in its weak form.

1. Final **ā** mostly becomes **ī**; e. g. **dā** *give*: **dī-yá**; but it also remains; e. g. **jñā** *know*: **jñā-yá.**

2. Final **i** and **u** are lengthened; e. g. **ji** *conquer*: **jī-yá-te**; **śru** *hear*: **śrū-yá-te.**

3. Final **ṛ** becomes **ri**; e. g. **kṛ** *make*: **kri-yá-te.**[1]

4. Final **ṝ** becomes **īr**; e. g. **śṝ** *crush*: **śīr-yá-te.**[2]

5. Roots ending in a consonant preceded by a nasal, lose the nasal; e. g. **añj** *anoint*: **aj-yá-te**; **bandh** *bind*: **badh-yá-te**; **bhañj** *break*: **bhaj-yá-te**; **vañc** *move crookedly*: **vac-yá-te**; **śaṃs** *praise*: **śas-yá-te.**

---

[1] The only two roots in which **ṛ** is preceded by two consonants and which form a passive are **stṛ** *strew* and **smṛ** *remember*. Their passives do not occur in the Saṃhitās, but in B. are found **stri-yá-te** and **smar-yá-te.**

[2] The passive of **pṝ** *fill* does not occur in the Saṃhitās, but in B. it is **pūr-yá-te** (the **ṝ** being preceded by a labial).

6. **Roots** liable to Samprasāraṇa (17 note 1) take it; e. g. **vac** *speak*: **uc-yá-te**; **vad** *speak*: **ud-yá-te**; **vah** *carry*: **uh-yá-te**; **grah** *seize*: **gṛh-yá-te**.

a. Derivative verbs in **aya** (causatives) drop the suffix while retaining the strong radical vowel. Only one such stem has been noted in the Saṃhitās: **bhāj-yá-te** *is caused to share* (from **bhāj-áya** causative of **bhaj** *share*).

a. The forms of the present indicative passive occurring, if made from **hū** *call*, would be:

Sing. 1. **hū-yé**. 2. **hū-yá-se**. 3. **hū-yá-te**. Du. 3. **hū-yé-te**. Pl. 1. **hū-yā́-mahe**. 3. **hū-yá-nte**.

b. As regards the moods only two certain subjunctive forms (s. 3. **uh-yā́-te, bhri-yā́-te**) and one injunctive (s. 3. **sū-ya-ta**: **sū** *bring forth*) occur. No optative forms occur in the RV. or AV.[1] There are, however, nearly thirty imperative forms occurring in the 2. 3. s. pl. These forms, illustrated by **hū** *call*, are: s. 2. **hū-yá-sva**. 3. **hū-yá-tām**. Pl. 2. **hū-yá-dhvam**. 3. **hū-yá-ntām**.

c. Of the participle over forty examples occur; e. g. **hū-yá-māna** *being called*. Of the imperfect only about eight forms have been noted, occurring only in the 3. s. and pl.: **á-hū-ya-ta** and **á-hū-yanta**.

Irregularities.

d. **tan** *stretch* forms its passive from **tā**: **tā-yá-te**[2]. Similarly **jan** *beget* becomes **jā́-ya-te** *is born*, which, however, in form belongs to the radically accented fourth class. **mri-yá-te** *dies* (√**mṛ**) and **dhri-yá-te** (√**dhṛ**) *is steadfast*, while passive in form, are intransitive in sense.

Aorist Passive.

155. Outside the present system the passive has no special finite form except in the **3. sing. aor.** This is a peculiar middle form (made from about forty-five roots in

---

[1] But they are met with in the Brāhmaṇas.

[2] In B. **khā-yá-te** is formed from **khan** *dig*.

the Saṃhitās)[1] which is used with a predominantly passive meaning. When it is formed from verbs with a neuter sense, like **gam** *go*, that sense remains unchanged (as in the past passive participle). It is a 3. s. ind. in which the augmented root takes the ending **i**. The characteristic feature of this form is the strengthening of the root as compared with other middle forms; e.g. **á-kār-i** beside **á-kr-i** (1. s. mid.). Prosodically short medial **i, u, ṛ** take Guṇa, and medial **a** is normally lengthened; final **i, u, ṛ** take Vṛddhi, while final **ā** interposes a **y** before the ending. The accent of unaugmented forms is always on the root. Examples are: **á-ved-i** (**vid** *find*), **á-bodh-i** (**budh** *wake*), **á-darś-i** (**dṛś** *see*), **á-vāc-i** (**vac** *speak*); **á-śrāy-i** (**śri** *resort*), **á-stāv-i** (**stu** *praise*), **á-kār-i** (**kṛ** *do*), **á-dhā-y-i** (**dhā** *put*).

More than twenty unaugmented forms are also used injunctively; e.g. **śrā́v-i** *let be heard*.

Irregularities.

a. 1. The medial **a** is not lengthened in **á-jan-i**, the unaugmented **ján-i** (beside **jā́n-i**), and **á-vah-i**.

2. From the denominative stem **jāraya** *play the lover* the unique form **jārayā́-y-i** *let him be embraced* is formed.

PARTICIPLES, GERUNDS, AND INFINITIVE.

I. Active Participles.

156. The stem of the present (except the reduplicating class), the future, and the aorist active participle is formed with the suffix **ant**.[2] The strong stem may be obtained by dropping the **i** of the 3. pl. ind. act.; e.g. **bháv-ant, kṣip-ánt, ás-yant; duh-ánt, kṛṇv-ánt, bhind-ánt, prī-ṇánt.**

---

[1] About a dozen more are found in B.

[2] On the declension of participles in **ant** see 85; on the formation of their fem. stems, 95 *a*.

Stems of the reduplicating class do not distinguish strong forms because they drop the **n**: e. g. **júhv-at** (3. pl. **júhv-ati**).

The strong stem of the future participle may similarly be obtained by dropping the **i** of the 3. pl. act.: **bhaviṣyánt, kariṣyánt.**

The active participle is formed by the root aorist, the **a** aorist, and the **s** aorist, from the unaugmented tense stem in the latter two; e. g. **vidá-nt, sák-ṣ-ant** (**sah** *prevail*); and from the weakened or unmodified root in the former; e. g. **ṛdh-ánt, kr-ánt** (**kṛ** *make*), **gm-ánt** (**gam** *go*), **pā́nt** (**pā** *drink*).

a. **Irregularities.**—In the pres. part. the initial **a** of **as** *be* and the medial **a** of **han** *slay* are lost: **sánt** (3. pl. **sánti**), **ghn-ánt** (3. pl. **ghn-ánti**); while the **n** of the suffix is lost in **dā́ś-at** *worshipping* and **śā́s-at**[1] (3. pl. **śā́s-ati**). The **n** is also lost in the **s** aor. part. of **dah** *burn*: **dákṣ-at** and **dhákṣ-at.** Whether it was also lost in **sákṣ-at,** the part. of the same aor. from **sah** *prevail*, is uncertain because it is only met with in a weak case.

157. The reduplicated perfect participle is formed from the weak (but uncontracted or unsyncopated) stem to which the suffix **vāṃs** is directly added. There are more than fifty such stems. Examples are: **cakṛ-vā́ṃs, jagan-vā́ṃs** (**gam** *go*), **tastabh-vā́ṃs** (**stambh** *prop*), **tasthi-vā́ṃs** (**sthā** *stand*), **dadṛś-vā́ṃs, dad-vā́ṃs** (**dā** *give*), **ba-bhū-vā́ṃs, vavṛt-vā́ṃs, sasa-vā́ṃs** (**san** *gain*), **suṣup-vā́ṃs** (**svap** *sleep*).

a. Some half-dozen of these participles are formed by adding the suffix with connecting **i** to the reduplicated stem contracted to a single syllable: **ī-y-i-vā́ṃs** (**i** *go*); **ūṣ-i-vā́ṃs** (**vas** *dwell*); **ok-i-vā́ṃs**[2] (**uc** *be pleased*); **papt-i-vā́ṃs** (**pat** *fall*); **saśc-i-vā́ṃs** (**sac** *follow*); in the later Saṃhitās also

---

[1] Both **dāś** and **śās** belong to the root, and not the reduplicating class.

[2] With strong radical vowel and reversion to the original guttural.

jakṣ-i-vā́ṃs (**ghas** *eat*).[1] The only certain example of a perf. part. adding the suffix with connecting **i** to the fully reduplicated stem is **viviś-i-vā́ṃs** (TS.).[2]

b. A few perfect participles are formed by attaching **vāṃs** to the unreduplicated stem: **dāś-vā́ṃs** *worshipping*, **vid-vā́ṃs** *knowing*, **sāh-vā́ṃs** *prevailing*, and perhaps **khid-vā́ṃs**[3] *oppressing*. Similarly formed is **mīḍh-vā́ṃs** *bountiful*, though the root does not occur in independent use. Three unreduplicated roots take connecting **i** in the later Saṃhitās: **dāś-i-vā́ṃs** (SV.) *worshipping*, **viś-i-vā́ṃs** (AV.) *entering*, **varj-i-vā́ṃs**[4] (AV.) *having twisted*.

a. **Irregularities.**—In seven stems the palatal reverts to the original guttural: **cikit-vā́ṃs** (√**cit**), **jigī-vā́ṃs** (√**ji**), **ririk-vā́ṃs** (√**ric**), **ruruk-vā́ṃs** (√**ruc**), **vivik-vā́ṃs** (√**vic**), **śuśuk-vā́ṃs** (√**śuc**), **ok-i-vā́ṃs** (√**uc**). The radical vowel is strong in **dadā-vā́ṃs** (AV.), **ok-i-vā́ṃs**, **sāh-vā́ṃs**; while the reduplicative vowel is long in **sāsah-vā́ṃs** and **śūśu-vā́ṃs** (√**śū**).

II. Middle and Passive Participles.

158. The participles of the future middle, of the present passive, and the present middle of the **a** conjugation are formed by adding the suffix **māna** to the stem (which always ends in **a**); e. g. fut. mid. **yakṣyá-māṇa** (√**yaj**); pres. pass. **kriyá-māṇa** (√**kṛ**); pres. mid. **yája-māna**.

a. Verbs of the second conjugation add the suffix **āna** to the weak stem in the pres. mid.; e. g. **bruv-āṇá** (√**brū**), **júhv-āna** (√**hu**), **rundh-āná** (√**rudh**), **kṛṇv-āná** (√**kṛ**), **pun-āná** (√**pū**).

a. There are several irregularities in the formation of the middle participles of the root class. 1. The root **ās** *sit* optionally takes the anomalous suffix **īna**: **ā́s-īna** beside **ās-āná**. 2. The final of the root

---

[1] **jakṣ** syncopated for **jagh(a)s**.

[2] In B. are also found **dadṛś-i-vāṃs** and **cichid-i-vāṃs**.

[3] Occurring only in the voc. **khidvas**.

[4] Presupposed by the fem. **varjuṣī**.

duh *milk* optionally reverts to the original guttural: **dúgh-āna** beside the regular **dúh-āna**. 3. A few roots take Guṇa: **oh-āná** (√ūh), **yodh-āná** (√yudh), **śáy-āna** (√śī), **stav-āná** (√stu). 4. Several of these participles optionally accent the radical syllable instead of the final vowel of the suffix; e. g. **víd-āna** beside **vid-āná**.

159. The **Perfect Middle Participle** is formed by adding the suffix **-āná** to the weak form of the stem as it appears before the ending of the 3. pl. mid. **re** (**ire**, **rire**). It is common, more than eighty examples occurring. The following are some of them: **ānaj-āná** (√**añj**), **ānaś-āná** (√**aṃś**), **ār-āṇá** (√**ṛ**), **īj-āná** (√**yaj**), **ūc-āná** (√**vac**), **cakr-āṇá** (√**kṛ**), **cikit-āná** (√**cit**), **jagm-āná** (√**gam**), **tasth-āná** (√**sthā**), **tistir-āṇá** (√**stṝ**), **tep-āná** (√**tap**), **pap-āná** (**pā** *drink*), **paspaś-āná** (√**spaś**), **bhej-āná** (√**bhaj**), **yem-āná** (√**yam**), **lebh-āná** (√**labh**), **vāvas-āná** (**vas** *wear* and *dwell*), **śiśriy-āṇá** (√**śri**), **siṣmiy-āṇá** (√**smi**), **suṣup-āṇá** (√**svap**).

a. **Irregularities.**—1. This participle of **śī** *lie* has the double anomaly of reduplicating with **a** and of strengthening the radical syllable:[1] **śaśay-āná**. 2. The root **sah** *prevail* adds the suffix to a reduplicated as well as to a contracted stem: **sāsah-āná** and **seh-āná**. 3. The radical vowel of **kam** *love* and **śam** *labour* is not syncopated: **cakam-āná** and **śaśam-āná**. 4. Four of these participles have the intensive accent on the reduplicative syllable: **tū́tuj-āna**[2], **śū́śuj-āna**, **śū́śuv-āna** (√**śū**), and **śā́śad-āna**[3] (**śad** *prevail*).[4]

160. The **Perfect Passive Participle** is formed by adding, in the great majority of instances, the suffix **tá** (with or without connecting **i**) or, far less commonly, the suffix **ná** (directly) to the root.

---

[1] Cp. a similar irregularity of **śī** in 134, 1 *b*.

[2] Also normally, but less frequently, accented **tūtuj-āná**.

[3] Cp. the Gk. perf. mid. part. *κεκαδ-μένο-ς*.

[4] The first three cannot be accounted intensives because they have not the intensive reduplicative vowel (173, 1). Though the reduplicative vowel of **śā́śad-āna** may be that of either perfect or intensive, the occurrence of the perf. form **śāśadúr** beside it favours the view that it is a perf. participle.

1. **ná**, which is taken by primary verbs only, is attached to the (unweakened) root, which ends in a long vowel or one of the consonants **d** and (rarely) **c** or **j**. Before this suffix, **ī** and **ū** remain unchanged; **ā** remains or is reduced to **ī** or **i**; **ṝ** becomes **īr** or (generally when a labial precedes) **ūr**; **d** is assimilated to **n**; **c** and **j** revert to the original guttural. Thus **lī** *cling*: **lī-ná**; **dū** *burn*: **dū-ná**; **drā** *sleep*: **drā-ṇá**; **dā** *divide*: **di-ná**; **hā** *leave*: **hī-ná**; **gṝ** *swallow*: **gīr-ṇá**; **mṛ** *crush*: **mūr-ṇá**; **jṝ** *waste away*: **jūr-ṇá**; **bhid** *split*: **bhin-ná**; **skand** *leap*: **skan-ná**; **vraśc** *cut up*: **vṛk-ṇá**; **ruj** *break*: **rug-ṇá**.

a. Several roots take alternative forms in **ta**: **nun-ná** and **nut-tá** (√**nud**); **vin-ná** and **vit-tá** (**vid** *find*); **san-ná** and **sat-tá** (**sad** *sit*); **śī-ná** and **śī-tá** (**śyā** *coagulate*); **pṝ** *fill*: **pūr-ṇá** and **pūr-tá**; **śṝ** *crush*: **śīr-ṇá** and **śūr-tá**; **pṛc** *mix*: **-pṛg-ṇa** and **pṛk-tá**.

b. The final palatal of **pṛc** *mix*, **vraśc** *cut up* and **ruj** *break* reverts to the guttural (cp. 160, 1).

2. When **tá** is added direct the root tends to appear in its weak form: verbs liable to Samprasāraṇa take it; a medial or final nasal is lost; **ā** is often reduced to **ī** or **i**; **yā** sometimes to **ī**. Examples are: **yā-tá**, **ji-tá**, **bhī-tá**, **stu-tá**, **hū-tá**, **kṛ-tá**; **naṣ-ṭá** (√**naś** *be lost*), **sik-tá** (√**sic**), **yuk-tá** (√**yuj**), **gū-ḍhá** (√**guh**),[1] **dug-dhá** (√**duh**), **sṛṣ-ṭá** (√**sṛj**); **iṣ-ṭá** (√**yaj**), **vid-dhá** (√**vyadh**), **uk-tá** (√**vac**), **ū-ḍhá** (√**vah**),[2] **sup-tá** (√**svap**), **pṛṣ-ṭá** (√**prach**); **ak-tá** (√**añj**), **ta-tá** (√**tan**), **ga-tá** (√**gam**); **pī-tá** (**pā** *drink*), **sthi-tá** (√**sthā**); **vī-tá** (√**vyā**).

a. The root **dhā** *put* is doubly weakened in **hi-tá** beside **-dhi-ta**. Medial **ā** is reduced to **i** in **śiṣ-ṭá** (**śās** *order*). Syncopation and loss of **s** appear in **-g-dha** *eaten* (√**ghas**).[3]

b. Excepting the occurrence of the normal form **-dāta** in the compound **tvā́-dāta** *given by thee*, **dā** *give* regularly uses the weak pres.

---

[1] With cerebralization and aspiration of the suffix, loss of the radical final and lengthening of the radical vowel (cp. 62, 69 *c*).

[2] With the same changes as in **gūḍhá** after **vah-tá** has been reduced by Samprasāraṇa to **uh-tá**.

[3] Cp. p. 170, note 7.

stem **dad** in forming its past passive participle: **dat-tá**. The latter is further reduced to **-tta** in **deva-ttá** *given by the gods*, and when combined with certain prepositions: **vy-ā́-tta** *opened*, **pári-tta** *given away*, **práti-tta** *given back*. The same syncopation appears in the compound participle of **dā** *divide*: **áva-tta** *cut off*.

c. One root in **an** and three or four in **am** retain the nasal and lengthen the vowel: **dhvan** *sound*: **dhvān-tá**; **kram** *stride*: **krān-tá**; **śam** *be quiet*: **śān-tá**; **śram** *be weary*: **śrān-tá**; **dham** *blow* has the irregular **dhmā-tá** and **dham-i-tá**.

d. A few roots in **an** have **ā**[1]: **khan** *dig*: **khā-tá**; **jan** *be born*: **jā-tá**; **van** *win*: **-vā-ta**; **san** *gain*: **sā-tá**.

3. **i-ta** is taken by a considerable number of roots ending not only in conjunct consonants or in single consonants difficult to combine with t, but also in simple consonants, especially sibilants, which present no such difficulty. The root is not weakened (excepting four instances of Samprasāraṇa). Secondary verbs (almost without exception causatives)[2] take **ita** exclusively (after dropping **aya**).[3]

Examples are: **nind-itá**, **rakṣ-itá**; **grath-itá**, **īḷ-itá**, **car-itá**, **jīv-itá**; **pat-itá**, **pan-itá**; **kup-itá**, **stabh-itá**; **muṣ-itá**; **arp-itá**[4] (**arp-áya** *cause to go*), **cod-itá** (**cod-áya** *set in motion*).

a. The roots taking Samprasāraṇa are: **grabh** and **grah** *seize*: **gṛbh-ī-tá** and **gṛh-ī-tá** (AV.);[5] **vakṣ** *increase*: **ukṣ-itá**; **vad** *speak*: **ud-itá**; **śrath** *slacken*: **śṛth-itá**.

161. There is once found in the AV. a perfect passive participle extended with the possessive suffix **vant**, which gives it the sense of a perfect participle active: **aśitá-vant** *having eaten*.[6]

---

[1] Representing the long sonant nasal.

[2] Only one perfect participle passive has been noted from a desiderative: **mīmāṃ-s-itá** *called in question*, and one from a denominative: **bhām-itá** *enraged*.

[3] In B. **jñapaya**, causative of **jñā** *know*, forms its part. without connecting **i**: **jñap-tá**.

[4] Usually (and abnormally) accented **árp-ita**.

[5] With **ī** for **i** as in some other forms from this root.

[6] This type of participle hardly occurs even in the Brāhmaṇas.

162. The **Future Passive Participle** is in the RV. formed with four suffixes: one with the primary suffix **ya**, which is common, the rest with the secondary suffixes **áy-ya, én-ya,** and **tv-a,** each of which occurs about a dozen times. In the AV. there begin to be used two other gerundives, formed with **tavyà** and **aníya,** each occurring twice. All these participles correspond in sense to the Lat. gerundive in *-ndus.*

1. In the RV. about forty examples of the gerundive in **ya** occur, and about twenty more in the AV. The suffix is nearly always to be read as **ia,** which accounts for the treatment before it of final radical vowels. The root, being accented, appears in a strong form excepting a few examples which have the short radical vowel **i, u,** or **ṛ.**

a. Final **ā** coalesces with the initial of **ia** to **e,** between which and the following **a** a phonetic **y** is interposed: **dā** *give*: **déya** (= **dá-i-y-a**) *to be given.*

b. Final **ĭ, ŭ, ṛ** regularly take Guṇa or Vṛddhi, the final element of which always appears as **y, v, r,** as before a vowel; e. g. **lī** *cling*: **-láy-ya**; **nu** *praise*: **náv-ya**; **bhū** *be*: **bháv-ya** and **bhāv-yá** *future*; **hū** *call*: **háv-ya**; **vṛ** *choose*: **vár-ya.**

c. Medial **i, u, ṛ,** if followed by a single consonant, may take Guṇa and **a** may be lengthened; e. g. **dviṣ**: **dvéṣ-ya** *hateful*; **yudh**: **yódh-ya** *to be subdued*; **ṛdh**: **árdh-ya** *to be accomplished*; **mṛj**: **márj-ya** *to be purified*; **vac**: **vác-ya** *to be said*; but also **gúh-ya** *to be concealed*; **-dhṛṣ-ya** *to be assailed*; **-sád-ya** *to be seated.*

d. A final short vowel sometimes remains unchanged, a **t** being then interposed: **í-t-ya** *to be gone*; **śrú-t-ya** *to be heard*; **-kṛ-t-ya** *to be made*; **carkṛ́-t-ya** *to be praised.*

2. The suffix **áyya,** nearly always to be read **áyia,** is almost restricted to the RV.; e. g. **pan-áyya** *to be admired*; **vid-áyya** *to be found*; **śrav-áyya** *glorious.* It is sometimes attached to secondary stems; to a causative: **panay-áyya** *admirable,* **spṛhay-áyya** *desirable*; to a desiderative: **di-dhi-ṣ-áyya** *to be conciliated* (√ **dhā**); to an intensive: **vi-tan-tas-áyya** *to be hastened.*

3. **énya** (generally to be read **énia**) is attached to the root,

which remains unaltered except when it ends in a vowel: thus **dviṣ-éṇya** *malignant*, **yudh-énya** *to be combatted*, **dṛś-énya** *worthy to be seen*; but **vár-eṇya** *choiceworthy* (**vṛ** *choose*). It is once added to an aor. stem: **yaṃ-s-énya** *to be guided* (√**yam**). Secondary verbs also take this suffix; desideratives: **didṛkṣ-éṇya** *worthy to be seen*, **śuśrūṣ-éṇya** *deserving to be heard*; intensives: **marmṛj-énya** *to be glorified*, **vāvṛdh-énya** *to be glorified*; denominatives: **sapar-éṇya** *to be adored*.

4. **tv-a**, almost restricted to the RV.[1] and generally to be read **tua**, is added to the strong form of the root, which is accented. Thus **kár-tva** *to be made*, **hé-tva** *to be driven on* (√**hi**), **só-tva** *to be pressed* (√**su**), **vák-tva** *to be said*; with connecting **i**: **sán-i-tva** *to be won*; with connecting **ī**: **bháv-ī-tva**[2] *future*.

5. The only two examples in V. (both occurring in AV.) of the gerundive in **tavyà**, which in both cases is added with connecting **i**, are **jan-i-tavyà** *to be born* and **hiṃs-i-tavyà** *to be injured*.[3]

6. The only examples of the gerundive in **anīya** (both appearing in the AV.) are **upa-jīv-anī́ya** *to be subsisted on* and **ā-mantr-aṇī́ya** *worthy to be addressed*.[4]

III. Gerund or Indeclinable Participle.

163. More than 120 examples of the gerund occur in the RV. and AV. It expresses an action which accompanies or more often precedes that of the finite verb. It is formed with the three suffixes **tvī́**, **tvā́**, **tvā́ya** (all old cases of stems

---

[1] A few examples occur in the Brāhmaṇas: **jé-tva** (**ji** *conquer*), **snā́-tva** (**snā** *bathe*), **hán-tva** (**han** *slay*).

[2] With ī instead of i.

[3] This gerundive has become not uncommon in B., where it is formed not only from the root, but from secondary stems.

[4] In B. nearly a dozen examples have been met with.

in **tu** which is also used to form infinitives) attached to the simple root.

1. The form in **tvī́**, which is almost restricted to the RV.,[1] is the commonest of the three in that Saṃhitā, where fifteen examples occur. It probably represents an old locative of stems in **tu**. It is as a rule added directly to the root, which has the same form as in the perf. pass. participle in **ta**. Examples are: **kṛ-tvī́** *having made*, **ga-tvī́** *having gone*, **gū-ḍhvī́** *having hidden*, **bhū-tvī́** *having become*, **vṛk-tvī́** *having overthrown* (√**vṛj**), **hi-tvī́** *having abandoned* (√**hā**). There are two forms in which the suffix is added with the connecting vowel **i**: **jan-i-tvī́** *having produced* and **skabh-i-tvī́** *having propped*.

2. The suffix **tv-ā́** (an old inst. sing. of a verbal noun in **tu**) is taken by nine roots in the RV. and about thirty more in the AV. The root has the same form as before the **ta** of the perf. pass. participle. The forms occurring in the RV. are: **pī-tvā́** (**pā** *drink*), **bhit-tvā́** *having shattered*, **bhū-tvā́** *having become*, **mi-tvā́** *having formed* (√**mā**), **yuk-tvā́** *having yoked*, **vṛ-tvā́** *having covered*, **śru-tvā́** *having heard*, **ha-tvā́** *having slain*, **hi-tvā́** *having abandoned*. Some of the forms from the AV. are: **iṣ-ṭvā́** *having sacrificed* (√**yaj**), **jag-dhvā́** *having devoured* (√**jakṣ**), **tīr-tvā́** *having crossed* (√**tṝ**), **tṛ-ḍhvā́** *having shattered* (√**tṛh**), **dat-tvā́** *having given* (√**dā**), **pak-tvā́** *having cooked* (√**pac**), **bad-dhvā́** *having bound* (√**bandh**), **bhak-tvā́** *having divided* (√**bhaj**), **rū-ḍhvā́** *having ascended* (√**ruh**), **vṛṣ-ṭvā́** *having cut up* (√**vraśc**), **sup-tvā́** *having slept* (√**svap**); three take the connecting vowel **i**: **cāy-i-tvā́** *noting* (√**cāy**), **hiṃs-i-tvā́** *having injured*, **gṛh-ī-tvā́** *having seized*; a few also are formed from secondary stems in **aya** (which is retained); e. g. **kalpay-i-tvā́** *having arranged*.

3. The rarest gerund is that in **tvā́ya**, which is formed

---

[1] This gerundive is not found in the AV., but it has not entirely disappeared in the Brāhmaṇas.

from only eight roots in the RV.[1]: **ga-tvā́ya** *having gone*, **jag-dhvā́ya** *having devoured*, **dat-tvā́ya** *having given*, **dṛṣ-ṭvā́ya** *having seen*, **bhak-tvā́ya** *having attained*, **yuk-tvā́ya** *having yoked*, **ha-tvā́ya** *having slain*, **hi-tvā́ya** *having abandoned*; three more of these gerunds appear in the Yajurveda: **kṛ-tvā́ya** *having done*, **ta-tvā́ya** *having stretched*, **vṛ-tvā́ya** *having covered*.

164. When the verb is compounded the suffix is regularly either **yă** or **tyă**. In at least two-thirds of such forms the vowel of the suffix is long in the RV. The root is always accented.

1. **yă** is added (but never with **i**) to the root, which has the same form as before **tvā**, except that final **ā** and **am** remain unchanged. Nearly forty roots in the RV. and about thirty more in the AV. form these compound gerunds. Examples from the RV. are: **ā́c-yā** *bending* (= **ā́-ac-**), **abhy-úp-ya** *having enveloped* (√**vap**), **abhi-krám-ya** *approaching*, **abhi-gū́r-yā** *graciously accepting* (**gṛ** *sing*), **saṃ-gṛ́bh-yā** *gathering*, **ni-cā́y-yā** *fearing*, **vi-tū́r-yā** *driving forth* (√**tṝ**), **ā-dā́-ya** *taking*, **ati-dī́v-ya** *playing higher*, **anu-dṛ́ś-ya** *looking along*, **ā-rábh-ya** *grasping*, **ni-ṣád-yă** *having sat down*; from a causative stem: **prā́rp-ya** *setting in motion* (**prá-arpaya**). Examples from the AV. are: **ud-úh-ya** *having carried up* (√**vah**), **saṃ-gī́r-ya** *swallowing up* (√**gṝ**), **upa-dád-ya** *putting in* (√**dā**), **saṃ-bhū́-ya** *combining*, **ut-thā́-ya** *arising* (√**sthā**), **saṃ-sī́v-ya** *having sewed*; from a causative stem: **vi-bhā́j-ya** *having apportioned* (√**bhaj**).

a. Three roots are found in the RV. compounded with adverbs or substantives: **punar-dā́-ya** *giving back*, **mitha-spṛ́dh-ya** *vying together*, **karṇa-gṛ́h-ya** *seizing by the ear*, **pāda-gṛ́h-ya** *grasping by the foot*, **hasta-gṛ́h-ya** *grasping by the hand*.

---

[1] This gerund occurs twice in the AV. and about half a dozen times in B. It is once formed from a causative stem in the ŚB.: **spāś-ay-i-tvā́ya** (√**spaś**).

165. 2. **tyă** (nearly always with long vowel in the RV.) is added instead of **yă** to compound verbs ending in a short vowel;[1] e. g. **é-tyā** *having come* (**ā́-i**), **abhi-jí-tya** *having conquered*, **ā-dṛ́-tyā** *regarding*, **apa-mí-tya**[2] *having borrowed*, **upa-śrú-tya** *having overheard*; with adverbial or nominal prefix: **araṃ-kṛ́-tyā** *having made ready*, **akhkhalī-kṛ́-tya** *shouting*, **namas-kṛ́-tya** (AV.) *paying homage*.

a. The analogy of these verbs is followed by some roots ending in **n** or **m** preceded by **a**, which drop the nasal as in the perf. pass. part.: **vi-há-tyā** *having driven away* (√**han**), **ā-gá-tyā** *having come* (√**gam**), **ud-yá-tya** (AV.) *lifting up* (√**yam**).

166. The accusative in **am** of certain verbal nouns, though not yet construed like a gerund in the Saṃhitās, is not infrequently so construed in the Brāhmaṇas and Sūtras. Before the suffix, the root (which is almost always compounded) appears in the form it assumes before the **i** of the 3. s. aor. pass. (155); e. g. **śā́khāṃ sam-ā-lámbh-am** *taking hold of a branch* (ŚB.); **mahānāgám abhi-saṃ-sā́r-am** *running together around a great snake* (ŚB.).

IV. Infinitive.

167. The infinitive, all the forms of which are old cases of verbal nouns, acc., dat., abl.-gen., or loc., is very frequent, occurring about 700 times in the RV. Only the acc. and dat. forms are common, but the datives outnumber the acc. in the proportion of 12 to 1 in the RV. and 3 to 1 in the AV. It is a remarkable fact that the infinitive in **tum**, the only form surviving in Sanskrit, occurs not more than five times in the RV., while the dative infinitive, which in the RV. is more than seven times as common as all the rest put together, has already for the most part disappeared in the Brāhmaṇas.

---

[1] Sometimes not original but reduced from a long vowel.

[2] Here **mi** is reduced from **mā** *measure*.

a. The infinitive is as a rule formed from the root, not being connected with any tense stems or ever showing the distinctions of voice. The forms in **dhyai, áse** and **sáni** are, however, not infrequently connected with a present stem; that in **dhyai** is once formed from a perfect stem, and is also in several instances taken by causative stems. The forms in **dhyai** and **taváí** are at once recognizable as infinitives by their abnormal endings; that in **sáni**, though it has an ordinary case-ending, by its isolated stem-formation. The acc. inf. in **tum** and **am** and the abl. gen. inf. show their infinitive character by their power of combining with prepositions and their verbal construction. Some infinitives, however, cannot be distinguished from ordinary cases of verbal nouns: they are not to be regarded as genuine infinitives unless they are isolated case forms or have a verbal construction.

1. Dative Infinitive.

This infinitive[1] ends in **e**, which with the final **ā** of a root or stem combines to **ai**.[2] It is formed from:

a. roots, about sixty forms occurring. About a dozen are formed from roots ending in long vowels and from one in **i**, all of them (except an alternative form of **bhū**) being compounded with prefixes; e.g. **parā-dái** *to give up*, **pra-hyè** *to send* (√**hi**); **-míy-e** *to diminish* (√**mī**), **-bhv-é** and **bhuv-é** *to be*; **-tír-e** *to cross*.

The rest are from roots ending in consonants. About a dozen are uncompounded, as **mah-é** *to be glad*, **mih-é** *to shed water*, **bhuj-é** *to enjoy*, **dṛś-é** *to see*. But the compounded forms are commoner; e.g. **-grábh-e** *to seize*, **-ídh-e** *to kindle*, **-núd-e** *to thrust*, **-pṛ́ch-e**[3] *to ask*, **-vā́c-e**[4] *to speak*, **-vídh-e**[3] *to pierce*, **-syád-e**[5] *to flow*.[6]

---

[1] The only dat. inf. in ordinary use in B. is that in **taváí**. Otherwise only five or six in **e** (see note 6); two in **tave**, **áv-i-tave** and **stár-tave**, and one in **dhyai**, **sā́-ḍhyai** *to conquer* (√**sah**) have been noted in B. Loc. infinitives have disappeared.

[2] Except **śrad-dhé** *to trust* and **pra-mé** *to form*, which drop the **ā**.

[3] With Samprasāraṇa.

[4] With lengthened vowel.

[5] With loss of nasal (√**syand**).

[6] In B. have been noted half a dozen infinitives in **e** from roots

b. verbal nouns derived with nine different suffixes. These in the aggregate are more numerous.

1. Some twenty-five are datives of stems in **as**;[1] e.g. **áy-as-e** *to go*, **cákṣ-as-e** *to see*, **car-ás-e** *to fare*, **puṣy-ás-e** *to thrive*, **bhiy-ás-e** *to fear*, **śriy-ás-e** *to be resplendent.*

2. Five or six datives of stems in **i** are found in the RV., and one or two in other Saṃhitās; **tuj-áye** *to breed*, **dṛś-áy-e** *to see*, **mah-áy-e** *to rejoice*, **yudh-áy-e** *to fight*, **san-áy-e** *to win*; **gṛh-aye** *to seize* (K.), **cit-áye** *to understand* (VS.).

3. Four or five are datives of stems in **ti**: **iṣ-ṭáy-e** *to refresh*, **pī-táy-e** *to drink*, **vī-táy-e** *to enjoy*, **sā-táy-e** *to win.*

4. More than thirty are datives of stems in **tu**[2] (added to the gunated root, sometimes with connecting **i**); e.g. **át-tav-e** *to eat*, **é-tav-e** *to go*, **ó-tav-e** *to weave* (√**ū** = **vā**), **kár-tav-e** *to make*, **gán-tav-e** *to go*, **pā́-tav-e** *to drink*, **bhár-tav-e** *to bear away*, **yáṣ-ṭav-e** *to sacrifice*, **vák-tav-e** *to speak*, **vás-tav-e** *to shine*, **vó-ḷhav-e** *to convey* (√**vah**); **áv-i-tav-e** *to refresh*, **cár-i-tav-e** *to fare*, **sáv-i-tav-e** *to bring forth* (√**sū**), **sráv-i-tav-e** *to flow* (√**sru**), **háv-i-tav-e** *to call* (√**hū**); **jīv-ā́-tav-e** *to live*, **stár-ī-tav-e** (AV.) *to lay low* (√**stṝ**).

5. More than a dozen are datives of stems in **tavā́** (which is added like **tu** to the gunated root) and have the peculiarity of being **doubly accented**; e.g. **é-tavái** *to go*, **ó-tavái** *to weave*, **gán-tavái** *to go*, **pā́-tavái** *to drink*, **mán-tavái** *to think*, **sár-tavái** *to flow*; **yám-i-tavái** *to guide*, **sráv-i-tavái** *to flow.*

---

ending in consonants, all but one being compounded: **dṛś-é** (TS.) *to see*, **prati-dhṛ́ṣ-e** *to withstand* (TS.), **pra-mrad-é** *to crush* (ŚB.), **ā-rábh-e** *to take hold* (ŚB.), **ā-sád-e** *to sit upon* (AB.), **ati-sṛ́p-e** *to glide over* (MS.). All these except **pra-mrad-é** occur in the RV.

[1] Which is generally accented, but about half a dozen examples accent the root.

[2] The only examples of this infinitive noted in B. are **ávitave** and **stártave**.

a. This infinitive is still in regular use in B., where the following examples have been noted: **étavái** and **yā́tavái** *to go*, **kártavái** *to do*, **dédīyitavái** *to fly away*, **drógdhavái** *to plot*, **mántavái** *to think*, **mánthitavái** *to rule*, **stártavái** *to lay low*, **áti-caritavái** *to transgress*, **ā́-netavái** *to bring*, **nír-astavái** *to throw out*, **pári-starītavái** *to strew around*, **sáṃhvayitavái** *to call together*.

6. There is only one certain example of a dative infinitive from a stem in **tyā**: **i-tyái** *to go*.

7. More than thirty-five are datives (almost restricted to the RV.) of stems in **dhyā**, which is added to verbal stems ending in **a** (generally accented); e. g. **iyá-dhyai** *to go* (√i), **gáma-dhyai** *to go*, **cará-dhyai** *to fare*, **śayá-dhyai** *to lie* (√śī), **stavá-dhyai** *to praise* (√stu); **pibá-dhyai** *to drink* (√pā), **pṛṇá-dhyai** *to fill* (√pṝ), **huvá-dhyai** *to call* (√hū);[1] **vāvṛdhá-dhyai**[2] *to strengthen*; **nāśayá-dhyai**[3] *to cause to disappear*, **vartayá-dhyai**[3] *to cause to turn*.

a. Only one of these infinitives has been noted in B.: **sā́ḍhyai** *to conquer* (√sah). In the TS. occurs one example ending in **e** instead of **ai**: **gamá-dhye** *to go*.

8. Five are datives of stems in **man**: **trā́-maṇ-e** *to protect*, **dā́-man-e** *to give* (Gk. δόμεν-αι), **dhár-maṇ-e** *to support*, **bhár-maṇ-e** *to preserve*, **vid-mán-e** (Gk. ἴδ-μεν-αι) *to know*.

9. Three are datives of stems in **van**: **tur-váṇ-e** *to overcome* (√tṛ), **dā-ván-e** (Gk. δοῦναι = δόϝεναι) *to give*, **dhū́rvaṇ-e**[4] *to injure*.

2. Accusative Infinitive.

This infinitive is formed in two ways.

a. One of them (of which more than a dozen examples occur in the RV. besides several others in the AV.) is made with **am** added to the weak form of the root, which nearly

---

[1] The last three are made from regular present stems.

[2] From the reduplicated perfect stem.

[3] From the causative stem, from which about ten such infinitives are formed.

[4] With interchange of vowel and semivowel: ūr = vṛ. Cp. 171, 2.

always ends in a consonant (except **dhā, mī, tṝ**); e.g. **sam-ídh-am** *to kindle*, **sam-pṛ́ch-am** *to ask*, **ā-rábh-am** *to reach*, **ā-rúh-am** *to mount*, **śúbh-am** *to shine*; **pra-tír-am** *to prolong* (√**tṝ**), **prati-dhā́-m** *to place upon*, **pra-míy-am** *to neglect* (√**mī**).

b. The second form which is made from stems in **tu** (= Lat. supine) is much less common than the datives from the same stems. Only five examples occur in the RV. and about as many others in the AV.; RV.: **ó-tum** *to weave*, **dā́-tum** *to give* (Lat. *da-tum*), **práṣ-ṭum** *to ask*, **prá-bhar-tum** *to present*, **anu-prá-voḷhum** *to advance*; AV.: **át-tum** *to eat*, **kár-tum** *to make*, **dráṣ-ṭum** *to see*, **yā́c-i-tum** *to ask*, **spárdh-i-tum** *to contend with*; K., VS.: **khán-i-tum** *to dig*.

a. The acc. inf. has become nearly twice as frequent as the dat. in B. The form in **am** is not unusual, while that in **tum** is quite common.

3. Ablative-Genitive Infinitive.

This infinitive is rare, fewer than twenty examples occurring in the Saṃhitās. It is rather of the nature of a verbal noun than a genuine infinitive. Like the acc. infinitive it is formed in two ways: from a radical (consonant) stem and from a verbal noun in **tu**. It thus ends either in **as** or **tos**; and as each of these endings represents both the abl. and the gen., the cases can only be distinguished syntactically.

a. The **as** form has the abl. sense almost exclusively. There are six examples of it in the RV.: **ā-tṛ́d-as** *being pierced*, **ava-pád-as** *falling down*, **sam-pṛ́c-as** *coming in contact*, **abhi-śríṣ-as** *binding*, **abhi-śvás-as** *blowing*, **ati-ṣkád-as** *leaping across*. There seems to be one certain example of the gen.: **ni-míṣ-as** *to wink*.

b. Of the **tos** form the RV. has six examples in the abl. sense: **é-tos** and **gán-tos** *going*, **ján-i-tos** *being born*, **ní-dhā-tos** *putting down*, **śár-ī-tos** *being shattered*, **só-tos** *pressing*, **hán-tos** *being struck*. Three examples in the gen. sense are: **kár-tos** *doing*, **dā́-tos** *giving*, **yó-tos** *warding off*.

a. The abl. gen. inf. has become as common as the dat. in B.

4. Locative Infinitive.

This form of the infinitive is rare; hardly more than a dozen examples occur even if several doubtful forms are included.

a. Five or six are locatives of radical stems: **vy-úṣ-i** *at the dawning,* **saṃ-cákṣ-i** *on beholding,* **dṛś-í** and **saṃ-dṛ́ś-i** *on seeing,* **budh-í** *at the waking.* As these forms, however, have nothing distinctive of the infinitive and govern the genitive only, they are rather to be regarded as ordinary locatives of verbal nouns.

b. From a stem in **ṭar** are formed **dhar-tár-i** *to support* and **vi-dhartár-i** *to bestow*; it is, however, doubtful whether these forms are genuine infinitives.

c. The RV. has eight locatives from stems in **san**, with a genuine infinitive sense: **ne-ṣáṇ-i** *to lead,* **par-ṣáṇ-i** *to pass,* **abhi-bhū-ṣáṇ-i** *to aid,* **śū-ṣáṇ-i** *to swell,* **sak-ṣáṇ-i** *to abide* (√**sac**); with connecting **ī**: **tar-ī-ṣáṇ-i**; from present stems: **gṛ-ṇī-ṣáṇi** *to sing,* **stṛ-ṇī-ṣáṇ-i** *to spread.*

DERIVATIVE VERBS.

I. Causatives.

168. This is by far the commonest of the secondary conjugations, being formed from more than two hundred roots in the Saṃhitās and from about a hundred additional ones in the Brāhmaṇas. Of about 150 causative stems in the RV., however, at least one-third have not a causative, but an iterative sense. The whole formation may indeed originally have had an iterative meaning. This perhaps explains how an iterative formation, the reduplicated aorist, specially attached itself to the causative. The same root occasionally forms both the iterative and the causative, as **pat-áya-ti** *flies about* and **pāt-áya-ti** *causes to fly* beside the simple verb **páta-ti** *flies.*

The causative is formed by adding the suffix **áya** to the root, which is usually strengthened.

1. Initial or medial i, u, ṛ, ḷ (if not long by position) take Guṇa; e.g. **vid** *know*: **ved-áya** *cause to know*; **krudh** *be angry*: **krodh-áya** *enrage*; **ṛd** *dissolve* (intr.): **ard-áya** *destroy*; **tṛp** *be pleased*: **tarp-áya** *delight*; **kḷp** *be adapted*: **kalp-áya** *arrange*.

a. Several roots, mostly lacking the causative meaning, leave the radical vowel unchanged; e.g. **ruc** *shine*: **ruc-áya**, *id.* (but **roc-áya** *illumine*).

b. Initial or medial **a** (if not long by position) is lengthened in about thirty roots; e.g. **am** *be injurious*: **ām-áya** *suffer injury*; **naś** *be lost*: **nāś-áya** *destroy*.

a. In the following roots the **a** optionally remains short in the causative: **gam** *go*, **das** *waste away*, **dhvan** *disappear*, **pat** *fly*, **mad** *be exhilarated*, **ram** *rest*; thus **pat** *fly*: **pat-áya** *fly about*, once *cause to fly*, and **pāt-áya** *cause to fly*.

β. In about twenty-five roots the **a** always remains short, the causative meaning being mostly absent; e.g. **dam** *control*: **dam-áya** *id.*; **jan** *beget*: **jan-áya** *id.*

c. Final i, ŭ, ṛ take Guṇa or Vṛddhi; e.g. **kṣi** *possess*: **kṣay-áya**[1] *cause to dwell securely*; **cyu** *waver*: **cyāv-áya** *shake*; **bhū** *be*: **bhāv-áya** *cause to become*; **ghṛ** *drip*: **ghār-áya** *cause to drip*; **śru** *hear*, **jṝ** *waste away*, and **sṛ** *flow* have Guṇa as well as Vṛddhi: **śrav-áya** and **śrāv-áya** *cause to hear*; **jar-áya** and **jār-áya** *wear out*, **sar-áya** and **sār-áya** *cause to flow*; **dṛ** *pierce* has Guṇa only: **dar-áya** *shatter*.

d. Roots ending in **ā** add **páya**;[2] e.g. **dhā** *put*: **dhā-páya** *cause to put*.

e. The causative retains the suffix throughout the conjugation even outside the present system. Its inflexion is identical with that of the primary verbs of the first conju-

---

[1] The only example of a causative from a root in final i (except the irregular **jāpáya** from **ji** *conquer* and **śrāpáya** from **śri** *resort*).

[2] As to other roots taking **paya** see 'Irregularities', 2.

gation (132). Subjunctive,[1] imperative,[2] injunctive, imperfect, and present participle forms are common; but the optative is very rare in the active and does not occur at all in the middle. Only four future forms occur in the RV. and the AV.: **dūṣay-iṣyā́mi** *I shall spoil*, **dhāray-iṣyáti** *will support*, **vāsay-iṣyáse** *thou wilt adorn thyself*, **vāray-iṣyáte** *will shield*. In the perfect only one periphrastic form (139, 9 *a*) occurs: **gamayā́ṃ cakā́ra**[3] (AV.). Reduplicated aorist forms are connected with only six causative stems (p. 175, *a*. 3). There are also three **iṣ** aorists formed from the causative stem: **vyathay-īs** from **vyath-áya** *disturb*; **ailay-īt** from **il-áya** *quiet down*; **dhvanay-īt** from **dhvan-áya** *envelope*.[4]

f. Of nominal derivatives the following are examples: a pres. pass. part. **bhāj-yá-māna**; a few perf. pass. participles: **ghār-i-tá** *smeared*, **cod-i-tá** *impelled*, **veś-i-tá** *caused to enter*; a few gerundives in **āyya** (162, 2): **trayay-ā́yya** *to be guarded*; **panay-ā́yya** *admirable*; **spṛhay-ā́yya** *desirable*; ten infinitives in **dhyai**: **nāśayá-dhyai** *to destroy*, &c. (p. 193, 7); four gerunds in the AV.: **arpay-i-tvā́** *having delivered up*, **kalpay-i-tvā́** *having arranged*, **sāday-i-tvā́** *having set down*, **sraṃsay-i-tvā́** *letting fall*.

Irregularities.

1. Three causatives in the AV. shorten the **ā** before **paya**: **jña-páya** *cause to know*, **śra-páya** *cook*, **sna-páya** *bathe* beside **snā-páya** (RV.).

2. Four roots in vowels other than **ā**, that is, in **ṛ** or **i**, take **paya**; **ṛ** *go*: **ar-páya** *cause to go*; **kṣi** *dwell*: **kṣe-páya** *cause to dwell* (beside

---

[1] The only du. mid. form occurring is 3. **mādáyaite**; and the only mid. form in **ai** (except 1. du.) in the RV. is **mādayādhvai**.

[2] The 2. s. in **tāt** occurs in both V. and B.; and from **vṛ** *cover* occurs the unique 2. pl. **vāraya-dhvāt** in K.

[3] In B. such forms are still uncommon except in the ŚB., where they are numerous.

[4] In B. desideratives are formed from about a dozen causative stems; e.g. **di-drāpay-iṣa** *desire to cause to run*.

kṣay-áya); ji *conquer* and **śri** *resort* substitute **ā** for **i**: **jā-páya** *cause to conquer*, **śrā-páya** *raise*.[1]

3 The root **bhī** *fear* forms the quite anomalous causative stem **bhī-ṣ-áya** *frighten*.

4. The roots **pā** *drink* and **pyā** *swell* add **aya** with interposed **y**: **pāy-áya** *cause to drink* and **pyāy-áya** *fill up*. This is probably to be explained by the assumption that the original form of these roots was pai and pyai.

5. The vowel of **grabh** *grasp* is weakened by Samprasāraṇa: **gṛbh-áya** *grasp*; while that of **duṣ** *spoil* is lengthened: **dūṣ-áya**, *id*. The root **pṝ** *fill*, owing to its initial labial, forms its causative with medial ū for ā: **pūr-áya** *fulfil*.

II. Desideratives.

169. The desiderative, which is the least common of the secondary conjugations, is formed from the root with an accented reduplicative syllable and the suffix **sa**. This **sa** is never added with a connecting i in the RV., nor, with the single exception of **pí-pat-i-ṣa**, in the AV., **jí-jīv-i-ṣa** in the VS., and **jí-gam-i-ṣa** in the TS.[2] The desiderative is formed from fewer than sixty roots in the Saṃhitās and from more than thirty additional ones in B. It is inflected like verbs of the first conjugation (132).

The accent being on the reduplicative syllable, the root as a rule remains unchanged; e.g. **dā** *give*: **dí-dā-sa** *desire to give*; **bhid** *cleave*: **bí-bhit-sa**; **nī** *lead*: **ní-nī-ṣa**; **guh** *hide*: **jú-guk-ṣa** (62 *a*, 69 *a*); **bhū** *be*: **bú-bhū-ṣa**; **dṛś** *see*: **dí-dṛk-ṣa**. But

1. final i and u are lengthened, and **ṛ** becomes **īr**; e.g. ji *conquer*: **jí-gī-ṣa**; **śru** *hear*: **śú-śrū-ṣa**; **kṛ** *make*: **cí-kīr-ṣa**.

2. final **ā** is in three roots reduced (cp. 171, 3) to **ī** and in

---

[1] In B. the root **ruh** *rise*, even though ending in a consonant, takes **paya** after dropping its **h**: **ro-paya** *raise* (beside **roh-áya**).

[2] In B. about a dozen other roots form their desiderative stem thus; e.g. **ci-kram-i-ṣa**, **ji-grah-ī-ṣa**, **vi-vid-i-ṣa** (**vid** *know*), &c.

one to i: **gā** *go*: **jí-gī-ṣa** (SV.); **pā** *drink*: **pí-pī-ṣa** (beside **pí-pā-sa**); **hā** *go forth*: **jí-hī-ṣa**; **dhā** *put*: **dí-dhi-ṣa** (beside **dhít-sa**).

Special Rule of Reduplication.

170. The characteristic reduplicative vowel is **i**, which appears in all stems except those formed from roots containing **ŭ** (which reduplicate with **u**); e. g. **jyā** *overpower*: **jí-jyā-sa**; **miś** *mix*: **mí-mik-ṣa**; **prī** *love*: **pí-prī-ṣa**; **vṛt** *turn*: **ví-vṛt-sa**; but **guh** *hide*: **jú-guk-ṣa**; **bhū** *be*: **bú-bhū-ṣa**.

Irregularities.

171. 1. Five roots with medial **a** followed by **m** or **n** lengthen the vowel: **gam** *go*: **jí-gāṃ-sa**; **han** *smite*: **jí-ghāṃ-sa** (66 A 2); **man** *think* lengthens the reduplicative vowel also: **mí-māṃ-sa** (66 A 2); **van** *win* and **san** *gain* drop the nasal: **ví-vā-sa** and **sí-ṣā-sa**.

2. **dhvṛ** *injure*, after interchange of semivowel and vowel to **ur**, lengthens its **u**: **dú-dhūr-ṣa**. Cp. p. 193, note 4.

3. Half a dozen roots containing **ā** or **a** shorten the radical syllable by a kind of syncopation: **dā** *give* and **dhā** *put* lose their vowel: **dí-t-sa** (= **dí-d[ā]-sa**) beside **dí-dā-sa**; **dhí-t-sa** (= **dí-dh[ā]-sa**) beside **dí-dhi-ṣa**; **dabh** *harm*, **labh** *take*, **śak** *be able*, **sah** *prevail* lose their initial radical consonant and their vowel: **dí-p-sa**[1] (= **dí[da]bh-sa**), **líp-sa**[2] (= **lí[la]bh-sa**), **śík-ṣa** (= **śí[śa]k-ṣa**), **sík-ṣa**, with lengthened reduplicative vowel (= **sí[sa]k-ṣa**).[3]

a. **āp** *obtain* and **ṛdh** *thrive* (treated as **ardh**) contract the reduplicated **i** with the radical initial to **ī**: **íp-sa** (= **i-āp-sa**) and **írt-sa** (= **i-ardh-sa**).

4. In **ci** *note*, **cit** *perceive*, **ji** *conquer*, **han** *slay*, the radical initial reverts to the original guttural: **cí-kī-ṣa**, **cí-kit-sa**, **jí-gī-ṣa**, **jí-ghāṃ-sa**.

---

1 Also **dhīpsa** in B.

2 Also **līpsa** in B.

3 In B. are similarly formed **dhīkṣa** (**dah** *burn*), **pitsa** (**pad** *go*), **ripsa** (**rabh** *grasp*).

5. **ghas** *eat* changes its final **s** to **t** (66 B 1): **jí-ghat-sa** (AV.) *be hungry*.

6. Three roots reduplicate with a long vowel: **tur** *cross* (= **tṝ**): **tū́-tur-ṣa**; **bādh** *oppress*: **bī-bhat-sa**;[1] **man** *think*: **mī-mām̐-sa**.[2] On the other hand the reduplicative syllable is reduced in the desiderative f **yaj** *sacrifice* and **naś** *attain* by loss of the initial consonant: **í-yak-ṣa** (for **yí-yak-ṣa**) and **í-nak-ṣa** (for **ní-nak-ṣa**). In one form from **āp** *obtain* the reduplication is dropped altogether: **ap-santa**.

a. The two roots with initial vowel **aś** *eat* and **edh** *increase* form their desiderative stem with the reduplicative vowel in the second syllable: **aś-iś-i-ṣa** (B.) and **ed-idh-i-ṣa** (VS.).

In the inflexion of the desiderative all the moods of the present system, besides the imperfect, are represented, though not fully; and of present participles more than twenty-five examples are met with. The forms occurring, if made from **ví-vā-sa** *desire to win*, would be:

Present ind. act. sing. 1. **vívāsāmi**. 2. **vívāsasi**. 3. **vívāsati**. Du. 2. **vívāsathas**. 3. **vívāsatas**. Pl. 1. **vívāsāmas**. 3. **vívāsanti**.

Mid. sing. 1. **vívāse**. 2. **vívāsase**. 3. **vívāsate**. Pl. 1. **vívāsāmahe**. 3. **vívāsante**.

Subj. act. sing. 1. **vívāsāni**. 3. **vívāsāt**. Pl. 3. **vívāsān**.

Inj. act. sing. 3. **vívāsat**. Mid. pl. 3. **vívāsanta**.

Opt. act. sing. 1. **vívāseyam**. 3. **vívāset**. Pl. 1. **vívāsema**. Mid. sing. 1. **vívāseya**.

Impv. act. sing. 2. **vívāsa** and **vívāsatāt**. 3. **vívāsatu**. Du. 2. **vívāsatam**. 3. **vívāsatām**. Pl. 2. **vívāsata**. 3. **vívāsantu**.

Part. act. **vívāsant**. Mid. **vívāsamāna**.

Impf. act. sing. 2. **ávivāsas**. 3. **ávivāsat**. Pl. 3. **ávivāsan**.

---

[1] With shortening of the radical vowel.

[2] With lengthening of the radical vowel.

a. Outside the present system only two desiderative verbal forms[1] have been met with, two iṣ aorists in the AV.: á-cikits-īs and īrts-īs.[2] Three participial forms have also been noted: the perf. pass. part. mīmāṃs-i-tá[3] and the gerundives didṛkṣ-éṇya *worthy to be seen* and śuśrūṣ-éṇya *worthy to be heard*.[4] Finally, over a dozen verbal adjectives formed with u from the desiderative stem occur in the RV., e. g. iyakṣ-ú *wishing to sacrifice*. They have the value of a pres. part. governing a case.

III. Intensives (Frequentatives).

172. These verbs are meant to convey intensification or frequent repetition of the action expressed by the simple root. They are common, being formed from over ninety roots in the Saṃhitās, and about twenty-five others in the Brāhmaṇas. The formation is restricted to roots with initial consonants, nor is it ever applied to derivative verbs.

The stem, of which a peculiar form of strong reduplication is characteristic, has two forms. The primary type, which is by far the commonest, adds the personal endings immediately to the reduplicated stem (accented on the first syllable in strong forms: App. III. 12 *e*). It is inflected, in both active and middle, like a verb of the third or reduplicated class (132); e. g. **nij** *wash*: 3. sing. **né-nek-ti**. The secondary form, which is rare, adds accented **yá** in the same way as the passive (154) to the reduplicated stem. It is conjugated in the middle only, like the passive; e. g. **vij** *tremble*: **ve-vij-yá-te** *trembles violently*.

---

[1] In B. periphrastic perfect forms from five or six desiderative stems have been noted.

[2] In B. iṣ aorists from half a dozen desiderative stems occur; e. g. aips-īt, aips-iṣ-ma, a-jighāṃs-is, a-mīmāṃs-iṣ-ṭhās. One or two simple and periphrastic futures also occur in B., as titikṣ-iṣyate (tij *be sharp*), didṛkṣ-i-tắras (dṛś *see*).

[3] In B. also jijyūṣ-i-tá (jīv *live*), dhīkṣ-i-tá (dah *burn*), śuśrūṣ-i-tá (śrū *hear*).

[4] In B. also līps-i-tavya (labh *take*), didhyās-i-tavyà (dhyā *think*), jijñās-yà (jñā *know*).

a. The primary intensive optionally inserts **ī** between the root and terminations beginning with consonants. This **ī** is found in the 1. 3. s. ind. act. and the 2. 3. s. impv. and impf. act.; e. g. ind. **cā́kaś-ī-mi, cā́kaś-ī-ti**; impv. 2. **cākaś-ī-hi.** 3. **jóhav-ī-tu**; impf. 3. **á-johav-ī-t.**

Special Rules of Reduplication.

173. 1. Radical **ĭ** and **ŭ** are reduplicated with the respective Guṇa vowels **e** and **o**; e. g. **diś** *point*: **de-diś**; **nī** *lead*: **ne-nī**; **śuc** *shine*: **śo-śuc**; **nu** *praise*: **no-nu**; **bhū** *be*: **bo-bhū.**

2. Radical **ă** and **ṛ̆** are reduplicated in two ways:

a. More than a dozen roots with medial **ă** (ending in mutes or sibilants, and one in **m**) as well as three with final **ṛ**, reduplicate with **ā**: **kāś** *shine*: **cā-kaś**; **pat** *fall*: **pā-pat**; **gam** *go*: **jā-gam**; **gṛ** *wake*: **jā-gṛ**; **dṛ** *split*: **dā-dṛ**; **dhṛ** *hold*: **dā-dhṛ**; also **cal** *stir*: **cā-cal.**

b. All other roots containing **ṛ** (**dṛ** and **dhṛ** also alternatively) and those with medial **a** followed by **r**, **l**, or a nasal, reduplicate with **ar, al, an** or **am**; e. g. **kṛ** *commemorate*: **car-kṛ** and **car-kir**; **kṛṣ** *drag*: **car-kṛṣ**; **dṛ** *split*: **dar-dṛ** and **dar-dir** (beside **dā-dṛ**); **dhṛ** *hold*: **dar-dhṛ** (beside **dā-dhṛ**); **hṛṣ** *be excited*: **jar-hṛṣ**; **car** *move*: **car-car**; **phar** *scatter*: **par-phar**; **cal** *stir*: **cal-cal** (beside **cā-cal**); **gam** *go*: **jaṅ-gam** (beside **jā-gam**); **jambh** *chew up*: **jañ-jabh**; **daṃś** *bite*: **dan-daś**; **tan** *thunder*: **taṃ-stan** (66 A 2).

3. Over twenty roots with final or penultimate nasal, **ṛ** or **ū**, interpose an **ī** (or **i** if the vowel would be long by position) between the reduplicative syllable and the root; e. g. **gam** *go*: **gan-ī-gam** (but **gan-i-gm-at**); **han** *slay*: **ghan-ī-ghan**; **krand** *cry out*: **kan-i-krand** and **kan-i-krad**; **skand** *leap*: **kan-i-ṣkand** and **can-i-ṣkad**; **bhṛ** *bear*: **bhar-ī-bhṛ**; **vṛt** *turn*: **var-ī-vṛt**; **nu** *praise*: **nav-ī-nu**; **dhū** *shake*: **dav-i-dhv**; **dyut** *shine*: **dav-i-dyut.**

Irregularities.

174. The radical vowel is shortened in roots with medial ā: **kāś** *shine*: **cā-kaś**; **bādh** *oppress*: **bā-badh**; **vāś** *bellow*: **vā-vaś**. In a few roots containing ṛ or r the radical syllable varies; thus **gṛ** *swallow*: **jar-gur** and **jal-gul**; **car** *move*: **car-cur** beside **car-car**; **tṝ** *cross*: **tar-tur** beside **tar-tar**.

a. The root **ṛ** *go* reduplicates with **al**: **al-ar** (dissimilation); **gāh** *plunge*, with a nasal: **jaṅ-gah**;[1] **bādh** *oppress*, with its final mute:[2] **bad-badh** (beside **bā-badh**); **bhṛ**[3] *bear* and **bhur** *quiver*, with a palatal: **jar-bhṛ**, **jar-bhur**; **bhur** and **gur** *greet* reduplicate **u** with **a**: **jar-bhur**, **jar-gur**.

b. Roots with initial guttural, if interposing ī̆ before the root, reduplicate with the same guttural; thus **krand** *cry out*: **kan-i-krand**; **gam** *go*: **gan-ī-gam**; **han** (for **ghan**) *slay*: **ghan-ī-ghan**; **kṛ** *make* has both **kar-i-kṛ**[4] and **car-i-kṛ**;[4] **skand** *leap* has both **kan-i-ṣkand** and **can-i-ṣkad**.

A. The forms of the **primary type** that occur, if made from **nij** *wash*, would be the following:

1. **Pres. ind.** act. sing. 1. **nénej-mi, nénej-ī-mi.** 2. **nének-ṣi.** 3. **nének-ti, nénej-ī-ti.** Du. 2. **nenik-thás.**[5] 3. **nenik-tás.** Pl. 1. **nenij-más, nenij-mási.** 3. **nénij-ati.**

Mid. sing. 1. **nenij-é.** 3. **nenik-té.** Du. 3. **nénij-āte.** Pl. 3. **nénij-ate.**

2. **Subj.** act. sing. 1. **néníj-āni.**[6] 2. **nénij-a-s.** 3. **nénij-a-t.** Du. 1. **nénij-ā-va.** Pl. 1. **nénij-ā-ma.** 3. **nénij-a-n.** Mid. du. 3. **nénij-aite.** Pl. 3. **nénij-a-nta.**

---

[1] In B. also **jañ-jap-yá-te** (**jap** *mutter*). Here also **vah** *carry* reduplicates with **n** (together with interposed ī) though there is no trace of a nasal in the root: **van-ī-vāh-yáte.**

[2] This is the only example of such reduplication.

[3] This root shows the same peculiarity in the perfect (139, 4).

[4] The intensive of this root occurs only in the participle **karikr-át** and **carikr-át.**

[5] The only form occurring in this person has the interposed ī and strong radical syllable: **tar-tar-ī-thas.**

[6] The only form actually occurring in this person is **jaṅghán-āni** (accented like the subj. of the reduplicating present).

3. **Opt.** No certain forms occur in the RV. and only two active forms in other Saṃhitās: sing. 3. **veviṣ-yāt** (AV.), pl. 1. **jā-gṛ-yāma** (VS., MS., TS.), **jāgri-yāma** (TS.). The 3. s. mid. **nenij-īta** occurs in K.

4. **Impv.** About twenty active (but no middle)[1] forms occur. Made from **jāgṛ** these would be: sing. 2. **jāgṛ-hí, jāgar-ī-hi, jāgṛ-tā́t.** 3. **jā́gar-tu, jā́gar-ī-tu.** Du. 2. **jāgṛ-tám.** 3. **jāgṛ-tā́m.** Pl. 2. **jāgṛ-tá.**[2]

5. Of the **participle** over forty stems occur, about two-thirds of them being active. Examples are: act. **kánikrad-at, cékit-at, jáṅghan-at, jā́gr-at, dárdr-at, nā́nad-at, róruv-at**; mid. **járbhur-āṇa, dándaś-āna, yóyuv-āna** (**yu** *join*), **sársr-āṇa.**

6. **Impf.** Fewer than thirty forms of this tense occur, only three of them being middle. Examples of the persons occurring are:

Act. sing. 1. **á-cākaś-am.** 2. **á-jāgar.** 3. **á-dardar, á-var-ī-var, á-johav-ī-t; dáv-i-dyot, náv-ī-no-t.** Du. 2. **á-dardṛ-tam.** Pl. 1. **marmṛj-má.** 3. **á-carkṛṣ-ur, á-dardir-ur, á-nonav-ur.**

Mid. sing. 3. **á-dediṣ-ṭa, á-nan-na-ta.**[3] Pl. 3. **mármṛj-ata.**

a. Outside the present system few intensive forms occur. There are four act. perfect intensives with present sense: sing. 1. **jāgara.** 3. **jāgā́r-a** (ἐγρήγορε), **davidhāv-a** (**dhū** *shake*), **nónāv-a** (**nu** *praise*); also **dodrāv-a** (**dru** *run*: TS.), **yoyāv-a** (**yu** *separate*: MS.), **leláy-a** (**lī** *be unsteady*: MS.). There is besides the perf. part. **jāgṛ-vā́ṃs.** A causative intensive appears once in the participial form **var-ī-varj-áyant-ī** *twisting about.*[4]

---

[1] In B. occurs the 2. s. mid. form **nenik-ṣva** (√**nij**).

[2] The RV. has no impv. forms with interposed **ī**, but the AV. and VS. have a few in the 2. 3. s., as **cākaś-ī-hi, johav-ī-tu.** A few examples occur in B. also.

[3] From **nam** *bend*, with loss of nasal (**a** = sonant nasal), for **á-nan-nan-ta.**

[4] In B. also occur the causative stems from intensives **jāgar-áya** and **dādhār-áya** (**dhṛ** *hold*).

B. The forms of the secondary type, which is indistinguishable from a passive in form, number only about a dozen. They occur only in the 2. 3. s. and 3. pl. ind. pres., besides a few participles. They are:

Pres. ind. sing. 2. co-ṣkū-yá-se (sku *tear*). **3. dediś-yá-te, ne-nī-yá-te, marmṛj-yá-te, rerih-yá-te, vevij-yáte, vevī-yáte (vī** *enjoy*). **Pl. 3. tartūr-yánte (√tṝ), marmṛj-yánte.**

Part. carcūr-yá-māṇa (√car), nenī-yá-māna, marmṛj-yá-māna.

IV. Denominatives.

175. These verbs, inflected like those of the **a** conjugation (132), are derived, almost exclusively with the suffix **ya**, from nouns, to which they express some such relation as 'be or act like', 'treat as', 'turn into', or 'use as', 'wish for'. More than a hundred denominative stems occur in the RV. and about fifty in the AV.[1] The suffix is normally accented, but a certain number of undoubted denominatives, such as **mantrá-ya** *utter a prayer*, **arthá-ya** *make an object of, desire*, have the causative accent, thus forming a connecting link between the regular denominatives and the causatives.

A. Before the suffix **ya**:

1. final **i**[2] and **u** are lengthened;[3] e. g. **kavī-yá** *be wise* (**kaví**), **rayī-yá** *desire wealth* (**rayí**); **ṛjū-yá** *be straight* (**ṛjú**); **vasū-yá** *desire wealth* (**vásu**); **śatrū-yá** *play the enemy* (**śátru**), *be hostile*.

2. final **a** usually remains unchanged, but is often lengthened; it is sometimes changed to **ī**; and even dropped;

---

[1] Denominatives are less common in B.; thus the AB. has hardly twenty, and the ŚB. about a dozen.

[2] Except **arāti-yá** *act like an enemy, be hostile* beside **arātī-yá**, and **jani-yá** *seek a wife* beside **janī-yá**; **gātu-yá** *set in motion* (**gātú**).

[3] In the Pada text the **ī** is usually, the **ū** is always, written short.

e. g. **jāra-yá** *treat like a lover*, **deva-yá** *serve the gods*, **ṛtá-ya**[1] *act according to sacred order*; **aśvā-yá** *desire horses*, **ṛtā-yá** *observe sacred order* (beside **ṛtá-ya**), **yajñā-yá** *sacrifice*; **adhvarī-yá** *perform the sacrifice* (**adhvará**), **putrī-yá**[2] *desire a son* (**putrá**), **rathī-yá**[2] *drive in a car* (**rátha**); **adhvar-yá** *perform sacrifice* (beside **adhvarī-yá**), **taviṣ-yá** *be mighty* (**taviṣá**: beside **taviṣī-yá**).

3. final ā remains unchanged; e. g. **gopā-yá** *act as herdsman, protect*, **pṛtanā-yá**[3] *fight*. Final **o**, in the only example occurring, becomes **av**: **gav-yá** *desire cows*.

4. Consonant stems, the commonest being those in **as**, nearly always remain unchanged; e.g. **bhiṣaj-yá** *play the physician, heal*; **ukṣaṇ-yá** *act like a bull* (**ukṣán**); **vadhar-yá** *hurl a bolt* (**vádhar**); **su-manas-yá** *be gracious* (**su-mánas**); **taruṣ-yá** *engage in fight* (**tárus**).

a. A few denominative forms are made without a suffix, direct from nominal stems, but nearly always beside regular denominatives in **yá**; e. g. **bhiṣák-ti** from **bhiṣáj** *act as physician* beside **bhiṣaj-yá**; and the forms **taruṣe-ma, taruṣa-nte, taruṣa-nta** (from **táruṣa** *conqueror*) beside **taruṣ-yá**.

Inflexion.

B. All the tenses, moods, and participles of the present system are represented. If made from **namas-yá** *pay homage* the forms occurring would be:

1. **Pres.** ind. act. sing. 1. **namasyā́mi**. 2. **namasyási**. 3. **namasyáti**. Du. 2. **namasyáthas**. 3. **namasyátas**. Pl. 1. **namasyā́-masi, -mas**. 2. **namasyátha**. 3. **namasyánti**.

Mid. sing. 1. **namasyé**. 2. **namasyáse**. 3. **namasyáte**.

---

[1] With causative accent.

[2] The Pada text in this and nearly every example has **ī-yá**. Even the Saṃhitā text of the AV. has **putri-yá**.

[3] The ā may also be dropped: **pṛtan-yá** *fight against*.

Du. 2. **namasyéthe.** 3. **namasyéte.** Pl. 1. **namasyā́mahe.** 3. **namasyánte.**

2. **Subj.** act. sing. 1. **namasyā́.** 2. **namasyā́s.** 3. **namasyā́t.** Du. 3. **namasyā́tas.** Pl. 3. **namasyā́n.**

Mid. sing. 2. **namasyā́se.** 3. **namasyā́te.**

3. **Inj.** act. sing. 2. **namasyás.** Pl. 3. **namasyán.**

4. **Opt.** act. sing. 2. **namasyés.** 3. **namasyét.** Pl. 1. **namasyéma.**

Mid. sing. 3. **namasyéta.**

5. **Impv.** act. sing. 2. **namasyá.** 3. **namasyátu.** Du. 2. **namasyátam.** 3. **namasyátām.** Pl. 2. **namasyáta.** 3. **namasyántu.**

Mid. sing. 2. **namasyásva.** Pl. 2. **namasyádhvam.** 3. **namasyántām.**

6. **Part.** act. **namasyánt.** Mid. **namasyámāna.**

7. **Impf.** act. sing. 2. **ánamasyas.** 3. **ánamasyat.** Du. 3. **namasyátām.** Pl. 3. **ánamasyan.**

Mid. sing. 3. **ánamasyata.** Du. 2. **ánamasyethām.** Pl. 3. **ánamasyanta.**

a. The only finite forms occurring outside the present system are four aorists. Two are injunctives: 2. s. **ūnay-īs** (RV.) from **ūnaya** *leave unfulfilled* (**ūna**); 2. pl. **pā́pay-iṣ-ṭa** (TS.) from **pāpaya** *lead into evil* (**pāpa**); and two indicatives: 3. s. **ásaparyait** (AV.) *has worshipped* (an irregular form, probably = **á-sapary-īt**); 3. pl. **á-vṛṣāy-iṣ-ata** (VS.) *they have accepted.*[1] The TS. has also the three fut. participles **kaṇḍūy-iṣyánt** *about to scratch*, **meghāy-iṣyánt** *about to be cloudy*, **śīkāy-iṣyánt**[2] *about to drip*, with the corresponding perf. pass. part. **kaṇḍūyitá, meghitá, śīkitá.**[3]

---

[1] In B. also occurs the iṣ aor. **ásūyīt** *has murmured.*

[2] In B. also occurs the future **gopāy-iṣyati.**

[3] In B. there are also a few other past pass. participles and a few gerunds.

CHAPTER V

INDECLINABLE WORDS

Prepositions.

176. Two classes of prepositions have to be distinguished. The first comprises the genuine or adverbial prepositions. These are words with a local sense which, primarily used to modify the meaning of verbs, came to be connected independently with the cases governed by the verbs thus modified. They show no signs of derivation from inflexional forms or (except **tirás** and **purás**) forms made with adverbial suffixes. The second class has been called adnominal prepositions because they are not compounded with verbs, but govern cases of nouns only. They almost invariably end in case terminations or adverbial suffixes.

1. Adverbial Prepositions.

There are fourteen or (if **sám** is included) fifteen genuine prepositions which, when used independently of verbs, define the local meaning of cases. They are almost entirely restricted to employment with the acc., loc., and abl. As their connexion with the abl. is only secondary, the genuine prepositions appear to have been originally connected with the acc. and loc. only. As a rule these prepositions follow, but also often precede, their case.

1. The accusative is exclusively taken by **ácha** *towards*, **áti** *beyond*, **ánu** *after*, **abhí** *towards*, **práti** (Gk. *προτί*) *against*, and **tirás** *across* (cp. Lat. *trans*).

a. **pári** (Gk. *περί*) *around* takes the acc. primarily, but secondarily and more frequently the abl. in the sense of *from* (*around*).

b. **úpa** *to* (with verbs of motion) takes the acc. primarily, and less frequently the loc. in the sense of *beside, upon, at.*

2. The **locative** is exclusively taken by **ápi** (Gk. ἐπί) *upon* and primarily by **ádhi** *upon*, **antár** (Lat. *inter*) *between*, **á́** *on, in, at, to*, **purás** *before.*

a. **ádhi** takes the abl. secondarily and less commonly in the sense of *from* (*upon*).

b. The last three secondarily take both abl. and acc.; **purás** does so without change of meaning.

antár with abl. means *from* (*within*); with acc., *between.*

á́ with acc. means *to*, expressing the goal with verbs of motion. With the abl., if following,[1] it means *from* (*on*); if preceding, *up to.*[2]

3. The **ablative** seems to be used once or twice independently with **áva** in the sense of *down from.*

2. Adnominal Prepositions.

177. These prepositions, being adverbs in origin, govern oblique cases (except the dat.) independently. Several of them govern the genitive and the instrumental, cases that are practically never connected with the genuine prepositions in the Saṃhitās. In the following list these prepositions are grouped under the cases which they accompany:

1. **Acc.**: **adhás** *below* (also with abl. or gen.), **antarā́** *between*, **abhí-tas** *around*, **upári** *above, beyond*, **parás** *beyond* (also with abl., more often inst.), **parí-tas** *around* (AV.), **sanitúr** *apart from.*[3]

2. **Instr.**: **sahá** *with*, **sākám** *with*, **sumád** *with*, **smád** *with*; **avás** *below* (also abl.), **parás** *outside* (also acc. and abl.).

3. **Abl.**: **adhás** *below* (also acc. and gen.), **avás** *down from*

---

[1] It sometimes also precedes the abl. in this sense.

[2] This is almost the only use of **á́** in B.; in C. it means both *from* and *up to.*

[3] In B. several adverbial instrumentals expressing situation or direction govern the acc.: **ántareṇa** *between*, **ávareṇa** *below*, **páreṇa** *beyond*; **úttareṇa** *to the north of*, **dákṣiṇena** *to the south of.*

(also instr.), **āré** *far from* (also gen.), **ṛté** *without*, **parás** *apart from* (also acc. and inst.), **purā́** *before*, **bahir-dhā́** *from out*, **sanutár** *far from.*

4. **Gen.:** **purás-tād** *in front of.*[1]

5. **Loc.:** **sácā** (*in association*) *with*, *beside*, *at*, *in*.

Adverbial Case-forms.

178. Many case-forms of nominal and pronominal stems, often not otherwise in use, are employed as adverbs. Examples of all the cases appear with adverbial function.

1. **Nom.:** **prathamá-m** *firstly*, **dvitī́ya-m** *secondly*. Such adverbs were originally used in apposition to the verbal action.

2. **Acc.:** these adverbs find their explanation in various meanings of the case. They represent (*a*) the cognate acc.; e. g. **bhū́yas** *more*, and comparatives in **taram** added to verbal prefixes, as **vi-tarám** (**kram**) (*stride*) *more widely*; (*b*) the appositional acc.; e. g. **nā́ma** *by name*, **rūpám** *in form*, **satyám** *truly*; (*c*) the acc. of direction; e. g. **ágram** (**i**) (*go*) *to the front of, before*, **ástam** (**gam**) (*go*) *home*; (*d*) the acc. of distance and time; e. g. **dūrám** *a long way off, far*; **náktam** *by night*, **sāyám** *in the evening*, **nityám** *constantly*, **pū́rvam** *formerly*.

a. There are also some acc. adverbs derived from obsolete nominal stems, as **ára-m** *sufficiently*, **nū-nám** *now*; others from pronominal stems, as **adás** *there*, **i-dám** *here, now*, **kí-m** *why?*, **yád** *when*.

3. **Instr.:** adverbs with the ending of this case (sometimes pl.) are formed from substantives, adjectives, and pronouns. They usually express manner or accompanying circumstances, as **sáhas-ā** *forcibly*, **návyas-ā** *anew*, **enā́** *in this way*; also not

---

[1] In B. the gen. is governed by this adverb as well as by **paras-tād** *after*; e. g. **sūktasya purastāt** *before the hymn*; **saṃvatsarasya parastāt** *after a year*.

infrequently extension of space or time, as **ágreṇa** *in front*, **aktú-bhis** *by night*, **dív-ā** *by day*.

a. The substantive instrumentals are chiefly formed from feminines in ā not otherwise used, as **ṛtayā́** *in the right way*, **naktayā́** *by night*.

b. The adjective instrumentals are formed from stems in a and a few in c; e.g. **uccā́** and **uccaís** *on high*, **paścā́** *behind*, **madhyā́** *in the midst*, **śánais** *slowly*; **prāc-ā́** *forwards*. There are also several anomalous feminines from stems in u and one or two in ī; e.g. **āśu-y-ā́** *swiftly*, **raghu-y-ā́** *rapidly*, **sādhu-y-ā́** *straight*, **urviy-ā́** *far*.

c. The pronominal instrumentals are formed from stems in a and one in u; e.g. **anā́** *thus*, **amā́** *at home*, **ayā́** *thus*, **kayā́** *how?*, **ubhayā́** *in both ways*; **amu-y-ā́** *in that way*.

4. **Dat.**: the adverbial use of the dat. is rare: **aparā́ya** *for the future* (from **ápara** *later*), **várāya** *according to wish* (**vára** *choice*).

5. **Abl.**: these adverbs are seldom formed from substantives, as **ārā́t** *from a distance*, **āsā́t** *from near*; or from pronouns, **amā́t** *from near*, **ā́t** *then*, **tā́t** *thus*, **yā́t** *as far as*; but they are fairly often formed from adjectives, as **uttarā́t** *from the north*, **dūrā́t** *from afar*, **paścā́t** *from behind*, **sanā́t** *from of old*, **sākṣā́t** *visibly*.

6. **Gen.**: such adverbs are very rare: **aktós** *by night*, **vástos** *in the morning*.

7. **Loc.**: **ágre** *in front*, **astám-īké** *at home*, **āké** *near*, **āré** *afar*, **ṛté** *without*, **dūré** *afar*; **aparī́ṣu** *in future*.

Adverbs formed with Suffixes.

179. The suffixes more or less commonly used in the formation of adverbs may be grouped under the senses expressed by the instr., abl., and loc. cases.

1. **Instr.**: **thā** forms adverbs of manner especially from pronominal stems: **á-thā** and more commonly (with shortened vowel) **á-tha** *then*, **i-t-thā́** *thus*, **imá-thā** *in this manner*, **ka-thā́** *how?*, **tá-thā** *thus*, **yá-thā** *in which manner*, **anyá-thā** *otherwise*, **viśvá-thā** *in every way*; **ūrdhvá-thā** *upwards*,

pūrvá-thā *formerly*, **pratná-thā** *as of old*; **ṛtu-thā́** *regularly*, **nāmá-thā** *by name*; **evá-thā** *just as.*

a. **tham** is similarly used in **it-thám** *thus* and **ka-thám** *how?*

dhā forms adverbs of manner from numerals or cognate words: **eka-dhā́** *singly*, **dví-dhā** *in two ways*, **kati-dhā́** *how many times*, **puru-dhā́** *variously*, **bahu-dhā́** and **viśvá-dhā** *in many ways*, **śaśva-dhā́** *again and again.* It also forms adverbs from a few nouns, adverbs, and pronouns: **priya-dhā́** *kindly*, **mitra-dhā́** *in a friendly way*; **bahir-dhā́** *outward*; **á-dhā** *then*, **a-d-dhā́** (*thus* =) *truly.* The same suffix, with its vowel shortened, forms **sa-dha** (*in one way* =) *together*, which appears as the first member of several compounds, and as an independent word assumes the form of **sahá** *with.*

β. The suffix **ha** probably also represents original **dhā** in **i-há** *here* (Prākrit **i-dha**), **kú-ha** *where?* **viśvá-ha** and **viśvá-hā** *always*, **sama-ha** *in some way or other.*

va, expressing similarity of manner, forms the two adverbs **i-va** *like, as*, and **e-vá** (often **e-vā́**) *thus.* **vam** appears in **e-vám** *thus*, the later form of **evá**.

vat forms adverbs meaning *like* from substantives and adjectives; e. g. **manu-vát** *like Manu*; **purāṇa-vát**, **pūrva-vát**, **pratna-vát** *as of old.*

śas forms adverbs of manner with a distributive sense: **śata-śás** *by hundreds*, **sahasra-śás** *by thousands*, **śreṇi-śás** *in rows*; **ṛtu-śás** *season by season*, **deva-śás** *to each of the gods*, **parva-śás** *joint by joint*, **manma-śás** *each as he is minded.*

s forms two or three multiplicative adverbs: **dví-s** *twice*, **trí-s** *thrice.* It also appears in a few other adverbs: **adhá-s** *below*, **avá-s** *downwards*; **dyú-s** (from **dyu** *day*) in **anye-dyú-s** *next day* and **ubhaya-dyú-s** *on both days.*

2. **Abl.**: **tas** forms adverbs in the ablative sense from pronouns, nouns, and prepositions; e. g. **á-tas** *hence*, **amú-tas** *thence*, **i-tás** *from here*, **mat-tás** *from me*; **dakṣiṇa-tás** *from the right*, **hṛt-tás** *from the heart*; **abhí-tas** *around*, **parí-tas**

round about. These adverbs are sometimes equivalent to ablatives; e. g. **áto bhū́yas** *more than that.*

tāt (an old abl. of **ta** *that*) forms adverbs with an abl. sense (sometimes merging into the loc.); e. g. **adhás-tāt** *below*; **ārā́t-tāt** *from afar*; **paścā́-tāt** *from behind*; **purás-tāt** *in* or *from the front*; **prā́k-tāt** *from the front.*

3. **Loc.**: **as** forms adverbs chiefly of a local or temporal sense: **tir-ás** *across*, **par-ás** *beyond*, **pur-ás** *before*; **sa-dív-as** and **sa-dy-ás** *to-day*, **śv-ás** *to-morrow*, **hy-ás** *yesterday*; also **mith-ás** *wrongly.*

trā or **tra** forms adverbs with a local sense, mostly from pronominal or cognate stems: **á-tra** *here*, **anyá-tra** *elsewhere*, **viśvá-tra** *everywhere*; **asma-trā́** *among us*, **sa-trā́** *in one place*, **dakṣiṇa-trā́** *on the right*, **puru-trā́** *in many places*, **bahu-trā́** *amongst many*; **deva-trā́** *among the gods*, **martya-trā́** *among mortals*, **śayu-trā́** *on a couch.*

a. These adverbs are sometimes used as equivalents of locatives, e. g. **hásta ā́ dakṣiṇatrā́** *in the right hand.*

dā forms adverbs of time almost exclusively from pronominal roots: **i-dā́** *now*, **ka-dā́** *when?* **ta-dā́** *then*, **ya-dā́** *at what time*, **sá-dā** and **sarva-dā́** *always.*

β. **dam** occurs beside **dā** in **sá-dam** *always*; and **dā-nīm**, an extended form of **dā**, in **i-dā́-nīm** *now*, **ta-dā́-nīm** *then*, **viśva-dā́-nīm** *always.*

γ. There are also various miscellaneous adverbs, mostly of obscure origin, formed with other suffixes of rare occurrence; e. g. **pur-ā́** *before*, **míth-u** *wrongly.*

Conjunctive and Adverbial Particles.

180. **aṅgá** emphasizes a preceding word (sometimes separated from it by short particles like **hí** and **īm**) in such a way as to express that the action especially or exclusively applies to that word, = *just, only, else*; e. g. **yó aṅgá** *just he who*; **yád aṅgá** *just when, just because*; **tvám aṅgá** *thou only*; **kím aṅgá** *how else, why else?*

a. In B. **aṅgá** never has this meaning; but it sometimes there begins a sentence with an adhortative sense, accentuating the verb: **aṅgá no yajñáṃ vyācákṣva** *pray explain the sacrifice to us* (MS.).

átra sometimes occurs as the correlative to **yád** *when*; e.g. **víśve yád asyāṃ raṇáyanta deváḥ, prá vo 'tra sumnám aśyām** *when all the gods shall rejoice in it, then may I obtain your favours.*

átha, a collateral form of **ádha**, occurs chiefly in the more recent hymns of the RV., and entirely supplants the older doublet in the later Vedas. Connecting sentences and clauses it expresses a temporal or logical sequence. It may generally be translated by (*and*) *then*, (*and*) *so*; when there is a contrast, especially after a negative, it is equivalent to *but.* It often corresponds to a **yádā** *when* or **hí** *since, as*, in the antecedent clause. With very few exceptions **átha** begins the sentence or clause. Examples are: **marúdbhir, indra, sakhyáṃ te astu, áthemā́ víśvāḥ pṛ́tanā jayāsi** *be friends with the Maruts, O Indra, then thou shalt win all these battles* (viii. 96[7]); **huvé vām, átha mā́ (= mā ā́) gatam** *I call you, so come to me* (viii. 10[5]); **yádéd ádevīr ásahiṣṭa māyā́, athā́bhavat kévalaḥ sómo asya** *when he had overcome the godless wiles, Soma became exclusively his* (vii. 98[5]); **mā́kir neśan, mákīṃ riṣan, mā́kīṃ sáṃ śāri kévaṭe, áthā́riṣṭābhir ā́ gahi** *let none be lost, let none suffer harm, none incur fracture in a pit, but come back with them uninjured* (vi. 54[7]). From B.: **pátiṃ nú me púnaryuvāṇaṃ kurutam, átha vāṃ vakṣyāmi** *make my husband young again, then I shall tell you* (ŚB.); **ahám durgé hántā‿ity, átha kás tvám iti** *I am called the slayer in danger, but who are you?* (TS.).

a. **átha** is also occasionally used after gerunds (which are equivalent to an antecedent clause): **sáubhāgyam asyai dattvā́ya‿átha‿ástaṃ ví páretana** *having wished her luck, then go home* (x. 85[33]). This use is common in B., where it also occurs after present participles and locatives absolute.

b. **átha** in the sense of *also* connects substantives, but this use represents an abridged sentence; e.g. **imé sómāso ádhi turváśe,**

yádau, imé káṇveṣu vām átha *these Somas are beside Turvaśa, beside Yadu, (they are) also beside the Kaṇvas for you* (viii. 9[14]). From B.: **idám hí pitā́‿evá‿ágré 'tha putró 'tha páutraḥ** *for here first comes the father, then the son, then the grandson* (ŚB.).

c. In B. **átha** also connects the verbs of a compound relative clause: **yásya pitā́ pitāmaháḥ púṇyaḥ syā́d, átha tán ná prāpnuyā́t** *whose father and grandfather are pious, but who cannot attain to this* (TS.).

átho (= **átha u**) generally means *and also, moreover*: **arvāváto na ā́ gahy átho, śakra, parāvátaḥ** *come to us from near, and also, O mighty one, from afar* (iii. 37[11]). From B.: **sám inddha ā́ nakhébhyo 'tho lómabhyaḥ** *he kindles himself completely up to his nails and also his hair* (ŚB.).

a. In B. **átho** sometimes has the sense of *but also*, e.g. **té vái dvé bhavataḥ . . . átho ápi trī́ṇi syuḥ** *there are two of them, but there may also be three* (ŚB.).

ádha occurs in the RV. only, and almost exclusively, as compared with **átha**, in the earlier hymns. Like the latter it means *then*, expressing both a temporal and a logical sequence; when there is a contrast, *but*. **ádha...ádha** *both... and*; **ádha dvitā́** *and that particularly*; **ádha nú** *just now*; *now at last*; *and even*; **ádha sma** *especially then*. Unlike **átha** it is never used with **u**.

ápi meaning *also, even* generally precedes the word it emphasizes: **yó gopā́ ápi tám huve** *he who is the herdsman, him too I call* (x. 19[4]); **óṣadhīr bápsad agnír ná vāyati, púnar yán táruṇīr ápi** *Agni tires not of chewing plants, returning even to the young ones* (viii. 43[7]). From B.: **tád dhaitád ápy ávidvāṃsa āhuḥ** *even those who do not know say this* (ŚB.); **adyā́pi** *even to-day* (AB.).

áram is an adverb meaning *suitably, in readiness*. Sometimes used like an adjective, it is construed with the dative; e. g. **tā́vāñ ayám pā́tave sómo astu, áram mánase yuvábhyām** *such let this Soma be (for you) to drink, according to (your) mind for you two* (i. 108[2]); **sā́smai‿áram** *it is ready for him*. In combination with **kṛ** it means *serve, prepare* (anything) *for*, with **gam**, *serve*, with **bhū**, *accrue* (to any one) *suitably* or *sufficiently*, always taking the dative.

a. **álam**, the form in which the preceding word appears in B., is there often similarly used; e. g. **sá nā́lam ā́hutyā āsa nā́laṃ bhakṣáya** *it was not fit for offering, nor fit for consuming* (ŚB.).

áha in the RV. and AV. emphasizes a preceding word whether it be verb, substantive, pronoun, adjective, adverb, or preposition. Its sense may generally be expressed by *surely*, *certainly*, *indeed*, *just*, or merely by stress. It also appears after other emphasizing particles such as **íd**, **ghéd**, **utó**, **īm**. Examples of its use are: **kvā́ha** *where pray?* (x. 51[2]); **nā́ha** *not at all* (i. 147[3]); **yásyā́ha śakráḥ sávaneṣu ráṇyati** *in the pressings of whomsoever the mighty one rejoices* (x. 43[6]).

In B. this use of **áha** is still found. But here it generally occurs in the first of two slightly antithetical sentences, the verb of the first being then nearly always accented, while the antithesis in the second sentence is either not expressed at all, or is indicated by the particles **átha**, **u**, or **tú**; e.g. **párācy áha devébhyo yajñáṃ váhaty arvā́cī manuṣyā̀n avati** *turned away it takes the sacrifice to the gods; turned hither it advances men* (ŚB.). Sometimes (in MS. and TS.) **áha** is thus used with the first of two **vā**'s; e. g. **kásya vā́hedáṃ śvó bhavitā́ kásya vā** *this will to-morrow belong either to the one or the other* (MS.).

ā́ (otherwise a preposition) appears in V. fairly often emphasizing, in the sense of completeness, words expressive of number or degree, or sometimes even ordinary adjectives and substantives; e. g. **trír ā́ diváḥ** *three times each day* (i. 142[3]); **kó vo várṣiṣṭha ā́, naraḥ** *who is the very mightiest of you, heroes?* (i. 37[6]); **prá bodhayā púraṃdhiṃ jārá ā́ sasatī́m iva** *awake the wise man, just as a lover a sleeping maiden* (i. 134[3]).

ā́d (originally an abl. of the pronoun **a** = *from* or *after that*) is used as an adverb expressing sequence of time = *thereupon*, *then*, often as a correlative to **yád**, **yadā́** or **yádi** *when*, sometimes to the relative when equivalent to those conjunctions: **yadéd áyukta harítaḥ sadhásthād ā́d rā́trī**

vā́sas tanute *as soon as he has yoked his steeds from their stall, then night spreads her garment* (i. 115⁴); **ádhā yó víśvā bhúvanābhy ávardhata, ā́d ródasī jyótiṣā váhnir ā́tanot** *now (who =) when he surpassed all beings, then the charioteer overspread the two worlds with light* (ii. 17⁴).

a. It sometimes connects words and clauses in the sense of *and, moreover*: **asáu ca yā́ na urvárā ā́d imā́ṃ tanvàṃ máma** *that field of ours and this my body* (viii. 91⁶); **yád, indra, áhan prathamajā́m áhīnām, ā́n māyínām áminā̄ḥ prótá māyā́ḥ** *when, O Indra, thou didst slay the firstborn of the serpents and then didst bring to nought the wiles of the wily* (i. 32⁴).

b. It is sometimes used with interrogatives, when it means *then, pray*: **kím ā́d ámatraṃ sakhyám** *how mighty then is the friendship?* (iv. 23⁶).

c. Unless used with interrogatives, **ā́d** almost invariably begins the Pāda.

d. **ā́d** is often followed by **íd**, when it means *just then, then at once, then more than ever.*

íti *thus* is used with verbs of speaking and thinking, which have sometimes to be supplied. The particle generally concludes the speech and is followed by the verb: **yá índrāya sunávāma íti āha** *who says 'we will press Soma for Indra'* (iv. 25⁴); **néndro asti íti néma u tva āha** *'Indra does not exist' one and another says* (viii. 100³). Less commonly the verb precedes: **jyeṣṭhá āha camasā́ dvā́ karā íti** *the eldest said 'I will make two cups'* (iv. 33⁵). Very rarely both **íti** and the verb precede the speech: **ví pṛchad íti mātáraṃ, ká ugrā́ḥ** *he asked his mother, 'who are the strong ones?'* (viii. 77¹). The verb is occasionally omitted: **tváṣṭā duhitré vahatúṃ kṛṇoti íti idáṃ víśvaṃ bhúvanaṃ sám eti** *'Tvaṣṭṛ prepares a wedding for his daughter'* (thinking) *thus this whole world comes together* (x. 17¹). Thus a principal sentence as direct speech is used with **íti** where in other languages a subordinate sentence would be employed.

1. In B. the use of **íti** is much the same, only that **íti** regularly follows and seems seldom to be omitted; the verbs of saying and thinking, too, with which it is employed, are more numerous: **táthā íti devá abruvan** *'yes', said the gods* (ŚB.).

2. There are in B. also some additional uses:

a. Very often the quotation is only an appellative that may be expressed by inverted commas: **yā́ṃs tv ètád devā́ ādityā́ íti‿ā-cákṣate** *whom they call thus: 'the divine Ādityas'* (ŚB.).

b. Sometimes íti is used at the end of an enumeration to express that it forms a well-known aggregate: **etad vai śiraḥ samṛddhaṃ yasmin prāṇo vāk cakṣuḥ śrotram iti** *that is a complete head in which are breath, speech, eye, ear* (KB.).

c. The particle is also often used in a special sense with reference to a ritual act to indicate how it is done: **íti‿ágre kṛṣati‿átha‿íti‿átha íti‿átha‿íti‿átha‿íti** (ŚB.) *so he first draws the furrow, then so, then so, then so, then so* (= *as you see*).

d. Sometimes a conjunction is introduced before the quotation that ends with íti, but without changing the construction: **sá ṛtám abravīd yáthā sárvāsv evá samā́vad vásāni‿íti** (MS.) *he swore* (*that*) *'I will dwell with all equally'* (= *that he would*).

itthā́ primarily means *so*: **gántā nūnáṃ .. yáthā purā́‿itthā́** *as before, so come ye now* (i. 39[7]); **satyám itthā́** *truly so* (viii. 33[10]). Secondarily it comes to mean (just *so* as it should be =) *truly*: **kṛṇóti‿asmai várivo yá itthā́‿índrāya sómam uśaté sunóti** *he* (Indra) *gives ease to him that truly presses Soma for Indra who desires it* (iv. 24[6]). In this sense the word is sometimes used like an adjective: **itthā́ sákhibhyaḥ** *for* (those who are *truly* =) *true friends* (iii. 32[16]).

íd (n. of the pron. stem i, Lat. *i-d*) is a very common particle in the RV., is much less frequent in the AV., and is comparatively rare in B.[1] It emphasizes preceding words of all kinds, including the finite verb (which it accents), and may usually be rendered by *just* or stress only, sometimes by *even*; e. g. **tád ín náktaṃ tád íd dívā máhyam āhuḥ** *this is what they tell me by night, this by day* (i. 24[12]); **syā́ma íd índrasya śármaṇi** *may we be in Indra's care* (i. 4[6]); **ádha smā no maghavañ carkṛtā́d ít** *then especially think of us, O Bounteous One* (i. 104[5]); **sadṛ́śīr adyá sadṛ́śīr íd u śváḥ** *alike to-day, alike even to-morrow* (i. 123[8]). When the verb is

---

[1] In classical Sanskrit íd survives only in the compound particle **ced** *if* = **ca-id**.

compound, the particle regularly follows the preposition, not the verb itself: **ulū́khala-sutānām áva‿íd v, indra, jalgulaḥ** *gulp eagerly down, O Indra, the drops shed by the mortar* (i. 28[1]).

a. In B. the particle is similarly used: **ná tā́ ít sadyò 'nyásmai áti diśet** *he should not assign* (*just those* =) *the same* (*cows*) *to another on the same day* (ŚB.); **táthā‿ín nūnáṃ tád āsa** *now thus it came to pass* (ŚB.).

iva is an enclitic particle with two uses:

1. It means *as if, as, like* in abbreviated similes in apposition, never introducing a clause like **yáthā**. It follows the word with which comparison is made; if the comparison consists of several words, the particle generally follows the first, less commonly the second. The comparison is usually complete, but not infrequently it is only partially expressed. This employment of **iva** is very common in V., but comparatively rare in B. Examples of this use are: **dūré cit sán taḷíd ivā́ti rocase** *even though far away, thou shinest brightly as if near at hand* (i. 94[7]); **tát padáṃ paśyanti divìva cákṣur ā́tatam** *they see that step like an eye fixed in heaven* (i. 22[20]); **sá naḥ pitā́‿iva sūnáve ágne sūpāyanó bhava** *as such be accessible to us, O Agni, as a father to his son* (i. 1[9]); **dvíṣo no áti nāvā́‿iva pāraya** *take us across our foes as* [across the ocean] *in a ship* (i. 97[7]); **tābhī rājānaṃ parigṛhya tiṣṭhati samudra iva bhūmim** *with these he keeps embracing the king, as the sea the earth* (AB.).

2. It modifies a statement not intended to be understood in its strict sense, meaning *as it were.* It chiefly follows adjectives, adverbs, prepositions or verbs. This use of **iva** is rare in V., but very common in B. Examples are: **ihá‿iva śṛṇve** *I hear close at hand as it were* (i. 37[3]); **tád, indra, prá‿iva vīryàṃ cakartha** *that heroic deed, O Indra, thou didst perform* (*as it were*=) *quite pre-eminently* (i. 103[7]); **yā́ prá‿iva náśyasi** *who* (*as it were* =) *almost losest thyself* (i. 146[1]); **yádi tán ná‿iva háryatha** *if ye are not quite pleased with that* (i. 161[8]). From B.: **tásmāt sá babhruká iva** *hence he* (*is as*

it were=) may be called brown (ŚB.); **rebhati͜iva** *he seems to chatter* (AB.); **tán na sárva iva͜abhiprá padyeta** *not exactly every one should have access to that* (ŚB.); **upári͜iva vái tád yád ūrdhvám̐ nā́bheḥ** *above may be called what is higher than the navel* (ŚB.).

īm (an old enclitic acc. of the pron. root i) occurs in V. only, and is almost restricted to the RV.

1. It is generally employed as an acc. sing. of all genders = *him, her, it,* sometimes even as an acc. du. or pl. It either takes the place of a noun, or prepares for a following noun, or is accompanied by other pronouns (**tám, yám, enam, enān**); e. g. **ā́ gachanti͜īm ávasā** *they come to him with aid* (i. 85[11]); **ā́͜īm āśúm āśáve bhara** *bring him, the swift, to the swift* (i. 4[7]); **tám īṃ hinvanti dhītáyaḥ** *him devotions impel* (i. 144[5]); **yád īm enā̆̄n uśató abhy ávarṣīt** (vii. 103[3]) *when it has rained upon them that longed* (for rain).

2. **īm** also appears as a generalizing particle with relatives (*whoever*), with **yád** (*whenever*), with interrogatives (*who, pray?*), with **kíṃ caná** (*nothing at all*); e. g. **yá īṃ bhávanti ājáyaḥ** *whatever conflicts take place* (vii. 32[17]); **ká īṃ vyàktā náraḥ** *who, pray, are the radiant men?* (vii. 56[1]).

u is an enclitic particle, often written **ū** where the metre requires or favours a long syllable, especially in the second syllable of a Pāda, before a single consonant. It often appears contracted to **o** (cp. 24) with a preceding **a** or **ā** (mostly the final of particles or prepositions, also of the pron. **eṣā́**, sometimes of verbal forms). It has two main uses in the RV.:

1. It is employed deictically with verbs and pronouns.

a. With verbs it expresses the immediate commencement of an action: with a present = *now, already*; with a past tense = *just*; with an imperative, injunctive, or optative used in an impv. sense = *at once*; **sú** is here very often added, **ū ṣú** being = *instantly*. When the verb is accompanied by a preposition, the particle regularly follows the latter. Examples of its use are: **úd u tyáṃ jātávedasaṃ deváṃ vahanti ketávaḥ** *his beams now bear aloft the god that knows all creatures* (i. 50¹); **ábhūd u bhā́ḥ** *the light has just arisen* (i. 46¹⁰); **tápa‿u ṣv àgne ántarām̐ amítrān** *burn instantly, O Agni, our neighbouring foes* (iii. 18²).

a. This use of u with verbal forms does not seem to be found in B.

b. It emphasizes deictic pronouns, which may then be rendered by stress, and interrogative pronouns, when it may be translated by *pray*; e.g. **ayám u te, sarasvati, vásiṣṭho dvā́rāv ṛtásya subhage vy àvaḥ** *this Vasiṣṭha has opened for thee, O bountiful Sarasvatī, the two doors of sacrifice* (vii. 95⁶); **ká u śravat** *who, pray, will hear?* (iv. 43¹).

a. In B. this use is very rare with deictic pronouns, but not infrequent with interrogatives; e.g. **idám u no bhaviṣyati yádi no jeṣyánti** *this at least will remain to us, if they conquer us* (TS.); **kím u sá yajñéna yajeta yó gā́m iva yajñáṃ ná duhītá** *what sort of sacrifice, pray, would he offer if he were not to milk out the sacrifice like a cow?* (MS.).

2. The particle u is used anaphorically to connect sentences, when a word (usually the first) is repeated in the second, in the sense of *also*; e.g. **trír náktaṃ yāthás, trír u, aśvinā, dívā** *thrice by night ye come, thrice also, O Aśvins, by day* (i. 34²); **tváṃ trātā́ tvám u no vṛdhé bhūḥ** *thou be our protector, thou, too, be for our increase* (i. 178⁵). The repeated word need not always have the same form: **yó no dvéṣṭy ádharaḥ sás padīṣṭa, yám u dviṣmás tám u prāṇó jahātu** *may he who hates us fall downward; whom also we hate, him too let his breath forsake* (iii. 53²¹). The u sometimes appears in both sentences, sometimes in the first only: **vayám u tvā dívā suté, vayáṃ náktaṃ havāmahe** *we call thee by day to the pressed Soma, we also by night* (viii. 64⁶).

a. It is sometimes used without referring back definitely, but simply adding some similar quality or activity with reference to the same thing = *and also, and*; e.g. **sá devó devā́n práti paprathe pṛthú, víśvéd u tā́ paribhū́r bráhmaṇas pátiḥ** *he, the god, has extended himself widely to the gods, and he, Lord of Prayer, embraces all this universe* (ii. 24¹¹).

b. It also, in the same sentence, expresses a contrast = *on the contrary*, or, more frequently, with the demonstrative **tá** corresponding to the relative **yá** = *again, in return*; e. g. **stríyaḥ satī́s tā́m̐ u me puṃsá āhuḥ** *those who are women, them on the contrary they speak of to me* (as) *men* (i. 164[16]); **yó adhvaréṣu hótā .. tám u námobhir ā́ kṛṇudhvam** *him who is priest at sacrifices, in return bring hither with devotions* (i. 77[2]).

a. In B. the anaphoric use is common, prevailing chiefly in the ŚB.; e.g. **tásmād vā́ índro 'bibhet, tásmād u tváṣṭābibhet** *of that Indra was afraid, of that also Tvaṣṭṛ was afraid* (MS.).

α. The demonstrative here often refers back with **u** to previous statements: **utò pañcāvattám evá bhavati : pā́ṅkto yajñáḥ, pā́ṅktaḥ paśúḥ, pañcartávaḥ saṃvatsarásya : eṣā́‿u pañcāvattásya sampát** : *but it is also divided into five parts : the sacrifice is fivefold, cattle are fivefold, the seasons of the year are five : this is the sum of what is divided into five parts* (ŚB.). Similarly used are the phrases **tád u ha smāha** *with reference to this he used to say*, **tád u hovāca** *with reference to this he said*; **tád u táthā ná kuryāt** *that one should not do thus*.

β. A slight contrast is expressed by **u** in the second sentence: **yádi nàśnā́ti pitṛdevatyò bhavati, yády v aśnā́ti devā́n áty aśnāti** *if he does not eat, he becomes a worshipper of the Manes, but if he does eat, he eats before the gods* (ŚB.).

γ. Used in combination with **kím**, **u** expresses a climax in the second clause = *how much more* : **manuṣyà ín nvā́ úpastīrṇam ichánti, kím u devā́ yéṣāṃ návāvasānam** *even men wish for something spread out, how much more the gods whose is a new dwelling* (TS.).

utá in the RV. means *and*, connecting two or more words or sentences.

a. The particle commonly couples two words; e. g. **yáḥ .. pṛthivī́m utá dyā́m éko dādhā́ra** *who alone has supported heaven and earth* (i. 154[4]). When there is an enumeration of more than two objects, **utá** comes after the last; e. g. **ádite, mítra, váruṇa‿utá** *O Aditi, Mitra, and Varuṇa* (ii. 27[14]). When a word is repeated from the beginning of a clause, **utá** (like **u**) follows the repeated word: **tríḥ saubhagatvám trír utá śrávāṃsi naḥ** *thrice* (grant) *us prosperity and thrice fame* (i. 34[5]).

b. When **utá** connects a sentence with a preceding one, it is placed at the beginning: **eténāgne bráhmaṇā vāvṛdhasva . . utá prá neṣy abhí vásyo asmā́n** *with this prayer, O Agni, strengthen thyself, and lead us onward to greater fortune* (i. 31¹⁸).

c. **utá...utá** means *both...and*; **utá vā** *or*; **utá vā...utá vā** *either...or*; e. g. **utá‿idā́nīm bhágavantaḥ syāma‿utá prapitvá utá mádhye áhnām** *both now may we be fortunate and at eventide and at midday* (i. 41⁴); **samudrā́d utá vā divás pári** *from the ocean or from heaven* (i. 47⁶); **yā́ ā́po divyā́ utá vā srávanti khanítrmāḥ** *either the waters that are celestial or that flow in channels* (i. 49²).

a. In B. **utá** does not mean *and*, but *also, even*, emphasizing the assertion generally and not (like **ápi**) a single notion in the sentence: **utá yádi‿itā́sur bhávati jī́vaty evá** *even when his breath is gone, he still lives* (TS.). Even when preceding a substantive **utá** seems to refer to the whole statement: **utá mátsya evá mátsyaṃ gilati** *it is also the case that one fish devours another* (ŚB.).

β. With the optative **utá** expresses that an action might *after all* take place: **utá‿evám cid devā́n abhí bhavema** *after all we might thus overcome the gods* (ŚB.).

b. **utá...utá** in B. (as well as in V.) means *both...and*: **utá ṛtáva utá paśáva íti brūyāt** *he should say 'both the seasons and the animals'* (ŚB.).

γ. **utá** is regularly the first word in the sentence except that **kím** or forms of **tá** or **yá** precede it: **tásmād utá bahúr apaśúr bhavati** *therefore even though rich he becomes cattleless* (ŚB.).

utó (= **utá u**) in the RV. means *and also*: **utó no asyā́ uṣáso juṣéta hí** *and may he also be pleased with us this morning* (i. 131⁶).

a. In B. **utó** has the sense of *but also* or *also*: **āhavanī́ye havíṃṣi śrapayeyuḥ . . . utò gā́rhapatya evá śrapayanti** *they should cook the oblation on the Āhavanīya fire, but they also cook it on the Gārhapatya* (ŚB.).

evá has two uses in the RV. and the AV.:

1. At the beginning of sentences or clauses it means *thus*, referring either to what precedes or follows; e. g. **evā́gnír gótamebhir astoṣṭa** *thus Agni has been praised by the Gotamas* (i. 77⁵); **evā́ tám āhur: índra éko vibhaktā́** *thus they speak of him: 'Indra is the one dispenser'* (vii. 26⁴).

It often appears as the correlative of **yáthā** *as*: **yáthā ná pū́rvam áparo jáhāty, evā́, dhātar, ā́yūṃṣi kalpayaiṣām** *as the later abandons not the earlier, so, Creator, arrange their lives* (x. 18⁵). With the impv. **evá** = *so, then*: **evā́ vandasva váruṇaṃ bṛhántam** (viii. 42²) *then praise the lofty Varuṇa* (who has done these great deeds).

2. As an emphasizing particle following the word on which stress is laid, **evá** may be variously rendered *just, quite, alone*, &c., or by stress; e. g. **tám evá** *him only*; **éka evá** *quite alone*; **átraivá** *just here*; **svayám evá** *quite spontaneously*, **jātá evá** *scarcely born*, **ná͜ evá** *not at all*.

a. In B. the first of the above uses has entirely disappeared (**evám** here taking the place of **evá**), while the second is extremely common. The particle follows all kinds of words requiring emphasis for any reason; this is especially the case when a word is repeated; e. g. **yám ágre 'gníṃ hotrā́ya prā́vṛṇata, sá prádhanvad, yáṃ dvitī́yaṃ prā́vṛṇata, sá prá͜evá͜adhanvat** *the Agni whom they first chose for the priesthood, perished; he whom they chose the second time, likewise perished* (ŚB.). When two notions are connected by way of contrast or otherwise, **evá** may follow either the first or the second; e. g. **amū́m evá devā́ upā́yan, imā́m ásurāḥ** (ŚB.) *the gods inherited that world* (heaven), *the Asuras this one* (the earth); **sómo yuṣmā́kaṃ, vā́g evàsmā́kam** (let) *Soma* (be) *yours, Vāc ours* (ŚB.).

evám *thus* occurs only once in the RV. (as correlative to **yáthā** *as*) and in the AV. not at all with **yáthā**, but only as an adverb with the verb **vid** *know*: **yá eváṃ vidyā́t** *he who may possess such knowledge*.

In B. **evám** is very common, having two uses:

1. It is correlative to **yáthā** *as*, being often accompanied by a form of the same verb as the latter; e. g. **yáthā vái parjányaḥ súvṛṣṭiṃ várṣaty, eváṃ yajñó yájamānāya varṣati** *as Parjanya rains heavily, so the sacrifice rains for the sacrificer* (TS.). When the second verb is omitted, **yáthā...evám** is equivalent to **iva**; e. g. **té devā́ abhy àsṛjyanta yáthā víttiṃ vetsyámānā evám** *the gods rushed up like those wishing to obtain property* (ŚB.).

2. It accompanies verbs as an adverb, especially in the very frequent phrase **yá eváṃ véda** *he who possesses such knowledge*; **utá͜ eváṃ cin nā́ labheran** *after all they will thus not touch it* (ŚB.).

kam appears both as an accented and an unaccented particle. The former use is found in both V. and B., the latter in the RV. only.

1. *a.* **kám** as an adv. with the full meaning *well* (equivalent to the Vedic **śám**) appears in B. only; e. g. **kám me 'sat** *may it be well with me* (ŚB.); it also occurs in a negative form: **á-kaṃ bhavati** *he fares not well* (TS.).

b. **kám** has the same meaning attenuated after datives (generally at the end of a Pāda) either of persons = *for the benefit of* (dat. commodi) or of abstract nouns (final dative); e. g. **yuvám etáṃ cakrathuḥ síndhuṣu plaváṃ taugryā́ya kám** *ye two have placed that ship in the waters for the benefit of the son of Tugra* (i. 182[5]); **tvā́ṃ devā́so amṛ́tāya káṃ papuḥ** *thee the gods have drunk for the love of immortality* (ix. 106[8]); **samānám añjy àñjate śubhé kám** (vii. 57[3]) *with the same hue they adorn themselves in order to shine* (*well*). From B.: **kásmai kám agnihotrám hūyata íti** *for whose benefit is the Agnihotra offered?* (MS.); **téjase káṃ pūrṇámā ijyate** *for the sake of splendour the full moon sacrifice is offered* (MS.).

2. The unaccented **kam** occurs in the RV. only excepting one independent passage of the AV. It always appears as an enclitic following the particles **nú, sú, hí.** It means *willingly, gladly, indeed,* but the sense is generally so attenuated as to be untranslatable. **nú kam** appears with the inj., impv., subj., ind., also in relative clauses; e. g. **áso nú kam ajáro várdhāś ca** *be unaging and grow* (x. 50[5]). **sú kam** appears with the imperative only: **tíṣṭhā sú kaṃ, maghavan, mā́ párā gāḥ** *pray stand still, bounteous god, go not further* (iii. 53[2]). **hí kam** generally appears with the ind. (occasionally omitted), sometimes with impv. or subj.: **rā́jā hí kaṃ bhúvanānām abhiśrī́ḥ** *for he indeed is the king who rules over beings* (i. 98[1]).

kím (n. of **kí** = **ká**) has two uses. In the first place it means *why?* e. g. **kím u śréṣṭhaḥ kíṃ yáviṣṭho na ā́jagan**

why has the best, why has the youngest come to us? (i. 161[1]). It is also a simple interrogative particle (equivalent to a mark of interrogation); e. g. **kíṃ me havyám áhṛṇāno juṣeta** *would he, free from anger, enjoy an oblation of mine?* (vii. 86[2]); **kíṃ rájasa enā́ paró anyád ásti** *is there anything else beyond the welkin?* (AV. v. 11[5]).

a. In B. **kím** is similarly used. With following **u** it here adds a climax in a second sentence = *how much more* (see **u**); with following **utá** and the optative it means *why after all*; e. g. **kím utá tvareran** *why, after all, should they hasten?* (ŚB.).

kíla, an uncommon particle in V., meaning *indeed, certainly*, strongly emphasizes (in RV. and AV.) the preceding word (noun, pronoun, adjective, and the negative **ná**); e. g. **svādúṣ kíla‿ayám** (vi. 47[1]) *sweet, indeed, is this* (Soma); **tādī́tnā śátruṃ ná kílā vivitse** *then thou didst find no foe at all* (i. 32[4]).

a. In B. the use is similar; e. g. **kṣiprám kíla‿ā́ stṛṇuta** (ŚB.) *quickly, then, spread* (the barhis). But here **kíla** usually follows other particles, **vái** or (**ha**) **vā́vá**: **eṣá vái kíla havíṣo yā́maḥ** *this, indeed, is the course of the sacrifice* (ŚB.); **tava ha vāva kila bhagava idam** *Sir, this belongs to you only* (AB.).

kuvíd, a pronominal interrogative particle, introduces sentences which, though apparently independent, are treated as dependent, since the verb (except twice in the RV.) is regularly accented. This use seems to have arisen from the particle's having been employed as an elliptical expression of doubt such as might be rendered by 'I wonder (whether)'; e. g. **tám, indra, mádam ā́ gahi kuvín nv àsya tṛpṇávaḥ** *come, Indra, to this carouse* (to see) *whether you shall enjoy it* (iii. 42[2]); **kuvít sómasya ápām íti** *have I, indeed, drunk Soma* (x. 119[1]) = (I wonder) *whether I have drunk Soma.*

a. In B. **kuvíd** is similarly used; e. g. **kuvín me putrám ávadhīt** *has he actually killed my son?* (ŚB.): **kuvít tūṣṇī́m ā́ste** *does he indeed sit silent?* (ŚB.).

khálu *indeed, in truth*, does not occur at all in the AV., and only once in the RV., where it emphasizes an imperative: **mitrám kṛṇudhvaṃ khálu** *pray, conclude friendship* (x. 34[14]).

a. In B. the particle is common. It is rarely used alone, but often with other particles.

a. It appears alone with the impv., subj., or ind.; e.g. **átra khálu ramata** *here, pray, remain* (ŚB.); **ṛdhnávat khálu sá yó maddevatyàm agním ādádhātai** *he indeed shall prosper who shall establish a fire consecrated to me* (TS.); **asmākám evá‿idám khálu bhúvanam** *to us alone indeed this world belongs* (ŚB.).

b. After the particles **u** or **átho** and before or after **vái**, it emphasizes the word preceding the combined particles; e.g. **tád u khálu mahā-yajñó bhavati** *thus, indeed, the great sacrifice arises* (ŚB.).

a. **átho khálu** is used either to express an (usually preferred) alternative = *or else, or rather, but surely rather*; or to introduce an objection; e.g. **vaiśvadevám íti brūyād, átho khálu aindrám íti brūyāt** *'for all gods' one should say, or else one should say 'for Indra'* (TS.); **dīkṣitena satyam eva vaditavyam; atho khalv āhuḥ: ko 'rhati manuṣyaḥ sarvaṃ satyaṃ vaditum iti** *an initiated man should speak the truth only; now they make the objection: 'what man can speak the whole truth?'* (AB.).

β. **vái khálu** can only be distinguished from **vái** alone as an emphatic **vái**. But **khálu vái** in the TS. and AB. has the special use of introducing a second causal protasis after a first beginning with simple **vái**, the conclusion then following with **evá**; e.g. **prājāpatyó vái púruṣaḥ; prajā́patiḥ khálu vái tásya veda: prajā́patim evá svéna bhāgadheyéna upa dhāvati** *now man comes from Prajāpati; again Prajāpati knows about him: so he approaches Prajāpati with the portion* (of the sacrifice) *belonging to him* (TS.). This use occasionally occurs even though the preceding clause does not begin with **vái**.

gha is an enclitic particle, almost restricted to the RV. Generally occupying the second place in the Pāda, it is with few exceptions metrically lengthened to **ghā**. It emphasizes the preceding word, which is nearly always either the negative **ná**, or a pronoun (demonstrative or personal), or a verbal preposition, the meaning being variously rendered by *just, only, very*, or merely stress. It emphasizes a noun only twice and a verb only once in the RV.: **tṛtī́ye ghā sávane** *at least at the third Soma libation* (i. 161[8]); **uśánti ghā té amṛ́tāsa etát** *those immortals desire this* (x. 10[3]).

ca (Gk. τε, Lat. *-que*) *and* is an enclitic conjunction used to connect both words and sentences. It regularly follows an accented word, and when it adds a clause, the first word of that clause.

1. **ca** connects substantives (including pronouns and numerals) and adverbs; e. g. **mitrám̐ huve váruṇam ca** *I invoke Mitra and Varuṇa* (i. 2^{7}); **maghávāno vayám̐ ca** *the patrons and we* (i. 73^{8}); **śatám ékam̐ ca** *a hundred and one* (i. 117^{18}); **adyá̄ nūnám̐ ca** *to-day and now* (i. 13^{6}). In a few passages (but never in B.) the **ca** follows the first word instead of the second: **náktā ca . . uṣásā** *night and morning* (i. 73^{7}).

a. **ca...ca** are used much in the same way; e. g. **giráyaś ca dyá̄vā ca bhū́mā** *the mountains and heaven-and-earth* (i. 61^{14}); **diváś ca gmáś ca** *of heaven and of earth* (i. 37^{6}); **asmá̄ñ ca tá̄m̐ś ca** *us and them* (ii. 1^{16}); **náva ca navatím̐ ca** *nine and ninety* (i. 32^{14}); **á̄ ca párā ca cárantam** *moving hither and away* (i. 164^{31}).

Similarly in B.: **devá̄ś ca‿ásurāś ca** *gods and Asuras* (ŚB.); **ṣaṣṭíś ca tríṇi ca śatá̄ni** *sixty and three hundred*; **purástāc ca‿upáriṣṭāc ca** *from before and from behind*.

β. **ca...ca** sometimes also express a contrast: **náktā ca cakrúr uṣásā vírūpe : kṛṣṇám̐ ca várṇam aruṇám̐ ca sám̐ dhuḥ** *they have made night and morning of different aspect: they have put together the black colour and the ruddy* (i. 73^{7}).

Similarly in B.: **ubháyam̐ grāmyám̐ ca‿āraṇyám̐ ca juhoti** *he sacrifices both: what is tame and what is wild* (MS.).

a. A peculiar use of **ca** in the RV. is to add a second vocative in the form of a nominative; e. g. **vá̄yav índraś ca . . á̄ yātam** *O Vāyu and Indra, come* (i. 2^{6}).

b. Another peculiar use of **ca**, both in V. and B., is to add one noun (nearly always in the nom.) to another which has to be supplied; e. g. **á̄ yád índraś ca dádvahe** *when we two,* (I) *and Indra, receive* (viii. 34^{16}); **índraś ca sómam̐ pibatam̐, bṛhaspate** *do ye,* (thou), *O Bṛhaspati, and Indra, drink* (iv. 50^{10}).

From B.: **tá̄ bṛ́haspátiś ca‿anvávaitām** *they two,* (*he*) *and Bṛhaspati, followed them* (TS.); **tát samjñá̄m̐ kṛṣṇājiná̄ya ca**

vadati *so he pronounces harmony* (between it) *and the black antelope skin* (ŚB.).

a. In B. **ca** is used to add a single word at the end of a sentence in the sense of *and* (*so did*); e. g. **śrámeṇa ha sma vái tád devā́ jayanti yád eṣāṃ jáyyam ā́sa‿ṛ́ṣayaś ca** *by penance the gods were wont to win what was to be won by them, and so did the seers* (ŚB.).

c. **ca** following the interrogative **ká**, or the relative **yá** and the interrogative **ká** combined, gives them an indefinite sense: **káś ca** or **yáḥ káś ca** *any one, whoever* (cp. 119 *b*).

2. **ca** also connects both principal sentences and relative clauses: **ā́ devébhir yāhi yákṣi ca** *come with the gods and sacrifice* (i. 14^{1}); **yā́ vyūṣúr yā́ś ca nūnáṃ vyuchā́n** *that have shone forth and that shall now shine forth* (i. 113^{10}); **yò 'smā́n dvéṣṭi yáṃ ca vayáṃ dviṣmáḥ** *who hates us and whom we hate* (ŚB.).

a. **ca...ca** connect sentences to express a contrast by means of parallel verbal forms which are either identical or at least appear in the same number and person, the first verb being then always accented: **párā ca yánti púnar ā́ ca yanti** *they go away and come again* (i. 123^{12}).

a. In B. the use of **ca...ca** is similar; e. g. **vatsáṃ ca‿upāvasṛjáty ukhā́ṃ ca‿ádhi śrayati** *he admits the calf and puts the pot on the fire* (TS.). The rule of accentuation applies even when the second verb is omitted: **agnáye ca havíḥ paridádāti gúptyā asyái ca pṛthivyái** *he delivers the oblation for protection to Fire and to this Earth* (ŚB.). This connecting use is particularly common in parallel abridged relative sentences: **sárvān paśū́n ní dadhire yé ca grāmyā́ yé ca‿āraṇyā́ḥ** *they laid down all animals, those that are tame and those that are wild* (ŚB.).

3. **ca** is used a few times in V. in the sense of *if* with the subjunctive or the indicative: **índraś ca mṛḷáyāti no, ná naḥ paścā́d aghám naśat** *if Indra be gracious to us, no calamity will hereafter befall us* (ii. 41^{11}); **imā́ṃ ca vā́caṃ pratiháryathā, naro, víśvéd vāmā́ vo aśnavat** *if ye graciously accept this song, O heroes, it will obtain all goods from you* (i. 40^{6}).

caná, properly meaning *not even*, is most usually employed after a negative; e.g. **tṛtī́yam asya nákir ā́ dadharṣati, váyaś caná patáyantaḥ patatríṇaḥ** *no one dares approach his third* (step), *not even the winged birds though they fly* (i. 155⁵). From its use in such supplementary clauses, where it may also be translated by *even*, the latter sense comes to be the natural or even necessary one after a negative in a single clause sentence; e.g. **yásmād ṛté ná sídhyati yajñó vipaścítaś caná** *without whom the sacrifice does not succeed* [not] *even of the wise man* (i. 18⁷); **índraṃ ná mahnā́ pṛthivī́ caná práti** *even the earth is not equal to Indra in greatness* (i. 81⁵). As one of the two negatives is superfluous in a single clause sentence, **caná** alone occasionally does duty for the negative: **mahé caná tvā́ṃ párā śulkā́ya deyām** *not even for a great reward would I give thee away* (viii. 1⁵).

a. In a few passages, even when there is no accompanying negative, **caná** throwing off its own negative sense, means *even, also*: **aháṃ caná tát sūríbhir ānaśyām** *I too would acquire this with the patrons* (vi. 26⁷); **ádhā caná śrád dadhati** *therefore also they believe* (i. 55⁵).

a. In B. **caná** appears only after a negative in single clause sentences, in which **ná caná** means *not even*; e.g. **ná hainaṃ sapátnas túṣṭūrṣamāṇaś caná stṛṇute** *no enemy fells him even though desiring to fell him* (ŚB.).

b. **caná** gives the interrogative an indefinite sense: **káś caná** *any one*, **ná káś caná** *no one* (cp. 119 *b*).

cid is an enclitic particle very frequently used to emphasize the preceding word. It has two senses:

1. expressing that the statement is not to be expected in regard to the word emphasized: *even*; e.g. **ā́ dṛḍháṃ cid árujo gávyam ūrvám** *even the firm cowstall thou hast broken through* (iii. 32¹⁶). This sense is, however, sometimes so attenuated as to be capable of being rendered by stress only; e.g. **tváṃ cin naḥ śámyai bodhi svādhī́ḥ** *be thou attentive to our endeavour* (iv. 3⁴).

2. generalizing = *any, every, all*; e.g. **kṛtám cid énaḥ prá mumugdhy asmát** (i. 24⁹) *remove from us any* (every, all) *sin committed* (by us). Similarly, with interrogatives = *any*, with relatives = *ever*; thus **káś cid** *any one*: **śṛṇóti káś cid eṣām** *any one* (= every one) *hears them* (i. 87¹³); **sunvádbhyo randhayā kám cid avratám** *subject every impious man to those that press Soma* (i. 132⁴); **ná** or **mā́ káś cid** (*not any* =) *no one*; **kadā́ cid** *ever* = *at any time* or *always*; **yáś cid** *whoever*; **yác cid** *if ever*; **yáthā cid** *as ever*.

a. In B. the only use that survives is the generalizing sense with interrogative pronouns = *any, some*; e.g. **átha kám cid āha** *then he says to some one* (ŚB.); **yát te káś cid ábravīt** *what any one said to you* (ŚB.).

céd (= **ca íd**) *if* occurs only three times in the RV., but later becomes commoner. In the RV. and AV. it is found with the ind. pres. and aor.; in the AV. it also occurs once with the opt. Thus: **ví céd uchánty, aśvinā, uṣā́saḥ, prá vām bráhmāṇi kā́ravo bharante** *when the Dawns shine forth, O Aśvins, the singers offer prayers to you* (vii. 72⁴); **brahmā́ céd dhástam ágrahīt sá evá pátir ekadhā́** *if a Brahman has taken her hand, he alone is her husband* (AV. v. 17⁸); **íti manvīta yācitáḥ vaśā́m céd enam yā́ceyuḥ** *thus one would think who has been requested, if they were to request a cow of him* (AV. xii. 4⁴⁸).

a. In B. **céd** is used with the ind. pres., aor., fut. and with the opt.; e.g. **átaś céd evá náiti nā́sya yajñó vyathate** *if he does not go away from there, his sacrifice does not fail* (MS.); **sá hovāca túrīyam-turīyam cén mā́m ábībhajaṃś túrīyam evá tárhi vā́ṅ níruktam vadiṣyatī́ti** *he said 'if they have given me only one-fourth each time, then Vāc will speak distinctly only to the extent of one-fourth'* (ŚB.); **tám cén me ná vivákṣyasi, mū́rdhā te ví patiṣyati** *if you cannot explain this* (riddle) *to me, your head will burst* (ŚB.); **etám céd anyásmā anubrūyā́s táta evá te śíraś chindyām** *if you were to tell this to another, I would strike off your head* (ŚB.).

tátas occurs in the RV. several times adverbially in the local sense of the ablative = *thence*; e.g. **táto viṣám prá vāvṛte** *thence the poison has turned away*. It also, but very rarely, has the temporal sense of *thereupon, then*; e. g. **yajñáir átharvā prathamáḥ patháś tate, tátaḥ sūryo . . ájani** *with sacrifices Atharvan first extended the paths, then the sun was born* (i. 83⁵).

a. In B., on the other hand, the temporal sense of *thereupon* is extremely common. Here it also often appears at the beginning of a sentence connected with a preceding one in the sense of *therefore, consequently*; e. g. **sá yajñám evá, yajñapā́trāṇi prá viveśa; táto hainām ná śekatur nírhantum** *it entered into the sacrifice itself, into the sacrificial vessels; consequently those two were unable to expel it* (ŚB.).

táthā occurs in the RV. in the sense of *so, thus*; e. g. **tátha ṛtúḥ** *such is the rule* (i. 83¹⁰). It also appears as a correlative (though less often than **evá**) to **yáthā**; e. g. **śyāvā́śvasya sunvatás táthā śṛṇu yáthā́śṛṇor átreḥ** *listen to the sacrificing Śyāvāśva as thou didst listen to Atri* (viii. 36⁷).

a. In B. the use is similar; e. g. **táthā‿ín nūnám tád āsa** *so, indeed, it came to pass* (ŚB.); as correlative (though less often than **evám**) to **yáthā**: **ná vái táthā‿abhūd yáthā‿ámamsi** *it has not come about as I had thought* (ŚB.).

b. **tátho** (= **táthā‿u**) occurs in B., meaning *and in the same way, but so*; e. g. **tátho evóttare ní vapet** *and in the same way he should assign the last two* (TS.); **sá yád dakṣiṇá-pravaṇā syā́t, kṣipré ha yájamāno 'múm lokám iyāt, tátho ha yájamāno jyóg jīvati** *if it* (the altar) *were sloping to the south, the sacrificer would quickly go to yonder world, but thus* (as it is) *the sacrificer lives a long time* (ŚB.).

tád is often used adverbially in the RV. It then has three different senses:

1. It frequently means *then* as correlative to **yád** *when*; e. g. **yáj jā́yathā vṛtrahátyāya tát pṛthivī́m aprathayaḥ** *when thou wast born for the Vṛtra-fight, thou didst spread out the earth* (viii. 89⁵).

2. It is also often used in the sense of *thither* (acc. of the goal); e. g. **tád ít tvā yuktā́ hárayo vahantu** *thither let the yoked bays waft thee* (iii. 53⁴).

3. Occasionally it has the sense of *therefore*; e. g. **tád vo devā́ abruvan, tád va ā́gamam** *that the gods said to you,*

therefore I have come to you (i. 161²); **prá tád víṣṇuḥ stavate vīryèṇa** *therefore Viṣṇu is praised for his heroism* (i. 154²).

a. In B. **tád** has four different adverbial uses:

1. as a correlative to **yád** (*when, inasmuch as*) = *thereby*, and to **yátra** (*where*) = *there*; e. g. **yán nv èvá rā́jānam abhiṣuṇvánti, tát tám ghnanti** *now when they press the king* (soma), *they kill him thereby* (ŚB.); **yátrānyā́ óṣadhayo mlā́yanti tád eté módamānā vardhante** *where other plants wither, it* (the wheat) *grows merrily* (ŚB.).

2. in the sense of *thereupon, then*; e. g. **átha‿itithī́ṃ sámāṃ tád aughá āgantā́, tán mā nā́vam upakálpya‿úpāsāsai** *now in such and such a year a flood will then come, then having built a ship you shall turn to me* (ŚB.).

3. constantly with reference to a preceding statement in the sense of *as to that, thereby, thus*; e.g. **yajñám evá tád devā́ upā́yan** *the gods thus obtained the sacrifice* (ŚB.); **tát tád avakḷptám evá yád brāhmaṇò 'rājanyáḥ syā́t** *so it is quite suitable that a Brahman should be without a king* (ŚB.); **tád āhuḥ** *as to that they say*; **tád u tát** *now as to this* (ŚB.).

4. before **yád** with reference to a preceding statement to add an explanation, and may be rendered by *that is to say, now*; e. g. **tád yád eṣá etát tápati téna eṣá śukráḥ** *now, inasmuch as he burns here, therefore he is bright* (ŚB.). Similarly in the phrase **tád yát táthā** *that is to say, why it is so* (is as follows) = *the reason for this is as follows* (ŚB.).

tárhi *at that time, then*, occurs only once in the RV., but several times in the AV.: **ná mṛtyúr āsīd amṛ́taṃ ná tárhi** *there was not death nor immortality then* (x. 129²). In the AV. the word appears as correlative to **yádā** *when*, and in B. to **yátra, yád, yádā, yárhi** *when*, and **yádi** *if*; e. g. **rakṣāṃsi vā enaṃ tarhy ā labhante yarhi na jāyate** *the Rakṣases then seize him when* (the fire) *does not arise* (AB.); **yádi vā́ ṛtvíjo 'lokā́ bhávanty aloká u tárhi yájamānaḥ** *if the priest is without a place, the sacrificer is then also without a place* (ŚB.).

tásmād *therefore* is not found as an adverb in the RV., but occurs several times as such in the AV., and is constantly so used in B. As correlative to **yád** *because* it appears once in the AV. and is very common in B.; e. g. **yád vái tád váruṇagṛhītābhyaḥ kám ábhavat tásmāt kāyáḥ** (MS.) *because those who were seized by Varuṇa felt well, therefore it is called kāya (body).*

tú, though accented, never commences a sentence or Pāda. It has two uses:

1. It is an emphasizing particle. In the RV., where it occurs nearly fifty times, it seems to be restricted to this sense.

a. In about two-thirds of its occurrences **tú** emphasizes an exhortation in the 2. pers. impv. (rarely the 3. pers., or the subj. in an impv. sense) = *pray, then*; e.g. **ā́ tv étā, ní ṣīdata** *pray come, sit you down* (i. 5[1]); **ná te dūré paramā́ cid rájāṃsy, ā́ tú prá yāhi háribhyām** *even the highest spaces are not far to thee; come hither, then, with thy two bays* (iii. 30[2]).

b. In several passages **tú** emphasizes assertions (generally following the demonstrative **tá**) in the sense of *surely, indeed*; e.g. **tát tv àsya** *that surely is his work* (iii. 30[12]).

2. It is an adversative particle meaning *but*. This is its sense in the only passage of the AV. in which it occurs, and is its only meaning in B.; e.g. **cakā́ra bhadrám asmábhyam ātmáne tápanaṃ tú sáḥ** *he has done what is good for us, but painful to himself* (AV. iv. 18[6]); **tád eváṃ véditor ná tv eváṃ kártavái** *that one should know thus, but not do thus* (MS.). With **áha** or **nú** in the preceding clause, it expresses the sense *it is true...but*; e.g. **tád áha téṣāṃ váco, 'nyā́ tv èvā́taḥ sthítiḥ** *this indeed is what they say, but the established practice is different therefrom* (ŚB.).

téna occurs in B. as an adverb correlative to **yád** *because*; e.g. **yád grāmyásya ná‿áśnāti téna grāmyā́n áva runddhe** *because he does not eat any tame animal, therefore he gains tame animals for himself* (MS.).

tvā́vá (compounded of **tú vā́vá**), a particle sometimes occurring in B., does not perceptibly differ in sense from **vā́vá** (q. v.); e.g. **tráyo ha tvā́vá paśávo 'medhyā́ḥ** *there are just three kinds of animals unfit for sacrifice* (ŚB.).

tvái (compounded of **tú vái**) is sometimes found in B. meaning *but indeed*.

dvitā́, a particle occurring about thirty times, is restricted to the RV. There can be no doubt that it is an old instrumental, etymologically meaning *doubly*. This sense taken either literally = *in two ways*, or figuratively = *emphatically, especially, more than ever*, seems to suit all the passages in which the word occurs; e. g. **bharádvājāya‿áva dhukṣata dvitā́ dhenúṃ ca viśvádohasam íṣaṃ ca viśvábhojasam** *on Bharadvāja do ye* (Maruts) *milk down doubly, both the all-milking cow and all-nourishing food* (vi. 48[13]); **rā́jā devā́nām utá mártyānāṃ dvitā́ bhuvad rayipátī rayīṇā́m** *as king of gods and mortals may he be doubly lord of riches* (ix. 97[24]); **dvitā́ yó vṛtrahántamo vidá índraḥ śatákratuḥ úpa no háribhiḥ sutám** *may he who above all is known as the best Vṛtra-slayer, Indra Śatakratu,* (come) *to our pressed Soma with his bays* (viii. 93[32]); **gavā́m éṣe sakhyā́ kṛṇuta dvitā́** (x. 48[9]) *in the search for the cows he especially concluded friendship* (with me).

a. The word occurs several times with **ádha**, meaning *and that too doubly or especially*, e. g. **ví tád vocer ádha dvitā́** *explain this, and* (do so) *particularly* (i. 132[3]).

ná has two senses in V. (but only the first of the two in B.):

1. As a negative particle meaning *not* it denies an assertion, appearing in principal sentences with the ind. of all tenses, with the subj., the opt., the inj. (in the sense of a fut.), but not with the impv.; it is also employed in relative and conjunctional clauses. It negatives either the assertion of the whole sentence (when it appears as near the beginning as possible, in V. even before the relative) or only the assertion of the verb. It can only be used in a sentence which contains a finite verb or in which one is to be supplied. There seems to be no undoubted example of its negativing any word (such as a participle or adjective) other than the verb. The employment of this negative **ná** is much the same in B. as in V.

a. A verb (such as **asti** *is*) has often to be supplied with this negative in simple sentences, especially with the gerundive, the infinitive, or a dative equivalent to an infinitive; e.g. **tán ná súr-kṣyam** *that* (is) *not to be troubled about* (MS.); **ná yó várāya** *who* (is) *not for hindering* = *who is irresistible* (i. 143[5]). Or the verb has to be supplied in a second sentence from the first; e.g. **náktam úpa tiṣṭhate, ná prātáḥ** *he worships at night,* (he does) *not* (worship) *in the morning* (TS.).

b. Two negatives express a strong positive; e.g. **ná hí paśávo ná bhuñjanti** *for cattle always eat* (MS.).

2. **ná** is used in V. (very commonly in RV., comparatively rarely in AV., but never in B.) as a particle of comparison, exactly like **iva** *as, like.* This meaning seems to be derived from *not* as negativing the predicate of a thing to which it properly belongs; e.g. 'he (neighs), not a horse neighs' = 'he, though not a horse, neighs' = 'he neighs like a horse'. This **ná**, being in sense closely connected with the preceding word, never coalesces in pronunciation (though it does in the written Sandhi) with a following vowel, whereas **ná** *not* generally does. This **ná** always follows the word of comparison to which it belongs; or if the simile consists of several words, the **ná** generally follows the first word, less commonly the second; e.g. **arā́n ná nemíḥ pári tā́ babhūva** *he surrounds them as the felly the spokes* (i. 32[15]); **pakvā́ śā́khā ná** *like a branch with ripe fruit* (i. 8[8]).

a. When the object compared is addressed in the voc. (which is sometimes to be supplied), the object with which it is compared is sometimes also put in the voc. agreeing with it by attraction; e.g. **úṣo ná śubhra ā́ bharā** *like brilliant Dawn,* (O sacrificer) *bring* (i. 57[3]); **áśve ná citre, aruṣi** *like a brilliant mare, O ruddy Dawn* (i. 30[21]).

b. When the object compared is not expressed, **ná** means *as it were*; e.g. **śivā́bhir ná smáyamānābhir ā́gāt** *he has come with gracious smiling women as it were* (i. 79[2]).

c. **ná** sometimes interchanges with **iva**; e.g. **rátham ná táṣṭeva tátsināya** *as a carpenter* (fashions) *a car for him who desires it* (i. 61[4]).

ná-kis[1] (*not any one*) is found in V. only, being almost restricted to the RV., where it frequently occurs. It properly

[1] N. sing. of interrogative **kí** (Lat. *qui-s*) of which the n. **kí-m** is in regular use (cp. 113).

means *no one*; e.g. **nákir indra tvád úttaraḥ** *no one, O Indra, is superior to thee* (iv. 30¹); **yáthā kṛmīṇāṃ nákir ucchiṣyā́tai** *that none of the worms shall be left* (AV. ii. 31³). Losing its N. sense,[1] it comes to be used, though less often, as a strong negative adverb meaning *not at all, never*; e.g. **yásya śárman nákir devā́ vārā́yante ná mártāḥ** *in whose protection gods never hinder him nor mortals* (iv. 17¹⁹). Cp. **mā́kis.**

ná-kīm[2] occurs only twice in one hymn of the RV. in the sense of a strong negative adverb = *not at all, never*: **nákīm índro níkartave** *Indra can never be subdued* (viii. 78⁵).

ná-nu occurs only twice in the RV. where it has the sense of a strong negative = *by no means, never.* In B. it occurs a few times as an interrogative expecting assent (= *nonne*), *not?*; e.g. **nánu śuśruma** *have we not heard?* (ŚB.).

na-hí, as the compounded form of **ná hí**, occurs only in V., where it sometimes has the sense of *for not*; e.g. **nahí tvā śátruḥ starate** *for no foe strikes thee down* (i. 129⁴). More commonly it emphatically negatives a statement as something well known = *certainly not, by no means*, as appears most clearly at the beginning of a hymn; e.g. **nahí vo ásty arbhakó, dévāsaḥ** *not one of you, O gods, is small* (viii. 30¹).

a. This compounded form never occurs in B., where **ná hí** alone is found. On the other hand, **ná hí** seems never to occur in V.

nā́ma is used adverbially in the following two senses:

1. *by name*; e.g. **sá ha śrutá índro nā́ma deváḥ** *that god famous as Indra by name* (ii. 20⁶); **kó nā́ma‿asi** *who art thou by name?* (VS. vii. 29). 2. *namely, indeed, verily*; e.g. **ájasro gharmó havír asmi nā́ma** *I am constant heat, namely the oblation* (iii. 26⁷); **mā́ṃ dhur índraṃ nā́ma devátā** *they have placed me among the gods verily as Indra* (x. 49²).

---

[1] Probably because the N. has no longer an independent existence coupled with the fact that the pronoun **kí** has gone out of use except in the one form **kí-m.**

[2] Probably A. n. of **ná-kis** with lengthened vowel.

nú[1] or **nū́**[2] means 1. *now*; e.g. **sá nv īyate** *he is now implored* (i. 145[1]); **índrasya nú vīryā̀ṇi prá vocam** *I will now proclaim the heroic deeds of Indra* (i. 32[1]); **yójā nv, indra, te hárī** *yoke now* (= at once), *O Indra, thy two bays* (i. 82[1]); **uvā́soṣā́ uchā́c ca nú** (i. 48[3]) *Dawn has shone* (in the past) *and she shall shine now* (= henceforth); **asmā́bhir ū nú praticákṣyā‿abhūt** *to us she has just now become visible* (i. 113[11]). 2. *still*: **páśyema nú sū́ryam uccárantam** *we would still see the sun rising* (vi. 52[5]); **mahā́ñ índraḥ paráś ca nú** *great is Indra and still more* (i. 8[5]). 3. *pray* with interrogatives: **kadā́ nv àntár váruṇe bhuvāni** *when, pray* (= at last), *shall I be in* (communion with) *Varuṇa* (vii. 86[2]). 4. *ever* with relatives: **yā́ nú kṛṇávai** *whatever* (deeds) *I shall accomplish* (i. 165[10]). 5. *ever, at all* with negatives: **ná‿asya vartā́ ná tarutā́ nv ásti** *there is none at all to obstruct, none to overcome him* (vi. 66[8]). 6. with **cid** it means (*a*) *even now, still*; e.g. **nū́ cid dadhiṣva me gíraḥ** *even now take to thyself my songs* (i. 10[9]); **daśasyā́ no, maghavan, nū́ cit** *favour us still, Bountiful one* (viii. 46[11]); (*b*) *never*; e.g. **nū́ cid dhí parimamnā́the asmā́n** *for never have ye despised us* (vii. 93[6]).

a. The senses of **nú** found in B. are the following:

1. *Now actually* in affirmative sentences, often correcting a previous statement; e.g. **nirdaśo nv abhūd, yajasva mā‿anena** *now he is actually more than ten days old: sacrifice him to me* (AB.). 2. *then, pray,* in exhortations with the subj., the impv., or **mā́** with the inj., e.g. **śraddhā́devo vái mánur: āvā́ṃ nú vedāva** *Manu is godfearing; let us two then try him* (ŚB.); **mā́ nu me prá hārṣīḥ** *pray, do not strike at me* (ŚB.). When **átha** follows such sentences, **nú** may be translated by *first*: **nirdaśo nv astv, atha tvā yajai** *let him* (the victim) *first be more than ten days old, then I will sacrifice him to you* (AB.). 3. *pray,* in questions with or without an interrogative; e.g. **kvà nu víṣṇur abhūt** *what, pray, has become of Viṣṇu?* (ŚB.); **tvā́ṃ nú khálu no bráhmiṣṭho 'si** *are you, pray, indeed the wisest of us?* (ŚB.). 4. *now,* after **íti** followed by **átha** *next*: **iti nu pūrvaṃ paṭalam, athottaram** *this now is the first section; next follows the*

---

[1] Never begins a sentence.

[2] Often begins a sentence.

second (AB.). 5. *indeed*, in the first of two antithetical clauses, when the second is introduced with **tú** or **kím u**; e.g. **yó nv èvá jñātás tásmai brūyād, ná tv èvá sárvasmā iva** *he may indeed tell it to him who is known to him, but not to any and every one* (ŚB.).

nūnám *now* has three uses in the RV.:

1. With the ind. pres. it means *now* as opposed to *formerly* or *in future* (an opposition often expressed by **purā́** *before* and **aparám** *after*); e.g. **ná nūnám ásti nó śváḥ** *there is no now and no to-morrow* (i. 170[1]).

It is a few times used with the perfect in combination with **purā́** to express that an action has taken place in the past and still takes place; e.g. **purā́ nūnáṃ ca stutáya ṛ́ṣīṇāṃ paspṛdhrá índre** *formerly and now the praises of seers have striven to Indra* (vi. 34[1]).

2. With the subj., impv., opt., or inj., it expresses that an action is to take place at once; e.g. **ví nūnám uchāt** *she shall now shine forth* (i. 124[11]); **prá nūnáṃ pūrṇávandhuras stutó yāhi** *praised advance now with laden car* (i. 82[3]).

With the perfect it is a few times used in the RV. to express that an action has just been completed; e.g. **úpa nūnáṃ yuyuje hárī** *he has just yoked his two bay steeds* (viii. 4[11]).

3. It occurs sometimes with interrogatives = *pray*; e.g. **kadā́ nūnáṃ te dāśema** *when, pray, may we serve thee?* (vii. 29[3]).

a. In B. none of these uses seem to survive, while the new sense of *certainly, assuredly* (perhaps once already in the AV.) has appeared; e.g. **tathā́ ín nūnáṃ tád āsa** *just so assuredly it came to pass* (ŚB.).

néd (= **ná íd** and not treated as a compound by the Padapāṭha) has two uses in both V. and B.: 1. sometimes as an emphatic negative, *certainly not*; e.g. **anyó nét sūrír óhate bhūridā́vattaraḥ** *no other patron indeed is accounted more liberal* (viii. 5[39]); **áhaṃ vadāmi nét tvám** *I am speaking, not thou* (vii. 38[4]); **néd ánuhūtaṃ prā́śnāmi** *I certainly do not eat it before it is invoked* (ŚB.). 2. much more commonly as introducing a final clause *in order that not* with the subj.

(= Lat. *ne*); e. g. **vy ùchā, duhitar divo, nét tvā tápāti súraḥ** *shine forth, daughter of the sky, lest the sun scorch thee* (v. 79[9]); **nén mā rudró hinásat** *lest Rudra injure me* (ŚB.). In B. the verb may also be in the inj.: **néd idám bahirdhā́ yajñā́d bhávat** *lest it be outside the sacrifice* (ŚB.).

a. **nvái** (= **nú vái** as analysed by the Padapāṭha of the TS.) occurs not infrequently in B. in the sense of *indeed*; e.g. **íti nvā́ etád brā́hmaṇam udyate** *such indeed is the Brāhmaṇa that is told* (ŚB.).

mā́ is the prohibitive negative (Gk. μή) regularly used with the injunctive. It is never used with the impv.; with the opt. only in the single form **bhujema** (RV.); and with the subj. only once (ŚB.); e. g. **mā́ no vadhīḥ** *slay us not* (i. 104[8]); **mā́ hṛṇīthā abhy asmā́n** *be not enraged against us* (viii. 2[19]).

a. An interrogative following **mā́** in a few cases receives an indefinite sense in the RV.; e.g. **mā́ kásmai dhātam abhy àmitríṇe naḥ** *deliver us not to any foe* (i. 120[8]).

mā́-kis (*not any one*, Gk. μή-τις), occurring about a dozen times in the RV., to which it is restricted, is used in prohibitive sentences with the injunctive in two senses:

1. *no one*: **mā́kis tokásya no riṣat** *may no one of our offspring be injured* (viii. 67[11]).

2. more often an emphatic negative = *by no means, never*: **mā́kir devā́nām ápa bhūḥ** *be not at all away from the gods* (x. 11[9]). Cp. **ná-kis**.

mā́-kīm, used as an emphatic prohibitive particle with the injunctive, occurs only in two passages of the RV.: **mā́kīm sám śāri kévaṭe** *let none suffer fracture in a pit* (vi. 54[7]).

yátra is employed in two main senses: 1. usually as a relative adverb, meaning *where*, but sometimes *whither*, e. g. **yajñé . . náro yátra devayávo mádanti** *where pious men rejoice in sacrifice* (vii. 97[1]); **yátrā ráthena gáchathaḥ** *whither ye go with your car* (i. 22[4]). The correlative is generally **tátra**, sometimes **átra** or **tád**.

a. Occasionally as equivalent to the locative of the relative; e. g. **á gha tā́ gachān úttarā yugā́ni yátra jāmáyaḥ kṛṇávann ájāmi** *those later generations will come in which those who are akin will do what befits not kinsmen* (x. 10[10]).

2. not infrequently as a temporal conjunction, *when*, in both V. and B.; e. g. **yátra prá sudā́sam ā́vatam** *when ye helped Sudās* (vii. 83[6]). In V. **ádha, átra, tád** appear as correlatives; e. g. **yátra śū́rāsas tanvò vitanvaté . . ádha smā yacha tanvè táne ca chardíḥ** *when the heroes strain themselves* (in battle) . . *then especially bestow protection on us and our sons* (vi. 46[12]). In B. **tád** is generally the correlative, sometimes **tátas**; e. g. **tám yátra devā́ ághnaṃs, tán mitrám abruvan** *when the gods killed him, they said to Mitra* (ŚB.).

yáthā has two distinct uses in both V. and B.:

1. as a relative adverb meaning *as*; e. g. **nūnám yáthā purā́** *now as before* (i. 39[7]); **yáthā vayám uśmási tát kṛdhi** *as we wish that do* (x. 38[2]); **yáthā vái puruṣó jī́ryaty evám agnír ā́hito jīryati** *as a man grows old, so fire when it has been laid grows old* (TS.). When there is a correlative in the RV., it is usually **evá**, sometimes **táthā**; in B. usually **evám**, sometimes **táthā**.

2. as a conjunction meaning *in order that, so that*, introducing a posterior clause, generally with the subj., rarely the opt.; e. g. **havíṣ kṛṇuṣva subhágo yáthā͜ ásasi** *prepare the oblation that thou mayest be successful* (ii. 26[2]); **ā́ daívyā vṛṇīmahé 'vāṃsi, yáthā bhávema mīḷhúṣe ánāgāḥ** (vii. 97[2]) *we crave divine aids that we may appear sinless to the gracious god*; **tathā me kuru yathā͜ aham imām senām jayāni** *arrange it so for me that I may conquer this army* (AB.); **táthaivá hotavyàṃ yáthā͜ agním vyaveyā́t** *it must be poured so that it should divide the fire* (ŚB.).

a. In the RV. after verbs of knowing or saying **yáthā** introduces an explanation = *how*; e. g. **kás tád brūyād anudéyī yáthā͜ ábhavat** *who could tell us this,* (viz.) *how the gift was?* (x. 135[5]). Occasionally it is used thus even without such verbs: **ná pramíye savitúr dáivyasya**

tád yáthā víśvam bhúvanam dhārayiṣyáti *that (power) of the divine Savitṛ (is not to =) will not decay,* (viz.) *that he will support the whole world* (iv. 54[4]).

yád (n. of the relative **yá**) is used in four distinct senses: 1. *that*, expanding the meaning of a word in the preceding principal clause; e.g. **gṛṇé tád, indra, te śávo yád dháṃsi vṛtrám** *I praise this mighty deed of thine that thou slayest Vṛtra* (viii. 62[8]); **kím ā́ga āsa, varuṇa, jyéṣṭhaṃ yát stotā́raṃ jíghāṃsasi sákhāyam,** *what has been the chief guilt, O Varuṇa, that thou wishest to slay thy praiser* (who is) *thy friend?* (vii. 86[4]). This use is not common in V.

a. **yad** is similarly employed in B. with reference to a preceding **tád** (often omitted); e.g. **tád yát páyasā śrīṇā́ti : vṛtró vái sóma āsīt** *that* (= the reason why) *he mixes Soma with milk* (is) *this: Vṛtra was Soma* (ŚB.). This use is also found in B. after certain verbs: **áva kalpate** *it is suitable,* **út sahate** *is able,* **icháti** *desires,* **yuktó bhavati** *is intent on,* **véda** *knows,* and **īśvará** *it is possible*; e.g. **ná hí tád avakálpate yád brūyā́t** *for it is not suitable that he should say* (ŚB.).

2. *when* with the ind. pres., imp., perf., aor., fut., and with the subj.; e.g. **yád dha yā́nti márutaḥ sáṃ ha bruvate** *when the Maruts go along, they speak together* (i. 37[13]); **kám apaśyo yát te bhī́r ágachat** *whom didst thou see when fear came upon thee?* (i. 32[14]); **índraś ca yád yuyudhā́te áhiś ca, maghávā ví jigye** *when Indra and the serpent fought, the bountiful god conquered* (i. 32[13]); **citró yád ábhrāṭ** *bright when he has shone forth* (i. 66[6]); **tigmā́ yád aśánir pátāti, ádha no bodhi gopā́ḥ** *when the sharp bolt shall fly, then be our protector* (iv. 16[17]). It also occurs rarely in anacolutha with the pres. part. and the past pass. part. much as in English; e.g. **pácanti te vṛṣabhā́ñ, átsi téṣāṃ yán, maghavan, hūyámānaḥ** *they roast bulls for thee, thou eatest of them, O bounteous one, when being called* (x. 28[3]).

a. In B. **yád** occurs with the sense of *when* with the pres., fut., and aor., and in the sense of *whenever* or *while* with the impf.

3. *if* used with the ind. pres., the subj., or the opt.; e.g.

yád, indra, údaṅ nyàg vā hūyáse, ā́ yāhi tū́yam *if, O Indra, thou art called above or below, come quickly* (viii. 65[1]); **yád ūrdhvás tíṣṭhā dráviṇā‿ihá dhattād yád vā kṣáyaḥ** *if thou shalt stand upright, bestow treasures here, or if thou shalt lie* (iii. 8[1]). The opt. is used when it is assumed that the condition will not be fulfilled; e. g. **yád, agne, syā́m ahám tvám, tvám vā ghā syā́ ahám, syúṣ ṭe satyā́ ihá‿āśíṣaḥ** *if, O Agni, I were thou, or if thou wert I, thy prayers here would be fulfilled* (viii. 44[23]).

a. In B. **yád** is used with the opt. as in V. (while with **yádi** the fulfilment of the condition is usually assumed) and with the conditional; **sá yád bhídyeta‿ā́rtim ā́rched yájamānaḥ** *if it were to break, the sacrificer would fall into misfortune* (TS.); **yád evám ná‿ávakṣyo mūrdhā́ te vy àpatiṣyat** *if thou hadst not spoken thus, thy head would have fallen to pieces* (ŚB.).

4. *in order that*, in posterior clauses, with the subj., very rarely with the opt. in V.; e. g. **ā́ vaha devátātiṃ śárdho yád adyá divyáṃ yájāsi** *bring hither the host of the gods that thou mayest adore the divine throng* (iii. 19[4]); **yán nūnám aśyā́ṃ gátiṃ, mitrásya yāyāṃ pathā́** *that I may now obtain refuge, I would go on Mitra's path* (v. 64[3]).

a. In B. this use of **yád** is very rare, occurring only a few times with the subj.; e. g. **tát prā́pnuhi yát te prāṇó vā́tam apipádyātai** *obtain thou this, that thy breath may pass into the wind* (ŚB.).

yadā́ *when* is used in V. and B. with the ind. perf., impf., pres., and with the subj.; with the aor. ind. and the inj. in V. only; and with the fut. and opt. in B. only. The correlative word (when there is one) is in V. **ā́d, átha, ádha, tád, tárhi**; in B. **átha** and **tárhi**.

1. **yadā́** is most commonly used in the RV. with the aor. ind., when as the beginning of the action is emphasized, the sense is *as soon as*; e. g. **yadéd ádevīr ásahiṣṭa māyā́, átha‿abhavat kévalaḥ sómo asya** *as soon as he had overcome the ungodly wiles, then Soma became his exclusively* (vii. 98[5]); **abhí gṛṇanti rā́dho yadā́ te márto ánu bhógam ā́naṭ** *they*

praise thy wealth as soon as the mortal has obtained thy reward (x. 7[2]). When the principal clause contains a historical tense, the aor. with **yadā́** has the value of a pluperfect.

a. The injunctive is found only once with **yadā́** in the RV.: **yadā́ máhyam dī́dharo bhāgám, indra, ā́d ín máyā kr̥ṇavo vīryā̀ṇi** *when thou shalt have secured for me my share, O Indra, then thou shalt perform heroic deeds with my help* (viii. 100[1]).

2. *a.* with the impf. and perf.; e.g. **yadā́ víṣṇus trī́ṇi padā́ vicakramé, yadā́ sū́ryam diví . . ádhāraya, ā́d ít te hárī vavakṣatuḥ** *when Viṣṇu took his three steps, when thou didst fix the sun in the sky, then thy two bays grew in strength* (viii. 12[27-30]); **tásya yadā́ márma‿ágachann átha‿aceṣṭat** *as soon as they touched his weak spot, he quivered* (MS.); **sá yadā́‿ābhyām anūvā́ca‿átha‿asya tád índraḥ śíraś ciccheda** *as soon as he had told them, Indra cut his head off* (ŚB.).

b. with the pres. ind.: **yadā́ satyám kr̥ṇuté manyúm índro, víśvam dr̥ḷhám bhayate éjad asmāt** *when Indra shows his true anger, all that is firm, trembling, is afraid of him* (iv. 17[10]); **yadā vai paśur nirdaśo bhavaty atha sa medhyo bhavati** *as soon as the victim is more than ten days old, it becomes fit for sacrifice* (AB.); **sá yadā́ keśaśmaśrú vápaty átha snāti** *when he has cut off his hair and beard, he bathes* (ŚB.).

c. with the subj. (here = future perfect): **yadā́ śr̥tám kr̥ṇávo 'tha‿īm enam prá hiṇutāt pitŕ̥bhyaḥ** *when thou shalt have made him done, then deliver him to the fathers* (x. 16[1]); **yadā́ tā́m ativárdhā, átha karṣū́m khātvā́ tásyām mā bibharāsi** *when I shall have grown too big for it, you shall, having dug a pit, keep me in it* (ŚB.).

3. *a.* with the fut.: **yadaiva hotā paridhāsyaty atha pāśān prati mokṣyāmi** *when the Hotr̥ shall have concluded, I shall tighten the cords* (AB.).

b. with the opt.: **sá yadā́ saṃgrāmám jáyed átha‿aindrāgnám nír vapet** *as soon as he may have won a battle, he should sacrifice to Indra and Agni* (MS.).

yádi *if* (sometimes *when* with a past tense) is found with perf. and impf. in V. only; with the ind. pres., aor., fut., and with the subj. in V. and B.; and with the opt. in B. only.

1. With the perf. used historically and with the impf. **yádi** means *when*, the verb then having the force of a pluperfect; e. g. **úd astambhīt samídhā nákam agnír yádī bhŕgubhyaḥ pári mātaríśvā havyavā́haṃ samīdhé** *Agni supported the vault with fuel when Mātariśvan from the Bhṛgus had kindled the oblation-bearer* (iii. 5[10]); **yádi sahásraṃ mahiṣā́ñ ághaḥ, ā́d ít ta indriyáṃ máhi prá vāvṛdhe** *when thou hadst eaten a thousand bulls, thy might grew great* (viii. 12[8]). But when the perf. has the pres. perf. sense, **yádi** has its ordinary meaning of *if*: **grā́hir jagrā́ha yádi vaitád enaṃ, tásyā, indrāgnī, prá mumuktam enam** *or if illness has seized him, from that release him, Indra and Agni* (x. 161[1]).

2. *a.* with the pres.: **yádī mánthanti bāhúbhir ví rocate** *when they rub with their arms, he shines* (iii. 29[6]); **adyā́ murīya yádi yātudhā́no ásmi** *to-day I would die, if I am a sorcerer* (vii. 104[15]); **yádi ná aśnā́ti pitṛdevatyò bhavati** *if he does not eat, he becomes dedicated to the Manes* (ŚB.).

b. with the aor.: **yádī mātúr úpa svásā . . ásthita, adhvaryúr modate** *if the sister* (coming) *from the mother has approached, the priest rejoices* (ii. 5[6]); **yády áha‿enaṃ prā́ñcam ácaiṣīr, yáthā párāca ā́sīnāya pṛṣṭhatò 'nnā́dyam upāháret** *if you have piled it frontways, it is as if one handed food from behind to one sitting with averted face* (ŚB.).

c. with the fut.: **yády evā́ kariṣyátha, sākáṃ deváir yajñíyāso bhaviṣyatha** *if ye will act thus, ye shall become objects of worship together with the gods* (i. 161[2]); **yádi vā́ imám abhimaṃsyé kánīyó 'nnaṃ kariṣye** *if I shall plot against him, I shall procure less food* (ŚB.).

d. with the subj.: **yájāma devā́n yádi śaknávāma** *we will worship the gods, if we shall be able* (i. 27[13]); **yádi stómaṃ máma śrávad, asmā́kam índram índavaḥ . . mandantu** *if he shall hear my song of praise, let our drops gladden Indra* (viii. 1[15]); **yádi tvā‿etát púnar brávatas, tvám̥ brūtāt** *if they two shall say that to thee again, do thou say* (ŚB.).

a. With the opt. **yádi** is (excepting one occurrence in the SV.) found in B. only, where this use is very common. Here a case is usually supposed with a rule applicable to it in the principal clause; e. g. **yadi na śaknuyāt, so 'gnaye puroḷāśam̥ nir vapet** *if he should not be able to do it, he should offer a cake to Agni* (AB.).

3. after the verb **vid** *know*, **yádi** is used in the sense of *whether* in one passage of the RV. (x. 129[7]) and often in B.; e. g. **hánta na éko véttu yádi ható vā vr̥tró jívati vā** *come, let one of us find out whether Vr̥tra is dead or whether he is alive* (ŚB.).

a. **yádi vā** is not only used after a preceding **yádi** in the sense of *or if*, but also alone in the sense of *or*, nearly always without a verb; e. g. **só aṅgá veda yádi vā ná véda** *he alone knows or he does not know* (x. 129[7]); **yám̥ váhanti śatám áśvā yádi vā saptá** *whom a hundred horses draw, or seven* (AV. xiii. 2[7]); **yádi vā‿itárathā** *or conversely* (ŚB.).

yárhi (*at the time*) *when* occurs only in B., where it is used with the pres. or past ind., and with the opt. It has almost invariably **tárhi** or **etárhi** *then* as a correlative; e. g. **sá tárhy evá jāyate yárhy agním ādhatté** *he is born at the moment when he lays his fire* (MS.); **yárhi prajáḥ kṣúdham̥ nigácheyus tárhi navarātréṇa yajeta** *when his people should suffer from hunger, he should sacrifice with the rite of nine nights* (TS.).

yásmād does not occur as a conjunction in V., but it sometimes appears as such in B. meaning *why*; e. g. **átha yásmāt samiṣṭa-yajúm̥ṣi nā́ma** *now* (follows the reason) *why they are called Samiṣṭayajus* (ŚB.).

yā́d (an old abl. of **yá**) is found in V. only. It is used with the indicative pres. or past, and with the subj. With the ind. it means *as far as* in the RV.; e. g. **árcāmasi yā́d evá vidmá tā́t tvā mahā́ntam** (vi. 21[6]) *we praise thee, the great, as far as we know* (how to); it seems to mean *since* in the AV.: **yá ā́kṣiyan pr̥thivím̥ yā́d ájāyata** *who ruled the earth since it arose* (AV. xii. 1[57]). With the subj. **yā́d** means *as long as*; e. g. **anānukr̥tyám apunáś cakāra yā́t sū́ryāmā́sā mithá uccárātaḥ** *he has once for all done what is inimitable as long as sun and moon alternately shall rise* (x. 68[10]).

yā́vat already appears in V. as an adverb meaning *as far as, as long as*, an extension of its acc. use; e. g. **yā́vad dyā́vāpṛthivī́ tā́vad ít tát** (x. 114⁸) *as far as heaven and earth, so far it* (extends); **juhómi havyáṃ yā́vad ī́śe** *I offer oblation as long as I am able* (iii. 18³); **ájāto vái tā́vat púruṣo yā́vad agníṃ ná‿ādhatté** *man is so long unborn, as he does not lay his fire* (MS.).

vā *or* is employed much in the same way as **ca** *and*. It is enclitic, following the word to which it belongs; and it connects words, clauses, or sentences; e. g. **áta ā́ gahi divó vā rocanā́d ádhi** *come from here or from the shining realm of heaven* (i. 6⁹); **yasya bhāryā gaur vā yamau janayet** *whose wife or cow bears twins* (AB.); **práti yáḥ śā́sam ínvati, ukthā́ vā yó abhigṛṇā́ti** *who promotes the law or welcomes songs of praise* (i. 54⁷).

a. **vā...vā** is frequently used in the same way; e. g. **śáktī vā yát te cakṛmā́ vidā́ vā** *that we have offered to thee according to our power or knowledge* (i. 31¹⁸); **náktaṃ vā hí dívā vā várṣati** *for it rains by night or by day* (TS.); **yád vā‿ahám abhidudróha yád vā śepá utá‿ánṛtam** *what evil I have plotted or what I have sworn falsely* (i. 23²²).

b. But **vā...vā** also mean *either...or*. When they contrast two principal sentences in this sense, implying exclusive alternatives, the verb of the first is accented even when the second is incomplete; e. g. **áhaye vā tā́n pradádātu sóma ā́ vā dadhātu nírṛter upásthe** *let Soma either deliver them to the serpent or place them in the lap of dissolution* (vii. 104⁹); **tád vā jajñáu tád vā ná jajñau** *she either agreed to it or did not agree to it* (ŚB.); **tásya vā tváṃ mána ichā́ sá vā táva** *either do thou seek his heart, or he thine* (x. 10¹⁴).

vāvá (doubtless a contraction of two particles) is found in B. only. It emphasizes the preceding word in the sense of *certainly, just*, being particularly frequent in the first of two correlated clauses; e. g. **eṣá vāvá sò 'gnír ity āhuḥ** *that is certainly the same Agni, they say* (TS.).

vái is an emphasizing particle meaning *truly, indeed*.

1. In the RV. this particle occurs only in 28 passages, in all but three of which it follows the first word of the sentence; e. g. **bhadráṃ vái váraṃ vṛṇate** *truly they make a good choice* (x. 164²); **íti vā íti me mánaḥ** *so, indeed, so is my mind* (x. 119¹); **ná vái strái̇ṇāni sakhyā́ni santi**

there are, indeed, no friendships with women (x. 95[15]). The stress is laid on the whole sentence, not on any particular word. The particle is often followed by **u** (**vā́ u**) without any perceptible change of meaning.

a. In the AV. the use is similar except that here the particle often appears after a demonstrative or a relative; e. g. **tásmād vái sá párābhavat** *therefore, indeed, he perished* (xii. 4[49]); **yó vái tā́ vidyā́t pratyákṣam, sá vā́ adyá mahád vadet** *whoever may know them plainly, he, verily, may speak aloud to-day* (xi. 8[3]).

2. In B. **vái** usually occupies the same position, but often yields the second place to **céd, hí, khálu,** and of course always to the enclitics **iva, u, ca, sma, ha.** When **átho** begins a sentence **vái** occupies the second place.

Here the use of **vái** in the first sentence of a narrative is typical; e. g. **yámo vā́ amriyata: té devā́ yamyā́ yámam ápābruvan** *Yama died: the gods* (then) *dissuaded Yamī from* (thinking of) *Yama* (MS.).

a. The particle often appears in the concluding sentence in discussions; e. g. **tásmād vā́ ápa úpa spṛśati** *that is, indeed, why he sips water* (ŚB.).

b. It is very often placed after the first word of a sentence that gives the reason for the one that follows; e. g. **śraddhā́devo vái mánur: āvā́ṃ nú vedāva** *now Manu is god-fearing: we two will therefore ascertain* (ŚB.). When **vái** is used in this way the clause containing it is often equivalent to a parenthetical one; e. g. **té vāyúm abruvan (ayáṃ vái vāyúr yó 'yáṃ pávate) vā́yo tvám idáṃ viddhi‿íti** *they said to Vāyu (now Vāyu is he who blows), 'Vāyu, ascertain this'* (ŚB.). In this sense **vái** is especially frequent in periods of three clauses, when that with **vái** contains the reason, and that with **evá** the conclusion; e. g. **tā́ etā́bhis tanū́bhiḥ sám abhavan; paśávo vái devā́nāṃ priyā́s tanvàḥ: paśúbhir éva sám abhavan** *they were together with these bodies; now animals are the bodies dear to the gods: they were therefore together with animals* (MS.).

c. The differences between the use of **vái** and of **evá** in B. are the following: **vái** coming after the first word emphasizes the whole sentence, while **evá** emphasizes a particular word in any part of the sentence; **vái** follows the first word of a sentence beginning a narrative, **evá** never does; in a period **vái** is typical in the clause stating a reason, **evá** in that expressing the conclusion.

sá is often used pleonastically before relatives in B.; e.g. **sá yó no vā́cam vyāhṛtām mithunéna ná‿anunikrā́māt, sá sárvaṃ párā jayātai** *he who shall not follow the word uttered by us with* (another of) *the corresponding gender, he shall lose everything* (ŚB.). This use led to **sá** being employed in a formulaic way not only pleonastically but also without reference to gender or number; e.g. **tásya tā́ni śīrṣā́ṇi prá cicheda. sá yát somapā́nam āsa tátaḥ kapíñjalaḥ sám abhavat** *he struck off his heads. Now that which had been Soma-drinking, from that arose the francoline partridge* (ŚB.); **sá yádi ná vindánti kím ā́ driyeran** *now if they do not find it, why should they mind?* (ŚB.).

sīm is an enclitic particle restricted to the RV. Originally the acc. sing. of a pronoun, related to **sá** as **kīm** to **ká**, it is generally used (much like **īm**) as an acc. of all numbers and genders in the third person—*him, her, it, them,* representing a substantive (which sometimes follows) and frequently placed between a preposition and its verb, occasionally also after a relative; e.g. **pári ṣīṃ nayanti** *they lead him around* (i. 95²); **prá sīm ādityó asṛjat** *the Āditya made them* (the streams) *to flow* (ii. 28⁴); **ní ṣīṃ vṛtrásya mármaṇi vájram índro apīpatat** *Indra has caused it, his bolt, to fall on Vṛtra's vital spot* (viii. 100⁷); **yáṃ sīm ákṛṇvan támase vipṛ́ce, táṃ sū́ryam** *whom they created to disperse the darkness, that sun* (iv. 13³).

a. **sīm** sometimes gives the relative the sense of *ever*; e.g. **yát sīm ā́gaś cakṛmā́, śiśráthas tát** *whatever sin we have committed, remove that* (v. 85⁷).

sú, sū́ *well*, used asseveratively = *thoroughly, fully, verily* and always referring to the verb, is almost restricted as an independent particle to the Saṃhitās, being common in the RV., but rare in the others; e.g. **juṣásva sū́ no adhvarám** *thoroughly enjoy our sacrifice* (iii. 24²); **námaḥ sú te** *homage verily* (be) *to thee* (VS. xii. 63); **jarā́ṃ sú gacha** *go safely to old age* (AV. xix. 24⁵).

a. With preceding u the particle means *right well*: **imā́ u ṣú śrudhī gíraḥ** *hear these songs right well* (i. 26[5]); **vidmó ṣv asya mātáram** *we know full well his mother* (AV. i. 2[1]).

b. With preceding **mā́** it = *by no means, not at all, never*; e.g. **mó ṣú tvā . . . asmā́n ní rīraman** *let none by any means keep thee from us* (vii. 32[1]).

c. **sú kam** is used like the simple **sú** except that it appears with the impv. only; e.g. **tiṣṭhata . . . sú kam** *stand quite still* (i. 191[6]).

sma, an enclitic, slightly emphasizing particle, has two senses in the RV.:

1. It generally emphasizes:

a. demonstrative or personal pronouns, relatives, or nouns, and may be rendered by *just, especially*, or simply by stress; e.g. **tásya sma prāvitā́ bhava** *be his helper* (i. 12[8]); **sá śrudhi yáḥ smā pṛ́tanāsu kā́su cit . . . śū́raiḥ svàḥ sánitā** *hear thou, who especially in all battles with heroes dost win the light* (i. 129[2]).

b. the verb, which or (if it is compounded) the preposition of which it follows (generally at the beginning of the sentence); e.g. **smási ṣmā vayám eṣām** *we are indeed theirs* (i. 37[15]); **ā́ smā rátham tiṣṭhasi** *thou mountest indeed upon thy car* (i. 51[12]). The verb is in the present ind. or the impv., rarely the perf.; it appears to have been accented before **sma** judging by the only example (vi. 44[18]) in which it is not the first word in the sentence (App. III, 19 A).

c. adverbs and particles; e.g. **utá sma** *and especially*; **ná sma** and **mā́ sma** *by no means*.

a. In the AV. these emphasizing uses are similar; but in B. they have entirely disappeared.

2. In a few instances **sma** occurs in the RV. before **purā́** with the pres. ind. to express that an action has habitually taken place in the past down to the present time; e.g. **yé smā purā́ gātūyánti** *who have always aided = who aids now and formerly did so* (i. 169[5]).

a. This use is not found in the AV., but has become extremely common in B., where **sma** is always preceded by **ha**. The meaning here expressed is that something habitually took place in the past (but does not as in the RV. include the present); e.g. **ná ha sma vái purā́ agnír aparaśuvṛkṇaṃ dahati** *formerly Agni used not to burn what was not lopped off with the axe* (TS.).

b. Much more frequently, however, **purā́** is left out and the particles **ha sma**, from their frequent association with it, assume its meaning; e.g. **té ha sma yád devā́ ásurāñ jáyanti, táto ha sma evá enān púnar upóttiṣṭhanti** *as often as the gods defeated the Asuras, the latter always opposed them again* (ŚB.). This use of **ha sma** is very common with the present perfect **āha**; e.g. **etád dha sma vā́ āha nāradáḥ** *with regard to this Nārada used to say* (MS.). Other tenses than the present with **ha sma** are found in the AB. where, in two or three passages, the perf. and the impf. are used with them in the same sense.

svid is an enclitic particle emphasizing the first word of a sentence, usually an interrogative pronoun or adverb. It may generally be translated by *pray*; e.g. **káḥ svid vṛkṣó níṣṭhito mádhye árṇasaḥ** *what tree, pray, was that which stood in the midst of the sea?* (i. 182[7]). In one passage of the RV. this particle gives the interrogative an indefinite meaning: **mātā́ putrásya cárataḥ kvà svit** *the mother of the son that wanders who knows where* (x. 34[10]). Very rarely (in double questions) the particle appears without an interrogative: **ásti svin nú vīryàṃ tát ta, indra, ná svid asti: tád ṛtuthā́ ví vocaḥ** *is this thy heroic deed, O Indra, or is it not: that declare in due season* (vi. 18[3]).

a. In a few instances **svid** appears in non-interrogative sentences: **tváyā ha svid yujā́ vayám abhí ṣmo vā́jasātaye** *with thee as companion we are equipped for the obtainment of booty* (viii. 102[3]).

b. The employment of **svid** in B. is similar; e.g. **kám u ṣvid átó 'dhi váraṃ variṣyāmahe** *what boon, pray, beyond this shall we choose?* (MS.); **tváṃ svin no bráhmiṣṭho 'si** *art thou, pray, the most learned of us?* (ŚB.); **yád áṅgāreṣu juhóti tát svid agnáu juhoti** *what he pours on the coals, that itself he pours on the fire* (MS.).

ha, an enclitic particle occurring after all words capable of beginning a sentence, has a slightly emphasizing and asseverative force. It is probably identical in origin with **gha**, but unlike that particle hardly ever (only twice) appears in the RV. with its vowel lengthened. It is common in the RV., occurring after personal, demonstrative, interrogative, and relative pronouns, nouns, verbs, verbal prepositions, and adverbs.

a. In B. the use of this particle varies in frequency: it is comparatively rare in the TS., where it generally appears with **sma** or with perfects; while in the ŚB. it is extremely frequent. It lays stress on the first word of sentences so as to emphasize the connexion or to mark a new or important step in the narrative; e.g. **iti marīmṛjyeta: ājarasaṃ ha cakṣuṣmān bhavati ya evaṃ veda** *with these words he should wipe* (his eyes): *so till old age he who knows this becomes possessed of vision* (AB.).

b. It is very often used after the first word of a story with or without **vái**. It appears predominantly with the perfect in those parts of the ŚB. and the AB. that narrate with the perfect, mostly with verbs of speaking. Thus **sa ha‿uvāca** appears here, while **so 'bravīt** is said elsewhere.

hánta occurs three times in the RV. as an interjection in exhortations; e.g. **yájāmahai yajñíyān hánta devā́n** *come, we will worship the adorable gods* (x. 53²).

a. It is similarly used in B.: **hanta‿imaṃ yajñaṃ sambharāma** *well, we will prepare the sacrifice* (AB.).

hí, in origin probably an emphasizing particle, is used throughout as a subordinating conjunction which regularly throws the accent on the verb. It nearly always follows the first word of the sentence, or the second when the first two are closely connected. In V. it is used in two ways:

1. in indicative sentences (the verb having sometimes to be supplied) to express the reason (like γάρ), meaning either *for*, if the clause containing it follows, or *because, since*, if it precedes; e.g. **bálaṃ dhehi tanū́ṣu no, tváṃ hí baladā́ ási** *bestow strength on our bodies, for thou art a giver of strength* (iii. 53¹⁸); **śruṣṭīvā́no hí dāśúṣe devā́s, tā́n ā́ vaha** *since the gods give ear to the pious man, bring them hither* (i. 45²).

2. in exhortative sentences, mostly with the impv., as an emphatic particle = *pray, indeed*; e.g. **yukṣvā́ hí keśínā hárī** *pray harness thy two long-maned bay steeds* (i. 10³).

a. In B. three uses of **hí** may be distinguished:

1. it expresses the reason, as in the first use in V., only that the clause containing **hí** always follows (= *for* only), and the verb is much oftener omitted than expressed; e.g. **tád índro 'mucyata, devó hí sáḥ** *from that Indra freed himself, for he* (is) *a god* (ŚB.). The particle **vái** is often added to strengthen **hí**; e.g. **vájro hí vā́ ā́paḥ** *for water is indeed a thunderbolt* (ŚB.).

2. it is sometimes employed to emphasize an interrogative = *pray*; e.g. **katháṃ hí kariṣyási** *how, pray, wilt thou do it?* (ŚB.).

3. it expresses assent in answers after a word repeated from a preceding question; e.g. **tám eva tváṃ paśyasi‿íti; táṃ hí** '*do you see him?*' *Yes,* (I see) *him* (ŚB.).

a. In B., when **hí** appears in the relative clause of a period explaining a previous statement, the verb of the principal clause (to which **hí** properly applies) is sometimes irregularly unaccented; e.g. **idáṃ hí yadā́ várṣaty átha‿óṣadhayo jāyante** *for, when it rains here, then the plants spring up* (ŚB.).

181. A certain number of words having the nature of interjections occur in the Saṃhitās. They are of two kinds, being either exclamations or imitative sounds.

a. The exclamations are: **báṭ** (RV.) *truly,* **bata** (RV.) *alas!* **hánta** *come,* used exhortatively with the subjunctive and **hayé** *come* before vocatives; **híruk** and **hurúk** (RV.) *away!* **hái** (AV.) *ho!*

b. Interjections of the onomatopoetic type are: **kikirā́** (RV.) used with **kṛ** = *make the sound* **kikirā́** = *tear to tatters*; **kikkiṭā́** (TS.) used in invocations; **ciścā́** (RV.) *whiz!* (of an arrow), used with **kṛ** *make a whizzing sound*; **pháṭ** (AV., VS.) *crash!* **phál** (AV.) *splash!* **bā́l** (AV.) *dash!* **bhúk** (AV.) *bang!* **śál** (AV.) *clap!*

CHAPTER VI

NOMINAL STEM FORMATION AND COMPOUNDS

A. Nominal Stems.

182. Declinable stems, though they often consist of the bare root (either verbal or pronominal), are chiefly formed by means of suffixes added to roots. These **suffixes** are of two kinds: **primary**, or those added directly to roots (which may at the same time be compounded with verbal prefixes); and **secondary**, or those added to stems already ending in a suffix and to pronominal roots (which are thus treated as primary stems).

1. **Primary Derivatives** as a rule show the root in its strong form; e. g. **véd-a** m. *knowledge* (**vid** *know*); **sár-aṇa** n. *running* (√**sṛ**); **kār-á** *making* (√**kṛ**); **grābh-á** m. *seizer* (√**grabh**). In meaning they may be divided into the two classes of abstract action nouns (cognate in sense to infinitives) and concrete agent nouns (cognate in sense to participles) used as adjectives or substantives; e. g. **ma-tí** f. *thought* (**man** *think*); **yodh-á**, m. *fighter* (**yudh** *fight*). Other meanings are only modifications of these two; e. g. **dā́na** (= **dā́‿ana**) n. *act of giving*, then *gift*.

a. When the **bare root** is used as a declinable stem, it usually remains unchanged; e. g. **dā́** m. *giver*, **bhíd** f. *destroyer*, **yúj** m. *companion*, **spáś** m. *spy*, **vṛdh** adj. *strengthening*. Roots ending in **i** or **u** take a determinative **t**; e. g. **mí-t** f. *pillar*, **stú-t** f. *praise*. The root may appear in a reduplicated form; e. g. **cikít** *wise*, **jó-gū** *singing aloud*.

b. Several primary nominal suffixes connected with the verbal system have already been sufficiently dealt with, viz. those of the pres. and fut. participles: **ant** (85; 156), **āna** and **māna** (158); of the perf. act. part.: **vāṃs** (89; 157); of the perf. pass. part.: **ta** and **na** (160); of the gerundive: **ya, āyya, enya, tva, tavyà**[1] and **anīya**[2] (162). The formation of stems to which the primary suffixes of the comparative and superlative, **īyāṃs** and **iṣṭha**, are added has also been explained (88; 103, 2). Of the rest the following in alphabetical order are the most usual and important:

a: e.g. **bhāg-á** m. *share* (√**bhaj**); **megh-á** m. *cloud* (**mih** *discharge water*); **cod-á** m. *instigator* (√**cud**); **sárg-a** m. *emission* (√**sṛj**); **nāy-á** m. *leader* (√**nī**), **priy-á** *pleasing* (√**prī**); **hav-á** m. *invocation* (√**hū**); **jār-á** m. *lover* (√**jṝ**); **ve-vij-á** *quick* (**vij** *dart*), **carā-car-á** *far-extending*. The substantives are almost exclusively m.; but **yug-á** n. (Gk. *ζυγ-ό-ν*; Lat. *jug-u-m*).

an: m. agent nouns and about a dozen defective n. stems; e.g. **ukṣ-án** m. *ox*, **mūrdh-án** m. *head*, **rā́j-an** m. *king*; **ás-an** n. *blood*, **áh-an** n. *day*, **ud-án** n. *water*, **ū́dh-an** n. *udder*.

ana: n. action nouns: **bhój-ana** n. *enjoyment* (√**bhuj**), **sā́d-ana** n. *seat* (√**sad**); **kár-aṇa** n. *deed* (√**kṛ**); **háv-ana** n. *invocation* (√**hū**); **bhúv-ana** n. *being* (√**bhū**), **vṛj-ána** n. *enclosure*; also m. agent nouns: e.g. **kar-aṇá** *active*, **mā́d-ana** *gladdening* (√**mad**), **saṃ-gám-ana** *assembling*; **tur-áṇa** *speeding*.

anā: f. action nouns: **jar-aṇā́** *old age*, **yóṣ-aṇā** *woman*, **vadh-ánā** *slaughter*. This is also the f. form of adjectives in **ana**; e.g. **tur-áṇā** *speeding*.

ani: f. action nouns, and m. f. agent nouns; e.g. **ar-áṇi** f. *fire-stick*, **vart-aní** f. *track*; **carṣ-aṇí** *active*; **ruruks-áṇi** *willing to destroy* (from des. stem of **ruj** *destroy*).

---

[1] The second part, **ya**, of this suffix is secondary (182, 2), but the whole is employed as a primary suffix (162, 5). The first part, **tav**, is probably derived from the old infinitive ending **tave** (p. 192, 4).

[2] The second half of this suffix, **īya**, is secondary, but the whole is employed as a primary suffix (162, 6).

as: n. action nouns (with accented root) and agent nouns (with accented suffix); e. g. **áp-as** n. *work* (Lat. *ŏp-us*), **ap-ás** *active*; **rákṣ-as** n. *demon*, **rakṣ-ás** m. *id.*

ā: f. action nouns (from roots and secondary conjugation stems); e. g. **nind-ā́** *blame*; **ji-gī-ṣ-ā́** *desire to win*; **gam-ay-ā́** *causing to go*; **aśva-y-ā́** *desire for horses.*

i: action nouns (nearly always f.); agent nouns (adj. and subst.); and a few neuters of obscure origin; e. g. **kṛṣ-í** f. *tillage*, **āj-í** m. f. *contest*; **cákr-i** *active* (√**kṛ**), **śúc-i** *bright*; **pāṇ-í** m. *hand*; **ákṣ-i** n. *eye*, **ásth-i** n. *bone*, **dádh-i** n. *sour milk.*

is: n. action nouns (mostly with concrete sense); e. g. **arc-ís** *flame*, **jyót-is** *light*, **ā́m-is** *raw flesh*, **barh-ís** *straw.*

u: agent nouns, adj. and subst. (mostly m., but several f. and n.); e. g. **tan-ú** *thin* (Lat. *ten-u-i-s*); **bāh-ú** m. *arm* (Gk. *πῆχ-υ-ς*), **pād-ú** m. *foot*; **hán-u** f. *jaw*; **jā́n-u** n. *knee* (Gk. *γόν-υ*).

una: adj. and m. n. subst.; e.g. **tár-uṇa** *young*, **dhar-úṇa** *supporting*, m. n. *support*, **mith-uná** *forming a pair*, m. *couple*; **vár-uṇa** m. a god, **śak-uná** m. *bird.*

us: n. action nouns and m. agent nouns; e. g. **dhán-us** n. *bow*; **jay-ús** *victorious*; **van-ús** m. *assailant.*

ū: f., mostly corresponding to m. and n. in **u**; e. g. **tan-ū́** *body*; **dhan-ū́** *sandbank* (n. **dhán-u**); independently formed: **cam-ū́** *dish*, **vadh-ū́** *bride.*

ka (rare as a primary, but very common as a secondary suffix): adj. and m. subst.: **śúṣ-ka** *dry*; **át-ka** m. *garment*, **śló-ka** m. *call*, **sto-ká** m. *drop*; **vṛ́śc-i-ka** m. *scorpion.*

ta: besides ordinarily forming perf. pass. participles, appears, in a more general sense, as the suffix of a few adjectives and of substantives with concrete meaning; e. g. **tṛṣ-ṭá** *rough*, **śī-tá** *cold*; **dū-tá** m. *messenger*, **gár-ta** m. *car-seat*, **már-ta** m. *mortal*, **hás-ta** m. *hand*; **ghṛ-tá** n. *ghee*, **nák-ta** n. *night*; with connecting **i**: **ás-i-ta** *black*, **pal-i-tá** *grey*, **róh-i-ta** *red.*

ti: chiefly f. action nouns; e. g. **iṣ-ṭí** *desire*, **ū-tí** *aid* (√**av**), **kīr-tí** *praise* (**kṛ** *commemorate*), **rā-tí** *gift*; **íṣ-ṭi** *offering*, **gá-ti** *motion*, **dā́-ti**[1] *gift*; **dī́dhi-ti** *devotion* (**dhī** *think*); **aṃh-a-tí** *distress*, **ám-a-ti** *indigence*. It also forms some twenty agent nouns used either as adjectives or as m. substantives; e. g. **rā-tí** *willing to give*, **váṣ-ṭi** *eager*; **jñā-tí** m. *relative*, **dṛ́-ti** m. *skin*, **dhū́-ti** m. *shaker*, **múṣ-ṭi** m. *fist*, **sáp-ti** m. *steed*, **abhi-ṣṭí** m. *helper* (but **abhí-ṣṭi** f. *help*); **ám-a-ti** *poor*, **ar-a-tí** m. *servant*, **vṛk-á-ti** m. *murderer*.

tu: chiefly forms the stem of dat., abl.-gen., and acc. infinitives; e. g. **dā́-tu**: D. **dā́-tave** and **dā́tavái**; Ab.G. **dā́-tos**; A. **dā́-tum**; also a few independent action nouns and still fewer agent nouns: **ó-tu** m. *weft* (**vā** *weave*), **tán-tu** m. *thread*; **ak-tú** m. *ray* (**añj** *anoint*), **ṛ-tú** m. *season*, **jan-tú** m. *creature*; **vás-tu** f. *morning* (**vas** *shine*); **vā́s-tu** n. *abode* (**vas** *dwell*: Gk. *ἄσ-τυ*).

tṛ: agent nouns, often used participially governing an acc. (when the root is generally accented); e. g. **gán-tṛ** *going to* (acc.), but **kar-tṛ́** m. *doer*, **yaṣ-ṭṛ́** *sacrificer* (√**yaj**), **uṣ-ṭṛ́** *ploughing bull*; less commonly with connecting vowel: **cod-i-tṛ́** *instigator*, **sav-i-tṛ́** *stimulator*; **ā-mar-ī-tṛ́** *destroyer*; **tár-u-tṛ** *winning*, **tar-u-tṛ́** m. *conqueror*; **var-ū-tṛ́** *protector*; **man-ó-tṛ** and **man-o-tṛ́** *inventor*. This suffix also forms several names of relationship; e. g. **pi-tṛ́** m. *father*, **mā-tṛ́** f. *mother* (101).

tnu forms more than a dozen agent nouns, mostly adj.; e. g. **kṛ-tnú** *active*; **pīy-a-tnú** *reviling*; **māday-i-tnú** *intoxicating*, **stanay-i-tnú** m. *thunder*.

tra: agent nouns, a few of them adjectives, the rest nearly all n. substantives, expressing the instrument or means;

[1] This word when the final number of a compound is reduced by syncope to tti: **bhága-tti** f. *gift of fortune*, **maghá-tti** f. *receipt of bounty*, **vásu-tti** f. *receipt of wealth*.

e. g. **jái-tra** *victorious*, **yáj-a-tra** *adorable*; **kṣé-tra** n. *field*, **pā́-tra** n. *cup*, **vás-tra** n. *garment*; **khan-í-tra** n. *shovel*. There are also a few masculines, as **dáṃṣ-ṭra** *tusk* (**daṃś** *bite*), **mán-tra** *prayer*, **mi-trá** *friend* (but n. *friendship*).

trā: occurs a few times as the f. form of the preceding: **áṣ-ṭrā** *goad* (**aś** *reach*), **mā́-trā** *measure* (Gk. μέ-τρο-ν).

tha: action nouns, more often m. than n.; e. g. **gā-thá** m. *song*, **bhṛ-thá** m. *offering*, **rá-tha** m. *car*, **há-tha**, m. *slaughter*; **ár-tha**[1] n. *goal*, **uk-thá** n. *saying* (√**vac**), **tīr-thá** n. *ford* (√**tṝ** *cross*), **rik-thá** n. *inheritance* (√**ric**); with connecting vowel: **uc-á-tha** n. *praise*, **stav-á-tha** m. *praise*.

thā: occurs a few times as the f. form of **tha**: **kā́ṣ-ṭhā** *course*, **gā́-thā** *song*, **nī́-thā** *trick*.

na: besides ordinarily forming perf. pass. participles (160, 1) appears as the suffix of a number of adjectives (f. **nā**) and substantives, the latter mostly m., a few n.; e. g. **uṣ-ṇá** *hot*, **kṛṣ-ṇá** *black*, **nag-ná** *naked*; **budh-ná** m. *bottom*, **yaj-ñá** m. *sacrifice*, **vár-ṇa** m. *colour*; **par-ṇá** n. *wing*, **vas-ná** n. *price*.

nā: as the f. form of **na** makes a few substantives: **tṛ́ṣ-ṇā** *thirst*, **dhé-nā** *cow*, **sé-nā** *missile*, **sthū́-ṇā** *post*.

ni: m. and f. action and agent nouns (some of the latter adj.): **yó-ni** m. *receptacle*, **jūr-ṇí** f. *heat*; **pṛ́ś-ni** *speckled*, **pre-ṇí** *loving* (√**prī**), **bhū́r-ṇi** *excited*; **ag-ní** m. *fire*, **váh-ni** m. *draught animal*.

nu: action and agent nouns (including some adjectives), nearly always m.; e. g. **kṣep-ṇú** m. *jerk*, **bhā-nú** m. *light*, **sū-nú** m. *son*; **dhe-nú** f. *cow*; **dā́-nu** n. *drop* (m. f. *demon*).

ma: adj. and (almost exclusively m.) substantives; e. g. **jih-má** *oblique*, **śag-má** *mighty*; **idh-má** m. *fuel*, **ghar-má** m. *heat*, **stó-ma** m. *praise*, **hi-má** m. *cold*; **bíl-ma** n. *chip*; **hí-mā** f. *winter*.

man: action nouns (very numerous), most of which are n.

---

[1] **ártha** occurs often in the RV., but appears only three times (in Maṇḍala X) as a m.; in the later language it is m. only.

accented on the root, while a good many are m. accented on the suffix; e.g. **áj-man** n. *course* (Lat. *ag-men*), **nā́-man** n. *name* (Lat. *no-men*), **bhū́-man** n. *world*, **śás-man** n. *praise* (Lat. *car-men*); **ján-i-man** n. *birth*; **vár-ī-man** n. *expanse*; **bhū-mán** m. *abundance*, **vid-mán** m. *knowledge*, **prath-i-mán** m. *breadth*; also a few rarely used m. agent nouns, mostly accented on the suffix; e.g. **vad-mán** m. *speaker*, **sad-mán** m. *sitter*; **áś-man** m. *stone* (Gk. ἄκ-μων); **jé-man** *victorious*; some of these differ in accent only from corresponding n. action nouns (cp. **as**): **dā-mán** m. *giver*: **dā́-man** n. *gift*; **dhar-mán** m. *ordainer*: **dhár-man** n. *ordinance*; **brah-mán** m. *priest*: **bráh-man** n. *worship*; **sad-mán** m. *sitter*: **sád-man** n. *seat*.

mi: adj. and m. (also one f.) subst.: **jā-mí** *related*; **ūr-mí** m. *wave*, **raś-mí** m. *ray*; **bhū́-mi** f. *earth*.

mī: a few f. substantives: **bhū́-mī** *earth*, **lakṣ-mī́** *sign*, **sūr-mī́** *tube*.

yu: a few adjectives and m. substantives: **yáj-yu** *pious*, **śundh-yú** *pure*, **sáh-yu** *strong*; **man-yú** m. *anger*, **mṛt-yú** m. *death*; **dás-yu** m. *enemy*, **śím-yu** m. *enemy*.

ra: many adjectives, mostly accented on the suffix; e.g. **ug-rá** *mighty*, **pat-a-rá** *flying*, **aj-i-rá** *swift*; **gṛ́dh-ra** *greedy*; **víp-ra** *inspired*; also several substantives of different genders (f. **rā**); e.g. **kṣu-rá** m. *razor*, **vam-rá** m. *ant*; **khad-i-rá** m. a tree; **áj-ra** m. *field* (Gk. ἀγ-ρό-ς), **váj-ra** m. *thunderbolt*, **śū́-ra** m. *hero*; **abh-rá** n. *cloud*, **kṣī-rá** n. *milk*; **ág-ra** n. *point*, **rándh-ra** n. *hollow*; **śár-ī-ra** n. *body*; **dhā́-rā** f. *stream*, **sú-rā** f. *intoxicating liquor*.

ri: adj. and m. f. subst.; e.g. **bhū́-ri** *abundant*, **vádh-ri** *emasculated*; **jás-u-ri** *exhausted*; **áṅgh-ri** m. *foot*, **sū-rí** m. *patron*; **áś-ri** f. *edge*, **ús-ri** f. *dawn*; **aṅg-ú-ri** f. *finger*.

ru: adj. and a few n. substantives: **cā́-ru** *dear* (Lat. *ca-ru-s*), **bhī-rú** *timid*; **pat-á-ru** *flying*; **vand-ā́-ru** *praising*; **san-é-ru** *obtaining*; **áś-ru** n. *tear*, **śmáś-ru** n. *beard*.

va: adj. and (mostly m.) substantives; e.g. **ūrdh-vá**

(Gk. ὀρθ-ό-ς), **pak-vá** *ripe*, **pū́r-va** *preceding*, **sár-va** *all* (Lat. *sal-vu-s*); **áś-va** m. *horse* (Lat. *eq-uu-s*), **sru-vá** m. *ladle*; **ám-ī-vā** f. *disease*.

van: adj. and subst. (mostly m., few n.); e.g. **ṝ́k-van** *praising*, **kṝ́t-van** *active*, **yáj-van** *sacrificing*; **ádh-van** m. *road*, **grā́-van** m. *stone*; **pár-van** n. *joint*.

sa: adj. and subst. (all genders); e.g. **gṝ́t-sa** *adroit*, **pṛk-ṣá** *dappled* (√**pṛc**); **mah-i-ṣá** *mighty*; **ṛj-ī-ṣá** *rushing*; **ar-u-ṣá** *red*; **út-sa** m. *fountain*, **drap-sá** m. *drop*, **púru-ṣa** m. *man*; **púr-ī-ṣa** n. *rubbish*; **man-ī-ṣā́** f. *devotion*.

snu: adj. (from root or caus. stem); e.g. **ji-ṣṇú** *victorious*; **vadh-a-snú** *murderous*; **car-i-ṣṇú** *wandering*; **māday-i-ṣṇú** *intoxicating*.

2. **Secondary nominal Suffixes.**

The great majority of these form adjectives with the general sense of *relating to* or *connected with*.

a: forms a large number of adjectives expressing the sense of relation to or connexion with the primitive word; many of them have in the m. become appellatives and in the n. abstract nouns. The first syllable in the great majority of instances is strengthened with Vṛddhi (the f. then always takes ī); e.g. **mā́rut-a** *relating to the Maruts* (**marút**); **dáiva** *divine* (**devá** *god*); **pā́rthiva** *earthly* (**pṛthiv-ī́** *earth*); **mānav-á** *belonging to man* (**mán-u**), m. *human being*; **tā́nv-a** *belonging to the body* (**tanū́**); **dāśarājñ-á** n. *battle of the ten kings* (**daśa-rājan**); **mā́ghon-a** n. *bountifulness* (**maghá-van** *bountiful*); without Vṛddhi: **bheṣaj-á** adj. *healing*, n. *medicine*; **sakhy-á** n. *friendship* (**sákhi** *friend*); **hotr-á** n. *office of priest* (**hótṛ**).

ā: forms the f. of adjectives which in m. and n. end in **a**; e.g. **návā** f., **náva** m. n. *new*; **priy-ā́** f., **priy-á** m. n. *dear*; **gatā́** f., **gatá** m. n. *gone*.

ānī: forms the f. of names of male beings in **a**, or f. personifications; e.g. **indr-ā́ṇī** *wife of Indra*, **mudgal-ā́nī**

wife of Mudgala; **araṇy-ānī́** *nymph of the Forest* (**áraṇya**); **ūrj-ā́nī** *Strength* (**ū́rj** *strength*).

āyana: forms m. patronymics with initial Vṛddhi; e.g. **kāṇv-āyana** *descendant of Kaṇva.*

i: forms m. patronymics, with initial Vṛddhi, from nouns in **a**; e.g. **páurukuts-i** *descendant of Purukutsa*; **sā́ṃvaraṇ-i** *descendant of Saṃvaraṇa.* Similarly formed is **sā́rath-i** m. *charioteer* (from **sa-rátha** *driving on the same chariot*).

in: forms numerous adjectives, in the sense of *possessing*, almost exclusively from stems in **a**; e.g. **ark-ín** *praising* (**ar-ká** *praise*); from other stems: **arc-ín** *radiant* (**arc-í** *beam*), **var-m-ín** *clad in armour* (**vár-man**); irregularly formed: **ret-ín** *abounding in seed* (**rét-as**), **hiraṇ-ín** *adorned with gold* (**híraṇ-ya**).

iya (= **ya** after conjunct consonants): forms adjectives of relation; e.g. **abhr-iyá** *derived from the clouds* (**abhrá**), **indr-iyá** *belonging to Indra*, **samudr-íya** *oceanic.*

ī: forms the f. of m. stems made with suffixes ending in consonants (95), or with **tṛ** (101 *e*), and often of stems in **u** (98 *c*) or in **a** (always when formed with Vṛddhi); e.g. **ad-at-ī́** *eating*, **av-i-tr-ī́** *protectress*, **pṛthv-ī́** *broad* (**pṛthú**), **dev-ī́** *goddess* (**dev-á**). Cp. 107.

īna: forms adjectives, chiefly expressive of direction, from the weak stem of derivatives in **añc**; e.g. **arvāc-ī́na** *turned towards* (**arvā́ñc** *hitherward*); also others expressing the general sense of relation; e.g. **viśvajan-ī́na** (AV.) *containing all kinds of people.*

īya: forms general adjectives, chiefly in the later Saṃhitās; e.g. **gṛhamedh-ī́ya** *relating to the domestic sacrifice*, **parvat-ī́ya** *mountainous*; **āhavan-ī́ya** *used for the oblation* (**ā-hávana**), as a m. *sacrificial fire* (AV.).

eya: forms m. patronymics as well as a few general adjectives; e.g. **ādit-eyá** m. *son of Aditi*; **páuruṣ-eya** *relating to man* (**púruṣa**).

ka: forms adjectives and diminutives; e.g. **ánta-ka** *making an end* (**ánta**), **dūra-ká** *distant*, **máma-ka** *my*; **pāda-ka** m. *little foot*, **rāja-ká** m. *kinglet*; with Vṛddhi and connecting i: **vā́sant-i-ka** *belonging to the spring* (**vasantá**). The f. of some of the diminutives is formed with **ikā**; e.g. **kumār-ikā́** f. *little girl* (**kumāra-ká** m. *little boy*).

tana and (its syncopated form) **tna**: form adjectives with a temporal sense from adverbs and prepositions; e.g. **nū́-tana** and **nū́-tna** *present* (**nū́** *now*); **sanā-tána** and **saná-tna** *eternal* (**sánā** *from of old*); **pra-tná** *ancient* (**prá** *before*).

tama: forms superlatives (from nominal stems and the prep. **úd**) and ordinals; e.g. **puru-táma** *very many*; **ut-tamá** *highest*; **śata-tamá** *hundredth*.

tara: forms comparatives from adjectives, substantives, and the prep. **úd**: **tavás-tara** *stronger*; **rathī́-tara** *better charioteer*; **út-tara** *higher*.

tā: forms abstract f. substantives with the sense conveyed by the English suffixes *-ship* and *-ness*; e.g. **bandhú-tā** *relationship*, **vasú-tā** *wealthiness*; **devá-tā** *divinity*, **puruṣá-tā** *human nature*.

tāti and (less often) **tāt**: form abstract f. substantives (like **tā**); e.g. **jyeṣṭhá-tāti** *superiority*, **sarvá-tāti** *complete welfare* (Lat. *salu-tāti-*); **devá-tāt** *divine service*, **sarvá-tāt** *completeness* (Lat. *salu-tāt-*).

tya: forms a few substantives and adjectives from adverbs and prepositions: **amā́-tya** m. *companion* (**amā́** *at home*); **ápa-tya** n. *offspring*; **ní-tya** *constant*, **níṣ-ṭya** *foreign* (**nís** *out*).

tva: forms n. abstract substantives (like **tā**); e.g. **amṛta-tvá** n. *immortality*, **maghavat-tvá** *liberality*.

tvana (= **tva-na**): forms n. abstract substantives (nearly all of them duplicates of others in **tva**); e.g. **jani-tvaná** *wifehood*, **sakhi-tvaná** *friendship*.

tha: forms a few ordinals as well as adjectives (from pronominal stems) with a general numerical sense; e.g.

catur-thá *fourth*, **saptá-tha** *seventh*; **kati-thá** *the how-manieth?*

nī: forms the f. of **páti** *lord* and of **paruṣá** *knotty*, as well as of several adjectives in **ta** denoting colours; thus **pát-nī** *mistress* (Gk. *πότ-νια*), **páruṣ-ṇī** a river; **é-ṇī** *variegated* (**é-ta**). In a few of the colour adjectives **nī** is substituted for the final **a**, while **k** takes the place of **t**; e. g. **ásik-nī** *black* (**ás-i-ta**).

bha: forms m. names of animals; thus **ṛṣa-bhá** and **vṛṣa-bhá** *bull*; **garda-bhá** and **rā́sa-bha** *ass*.

ma: forms superlatives (partly from prepositions) and a few ordinals; e. g. **ava-má** *lowest*; **madhya-má** *middlemost*; **nava-má** *ninth* (Lat. *novi-mu-s*), **daśa-má** *tenth* (Lat. *deci-mu-s*).

mant: forms adjectives in the sense of *possessing* from substantives (except stems in **ă**); e. g. **aśáni-mant** *possessing the thunderbolt*, **krátu-mant** *powerful*; **gó-mant** *rich in cows*, **cákṣuṣ-mant** *possessed of eyes*.

maya: forms adjectives (f. **ī**) in the sense of *consisting of*; e. g. **manas-máya** *spiritual*, **mṛn-máya** *made of clay* (**mṛ́d**).

mna: forms a few n. abstracts from nouns or particles: **dyu-mná** *brightness*, **su-mná** *welfare*.

ya: forms adjectives of relation, m. patronymics and n. abstracts. Most of the latter two classes take Vṛddhi of the first syllable, but only about one-fourth of the adjectives do so; e. g. **paśav-yà** *relating to cattle* (**paśú**); **ādityá** m. *son of Aditi*; **taugryá** m. *son of Tugra*, but also **túgr-ya**; **ā́dhipa-tya** n. *lordship* (**ádhipati** *overlord*).

ra: forms comparatives (from prepositions) and ordinary nouns, mostly adjectives; e. g. **áva-ra** *lower*; **dhūm-rá** *grey* (**dhūmá** *smoke*); **rath-i-rá** *riding in a car* (**rátha**).

la: forms adjectives and a few m. diminutives; e. g. **kapi-lá** (*monkey-coloured* =) *brown*, **bahu-lá** *abundant*; **vṛṣa-lá** m. *little man*, **śiśū́-la** m. *little child*.

vat: forms a few f. abstract substantives, almost exclusively from prepositions, expressing local position; e. g. **ud-vát** *height*, **ni-vát** *depth*.

van: forms adjectives in the sense of *possessing* and a few m. substantives; e. g. **maghá-van** *bountiful*, **śruṣṭī-ván** *obedient*, **samád-van** *warlike*; **áthar-van** m. *fire-priest*.

vant: forms adjectives, from every kind of nominal stem, in the sense of *possessing*; e. g. **áśvā-vant** and **áśva-vant** *owning horses*; **sákhi-vant** *having friends*; **víṣṇu-vant** *accompanied by Viṣṇu*; **rómaṇ-vant** *hairy*; **páyas-vant** *containing milk*. Some of these derivatives, especially those formed from pronominal stems, have the sense of *resembling*; e. g. **mā́-vant** *like me*; **nṛ-vánt** *manly*. From this sense is derived the use of the n. acc. as an adv. of comparison; e. g. **manuṣ-vát** *like Manus*.

vin: forms adjectives from stems ending in **a** (which is lengthened), ā, and **as**; e. g. **ubhayā-vín** *partaking of both* (**ubháya**), **aṣṭrā-vín** *obedient to the goad*, **yaśas-vín** *glorious*. Exceptionally formed are **dhṛṣad-vín** *bold* (**dhṛṣát**) and **vāg-vín** *eloquent* (**vā́c**).

śa: forms adjectives and m. substantives, sometimes without change of meaning; e. g. **éta-śa** *variegated* (**éta** *id.*), **yuva-śá** *youthful* (**yúvan** *id.*), **roma-śá** *hairy* (**róman** *hair*); **aṅku-śá** m. *hook*, **kalá-śa** m. *jar*.

183. The above lists of suffixes practically supply the **rules of gender** for the Vedic noun. These may be summarized as follows:

Speaking generally, bare roots as stems, if action nouns, are f., if agent nouns, m.

Derivative stems in **ā, ī, ū** are f.; stems in **a, t, n** may be m. or n.; stems in **i** and **u** may be of any gender.

a. **Feminine** are all stems formed with the suffixes **ā, ī,**[1] **ū; tā, tāt, tāti, ti,**[2] **trā.**

---

[1] Except seven m. stems in ī; see 100, I *b*.

[2] But when stems in ti appear as agent nouns they are m., and m. f. as adjectives.

b. **Neuter** are all stems formed with **is, tva, tvana,** and, unless adjectives[1] or agent nouns,[2] those formed with **ana, as, us.**

c. **Masculine** are (in so far as not used adjectivally) all stems formed with the suffixes **yu, va; āyana, i,**[3] **ka, bha, la.**

d. **Masc.** or **fem.** are stems formed with the suffixes **ni, nu, mi, tṛ**[4]; also stems formed with the bare root.[5]

e. **Masc.** or **neut.** are stems formed with the suffixes **a, ta, tha, na, una, ma, ya, ra, tya, tra, tu, an, man, van**; also adjectives formed with **in, vin, īna, īya, tana, tama, tara, maya, mant, vant.**

f. **Masc., fem., neut.** are stems formed with **i** or **u.**

B. Compounds.

184. **I. Verbal Compounds** are formed by combining roots with twenty prepositions and a few adverbs. The compound verb (which, however, in finite forms is actually compounded only in subordinate clauses when the preposition immediately precedes the verb) is conjugated like the simple verb. Thus **gam** *go* combines with **sam** *together* to **saṃ-gám** *go together, unite*; 3. s. **saṃ-gáchati.** The compound root can be used to form nominal stems by means of the primary suffixes enumerated above (182, 1); e. g. **saṃ-gam-á** m. *union.*

a. The prepositions which are compounded with roots are the following: **ácha** *towards,* **áti** *beyond,* **ádhi** *upon,* **ánu** *after,* **antár** *between,* **ápa** *away,* **ápi** *on,* **abhí** *against,* **áva** *down,* **ā́**[6] *near,* **úd** *up,* **ní** *down, into,* **nís** *out,* **párā** *away,*

---

[1] When they are of course m. as well as n.

[2] When they are m.

[3] In patronymics.

[4] Stems in **tṛ** are always m. when they are agent nouns.

[5] These when used as adj. are occasionally neuter.

[6] The preposition **ā** reverses the sense of verbs of going or giving; e. g. **ā-gám** *come,* **ā-dā́** *take.*

pári *around*, **prá** *forth*, **práti** *towards*, **ví** *asunder*, **sám** *together*.

b. A few adverbs are also compounded with a limited number of verbs:

áram *at hand* is combined with **kṛ** = *serve* (dat.), *prepare* (acc.); with **gam** = *serve*; with **bhū** = *serve, conduce to* (dat.).

āvís *openly* is combined with **as**, **bhū** and **kṛ** only; with the two former it means *become visible, appear*; e. g. **āvís sánti** *being manifest*; **āvír agnír abhavat** *Agni became manifest*; with **kṛ** it means *make visible*, e. g. **āvíṣ karta** *make manifest*.

tirás *aside* is combined with **bhū** *be* and **dhā**[1] *put* only; e. g. **mā́ tiró bhūt** *may it not disappear*.

purás *in front* is combined with **kṛ** *do* and **dhā** *put* only; e. g. **kṛṇótu rathám̐ puráḥ** *may he place* (our) *car in the forefront*.

śrád, an old word meaning *heart* (Gk. *καρδ-ία* and *κραδ-ίη*, Lat. *cord-*), having acquired the character of an adverb, is once combined with **kṛ** and often with **dhā** *put* in the sense of *put faith in, credit* (= Lat. *crēdo* for *cred-do*), but is nearly always separated from the verb by other words; e. g. **śrád asmai dhatta** *believe in him*; **śrád víśvā vā́ryā kṛdhi** *entrust all boons* (to us).

prā-dúr (*before the door*) begins to appear in the AV. in combination with **bhū** = *become manifest, appear*.

c. A few substantives, after assuming an adverbial character, appear compounded, like verbal prefixes, with participial forms in the AV. These are: **ásta-m**[2] *home* with **i** *go*: **astam-yánt** *setting*, **astam-eṣyánt** *about to set*, **ástam-ita** *set*; **námas** *obeisance* with the gerund of **kṛ** *make*: **namas-kṛ́tya** *doing homage*.

---

[1] In the ŚB. and later **tirás** is also combined with **kṛ** *do*.

[2] This word is still a substantive in the RV.

In the RV. a few substantives designating parts of the body are compounded with the gerund of **grah** *seize*: **karṇa-gṛ́hya** *seizing by the ear*, **pāda-gṛ́hya** *seizing by the foot*, **hasta-gṛ́hya** *grasping by the hand*.

d. The interjection **híṅ** is compounded with **kṛ** in the sense of *utter the sound* **híṅ**, *murmur*; e. g. **hiṅ-kṛṇvatī́** *lowing*. There are also a few reduplicated interjectional words, mostly onomatopoetic and nearly always ending in **ā**, that appear compounded with **bhū** and **kṛ**: **alalā-bhávant** *sounding merrily*; **jañjanā-bhávant** *sparkling*; **malmalā-bhávant** *glittering*; **bharbharā́-bhavat** *became confounded*; **bibibā-bhávant** *crackling*; **kikirā́ kṛṇu** *tear to tatters*; **maṣmaṣā́ karam** *I have crushed*; **masmasā́ kuru** and **mṛsmṛsā́ kuru** *crush*; **akhkhalī-kṛ́tya** *croaking*.

a. The latter compound is the only example in the RV. of **ī** appearing instead of **ā** before **kṛ** or **bhū**. The AV. has **vātī́-kṛta** n. a disease (from **vā́ta** *wind*).

II. Nominal Compounds.

185. From the Indo-European period the Vedic language has inherited the power of combining two or more words into one treated like a simple word as regards accent, inflexion, and construction. Both in the frequency and in the length of compounds the Vedic language resembles the Greek of Homer. In the RV. and the AV. no compounds of more than three independent members are met with, and those in which three occur are rare, such as **pūrva-kāma-kṛ́tvan** *fulfilling former wishes*.

The two characteristic features of a compound are unity of accent and employment of the uninflected stem in the first member (or members); but there are exceptions to both these rules. Occasionally tmesis of a compound occurs.[1]

---

[1] Chiefly in dual compounds, as **dyā́vā ha kṣā́mā** *heaven and earth*; also in a few others, as **nárā vā śáṃsam**, for **nárā-śáṃsam**. It takes place only when the compound is doubly accented.

The Sandhi between the members is, moreover, sometimes different from that between words in a sentence.

a. The gender of compounds, if they end in substantives, is with few exceptions that of the last member; the gender of collectives is always neuter. The number in compounds depends on the sense; that in collectives is always singular. When the word appearing as the first member has two stems, the weak stem is used; when it has three, the middle stem (73 *a*). In substantive compounds the last member retains, as a rule, its gender, form, and inflexion; while in adjectival compounds the gender and inflexion of the last member are of course variable.

b. **Classification.** Vedic compounds may be divided into three main classes according to their syntactical relations: 1. **Co-ordinatives**, or those in which the members are co-ordinated; 2. **Determinatives**, or those in which the first member determines or limits the sense of the last; 3. **Possessives**, or adjectives the general meaning of which implies possession (as **bahv-anná** *possessing much food*). To these must be added, in order to classify Vedic compounds exhaustively, three lesser groups: 4. **Governing compounds**, or adjectives in which the first member governs the last in sense (as **kṣayád-vīra** *ruling men*); 5. **Syntactical compounds**, or irregular formations arising from the juxtaposition of two words in a sentence; 6. **Iteratives**, or repeated words treated as compounds in the Saṃhitās inasmuch as they have only one accent and a special meaning when thus combined.

1. Co-ordinative (Dvandva)[1] Compounds.

186. These consist of two substantives, far less commonly adjectives, connected in sense with 'and'.

---

[1] This term applied to co-ordinatives by the later Hindu grammarians, means *pair* or *couple*.

A 1. The most numerous group (about three-fourths of all the Dvandvas) in the Rigveda comprises those compounds (nearly always names of deities) in which **each member is dual** in form and has a separate accent; e. g. **mitrā́-váruṇā** *Mitra and Varuṇa*; **mātárā-pitárā** *mother and father*; **dyā́vā-pṛthivī́** *heaven and earth*. In the RV. the two duals are often separated, as in the line **ā́ náktā barhíḥ sadatām uṣā́sā** *let Night and Dawn seat themselves upon the litter*. The proper genitive of such compounds is e. g. **mitráyor váruṇayoḥ**. But as these co-ordinate duals early came to be regarded as a unit, the commonest ending of the first member, that of the N. A., came to be retained unaltered in the other cases: G. **mitrā́-váruṇayoḥ**, I. **mitrā́-váruṇābhyām**. A further step towards unification is taken in a minority of cases in which the first member loses its accent and the last syllable of the final member (irrespectively of its original accent) receives the acute, as **sūryā-candramás-ā** *sun and moon* (**candrá-mas**). The last stage in the Rigveda appears in four examples in which the first member assumes the stem-form, e. g. **indra-vāyū́** *Indra and Vāyu*. In the later Saṃhitās and in B. this is the prevailing type in new formations, e. g. **dakṣa-kratū́** m. *will and understanding* (TB.).

2. Another type is represented by the **plural Dvandvas**[1] which express pairs of groups. These show the stem-form in the first member and the accent on the final syllable of the last. The only examples in the RV. occur in Book X; e. g. **aho-rātrā́ṇi**[2] *days and nights*, **ajāváyas** *goats* (**ajá**) *and sheep* (**ávi**); but in the later Saṃhitās this type becomes quite general, e. g. **bhadra-pāpā́ḥ** (AV.), *the good and the bad*.[3]

---

[1] Cp. Latin *su-ove-taurilia*, a later type representing three groups.

[2] This Dvandva shows a double irregularity: the gender of the first member has prevailed over that of the second, and the f. stem **rātrī** has been changed to **rātra**.

[3] Several of the cardinal numerals are old Dvandvas, e. g. **dvā́-daśa** *twelve* (*two and ten*), **dvā́** being an old dual; **tráyo-daśa** *thirteen* (*three and ten*).

3. There occur in the Saṃhitās a few **singular Dvandvas** which express a collective sense and are always neuter,[1] and accent the final syllable; e. g. **iṣṭā-pūrtám**[2] *what has been offered or given*; **kṛta‿akṛtám** (AV.) *what has been done and not done*; **keśa-śmaśrú** n. *hair and beard* (AV.); **bhadra-pāpám** (AV.) *good and evil*; **samiṣṭa-yajús** (VS.) *sacrifice and sacrificial formula.*

B. Dvandvas consisting of adjectives are rare. They are of three types:

1. The adjectives designate colours, their combination expressing a mixture of the two, as **nīla-lohitá** *dark blue and red = dark red.*

2. They express a contrast, as **utkūla-nikūlá** (VS.) *going uphill and downhill.*

3. They are used with dual substantives to express that each is an attribute of one unit of the kind, as **pad-bhyā́ṃ dakṣiṇa-savyā́bhyām** (AV.) *with the two feet, the right and the left.*

a. The old dual Dvandvas (A 1) are frequently represented by elliptical duals which put one of a pair in the dual to express both, as **dyā́vā** = *heaven and earth*; **mitrā́** = *Mitra and Varuṇa*; **pitárā** = *father and mother*; **mātárā** = *mother and father, parents.*

2. Determinatives.

187. This numerous class of compounds comprises two groups. In the larger group (2 *a*) the first member has the value of a substantive dependent, in the sense of an oblique case, on the second, which may be either a verbal noun or an ordinary substantive. This may be called the dependent determinative group (named Tatpuruṣa by the later Hindu grammarians). In the other group (2 *b*) the final member,

---

[1] Cf. the Greek νυχθήμερον.

[2] Originally doubtless **iṣṭā́pūrtā́**, dual in both members.

if an ordinary substantive, is described adjectivally, or, if a verbal noun, adverbially, by the first member. This may be called the descriptive determinative group (called Karmadhāraya by the later Hindu grammarians).

2 *a*. Dependent (Tatpuruṣa) Determinatives.

A. The first member (substantive or pronoun) may have the sense (and often even the form) of any oblique case. When it has an acc., inst., abl., or loc. sense, the final member is mostly a verbal noun;[1] when it has a dat.[2] or gen.[3] sense, it is always an ordinary noun.[4] The compound may be a substantive or an adjective, according as the last member is one or the other.

1. In acc. dependents the final member is always a verbal noun; e.g. **havir-ád** *eating the oblation*; **go-ghná** *cow-slaying*, **aśva-hayá**[5] *urging on steeds*; **deva-mā́dana** *exhilarating the gods*; **gara-gīrṇá** (AV.)[6] *having swallowed poison*; **bhūri-dā́van** *giving much*; **bhadra-vādín** *uttering an auspicious cry*; **vā́ja-sāti** f. *act of winning booty*; **vṛtra-hátya** n. *act of slaying Vṛtra*.

2. Inst.: **indra-pā́tama** *most drunk by Indra*; **agni-dagdhá** *burnt with fire*; **devá-tta**[7] *given by the gods*; **aritra-páraṇa**, adj. *crossing with oars*; **tanū́-śubhra** *shining* (*with* =) *in body*; **bala-vijñāyá** *to be recognized by his strength*.

---

[1] The subdivision ending in verbal nouns may be called 'verbal dependents'.

[2] Examples of this sense are very rare. The final member is an ordinary adjective or substantive.

[3] The final member of genitive dependents is always an ordinary substantive.

[4] The subdivision ending in ordinary substantives may be called 'nominal dependents'.

[5] Cf. Greek *ἱππό-δαμο-ς horse-taming*.

[6] An example of the rare use of a past pass. part. in a transitive sense.

[7] tta for datta (160, 2 *b*).

3. Dat.: **vakmarā́ja-satya** *faithful to the ordainers of hymns*; **viśvá-śambhū** *salutary for all.*

4. Abl.: **go-jā́** *produced from cows*; **tīvra-sú-t** *pressed from the fermenting mass.*

5. Gen. (the commonest sense): **rāja-putrá** *king's son*; **viś-páti** *lord of the clan*; **deva-kilbiṣá** m. *offence against the gods*;[1] **dru-padá** n. *post of wood.*[2]

6. Loc.: **áhar-jāta** (AV.) *born in the day*; **uda-plutá** (AV.) *swimming in the water*; **puru-bhū́** *being in many places*; **bandhu-kṣít** *dwelling among relatives.*

a. In their first member many dependent compounds retain the case-ending, most commonly the acc., often the loc., but the rest rarely. Sing. endings (acc. and inst.) may express a plur. sense. Plur. endings (acc. and loc.) sometimes occur, but du. endings never in these compounds.

The **acc.** generally expresses the object of a transitive verb. The form in **am** is, in the RV., the rule before the verbal nouns **-kara** *making*, **-caya** *collecting*, **-jaya** *conquering*, **-tara** *overcoming*, **-dara** *cleaving*, **-bhara** *bearing*, **-ruja** *breaking*, **-sani** *winning*, **-saha** *overwhelming*; e.g. **abhayaṃ-kará** *procuring security*, **dhanaṃ-jayá** *winning booty*, **pur-aṃ-dará**,[3] *destroying forts*, **sutaṃ-bhará**[4] *receiving pressed Soma*; it also occurs before other verbal nouns, not infrequently before such as begin with vowels; e.g. **dhiyaṃ-dhā́** *devout*, **viśvam-invá** *all-moving*, **áśvam-iṣṭi**[3] *seeking horses*. An example of a cognate acc. is **śubhaṃ-yā́** *moving in brilliance*, and of an adverbial acc., **ugraṃ-paśyá** (AV.) *looking fiercely*. Examples of an acc. pl. ending are **kā-cit-kará** *doing all manner of things*; **páśva-iṣṭi**[5] *desiring kine.*

---

1 An example of an objective genitive.

2 Here the genitive expresses the material.

3 The singular acc. form with plural sense.

4 Also im in **puṣṭiṃ-bhará** *bringing prosperity* and **hariṃ-bhará** *bearing the tawny* (bolt).

5 This and **áśvam-iṣṭi** are Tatpuruṣa possessives (189, 2).

Inst.: **girā-vṛ́dh** *rejoicing in song*; **śúneṣita** *driven by dogs*[1] (**śúnā**); **vidmanā́pas** *working* (**apás**) *with wisdom* (**vidmánā**); **kṣudhā-mārá** (AV.) m. *death by hunger*; **vācā́-stena**[2] *thief by speech, secretly injuring by words.*

Dat.: the only example seems to be found in the loose syntactical compound **dásyave vṛ́ka** *wolf to the Dasyu*, used as a proper name.

Abl.: **divo-jā́** *produced from heaven*; **divo-rúc** *shining from the sky.*

Gen.: very common before **páti** *husband* or *lord*, as **gnā́-s-páti** *husband of a divine woman*; **jā́-s-páti** *lord of a family*; **bráhmaṇas-páti** *lord of prayer.*[3] It also occurs in the proper names **dívo-dāsa** *servant of heaven* and **śúnaḥ-śépa** *Dog's-tail.*

Loc.: common in the RV. before agent nouns formed from the simple root; e. g. **divi-yáj** *worshipping in heaven*; **rathe-ṣṭhā́** *standing on a car*; also before several formed with **a**; e. g. **divi-kṣayá** *dwelling in heaven.* There are also several examples of plurals, as **apsu-ṣád** *dwelling in the waters*; **goṣu-yúdh** *fighting in* (= *for*) *kine*; **hṛtsv-ás** *piercing the heart.* The singular also occurs a few times before an ordinary adj. or subst., as **máde-raghu** *quick in exhilaration*; **svapne-duḥṣvapnyá** (AV.) n. *evil dream in sleep.*

a. If a root forms the last member of a Tatpuruṣa, final long vowels (**ā, ī, ū**) undergo no change, while short vowels[4] (**i, u, ṛ**) usually add a determinative **t**; e. g. **agre-pā́** *drinking first*; **yajña-nī́** *leading the*

---

[1] Singular ending with plural sense.

[2] A rare example of an inst. with an ordinary substantive as final member.

[3] By the false analogy of these words are also formed from a stems **ṛta-s-pati** *lord of pious works* and **rátha-s-páti** *lord of the car.* **Dám-pati** *lord of the house* probably = **dám-s-pati.**

[4] Radical **a**, as a shortened form of **ā**, often appears as a final, hciefly in the later Saṃhitās, as **agre-gá** *going in front*, **nāma-dhá** (AV.) *name-giving.*

sacrifice; **rāja-sú** *king-creating*; but **divi-kṣí-t** *dwelling in heaven*; **soma-sú-t** *Soma-pressing*; **jyotiṣ-kṛ́-t** *light-creating*. There is, however, no t added in **vanar-gú** *forest-roaming*.[1]

2 *b*. Descriptive (Karmadhāraya)[2] Compounds.

188. This class of Determinatives is comparatively rare in the Saṃhitās. The last member is generally an ordinary substantive, but is sometimes a verbal or an ordinary adjective. The relation of the first member to the last is appositional, attributive, or adverbial. It is expressed in three ways:

1. **By a Substantive.** If followed by a subst., it has an attributive sense equivalent to an adj. expressing sex or a compound nature; e. g. **puruṣa-mṛgá** (VS.) m. (*man* =) *male antelope*; **úlūka-yātu** m. *owl demon*, i. e. demon in form of an owl; **puruṣa-vyāghrá** (VS.) m. *man-tiger*, a kind of demon; **vṛṣā́-kapi** m. *man-ape*.

If followed by a verbal adj., the preceding subst. is usually appositional in sense; e. g. **īśāna-kṛ́t** *acting as a ruler*; **stóma-taṣṭa** *fashioned as a hymn of praise*. But sometimes it is adverbial; e. g. **ṛtv-íj** *sacrificing in season = regularly*; **sárga-takta** *speeding with a rush*.

a. Before a verbal noun a substantive sometimes implies a comparison; e. g. **dhāra-vāká** *sounding like a stream*, **śyená-jūta** *speeding like an eagle*. Similarly before an ordinary adjective: **śúka-babhru** (VS.) *reddish like a parrot*.

2. By an **Adjective**. If followed by an ordinary subst., the adj. has the usual attributive sense; e. g. **candrá-mās** m. (*bright*) *moon*; **kṛṣṇa-śakuní** (AV.) m. *raven* (lit. *black*

---

[1] Final u sometimes appears as a shortened form of ū in some Tatpuruṣas, as **dhī-jú** *inspiring the mind*; **puru-bhú** *appearing in many places*.

[2] This is the term applied to this class of compounds by the later Hindu grammarians.

bird); **nava-jvārá** m. *new pain*; **mahā-grāmá**[1] m. *great host*; **yāvayat-sakhá** m. *protecting friend.*[2] Sometimes the qualifying adj. indicates a part of what the last member expresses; e. g. **adhara-kaṇṭhá** (VS.) m. *lower* (part of the) *neck*; **ardha-devá** m. *demi-god*; **pūrvāhṇá**[3] m. *forenoon*; **madhyám-dina**[4] m. *midday.*

If followed by a verbal noun, the preceding adj. is adverbial in sense;[5] e. g. **āśu-pátvan**[6] *swift-flying*, i. e. *flying swiftly*; **āśu-héman** *swiftly-speeding*; **sana-jā́** *born of old* (= **sánā**); **satya-yáj** *sacrificing truly* (= **satyám**), **dvi-já** (AV.) *born twice.*[7] Similarly before ordinary adjectives: **viśvá-ścandra** *all-glittering*; **hári-ścandra** *glittering yellow*; **try-àruṣa**[7] (AV.) *ruddy in three places.*

a. At the end of Karmadhārayas the final n of an stems is dropped[8] in **eka-vṛṣá** (AV.) m. *only bull*, **mahā-vṛṣá** (AV.) m. *great bull*, **bhadrāhá**[9] (AV.) n. *auspicious day.*

3. By an **Adverb** (inclusive of particles and prepositions): **akṣṇayā-drúh** *injuring wrongly*; **amutra-bhū́ya** (AV.) n. *state of being there*; **evā́ra** *quite* (**evá**) *ready* (**ára**); **púnarnava** *renewing itself*; **punar-bhū́** *arising again*; **puro-yā́van** *going before*; **puró-hita** *placed in front*; **sató-mahat** *equally* (**sa-tás**) *great*; **satyám-ugra** *truly mighty*; **sāyam-bhavá**

---

[1] As first member of Karmadhārayas (and Bahuvrīhis) **mahát** appears as **mahā**; but the AV. has **mahat-kāṇḍá** *great section.*

[2] Here **sákhi** *friend* becomes **sakha**. Cf. 189, 4 *d* and 189 A. 2 *a.*

[3] Here **áhan** *day* is syncopated and extended with **a**; also in **aparāhṇá** (AV.) *afternoon*, **ny-áhn-a** (AV.) *decline of day.*

[4] With case-ending retained in the first member.

[5] The sense is rather appositional in **pūrva-pā́** *drinking* (as) *first*, **vāmá-jāta** *born as one dear*, i. e. *dear by nature.*

[6] Cf. Gk. ὠκυ-πέτης *swift-flying.*

[7] Here the cardinals are used for the numeral adverbs **dví-s**, **trí-s**.

[8] This is much commoner in Bahuvrīhis (189, 4).

[9] Also in **ṣaḍ-ahá** (AV.) m. *period of six days* (189, 4).

(AV.) m. *becoming evening*; **paścā[1]-dośá** (VS.) m. *later part of the evening*; **idā-vatsará**[1] (AV.) m. *the present year*; **puró-agni**[1] (VS.) m. *fire in front*; **su-dā́** *giving willingly*; **duḥ-śéva** *unfavourable*; **a-mítra** m. *non-friend, enemy*; **su-vasaná** n. *fair garment*; **áti-kṛṣṇa** *excessively dark*; **prá-ṇapāt** m. *great grandson*; **adhi-rājá** m. *supreme king*; **prá-vīra** m. *great hero*; **saṃ-vatsará** m. *full year*.

3. Possessive (Bahuvrīhi) Compounds.

189. These compounds are secondary adjectives. They are determinatives (generally Karmadhārayas), ending in substantives, which have been transformed into adjectives agreeing in gender, number, and case with another substantive expressed or understood. The transformation is accompanied by a shift of accent from the final member to the first. The term 'possessive' is probably the most appropriate as applied to these compounds, for it expresses their general meaning in the vast majority of cases; in a few instances the more comprehensive sense of 'connected with' is required to indicate the relation between the substantive and the Bahuvrīhi compound agreeing with it; e.g. **viśvā́-nara** *belonging to all men*. Possessives are of two kinds:

1. **Karmadhāraya Possessives**, in which the first member is an attributive adj. (including participles), an appositional subst., or an adverb (including particles and prepositions): e.g. **ugrá-bāhu** *powerful-armed*; **hatá-mātṛ** *whose mother has been slain*; **rúśad-vatsa** *having a shining calf*; **áśva-parṇa** *horse-winged*, i.e. *whose wings are horses*; **índra-śatru** *having Indra as a foe*; **rājá-putra** *having kings as sons*; **híraṇya-nemi** *whose fellies are* (made of) *gold*; **aṣṭā́-pad**[2] *eight-footed*, **dvi-pád**[3] *two-footed*; **itthā́-dhī** *having such thought, devout*; **puro-rathá** *whose car is in front*; **ví-grīva** *wry-necked*;

[1] Here the adverbs preceding ordinary substantives are = adjectives.

[2] Gk. ὀκτώ-ποδ-.

[3] Lat. *bi-ped-*.

an-udrá[1] *waterless*; **a-pád** *footless*; **kú-yava** *causing a bad harvest*; **duṣ-pád** *ill-footed*; **su-parṇá** *beautiful-winged.*

a. In some possessives based on appositional Karmadhārayas a comparison of the first with the final member is implied; e. g. **varṣā́jya** (AV.) *whose rain is* (like) *butter*; **vṛkṣá-keśa** *whose trees are* (like) *hair*, *tree-haired* = *wooded* (mountain).

b. The superlatives **jyéṣṭha** *chief* and **śréṣṭha** *best*, the comparative **bhū́yas** *more*, and **pára** *higher*, are used substantively as final member of possessives: **índra-jyeṣṭha** *having Indra as chief*, **yamá-śreṣṭha** (AV.) *of whom Yama is best*, **ásthi-bhūyāṃs** (AV.) *having bone as its chief part* = *chiefly bone*, **avara-s-pará**[2] (VS.) *in which the lower is higher, topsy-turvy.*

2. In **Tatpuruṣa Possessives** the first member most commonly has a gen., not infrequently a loc., but rarely an inst. or acc. sense. The case-ending is in several instances retained. Examples are: **rāyás-kāma** *having a desire for wealth*; **diví-yoni** *having* (*his*) *origin in heaven*; **bhāsá-ketu** *recognizable by light*; **tvā́ṃ-kāma** *having a desire for thee.*

a. In possessives based on gen. Tatpuruṣas, the first member often implies a comparison, but never with a case-ending; as **agní-tejas** (AV.) *having the brightness of fire*, *fire-bright*; **ṛ́kṣa-grīva** *bear-necked*; **gó-vapus** *cow-shaped*; **máno-java** *having the swiftness of thought*, *swift as thought*; **mayū́ra-roman** *having the plumes of peacocks.*

b. When a loc. sense is intended, parts of the body appear as the last member; e. g. **aśru-mukhá** (AV.) *having tears on her face*, *tear-faced*; **ghṛtá-pṛṣṭha** *having butter on his back*, *butter-backed*; **pā́tra-hasta** (AV.) *having a vessel in his hand*; **maṇi-grīvá** *having pearls on the neck*; **mádhu-jihva** *having honey on his tongue*; **vájra-bāhu** *having a bolt on his arm.*

3. Bahuvrīhis come to be used substantively, when the noun with which they agree is dropped: thus **su-parṇá** *fair-winged*, m. *bird*. Of this use there are three applications:

a. These compounds very frequently appear as m., sometimes as f., proper names, the adjectival sense often not

---

[1] Gk. ἄν-υδρο-ς.

[2] Here the **s** of the nom. survives from the use of the two words in syntactical juxtaposition. Cp. the later **para-s-para** and **anyo-'nya.**

occurring at all. Thus **bṛhád-uktha** adj. *having great praise*, m. a seer; **bṛhád-diva** adj. *dwelling in high heaven*, m. a seer, f. **bṛhad-divā́** a goddess; m. as names only, **Priyá-medha** (*to whom sacrifice is dear*) and **Vāmá-deva** (*to whom the gods are dear*).

b. They appear not infrequently as n. substantives with an abstract (sometimes a collective) sense, especially when the first member is the privative particle **a-** or **an-**, or the adjective **sárva** *all*; e. g. **an-apatyá**, adj. *childless* (AV.), n. *childlessness*; **sarva-vedasá** (AV.) n. *whole property*; **ni-kilbiṣá** n. *deliverance from sin*; **mātṛ-bandhú** (AV.) n. *maternal kinship*.

c. With numerals, from **dvi** *two* upwards, as their first member, they form sing. neuters[1] (always ending in accented **á**) with a collective sense; e. g. **tri-yugá** n. *period of three lives*; **dvi-rājá** (AV.) n. *battle of two kings*; **daśāṅgulá** n. *length of ten fingers* (4 *d*).

4. The final member of Bahuvrīhis is liable to various changes tending to make it end in **a**.

a. The **n** of several words in **an**, **kárman**,[2] **dhā́man**, **nā́man**, **párvan**, **vṛ́ṣan**, **sakthán**, is frequently dropped in ordinary Bahuvrīhis, and that of **áhan** in numeral collectives; e. g. **viśvá-karma**[3] *performing all work*, **priyá-dhāma** *occupying desirable places*, **chando-nāmá** (VS.) *named metre, metrical*, **ví-parva**[4] *jointless*, **dvi-vṛṣá** (VS.) *having two bulls*, **lomaśá-saktha** (VS.) *having hairy thighs*; **ṣaḍ-ahá** (AV.) m. *period of six days*.

b. The suffixes **a** and **ya** are frequently added, and sometimes **ka**; e. g. **catur-akṣ-á** *four-eyed*, **su-gáv-a** *having fine cows*, **anyódar-ya** *born from another womb* (**udára**), **dáśa-mās-ya** *ten months old*, **mádhu-hast-ya** *honey-handed*, **try-àmba-ka** *having three mothers*, **ví-manyu-ka** (AV.) *free from anger*, **a-karṇá-ka** (TS.) *earless*.

c. The suffix **in** (*possessing*) is sometimes pleonastically added: **mahā-hast-ín** *having large hands*, **ku-nakh-ín** (AV.) *having bad nails*,

---

[1] Except those formed with **ahá** *day*, which are m., as **ṣaḍ-ahá** m. *series of six days*.

[2] But this word retains its n in seven compounds in the RV.

[3] But also **viśvá-karman**.

[4] But **a-parván** and **vṛ́ṣa-parvan**.

yaśo-bhag-ín (VS.) *rich in glory*, **sa-rath-ín** (VS.) *riding in the same chariot.*

d. **a** is substituted for **i** in **kavā-sakhá**[1] *having a niggard for a friend*, and in **daśāṅgulá** n. *length of ten fingers* (**aṅgúli**). On the other hand, **i** is substituted for **a** in some compounds of **gandhá** *smell*, and in a few others: **dhūmá-gandhi** *smelling of smoke*, **kṛṣṭá-rādhi** (AV.) *attaining success* (**rādha**) *in agriculture*, **práty-ardhi** *to whom the half* (**árdha**) *belongs.*

e. In the f. of Bahuvrīhis **páti** *husband* or *lord*, instead of remaining unchanged, takes the f. form of the subst. (**pátnī** *wife*) in **dāsá-patnī** *having a demon as master*, **devá-patnī** *having a god as a husband*, **vṛ́ṣa-patnī** *ruled by a mighty one*, **śū́ra-patnī** *having a hero as a husband.*

4. Governing Compounds.

189 A. In this class, which embraces a considerable number of compounds, the first member, being either a preposition or a verbal noun, governs the last in sense. They resemble Bahuvrīhis in form[2] as well as in their adjectival character.

1. In the prepositional group, in which about twenty examples occur in the RV., the first member is a preposition capable of governing a case; e.g. **ati-rātrá**[3] *lasting overnight*; **anu-kāmá** *according to wish*; **ā́-pathi** and **ā-pathí** *being on the way*; **paro-mātrá** *going beyond measure, excessive.*

a. Like Bahuvrīhis, compounds of this type may become substantives; e.g. **upānas-á** adj. *being on a wagon*, n. (AV.) *space on a wagon.*

b. The final member, when it does not end in **a**, adds the suffix **a**, and **ya** sometimes even when it already ends in **a**; e.g. **ánu-path-a** *going along the road*, **adhas-pad-á** *being under the feet*, **paró-kṣ-a** (AV.) *away from the eye* (**ákṣ**), **puro-gav-á** m. *leader* (*going before the cows*);

---

[1] Otherwise **sakhi** remains unchanged in both Bahuvrīhis and Karmadhārayas (but 188, 2) in the RV.; cp. 189, 2 *a*.

[2] But the meaning is entirely different; for in the prepositional class the first member has the sense of a prep. (not an adj.), and in the verbal class, it has a transitive (not an intransitive) sense. In the latter class the final syllable of a part. is always accented (but in Bahuvrīhis only when that is the natural accent).

[3] Here **rātrī** *night* becomes **rātra**, as in the Dvandva **aho-rātrá** n. *day and night.*

ádhi-gart-ya *being on the car-seat* (**gárta**), **antaḥ-parśav-yá** (VS.) *being between the ribs* (**párśu**), **úpa-mās-ya** (AV.) *occurring every month* (**mā́sa**), **tiró-ahn-ya** (*being beyond a day*), *belonging to the day* (**áhan**) *before yesterday*.

2. In the verbally governing class the first member is an agent noun or an action noun governing the last member as an object. With a single exception[1] they never add a suffix. Three types (in all of which examples of proper names occur) may be distinguished.

a. In the commonest type, which is almost restricted to the RV., the first member is a participle ending in **át** formed from transitive present stems in **a**, **á**, or **áya**; e. g. **ṛdhád-vāra**[2] *increasing goods*, **tarád-dveṣas** *overcoming* (**tárat**) *foes*, **dhārayát-kavi** *supporting the wise*, **mandayát-sakha**[3] *gladdening his friend*. The following are used as proper names: **ṛdhád-ray**[2] (*increasing wealth*), **jamád-agni**[4] (*going to Agni*), **bharád-vāja** (*carrying off the prize*).

b. Only three or four examples occur of a second type, in which the first member consists of a simple present stem (probably representing an imperative): **radā-vasu**[5] *dispensing wealth*, **śikṣā-nar-á**[6] *helping men*; as the name of a man: **trasá-dasyu** (*terrify the foe*).

c. Some half dozen examples occur in the RV. of a third type, in which the first member is an action-noun in **ti**: **dā́ti-vāra** *giving treasures*, **vītí-rādhas** *enjoying the oblation*, **vṛṣṭí-dyāv** *causing the sky to rain*; as the name of a man: **púṣṭi-gu** m. (*rearing kine*).

5. Syntactical Compounds.

189 B. A certain number of irregular compounds are formed in a manner differing from that of any of the four classes described above. They may be treated as a class, since all of them have been produced by the same cause: frequent syntactical juxtaposition in a sentence.

---

[1] **śikṣā-nar-á**; see below, note 6.

[2] **ṛdhát** aor. part. of **ṛdh** *increase*.

[3] **sakhi** *friend* becomes **sakha** in two other governing compounds: **drāvayát-sakha** *speeding his friend* and **śrāvayát-sakha** *making his friend famous*. Cf. 188, 2, note 2.

[4] **jamat** is a palatalized form of an aor. part. of **gam** *go*.

[5] In this and the following example the **a** of **radā** and **śikṣa** is metrically lengthened.

[6] Here the stem of the final member is extended with **a**.

a. The relative adverb **yád** (a nominally formed abl.) *in so far as* has come to be compounded with a superlative in the adj. **yāc-chreṣṭhá** *the best possible* (lit. *in so far as best*), and with a gerundive in the adv. **yād-rādhyàm** *as quickly as possible* (lit. *in so far as attainable*).

b. The initial words of a text begin to be compounded in the later Saṃhitās as a substantive to designate that text. Thus **ye-yajāmahá** (VS.) m., used in the N. pl., means the text beginning with the words **yé yájāmahe.**

c. Several subst. or adj. compounds have resulted from phrases consisting of two words in juxtaposition. Thus **aham-uttará** (AV.) n. *dispute for precedence* (from **ahám úttaraḥ** *I* am *higher*); **mama-satyá** n. *dispute as to ownership* (from **máma satyám** it is *certainly mine*); **māṃ-paśyá** (AV.) designation of an aphrodisiac plant (from **mā́ṃ paśya** *look at me*); **kuvít-sa** *some one* (from **kuvít sá** is *it he?*); **áhaṃ-sana** (voc.) *rapacious* (from **aháṃ sanā** *I will obtain*); **ahaṃ-pūrvá** *eager to be first* (from **aháṃ pūrváḥ** *I* should be *first*); **kiṃ-tvá** (VS.) *asking garrulously* (from **kíṃ tvám** *what* are *you* doing?).

6. Iterative Compounds.

189 C. Substantives, adjectives, pronouns, numerals, adverbs, and prepositions are often repeated. They are then treated as compounds, the second member losing its accent and the two words being written in the Pada text with the Avagraha between them, as in other compounds. This class resembles other compounds in having a single accent, but differs from them in having not the stem but the fully inflected form of nominal words in the first member. In the RV. the iteratives number over 140, rather more than half of them being substantives. The sense conveyed by the repetition is frequency, or constant succession in time, or distribution in space. Examples of the various kinds of iteratives are the following:

a. **Substantives: áhar-ahar,**[1] **divé-dive,**[2] **dyávi-dyavi** *every day*, **māsí-māsi** *month after month*; **gṛhé-gṛhe, dáme-dame, viśé-viśe**[2] *in every house*; **áṅgād-aṅgāt** *from every limb*; **diśó-diśaḥ** (AV.) *from every quarter*; **yajñásya-yajñasya** *of every sacrifice*; **párvaṇi-parvaṇi** *in every joint*; **agním-agnim (duvasyata)**, (*worship*) *Agni again and again*; **ánnam-annam** (AV.) *food in perpetuity*.

b. **Adjectives: pányaṃ-panyaṃ . . sómam** *Soma who is again and again to be praised*; **prā́cīṃ-prācīṃ pradíśam** *each eastern direction*; **úttarām-uttarāṃ sámām** (AV.) *each following year*.

c. **Pronouns: tváṃ-tvam aharyathāḥ** *thou didst ever rejoice*; **yád-yad yā́mi** *whatever I ask*; **tát-tad . . dadhe** *he always bestows that*.[3]

d. **Numerals: páñca-pañca** *five each time*; **saptá-sapta (tredhā́** *three times*) *seven in each case* (= 21).[4]

e. **Adverbs:**[5] **yáthā-yathā** *as in each case*; **adyā́dyā śváḥ-śvaḥ** *on each to-day, on each to-morrow*.

f. **Prepositions**: the four which are found used thus are **úpa, párā, prá, sám**; e.g. **prá-pra . . śasyate** *it is ever proclaimed*.

g. The only example of a verbal form occurring as an iterative is **píba-piba** *drink, drink*.[6] Otherwise a repeated verb is treated independently; e.g. **stuhí stuhí** *praise, praise*.

---

[1] **áhar-divi** *day after day*, is a kind of mixed iterative.

[2] For **diví-divi** and **viśí-viśi**, owing to the influence of the frequent loc. in **e** from **a** stems.

[3] In the ŚB. such words are repeated with **vā: yā́vad vā yāvad vā** and **yatamé vā yatame vā**.

[4] Such iteratives led to the formation of regular compounds in B.: **éka-ekaḥ** (AV.): **ékaikaḥ** (ŚB.); **dvā́-dvā** (RV.): **dvan-dvám** (MS.) *in twos*, **dvan-dvá** *pair* (B.).

[5] In a few instances repeated adverbs are not treated as compounds, both words being accented: **nū́ nú** *now, now*; **ihéhá** (AV.) *here, here*, but always **ihéha** in RV.

[6] In the ŚB. also occurs **yájasva-yajasva**.

CHAPTER VII

OUTLINES OF SYNTAX

190. Having in the preceding parts of the present grammar dealt with single words in their phonetic, their derivative, and their inflexional aspects, we now turn to their treatment in syntax, which regards their arrangement and mutual meaning when they are combined to form a sentence, which is the expression of a connected and definite unit of thought. The parts of which the sentence may consist are either inflected words: the noun (substantive and adjective) and the verb, the participle which shares the nature of both, and the pronoun; or uninflected words: prepositions, adverbs, and conjunctions. A comparison of the syntax of the RV. with that of classical Sanskrit shows (1) that the use of the middle voice, the tenses, the moods, the inflected participles, the infinitives, and the genuine prepositions is much fuller and more living in the former, while (2) that of the passive voice and of indeclinable participles is much less developed, that of absolute cases and of adverbial prepositions with case-endings is only incipient, and that of periphrastic verbal forms is non-existent. The later Saṃhitās and the Brāhmaṇas exhibit a gradual transition by restriction or loss in the former group and by growth in the latter to the condition of things prevailing in classical Sanskrit.

The Order of Words.

191. Since metrical considerations largely interfere with the ordinary position of words in the Saṃhitās, the normal order is best represented by the prose of the Brāhmaṇas, and as it there appears is, moreover, doubtless the original one.

The general rule is that the subject begins the sentence and the verb ends it, the remaining members coming between.

a. The **subject** begins the sentence; e. g. **víśaḥ kṣatríyāya balím haranti** *the peasants pay tribute to the prince* (ŚB.). It may, however, be preceded by a particle like **utá** or occasionally by any other member of the sentence intended to be strongly emphasized; e. g. **prayājáir vái devā́ḥ svargám lokám āyan** *by means of the Prayājas the gods went to the heavenly world* (ŚB.).

b. The **verb** occasionally moves to the beginning of the sentence when it is strongly emphasized; e. g. **yánti vā́ ā́pa, éty ādityá, éti candrámā, yánti nákṣatrāṇi** *the waters move, the sun moves, the moon moves, the stars move* (ŚB.). A predicative noun with the copula (which may be omitted) being equivalent to a verb, naturally occupies the same position; e. g. **sárve ha vái devā́ ágre sadṛ́śā āsuḥ** *all the gods in the beginning were similar* (ŚB.); **mitró vái śivó devā́nām** *Mitra, indeed,* is *the kindly one among the gods* (TS.). Nevertheless the predicative noun, being emphatic, is as a rule the first word in the sentence; e. g. **mártyā ha vā́ ágre devā́ āsuḥ** *the gods were originally mortals* (ŚB.); **púruṣo vái yajñáḥ** *the sacrifice* (is) *a man* (ŚB.).

c. As regards **the cases**, the acc. is placed immediately before the verb; e.g. **chándāṃsi yuktā́ni devébhyo yajñáṃ vahanti** *the metres, when they are yoked, take the sacrifice to the gods* (ŚB.). Adverbs and indeclinable participles occupy a similar position. Occasionally such words move to the beginning; e. g. **diví vái sóma ā́sīd, átha‿ihá devā́ḥ** *in heaven was Soma, but here the gods* (SB.).

d. The **apposition**, including patronymics and participles, follows the word which it explains or defines; e. g. **sómo rā́jā** *Soma, the King.* A participle, in its proper sense, if emphatic may be placed at the beginning; e. g. **svapántam vái dīkṣitám rákṣāṃsi jighāṃsanti** *it is when he sleeps that the Rakṣases seek to slay the initiated man* (TS.).

e. The **attribute**, whether adjective or genitive, precedes its substantive; e. g. **hiraṇyáyena ráthena** *with golden car* (i. 35²); **devā́nām hótā** *the priest of the gods.* Only when adjectives are used in apposition, especially as epithets of the gods, do they follow; e. g. **mitrā́ya satyā́ya** *to Mitra, the true* (TS.). Also adjectives designating the colours of certain animals, especially horses and cows, are found after the subst. The subst. belonging to a gen. is placed before the latter only when it is emphatic.

f. The **preposition** belonging to a verb precedes it, always in B., generally in V., where, however, it also sometimes follows; e. g. **jáyema sám yudhí spṛ́dhaḥ** *we would conquer our foes in battle* (i. 8³). The preposition as a rule immediately precedes the verb, but is often also separated from it by one or more words; e. g. **ā́ sā́yakam maghávā‿adatta** *the Bounteous One seized his missile* (i. 32³); **ápa támaḥ pāpmā́nam hate** *she drives away darkness and sin* (TS.). When a compound verb is emphatic, the preposition alone as a rule moves to the front óccupying the position that the simple verb would occupy; e. g. **prá prajáyā jāyeya** *I would increase with progeny* (TS.).

When used with substantives the genuine prepositions as a rule follow their case, while the prepositional adverbs precede it. The reason of this doubtless is that the former supplement the sense of the case, while the latter modify the sense much more emphatically.

g. **Multiplicative adverbs** precede their genitive; e. g. **tríḥ saṃvatsarásya** *three times a year.*

h. **Enclitics** cannot, of course, begin a sentence. If they belong to a particular word they follow it; otherwise they tend to occupy the second position in the sentence. The enclitic particles that follow the word with which they are most closely connected are **ca, vā, iva, cid**; **kam** is restricted to following **nú, sú, hí** in V., and **sma** to following **ha** in B. The other unaccented particles, **u, gha, ha, svid**, which refer to the statement of the whole sentence, occupy the second (or third) position in the sentence.

i. Even **accented particles** for the most part cannot begin a sentence. They either follow the word they emphasize in any position in the sentence: **ā́, evá, kám**; or they occupy the second position in the sentence, as emphasizing the whole statement: **aṅgá, áha, íd, kíla, khálu, tú, nú, vái, hí.**

The only particles that can begin the sentence are **átha, ápi, utá**; also **ná** if it negatives the whole sentence, but if it negatives the verb only, it follows that.

j. Forms of the pronoun **tá** tend in B. to occupy the first position, especially **sá** when it anticipates a proper name in dialogues, or **tád** as an acc. when famous authorities are quoted; e. g. **sá hovāca gā́rgyaḥ** (ŚB.) *Gārgya spoke* (as follows); **tád u hovāca‿ā́suriḥ** *with regard to this Āsuri said* (ŚB.). The order is similar when **átha** or **ápi** are used: **ápi hovāca yā́jñavalkyaḥ** (ŚB.).

k. In **relative** and **interrogative** sentences there is nothing peculiar except that, as these two classes of words tend to begin the sentence, cases of them come to occupy the first position which in ordinary sentences do not occupy it; e. g. **kíṃ hí sá táir gṛháiḥ kuryā́t** *what indeed should he do with this house?* (ŚB.).

a. The last position in the sentence is exceptionally occupied in the following ways: 1. very often by final datives as a supplement to the sentence; e. g. **tát paśū́n evá‿asmai pári dadāti gúptyai** *thus he hands the cattle over to him for protection* (ŚB.); 2. by the subject either when it is the name of an authority quoted or when it is equivalent to a relative clause; e. g. **sá ha‿uvāca gā́rgyaḥ** *so said Gārgya*; **aindrā́ṃ carúṃ nír vapet paśúkāmaḥ** *one* (who is) *desirous of cattle should assign a pap for Indra* (TS.).

192. There is neither an indefinite nor a definite article in the Vedic language. Their meaning is inherent in the substantive much as personal pronouns are in forms of the definite verb. Whether the one or the other is meant is made sufficiently clear by the context; e. g. **agním īḷe puróhitam** *I praise Agni the domestic priest* (i. 1¹); **agním manye pitáram** *Agni I deem a father* (x. 7³). In B. the anaphoric use of **tá** is sometimes very nearly equivalent to the definite article (cp. 195 B 3 *b*, p. 294).

Number.

193. 1. Singular words with a plural or a collective sense are always treated strictly as singulars, being never construed with a plural form of the verb (cp. 194).

2. The dual number is in regular use and, generally speaking, in strict application. But in certain parts of the RV. the plural is often used instead of the dual of natural pairs; sometimes also otherwise; e. g. **sám añjantu víśve devā́ḥ, sám ā́po hṛ́dayāni nau** *let all the gods, let the waters unite the hearts of us two* (x. 85⁴⁷).

a. A m. or f. du. is sometimes used to express a male and female of the same class; e. g. **pitárā** = *father and mother*; **mātárā** = *mother and father*. This type of the dual has its widest application in naming pairs of deities by means of one of them and is equivalent to dual compounds containing both names; e. g. **dyā́vā** *heaven and earth* (= **dyā́vā-pṛthivī́**); **uṣā́sā** *Dawn and Night* (= **uṣā́sā-náktā**); **mitrā́** *Mitra and Varuṇa* (= **mitrā́-váruṇā**). Sometimes the other member of the pair is added in the N. sing.; e. g. **mitrā́ tánā ná rathyā̀ váruṇo yáś ca sukrátuḥ** *Mitra (and Varuṇa) and the very wise Varuṇa, like two constant charioteers* (viii. 25²).

3. *a.* The plural is sometimes used (analogously to the dual) so as to include the other two of a group of three; e. g. **dyā́vaḥ** *the* (three) *heavens* = *heaven, air, and earth*;

pṛthivī́ḥ *the* (three) *earths* = *earth, air, and heaven.*[1] This inclusive plural is also found with the names of the two other members of the group added in the N. sing.; thus **abhí samrā́jo váruṇo gṛṇanty, abhí mitrā́so aryamā́ sajóṣāḥ** *to it the universal sovereigns Varuṇa, to it the Mitras* (= Mitra, Varuṇa, Aryaman), *and Aryaman, accordant, sing* (vii. 38[4]).

b. The 1. pers. pl. is sometimes loosely used instead of the sing. or du.; thus Yama in his dialogue with Yamī says **ná yát purā́ cakṛmā́ kád dha nūnám ṛtā́ vádanto ánṛtam rapema** *how pray can we, what we have never done before, speaking of righteous things now talk of what is unrighteous?* (x. 10[4]). The plur. of personal pronouns is also occasionally used in a similar way; thus in the dialogue of Yama and Yamī (x. 10[4]) **nas** alternates with the correct **nau**: **sā́ no nā́bhiḥ, paramáṃ jāmí tán nau** *that is our bond of union, that our highest kinship.* This occasional looseness is probably due to the situation for the moment being regarded more generally so as to include others; *we* would then mean *I and those present, we two and others in like circumstances.* In B. the use of the pl. for the sing. of the first pers. of the personal pronoun is not infrequent both when the pronoun is expressed and when it is latent in the verb; e. g. **sá ha‿uvāca: námo vayáṃ bráhmiṣṭhāya kurmaḥ** *he replied: we* (= *I*) *show reverence to the most learned man* (ŚB.); **váram bhávate gautamā́ya dadmaḥ** *we* (= *I*, Jaivali) *offer a boon to his Honour Gautama* (ŚB.).

Concord.

194. The rules of concord in case, person, gender, and number are in general the same as in other inflexional languages.

---

[1] To this use is probably due the conception of the three heavens and three earths in Vedic cosmology.

A. 1. To the rule that the **verb agrees** with its substantive in person and number the exceptions are very rare. Thus the sing. of the word **tva** *many*, having a pl. sense, appears once with a pl. verb: **jáyān u tvo juhvati** *many a one sacrifices for victories* (MS.). On the other hand, there are a few examples in the RV. of a neut. pl. taking a verb in the sing.; e. g. **dhṛṣṇáve dhīyate dhánā** *to the bold man booty accrues* (i. 81^3).

2. *a.* When two sing. subjects have one verb, the latter in most cases is in the dual; e. g. **índraś ca yád yuyudhā́te áhiś ca** *when Indra and the dragon fought* (i. 32^{13}); **ū́rjaṃ no dyáuś ca pṛthivī́ ca pinvatām** *may heaven and earth increase our strength* (vi. 70^6); **índraś ca sómaṃ pibataṃ bṛhaspate** *do ye two, Indra and* (*thou*), *O Bṛhaspati, drink Soma* (iv. 50^{10}).

When one only of two subjects is expressed, the other having to be supplied, the verb is also in the dual; e. g. **ā́ yád índraś ca dádvahe** *when* (I) *and Indra receive* (viii. 34^{16}); **bṛ́haspate yuvám índraś ca vásvo divyásya‿īśāthe** *O Bṛhaspati, ye two,* (thou) *and Indra, dispose of heavenly wealth* (vii. 97^{10}). In B. this usage seems to be found only when the verb is in the third person; e. g. **prajā́patiḥ prajā́ asṛjata: tā́ bṛ́haspátiś ca‿anvávaitām** *Prajāpati created beings:* (he) *and Bṛhaspati followed them* (TS.).

α. In a minority of cases two sing. subjects take a sing. verb when they are equivalent in sense to a du. compound; e. g. **tokáṃ ca tásya tánayaṃ ca vardhate** *his offspring and family prosper* (ii. 25^2).

β. In B. when two sing. subjects are connected by **ca** the verb is in the du.; but if a contrast is intended, in the sing.; e. g. **tásyā dhātā́ ca‿aryamā́ ca‿ajāyetām** *from her Dhātṛ and Aryaman were born* (MS.); but **pṛthivyā́ vái médhyaṃ ca‿amedhyáṃ ca vyúd akrāmat** *from the earth there issued on the one hand the pure and on the other the impure* (MS.).

b. When there are more than two subjects the verb is not necessarily in the pl., but may agree with only one of them.

1. If each of the subjects is sing. the verb is sing.; e. g.

mitrás tán no várunọ ródasī ca dyúbhaktam índro aryamā́ dadātu *let Mitra, Varuṇa, Rodasī, Indra and Aryaman give us this divine wealth* (vii. 40[2]).

2. If the subjects are of different numbers the verb may agree with either one or the other; e.g. **ā́vad índram yamúnā tṛ́tsavaś ca** *Yamunā and the Tṛtsus helped Indra* (vii. 18[19]); **índro vidur áṅgirasaś ca** *Indra and the Aṅgirases know it* (x. 108[10]).

The du. and pl. take the du. or the pl.; e.g. **giráyaś ca dṛḷhā́ dyā́vā ca bhū́mā tujete** *the firm mountains and heaven and earth trembled* (i. 61[14]); **dyā́vā ca yátra pīpáyann áhā ca** *where heaven and earth and the days have given abundance* (vii. 65[2]).

a. In B. a sing. and a du. subject take a verb in the sing. or pl.; e.g. **vyāmamātráu pakṣáu ca púcham ca bhavati** *both the wings and the tail are a fathom in length* (TS.); **tā́v aśvínau ca sárasvatī ca͜apā́m phenám vájram asiñcan** *the Aśvins and Sarasvatī moulded the foam of the waters into a bolt* (ŚB.); a sing. and a pl. take the verb in the pl.; e.g. **devā́ś ca vái yamáś ca͜asmin lokè 'spardhanta** *the gods and Yama fought for* (the possession of) *this world* (TS.).

β. In B. **anyò 'nyá** *one another* takes the verb in the sing., du., or pl. according as one, two, or several agents are intended; e.g. **tā́bhyaḥ sá nír ṛchād yó naḥ prathamò 'nyò 'nyásmai drúhyāt** *of these he shall be deprived who first of us may cheat another* (TS.); **néd anyò 'nyám hinásātaḥ** *lest they injure each other* (ŚB.); **tā́ni sṛṣṭā́ny anyò 'nyéna͜ aspardhanta** *being created they fought with one another* (ŚB.).

3. When two or more subjects of different persons take a verb in the du. or pl. the first person is preferred to the second or third, the second to the third; e.g. **ahám ca tvám ca sám yujyāva** *I and thou will unite together* (viii. 62[11]); **tám yūyám vayám ca͜aśyā́ma** *may you and we obtain him* (ix. 98[12]). Occasionally, however, the third person is preferred to the first; e.g. **amī́ ca yé magháváno vayám ca míham ná sū́ro áti níṣ ṭatanyuḥ** *may these patrons and we pierce through as the sun the mist* (i. 141[13]).

B. 1. An attributive adjective agrees with its substantive in gender, number, and case. The exceptions are few and unimportant, being chiefly due to the exigencies of metre.

a. The cardinals from *five* to *nineteen*, being adjectives, show some peculiarities of concord: in the oblique cases they appear in V. not only in their inflected form, but often also the uninflected form of the nom. and acc.; e.g. **saptábhiḥ putráiḥ** and **saptá hótṛbhiḥ**, **pañcásu jáneṣu** and **páñca kṛṣṭíṣu**. In B. only the inflected forms are used.

b. The cardinals from 20 upwards being substantives in form may govern a G.; e.g. **ṣaṣṭím áśvānām** *sixty horses*, **śatáṃ gónām** *a hundred kine*, **sahásrāṇi gávām** *thousands of kine*. They are, however, generally treated like adjectives; but being collectives they take sing. endings in concord with pl. cases; e.g. **triṃśád deváḥ** *thirty gods*, **triṃśátaṃ yójanāni** *thirty yojanas* (acc.), **triṃśátā háribhiḥ** *with thirty bays*, **trayastriṃśato devānām** *of thirty gods* (AB.). **śatám** *hundred* and **sahásram** *thousand* are used as the nom. acc. form in agreement with plurals; e.g. **śatáṃ púraḥ** *a hundred forts*, **sahásraṃ hárayaḥ** *a thousand bays*, **sahásraṃ paśún** *a thousand beasts* (TS.); they also appear in the same sense in the plural; e.g. **śatá púraḥ** *a hundred forts*, **sahásrāṇy ádhirathāni** *a thousand wagon loads* (x. 98[9]). **śatám** and **sahásram** are also found (but not in B.) with an inst. pl., as **śatáṃ pūrbhíḥ** *with a hundred forts* beside **śaténa háribhiḥ** *with a hundred bays*, **sahásram ṛ́ṣibhiḥ** *with a thousand seers*. The noun accompanying **sahásra** occasionally appears by a kind of attraction in the sing.: **śúnaś cic chépaṃ níditaṃ sahásrād yū́pād amuñcaḥ** *thou didst deliver Śunaḥśepa, who was bound, from a thousand posts* (v. 2[7]): this use does not seem to occur in B.

2. A predicative adjective used with as or bhū (often to be supplied) agrees in gender and number with its subject.

a. The nom. of **īśvará** *capable* used thus in B. is equivalent to a verb = *be able*. The concord here is in the majority of cases normal; e.g. **īśvaró vá áśvó 'yató 'pratiṣṭhitaḥ páram parāvátaṃ gántoḥ** *a horse if unbridled and unobstructed can go to an extreme distance* (TS.); **sá‿enam īśvará pradáhaḥ** *she can burn him* (TS.); **īśvaráu vá etáu nirdáhaḥ** *both of them can burn* (ŚB.); **tány enam īśvarāṇi pratinúdaḥ** *they can drive him away* (MS.). Sometimes, however, the concord of either number or gender, or of both, is neglected; e.g. **tám īśvaráṃ rákṣāṃsi hántoḥ** *the demons can kill him* (TS.); **tásya‿īśvaráḥ prajá pápīyasī bhávitoḥ** *his offspring can degenerate* (ŚB.); **īśvaró ha‿etá ánagnicitaṃ saṃtáptoḥ** *these* (f. pl.) *are liable to weigh heavily upon one who has not built a fire altar* (ŚB.). In the last two examples quoted and in others the masc. sing. has become stereotyped as a nom. of all genders and numbers.

b. The use of a predicative adjective referring to two or more substantives differing in gender is very rare; it then seems to agree in gender with the subst. nearest it, or the masc. seems to have been preferred to the neut.; e. g. **trayā́ vái náirṛtā akṣā́ḥ stríyaḥ svápnaḥ** (MS.) *dice, women, and sleep* (are) *the treble pernicious* (things); **evá hy àsya kā́myā stóma ukthā́m ca śáṃsyā** *thus indeed his two favourites, stoma and uktha, are to be recited* (i. 8[10]). A predicative adj. dependent on **kṛ** agrees with its subst.; if there are two, the du. is used; e.g. **dáivīṃ ca vā́vá‿asmā etád víśaṃ mānuṣī́ṃ ca‿ánuvartmānau karoti** *so he makes the divine and the human folk obedient to him* (MS.).

3. As in Greek and Latin, a demonstrative pronoun agrees with a predicative noun in gender and number; e. g. **ye tuṣā́ḥ sā tvak** *what* (are) *the husks* (*that* =) *those* (are) *the skin* (AB.); **yád áśru sáṃkṣāritam ā́sīt tā́ni vā́yāṃsi‿abhavan** *what was the concentrated tear* (*those* =) *that became the birds* (ŚB.).

Pronouns.

195. A. Personal. *a.* Owing to its highly inflexional character the Vedic language, like Latin and Greek, uses the nominatives of personal pronouns far less frequently than modern European languages do. Being already inherent in the first and second persons of the finite verb such pronouns are expressed separately only when they require emphasizing.

b. The unaccented forms of **ahám** and **tvám** (109 *a*) being enclitic, can be used neither at the beginning of a sentence or metrical line (Pāda), nor after vocatives, nor before emphasizing, conjunctive or disjunctive particles.

c. **Bhavān** *Your Honour*, the polite form of **tvám**, which first comes into use in B., properly takes a verb in the 3. sing. But being practically equivalent to a personal pronoun of the 2. pers., it occasionally appears with a verb in that person; e. g. **íti vā́vá kíla no bhávān purā́‿**

anuśiṣṭā́n ávocaḥ (ŚB.) *in this sense then you have formerly spoken of* (*us* =) *me as instructed* (cp. 194, 1).

B. Demonstrative. 1. **ayám** *this* (*here*) is a deictic pronoun used adjectivally of what is in the neighbourhood, presence, or possession of the speaker, and may often be translated by *here*; e.g. **ayáṃ ta emi tanvā̀ purástāt** *here I come with my body before thee* (viii. 100[1]); **iyáṃ mátir máma** *this my hymn*; **ayáṃ vā́taḥ** *the wind here* (on earth); **ayáṃ jánaḥ** *the people here* (vii. 55[5]); **idáṃ bhúvanam** *this world*; **ayám agníḥ** *Agni here* (present). In the RV. **ayám** is sometimes used even with **div** *heaven* and **ādityá** *sun* as if they were included in the environment of the speaker.

2. Opposed to **ayám** is **asáu** *that* (*there*), applied to objects remote from the speaker, as heaven and its phenomena, immortals, persons who are not present or are at a distance; e.g. **amī́ yé devā sthána triṣú‿ā́ rocané diváḥ** *ye, O gods, who are there, in the three bright realms of heaven* (i. 105[5]); **amī́ ca yé maghávāno vayáṃ ca** *those* (absent) *patrons and we* (i. 141[13]); **asáu yá éṣi vīrakáḥ** *you who go there, a mannikin* (viii. 91[2]).

a. In B. the usage is similar, only the contrast is more definite: it is typical in referring to the earth (**iyám**) and the heavenly world (**asáu**), and in the phrases **yò 'yáṃ pávate** *he who blows here* (= Wind), and **yò 'sáu tápati** *he who burns there* (= Sun), and **asā́v ādityáḥ** *the sun there.* In B. **asáu** is besides used in a formulaic way (= *so and so*) when the actual name is to be substituted; e.g. **asáu nā́ma‿ayám idáṃrūpaḥ** *he here, having this form, is so and so by name* (ŚB.). In addressing a person the voc. form **ásau** is also used thus: **yáthā vā́ idáṃ nāmagrā́ham ásā ásā íti hváyati** *as one here* (= in ordinary life) *by way of mentioning the name calls: 'you there, you there'* (MS.).

3. **tá**, like **asáu**, can be translated by *that*, but in a different sense. It is not like **asáu** essentially deictic and local, nor does it imply a contrast (*that there* as opposed to *this here*); but it refers to something already known either as just mentioned or as generally familiar.

a. A very frequent application of this meaning is its

reference as a **correlative** to what is made known by an antecedent relative clause; e.g. **yáṃ yajñáṃ paribhū́r ási, sá íd devéṣu gachati** *the sacrifice that thou encompassest, that certainly goes to the gods* (i. 1[4]). Often, however, an antecedent clause is lacking and must be mentally supplied in some such form as *whom we have in mind.* Then **tá** is equivalent to *the well known.* This use comes out most clearly in the first verse of a hymn; e.g. **sá pratnáthā sáhasā jā́yamānaḥ, sadyáḥ kā́vyāni báḷ adhatta víśvā** (i. 96[1]) *he* (who is in our thoughts, the famous Agni) *being engendered in the ancient way with strength, lo! has straightway assumed all wisdom*; **tā́ vāṃ víśvasya gopā́ yajase** (viii. 25[1]) *you two famous guardians of the universe I worship.*

b. **tá** has a very frequent **anaphoric** use, referring back to a noun or a pronoun of the third or second person (in B. also of the first), and may then be translated by *as such, so*; e.g. **tváṃ vā́jasya śrútyasya rājasi: sá no mṛḷa** *thou rulest over glorious spoil: as such be gracious to us* (i. 36[12]); **sā tathā‿ity abravīt: sā vai vo varaṃ vṛṇā iti** *she said, yes: I as such* (= in the proposed circumstances) *will choose a boon of you* (AB.). This usage is a prominent and somewhat monotonous feature of the narrative style in B.; e.g. **prajā́pates tráyastṛṃśad duhitára āsan, tā́ḥ sómāya rā́jñe 'dadāt, tā́sāṃ róhiṇīm úpait, tā́ ī́rṣyantīḥ púnar agachan** *Prajāpati had thirty daughters; he gave them to King Soma; of them he visited Rohiṇī* (only); *they* (the others), *being jealous, went back* (TS.). When this **tá** is widely separated from the antecedent noun to which it refers (sometimes only indirectly) it may be translated by the definite article; thus the opening of the story of Urvaśī: **urváśī ha‿apsarā́ḥ purūrávasam aiḍáṃ cakame** *an Apsaras Urvaśī loved Purūravas, the son of Iḍā* is some sentences later referred to with: **tád dha tā́ apsarása ātáyo bhūtvā́ pári pupluvire** *then the Apsarases swam about in the form of water birds* (ŚB.).

a. In its anaphoric use **tá** is frequently followed by personal pronouns of all persons (regularly in their enclitic form when they have one); e. g. **tám mā sám sṛja várcasā** *unite me as such with glory* (i. 23[23]), **mā́m yajñā́d antár agāta : sā́ vo 'hám evá yajñā́m amūmuham** *ye have excluded me from the sacrifice; so I have thrown your sacrifice into confusion* (ŚB.); **havíṣmanto vidhema te : sá tvā́m no adyá sumánā ihá͜avitā́ bháva** *bringing oblations we would serve thee: so do thou be for us to-day a benevolent helper* (i. 36[2]); **yádi tvā͜etát púnar brávataḥ, sā́ tvā́m brūtāt** (ŚB.) *if they (two) shall say this to you again, then do you say* (to them); **asyá pītvā́ ghanó vṛtrā́ṇām abhavas . . . tā́m tvā vājáyāmaḥ** *having drunk of this thou becamest a slayer of Vṛtras: so we strengthen thee* (i. 4[9]). Similarly used are: sing. A. **tā́m tvā́m** (here exceptionally not enclitic), D. **tásmai te,** G. **tásya te, tásyās te**; du. **tā́ vām**; pl. A. **tā́n vas,** G. **téṣām vas.**

β. Four demonstrative pronouns are found following **tá** in this way: **idám, adás, tá** itself, and oftenest of all **etád**; e. g. **sā́͜iyám asmé sanajā́ pítryā dhī́ḥ** *this here is among us an ancient hymn of our forefathers* (iii. 39[2]); **tásya vā́lo ny àsañji : tám amúm vā́to dhunoti** *its tail hangs down: that the wind tosses to and fro* (ŚB.); **tā́m ha͜evá ná͜áti dadāha : tā́m ha sma tā́m purā́ brāhmaṇā́ ná taranti** *that* (river) *he* (Agni) *did not burn across: that same one the Brāhmans used not formerly to cross* (ŚB.), **bhavaty asya͜anucaro ya evam veda : sa vā eṣa ekātithiḥ, sa eṣa juhvatsu vasati** *he who knows this has a follower; that* (follower) *is this one guest; this same* (follower, the Sun) *abides among the sacrificers* (AB.).

γ. The N. sing. **sá** is sometimes used adverbially in B. (see 180, p. 249).

4. **etá** *this* is used like **tá** but is more emphatic. It refers to something known to the listener as present either to his senses or his thoughts.

a. The correlative use of **etá** seems to be limited to B., the relative clause here usually following; e. g. **patho vā eṣa praiti, yo yajñe muhyati** *he diverges from the path who goes wrong in the sacrifice* (AB.). It is somewhat peculiar when the relative in the neuter sing. and without a verb is added solely for the purpose of emphasizing a particular word; e. g. **svargam vā etena lokam upapra yanti yat prāyaṇīyaḥ** *people go to the heavenly world with that which* (is) *the preliminary sacrifice* (AB.). In these circumstances **etá** when alone always agrees in gender with the noun in the relative clause; but when it is accompanied by a substantive, with the latter; e.g. **paśavo vā ete yad āpaḥ** *water is equivalent to cattle* (AB.). In this usage **yád** often loses its inflexional character to such an extent that it becomes like an explanatory particle (= *that is to say*), the substantive that follows it agreeing in case with that which precedes; e.g. **etáir átra‿ubháyair ártho bhavati yád deváiś ca brāhmaṇáiś ca** *there is need here of both, that is, of the gods and the Brāhmans* (ŚB.).

The use of **etá** without an antecedent, parallel to that of **tá**, is common both in V. and B.; e.g. **eṣó uṣā́ vy ùchati** *this Dawn* (whom we see before us) *has shone forth* (i. 46[1]); **té ha‿ásurā asūyánta iva‿ūcur: yā́vad evàiṣá víṣṇur abhiśéte tā́vad vo dadma íti** *the Asuras said somewhat displeased: as much as this Viṣṇu* (here present) *covers lying down, so much we give you* (ŚB.); **yuvám etám cakrathuḥ síndhuṣu plavám** *ye two have made that boat* (present to our thought) *in the ocean* (i. 182[5]); **téna‿etám uttarám girím áti dudrāva** *therewith he passed over that* (well known) *northern mountain* (ŚB.); **tá eté māyé asṛjanta suparṇī́m ca kadrū́m ca** *they created these two* (well-known) *miraculous beings, Suparṇī and Kadrū* (ŚB.). In the last example **ete** requires the addition of the two following names to supplement its sense.

a. Somewhat similarly this pronoun is sometimes followed in B. by words or a sentence explaining it; e.g. **sá etā́bhir devátābhiḥ sayúg bhūtvā́ marúdbhir viśā́‿agnínā‿ánīkena‿upaplā́yata** *he, united with these deities, the Maruts as the fighting folk and Agni as the head, approached* (MS.); **sá ha‿etád evá dadarśa:‿anaśanátayā vái me prajā́ḥ párā bhavanti‿íti** *he saw this: in consequence of hunger my creatures are perishing* (ŚB.).

b. In its **anaphoric** use **etá** expresses identity with that to which it refers back, more emphatically than **tá** does; e.g. **ápeta vī̀ta ví ca sarpata‿áto: asmā́ etám pitáro lokám akran** *go away, disperse, depart from hence: this place* (on which you have been standing) *the fathers have prepared for him* (x. 14[9]); in the final verse the expression **eṣá stóma indra túbhyam** (i. 173[3]) *this praise is for thee, O Indra,* refers to the whole preceding hymn; **tád ubháyaṃ sambhṛ́tya mṛ́daṃ ca‿apáś ca‿íṣṭakām akurvaṃs : tásmād etád ubháyam íṣṭakā bhavati mṛ́c ca‿ā́paś ca** *having brought both those together, clay and water, they made the brick : therefore a brick consists of both these, clay and water* (ŚB.).

5. **tyá** occurs only in the sense of *that* (*well known*); e. g. **kvà tyā́ni nau sakhyā́ babhūvuḥ** *what has become of those friendships of us two?* (vii. 88[5]). It often follows forms of the demonstrative pronouns **etá** and **idám**; e. g. **eté tyé bhānáva uṣása ā́guḥ** *here those* (familiar) *beams of Dawn have come* (vii. 75[3]); **imám u tyám atharvavád agníṃ manthanti** *they, like Atharvan, rub forth that* (famous) *Agni here* (vi. 15[17]). The neuter **tyád** is sometimes used after the relative **yá**, and often after the particle **ha**, in an adverbial sense; e. g. **yásya tyác chámbaraṃ máde dívodāsāya randháyaḥ** *in the exhilaration of which* (Soma) *thou didst at that time subject Śambara to Divodāsa* (vi. 43[1]).

6. The pronoun **a** *that* in its substantive sense (= *he, she, it, they*), when it is unaccented, not infrequently appears as an unemphatic correlative (while the accented form is a deictic adjective); e. g. **yásya deváir ā́sado barhír agne, áhāni asmai sudínā bhavanti** *on whose litter thou, O Agni, hast sat down, fair days arise for him* (vii. 11[2]); **yā́ vāṃ śatáṃ niyútaḥ sácante, ā́bhir yātam arvā́k** *the hundred teams that accompany you, with them do ye two come hither* (vii. 91[6]); **nákir eṣāṃ ninditā́ mártyeṣu, yé asmā́kaṃ pitáro góṣu yodhā́ḥ** *there is among mortals no reproacher of them who, (being) our fathers, were fighters for cows* (iii. 39[4]).

THE CASES.

Nominative.

196. The nominative, as in other languages, is mainly used as the subject of a sentence.

a. A second nominative is employed as a predicate with certain verbs beside the subject, that is, with verbs meaning *be, become, seem* or *be accounted, think oneself*; e. g. **tváṃ hí ratnadhā́ ási** *for thou art a bestower of treasure* (i. 15[3]); **śivā́saḥ sánto áśivā abhūvan** *being friendly they have become unfriendly* (v. 12[5]); **ékaviṃśatiḥ sáṃ padyante** *they become twenty-one* (TS.);[1] **gókāmā me achadayan** *they seemed to me desirous of cows* (x. 108[10]); **ṛ́ṣiḥ kó vípra ohate** *who counts as a seer, as a singer?* (viii. 3[14]); **apratír mányamānaḥ** *thinking himself irresistible* (v. 32[3]); **sómaṃ manyate papivā́n** *he believes he has drunk Soma* (x. 85[3]); **parābhaviṣyánto manāmahe** *we think we are about to perish* (TS.).

a. In B. the predicative nom. also appears with verbs meaning to *call oneself* (**brū, vac, vad** in the middle); e. g. **índro brāhmaṇó bruvāṇáḥ** *Indra calling himself a Brāhman* (TB.); **hántāvocathāḥ** *thou hast described thyself as a slayer* (TS.).

β. With verbs of naming the predicative acc. may also be expressed in B. by the nom. with **íti**; e. g. **rásabha íti hy ètám ṛ́ṣayó 'vadan** *for the seers called him 'ass'* (TS.).

b. With passive verbs the predicative nom. takes the place of the acc. object of the active verb; e. g. **tvám . . ucyase pitā́** *thou art called a father* (i. 31[14]).

c. Instead of the predicative nom. the voc. is sometimes used; e. g. **yūyáṃ hí ṣṭhā́, sudānavaḥ** *for ye are liberal* (i. 15[2]); **ábhūr éko, rayipate rayīṇā́m** *thou alone hast been*

---

[1] In B. the phrase **rūpáṃ kṛ** *to assume a form*, because it is equivalent to **bhū** *become*, takes a predicative nom.; e. g. **víṣṇū rūpáṃ kṛtvā́** *assuming the form of Viṣṇu* (TS.).

the lord of riches (vi. 31[1]); **gáutama bruvāṇa** *thou who callest thyself Gautama* (ŚB.). (Cp. 180 under **ná**, 2 *a*.)

a. Since apparently two vocatives cannot be connected with **ca**, the nom. often appears instead of the first or the second vocative; e. g. **vā́yav índraś ca cetathaḥ** *O Vāyu and Indra, ye know* (i. 2[5]); **índraś ca sómam pibatam bṛhaspate** *Indra and Bṛhaspati, drink the Soma* (iv. 50[10]). Cp. 180 under **ca**, 1 *a*, *b*.

Accusative.

197. A. This case is usually employed in connexion with verbs in various ways. Besides its ordinary use of denoting the object of transitive verbs, the acc. is employed to express:

1. the **goal** with verbs of motion, chiefly **gam**, also **i**, much less often **yā**, **car**, and **sṛ** and some others. The acc. may be a person, a place, an activity or a condition; e. g. **yamáṃ ha yajñó gachati** *to Yama goes the sacrifice* (x. 14[13]); **devā́m̐ íd eṣi pathíbhiḥ sugébhiḥ** *to the gods thou goest by paths easy to traverse* (i. 162[21]); **índraṃ stómāś caranti** *to Indra fare the songs of praise* (x. 47[7]); **sáraj jāró ná yóṣaṇām** *he sped like a lover to a maiden* (ix. 101[14]); **mā́ tvát kṣétrāṇy áraṇāni ganma** *may we not go from thee to strange fields* (vi. 61[14]); **sabhā́m eti kitaváḥ** *the gambler goes to the assembly* (x. 34[6]); **jaritúr gachatho hávam** *ye two go to the call of the singer* (viii. 35[13]); **táva krátubhir amṛtatvám āyan** *by thy mental powers they (went to =) attained immortality* (vi. 7[4]).

a. The usage in B. is similar; e.g. **prajā́patiḥ prajā́ asṛjata, tā́ várunam agachan** *Prajāpati created creatures; they went to Varuṇa* (TS.); **sá ná dívam apatat** *he did not fly to heaven* (ŚB.); **śríyam gacheyam** *may I (go to =) attain prosperity* (ŚB.).

2. **duration** of **time** (in origin only a special form of the cognate acc.); e. g. **śatáṃ jīva śarádo várdhamānaḥ** *live prospering a hundred autumns* (x. 161[4]); **só aśvatthé saṃvatsarám atiṣṭhat** *he remained in the Aśvattha tree for a year*

(TB.); **tásmāt sárvān ṛtū́n varṣati** *therefore it rains during all the seasons* (TS.); **saṃvatsaratamī́ṃ rā́trim ā́ gachatāt** (ŚB.) *for the night a year hence thou shalt come* (to me).

3. **extension of distance** (in origin only a special form of the cognate acc.), a use rare in both V. and B.; e. g. **yád āśúbhiḥ pátasi yójanā purū́** *when with the swift ones thou fliest many leagues* (ii. 16³); **sá bhū́miṃ viśváto vṛtvā́‿áty atiṣṭhad daśāṅgulám** *he covering the earth on all sides extended beyond* (it) *a distance of ten fingers* (x. 90¹); **saptádaśa pravyādhā́n ājíṃ dhāvanti** *they run a race* (a distance of) *seventeen arrow-flights* (TB.).

4. the **cognate object** of intransitive verbs, which may be allied to the latter etymologically or only in sense; e. g. **samānám añjí‿añjate** *they deck themselves with like adornment* (vii. 57³); **yád agne yāsi dūtyàm** *when, O Agni, thou goest on a message* (i. 12⁴); **tváyā‿ádhyakṣeṇa pṛ́tanā jayema** *with thee as witness we would conquer in battles* (x. 128¹); **tásmād rā́jā saṃgrāmáṃ jitvā́‿udājám úd ajate** *therefore a king, having won a battle, chooses booty for himself* (MS.); **tisró rā́trīr vratáṃ caret** *he should perform a fast for three nights* (TS.).

a. Verbs meaning *to stream* or *to shine* in V. take a cognate acc. with a concrete sense; e. g. **ṛtásya jihvā́ pavate mádhu** *the tongue of the rite* (Soma) *streams mead* (ix. 75²), **tásmā ā́po ghṛtám arṣanti** *for him the waters stream ghee* (i. 125⁵), **ví yát sū́ryo ná rócate bṛhád bhā́ḥ** *when, like the sun, he beams forth lofty light* (vii. 8⁴).

5. an **adverbial sense.** Adverbs of this form all originated in various uses of the acc. which have acquired an independent character. They are formed from:

a. substantives; e. g. **náktam** *by night* (not *during the night* like the acc. of time); **kā́mam** *at will* (still rare in the RV.), e. g. **kāmaṃ tad dhotā śaṃsed yad dhotrakāḥ pūrvedyuḥ śaṃseyuḥ** *the Hotṛ may, as he likes, recite what the assistants of the Hotṛ may recite the day before* (AB.); **nā́ma** *by name*; e. g. **mā́ṃ dhur índraṃ nā́ma devátā**

(x. 49²) *me they have placed as Indra by name* (or *verily*) *among the gods.*

b. various kinds of adjectives. They have an attributive origin when they express the senses of *quickly* or *slowly* (**kṣiprám, cirám**), *much* or *greatly* (**bahú, bálavat**), *well* or *badly*, *boldly* (**dhṛṣṇú**), or direction (as **nyák** *downward*, &c.); e. g. **bálavad vāti** *it blows hard* (ŚB.); **bhadrám jī́vantaḥ** *living happily* (x. 37⁶).

a. The acc. adverbs from ordinals seem to have been appositional in origin; e. g. **tān vā etān sampātān viśvāmitraḥ prathamam apaśyat** (AB.) *these same Sampāta hymns Viśvāmitra invented first* (= as the first thing).

β. Several acc. adverbs are from comparatives and superlatives in **tara** and **tama** formed from prepositions and adverbs; e. g. **drā́ghīya ā́yuḥ pratarám dádhānāḥ** *obtaining longer life furthermore* (i. 53¹¹). A good many such have a fem. acc. form in later use, but there is only one found in the RV.: **saṃtarā́ṃ pādukáu hara** *put your two little feet closer together* (viii. 33¹⁹).

γ. A special class is formed by adverbs in **vat** expressing that an action takes place like that performed by the noun preceding the suffix; e.g. **tvā́dūtāso manuvád vadema** (ii. 10⁶) *having thee as our messenger we would speak like men* (= as men should speak: properly *something that belongs to men*).

δ. Another class of acc. adverbs is formed from various adjectival compounds. A number of these are formed with the privative particle **a**, being of the nature of cognate accusatives; e. g. **devā́ś chándobhir imā́ṃl lokā́n anapajayyám abhy ā́jayan** *the gods* (*unconquerably* =) *irrevocably conquered these worlds by means of the metres* (TS.).

ε. Another group comparatively rare in V., but very common in B., are those formed from prepositionally governing adjectival compounds; e.g. **anukāmám tarpayethām** *satisfy yourselves according to desire* (i. 17³), **adhidevatám** *with reference to the deity* (ŚB.). Probably following the analogy of some of these were formed others in which the first member of the compound is not a preposition, but an adverb derived from the relative **yá**; e. g. **yathā-kāmám ní padyate** *she turns in according to her desire* (x. 146⁵), **yāvaj-jīvám** (*as long as* =) *for life* (ŚB.). Some other adverbial compounds are used like gerunds in **am**; e.g. **stukā-sárgam sṛṣṭā́ bhavati** *it is plaited like a braid of hair* (ŚB.).

197. B. The acc. is largely used with verbal nouns. Besides being governed by all participles, active and middle, and by genuine infinitives, in V. it is used with agent nouns formed from the root or other verbal stems by means of about ten primary suffixes. Such nouns are made from the simple root (when compounded with a preposition), and with the suffixes **a** (when the stem is compounded with a preposition), **ani** (from the aor. or desid. stem), **i** (generally from the reduplicated root), **īyas** and **iṣṭha** (comparatives and superlatives), **u** (from desiderative stems), **uka** (very rare in V.), **tar** (when the root is accented), **van** (when compounded), **snu** (from causative stems); and a few with the secondary suffix **in**. Examples of the acc. with such agent nouns are: **devā́ṃs tvám paribhū́r asi** *thou encompassest the gods* (v. 13[6]); **dṛḷhā́ cid ārujáḥ** *breaking even what is firm* (iii. 45[2]); **tvám no víśvā abhímātīḥ sakṣáṇiḥ** *thou overcomest all our adversaries* (viii. 24[26]); **śatám púro rurukṣáṇiḥ** *ready to destroy a hundred forts* (ix. 48[2]); **índrā ha rátnaṃ váruṇā dhéṣṭhā** *Indra and Varuṇa bestow treasure most abundantly* (iv. 41[3]); **vatsā́ṃś ca ghā́tuko vṛ́kaḥ** (AV. xii. 4[7]) *and the wolf slays the calves*; **dā́tā rā́dhāṃsi śumbhati** *giving riches he shines* (i. 22[8]); **prātaryā́vāṇo adhvarám** *coming early to the sacrifice* (i. 44[13]); **sthirā́ cin namayiṣṇavaḥ** *O ye who desire to bend even what is rigid* (viii. 20[1]); **kāmī́ hí vīráḥ sádam asya pītím** *for the hero always desires a draught of it* (ii. 14[1]).

a. Some adjectives formed with **añc** from prepositions governing the acc. are also used with that case. Such are **pratyáñc** *facing*, **anváñc** *following*; e.g. **pratyáṅṅ uṣásam urviyā́ vi bhāti** *facing the Dawn* (the fire) *shines forth far and wide* (v. 28[1]), **tasmād anūcī patnī gārhapatyam āste** *hence the wife sits behind the Gārhapatya fire* (AB.). The acc. is found even with **samyáñc** *united*; e. g. **óṣadhīr evá‿enaṃ samyáñcaṃ dadhāti** *he puts him into contact with the plants* (MS.); but this adj. also takes the inst., the natural case with a compound of **sám**.

β. In B. the only nouns taking the acc. seem to be the des. adjectives in **u** and the ordinary adjectives in **uka** (which are very common) and those in **in**; e.g. **pāpmānam apajighāṃsuḥ** *wishing to drive away sin* (AB.), **sarpā́ enaṃ ghā́tukāḥ syuḥ** *the snakes might bite* *him* (MS.); **aprativādy enaṃ bhrātṛvyo bhavati** *his enemy does not contradict him* (PB.).

c. The acc. is governed by more prepositions than any other case. The genuine prepositions with which it is exclusively connected in both V. and B. are **áti** *beyond*, **ánu** *after*, **abhí** *towards*, **práti** *against*, **tirás** *across*; and in V. only **ácha** *towards*. It is also taken secondarily by others which primarily govern other cases (cp. 176. 1, 2). The acc. is further taken exclusively by the adnominal prepositions **antarā́** *between*, **abhítas** *around*, **upári** *above*, **sanitúr** *apart from*; and secondarily by some others (cp. 177. 1–3).

a. The preposition **vínā** *without, except*, which first occurs in B. (and there has only been noted once), takes the acc.; and **ṛté** *without*, which in the RV. governs the abl. only, in B. begins to take the acc. also (as it often does in post-Vedic Sanskrit).

β. In B. a number of adverbs (inst. of adjectives and substantives or formed with **tas** from pronouns expressive of some relation in space) take the acc.; such are **ágreṇa** *in front of*, **ántareṇa** *within, between*, **úttareṇa** *north of*, **dákṣiṇena** *to the right or the south of*, **páreṇa** *beyond*; **ubhayá-tas** *on both sides of*.

γ. In B. the acc. is taken by two interjections. One of them, **éd** *lo! behold!* (cp. Lat. *en*), is always preceded by a verb of motion, which, however, has sometimes to be supplied; e.g. **éyāya vāyúr: éd dhatáṃ vṛtrám** *Vāyu came* (to see): *behold, Vṛtra* (was) *dead* (ŚB.); **púnar éma íti devā́: éd agníṃ tiróbhūtam** '*we are coming back*', *said the gods*; (they came back, and) *behold! Agni* (had) *disappeared!* (ŚB.). The other interjection **dhik** *fie!*, used with the acc. of the person only, is still very rare in B.; e.g. **dhik tvā jālma‿astu** *fie on you, rogue!* (KB.).

Double Accusative.

198. A second acc. appears in apposition with various verbs; e.g. **púruṣaṃ ha vái devā́ ágre paśúm ā́ lebhire** *the gods in the beginning sacrificed a man as a victim* (ŚB.). It is further used:

1. predicatively with verbs of saying (**brū, vac**), thinking (**man**), knowing (**vid**), hearing (**śru**), making (**kṛ**), ordaining (**vi-dhā**), choosing (**vṛ**), appointing (**ni-dhā**) in both V.

and B.; e. g. **śvā́naṃ bastó bodhayitā́ram abravīt** *the he-goat said* (that) *the dog* (was) *the wakener* (i. 161[13]); **yád anyó 'nyáṃ pāpám avadan** *that the one called the other wicked* (ŚB.); **agníṃ manye pitáram** *Agni I think a father* (x. 7[3]); **mariṣyántaṃ céd yájamānaṃ mányeta** *if he thinks the sacrificer* (is) *going to die* (ŚB.); **cirā́ṃ tán mene** *he thought that too long* (ŚB.); **vidmā́ hí tvā purūvásum** *we know thee* (to be) *possessed of much wealth* (i. 81[8]); **ná vái hatáṃ vṛtráṃ vidmá ná jīvám** *we know not* (whether) *Vṛtra* (is) *dead nor* (whether he is) *alive* (ŚB.); **reväntaṃ hí tvā śṛṇómi** *I hear* (about) *thee* (that thou art) *rich* (viii. 2[11]); **śṛṇvánty enam agníṃ cikyānám** (TS.) *they hear* (about) *him having piled the fire* (altar); **asmā́n sú jigyúṣaḥ kṛdhi** *make us thoroughly victorious* (viii. 80[6]); **téṣāṃ pūṣáṇam adhipā́m akarot** *he made Pūṣan their lord* (MS.); **tásmā ā́hutīr yajñáṃ vy àdadhuḥ** *they made* (= ordained) *the oblations* (to be) *the sacrifice for him* (MS.); **agníṃ hótāraṃ prá vṛṇe** *I choose Agni priest* (iii. 19[1]); **ní tvā́m agne mánur dadhe jyótir jánāya śáśvate** *Manu has appointed thee, O Agni, as a light for every man* (i. 36[19]).

2. to express the person as a direct object beside the thing with verbs of addressing (**vac**), asking (**prach**), begging (**yāc**), approaching with prayer (**ī, yā**), milking (**duh**), shaking (**dhū**), sacrificing to (**yaj**), doing to (**kṛ**); e. g. **agníṃ mahā́m avocāmā suvṛktím** *to Agni we have addressed a great hymn* (x. 80[7]); **pṛchā́mi tvā páram ántaṃ pṛthivyā́ḥ** *I ask thee about the farthest limit of the earth* (i. 164[34]); **yā́jñavalkyaṃ dvā́u praśnā́u prakṣyāmi** *I will ask Yājñavalkya two questions* (ŚB.); **apó yācāmi bheṣajám** *I beg healing from the waters* (x. 9[5]); **tád agnihotry àgníṃ yācet** *that the Agnihotṛ should beg of Agni* (MS.); **vásūni dasmám īmahe** *we approach the wondrous one for riches* (i. 42[10]); **tát tvā yāmi** *I approach thee for this* (i. 24[11]); **duhánty ū́dhar divyā́ni** *they milk celestial gifts from the udder* (i. 64[5]); **imā́m evá sárvān kā́mān duhe** *from her he* (*milks* =) *obtains all desires* (ŚB.);

vṛkṣám phálaṃ dhūnuhi *shake down fruit from the tree* (iii. 45[4]); **yájā devā́m̐ ṛtáṃ bṛhát** *sacrifice to the gods the lofty rite* (i. 75[5]); **kíṃ mā karann abalā́ asya sénāḥ** *what can his feeble hosts do to me?* (v. 30[9]).

a. Of the above verbs **vac, ī** and **yā, dhū, yaj** and **kṛ** do not seem to be found with two acc. in B.; on the other hand **ā-gam** *approach*, **dhā** *milk*, **ji** *win*, **jyā** *wrest from* are so used there; e.g. **agnír vái váruṇaṃ brahmacáryam ā́ gachat** *Agni (approached =) asked Varuṇa for the position of a religious student* (MS.); **imā̐l lokān adhayad yaṃ-yaṃ kāmam akāmayata** *from these worlds he extracted whatever he desired* (AB.); **devā́n ásurā yajñám ajayan** *the Asuras won the sacrifice from the gods* (MS.); **índro marutaḥ sahasram ajināt** *Indra wrested a thousand from the Maruts* (PB.).

3. to express the agent[1] with causative verbs beside the acc. which would be taken by the simple verb also; e.g. **uśán devā́m̐ uśatáḥ pāyayā havíḥ** *eager thyself cause the eager gods to drink the libation* (ii. 37[6]); **tā́ yájamānaṃ vācayati** *he makes the sacrificer name them* (TS.). With verbs of motion the other acc. expresses the goal (which is, however, never a person)[2]; e.g. **párām evá parāvátām sapátnīṃ gamayāmasi** *to the extreme distance we cause the rival wife to go* (x. 145[4]); **yájamānaṃ suvargáṃ lokáṃ gamayati** *he causes the sacrificer to reach the celestial world* (TS.).

a. In B. the agent is frequently put in the inst. instead of the acc. with various causatives, especially that of **grah** *seize*; e.g. **tā́ váruṇena‿agrāhayat** (MS.) *he caused Varuṇa to seize them* (= he caused them to be seized by Varuṇa).

b. In B. a second acc. expresses the goal (with **nī** *lead*) or duration of time beside the acc. of the object; e.g. **evám evá‿enaṃ kūrmáḥ suvargáṃ lokáṃ nayati** *thus the tortoise leads him to the celestial world* (TS.), **tisró rā́trīr vratáṃ caret** *he should observe a fast for three nights* (TS.).

---

[1] Which would be expressed by the nom. with the simple verb; e.g. **devā́ havíḥ pibanti** *the gods drink the libation.*

[2] When the goal is a person it is expressed by the loc. or a loc. adverb; e.g. **agnā́v agníṃ gamayet** *he would send Agni to Agni* (ŚB.); **devatrā́‿evá enad gamayati** *he sends it to the gods* (ŚB.).

Instrumental.

199. A. The fundamental sense of this case is concomitance, which may variously be rendered by *with*, *by*, *through*, according as it expresses accompaniment, instrumentality or agency, causality, motion through space or duration of time.

1. In its **sociative sense** the instrumental expresses the companion or accompaniment of the subject in any activity; e. g. **devó devébhir ā́ gamat** *may the god come with the gods* (i. 1[5]); **índreṇa yujā́ nír apā́m aubjo arṇavám** *with Indra as thy companion thou didst release the flood of waters* (ii. 23[18]); **índro no rā́dhasā͜ ā́ gamat** *may Indra come to us with wealth* (iv. 55[10]).

a. Similarly in B.: **agnir vasubhir ud akrāmat** *Indra departed with the Vasus* (AB.); **yéna mántreṇa juhóti tád yájuḥ** *the spell to the accompaniment of which he offers the oblation is the Yajus* (ŚB.); **tád asya sáhasā͜ ā́ditsanta** *they tried to take it from him by force* (TS.).

2. In its **instrumental sense** it expresses the means (person or thing) by which an action is accomplished; e. g. **vayám índreṇa sanuyāma vā́jam** *we would win booty through Indra* (i. 101[11]); **áhan vṛtrám índro vájreṇa** *Indra smote Vṛtra with his bolt* (i. 32[5]).

a. Similarly in B.: **kéna vīréṇa** *by whom as champion* (ŚB.); **śīrṣṇā́ bī́jaṃ haranti** *they carry corn (with =) on the head* (ŚB.); **tásmād dákṣiṇena hástena͜ ánnam adyate** *therefore food is eaten with the right hand* (MS.).

3. In its **causal sense** it expresses the reason or motive of an action = *by reason of*, *on account of*, *for the sake of*; e. g. **sómasya pītyā́ . . . ā́ gatam** *come hither for the sake of the Soma draught* (i. 46[13]); **aśatrúr janúṣā sanā́d asi** *thou art by thy nature without foes from of old* (i. 102[8]).

a. Similarly in B.: **sá bhīṣā́ ní lilye** *he concealed himself through fear* (ŚB.).; **so nā́mnā** *by name.*

4. In its **local sense** of *through* or *over* it is used with

verbs of motion to express the space through or over which an action extends; e. g. divā́ yānti marúto bhū́myā‿agnír ayám vā́to antárikṣeṇa yāti *the Maruts go along the sky, Agni over the earth, the Wind here goes through the air* (i. 161[14]); antárikṣe pathíbhiḥ pátantam *flying along the paths in the air* (x. 87[6]).

a. In B. the inst. is constantly used in the local sense with words meaning *path* or *door*, but rarely with others; e. g. yáthā‿ákṣetrajño 'nyéna pathā́ náyet *as if one who does not know the district were to lead by a wrong road* (ŚB.); sárasvatyā yānti *they go along the Sarasvatī* (TS.).

5. In its temporal sense the inst. expresses the time *throughout* which an action extends; e. g. pūrvī́bhir dadāśimá śarádbhiḥ *we have worshipped throughout many autumns* (i. 86[6]). Sometimes, however, the sense of duration is not apparent, the inst. being then used like the loc. of time; thus ṛtúnā and ṛtúbhiḥ mean *in due season.*

a. In B. the temporal meaning is rare; e.g. sá vā́ iṣumātrám evā́hnā tiryáñṅ avardhata *he grew in the course of a day quite an arrow's length in width* (MS.).

6. Many instrumentals (chiefly of the sociative and local classes) have come to be used in a purely adverbial sense. Such are formed from either substantives or adjectives (of which sometimes no other form occurs); e. g. áñjasā *straightway,* máhobhiḥ *mightily,* sáhasā and sáhobhis *suddenly*; ántareṇa *within,* úttareṇa *to the north*; uccáis *above,* nīcáis *below,* parācáis *sideways,* prācáis *forwards,* śánais and śanáis, śanakáis *slowly.*

a. In a number of these instrumentals the adverbial use is indicated, not only by the sense, but by a shift of accent; e. g. dívā *by day*; dakṣiṇā́ *to the right*; madhyā́ *between*; naktayā́ *by night*; svapnayā́ *in a dream*; akṣṇayā́ *across* (B.); anomalously formed from u stems: āśuyā́ *quickly,* dhṛṣṇuyā́ *boldly,* raghuyā́ *swiftly,* sādhuyā́ *straightway,* mithuyā́ *falsely* (mithyā́ ŚB.), anuṣṭhuyā́ *immediately* (anuṣṭhyā́ B.); and from a pronoun, amuyā́ *in that way.*

199. B. Besides having the above general and independent uses the inst. also appears, in special connexion with different classes of words by which it may be said to be 'governed':

1. **with verbs expressing:**

a. association or contention with; in RV.: **yat** *marshal*, **yād** *combine*, **yuj** *join* (mid.), **sac** *accompany*; **yudh** *fight*, **spṛdh** *strive*, **hās** *race*, **krīḍ** *play*; in B.: **yudh** *fight*, **vi-ji** *contend victoriously* (*with*).

b. separation from (compounds with vi); in RV.: **vi-yu** *dissever from*, **vi-vṛt** *turn away from*, **vy-ā-vṛt** *separate* (intr.) *from*; in B.: **vy-ā-vṛt** *id.*, **vi-ṛdh** *be deprived of*, **vi-sthā** *be removed from*, **víṣvaṅṅ i** *go away from* = *lose*.

c. enjoyment; in RV.: **kan** *find pleasure in*, **mad** *be exhilarated with*, **uc** *be fond of*, **tuṣ** *be satisfied with*, **mah** *delight in*, **hṛṣ** *rejoice in*, **bhuj** *enjoy*; in B.: **tṛp** *be pleased with*, **nand** *be glad of*, **bhuj** *enjoy*.

d. repletion; in RV.: **pṝ** *fill* (acc.) *with*,[1] **pī** *swell with*; in B.: caus. of **pṝ**: **pūraya** *fill*, pass. **pūrya** *be filled with*.

e. purchase for (a price); in V.: **vi-krī** *bargain away for*; in B.: **niṣ-krī** *ransom for*.

f. adoration or sacrifice (the victim or object offered). With **yaj** *sacrifice to* the deity is in the acc. in both V. and B.; in B. the sacrificial date also is put in the (cognate) acc.; e. g. **amāvasyā̀ṃ yajate** *he celebrates the feast of new moon*.

g. procedure: the verb **car** in both V. and B.; e.g. **ádhenvā carati māyáyā** *he acts with barren craft* (x. 71⁵); **upāṃśu vācā carati** *he proceeds in a low tone with his voice* (AB.).

h. ability to do: the verb **kṛ** in both V. and B.; e.g. **kím ṛcā́ kariṣyati** *what will he do with a hymn?* (i. 164³⁹); **kíṃ sá táir gṛháiḥ kuryā́t** *what could he do with that house?* (ŚB.). In B. the phrase **ártho bhavati** *there is business with* = *there is need of* (Lat. *opus est aliqua re*) is similarly used;

---

[1] Sometimes also with the gen.: the past part. pass. **pūrṇá** with the gen. = *full of*, but with the inst. *filled with*.

e. g. **yarhi vāva vo mayārtho bhavitā** *if you* (gen.) *shall have need of me* (AB.).

i. dominion: only (in V.) the verb **patya** *be lord of* (lit. *by means of*); e. g. **índro víśvair vīryàiḥ pátyamānaḥ** *Indra who is lord of all heroic powers* (iii. 54[15]).

j. subsistence: only (in B.) the verb **jīv** *live on, subsist by*; e. g. **yáyā manuṣyà jī́vanti** (the cow) *on which men subsist* (TS.).

a. With passive forms of the verb (including participles) the inst. expresses either the means (as with the active verb) or the agent (the nom. of the active verb); e. g. **ghṛténa‿agníḥ sám ajyate** *Agni is anointed with ghee* (x. 118[4]); **uṣā́ uchántī ribhyate vásiṣṭhaiḥ** *Uṣas when she dawns is praised by the Vasiṣṭhas* (vii. 76[7]). Similarly in B.: **prajā́patinā sṛjyante** *they are created by Prajāpati* (MS.); **pā́trair ánnam adyate** *food is eaten with the aid of dishes* (MS.).

β. Nominal forms connected with the verb, when they have a passive sense, as gerundives and infinitives, take the same construction; e. g. **nṛ́bhir hávyaḥ** *to be invoked by men* (vii. 22[7]); **ripúṇā ná‿avacákṣe** *not to be observed by the enemy* (iv. 58[5]).

2. **with nouns:**

a. substantives and adjectives (especially those compounded with **sa-**) expressive of association or equality; e. g. **nā́sunvatā sakhyáṃ vaṣṭi śū́raḥ** *the hero desires not friendship with him who does not press Soma* (x. 42[4]); **ási samó deváiḥ** *thou art equal to the gods* (vi. 48[19]); **índro vái sadṛ́ṅ devátābhir āsīt** *Indra was equal to the* (other) *deities* (TS.); **ā́jyena miśráḥ** *mixed with butter* (ŚB.).

b. other adjectives, to express that by which the quality in question is produced; e. g. **úṣo vā́jena vājini** *O Dawn rich in booty* (iii. 61[1]); **bahúḥ prajáyā bhaviṣyasi** *thou wilt be rich in offspring* (ŚB.).

c. numerals accompanied by **ná**, to express deficiency; e. g. **ekáyā ná viṃśatíḥ** *not twenty by* (lack of) *one = nineteen.*

3. **with prepositions:** genuine prepositions are virtually not used with the instrumental. The only exceptions in

the RV. are the employment of **ádhi** with the inst. of **snú** *height*; of **úpa** in three passages with **dyúbhis** and **dhárma-bhis**; and possibly of **sám** *with* in a few passages with the inst. But prepositional adverbs are found thus used; in the RV. only **avás** *below* and **parás** *above*; and in both V. and B. **sahá** and **sākám** *with*. Cp. 177, 2.

Dative.

200. The dative expresses the notion with which an action is concerned. It is either connected with individual words or is used more generally as a complement to the whole statement.

A. Dative in a **special sense** with:

1. **verbs** (mostly as affecting persons) having the sense of *a. give*; in V. B. **dā** *give*, **yam** *extend*, **dhā** *bestow*, **bhaj** *apportion*; e. g. **dádhāti rátnaṃ vidhaté** *he bestows treasure on the worshipper* (iv. 12[3]); in V. also many other verbs expressing a modification of the sense of giving: **diś** *assign*, **áva-duh** *milk down on*, **pṝ** *bestow fully*, **pṛc** *bestow abundantly*, **maṃh** *give liberally*, **mā** *measure out*, **rā** *procure* (*for*), **ní-yu** *bestow permanently*, **vid** *find* (*for*), **san** *obtain* (*for*), **sū** *set in motion* (*for*), **sṛj** *shed* (*for*), and others.

b. sacrifice; in V. **ā-yaj** *offer to* (while **yaj** takes the acc.); and in V. B. **kṛ** when = *make an offering to*; in B. **ā-labh** (*catch and tie up* =) *offer*; e. g. **agníbhyaḥ paśū́n ā́ labhate** *he sacrifices the animals to the Agnis* (TS.).

c. say = *announce*, *explain* (but with acc. of person if = *address*): in V. B. **ah**, **brū**, **vac**, **vad** (in B. also **ā-cakṣ**); in V. also **arc** and **gā** *sing to*, **stu** *utter praise to*, **gir**, **rap**, **śaṃs** *praise* anything (acc.) *to*. In B. also: **ni-hnu** *apologize to*; e.g. **tád u devébhyo ní hnute** *thereby he craves pardon of the gods* (ŚB.).

d. hear: in RV. a few times **śru** = *listen to*; also **ram** *linger for* = *listen to*.

e. believe, have confidence in: **śrád dhā**; e. g. **śrád asmai dhatta** *believe in him* (ii. 12[5]); in B. also **ślāgh** *trust in.*

f. help, be gracious to, pay homage to: in V. **śak** *aid*, **sidh** *avail*; **sám-nam** *be complaisant to*; **daśasya** *pay honour to*, **saparya** *do anything* (acc.) *in honour of* (a god); **dāś, vidh, sac** *pay homage to* (a god), **śam** *serve* (a god); in V. and B.: **mṛḍ** *be gracious to.*

g. bring: **nī, bhṛ, vah, hi, hṛ**; e. g. **amā́ saté vahasi bhū́ri vāmám** *for him who is at home thou bringest much wealth* (i. 124[12]); **devébhyo havyáṃ vahanti** *they take the oblation to the gods* (TS.); **táṃ harāmi pitṛyajñā́ya devám** *that god I bring to the sacrifice for the Manes* (x. 16[10]); **víśaḥ kṣatríyāya balíṃ haranti** *the peasants bring the taxes to the nobility* (ŚB.). In V. only there are many other verbs, with this general sense, that take the dative, such as **ṛ, inv, cud** *set in motion for*, and figurative expressions such as **abhi-kṣar** *stream to*, **dī** and **śuc** *shine on*, **pruṣ** *sprinkle on*, **abhi-vā** *waft to*: in V. also the verb **i** *go* is used with the dat.; e. g. **prá víṣṇave śūṣám etu mánma** *let my strong hymn go forth in honour of Viṣṇu* (i. 154[3]).

h. please: **svad** *be sweet to* and **chand** *be pleasing to*; e. g. **svádasva‿índrāya pītáye** *be sweet to Indra as a draught* (ix. 74[9]); **utó tád asmai mádhv íc cachadyāt** *and may that mead be pleasing to him* (x. 73[9]).

i. succeed: in B. **ṛdh** and **kḷp**; e. g. **ná ha‿evá‿asmai tát sám ānṛdhe** *he did not succeed in that* (ŚB.); **kálpate 'smai** *he succeeds* (TS.).

j. subject to: **radh**; e. g. **asmábhyaṃ vṛtrā́ randhi** *subject our foes to us* (iv. 22[9]).

k. yield to: **radh** *succumb*, **nam** and **ni-hā** *bow before*, **sthā** *obey*, **mrad** and **kṣam** (B.) *yield to*, **ā-vraśc** *fall a victim to*; e. g. **mó aháṃ dviṣaté radham** *may I not succumb to my enemy* (i. 50[13]); **tasthúḥ savā́ya te** *they obey thy command* (iv. 54[5]).

l. be angry with: in V. **hṛ** (**hṛṇīte**); in V. and B.: **asūya** and **krudh**; in B. also **arātīya** *be hostile* and **glā** *be averse to.*

m. seek to injure: in V. and B. **druh**; e.g. **yád dudróhitha striyái puṃsé** *what mischief thou hast done to woman or man* (AV.).

n. cast at: V. **sṛj** *discharge*; V. B. **as** *throw*; B. **pra-hṛ** *hurl at*; e.g. **sṛjád ástā didyúm asmai** *the archer shot a lightning shaft at him* (i. 71[5]); **tásmai tā́m íṣum asyati** *he shoots the arrow at him* (MS.); **vájraṃ bhrā́tṛvyāya prá harati** *he hurls the bolt at the foe* (TS.).

o. exist or *be intended for, accrue to*: **as** *be*, **bhū** *become*; e.g. **gambhīré cid bhavati gādhám asmai** *even in deep water there is a ford for him* (vi. 24[8]); **índra túbhyam íd abhūma** *we have become thine own, O Indra* (TS.); **átha kó máhyaṃ bhāgó bhaviṣyati** *then what share will accrue to me* (ŚB.).

a. The dative is used with gerundives and infinitives to express the agent, and with the latter also the object by attraction instead of the acc.; e.g. **yáḥ stotṛ́bhyo hávyo asti** *who is to be invoked by singers* (i. 33[2]); **ví śrayantāṃ prayái devébhyaḥ** *let* (the doors) *open wide for the gods to enter* (i. 142[6]); **índram arkáir ávardhayann áhaye hántavā́ u** *they strengthened Indra with hymns to slay the serpent* (v. 31[4]).

2. The dative is used with a certain number of substantives.

a. Such are words that invoke blessings, especially **námas** *homage* (with the verbs **kṛ** *do* or **as** *be*, which are often to be supplied); e.g. **námo mahádbhyaḥ** *homage to the great* (i. 27[13]); **námo 'stu bráhmiṣṭhāya** *adoration to the greatest Brahman* (ŚB.). Similarly used are the sacrificial formulas **svā́hā, svadhā́, váṣaṭ** *hail! blessing!* e.g. **tébhyaḥ svā́hā** *blessing on them* (AV.).

a. The indeclinables **śám** in V. and **kám** in B. meaning *welfare* are used as nom. or acc. with the dat.; e.g. **yáthā śám ásad dvipáde cátuṣpade** *in order that there may be welfare for biped and quadruped* (i. 114[1]); **áhutayo hy agnáye kám** *for the oblations are a joy to Agni* (ŚB.); **ná‿asmā á-kaṃ bhavati** *it does not fare ill with him* (TS.).

β. In V. the substantives **kā́ma** *desire* and **gatú** *path* may perhaps be regarded as taking a dative without a verb to be supplied; e.g. **kṛṇvānā́so amṛtatvā́ya gātúm** *procuring for themselves a path to immortality* (i. 72[9]).

γ. In the name **Dā́syave vṛ́kaḥ** *Wolf to the Dasyu* (RV.) the dat. is to be explained as due to its use in the sentence *he is a very wolf to the Dasyu.*

3. The dative is used **with adjectives** meaning *dear, kind, agreeable, beneficial, willing, obedient, ill-disposed, hostile*; e.g. **śivā́ sákhibhya utá máhyam āsīt** *she was kind to friends and also to me* (x. 34[2]); **átithiś cā́rur āyáve** *a guest dear to man* (ii. 2[8]); **yád vā́vá jīvébhyo hitám̐ tát pitṛ́bhyaḥ** *what is good for the living is good for the Manes* (ŚB.); **sá rātámanā vráścanāya bhavati** (ŚB.) *he is ready for felling* (the tree); **pratyudyāmínīm̐ ha kṣatrā́ya víśam̐ kuryāt** *he would make the peasantry hostile to the nobility* (ŚB.).

a. The adj. **ánāgas** *sinless* often seems to take the dative of the name of a deity, but it is somewhat uncertain whether the case should not be connected with the verb; e.g. **ánāgaso áditaye syāma** *may we be sinless* (*to* =) *in the eyes of Aditi* (i. 24[15]) may perhaps mean *may we, as sinless, belong to Aditi.*

4. The dative is used **with a few adverbs**.

a. **áram** often takes the dat.; e.g. **yé áram̐ váhanti manyáve** *who drive in accordance with* (thy) *zeal* (vi. 16[43]). This use of **áram** is common in combination with the verbs **kṛ, gam,** and **bhū.** When used with the dat. **áram** is not infrequently equivalent to an adj.; e.g. **sā́smā áram** *he is ready for him* (ii. 18[2]); **ayám̐ sómo astu áram̐ mánase yuvábhyām** *let this Soma be agreeable to your heart* (i. 108[2]). In B. **álam** appears in the place of **áram** and is often similarly used; e.g. **nā́lam ā́hutyā ā́sa, nā́lam̐ bhakṣā́ya** *he was not suitable for sacrifice, nor suitable for food* (ŚB.).

b. The adverb **āvís** *visibly* is used with the dat. in V. and B., but only when accompanied by the verbs **kṛ, bhū** or **as** (the latter sometimes to be supplied); e.g. **āvír ebhyo abhavat sū́ryaḥ** *the sun appeared to them* (i. 146[4]); **tásmai vā́ āvír asāma** *we will appear to him* (ŚB.).

B. The dative also in a **general sense** complements the statement of the whole sentence.

1. It expresses the person for whose **advantage** or **disadvantage** the action of the sentence takes place; e. g. **devā́n devayaté yaja** *worship the gods for the benefit of the pious man* (i. 15[12]); **tásmā etám̧ vájram akurvan** *for him they made this bolt* (ŚB.); **tasmā upākṛtāya niyoktāram̧ na vividuḥ** (AB.) *for him when he had been brought near they could find no binder* (i.e. they could find no one willing to bind him).

2. It expresses the **purpose** for which an action is done (final dative); e. g. **ūrdhvás tiṣṭhā na ūtáye** *stand up for our help = in order to help us* (i. 30[6]); **ná súṣvim índro ávase mṛdhāti** *Indra will not leave the pious man in the lurch for help* (vi. 23[9]); **svargā́ya lokā́ya viṣṇukramā́ḥ kramyante** *the Viṣṇu steps are taken for the sake of* (= in order to gain) *heaven* (TS.); **agním̧ hotrā́ya prā́vṛṇata** *they chose Agni for the priesthood* = in order that he should be priest (ŚB.). The final sense is commonly expressed by abstract substantives (including in V. many infinitives); e. g. **ádhi śriyé duhitā́ sū́ryasya rátham̧ tasthau** *the daughter of the sun has mounted the car for beauty* = so as to produce a beautiful effect (vi. 63[5]); **téna‿evá‿enam̧ sám̧ sṛjati śā́ntyai** *with him* (Mitra) *he unites him* (Agni) *for appeasement* (TS.).

a. This final dat. is particularly used with **as** and **bhū**; e. g. **ásti hí ṣmā mádāya vaḥ** *there is* (something) *for your intoxication*, i. e. to intoxicate you (i. 37[15]); **mádāya sómaḥ** (sc. **asti**) *Soma* (*is for* =) *produces intoxication* (ŚB.).

3. The **dative** is used, though rarely, in expressions of time like the English *for*; e. g. **nūnám̧ na indra‿ aparā́ya ca syāḥ** *now and for the future mayst thou be ours, O Indra* (vi. 33[5]); **sam̧vatsarā́ya sám amyate** *for a year an alliance is made* (MS.).

a. The iterative compound **divé-dive** *day by day*, though apparently dat. of **div**, is probably in reality meant for the loc. of the transfer stem **divá**.

4. **Two datives** connected in sense often appear together. This occurs in V. when an acc. is attracted by a dative infinitive; e. g. **vṛtrā́ya hántave** = **vṛtrám hántave** *to slay Vṛtra* (cp. 200. A. 1 *o α*).

a. There is an analogous use in B., where, however, an abstract substantive takes the place of the infinitive; e. g. **yáthā‿idáṃ pāṇí-bhyām avanéjanāya‿āháranty evám** *just as they bring it for washing the hands* (ŚB.). Two datives are here often found with the verb **sthā**, one expressing the purpose, the other the person affected by the action; e.g. **devebhyaḥ paśavo 'nnādyāyālambāya na‿atiṣṭhanta** *the animals did not present themselves to the gods for food, for sacrifice* (AB.).

5. The **adverbial** use of the **dative** is very rare: **kā́māya** and **árthāya** *for the sake of* may be regarded as such; **kāmacārásya kā́māya** *for the sake of unrestrained motion* (ŚB.); **asmā́kā́rthāya jajñiṣe** *thou hast been born for our sake* (AV.).

Ablative.

201. The ablative, expressing the starting-point from which the action of the verb proceeds, may as a rule be translated by *from*. It is chiefly connected with various classes of words, but is also used independently.

A. In its **dependent use** the ablative appears with:

1. **verbs** *a.* expressing a local action, as *go, proceed, drive, lead, take, receive; pour, drink; call, loosen, ward off, exclude*; e. g. **īyúr gā́vo ná yávasād ágopāḥ** *they went like unherded kine from the pasture* (vii. 18[10]); **vṛtrásya śvasáthād ī́ṣa-māṇāḥ** *fleeing from the snorting of Vṛtra* (viii. 96[7]); **ásataḥ sád ajāyata** *from non-being arose being* (x. 72[3]); **abhrā́d íva prá stanayanti vṛṣṭáyaḥ** *from the cloud as it were thunder the rains* (x. 75[3]); **tváṃ dásyūm̐r ókasa ājaḥ** *thou drovest the enemies from the house* (vii. 5[6]); **bhujyúṃ samudrā́d ūha-thuḥ** *ye two have borne Bhujyu from the sea* (vi. 62[6]); **dáśo hiraṇyapiṇḍā́n dívodāsād asāniṣam** *ten lumps of gold I*

have received from Divodāsa (vi. 47[23]); **ápād dhotrā́d utá potrā́d amatta** *he has drunk from the Hotṛ's vessel and has intoxicated himself from the Potṛ's vessel* (ii. 37[4]); **máruto yád vo diváḥ hávāmahe** *O Maruts, when we call you from heaven* (viii. 7[11]); **śúnaś cic chépaṃ yū́pād amuñcaḥ** *thou didst release Śunaḥśepa from the post* (v. 2[7]); **yuyutám asmád ánirām ámīvām** *ward off from us sickness and calamity* (vii. 71[2]).

a. Examples from B. are: **yád dhā́ved annā́dyād dhāvet** *if he were to run, he would run away from his food* (TS.); **sá ráthāt papāta** *he fell from his car* (ŚB.); **divó vṛ́ṣṭir īrte** *rain comes from the sky* (TS.); **ṛṣayaḥ kavaṣam ailūṣaṃ somād anayan** *the seers led Kavaṣa Ailūṣa away from Soma*, i.e. excluded him from it (AB.); **enān asmāl lokād anudanta** *they drove them away from this world* (AB.); **tásmād ánasa evá gṛhṇīyāt** *therefore he should take it from the cart* (ŚB.); **keśavā́t púruṣāt sī́sena parisrútaṃ krīṇāti** *he buys the Parisrut from a long-haired man for lead* (ŚB.); **sá evá‿enaṃ varuṇapāśā́n muñcati** *he releases him from the fetter of Varuṇa* (TS.); **suvargā́l lokā́d yájamāno hīyeta** *the sacrificer would fall short of heaven* (TS.). The two verbs **antár dhā** *hide* and **ní-lī** *conceal oneself* are used with the abl. in B. only: **vájreṇa‿enaṃ suvargā́l lokā́d antár dadhyāt** *he would exclude him from heaven with the bolt* (TS.); **agnír devébhyo nílāyata** *Agni concealed himself from the gods* (TS.).

b. expressing *rescue, protect*; *fear, dislike*; *transcend, prefer*: verbs with the latter two senses as well as **uruṣya** *protect*, **rakṣ** *guard*, and **rej** *tremble* take this construction in V. only; **pā** and **trā** *protect* and **bhī** *fear* in both V. and B.; **gopāya** *protect*, **bībhatsa** *be disgusted with* in B. only; e. g. **áṃhaso no mitrá uruṣyet** *may Mitra rescue us from distress* (iv. 55[5]); **sá nás trāsate duritā́t** *he shall protect us from misfortune* (i. 128[5]); **índrasya vájrād abibhet** *she was afraid of Indra's bolt* (x. 138[5]); **prá síndhubhyo ririce, prá kṣitíbhyaḥ** *he reaches beyond rivers and beyond lands* (x. 89[11]); **sómāt sutā́d índro avṛṇīta vásiṣṭhān** *Indra preferred the Vasiṣṭhas to* (Pāśadyumna's) *pressed Soma* (vii. 33[2]).

a. With **bhī** two ablatives are found, the one being the object feared, the other the action proceeding from it; e. g. **índrasya vájrād abibhed abhiśnáthaḥ** *she was afraid of*

Indra's bolt, of its crushing (x. 138⁵), i. e. that it would crush her; **asurarakṣaséбhya āsaṅgā́d bibhayā́ṃ cakruḥ** *they were afraid of the Asuras and Rakṣasas, of their attachment* = that they would attach themselves to them (ŚB.).

2. **substantives** when derived from, or equivalent to, verbs used with the ablative; e. g. **śárma no yaṃsan trivárūtham áṃhasaḥ** *they shall grant us thrice-protecting shelter from distress* (x. 66[5]); **úpa chāyā́m iva ghṛ́ṇer áganma śárma te vayám** *we have entered thy shelter like shade* (that protects) *from heat* (vi. 16[38]); **rákṣobhyo vái tā́ṃ bhīṣā́ vā́cam ayachan** *they restrained their speech from fear of the demons* (ŚB.).

3. **adjectives**: in V. and B. comparatives and adjectives of cognate sense, when it means *than*; e. g. **ghṛtā́t svā́dīyaḥ** *sweeter than butter* (viii. 24[20]); **víśvasmād índra úttaraḥ** *Indra is greater than every one* (x. 86[1]); **jātā́ny ávarāṇy asmāt** *born later than he* (viii. 96[6]); **pū́rvā víśvasmād bhúvanād abodhi** *she has awakened earlier than every being* (i. 123[2]); **pā́pīyān áśvād gardabháḥ** *the ass is worse than the horse* (TS.); **brahma hi pūrvaṃ kṣatrāt** *the priesthood is superior to the warrior class* (PB.); **anyo vā ayam asmad bhavati** *he becomes other than we* (AB.).

a. In B. several local and temporal adjectives: **arvācī́na** *below*, **ūrdhvá** *above*, **jihmá** *aslant*; **arvā́ñc** *before*, **parā́ñc** *after*; e. g. **yát kíṃ ca‿arvācī́nam ādityā́t** *whatever is below the sun* (ŚB.); **etásmāc cā́tvalād ūrdhvā́ḥ svargáṃ lokám upód akrāman** *upward from that pit they ascended to heaven* (ŚB.); **yajñāj jihmā īyuḥ** *they (would go obliquely from* =) *lose the sacrifice* (AB.); **daśa vā etasmād arvāñcas trivrto, daśa parāñcaḥ** *ten Trivṛts occur before it and ten after it* (AB.).

b. in B. adjectives in **uka**, which with **bhū** are equivalent to a verb; e. g. **yajamānāt paśavo 'nutkrāmukā bhavanti** *the animals are not inclined to run away from the sacrificer* (AB.).

c. in B. numerals, both ordinals and cardinals: with the former the abl. expresses the point from which the reckoning is made; e.g. **īśvaro ha‿asmād dvitīyo vā tṛtīyo vā brāhmaṇatām abhyupaitoḥ** *the second or third* (in descent) *from him can obtain Brahminhood* (AB.); with the latter it expresses the figure by which the complete number is defective; e.g. **ékān ná śatám** *not a hundred by one = ninety-nine.*

Analogously with words meaning *incomplete* the abl. expresses the amount of the deficiency; e.g. **ékasmād akṣárād ánāptam** (a verse) *incomplete by one syllable* (TS.); **téṣām alpakā́d evá agnír ásaṃcita āsa** *their fire* (altar) *was not completely piled up by a little only*, i.e. was almost completely piled up (ŚB.).

4. adverbs meaning *before, beyond, outside, below, far from, without* are used prepositionally with the abl. Those occurring in V. only are: **adhás** *below*, **avás** *down from*, **āré** *without*, **purás** *before*; in V. and B.: **ṛté** *without*, **tirás** *apart from*, **parás** *outside*, **purā́** *before*; in B. only: **abhyardhás** *far from*; **bahís** *outside*. Cp. 177, 3.

a. In B. some other adverbs with a local or temporal sense; e.g. **dūrám ha vā́ asmā́n mṛtyúr bhavati** *death is far from him* (ŚB.); **tásmān madhyamā́c chaṅkór dakṣiṇā́ páñcadaśa vikramā́n prá krāmati** *he strides forward fifteen steps to the right of this middle peg* (ŚB.); **prāg ghomāt** *before* (making) *the oblation* (AB.).

B. The abl. is used **independently** of any particular class of word to express the **reason** of an action in the sense of *on account of*; e.g. **mā́ nas tásmād énaso deva rīriṣaḥ** *let us suffer no harm, O god, on account of this sin* (vii. 89[5]); **ánṛtād vái tā́ḥ prajā́ váruṇo 'gṛhṇāt** *by reason of their guilt Varuṇa seized creatures* (MS.). Similarly in B.: **tásmād** *therefore*; **kásmāt** *wherefore?*

Genitive.

202. The genitive is a dependent case, being in its main uses connected with verbs and substantives, but also appearing with adjectives and adverbs.

A. With **verbs** the gen. has a sense analogous to that of the acc., but differs here from the latter in expressing that the action affects the object not as a whole, but only in part. It is used with verbs having the following senses:

a. rule over, dispose of: always with **kṣi** and **rāj**, nearly always with **irajya** and **īś** (rarely acc.). In B. the only verb with this sense taking the gen. is **īś** *have power over*; e. g. **átha‿eṣāṃ sárva īśe** *then every one has power over them* (MS.).

b. *rejoice in*: always with **tṛp, prī, vṛdh**; optionally with **kan** and **mad** (also inst. and loc.), and with the caus. of **pan** (also acc.).

a. In B. the only verb of this group taking the gen. is **tṛp** in a partitive sense; e. g. **ánnasya tṛpyati** *he refreshes himself with (some) food* (ŚB.).

c. *take note of*: always with 2. **kṛ** *speak highly of* and **ā-dhī** *think about, care for*; alternatively with acc.: **cit** *observe, attend to,* **budh** *take note of*; **adhi-i, -gam, -gā** *attend to, care for*; **vid** *know about* (with acc. *know fully*); **śru** *hear* (gen. of person, acc. of thing, heard). In AV. **kīrtaya** *mention* and **smṛ** *remember* take the gen.

a. In B. only three verbs of this class are thus construed: **vid** and **śru** as in RV., and **kīrtaya** *mention*.

d. partitiveness (while the acc. with the same verbs expresses full extent):

1. *eat, drink*: **aś** *eat of,* **ad** *eat* (almost exclusively with acc.); **pā** *drink*; **ā-vṛṣ** *fill oneself full of,* **vī** and **juṣ** *enjoy.*

a. In B. only **aś** and **pā** besides **bhakṣ** *eat* (in RV. with acc. only) take the partitive gen.

2. *give, present, sacrifice*: **dā** *give of,* **ā-daśasya** and **śak** *present with*; **pṛc** *give abundantly of*; **yaj** *sacrifice* (acc. of person, gen. of offering), e. g. **sómasya tvā yakṣi** *I will worship thee* (with a libation) *of Soma* (iii. 53^2).

a. In B. **yaj** may be used without acc. of the person; e. g. **tásmād ā́jyasya‿evá yajet** *therefore he should sacrifice some butter* (ŚB.).

β. In B. several verbs having the general sense of giving and taking, not so used in V., come to be used with the gen. of the object in a partitive sense: **vap** *strew,* **hu** *offer,* **abhi-ghar** *pour upon,* **ava-dā** *cut off some of,* **ā-ścut** *drip,* **upa-stṛ** *spread over,* **ni-han** (AV.) and **pra-han** *strike,* **vi-khan** *dig up some of*; **grabh** *take of* and in the passive *be seized = suffer in* (a part of the body); e. g. **ná cákṣuṣo gṛhe** *he does not suffer in his eye* (MS.): **yó vācó gṛhītáḥ** *who suffers in his voice* (MS.).

γ. In B. **anu-brū** *invite* is used with the dat. of the god and the gen. of that to which he is invited; e. g. **agnī-ṣómābhyām médasó 'nu brūhi** *invite Agni and Soma to the fat* (ŚB.).

e. obtain, ask for: **bhaj** *participate in* (with acc. *obtain*); **bhikṣ** *beg for*: **ī** and **īḍ** *implore for* (generally acc. of thing as well as person); e. g. **tám īmahe índram asya rāyáḥ** *we implore Indra for some of that wealth* (vi. 22³); **īyate vásūnām** *he is implored for some of his riches* (vii. 32⁵); also **ā-yu** *take possession of*.

a. Of these verbs **bhaj** remains in use in B.: with gen. = *have a share in* (with acc. *receive as a share*).

f. belong to: **as** and **bhū**, with the gen. of the possessor in both V. and B.; e. g. **asmā́kam astu kévalaḥ** *let him exclusively be ours* (i. 7¹⁰); **átha‿abhavat kévalaḥ sómo asya** *then Soma became exclusively his* (vii. 98⁵); **mánor ha vā́ ṛṣabhá āsa** *Manu had a bull* (ŚB.); **tasya śatam jāyā babhūvuḥ** *he had a hundred wives* (AB.).

B. The genitive is used with two classes of substantives.

1. It depends on verbal substantives and is then allied to the gen. with verbs (especially those expressing possession).

a. The **subjective** gen., which is equivalent to the agent of the action expressed by the cognate verb; e. g. **uṣáso vyùṣṭau** *at the break of dawn* = when the dawn breaks; **apakramā́d u ha‿evá‿eṣām etád bibhayā́m cakāra** *he was afraid of their departure* (ŚB.) = that they would run away. It very often occurs with datives; e. g. **yajñásya sámṛddhyai** *for the success of the sacrifice* (TS.) = that the sacrifice might succeed.

b. The **objective** gen., which is equivalent to the object expressed by the cognate verb; e. g. **yógo vājínaḥ** *the yoking of the steed* = he yokes the steed; **purā́ vṛtrásya vadhā́t** *before the slaughter of Vṛtra* (ŚB.) = before he slew Vṛtra. It often occurs with datives; e. g. **yájamānasya‿áhiṃsāyai** *for the non-injury of the sacrificer* (MS.) = in order not to injure the sacrificer.

a. This genitive is common with agent nouns, especially those in **tṝ**; e.g. **rāyó dātā́** *giver of wealth* (vi. 23[10]); **pūṣā́ paśūnā́ṃ prajanayitā́** *Puṣan is the propagator of cattle* (MS.). But in V. the agent nouns in **tṛ** with few exceptions take the acc. when the root is accented; e.g. **dā́tā vásu** *one who gives wealth* (vi. 23[3]).

2. The gen. commonly depends on non-verbal substantives. It may then have two senses:

a. The **possessive** gen.; e.g. **véḥ parṇám** *the wing of the bird* = wing belonging to the bird; **devā́nāṃ dūtáḥ** *the messenger of the gods.* It also appears with abstract nouns derived from such words; e.g. **ā́d íd devā́nām úpa sakhyám āyan** *then they came to friendship with the gods* (iv. 33[2]) = then they became friends of the gods.

a. The gen. used with the perf. pass. part., felt to be the agent, is a variety of the possessive gen. Already appearing a few times in the RV. it is common in B.; e.g. **pátyuḥ krītā́** (MS.) *the bought* (wife) *of the husband* = (the wife) *bought by the husband.*

β. The gen. is similarly used with the gerundive; e.g. **anyasya balikṛd anyasya‿adyaḥ** *paying taxes to another, to be devoured by another* (AB.).

γ. The gen. is frequently used possessively where we would use a dative; e.g. **tasya ha putro jajñe** *a son of his was born* = *a son was born to him* (AB.).

δ. The gen. is occasionally used for the dative with **śrad dhā** *believe* and **dā** *give* in the AB. This use may have started from the possessive sense.

b. The **partitive** gen. expresses a part of the whole; e.g. **mitró vái śivó devā́nām** *Mitra is the kindly one among the gods* (TS.). If the gen. is a plural of the same word as that on which it depends it is equivalent to a superlative; e.g. **sákhe sákhīnām** *O friend among friends* = *best of friends* (i. 30[11]); **mantrakṛtāṃ mantrakṛt** *best of composers of hymns* (B.).

a. This gen. is in particular used with comparatives and superlatives (including **prathamá** *first*, **caramá** *last*, &c.); e.g. **ná párā jigye katarás canáinoḥ** *not either of the two of them conquered* (vi. 69[8]); **gardabháḥ paśūnā́ṃ bhārabharítamaḥ** *the ass is the best bearer of burdens among animals* (TS.).

β. It is used with numbers above *twenty* (in B. only with **sahásram**) and words expressive of a division or a measure; e. g. **ṣaṣṭím áśvānām** (an aggregate of) *sixty horses*; **gónām ardhám** *half of the cows*; **gávāṃ yūthā́ni** *herds of cows*. Sometimes this gen. is used by transference to express not a part, but the whole; as in **marútāṃ gaṇáḥ** *the host* (consisting) *of the Maruts*.

γ. The gen. sometimes expresses the material; e. g. **kṛṣṇā́nāṃ vrīhīṇā́ṃ carúṃ śrapayati** *he cooks a mess of black rice* (ŚB.); **etéṣāṃ vṛkṣā́ṇāṃ bhavanti** *they* (the fences) *are* (made of the wood) *of these trees* (ŚB.). It is used in this sense with the verb **kṛ**; e. g. **yá evá káś ca vṛkṣáḥ phalagráhis tásya kāryà** *whatever tree bears fruit, of* (a part of) *that it is to be made* (MS.).

C. The gen. is used **with** a few **adjectives** meaning *attached to, like, capable of, knowing, offering, abounding in*: **priyá** *dear*, **ánuvrata** *obedient*; **prátyardhi** *standing at the side of*; **ánurūpa** *similar*; **īśvará** *able to*, **návedas** *cognisant of*; **pápri** *bestowing abundantly* (partitive gen. of the thing offered, e. g. **ándhasaḥ** *of the juice* (i. 52[3]); and with the participles, used like adjectives, **pūrṇá** *full of*, **pīpivā́ṃs** *abounding in*.

D. The gen. is used **with** certain **adverbs** having 1. a local sense: in V. **agratás** *before* (AV.); in V. and B.: **dakṣiṇatás** *to the right of*; **avástād** *below*, **parástād** *above*, **purástād** *before*; in B.: **upáriṣṭād** *behind*, **paścā́d** *behind*, **purás** *before*; **antikám** *near*, **nédīyas** *nearer*, **nédiṣṭham** *nearest*.

a. In the RV. **āré** *far from* takes the gen. (also the abl.).

β. In B. the local adjective (like the local adverbs) **údañc** *northward of* takes the gen.

2. a temporal sense: **idā́** and **idā́nīm** *now* are used in V. with the genitives **áhnas** and **áhnām** = *at the present time of day*; **prātár** *early* with the gen. **áhnas** in V. and with **rā́tryās** in B.; e. g. **yásyā rā́tryāḥ prātár yakṣyámāṇaḥ syā́t** *in the morning of which night he may be about to sacrifice* (MS.).

3. a multiplicative sense: in V. **sakṛ́t** *once* with **áhnas** *once a day*; **trís** *thrice* in **trír áhnas, trír ā́ diváḥ** *thrice*

a day and **trír aktós** *three times a night*; in B.: **dvís** *twice* and **trís** *thrice* with **saṃvatsarásya**, *twice, thrice a year.*

a. The adverbial use in V. of the gen. in a temporal sense is perhaps derived from that with multiplicatives: **aktós, kṣápas** and **kṣapás** *of a night*; **vástos** and **uṣásas** *of a morning.*

Locative.

203. This case expresses the sphere in which an action takes place, or with verbs of motion the sphere which is reached by the action. Its sense includes not only locality (both concrete and abstract) but persons and time. It may therefore be variously translated by *in, on, at*; *beside, among, in the presence of*; *to, into.*

A. The loc. appears in a general and independent way in the following senses:

1. **Place**: *a.* concrete; e.g. **diví** *in heaven*, **párvate** *in* or *on the mountain* (i. 32^2); **sárasvatyām** *at the Sarasvatī* (iii. 23^4); **yudhí** *in battle* (i. 8^3), **saṃgrāmé** *id.* (ŚB.).

b. abstract: **asya sumatáu syāma** *may we be in his good graces* (viii. 48^{12}); **tád indra te váśe** *that, O Indra, is in thy power* (viii. 93^4); **yá ādityā́nāṃ bhávati práṇītau** *who is in the guidance of the Ādityas* (ii. 27^{13}); **vájrasya yát pátane pā́di śúṣṇaḥ** *when upon the flight of the bolt Śuṣṇa fell* (vi. 20^5); **ghṛtakīrtáu** *at the mention of* (the word) *ghee* (ŚB.).

2. **Persons**: e.g. **yát kíṃ ca duritáṃ máyi** *whatever sin there is in me* (i. 23^{22}); **pīpā́ya sá śrávasā mártyeṣu** *he abounds in fame among mortals* (vi. 10^3); **yát sthó druhyávy ánavi turváśe yádau, huvé vām** *whether ye two are beside* (with) *Druhyu, Anu, Turvaśa* (or) *Yadu, I call you* (viii. 10^5); **vayáṃ syāma váruṇe ánāgāḥ** *may we be guiltless in the eyes of Varuṇa* (vii. 87^7); **asmín puṣyantu gópatau** *let them prosper under this herdsman* (x. 19^3).

3. **Time**: here the loc. expresses that an action takes place within the limits of the time mentioned; e.g. **uṣáso**

vyùṣṭau *at the flush of dawn*; **uṣási** *in the morning* (in B. **prātár** is used instead); **dyávi-dyavi** *every day* (not used in B.); **trír áhan** *three times in the day* (in B. gen. only); **jāyate māsí-māsi** *he is born* (once) *in every* (successive) *month* (x. 52[3]).

a. This temporal use sometimes comes to mean that something happens at the end of the period; e. g. **saṃvatsaré idám adyā́ vy àkhyata** *ye have opened your eyes now to-day* (for the first time) *in a year* (i. 161[13]) = *at the end of a year*; **tátaḥ saṃvatsaré púruṣaḥ sám abhavat** *thence arose in* (= at the end of) *a year a man* (ŚB.).

4. **Adverbially.** A few substantives and adjectives are thus used; e. g. **ágre** often occurs in the sense of *in front* and *at first*, appearing even in compounds (e. g. **agre-gá** *going before*, **agre-pā́** *drinking first*); in ŚB. the loc. of **kṣiprá** *quick* is several times thus employed, e. g. **kṣipré ha yájamāno 'múṃ lokám iyāt** *the sacrificer would speedily go to yonder world.*

204. B. The loc. is connected with different classes of words by which it may be said to be governed.

1. It is specially connected with **verbs** expressing:

a. in V.: *rejoice in*; *grow, prosper*; *bless, injure in respect of*; *implore, invoke for* (ī, hū); *receive from*; e. g. **víśve devā haviṣi mādayadhvam** *do ye, O all-gods, rejoice in the oblation* (vi. 52[17]); **táviṣīṣu vāvṛdhe** *he grew in strength* (i. 52[2]); **yá eṣāṃ bhṛtyā́m ṛṇádhat sá jīvāt** *he who will succeed in their support, shall live* (i. 84[16]); **prā́va nas toké** *bless us in children* (viii. 23[12]); **mā́ nas toké rīriṣaḥ** *injure us not in our children* (i. 114[8]); **agníṃ toké tánaye śáśvad īmahe** *Agni we constantly implore for children and for grandchildren* (viii. 71[13]); **ádhā hí tvā hávāmahe tánaye góṣu͜apsú** *for we invoke thee for offspring, cows, water* (vi. 19[12]); **devéṣu͜ amṛtatvám ānaśa** *ye received immortality* (*among* =) *from the gods* (iv. 36[4]);

in V. and B.: *let share in* (**ā-bhaj**) and *struggle for* (**spṛdh**, rarely in V.); e. g. **yā́n ā́bhajo marúta indra sóme** *the*

Maruts whom thou, O Indra, didst allow to share in Soma (iii. 35[9]); **ánu no 'syā́ṃ pṛthivyā́m ā́ bhajata** *let us have a share in this earth* (ŚB.); **ādityāś ca ha vā aṅgirasaś ca svarge loke 'spardhanta** *the Ādityas and the Aṅgirases struggled for* (the possession of) *the heavenly world* (AB.);

in B.: *request* (**iṣ**), *ask* (**prach**), *call in question* (**mīmāṃs**); e. g. **sā́ ha‿iyáṃ devéṣu sutyā́yām apitvám īṣe** *she requested from the gods a share in the Soma feast* (ŚB.); **te deveṣv apṛchanta** *they inquired of the gods* (PB.).

b. in V. and B.: *motion*, to indicate the place that is reached. The case may here be translated by *to, into, upon.* Such verbs in V. are: *go* (**gam**), *enter* (**ā-viś**), *ascend* (**ā-ruh**), *descend* (**ava-vyadh**), *flow* (**arṣ, dhāv**), *pour* (**sic, hu**), *put* (**dhā, kṛ**); e. g. **sá íd devéṣu gachati** (i. 1[4]) *that goes to* (= reaches) *the gods* (while **devā́n gachati** would mean *goes in the direction of the gods*); **yó mártyeṣv ít kṛṇóti devā́n** *who brings the gods to mortals* (i. 77[1]); **vīryàṃ yájamāne dadhāti** *he puts energy into the sacrificer* (TS.); **ná vā́ eṣá grāmyéṣu paśúṣu hitáḥ** *he* (*is not placed among* =) *does not belong to the tame animals* (TS.). In B. verbs meaning to *throw at* are especially common with the loc.

c. desire, to indicate the goal or object aimed at: **gṛdh** *be eager*, **yat** *strive*, **ā-śaṃs** *hope*; e. g. **ánneṣu jāgṛdhur** *they are eager for food* (ii. 23[16]); **diví svanó yatate** *the sound soars to heaven* (x. 75[3]); **ā́ tū́ na indra śaṃsaya góṣv áśveṣu** *pray give us hope, Indra, of cows and horses* (i. 29[1]); **agnihotríṇi devátā ā́ śaṃsante** *the gods place their hope in the maintainer of the sacrificial fire* (MS.).

2. The loc. is also used to some extent connected with **nouns**:

a. verbal nouns (substantives and adjectives) derived from verbs taking that case; e. g. **ná tásya vācy ápi bhāgó asti** *he has no share in speech* (x. 71[6]); **sómo bhūtv avapā́neṣv ā́bhagaḥ** *let Soma be a participator in drinking bouts* (i. 136[4]); **sutá ít tváṃ nímiśla indra sóme** *thou art attached, O Indra,* *to the pressed Soma* (vi. 23[1]); **tásminn evá͜ etā́ nímiślatamā iva** *to him these* (women) *are most devoted* (ŚB.).

b. ordinary adjectives: in V. **priyá** and **cā́ru** *dear*; e. g. **priyáḥ sū́rye priyó agnā́ bhavāti** *he will be dear to Sūrya, dear to Agni* (v. 37[5]); **cā́rur mitré váruṇe ca** *dear to Mitra and Varuṇa* (ix. 61[9]); in B. **dhruvá** *firm*; e. g. **rāṣṭrám evá͜ asmin dhruvám akaḥ** *he has made the sovereignty established in him* (TS.).

3. The loc. is used **with** a few **prepositions**: in V. **ā́** *in, at, on*, and (rarely) **ápi** *near, in*, and **úpa** *near to, at, upon*, as well as the prepositional adverb **sácā** *beside, with*; in V. and B. **ádhi** *on* and **antár** *within* (cp. 176, 2; 177, 5).

Locative and Genitive Absolute.

205. 1. The absolute construction of the loc., in which the case is always accompanied by a participle, started from the ordinary use of the loc. Combined with a participle it came to be regarded as a temporal or qualifying clause where the case alone could not be employed. Thus beside **uṣási** *at dawn* could appear **uchántyām uṣási** *at dawn as it shines forth*, which then acquired the independent sense *when dawn shines forth* (i. 184[1]). As regards the participles used in this construction, the future never occurs; the perf. act. is quite isolated; the perf. pass. part. is somewhat doubtful in V., but undoubted in B.; while the pres. part. is in fully developed use in V. as well as B.

a. An example of the perf. part. act. in **vant** used absolutely is: **aśitā́vaty átithāv aśnīyāt** (AV. ix. 6[38]) *the guest having eaten, he may eat* (cp. 161).

b. The perf. part. pass. appears in the RV. in several expressions, such as **jāté agnáu, stīrṇé barhíṣi, suté sóme,** in which the loc. probably still has its ordinary sense; e. g. **víśvam adhāg ā́yudham iddhé agnáu** *he burnt every weapon in the kindled fire* (ii. 15[4]); **yó áśvasya dadhikrā́vṇo ákārīt**

sámiddhe agnā́ uṣáso vyùṣṭau *who has honoured the steed Dadhikrāvan beside the kindled fire at the flush of Dawn* (iv. 39³), possibly *when the fire is kindled.* In other examples the absolute sense seems more likely: **yád īm enām̐ uśató abhy ávarṣīt tṛṣyā́vataḥ prāvṛ́ṣy ā́gatāyām** *when it has rained upon the eager thirsty ones, the rainy season having come* (vii. 103³); especially in **yán marutaḥ sū́rya údite mádatha** *when ye, O Maruts, are exhilarated at the rising of the sun* (v. 54¹⁰). Here **sū́rye** could not be used alone,[1] while the loc. of time would be expressed by **úditā sū́ryasya** *at sunrise.*

a. In B. the absolute use with the perf. part. pass. is much more pronounced; e.g. **úditeṣu nákṣatreṣu vā́cam ví sṛjati** *when the stars have risen he sets free his voice* (TS.); **sá enāḥ śvó bhūté yajate** *he sacrifices to them when the morning has appeared* (TS.); **krīté sóme maitrāvaruṇā́ya daṇḍám prá yachati** *when the Soma has been bought he hands the staff to the Maitrāvaruṇa priest* (TS.); **tásmād gardabhé purā́‿ā́yuṣaḥ prámīte bibhyati** *therefore one is frightened when a donkey has died before its time* (TS.). The substantive has sometimes to be supplied; e.g. **sá hovāca: ható vṛtró; yád dhaté kuryā́ta tát kuruta‿íti** *he said: Vṛtra is dead; what you would do, if he were dead, that do* (ŚB.).

c. Of the pres. part. with the loc. in the absolute sense there are many examples in V.; e.g. **índram prātár havāmaha índram prayatí‿adhvaré** *Indra we invoke early, Indra when the sacrifice proceeds* (i. 16³); **sárasvatīm devayánto havante sárasvatīm adhvaré tāyámāne** *men devoted to the gods invoke Sarasvatī, Sarasvatī while the sacrifice is extended* (x. 17⁷); **tā́ vām adyá tā́v aparám huvema‿uchántyām uṣási** *so you two to-day, so you two in future we would invoke when Dawn shines forth* (i. 184¹).

a. Similarly in B: **yajñamukhé-yajñamukhe vái kriyámāṇe yajñám rákṣāṃsi jighāṃsanti** *always when the commencement of the sacrifice is being made, the Rakṣases seek to destroy the sacrifice* (TS.); **sóme hanyámāne yajñó hanyate** *when Soma is destroyed, the sacrifice is destroyed* (TS.);

---

[1] Because the sense *rejoice in the sun* would be unnatural, though the construction of **mad** with the loc. is normal (cp. 204, 1 *a*).

tásmād agnicíd várṣati ná dhāvet *therefore the fire-piler should not run when it rains* (TS.); **tám etát pratyāyatyā́ṃ rā́trau sāyám úpātiṣṭhanta** *so they approached him in the evening when night returned* (ŚB.).

2. The **genitive absolute** is unknown in V., but has already come into use in B. It arose from the possessive genitive which acquired an independent syntactical value when accompanied by a (pres. or perf. pass.) participle much in the same way as the loc. The substantive is sometimes omitted. Examples are: **tásya‿ā́labdhasya sā́ vā́g ápa cakrāma** *he being sacrificed, this voice departed* (ŚB.); **tásmād apā́ṃ taptā́nāṃ phéno jāyate** *therefore, when water is heated, foam arises* (ŚB.); **sá etā́ viprúṣo 'janayata yā́ īmā́ḥ skūyámānasya viprávante** *he* (Agni) *produced those sparks which dart about when* (the fire) *is stirred* (MS.); **teṣāṃ ha‿ uttiṣṭhatām uvāca** *while these stood up he said* (AB.). In the first three of the above examples the close relationship of the absolute to the possessive case is still apparent.

Participles.

206. Participles are of a twofold nature inasmuch as they share the characteristics of both noun and verb. In form they are adjectives both in inflexion and concord. On the other hand they not only govern cases like the verb, but also indicate differences of voice and generally speaking retain the distinctions of time expressed by the tenses to which they belong. They are as a rule used appositionally with substantives, qualifying the main action and equivalent to subordinate clauses. They may thus express a relative, temporal, causal, concessive, final, or hypothetical sense. The verbal character of participles formed directly from the root (and not from tense stems) is restricted (with certain exceptions) to the passive voice in sense, and to past and future time; while owing to their passive nature they are not construed with an acc. of the object, but only with the inst. of the agent or means.

207. The pres. part. is occasionally used in V. by anacoluthon as a finite verb; e.g. **asmā́d ahá̱ṃ taviṣā́d ī́ṣamāṇa índrād bhiyā́ maruto réjamānaḥ** *I* (am) *fleeing from this mighty one, trembling with fear of Indra, ye Maruts* (i. 171^4). This use does not seem to be found in B.

a. The pres. part. is used with the verbs i *go*, car *move*, ās *remain*, sthā *stand* as auxiliaries to express continued duration in V. and B.; e.g. **víśvam anyó abhicákṣāṇa eti** *the other* (Pūṣan) *goes on watching the universe* (ii. 40^5); **vicā́kaśac candrámā náktam eti** *the moon goes on shining brightly at night* (i. 24^{10}); **tè 'sya gṛhā́ḥ paśáva upamūryámāṇā īyuḥ** *his house and cattle would go on being destroyed* (ŚB.); **tvá̱ṃ hí . . . éko vṛtrā́ cárasi jíghnamānaḥ** *for thou alone goest on killing the Vṛtras* (iii. 30^4); **té 'rcantaḥ śrā́myantaś ceruḥ** *they went on praying and fasting* (ŚB.); **ṛcā́ṃ tvaḥ póṣam āste pupuṣvā́n** *the one keeps producing abundance of verses* (x. 71^{11}); **sómam evá‿etát píbanta āsate** *they thus keep on drinking Soma* (TS.); **ucchváñcamānā pṛthivī́ sú tiṣṭhatu** *let the earth keep on yawning wide* (x. 18^{12}); **vitṛṃhāṇā́s tiṣṭhanti** *they keep conflicting* (TS.).

208. The past passive participle in ta is very frequently used as a finite verb; e.g. **tatá̱ṃ me ápas tád u tāyate púnaḥ** *my work is done and it is being done again* (i. 110^1); **ná tvā́vām̐ indra káś caná ná jātó ná janiṣyate** *no one is like thee, O Indra, he has not been born, and he will not be born* (i. 81^5); used impersonally: **śráddhitaṃ te mahatá indriyā́ya** *confidence has been placed in thy great might* (i. 104^6).

Similarly in B.: **iṣṭā́ devátā átha katamá eté** *the gods have been worshipped, but which are these gods?* (TS.); also in subordinate clauses: **tásmin yád āpannaṃ, grasitám evá‿asya tát** *what has got into him, that has been devoured by him* (TS.).

a. The perf. pass. part. is not infrequently used with forms of as and bhū as auxiliaries constituting a periphrastic mood or tense in V.; e.g. **yuktás te astu dákṣiṇaḥ** *let thy right* (steed) *be yoked* (i. 82^5); **dhūmás te ketúr abhavad**

diví śritáḥ *the smoke, thy banner, (was raised =) arose to heaven* (v. 11[3]).

b. Such forms (pres. and aor. ind. of **bhū**, impf. and perf. ind. and opt. of **as**) make regular past and present tenses and the opt. mood in B.; e.g. **bhūyasībhir ha‿asya‿āhutibhir iṣṭaṃ bhavati** *by him sacrifice has been made with several offerings* (AB.); **devāsuráḥ sáṃyattā āsan** *the gods and Asuras were engaged in conflict* (TS.); **tád vā ṛ́ṣīṇām ánuśrutam āsa** *that was heard by the seers* (ŚB.); **tásmād vídhṛtā ádhvāno 'bhūvan** *therefore the roads have been divided* (TS.).

209. Future Participles Passive. There are six of these: one, that in **āyya** occurs in the RV. only; three, those in **enya, ya,** and **tva**, in V. and in B.; two, those in **tavya** and **anīya** in V. (but not in the RV.) and in B. The commonest sense expressed by these verbal nouns is necessity; but various allied meanings, such as obligation, fitness, certain futurity, and possibility, are also frequent. Four of them are construed with the inst. of the agent (the gen. and dat. sometimes appearing instead), while the forms in **tva** and **anīya** are never found connected with a case.

1. The commonest of these gerundives is that in **ya**; **sadyó jajñānó hávyo babhūva** *as soon as born he became one to be invoked* (viii. 96[21]). It often appears without a verb; e.g. **víśvā hí vo namasyàni vándyā nā́māni devā utá yajñíyāni vaḥ** *all your names, ye gods, are adorable, worthy of praise, and worshipful* (x. 63[2]). The agent may be expressed by the inst., dat., or gen.; e.g. **tváṃ nṛ́bhir hávyo viśvádhā‿asi** *thou art always to be invoked by men* (vii. 22[7]); **asmā́bhir ū nú praticákṣyā‿abhūt** *she has become visible (by =) to us* (i. 113[11]); **sákhā sákhibhya íḍyaḥ** *a friend to be praised by friends* (i. 75[4]); **yá éka íd dhávyaḥ carṣaṇīnā́m** *who alone is to be invoked of men* (vi. 22[1]).

a. In B. the agent may be in the inst. or gen., but not in the dat.; thus **tásmai déyam** means *to him gifts should be given* (ŚB.). This example also illustrates the impersonal use of this gerundive in B., a use unknown to the RV. This gerundive is always without a verb, being unaccompanied by forms of **as** or **bhū** in B.; e.g. **bahú déyam** *much* (is) *to be given* (MS.).

2. The gerundive in **tva** in the RV. implies necessity or possibility and is often used in contrast with the past; but it is not found accompanied by a verb (**as** or **bhū**) or a noun expressing the agent; e.g. **ripávo hántvāsaḥ** *the enemy are to be killed* (iii. 30[15]); **yó nántvāny ánaman ny ójasā** *who by his might bent what could be bent* (ii. 24[2]); **tád víśvam abhibhū́r asi yáj jātám yác ca jántvam** *thou surpassest all that has been born and that is to be born* (viii. 89[6]).

a. The only meaning that seems to be expressed by this gerundive in B. is possibility; e.g. **snā́tvam udakám** *water that can be bathed in* (ŚB.); **nó asya‿anyád dhótvam āsīt prāṇā́t** *and he had nothing else that could be offered but breath* (MS.).

3. The gerundive in **ā́yya**, found in the RV. only, sometimes appears accompanied by an agent in the inst. or the dat.; e.g. **dakṣā́yyo nṛ́bhiḥ** *to be propitiated by men* (i. 129[2]); **dakṣā́yyo dā́śvate dáma ā́** *who is to be propitiated by the pious man in his house* (ii. 4[3]).

4. The form in **enya**, almost restricted to the RV., may be accompanied by an agent in the inst.; e.g. **agnír īḷényo girā́** *Agni to be praised with song* (i. 79[5]); **abhyāyaṃsényā bhavataṃ manīṣíbhiḥ** *be willing to be drawn near by the devout* (i. 34[1]).

a. It is once or twice also found in B.; thus **vā́cam udyāsaṃ śuśrūṣéṇyām** *I would utter a speech worthy to be heard* (TS.).

5. The gerundive in **tavya**, which is not found in the RV. at all, occurs only twice in the AV.; thus **ná brāhmaṇó hiṃsitavyàḥ** *a Brahmin is not to be injured* (AV. v. 18[6]).

a. In B. it is frequent and used much in the same way as the form in **ya**; here it is also used impersonally and with the agent in the inst.; e.g. **putró yājayayitavyàḥ** *a son must be made to sacrifice* (MS.); **agnicítā pakṣíṇo ná‿aśitavyàm** *an Agnicit should not eat* (any part) *of a bird* (MS.); **paśúvratena bhavitavyàm** (MS.) *he should act after the manner of* *cattle* (more literally: *action should be taken by him as one following the manner of cattle*).

6. The form in **anīya**, which is rare in both V. and B., does not occur at all in the RV., and only twice in the prose of the AV. Expressing only suitability or possibility, and never used either with an inst. or impersonally, it has hardly attained the full value of a gerundive even in B.; e.g. **upajīvanī́yo bhavati** *he is one who may be subsisted on* (AV.); **abhicaraṇī́ya** *liable to be bewitched* (ŚB.); **āhavanī́ya** *suitable to be offered to* (AB.).

Gerund or Indeclinable Participle.

210. The forms of the gerund, ending in **tvī, tvā, tvāya** (cp. 163) and in **ya** or **tya** (164) are synonymous, expressing an action that is past before that of the finite verb begins. It regularly refers to what is regarded as the subject of the sentence; e.g. **gūḍhvī́ támo jyótiṣā‿uṣā́ abodhi** *having hidden away the darkness, Dawn has awakened with light* (vii. 80²); **yuktvā́ háribhyām úpa yāsad arvā́k** *having yoked* (them) *may he come hither with his two bays* (v. 40⁴); **stríyaṃ dṛṣṭvā́ya kitavám tatāpa** *having seen a woman it pains the gambler* (x. 34¹¹) = *the gambler, having seen a woman, is pained*; **píbā niṣádya** *drink, after having sat down* (i. 177⁴); **yó hánti śátrum abhī́tya** *who slays the foe after having attacked him* (ix. 55⁴).

a. The usage in B. is similar; e.g. **tásmāt suptvā́ prajā́ḥ prá budhyante** *therefore creatures awake after having slept* (TS.); **tám ha‿enaṃ dṛṣṭvā́ bhī́r viveda** *having seen him fear seized him* = *having seen him he became afraid* (ŚB.). The gerund is, however, here found loosely construed in various ways not occurring in V. Thus it refers in sense to the agent implied by the future part. pass. in **tavya** or **ya** used predicatively as a finite verb; e.g. **agnihotrahávanīṃ pratápya hásto 'vadhéyaḥ** *his hand* (is) *to be put into it* (by the holder) *after having heated the fire-sacrifice ladle* (MS.). Still looser is the connexion in such sentences as the following: **té paśáva óṣadhīr jagdhvā́‿apáḥ pītvā́ táta eṣá rásaḥ sáṃ bhavati** *the beasts having eaten the plants and drunk water*—

then this vital sap arises (ŚB.) = *then acquire this vital sap.* The past sense of the gerund is often emphasized by the particle **átha** *then* being placed immediately after it. The gerund is here sometimes equivalent to the finite verb of a subordinate clause; e. g. **ātithyéna vái devā́ iṣṭvā́ tā́nt samád avindat** *after the gods had sacrificed with the rite of hospitable reception, discord came upon them* (ŚB.); similarly with the verb **man** *think*: **etád vái devā́ḥ prā́pya rāddhvā́‿iva‿amanyanta** *the gods, having obtained this, thought that they had as good as won* (ŚB.).

b. The gerund in **am**, which is always a compound, and the first member of which is nearly always a preposition, expresses a simultaneous action performed by the subject of the finite verb of the sentence. Being a cognate acc. used adverbially it is only beginning to be used as a gerund in late V.; e. g. **tantrám yuvatī́ abhyākrā́mam vayataḥ** *the two maidens weave the web while going up to it* (AV.).

a. In B. it has become common; e. g. **abhikrā́mam juhoti** (TS.) *he sacrifices while approaching* (the fire). This gerund is sometimes used with **ās**, **i**, or **car** to express continued action; e. g. **té parāpā́tam āsata** *they kept flying away* (MS.).

Infinitive.

211. The normal use of this form is to supplement the general statement of the sentence in a final (*in order to*) or a consequential (*so as to*) sense. The infinitive is, however, sometimes dependent on a particular word in the sentence, usually a verb, occasionally a noun: it then loses some of its full meaning, as in other languages after an auxiliary. The object when it is expressed is generally in the accusative.

1. Dative Infinitive.

a. The various forms of this infinitive govern either an acc. or (by attraction) a dat., sometimes (according to the nature of the verb) another case; e. g. **índrāya‿arkám juhvā̀ sám añje, vīrám dānáukasam vandádhyai** *for Indra I with my tongue adorn a song, to praise the bountiful hero* (i. 61[5]); **tvám akṛṇor duṣṭárītu sáho víśvasmai sáhase sáhadhyai** *thou didst display irresistible power to overcome* *every power* (vi. 1[1]); **áva sya śūra‿ádhvano ná‿ánte 'smín nó adyá sávane mandádhyai** *unyoke, O hero, as at the end of a journey, to delight in this our Soma pressing to-day* (iv. 16[2]); **ábhūd u pārám étave pánthā** *the path has appeared, to* (enable us to) *go to the farther shore* (i. 46[11]); **ā́ no nāvā́ matīnā́ṃ yātáṃ pārā́ya gántave** *do ye two come to us with the boat of our hymns, to go to the farther shore* (i. 46[7]); **índraṃ codaya dā́tave maghám** *urge Indra to give bounty* (ix. 75[5]); **índram avardhayann áhaye hántavā́ u** *they strengthened Indra to slay the dragon* (v. 31[4]); **ā́ ta etu mánaḥ púnaḥ jīváse jyók ca sū́ryaṃ dṛśé** *let thy spirit return* (*to live* =) *that thou mayest live and long see the sun* (x. 57[4]); **śiśīte śṛ́ṅge rákṣase viníkṣe** *he sharpens his horns in order to pierce the demon* (v. 2[9]); **sadyáś cin máhi dāváne** *to give much at once* (viii. 46[25]); **prá yád bháradhve suvitā́ya dāváne** *when ye proceed to give welfare* (v. 59[4]); **amítrān pṛtsú turváṇe** *to overcome foes in battle* (vi. 46[8]); **átha‿úpa prá‿aid yudháye dásyum** *then he advanced to fight the demon* (v. 30[9]); **tā́v asmábhyaṃ dṛśáye sū́ryāya púnar dātām ásum** *may these two give us back our breath that we may see the sun* (x. 14[12]); **devó no átra savitā́ nú‿árthaṃ prā́sāvīd dvípat prá cátuṣpad ityái** *here god Savitṛ has now urged on our bipeds, on our quadrupeds to go to their work* (i. 124[1]); **ábodhi hótā yajáthāya devā́n** *the priest has awakened to worship the gods* (v. 1[2]).

b. The dat. inf. not infrequently depends on a particular word in the sentence; e. g. **tā́ vāṃ vā́stūni‿uśmasi gámadhyai** *we desire to go to those abodes of you two* (i. 154[6]); **dā́dhṛvir bháradhyai** *strong to carry* (vi. 66[3]); **cikíd nāśayádhyai** *understanding to destroy* (viii. 97[14]); **agníṃ dvéṣo yótavái no gṛṇīmasi** *we implore Agni to ward off hostility from us* (viii. 71[15]); **té hí putrā́so áditer vidur dvéṣāṃsi yótave** *for those sons of Aditi know how to ward off hostilities* (viii. 18[5]); **tvám indra sravitavā́ apás kaḥ** *thou, O Indra, hast made the waters to flow* (vii. 21[3]); **vidyā́ma tásya te**

vayám ákūpārasya dāváne *may we know this of thee who art inexhaustible to give* (v. 39[7]); **bhiyáse mṛgáṃ kaḥ** *he has made the monster to fear* (v. 29[4]); **jajanúś ca rājáse** *and they created* (him) *to rule* (viii. 97[10]); **kavī́m̐r ichāmi saṃdṛ́śe** *I wish to see the poets* (iii. 38[1]).

a. The dat. inf. has sometimes a passive force; e. g. **ā́ vo vā́hiṣṭho vahatu stavádhyai ráthaḥ** *may your most swift car bring you hither to be praised* (vii. 37[1]); **gīrbhíḥ sakhā́yaṃ gā́ṃ ná doháse huve** *with songs I call my friend like a cow to be milked* (vi. 45[7]); **eṣā́ purutámā dṛśé kám** *she here that constantly returns* (so as) *to be seen* (i. 124[6]). This sense is especially noticeable in the infinitives in **tavái, tave,** and **e,** which when used predicatively (as a rule with the negative **ná**) are equivalent to a future part. pass.[1] with the copula; e. g. **stuṣé sā́ vāṃ rātíḥ**[2] *that bounty of yours is to be praised* (i. 122[7]); **náiṣā́ gávyūtir ápabhartavā́ u** *this pasture* (is) *not to be taken away* (x. 14[2]); **yásya ná rā́dhaḥ páryetave** *whose treasure is not to be surpassed* (viii. 24[21]); **ná‿asmā́kam asti tát tára ā́dityāso atiṣkáde** *this our zeal, O Ādityas, is not to be overlooked* (viii. 67[19]); **ná pramíye savitúr dáivyasya tát** *this* (work) *of the divine Savitṛ* (is) *indestructible* (iv. 54[4]).

β. The agent (or instrument) of the action expressed by the inf. is put in the inst. or gen. when there is a passive sense; e. g. **ná‿anyéna stómo vasiṣṭhā ánvetave vaḥ** *your laudation, O Vasiṣṭhas, is not to be equalled by another* (vii. 33[8]); **ábhūd agníḥ samídhe mā́nuṣāṇām** *Agni has appeared to be kindled of men* (vii. 77[1]). When there is no passive sense the agent is expressed by the dat.; e. g. **ví śrayantāṃ prayái devébhyo mahī́ḥ** *may the great* (*gates*) *open* (*for the gods to* =) *that the gods may enter* (i. 142[6]); **dabhráṃ páśyadbhya urviyā́ vicákṣa uṣā́ ajīgar bhúvanāni víśvā** (i. 113[5]) *Dawn has wakened all creatures* (*for those who* now *see little to* =) *that those who see little* now *may look far and wide*; **aháṃ rudrā́ya dhánur ā́ tanomi brahmadvíṣe śárave hántavā́ u** *I stretch the bow for Rudra* (*for the arrow to* =) *that the arrow may strike the hater of prayer* (x. 125[6]).

γ. The infinitive in **dhyai** is not infrequently employed elliptically to express an intention, the subject being either expressed or requiring to be supplied in the first or third person[3]; e. g. **práti vāṃ rátham**

---

[1] In Latin the gerundive actually appears to have taken the place of the IE. predicative infinitive: see Brugmann, *Grundriss*, 4, 2, pp. 461 and 488.

[2] Which in Latin would be: *laudanda* (*est*) *vestra benignitas.*

[3] The inf. is similarly used in Greek in the sense of a 2. pers. impv.; e. g. *πάντα τάδ' ἀγγεῖλαι μηδὲ ψευδάγγελος εἶναι tell all this and be not a false messenger* (Homer, *Od.*); *εἰπέμεναί μοι, Τρῶες tell me, ye Trojans* (*ibid.*).

jarádhyai *the chariot of you two* (I purpose) *to invoke* (vii. 67[1]); **á va auśijó huvádhyai śáṃsam** *the son of Uśij* (intends) *to proclaim your praise* (i. 122[5]).

δ. In B. the inf. in **tavái** has three uses: 1. with a final sense; e.g. **taṃ pra harati yo 'sya stṛtyas tasmai startavai** *he hurls it in order to strike down him who is to be struck down by it* (AB.). 2. predicatively with **ná**, often with a passive sense, sometimes impersonally; e.g. **ná vái yajñá iva mántavái** *it is not to be regarded like a sacrifice* (ŚB.); **ná purá sū́ryasya údetor mánthitavái** *one should not rub fire before sunrise* (MS.); **tásmād eténa‿áśru ná kártavái** *therefore tears should not be shed by him* (MS.). 3. with a pass. sense after an acc. governed by **āha, uvāca** and **brūyāt**; e.g. **agníṃ páristarītavā́ āha** *he says that the fire is to be enclosed* (MS.); **gopālā́n sáṃhvayitavā́ uvāca** *he said that the cow-herds should be called together* (ŚB.); **tád aśvám ā́netavái brūyāt** *then he should order the horse to be brought* (ŚB.). Perhaps, however, the acc. here depends on the inf. alone: *he should give orders to bring the horse.*

2. Accusative Infinitive.

a. The form in **am** is used to supplement statements containing a verb of going or in dependence on verbs meaning *be able* (**arh, aś, śak**), *wish* (**vaś**), or *know* (**vid**); e.g. **úpo emi cikitúṣo vipṛ́cham** *I go to the wise to inquire* (vii. 86[3]); **iyétha barhír āsádam** *thou hast gone to seat thyself on the straw* (iv. 9[1]); **śakéma tvā samídham** *we would be able to kindle thee* (i. 94[3]); **sá veda devá ānámaṃ devā́n** *he, the god, knows* (how) *to guide hither the gods* (iv. 8[3]).

a. In B. this form of the inf. appears only in dependance on the verbs **arh, vid,** and **śak** when they are combined with the negative **ná**; e.g. **avarúndhaṃ ná‿aśaknot** *he was not able to keep back* (MS.).

b. The inf. in **tum** in the RV. expresses the purpose with verbs of motion[1] and also appears in dependence on the verbs **arh** *be able* and **ci** *intend*; e.g. **kó vidvā́ṃsam úpa gāt prá́ṣṭum etát** *who has gone to the wise man to ask him this?* (i. 164[4]); **bhū́yo vā dā́tum arhasi** *or thou canst give more* (v. 79[10]).

---

[1] The use of this inf. is restricted to dependence on such verbs in the Latin supine in *tum*.

a. In B. the use is similar, this inf. expressing the purpose with verbs of motion, or in dependence on the verbs **dhṛ** *intend* and (generally accompanied by the negative **ná**) **arh** and **śak** *be able*, **kam** *desire*, **dhṛṣ** *dare*, **ā-dṛ** *trouble*, **ā-śaṃs** *expect*; e. g. **hótum eti** *he goes to sacrifice* (TS.), **drā́ṣṭum ā́ gachati** *he comes in order to see* (ŚB.); **anyád eva kártuṃ dadhrire 'nyád vái kurvanti** *they have purposed to do one thing, but do another* (ŚB.); **katháṃ aśakata mád ṛté jīvitum** *how have you been able to live without me?* (ŚB.); **ná cakame hántum** *he did not wish to kill* (ŚB.).

3. Ablative-Genitive Infinitive.

a. The form in **as** (which is always compounded with prepositions) is almost exclusively abl. as is shown by its being used with words governing that case, viz. the prepositions **ṛté** *without*, **purā́** *before*, and the verbs **pā** *protect*, **trā** *rescue*, **bhī** *fear*; e. g. **ṛté cid abhiśríṣaḥ purā́ jatrúbhya ātṛ́daḥ** *without binding, before the cartilages being pierced* (viii. 1[12]); **trā́dhvaṃ kartā́d avapádaḥ** (ii. 29[6]) *save us from falling into the pit* (lit. *from the pit, from falling down*).

There is one example of its being a gen., as it is governed by the verb **īś**: **nahí tvád ārè nimíṣaś caná īśe** *for without thee I am not able even to blink* (ii. 28[6]).

a. In B. it appears only as a gen. governed by **īśvará**; e. g. **sá īśvaró yájamānasya paśū́n nirdáhaḥ** *he is able to burn the cattle of the sacrificer* (MS.).

b. The form in **tos** is abl. when it is governed by the prepositions **purā́** *before* and **ā́** *till* or by verbs of saving and preventing; e. g. **purā́ hántor bháyamāno vy ā̀ra** *fearing he withdrew, before being struck* (iii. 30[10]); **yuyóta no anapatyā́ni gántoḥ** *save us from coming to childlessness* (iii. 54[18]).

The gen. form is found only in dependence on the verb **ī́ś** *be able* (with the object by attraction in the gen.) or on the adverb **madhyā́** *in the midst of*; e. g. **ī́śe rāyáḥ suvī́ryasya dā́toḥ** *he can give wealth and heroic offspring* (vii. 4[6]);

mā́ no madhyā́ rīriṣata‿ā́yur gántoḥ *injure us not (in the midst of =) before our reaching old age* (i. 89[9]).

a. In B. the abl. inf. is found with prepositional words only. It usually occurs with **ā́** *till* and **purā́** *before*, both the subject and the object being in the gen. The object may, however, by attraction be in the abl., and a predicate is in the abl.; e.g. **ā́ sū́ryasya údetoḥ** (MS.) *till the sun's rising = till the sun rises*; **ā́ tisṛṇā́ṃ dógdhoḥ** (ŚB.) *till the milking of three* (cows) = *till three* (cows) *are milked*; **ā́ médhyād bhávitoḥ** *till becoming pure*; **purā́ sū́ryasya‿údetoḥ** *before the sun's rising* (MS.) = *before the sun rises*; **purā vāgbhyaḥ sampravaditoḥ** *before the voices' uttering* (PB.) = *before the voices are uttered*. The abl. form is also sometimes used with the prepositional adverbs **purástād** and **arvācī́nam** *before*; e.g. **purástād dhótoḥ** *before sacrificing* (MS.); **arvācī́nam jánitoḥ** *before being born* (MS.).

The gen. form occurs only in dependence on **īśvarā́** *able*, the object being in the acc. (sometimes by attraction in the gen.), and the predicate in the nom.; e.g. **sá īśvarā́ ā́rtim ā́rtoḥ** *he can fall into misfortune* (TS.); **tā́ īśvarā́ yájamānam híṃsitoḥ** *these two can injure the sacrificer* (MS.). Occasionally **īśvarā́** is omitted; e.g. **táto dīkṣitáḥ pāmanó bhávitoḥ** *hence the initiated man* (can) *become scabby* (ŚB.).

4. Locative Infinitive.

The only loc. forms to which a genuine inf. use (cp. 167, 4) can be attributed are the few in **sáni**. These supplement the general statement of the sentence or depend on a particular word in it, and (like the form in **dhyai**) express an intention or exhortation (with the ellipse of a verb in the 1., 2., or 3. pers.); e.g. **ví naḥ patháś citana yáṣṭave, asmábhyaṃ víśvā ā́śās tarīṣáṇi** *do ye open up for us the paths to sacrifice, (for us to =) that we may conquer all regions* (iv. 37[7]); **náyiṣṭhā u no neṣáṇi, párṣiṣṭhā u naḥ parṣáṇy áti dviṣáḥ** *the best guides to guide us, the best leaders to lead us through our foes* (x. 126[3]); **tád va ukthásya barháṇā‿índrāya‿upastṛṇīṣáṇi** *this song of praise* (I will) *spread out with power for your Indra* (vi. 44[6]); **priyáṃ vo átithiṃ gṛṇīṣáṇi** (do ye) *extol your dear guest* (vi. 15[6]); **ījānám bhū́mir abhí prabhūṣáṇi** (*let*) *Earth assist the sacrificer* (x. 132[1]).

TENSES AND MOODS.

212. Two or more roots of cognate meaning sometimes supplement each other in such a way as to be used for different tenses of what is practically one verb. Such are:

1. **as** and **bhū** *be*: the pres., impf., and perf. are formed by **as**; the fut. and aor. by **bhū** alone. In its proper sense **bhū** means *to become* (originally *to grow*), but unless opposed to **as** *be*, it has the same sense as the latter, the pres. and perf. of both being used promiscuously. The contrast appears clearly when the pres. is opposed to the aor.; e. g. **yamó vā́ idám abhūd yád vayáṃ smáḥ** *Yama has become that which we are* (TS.). It also appears in the impf.: **yā́ viprúṣā ā́saṃs tā́ḥ śárkarā abhavan** *what were sparks became gravel* (MS.).

2. **dhāv** and **sṛ** *run*: in the RV. occur the plup. **ádadhāvat** and the pres. **sísarti**; in B. the pres. **dhāvati**, the impf. **ásarat**, and the perf. **sasā́ra**.

3. **paś** and **dṛś** *see*: the former appears in the pres. only, the latter in the aor., fut., and perf. only; **khyā** *see* is used in the same tenses as **dṛś**, but as opposed to the latter means *discern*.

4. **brū** and **vac** *speak*: the former is used in the pres. stem only; the latter in the aor., fut., perf. (V. has also the pres. **vívakti**).

5. **han** and **vadh** *slay*: the former has the pres., impf., fut., perf. only, the latter the aor. only.

a. In B. a few additional pairs of roots supplement each other to some extent. Such are **ad** and **ghas** *eat*; **aj** and **vī** *drive*; **i** and **gā** (aor.) *go*; **pra-yam** and **pra-dā** *present*; **śad** and **śī** *fall*.

Present.

A. In V. a number of verbs form two or more present stems, in which, however, no differences of meaning are traceable. In B. this multiplicity is for the most part lost.

The only type here showing any development is that in **ya**, which tends to have an intransitive sense. Such present stems are formed in B. from more than a dozen roots that do not form it in the RV.; e. g. **tápyati** *grows hot* (RV. **tápati**).

1. As in other languages, the present is used to indicate an action that is taking place when the speaker makes his statement.

2. In the RV. the simple pres. is sometimes employed of past actions in narration to add a new statement in a vivid manner; e. g. **purutrā́ vṛtró aśayad vyàstaḥ: amuyā́ śáyānam áti yanti‿ā́paḥ** *Vṛtra lay scattered in many places: over him as he thus lies the waters flow* (i. 32[7]).

This use does not seem to occur in B.

a. **purā́** *formerly* is used with the pres. to indicate an action which has extended through the past down to the present; e. g. **kvà tā́ni nau sakhyā́ babhūvuḥ, sácāvahe yád avṛkám purā́ cit** *where has that friendship of us two gone, inasmuch as we have hitherto associated inoffensively* (vii. 88[5]); **sá ha‿agnír uvāca‿átha yán mā́m purā́ prathamám yájatha kvà‿ahám bhavāni‿íti** *so Agni said: now that you have hitherto honoured me at the sacrifice as the first where shall I be?* (ŚB.).

a. In B. **purā́** is also used without reference to the actual present from the speaker's point of view, to express a previous stage in typical conditions; e. g. **áhotā vā́ eṣá purā́ bhavati yadā́‿evá‿enam pravṛṇīté 'tha hótā** *he is previously a non-Hotṛ; as soon as he chooses him, then he is a Hotṛ* (ŚB.); **ánaddhā‿iva vā́ asya‿átaḥ purā́ jā́nam bhavati** *previously his origin is as it were uncertain* (ŚB.).

b. **sma purā́** with the pres. ind. expresses that something used to happen in the past; e. g. **saṃhotrám sma purā́ nā́rī sámanam vā́‿áva gachati** *formerly the woman used to go down to the common sacrifice or the assembly* (x. 86[10]).

a. The same usage is common in B. with **ha sma purā́**; e. g. **ná ha sma vái purā́‿agnír áparaśuvṛkṇam dahati** *formerly Agni used not to burn what was not cut off with the axe* (TS.). Here, however, the **purā́** is much more usually omitted, **ha sma** alone expressing the same sense, especially often with the pres. perf. **āha**; e.g. **etád dha sma vā́ āha nāradáḥ** (MS.) *with regard to this Nārada used to say.* (The AB. uses the perf. and the impf. with **ha sma** in the same sense.) The particles **ha sma**, which originally only accompanied it, have thus acquired, when used alone, the sense which is inherent in **purā́** only.

c. The pres. ind. is also sometimes used for the fut. or the subj.; e.g. **áham ápi hanmi‿íti ha‿uvāca** *he said: I too will slay him* (ŚB.); **indraś ca ruśamaś ca‿aṃśam prāsyetām: yataro nau pūrvo bhūmim paryeti sa jayati‿iti** *Indra and Ruśama proposed a wager: whichever of us shall go round the earth first shall win* (PB.).

Past Tenses.

213. Each of the past tenses (except the pluperfect) has a distinctive meaning of its own, though occasional examples of aor. and perf. forms occur that are almost indistinguishable in sense from the impf.

A. The **perfect** characteristically expresses the condition attained by the subject as the result of a preceding action. If that action (often a repeated or continuous one) is continued into the present so as to include the latter, it may be translated by the present; if it is regarded as concluded before the present, by the present perfect. It can express both these senses when accompanied by the adverbs **purā́** *formerly* and **nūnám** *now*; e.g. **purā́ nūnám ca stutáya ṛ́ṣīṇām paspṛdhre** *the praises of the seers have vied together in past times and* (do so) *now* (vi. 34^1); **śáśvad dhí va ūtíbhir vayáṃ purā́ nūnáṃ bubhujmáhe** *we have constantly enjoyed your aids and* (do so) *now* (viii. 67^{16}); the same sense appears with the adverb **satrā́** *always*; e.g. **túbhyam bráhmāṇi gíra indra túbhyaṃ satrā́ dadhire: juṣásva** *to thee prayers, O Indra, to thee songs have always been offered* (and still are): *accept them kindly* (iii. 51^6). But even without a particle this double sense is not infrequently apparent:

ná sóma índram ásuto mamāda (vii. 26[1]) *unpressed Soma has not* (in the past) *intoxicated Indra* (and does not now); **ná bhojā́ mamrur ná nyarthám īyur: ná riṣyanti ná vyathante ha bhojā́ḥ** *the liberal have not died* (and die not), *they have not fallen into calamity* (and do not now): *the liberal are not injured and waver not* (x. 107[8]); **índra . . . ubhé ā́ paprau ródasī mahitvā́** *Indra has with his greatness filled* (and still fills) *the two worlds* (iii. 54[15]).

a. Thus a number of perfects (since their action includes the present) can be translated by the present, as is indicated by their often occurring by the side of actual present forms. Such perfects are formed from verbs meaning to *know*; *be pleased, sad,* or *afraid*; *stand, sit, lie*; *rest upon, hold fast*; *have, possess*; *encompass*; *surpass*; *prosper*; *become*; *show oneself*; e. g. **kvà‿idā́nīṃ sū́ryaḥ : káś ciketa** *where is now the sun : who knows?* (i. 35[7]); **yán na índro jujūṣé yác ca váṣṭi** *what Indra likes from us and what he desires* (iv. 22[1]); **ká īṣate, tujyáte, kó bibhāya** *who flees* (and) *speeds, who is afraid?* (i. 84[17]); **ná methete ná tasthatuḥ** *they* (night and morning) *clash not and stand not still* (i. 113[3]); **váne-vane śiśriye takvavī́r iva** *on every tree he sits like a bird* (x. 91[2]); **yáthā‿iyáṃ pṛthivī́ mahī́ dādhā́ra‿imā́n vánaspátīn evā́ dādhāra te mánaḥ** *as this great earth holds these trees, so he holds thy spirit* (x. 60[9]); **ná te pū́rve ná‿áparāso ná vīryàṃ nū́tanaḥ káś caná‿āpa** *not earlier men, not future men, no man of the present* (*has attained* =) *equals thy heroism* (v. 42[6]); **prá hí ririkṣá ójasā divó ántebhyas pári, ná tvā vivyāca rája indra pā́rthivam** *thou extendest beyond the ends of heaven with thy might, the terrestrial space does not contain thee* (viii. 88[5]); **índreṇa śuśuve nṛ́bhir yás te sunóti** *through Indra he who presses* (Soma) *for thee prospers in men* (vii. 32[6]); **séd u rā́jā kṣayati carṣaṇīnā́m, arā́n ná nemíḥ pári tā́ babhūva** *he rules as king over men, he encompasses the worlds* (**tā́**) *as the felly the spokes* (i. 32[15]); **bhadrā́ dadṛkṣa urviyā́ vi bhāsi, út te śocír bhānávo dyā́m apaptan** *brilliant* *thou appearest, thou shinest afar, thy light, thy beams, have shot up to heaven* (vi. 64²).

b. Other perfects, which sum up past action but exclude the present, may be translated by the present perfect; e. g. **yát sīm ā́gaś cakṛmā́ tát sú mṛḷatu** *whatever sin we have committed, let him forgive that* (i. 179⁵); **yā́ vṛtrahā́ parāváti sánā návā ca cucyuvé, tā́ saṃsátsu prá vocata** *what old and new deeds the Vṛtra-slayer has set going in the distance, those proclaim in the assemblies* (viii. 45²⁵); **uvā́sa‿uṣā́ uchā́c ca nú** *Dawn has flushed* (in the past) *and she shall flush now* (i. 48³); **kím ā́ga āsa varuṇa jyéṣṭhaṃ, yát stotā́raṃ jíghāṃsasi sákhāyam** *what has that chief sin been* (in my past life) *that thou desirest to slay the praiser, thy friend?* (vii. 86⁴); **īyúṣ ṭé yé pū́rvatarām ápaśyan vyuchántīm uṣásaṃ mártyāsaḥ; ó [=ā́ u] té yanti yé áparīṣu páśyān** *those mortals have gone who saw flushing the earlier dawn; those are coming who shall see her in the future* (i. 113¹¹).

c. The perf. often expresses a single action that has been completed in the recent past, when it can be translated by the pres. perf.; e.g. **ā́ no yātaṃ divás pári: putráḥ káṇvasya vām ihá suṣā́va somyáṃ mádhu** *come to us from heaven: the son of Kaṇva has here pressed for you the Soma mead* (viii. 8⁴). This use of the perf. comes very near that of the aor. The distinction seems to be this: in the above passage the perfect means *come because the Soma has been pressed*, i. e. *is ready for you*; the aor. would mean *come because of the fact that the Soma has just been pressed for you.*

d. The perf. is not infrequently used of a single action in the remoter past, when it cannot be translated by the perf. pres. It occurs thus beside the impf. of narration, when the story is interrupted by a reflexion which often expresses the result of the action previously related. Thus in the story of the Vṛtra fight the poet says: **ájayo gā́ ájayaḥ śūra sómam; ávāsṛjaḥ sártave saptá síndhūn** *thou didst win the kine, thou didst win the Soma, O hero, thou didst let* *loose the seven streams to flow* (i. 32[12]); he then adds **índraś ca yád yuyudhā́te áhiś ca͜ utá͜ aparī́bhyo maghávā ví jigye** *when Indra and the serpent fought, the bounteous god conquered* (= remained conqueror) *for the future.* This use of the perf. is hardly distinguishable from the impf.

a. In B. the perf. ind. appears in three different uses:

1. in a present sense based on the pres. perf., chiefly in forms that have a strengthened reduplicative vowel and thus seem to have an intensive meaning. It is the pres. perf. that includes the present, expressing that an action takes place in the present as a result of its repetition in the past; e. g. **dādhāra** (*he has constantly held and now*) *holds*; e. g. **yát sāyám̐ juhóti rā́tryai téna dādhāra** *if he offers in the evening, he thereby holds* (*Agni*) *for the night* (MS.). Other perfects of this kind are: **dīdāya** *shines*; **upa dodrāva** *rushes at*; **yoyāva** *wards off*; **lelāya** *quivers*; **bībhā́ya** (beside **bibhā́ya**) *fears* (while the periphrastic **bibhayā́m̐ cakāra** has always a preterite sense). Besides these verbs **veda** *knows* and **āha** *says* always have a present sense.

Several other perfects with ordinary reduplication often have the present sense: **ānaśé** (*has obtained* =) *has* (MS., TS.); **párīyāya** (*has acquired* =) *possesses* (TS.); **babhū́va** (*has become* =) *is* (MS.); **vivyā́ca** (*has encompassed* =) *contains*; **dadṛśé** (*has been seen* =) *appears* (while **dadárśa** always has a past sense); also the perfect of **grah** and **pra-āp**: **yé hí paśávo lóma jagṛhús té médham̐ prā́puḥ** *the cattle which have hair have also fat* (MS.).

2. in a preterite sense, expressing that an action once occurred in the past (but not in the narrative sense of the impf.). This use most often appears in the form **uvāca**, which may be translated by *once said* or *has said*; e. g. **eténa vā́ úpakerū rarādha : ṛdhnóti yá eténa yájate** *by this sacrifice Upakeru once prospered; he who sacrifices with it prospers* (MS.). It often occurs in the AB. at the conclusion of a story related in the impf., in the phrase **tad etad ṛṣiḥ paśyann abhyanūvāca** *seeing this a seer has uttered with reference to it* (the following verse). A somewhat different connexion with the narrative impf. appears in the following example: **etā́m̐ ha vái yajñásenaś cítim̐ vidā́m̐ cakāra : táyā vái sá paśū́n ávārunddha** *this method of piling Yajñasena once invented: by means of it he acquired cattle* (TS.). This perfect is found contrasting what is past with the present and future in the following successive sentences: **yád vā́ asyā́m̐ kím̐ cā́rcanti yád ā́nṛcúr ; yád evá kím̐ ca vācā́͜ ā́nṛcúr yád ató 'dhi͜ arcitā́raḥ** *whatever prayers they offer on it* (the earth) *or have offered; whatever prayers they have offered with the voice or will offer in future* (TS.).

3. in an historical sense, equivalent to that of the impf. in narrative,

in certain parts of the AB. (vi–viii) and the ŚB. (i–v; xi, xii, xiv), while the impf. is used elsewhere in B. (MS., TS., K., TB., PB., AB. i–v; ŚB. vi–x, xiii). Thus in the former **uvāca** *said* and **devā́ś ca‿ásurāś ca paspṛdhire** *the gods and the Asuras were in conflict*, in the latter **abravīt** and **aspardhanta** would be used. There are, of course, exceptions in both groups.

B. The **imperfect** is the past tense of narration, never having any relation to the present as the perf. and the aor. have; e. g. **áhann áhim . . . prá vakṣáṇā abhinat párvatānām** *he slew the serpent; he pierced the bellies of the mountains* (i. 32[1]); **ná vái tvám̐ tád akaror yád ahám ábravam** *you did not do what I said* (ŚB.). The impf. has also to do duty for the pluperfect, as in the relative clause of the preceding example, which is equivalent to *what I had told you.*

C. The **aorist** ind. expresses that an action has occurred in the past with reference to the present. It neither describes nor indicates duration, but simply states a fact. It may nearly always be translated by the English present perfect.

The aor. usually expresses the immediate past; e. g. **práti divó adarśi duhitā́** *the daughter of heaven has appeared* (iv. 52[1]); **yásmād duṣvápnyād ábhaiṣma‿ápa tád uchatu** *let her* (Dawn) *drive away with her light the evil dream that we have feared* (viii. 47[18]).

a. In B. three uses of the aor. ind. may be distinguished: 1. it expresses what has occurred in the speaker's experience, very commonly in the statement made by the witness of an action; e. g. **táto ha gandharvā́ḥ sám ūdire: jyók vā́ iyám urváśī manuṣyèṣv avātsīt** *then the Gandharvas spoke together: this Urvaśī has dwelt long among men* (ŚB.). As compared with the impf. it never narrates; e. g. **yajño vai devebhya ud akrāmat; te devā abruvan: yajño vai na ud akramīt** *the sacrifice went away from the gods; the gods then said: the sacrifice has gone away from us* (AB.); **tā́ṃ yád ápṛchant sā́bravīd: adyá‿amṛta‿íti** *when they asked her, she said: he has died to-day* (MS.); **tám apṛchan: kásmai tvám ahauṣīr íti** *they asked him: to whom have you sacrificed?* (MS.); **tā́ṃ devā́ abruvan: mahā́n vā́ ayám abhūd yó vṛtrám ávadhīd íti** *the gods said of him: he has shown himself great who has slain Vṛtra* (TS.); **té ha‿ūcur: agnáye tiṣṭha‿íti tátas tasthāv, agnáye vā asthād íti tám agnā́v ajuhavuḥ** *they said: stand still for Agni; then* *it stood still; thinking it has stood still for Agni, they sacrificed it in Agni* (ŚB.).

2. it is employed by the author with regard to what from his own point of view has either just happened or has occurred in the more remote past; e.g. **sá bándhur śunāsīryàsya yám̐ pūrvám ávocāma** *this is the import of the Śunāsīrya oblation which we have explained above* (ŚB.); **puro vā etān devā akrata yat puroḷāśām̐s tat puroḷāśānāṃ puroḷāśatvam** *because the gods have made these cakes their castles, the cakes are so called* (AB.). The adverb **purā́** is not infrequently used with these aorists; e.g. **ná vā́ etásya brāhmaṇā́ḥ purā́‿ánnam akṣan** *Brahmins have never hitherto eaten his food* (TS.).

3. it expresses what results from a ritual act or is antecedent to it; e.g. **putrásya nā́ma gṛhṇāti : prajā́m evá‿ánu sám atanīt** *he gives his son a name : he has thus extended his race* (MS.); **etád vái tṛtī́yaṃ yajñám āpad yác chándāṃsi‿āpnóti** *thereby he has obtained the third sacrifice when he obtains the metres* (TS.); **yád dhí‿asya‿amedhyám ábhūt tád dhi‿asya‿etád avadhūnóti** *what has been impure in it, that in it he shakes off in this way* (ŚB.).

D. The **pluperfect**, as an augmented perfect, is equivalent to the corresponding Greek tense in form only. It cannot be distinguished in syntactical use from the impf. in some examples and from the aor. in others; e.g. **átrā samudrá ā́ gūḷhám ā́ sū́ryam ajabhartana** *then ye brought the sun hidden in the sea* (x. 72⁷); **úd u ṣyá deváḥ savitā́ yayāma hiraṇyáyīm amátiṃ yā́m áśiśret** *that god Savitṛ now has raised up the golden sheen which he has spread out* (vii. 38¹).

Future.

214. A. 1. The simple future is in comparatively rare use in V., being formed from only fifteen roots in the RV. and from rather more than twenty others in the AV. This limited employment is accounted for by its sense being partly expressed by the subjunctive and to some extent by the present. It means that, according to the opinion, expectation, intention, hope or fear of the speaker, an action is to take place in the near or the remote future. The sphere of the future includes that of the will, the specific meaning of the subjunctive, but the stress is here laid on the futurity rather than the purpose; e. g. **atha‿ataḥ paśor vibhaktis: tasya vibhāgaṃ vakṣyāmaḥ** *next* (comes) *the division of the* (sacrificial) *animal:* (now) *we will* (*shall*) *state its division* (AB.).

Examples from the RV. are: **staviṣyā́mi tvā́m ahám** *I shall praise thee* (i. 44⁵); **kíṃ svid vakṣyā́mi kím u nū́ maniṣye** *what pray shall I say, what shall I now think?* (vi. 9⁶); **yády evā́ kariṣyátha sākáṃ deváir yajñíyāso bhaviṣyatha** *if ye will do so, you will be partakers of the sacrifice with the gods* (i. 161²); **ná tvā́vām̐ indra káś caná ná jātó ná janiṣyate** *no one equal to thee, O Indra, has been born or will be born.*

2. In B. the simple future is frequently used after verbs of speaking, knowing, thinking, hoping, fearing, which are sometimes also to be supplied; e.g. **só 'bravīd: idáṃ máyi vīryàṃ, tát te prá dāsyāmi‿íti** *he said: here is heroism in me, that I will give thee* (TS.); **té ha‿ūcuḥ kéna rā́jñā, kéna‿ánīkena yotsyāma íti** *they said: with whom as king, with whom as leader shall we fight?* (ŚB.); **tátra vidyād: varṣiṣyati‿íti** *in regard to that he should know: it will rain* (ŚB.); **índro ha vā īkṣā́ṃ cakre: mahád vā́ itó 'bhváṃ janiṣyate** *Indra reflected: a great abuse will arise from this* (ŚB.); **sarvā devatā āśaṃsanta: mām abhi prati patsyati‿iti** *all the gods hoped: he will begin with me* (AB.); **yádi bibhīyā́d duścarmā bhaviṣyāmi‿íti** *if he should fear, 'I shall suffer from skin disease'* (TS.); **ásurā vā́ íṣṭakā acinvata: dívam ā́ rokṣyāma íti** *the Asuras built up the bricks* (thinking): *we shall scale heaven* (MS.).

a. After an impv., the fut. is often used with **átha**; e.g. **pátiṃ nú me púnar yúvānaṃ kurutam: átha vāṃ vakṣyāmi** (ŚB.) *make my husband young again: then I shall tell you* (*two*).

β. After the impv. of **ā-i** or **pra-i** the 1. pers. fut. is equivalent to an exhortation; e. g. **prá‿ita, tád eṣyāmaḥ** *come, we will go there* (ŚB.).

γ. With the negative **ná**, the 2. and even the 3. pers. may have the value of a prohibition; e. g. **devā́n rákṣāṃsi .. ajighāṃsan: ná yakṣyadhva íti** *the Rakṣases wished to slay the gods* (saying): *you shall not sacrifice* (ŚB.); **tān viśve devā anonudyanta neha pāsyanti neha‿iti** *all the gods drove them back* (saying): *they shall not drink here, not here* (AB.).

B. The **periphrastic future** though not occurring in V., is frequent in B. It expresses that something will take place at a definite point of time in the future. It is therefore often accompanied by such words as **prātár** *early in the morning*, **śvás** *to-morrow* (but never by **adyá** *to-day*). The point of time, however, need not be expressed by an adverb; it may be defined by a clause. Examples are: **saṃvatsaratamī́ṃ rā́trim ā́ gachatāt, tán ma ékāṃ rā́trim ánte śayitā́se, jātá u te 'yáṃ tárhi putró bhavitā́** *come for the night of this day year, then you* *will lie beside me for one night, then too this son of thine will be born* (ŚB.); **yádi purā́ saṃsthā́nād dī́ryeta‿adyā́ varṣiṣyati‿íti brūyād; yádi sáṃsthite śvó vraṣṭā́‿íti brūyāt** *if it* (the vessel) *should be broken before the completion* (of the sacrifice) *he should say: it will rain to-day; if it has been completed, he should say: it will rain to-morrow* (MS.); **yarhi vāva vo mayā‿artho bhavitā, tarhy eva vo 'haṃ punar āgantāsmi** *when you will have need of me, then* (on that particular occasion) *I will come back to you* (AB.).

a. Sometimes this form is used to express not that an action will take place at a definite time, but that it will take place with certainty; e.g. **sā́‿evā́‿iyám adyā́‿ápi pratiṣṭhā́, sā́‿u evā́‿ápi‿ātó 'dhi bhavitā́** *this is the foundation to-day, and it will also* (certainly) *be so in future* (ŚB.).

A. Imperative.

215. The only pure impv. forms are those of the 2. 3. sing. and 3. pl., represented by **bháva** and **bhávatāt, bhávasva; bhávatu; bhávantu, bhávantām.** The forms later regarded as imperatives of the 1. pers., **bhávāni, bhávāva, bhávāma** are subjunctives (cp. 131): while the 2. 3. du. and 2. pl. **bhávatam, bhávatām, bhávethām, bhávetām; bhávata, bhávadhvam,** are injunctives (cp. 122 *a a*).

a. The impv. does not express commands only, but also a desire in the widest sense, such as a wish, a request, advice, a direction; e.g. **devā́m̐ ihá‿ā́ vaha** *bring hither the gods* (i. 14[12]); **áheḷamāno bodhi** *be not angry* (i. 24[11]); **imā́ni‿asya śīrṣā́ṇi chinddhi** *cut off these heads of his* (MS.); **vṛkṣé nā́vaṃ práti badhnīṣva** *tie the ship to the tree* (ŚB.); **prá vām aśnotu suṣṭutíḥ** *may the hymn of praise reach you two* (i. 17[9]); **hánta na éko vettu** *come, let one of us find out* (ŚB.).

b. The sphere of the ordinary impv. is the present; it may, however, still be used for the later of two opposed actions; e.g. **váraṃ vṛṇīsva‿átha me púnar dehi** *choose a boon and then give it me back* (TS.). The form in **tād,** however, has a tendency in V. to express the more remote future, and in B. does so distinctly; e.g. **ihá‿evá mā tíṣṭhantam abhyéhi‿íti brūhi, tā́ṃ tú na ā́gatāṃ pratiprá**

brūtāt *tell her: come to me as I stand here; when she has come, you shall* (then) *tell it us* (ŚB.). As this form is only active, the subj. takes its place in middle verbs; thus **tám vṛṇīṣva** = *do thou choose it* (now) as opposed to **tám vṛṇāsai** *choose it then* (ŚB.).

a. The genuine impv. seems never to be found in negative sentences; thus it never appears in V. with the prohibitive particle **mā́** (which is used with injunctive forms only, and in B. almost exclusively with the aor. inj.). It is employed in positive principal clauses only; e.g. **ví no dhehi yáthā jī́vāma** *so dispose us that we may live* (ŚB.). A subordinate clause with ind., subj., or (very rarely) opt. may precede or follow; e.g. **yás tvā́m dūtám saparyáti, tásya sma prāvitā́ bhava** *be the promoter of him who adores thee as a messenger* (i. 12[8]); **sám vidúṣā naya yó . . anuśā́sati** *bring us together with one who knows, who may give us directions* (vi. 54[1]); **idám me haryatā váco yásya tárema tárasā śatám hímāḥ** *gladly accept this word of mine by the force of which we would pass a hundred winters* (v. 54[15]). In such periods the form with **tād** would regularly be used in B.

β. The RV. has a number of 2. sing. forms made with **si** added directly to the root, which are clearly used imperatively, as is indicated by their being generally accompanied by imperatives (sometimes by subjunctives and imperatives); e.g. **ā́ devébhir yāhi yákṣi ca** *come with the gods and sacrifice* (i. 14[1]). These forms are confined to the RV. (and passages borrowed from it) except **satsi** (AV. vi. 110[1]); and they are restricted to positive principal sentences.

B. Injunctive.

Formally this mood corresponds to an unaugmented past tense (including the 2. 3. du. and 2. pl. as represented by act. **bhávatam, bhávatām, bhávata**; mid. **bhávethām, bhávetām, bhávadhvam**, which later came to be regarded as imperatives). Its use constitutes one of the chief difficulties of Vedic grammar and interpretation, because it cannot always be distinguished from the subjunctive (e. g. **gamat** might be the subj. of **á-gan** or the inj. of **á-gamat**) or from an unaugmented indicative (e. g. **cáraḥ** might be = **á-caraḥ**). Judged by its uses the inj. probably represents a very primitive verbal form which originally expressed an action irrespective of tense or mood, the context showing which was meant. The addition of the augment gave the sense of a past tense to one set of forms, while the rest finally became incorporated with the impv. The general meaning of the inj. expresses a desire, combining the senses of the subj., the opt., and the impv. As compared with the subj., the inj. is essentially appropriate in principal clauses, though it sometimes appears in subordinate clauses introduced by relatives or the relative conjunctions **yád** and **yadā́**.

a. The first person expresses an intention the execution of which lies in the power of the speaker; e. g. **índrasya nú vīryā̀ṇi prá vocam** *now I will proclaim the heroic deeds of Indra* (i. 32[1]). Sometimes, however, the execution depends on another; e. g. **agním hinvantu no dhíyas: téna jeṣma dhánam-dhanam** *let our prayers urge Agni: through him we shall assuredly win booty after booty* (x. 156[1]).

b. The second person is used exhortatively, very often beside an impv.; e. g. **sugā́ naḥ supáthā kṛṇu; pū́ṣann ihá kratúṃ vidaḥ** *do thou make fair paths for us easy to traverse; O Pūṣan, here procure us wisdom*; **adyā́ no deva sāvīḥ sáubhagaṃ, párā duṣvápnyaṃ suva** *to-day, O god, procure us good fortune; drive away evil dream* (v. 82[4]). A parallel opt. is much less common; e. g. **eténa gātúṃ vido naḥ; ā́ no vavṛtyāḥ suvitā́ya** *by reason of that find for us the path; mayst thou bring us to welfare* (i. 173[13]).

c. The third person also is used exhortatively, very often beside an impv.; e. g. **sémā́ṃ vetu váṣaṭkṛtim; agnír juṣata no gíraḥ** *let him come to this Vaṣaṭ call; may Agni accept our songs* (vii. 15[6]); it is often accompanied by a 2. sing. impv.; e. g. **ā́‿idáṃ barhír yájamānasya sīda; áthā ca bhūd ukthám índrāya śastám** *seat thyself upon this straw of the sacrificer; and then may the hymn be sung to Indra* (iii. 53[3]). It appears less frequently with the subj.; e. g. **úpa bráhmāṇi śṛṇava imā́ no, áthā te yajñás tanvè váyo dhāt** *mayst thou listen to these our prayers, and then let the* *sacrifice bestow vigour on thyself* (vi. 40^4). A parallel opt. is not common; e.g. **pári no hetí rudrásya vṛjyāḥ, pári tveṣásya durmatír mahī́ gāt** *would that the dart of Rudra pass us by, let the great malevolence of the impetuous one avoid us* (ii. 33^{14}).

d. The injunctive is very frequently used alone (unaccompanied by any other modal form) in an impv. sense; e.g. **imā́ havyā́ juṣanta naḥ** *let them accept these oblations of ours* (vi. 52^{11}); the preceding verse has the regular impv.: **juṣántām yújyam páyaḥ** *let them accept the suitable milk.*

In negative sentences the inj. is the only mood (with the exception of the single opt. form **bhujema**) with which the prohibitive particle **mā́** can be used; e.g. **mā́ na indra párā vṛṇak** *do not, O Indra, abandon us* (viii. 97^7); **viśváyan mā́ na ā́ gan** *let not any swelling thing come near us* (vii. 50^1); **mā́ tántuś chedi** *let not the thread be cut* (ii. 28^5). The aor. form is commoner than the impf. form in the RV., but its relative predominance has greatly increased in the AV.

e. The inj. not infrequently expresses a future sense like the subj. (215 C) in two types of sentences:

1. in positive interrogative sentences; e.g. **kó no mahyā́ áditaye púnar dāt** *who will give us back to great Aditi?* (i. 24^1). The subj. itself is here sometimes found beside it; e.g. **kadā́ mártam arādhásam padā́ kṣúmpam iva sphurat, kadā́ naḥ śuśravad gíraḥ** *when will he spurn the niggardly mortal like a mushroom with his foot; when will he hear our songs?* (i. 84^8).

2. in negative sentences with **ná**; e.g. **yám ādityā abhi druhó rákṣathā, ném aghám naśat** *whom, O Ādityas, ye protect from harm, him misfortune will not reach* (viii. 47^1).

a. In B. the use of the inj. in positive sentences has almost entirely disappeared. The ŚB., however, preserves several examples; e.g. **devā́n avat** *let it refresh the gods*; also sometimes in subordinate clauses, especially with **néd**; e.g. **néd idám bahirdhā́ yajñā́d bhávat** *lest it be outside the sacrifice.*

On the other hand the inj. is very frequent in negative sentences, in which it constantly appears with **mā́**, in the vast majority of cases in the aor. form. Only a few examples of the impf. form occur: **mā́ vadhadhvam** *slay not* (TS.); **mā bibhīta** *fear not* (AB.); **kilbiṣam nu mā yātayan** *let them not reprove it as a fault* (AB.); and from the perfect: **mā́ suṣupthāḥ** *sleep not* (ŚB.).

C. Subjunctive.

The meaning of the subj. is best brought out by contrasting its use with that of the opt. From this it appears that the fundamental sense of the subj. is will, while that of the opt. is either wish or possibility (this mood being therefore alternatively called optative or potential). This distinction appears clearly from the fact that in the first person in independent sentences one group of verbs in the RV. employs the subj. exclusively or almost exclusively, while another employs the opt., because in the former the execution is dependent on the will of the speaker, while in the latter it is not in his control, but is only possible. With the subj. are thus used the verbs **han** *strike*, **kṛ** *make*, **su** *press*, **brū** *speak*. With the opt. on the other hand appear: **ji** *conquer*, **tṛ** *overcome*, **sah** *conquer*; **aś** and **naś** *obtain*, **vid** *acquire*, **īś** *be master of*; **sac** *be associated with*; **ā́-vṛt** *attract* (to the sacrifice); **śak** *be able*; **mad** *be happy*; **ṛdh** *prosper*; **paś** *live to see*; **as** *be* (with predicates such as *prosperous*, &c.); also certain sacrificial verbs: **idh** *kindle* (with the co-operation of the god), **dāś** *worship*, **vac** and **vad** *speak* (effectively), **vidh** *serve*, **sap** *please = obtain the favour of* (a god), **hū** *call* (= *bring hither*).

1. The meanings expressed by the different persons of the subj. are the following:

The first person declares the will of the speaker; e.g. **svastáye vā́yum úpa bravāmahai** *for welfare we will invoke Vāyu* (v. 51[12]). It is often accompanied by the particles **nú** and **hánta**; e.g. **prá nú vocā sutéṣu vām** *I will now praise you two at the libations* (v. 69[1]). The 1. du. and pl. may also express an exhortation to another to share an action with the speaker, an impv. usually then preceding; e.g. **dakṣiṇató bhavā me: ádhā vṛtrā́ṇi jaṅghanāva bhū́ri** *stand on my right: then we two will slay many foes* (x. 83[7]); or an exhortation to aid the speaker; e.g. **jéṣāma‿indra tváyā yujā́** *we will conquer* (= *let us conquer*) *with thee as our ally* (viii. 63[11]).

In B. the usage is the same; e.g. **váraṃ vṛṇai** *I will choose a boon* (TS.); **hanta‿imān bhīṣayai** *well, I will terrify them* (AB.); **vāyúṃ devā́ abruvan: sómaṃ rā́jānaṃ hanāma‿íti** *the gods said to Vāyu: let us slay king Soma* (TS.).

The second person is used exhortatively: **háno vṛtráṃ, jáyā apáḥ** *slay Vṛtra, win the waters* (i. 80[3]). It often follows a 2. pers. impv.; e.g. **agne śṛṇuhi; devébhyo bravasi** *hear, O Agni, do thou say to the gods* (i. 139[7]); sometimes it follows a 3. pers. impv.; e.g. **ā́ vāṃ vahantu .. áśvāḥ, pibātho asmé mádhūni** *let the horses bring you two; do ye drink the honied draughts beside us* (vii. 67[4]). When an expectation is indicated, the subj. is almost equivalent to a future; e.g. **áchānta me, chadáyāthā ca nūnám** *ye have pleased me and ye shall please me now* (i. 165[12]).

In B. the 2. pers. subj. is used only when the speaker makes a condition or gives a direction relating to the (not immediate) future; e.g. **atho etaṃ varam avṛṇīta: mayā‿eva prācīṃ diśaṃ pra janātha‿iti** *so he made this condition: through me ye shall* (in future) *discover the eastern quarter* (AB.).

The third person is as a rule used in exhortations to the gods, though the subject is not always the name of the deity; e.g. **imáṃ naḥ śṛṇavad dhávam** *he shall hear this our call* (viii. 43[22]); **pári ṇo héḷo váruṇasya vṛjyāḥ; urúṃ na índraḥ kṛṇavad u lokám** *may the wrath of Varuṇa avoid us; Indra shall procure us wide space* (vii. 84[2]); **sá devā́m̐ ā́‿ihá vakṣati** *he shall bring the gods hither* (i. 1[2]); **prá te sumnā́ no aśnavan** *thy good intentions shall reach us* (viii. 90[6]). The subj. sentence is sometimes connected with a preceding one; e.g. **agním īḷe: sá u śravat** *I praise Agni: he shall hear* (viii. 43[24]). The subj. here often approaches the future in sense, being then usually opposed with **nūnám** or **nú** to another verb: **úd u ṣyá deváḥ savitā́ . . asthāt: nūnáṃ devébhyo ví hí dhā́ti rátnam** *god Savitṛ has just arisen: he will now distribute bounty to the gods* (ii. 38[1]); **uvā́sa‿uṣā́ uchā́c ca nú** *Dawn has flushed* (in the past) *and she will flush now* (i. 48[3]). Sometimes there is no opposition; e.g. **ā́ ghā tā́ gachān úttarā yugā́ni, yátra jāmáyaḥ kṛṇávan ájāmi** *there shall come those later generations when those who are akin will do what befits not kinsmen* (x. 10[10]).

In B. the 3. pers. subj. is not found in the hortative sense, appearing only when a condition, promise, or curse is expressed; e.g. **vṛṇīṣva‿ ity abruvan; so 'bravīn: maddevatyā‿eva samid asad iti** *they said: choose a boon; he replied: the fuel shall be sacred to me* (MS.); **sā́‿abravīd: váraṃ vṛṇai; khātā́t parābhaviṣyántī manye: táto mā́ parā́ bhūvam íti; purā́ te saṃvatsarā́d ápi rohād íty abravīt** *she said: I will make a condition; I think I shall perish in consequence of digging; let me not perish. He replied: before the lapse of a year for you, it* (the wound) *shall heal up* (TS.); **devās tān aśapan: svena vaḥ kiṣkuṇā vajreṇa vṛścān iti** *the gods cursed them* (the trees): *they shall destroy you with your own handle, with a bolt* (TB.). The 3. pers. subj. often also expresses the purpose of a ceremony; e.g. **śṛṇā́d íti śaramáyaṃ barhír bhavati** (MS.) *the litter is made of reeds with the intention: it shall destroy him* (the adversary).

2. **The syntactical employment** of the subj. is twofold.

a. It appears in principal sentences:

α. with interrogatives, either the pronoun or the adverbs **kathā́** *how?* **kadā́** *when*, and **kuvíd**; e.g. **kím ū nú vaḥ kṛṇavāma** *what, pray, shall we do for you?* (ii. 29[3]); **kathā́ mahé rudríyāya bravāma** *how shall we speak to the great Rudra-host?* (v. 41[11]); **kadā́ naḥ śuśravad gíraḥ** *when will he hear our prayers?* (i. 84[8]). **kuvíd** nearly always accentuates the verb (which is thus treated as in a subordinate clause); e.g. **aśvínā sú ṛṣe stuhi: kuvít te śrávato hávam** *the Aśvins praise well, O seer: shall they hear thy call?* (viii. 26[10]).

In B. first persons only seem to be met with in this use, and an interrogative word is sometimes lacking.

β. In negative sentences with **ná** *not*; e.g. **ná tā́ naśanti**;

ná dabhāti táskaraḥ *they perish not; no thief shall* (can) *harm them* (vi. 28³).

In B. **ná** is similarly used; e. g. **ná͜ ató 'paraḥ káś caná sahá śárīreṇa͜ amŕ̥to 'sat** *from now onwards no one shall be immortal with his body* (ŚB.). Once only, in a command, is the subj. used with **mā́**: **akāmā́ṃ sma mā́ ní padyāsai** *you shall not approach me* (in future) *against my will* (ŚB.).

b. In dependent clauses the subj. is used either with a negative or with relatives (pronominal or adverbial):

α. in a final sense with the negative particle **néd** *that not, lest.* The antecedent clause has either an ind. or an impv.; e.g. **hotrā́d ahám varuṇa bíbhyad āyam, néd evá mā yunájann átra devā́ḥ** *fearing the office of Hotṛ, O Varuṇa, I went away, lest the gods should appoint me thereto* (x. 51⁴); **vy ùchā duhitar divo mā́ cirám tanuthā ápaḥ, nét tvā stenáṃ yáthā ripúṃ tápāti sū́ro arcíṣā** *shine forth, daughter of the sky, delay not long thy work, lest the sun scorch thee, like a hostile thief, with his ray* (v. 79⁹).

In B. the antecedent clause has either an ind. or an opt.; e. g. **átha yán ná prékṣate, nén mā rudró hinásad íti** *now* (the reason) *why he does not look is lest Rudra should injure him* (ŚB.); **tán ná dadbhíḥ khāded, nén ma idáṃ rudríyaṃ dató hinásad íti** *he should not chew it with his teeth, lest this that belongs to Rudra injure his teeth* (ŚB.). A gerundive in the antecedent clause has also been noted in the AB.

β. in relative clauses:

1. such a clause normally precedes if it contains a supposition determining the sense of the principal clause; the latter usually has an impv., not infrequently a subj., seldom an inj. or ind.; e.g. **yó naḥ pṛtanyā́d, ápa táṃ-tam íd dhatam** *whoever shall combat us, him do ye two slay* (i. 132⁶); **yás túbhyaṃ dā́śān ná tám áṃho aśnavat** *who shall serve thee, him no distress can reach* (ii. 23⁴); **utá nūnáṃ yád indriyáṃ kariṣyā́ indra páuṃsyam, adyā́ nákiṣ ṭád ā́ minat** *and what heroic, manly deed thou, Indra, shalt now do, that let no one belittle to-day* (iv. 30²³); **yásmai tváṃ sukŕ̥te jātaveda, u lokám agne kṛṇávaḥ syonáṃ, sá rayíṃ**

naśate svastí *the righteous man for whom thou shalt procure, O Agni Jātavedas, a comfortable place, he obtains riches for welfare* (v. 4[11]).

In B. the use of the subj. in relative clauses is similar; but here the subj. is by far the commonest form in the principal clause, the impv. and ind. (sometimes omitted) being rare; e.g. **tā́ny abruvan, váraṃ vṛṇāmahai : yád ásurāñ jáyāma, tán naḥ sahá͜asad íti** *they said, we will make a condition : what we shall win from the Asuras that shall be ours in common* (TS.); **yás tvā káś ca͜upā́yat, tūṣṇī́m evá͜āsva** *whoever shall come towards you, sit still*; **yád vindā́sai tát te 'gnihotrám kurmaḥ** *what thou shalt find, that we* (shall) *make thy fire-oblation* (MS.); **tád vái sámṛddhaṃ yáṃ devā́ḥ sādháve kármaṇe juṣántai** *that, indeed,* (is) *excellent, if the gods shall be pleased with him for a good work* (ŚB.). In the last example the relative clause exceptionally follows.

2. The relative clause follows if it expresses a final or consequential sense (*in order that, so that*) arising from the principal clause; the latter usually has an impv., but sometimes an inj., opt., or ind.; e.g. **sáṃ pūṣan vidúṣā naya, yó áñjasā͜anuśā́sati, yá evá͜idám íti brávat** *associate us, O Pūṣan, with a wise* (guide) *who shall at once direct us and who shall say: here it is* (vi. 54[1]); **asmábhyaṃ tád rā́dha ā́ gāt, śáṃ yát stotṛ́bhya āpáye bhávāti** *let that wealth come for us which shall be a blessing to thy praisers and thy kinsman* (ii. 38[11]); **tád adyá vācáḥ prathamáṃ masīya yéna͜ásurām̐ abhí devā́ ásāma** *I would to-day think of that as the first* (point) *of my speech whereby we gods shall overcome the Asuras* (x. 53[4]); **imáṃ bibharmi súkṛtaṃ te aṅkuśáṃ yéna͜ārujā́si maghavañ chaphārújaḥ** *I bring to thee this well-fashioned weapon* (*with which* =) *in order that thou shouldst break the hoof-breakers* (x. 44[9]). The subj. of these relative clauses sometimes comes to have a purely future sense; e.g. **ó** (=**ā́͜u**) **té yanti yé áparī́ṣu páśyān** *those are coming who in future days will see her* (i. 113[11]).

In B. this type of relative clause with the subj. is rare; e.g. **yán mā dhinávat tán me kuruta** *procure for me that which shall refresh me* (ŚB.); **hánta vayáṃ tát sṛjāmahai yád asmā́n anvásad íti** *come, let us create what shall come after us* (ŚB.).

γ. with relative conjunctions :

1. **yád,** which, if the clause is determinative, means *when* ; the dependent clause then precedes, while the principal clause usually contains an impv., but sometimes an inj., a subj., or an opt. ; the conjunction means *in order that, so that,* if the dependent clause is final or consequential ; the dependent clause then follows, while the principal clause contains an impv., a subj., or an ind., e. g.

if **yád** = *when* : **úṣo yád adyá bhānúnā ví dvā́rāv ṛṇávo diváḥ, prá no yachatād avṛkám** *O Dawn, when to-day with thy beam thou shalt open the doors of heaven, then bestow on us safe shelter* (i. 48[15]) ; **yád adyá bhāgáṃ vibháj-āsi nṛ́bhya, úṣo devó no átra savitā́ dámūnā ánāgaso vocati sū́ryāya** *when thou shalt to-day distribute a share to men, O Dawn, god Savitṛ, the house friend, shall declare us guiltless to Sūrya* (i. 123[3]) ; **yád va ā́gaḥ puruṣátā kárāma, mā́ vas tásyām ápi bhūma** *when we shall commit a sin against you after the manner of men, let us not have a part in that* (shaft) *of yours* (vii. 57[4]) ; **yád didyávaḥ pṛ́tanāsu prakrī́ḷān, tásya vāṃ syāma sanitā́ra ājéḥ** *when shafts shall play in battles, of that conflict of yours we would be the winners* (iv. 41[11]).

if **yad** = *in order that,* or *so that* : **sá ā́ vaha devátātiṃ yaviṣṭha, śárdho yád adyá divyáṃ yájāsi** *so bring hither the gods, O youngest, that thou mayst adore the heavenly host to-day* (iii. 19[4]) ; **tavéd u tā́ḥ sukīrtáyó 'sann utá práśastayaḥ, yád indra mṛḷáyāsi naḥ** *these laudations and praises shall be thine, that thou, O Indra, mayst be merciful to us* (viii. 45[33]) ; **ná pāpā́so manāmahe, yád ín nv índraṃ sákhāyaṃ kṛṇáv-āmahai** *we deem not ourselves wicked,* (*so*) *that we can now make Indra our friend* (viii. 61[11]). In such posterior clauses the **yád** sometimes comes to express the content of the principal clause ; e. g. **ná te sákhā sakhyáṃ vaṣṭy etát, sálakṣmā yád víṣurūpā bhávāti** (x. 10[2]) *thy friend wishes not this friendship, that she who is of the same type* (= *akin*) *shall become of a different kind* (= *not akin*). This **yád** may once be translated by *till*: **kíyāty ā́ yát samáyā bhavāti yā́ vyūṣúr yāś ca nūnáṃ vyuchā́n** *in what time will it be that* (= how long will it be till) *she shall be between those that have shone forth and those that shall now shine forth?* (i. 113[10]).

In B. the subj. is rarely found in these clauses with **yád**; e. g. **tát prāpnuhi yát te prāṇó vā́tam apipádyātai** *attain this that your breath shall transfer itself to the wind* (ŚB.).

2. **yátra** *when* seems not to occur in V. with the subj. when it is a genuine conjunction (that is, when it is not equivalent to the loc. of the relative pronoun).

In B., however, it is found with the subj. in the sense of a future perfect; e. g. **yátra hótā chándasaḥ pāráṃ gáchāt, tát pratiprasthātā́ prātaranuvākám upā́ kurutāt** *when the Hotṛ shall have got to the end of the metre, then let the Pratiprasthātṛ start a Prātaranuvāka* (ŚB.).

3. **yáthā** with the subj. as an antecedent clause means *as*, the principal clause containing an impv. or a subj.; as a posterior clause it has the sense of *in order that, so that*, the principal clause containing either a demand (generally impv., occasionally inj., opt., or gerundive) or a statement (ind. pres. or aor., act. or pass.). Examples of the first use are: **yáthā hotar mánuṣo devátātā yájāsi, evā́ no adyá yakṣi devā́n** *as thou canst, O priest, worship at the divine service of man, so do thou for us to-day worship the gods* (vi. 4[1]). This use does not seem to occur in B. Examples of the second use are: **gṛhā́n gacha gṛhápatnī yáthā‿ásaḥ** *go to the house that you may be mistress of the house* (x. 85[26]); **idā́nīm áhna upavā́cyo nṛ́bhiḥ, śréṣṭhaṃ no átra dráviṇaṃ yáthā dádhat** *at this time of day he is to be addressed by men that he may here bestow on us the best wealth* (iv. 54[1]); **mahatā́m ā́ vṛṇīmahé 'vo, yáthā vásu náśāmahai** *we implore the favour of the great, in order that we may obtain riches* (x. 36[11]); **idáṃ pā́tram apāyi mátsad yáthā saumanasā́ya devám** *this bowl has been drunk up, in order that it may exhilarate the god to benevolence* (vi. 44[16]). The negative in such clauses is **ná** or **nú**.

a. In B. the usage is similar: the principal clause here contains either an impv. or a subj.; e.g. **tathā me kuru yathā‿aham imām senām jayāni** *so arrange for me that I may conquer this army* (AB.); **saṃdhā́ṃ nú sā́m dadhāvahai yáthā tvā́m evá praviśā́nīti** *now let us two make an agreement in order that I may enter into thee* (MS.).

4. **yadā́** *when*, with the subj. (pres. or aor.), which then has the value of a fut. perf., is regularly antecedent, the principal clause containing an impv. or a subj.; e.g. **śṛtáṃ yadā́ kárasi jātavedo, átha‿īm enaṃ pári dattāt pitṛ́bhyaḥ** *when thou shalt have made him done, then deliver him to the fathers* (x. 16²); **yadā́ gácchāty ásunītim etā́m, átha devā́nāṃ vaśanī́r bhavāti** *when he shall have gone to that spirit world, then he shall become subject to the gods* (x. 16²). **yadā́ kadā́ ca** *whenever* seems to give the verb the same sense: **yadā́ kadā́ ca sunávama sómam, agníṣ ṭvā dūtó dhanvāty ácha** *whenever we shall have pressed Soma, Agni shall hasten to thee as a messenger* (iii. 53⁴).

a. The usage of B. is the same; e.g. **sá yadā́ tā́m ativárdhā, átha karṣū́ṃ khātvā́ tásyāṃ mā bibharāsi** *when I shall have outgrown that* (vessel), *then having dug a trench you shall keep me in it* (ŚB.).

5. **yádi** *if* with the subj. generally precedes the principal clause, which contains an impv., a subj., (rarely) an opt., or an ind. (sometimes to be supplied); e.g. **yádi stómaṃ máma śrávad, asmā́kam índram índavo mandantu** *if he shall hear my praise, let these drops of ours gladden Indra* (viii. 1¹⁵); **yájāma devā́n yádi śaknávāma** *we will adore the gods, if we shall be able* (i. 27¹³); **yádi práti tváṃ háryāḥ . . apá enā jayema** *if thou shalt accept* (it) *gladly, we might thereby win the waters* (v. 2¹¹); **índrā ha váruṇā dhéṣṭhā, yádi sómaiḥ . . mādáyaite** *Indra and Varuṇa* (are) *the most liberal, if they shall delight in the Soma offerings* (iv. 41³).

a. In B. the subj. with **yádi** is very rare; an example is: **yádi tvā‿etát púnar brávatas, tváṃ brūtāt** *if they two shall say this again to thee, do thou say* (ŚB.).

6. **yā́d** *so long as* occurs twice with the subj. in the RV.: **anānukṛtyám apunáś cakāra yā́t sū́ryāmā́sā mithá uccá-**

rātaḥ *he has once for all done what is inimitable so long as sun and moon alternately shall rise* (x. 68[10]); **vásiṣṭhaṃ ha váruṇo . . ŕ̥ṣiṃ cakāra . . yā́n nú dyā́vas tatánan, yā́d uṣā́saḥ** *Varuṇa has made Vasiṣṭha a seer, so long as the days shall extend, so long as the dawns* (vii. 88[4]). In B. **yā́d** does not occur.

δ. The subj. is sometimes used in an antecedent clause with **ca** in the sense of *if*, which is then treated as a subordinate conjunction and accentuates the verb; e.g. **índraś ca mr̥ḷáyāti no, ná naḥ paścā́d aghám naśat** *if Indra shall be gracious to us, no evil shall afterwards touch us* (ii. 41[11]).

D. Optative or Potential.

216. 1. The **meaning** of the opt. is predominantly a wish, which is modified according to the person of the verb.

The **first person**, which is very common, expresses the wish of the speaker, generally addressed to the gods; e.g. **úṣas tám aśyāṃ yaśásaṃ rayím** *O Dawn, I would obtain that glorious wealth* (i. 92[8]); **vidhéma te stómaiḥ** *we would worship thee with songs of praise* (ii. 9[3]); **vayáṃ syāma pátayo rayīṇā́m** *we would be lords of riches* (iv. 50[6]).

In B. the sense of the first person is similar, but its occurrence, owing to the nature of the subject-matter, is far less common; e.g. **viśé ca kṣatrā́ya ca samádaṃ kuryām** *I should like to create enmity between people and nobility* (MS.).

The **second person** is much less common. It is almost exclusively used to express a wish or a request addressed to a god; e.g. **ā́ no mitrā́váruṇā hotrā́ya vavr̥tyāḥ** *pray bring Mitra and Varuṇa to our oblation* (vi. 11[1]); **tyā́ me hávam ā́ jagmyātam** *so, pray, do ye two come to my call* (vi. 50[10]); **prá sū́ na ā́yur jīváse tiretana** *do ye, pray, extend fully our allotted span that we may live* (viii. 18[22]). We might here often rather expect the impv., which indeed frequently either precedes or follows the 2. opt.; e.g. **dhiṣvá vájraṃ rakṣohátyāya: sāsahīṣṭhā́ abhí spŕ̥dhaḥ** *take the bolt for* *the slaughter of the demons: mayst thou overcome our foes* (vi. 45[18]); **imā́m me samídham vaneḥ; imā́ ū ṣú śrudhī gíraḥ** *pray accept this my fuel; graciously hear these songs* (ii. 6[1]).

In B. the second person is used almost exclusively in wishes; e. g. **asmín yájamāne bahvyàḥ syāta** *may you be numerous beside this sacrificer* (ŚB.).

The **third** person is used in the three different senses of wish, precept, or supposition; e.g. **mīḍhvā́m̐ asmā́kam babhūyāt** *may he be bountiful to us* (i. 27[2]); **imám amŕ̥tam dūtám kr̥ṇvīta mártyaḥ** *this immortal the mortal should make his messenger* (viii. 23[19]); **pr̥ṇánn āpír ápr̥ṇantam abhí ṣyāt** *the friend who bestows would prevail over him who does not bestow* (x. 117[7]). In the sense of a supposition (regarded as possible or probable) the opt. seldom appears independently, but often in an apodosis.

In B. it is common in all three senses: expressing a wish; e.g. **apaśúḥ syāt** *may he be bereft of cattle* (TS.); a general precept (where a gerundive may also be used); e.g. **kṣáume vásānā agním ā́ dadhīyātām, té adhvaryáve déye** *wearing linen garments the two should lay the fire; the two* (garments) *should be given to the Adhvaryu* (MS.); a supposition in the apodosis of periods, but seldom independently; e.g. **ná‿asya tā́m rā́trīm apó gr̥hā́n prá hareyur; ā́po vái śā́ntiḥ: śamáyeyur eva** (MS.) *they should not during that night bring water into his house; for water is extinction: they would thus extinguish* (if they did this). The protasis in this example must be supplied.

2. The **syntactical employment** of the optative is twofold:

a. it appears in principal sentences (for the most part retaining the sense of a wish) with interrogatives, either the pronoun or the adverbs **kathā́** *how?* **kadā́** *when?* and **kuvíd**; e.g. **kásmai devā́ya havíṣā vidhema** *what god would we worship with oblation?* (x. 121[1]); **kadā́ na indra rāyá ā́ daśasyeḥ** *when wouldst thou, O Indra, bestow riches upon us?* (vii. 37[5]); **kuvít tutujyā́t sātáye dhíyaḥ** (i. 143[6]) *would he not stimulate our prayers for gain?* (cp. p. 354, 2 *a*). A possibility is sometimes thus repudiated; e.g. **kád dha nūnám**

ṛtā́ vádanto ánṛtam rapema *how could we now speaking righteous words utter unrighteousness?* (x. 10[4]).

In B. the optative with interrogatives may express a wish, precept, possibility, or the repudiation of a suggestion; e. g. **katháṃ nú prá jāyeya** *how should I propagate myself?* (ŚB.); **yāmīm eva pūrvāṃ śaṃset** *he should first pronounce the formula addressed to Yama* (AB.); **kíṃ máma tátaḥ syāt** (ŚB.) *what would then accrue to me* (if I did this)? **kás tád ā́ driyeta** *who would pay attention to that?* (ŚB.).

a. The opt. appears in negative sentences with **ná** *not*, sometimes **nū́ cid** *never*. The sense is either optative or potential; e.g. **ná riṣyema kadā́ caná** *may we never suffer harm* (vi. 54[9]); **nū́ cin nú vāyór amṛ́taṃ ví dasyet** *may the nectar of Vāyu never fail* (vi. 37[3]); **ná tád devó ná mártyas tuturyād yā́ni právṛddho vṛṣabháś cakā́ra** *no god, no mortal could surpass what the mighty bull has done* (viii. 96[2]). The only opt. form with which the prohibitive **mā́** occurs is **bhujema**: **mā́ va éno anyákṛtaṃ bhujema** *may we not suffer before you for a sin done by others* (vi. 51[7]).

In B. the opt. is used with **ná** to express either a general prohibition or a potential sense; e. g. **tásya‿etád vratám: ná‿ánṛtaṃ vaden, ná māṃsám aśnīyāt** *this is his vow: he should not speak the untruth, he should not eat meat*; **ná‿enaṃ dadhikrā́vā caná pāvayā́ṃ kriyāt** *Dadhikrāvan himself could not make him pure* (MS.).

b. In dependent clauses the opt. is used with relatives (pronominal or adverbial):

a. such a clause having a determining sense, usually precedes. This type is very rare in V.; e.g. **sūryā́ṃ yó brahmā́ vidyā́t, sá íd vā́dhūyam arhati** *a priest who should know Sūryā deserves the bridal garment* (x. 85[34]).

In B., on the other hand, clauses of this type, which always imply a supposition, are very common. The opt. here expresses a precept or a potential sense; the principal clause most often has the opt. also; e. g. **yáṃ dviṣyā́t, táṃ dhyāyet** *whom he may hate, he should think of* (TS.); **yó vā́ imám ālábheta, múcyeta‿asmā́t pāpmánaḥ** *he who were to offer this* (bull), *would be delivered from this sin* (TS.). In the principal clause a gerundive occasionally appears or the verb *to be* has to be supplied; e.g. **yó rāṣṭrā́d ápabhūtaḥ syā̀t tásmai hotavyā̀** *this should be offered for him who should be deprived of his kingdom* (TS.); **yasya‿agnayo grāmyeṇa‿agninā saṃdahyeran, kā tatra prāyaścittiḥ** *if any one's fires should be united with a village fire, what expiation* (is) *there?* (AB.).

β. the relative clause, if it has a final or consequential sense (*in order that, so that*) follows. The principal clause contains an impv., a subj., or an opt.; e.g. **revátīr naḥ sadhamā́da índre santu yā́bhir mádema** (i. 30[13]) *let our feasts beside Indra be rich* (*by which* =) *that we may rejoice* (in them); **dhā́satho rayíṃ yéna samátsu sāhiṣīmáhi** *bestow wealth on us* (*by which* =) *that we may be victorious in battles* (viii. 40[1]); **yáyā‿áti víśvā duritā́ tárema sutármāṇam ádhi nā́vaṃ ruhema** *we would ascend the rescuing ship* (*by which* =) *that we may cross over all misfortunes* (viii. 42[3]).

In B. final relative clauses with the optative are rare.

γ. with relative conjunctions:

1. **yád** *if*: in the antecedent clause of pres. conditional periods, the condition being generally regarded as unfulfilled. The apodosis normally contains a potential opt. (though isolated examples of the impv., inj., and ind. occur); e.g. **yád agne syā́m aháṃ tváṃ, tváṃ vā ghā syā́ ahám, syúṣ ṭe satyā́ ihá‿āśíṣaḥ** *if I, O Agni, were thou, and thou wert I, thy prayers would be fulfilled* (viii. 44[23]); occasionally the fulfilment of the condition is expected; e.g. **yác chuśruyā́ imáṃ hávaṃ durmárṣaṃ cakriyā utá, bháver āpír no ántamaḥ** *if thou shouldst hear this call and shouldst not forget it, thou wouldst be our most intimate friend* (viii. 45[18]). The temporal sense of *when* with the opt. seems to occur only once in the RV. (iii. 33[11]).

In B. (as in V.) **yád** *if* with the opt. is very common in the protasis, when the fulfilment of the condition is not expected (**yádi** with opt. being used when it is expected); e.g. **sá yád bhídyeta‿ā́rtim ā́rched yájamānaḥ** *if it should be broken, the sacrificer would fall into calamity* (TS.). The infinitive with **īśvará** may take the place of the opt. in the principal clause; e.g. **yad etāṃ śaṃsed īśvaraḥ parjanyo 'varṣṭoḥ** *if he were to repeat this* (*formula*), *Parjanya might not rain* (AB.). Sometimes the verb (opt. of **as** *be*) is omitted in the apodosis. The opt. with **yád** here rarely expresses a purely hypothetical case (that is, without the implication that the condition will not be fulfilled); e. g. **yán mā́m praviśéḥ kím mā bhuñjyāḥ** (TS.) *if you were to enter me, of what use would you be to me?* (afterwards he does enter Indra).

a. **yád** with the opt. in the final sense of *in order that* is very rare; e.g. **yán nūnám aśyā́m gátim, mitrásya yāyām pathā́** *in order that I might now obtain a refuge, I would go on the path of Mitra* (v. 64[3]).

β. In B. **yád** with the opt in the sense of *that* is frequently used after **áva kalpate** *is suitable*, **út sahate** *endures*, **icháti** *desires*, **véda** *knows*, **yuktó bhavati** *is intent*, in posterior clauses; e. g. **ná hí tád avakálpate yád brūyā́t** *for it is not fitting that he should say* (ŚB.); **ná vā́ ahám idám út sahe yád vo hótā syā́m** (ŚB.) *I cannot endure this that should be* (= *I cannot be*) *your Hotṛ*; **tád dhy èvá brā́hmaṇena‿eṣṭávyam yád brahmavarcasī́ syā́t** *for that is to be aimed at by the Brahmin, that he should be pious* (ŚB.); **svayám vā́ etásmai devā́ yuktā́ bhavanti yát sādhú vádeyuḥ** *for the gods themselves are intent on this, that they should say what is right* (ŚB.); **kás tád veda yád vratapradó vratám upotsiñcet** *for who knows (this that =) whether he who hands the fast-milk (should add =) adds* (fresh milk) *to it* (ŚB.). In the ŚB. **īśvará** also is used with this construction (in other Brāhmaṇas with the infinitive only) to express a possible consequence (though the **yád** is nearly always omitted); e. g. **párāṅ asmād yajñò 'bhūd íti‿īśvaró ha yát táthā‿evá syā́t** *the sacrifice has turned away from him: it is possible that this should be so* (ŚB.). Otherwise the phrase regularly appears in the form of **íti‿īśvaró ha táthā eva syāt**, perhaps because **īśvará** came to be regarded as a kind of adverb = *possibly this might be so.*

γ. In B. **yád** introducing a clause with the opt. accompanied by **ná** and ending with **íti**, dependent on a verb of fearing or similar expression, is equivalent to *lest*; e. g. **devā́ ha vái bibhayā́ṃ cakrur yád vái naḥ . . asurarakṣasā́ni‿imám gráham ná hanyúr íti** *the gods feared lest the Asuras and Rakṣases should destroy this draught* (ŚB.); **índro ha vā́ īkṣā́ṃ cakre yán mā tán ná‿abhibhávet íti** *Indra pondered* (fearing) *lest that should vanquish him* (ŚB.).

2. **yádi** *if* with the opt. does not occur in the RV. and AV. at all, and only once in the SV.

In B. it is very common, expressing a condition the fulfilment of which is assumed (while **yád** with opt. implies non-fulfilment of the condition). The clause with **yádi** generally precedes. The apodosis has :

a. usually the opt., which expresses a precept applicable when the condition is fulfilled ; e. g. **yádi purā́ saṃsthā́nād dīryeta‿adyá varṣiṣyati‿íti brūyāt** *if* (the vessel) *should be broken before the completion* (of the sacrifice), *he should say : it will rain to-day* (MS.); **yadi na śaknuyāt so 'gnaye puroḷāśaṃ nir vapet** *if he should not be able to do so, he should offer a cake to Agni* (AB.). The precept occasionally has a potential sense ; e. g. **yády ékatayīṣu dvayī́ṣu vā‿avagáched, aparódhukā enaṃ syuḥ** (MS.) *if he* (the banished man) *should return after one or two libations, they might exclude him from the sovereignty* (but not if he returns at the conclusion of the ceremony).

β. **īśvará** with the infinitive ; e. g. **īśvaro ha yady apy anyo yajeta‿atha hotāraṃ yaśo 'rtoḥ** *even if another should sacrifice* (instead of him), *it is possible that fame should come to the Hotṛ* (AB.).

γ. a gerundive ; **sa yadi na jāyeta, rākṣoghnyo gāyatryo 'nūcyāḥ** *if it* (the fire) *should not be kindled, the demon-slaying verses* are *to be repeated* (AB.).

δ. an ind. (sometimes omitted if it is a form of **as** *be*); e. g. **tasmād yadi yajña ṛkta ārtiḥ syād brahmaṇa eva ni vedayante** *therefore if at the sacrifice there should be any failure with regard to a Ṛc verse, they inform the Brahman priest* (AB.); **yadi no yajña ṛkta ārtiḥ syāt, kā prāyaścittiḥ** *if we shall have an accident at the sacrifice in regard to a Ṛc verse, what* (is) *the penance?* (AB.).

ε. The difference between **yád** and **yádi** with the opt. may be illustrated by the following example : **yán no jáyeyur imā́ abhyúpa dhāvema, yády u jáyema‿ímā́ abhyupā́ vartemahi‿íti** *if they were to conquer us* (not to be assumed), *we should take refuge with these* (friends), *but if* (as is to be assumed) *we should conquer, we could again betake ourselves to them* (MS.).

3. **yáthā** used in V. only in the sense of *in order that*, generally following the principal clause, which contains an impv., an inj., or an ind. ; e. g. **ápa víśvām̐ amitrān nudasva, yáthā táva śárman mádema** *drive away all foes that we may rejoice in thy protection* (x. 131[1]); **tváyā yáthā gṛtsamadā́so . . úparām̐ abhí ṣyúḥ, sūríbhyo gṛṇaté tád váyo dhāḥ** *bestow on the patrons and the singer this blessing that through thee the Gṛtsamadas may be superior to their neighbours* (ii. 4[9]);

ā dáivyā vṛṇīmahé 'vāṃsi, yáthā bhávema mīḷhúṣe ánāgāḥ *we implore the divine aids that we may be sinless before the gracious one* (vii. 97²).

a. In B. **yáthā** with the opt. has two uses : *α*. in antecedent clauses in the sense of *as, as if*, with a correlative meaning *so* in the principal clause, which contains an opt., an ind., or no verb ; e. g. **yathā‿eva chinnā naur bandhanāt plaveta,‿evam eva te plaveran** *just as a boat cut from its fastening would drift, so they would drift* (AB.); **sá yáthā nadyái pārám parāpáśyed evám svásya‿áyuṣaḥ pārám párā cakhyau** *as if he were looking across to the farther bank of a river, so he saw the end of his life from afar* (ŚB.) ; **átho yáthā brūyád etán me gopāya‿íti tādṛ́g evá tát** *then it* (is) *so as if he were to say : guard this for me* (TS.).

β. in posterior clauses in the sense of *how, so that* ; e. g. **úpa jānīta yáthā‿iyám púnar ágáchet** *do ye find out how she could come back* (ŚB.) ; **tát táthā‿evá hotavyàm yáthā‿agním vyaveyā́t** *hence it is to be so poured that it may divide the fire* (MS.).

4. **yátra** and **yadā́** are not found with the opt. in V., and **yárhi** does not occur at all in the RV. and AV.

In B. all three conjunctions are used hypothetically with the opt. in the sense of *when*.

a. **yátra**, besides having the sense of *when, in case*, often seems to mean *at the moment when, as soon as* ; the principal clause has the opt. or the ind. ; e. g. **mārutám saptákapālam nír vaped yátra víḍ rā́jānam jíjyāset** *he should offer a cake on seven dishes to the Maruts in case the people were to oppress the king* (MS.) ; **sá yátra prastuyā́t tád etā́ni japet** *as soon as he* (the priest) *begins to sing, one should mutter the following prayers* (ŚB.).

β. **yadā́** *as soon as* seems often to imply that the action of the opt. should be assumed to be past ; it seems always to be followed by **átha** *then* ; e. g. **sá yadā́ saṃgrāmám jáyed átha‿aindrāgnám nír vapet** *as soon as he may have won a battle, he should sacrifice to Indra and Agni* (MS.).

γ. **yárhi** *when* is generally followed by the correlative **tárhi** *then* in the principal clause, which usually has the opt. also ; e. g. **yárhi prajā́ḥ kṣúdham nigáchеyus, tárhi navarātréṇa yajeta** *when his people should be exposed to hunger, then he should sacrifice with the rite of nine nights* (TS.).

5. **céd** *if* is used with the ind. only in the RV. and only once with the opt. in the AV.

In B. it is used with the opt. like **yádi** (with which it may interchange) ; e. g. **etám céd anyásmā anubrūyā́s, táta evá te śíraś chindyām** *if you were to communicate this to another, I would cut off your head* (ŚB.).

Precative.

217. This form, which occurs in the RV. and AV. in principal clauses only, and never interrogatively, expresses a prayer or wish addressed to the gods almost exclusively, as is to be expected from the nature of those texts; e.g. **yó no dvéṣṭy ádharaḥ sás padīṣṭa** *may he who hates us fall to the ground* (iii. 53[21]). When a negative is used it is **ná**; e.g. **bhágo me agne sakhyé ná mṛdhyāḥ** *may my good fortune, O Agni, not relax in* (thy) *friendship* (iii. 54[21]).

In B. the precative is almost restricted to verse or prose formulas quoted and to paraphrases of such formulas; e.g. **bhū́yasīnām úttarāṃ sámāṃ kriyāsam íti gávāṃ lákṣma kuryāt** *would that I may do* (this) *to more next year: so saying he should make the mark of the cows* (MS.). **śatáṃ hímā íti śatáṃ varṣáṇi jīvyāsam íty evá‿etád āha** *by the expression 'a hundred winters' he says this: 'would that I may live a hundred years'* (ŚB.). It is, however, sometimes found in genuine prose narrative also; e.g. **sá ha vā́k prajā́patim uvāca: áhavyavāḍ evá‿ahám túbhyaṃ bhūyāsam** *Vāc said to Prajāpati: I would like not to be a conductor of sacrifice for thee* (ŚB.); **tám aśapad: dhiyā́-dhiyā tvā vadhyāsuḥ** *him* (Agni) *cursed* (saying): *I wish they may kill thee with repeated deliberation* (TS.).

Conditional.

218. In V. the conditional occurs only once (RV. ii. 30[2]) in a somewhat obscure passage, though the form **abhariṣyat** used after a past tense appears to mean *would take away* (in place of the future which would have been used after a present tense).

In B. the conditional is once found in a simple interrogative sentence: **táta evá‿asya bhayáṃ vìyāya: kásmād dhy ábheṣyat** *thereupon his fear departed: for of what should he have been afraid?* (ŚB.). Otherwise it occurs only in compound sentences:

1. usually in both protasis and apodosis of conditional sentences, expressing what might have happened in the past, but did not happen because the condition was not fulfilled. The conditional clause is generally introduced by **yád**, rarely by **yádi** (216); e.g. **sá yád dha‿ápi múkhād ádroṣyan, ná ha‿evá prā́yaścittir abhaviṣyat** *if it* (Soma) *had also flowed out of his mouth, there would not have been a penance* (ŚB.); **yád eváṃ ná‿ávakṣyo mūrdhā́ te vy àpatiṣyat** *if you had not spoken thus, your head would have split asunder* (ŚB.); **pā́dau te 'mlāsyatāṃ yádi ha ná‿ágamiṣyaḥ** *your feet would have withered, if you had not come* (ŚB.).

a. When **yád** is used with the opt. the supposed condition refers to the present (216).

2. in relative clauses dependent on negative principal clauses containing a past tense (always of **vid** *find*); e.g. **sá tád evá ná‿avindat prajā́patir yád áhoṣyat** *Prajāpati found nothing that he could sacrifice* (MS.); **sá vái tám ná‿avindad yásmai tāṃ dákṣiṇām áneṣyat** *he found no one to whom he should give this sacrificial fee* (TB.).

3. in a clause introduced by **yád** *that* dependent on a negative (or equivalent) clause; e.g. **cirám tán mene yád vā́saḥ paryádhāsyata** *he thought it too long* (*that* =) *till he should put on the garment* (ŚB.) = *he thought the time was not short enough till he should put on the garment.*

APPENDIX I

LIST OF VERBS.

The order of the parts of the verb, when all are given, is: Present Indicative (PR.), Subjunctive (SB.), Injunctive (INJ.), Optative (OP.), Imperative (IPV.), Participle (PT.), Imperfect (IPF.); Perfect (PF.); Pluperfect (PPF.); Aorist (AO.); Precative (PRC.); Future (FT.); Conditional (CO.), Passive (PS.), Present, Aorist, Past Participle (PP.); Gerundive (GDV.); Gerund (GD.); Infinitive (INF.); Causative (CS.); Desiderative (DS.); Intensive (INT.).

The Roman numerals indicate the conjugational class of the verb; P. signifies that the verb is conjugated in the Parasmaipada (active) only, Ā. that it is conjugated in the Ātmanepada (middle) only.

aṃś *attain*, V.: PR. **aśnóti**; SB. **aśnávat**; IPV. **aśnótu**; PT. **aśnuvánt**. PF. **ānáṃśa** and **ānā́śa**; **ānaśmá**, **ānaśá**, **ānaśúr**; **ānaśé**; SB. **anaśāmahai**; OP. **ānaśyā́m**; PT. **ānaśāná**; PF. also **ā́śa**, **āśátur**, **āśúr**; Ā. du. **āśā́the**, **āśā́te**. AO. root: Ā. 3. s. **ā́ṣṭa**, pl. **ā́śata**; INJ. **aṣṭa**, pl. **aśata**; OP. **aśyā́t**, PRC. 3. s. **aśyā́s** (=**aśyā́s-t**); s: SB. **ákṣat**; a: **aśét**. INF. **áṣṭave**.

akṣ *mutilate*, V.: PR. IPV. **akṣṇuhí**. PF. PT. **ākṣāṇá**. AO. iṣ: **ā́kṣiṣur**.

ac *bend*, I.: PR. **ácati**. IPV. 2. s. **áca**; **ácasva**. PS. **acyáte**; PT. **acyámāna**; IPF. **acyánta**; PP. **akná** (B.). GD. **-acya**.

aj *drive*, I.: PR. **ájati**, **ájate**; SB. **ájāni**, **ájāsi**, **ájāti**; OP. **ájeta**; IPV. **ájatu**; PT. **ájant**. IPF. **ā́jat**. PS. **ajyáte**; PT. **ajyámāna**. INF. **-áje**.

añj *anoint*, VII.: PR. **anákti**, **aṅkté**; SB. **anájat**; IPV. **aṅdhí** (= **aṅgdhí**), **anáktu**; PT. **añjánt**, **añjāná**. IPF. **ā́ñjan**. PF. **ānáñja**; **ānajé**, **ānajré**; SB. **anajā**; OP. **anajyā́t**; PT. **ānajāná**. PS. **ajyáte**; PT. **ajyámāna**; PP. **aktá**. GD. **aktvā́** (B.), **-ajya** (B.).

ad *eat*, II. : PR. ádmi, átsi, átti; adánti; SB. ádat, pl. ádān (AV.); OP. adyā́t; IPV. addhí, áttu; attám, attā́m; attá, adántu; PT. adánt, adāná. IPF. ā́dat. FT. atsyáti. PP. ánna n. *food*. GD. attvā́ya (B.). INF. áttum, áttave, áttos (B.). CS. ādáyati (B.).

an *breathe*, P. : I. ánati (AV.); VI. : anáti (AV.); II. : ániti; IPV. anihí; PT. anánt. IPF. ā́nīt. PF. ā́na. AO. ā́niṣur. FT. aniṣyáti (B.). PP. anitá (B.). -anya (B.). INF. ánitum (B.). CS. anáyati.

am *injure*, II. : PR. ámīṣi, ámīti; I. : PR. áme; INJ. ámanta; IPV. ámīṣva; PT. ámamāna. IPF. ā́mīt. PF. āmiré (B.). AO. ā́mamat. PS. amyáte. CS. āmáyati.

arc *praise*, I. : PR. árcati; SB. árcā, árcāt; árcāma, árcān; INJ. árcat; árcan; IPV. árcatu; PT. árcant. IPF. ā́rcan. PF. ānṛcúr; ānṛcé. PS. ṛcyáte; PT. ṛcyámāna. INF. ṛcáse. CS. arcáyati.

arh *deserve*, I. : PR. árhati; SB. árhāt; PT. árhant. PF. ānṛhúr (TS.); arhiré. INF. arháse.

av *favour*, I. P. : PR. ávati; SB. ávāt; INJ. ávat; OP. ávet; IPV. ávatu; PT. ávant. IPF. ā́vat. PF. ā́vitha, ā́va. AO. root : OP. 2. avyā́s; PRC. 3. avyā́s (=avyā́s-t); iṣ : ā́vīt; SB. áviṣat; INJ. ávīt; IPV. aviḍḍhí, áviṣṭu; aviṣṭám, aviṣṭā́m; aviṣṭána. FT. aviṣyáti; PT. aviṣyánt. PP. -ūta. GD. -avya. INF. ávitave.

aś *eat*, IX. : PR. aśnā́ti, aśnánti; aśnīté, aśnáte; OP. aśnīyā́t; IPV. aśāná; PT. aśnánt. IPF. ā́śnām, ā́śnāt; ā́śnan, aśnan. PF. ā́śa. AO. iṣ : ā́śiṣam, ā́śīs, ā́śīt; INJ. aśīt. FT. aśiṣyáti (B.). PS. aśyáte; PP. aśitá. GD. aśitvā́ (B.), -áśya (B.). CS. āśáyati (B.). DS. aśiśiṣati (B.).

1. **as** *be*, II. P. : PR. ásmi, ási, ásti; sthás, stás; smás, sthá and sthána, sánti; SB. ásāni, ásasi and ásas, ásati and ásat; ásathas; ásāma, ásatha, ásan; INJ. 3. pl. sán; OP. syā́m, syā́s, syā́t; syā́tam, syā́tām; syā́ma, syā́ta and syā́tana, syúr; IPV. edhí, ástu; stám, stā́m; stá, sántu; PT. sánt. IPF. ā́sam, ā́sīs, ā́s (=ā́s-t) and

ā́sīt; ā́stam, ā́stām; ā́san. PF. ā́sa, ā́sitha, ā́sa; āsáthur, āsátur; āsimá, āsúr.

2. as *throw*, IV.: PR. ásyāmi, ásyati and ásyate; ásyāmasi, ásyanti; IPV. ásya and ásyatāt, ásyatu; PT. ásyant. IPF. ā́syat. PF. ā́sa. FT. asiṣyáti. PS. asyáte; PP. astá. GD. -asya. INF. ástave, ástavái (B.).

ah *say*, P.: PF. ā́ha, ā́ttha (B.); āhátur (B.); āhúr.

āp *obtain*, V.: PR. āpnóti. PF. ā́pa, ā́pitha; āpiré; PT. āpāná. AO. red.: ā́pipan (B.); a: ā́pat; OP. apéyam (AV.). FT. āpsyáti, -te (B.); āptā (B.). PS. āpyáte (B.); AO. ā́pi (B.); PP. āptá. GD. āptvā́ (B.), -āpya (B.). INF. ā́ptum (B.). CS. āpáyati (B.). DS. ī́psati, ī́psate (B.); AO. áipsīt (B.); DS. of CS. āpipayiṣet (B.).

ās *sit*, II. Ā.: PR. ā́ste; ā́sāthe, ā́sāte; ā́smahe, ā́sate; SB. ā́sate; OPT. ā́sīta; IPV. s. 3. ā́stām, pl. 2. ā́dhvam; PT. āsāná and ā́sīna. IPF. pl. 3. ā́sata. PF. āsā́ṃ cakre (B.). AO. āsiṣṭa (B.). FT. āsiṣyáti, -te (B.). PP. āsitá (B.). GD. āsitvā́ (B.). INF. ā́situm (B.). CS. āsáyati (B.).

i *go*, II.: PR. éti; yánti; Ā. 1. s. iye, du. 3. iyāte, pl. 1. ī́mahe; SB. áyā, áyasi and áyas, áyati and áyat; áyāma, áyan; INJ. pl. 3. yán; OP. iyā́m, iyā́t; iyā́ma; IPV. ihí, étu; itám, itā́m; itá and eta, itána, yántu; PT. yánt, iyāná. IPF. ā́yam, áis, áit; áitam, áitām; áita, ā́yan; Ā. 3. pl. ā́yata. I.: áyati, áyate; INJ. áyanta; IPV. 3. du. áyatām, pl. áyantām. V.: PR. inóti; inviré. IPF. áinos, áinot.

PF. iyétha and iyátha, iyā́ya; īyáthur, īyátur; īyúr; PT. īyivā́ṃs. PPF. áiyes. FT. eṣyáti; ayiṣyati (B.); etā́ (B.). PP. itá. GD. itvā́, -ítya. INF. étum (B.); étave, étavái, ityái, iyádhyai, áyase; étos.

idh *kindle*, VII. Ā.: PR. inddhé; indháte and indhaté; SB. inádhate; IPV. indhā́m (= inddhā́m); indhvám (= inddhvám), indhátām; PT. índhāna. IPF. áindha. PF. īdhé; īdhiré. AO. SB. idhaté; OP. idhīmáhi; PT. idhāná. PS. idhyáte; IPV. idhyásva; PT. idhyámāna; PP. iddhá. INF. -ídham; -ídhe. From the nasalized root, indh, the iṣ AO. is formed in B.: IND. áindhiṣṭa; OP. indhiṣīya.

inv *go*, I. P. (=V. i-nu+a): PR. ínvasi, ínvati; ínvathas, ínvatas. SB. ínvāt; IPV. ínva, ínvatu; ínvatam, ínvatām; PT. ínvant.

1. **iṣ** *desire*, VI.: PR. icháti, -tə; SB. ichā́t; INJ. ichás; ichánta; OP. ichét; ichéta; IPV. ichá, ichátu; ichátа; ichásva, ichátām; PT. ichánt; ichámāna. IPF. áichat. PF. (B.) iyéṣa, īṣúr; īṣé, īṣiré. AO. (B.) áiṣīt; áiṣīṣur. FT. (B.) eṣiṣyáti, -te. PP. iṣṭá. GD. -íṣya. INF. éṣṭum (B.); éṣṭavái (B.).

2. **iṣ** *send*, IV.: PR. íṣyati, -te; IPV. íṣyatam; íṣyata; PT. íṣyant. IX.: PR. iṣṇā́ti; PT. iṣṇánt; iṣṇāná. VI.: PR. iṣé; INJ. iṣánta; OP. iṣéma; IPF. áiṣanta. PF. īṣáthur, īṣúr; īṣé, īṣiré. PP. iṣitá. GD. -iṣya (B.). INF. iṣádhyai. CS. iṣáyati, -te; INF. iṣayádhyai.

īkṣ *see*, I. Ā.: PR. ī́kṣe; PT. ī́kṣamāṇa. IPF. áikṣata; áikṣetām; áikṣanta. PER. PF. īkṣā́ṃ cakre (B.). AO. iṣ: áikṣiṣi. FT. īkṣiṣyáti, -te (B.). PP. īkṣitá (B.). GDV. īkṣeṇyà. GD. īkṣitvā́ (B.). CS. īkṣáyati, -te.

īṅkh *swing*: CS. īṅkháyati, -te; SB. īṅkháyātai (AV.), īṅkháyāvahai; IPV. īṅkháya; PT. īṅkháyant. PP. īṅkhitá.

īḍ *praise*, II. Ā.: PR. 1. ī́ḷe, 3. ī́ṭṭe; ī́ḷate; SB. ī́ḷāmahai and īḷāmahe; INJ. īḷata (3. pl.); OP. īḷīta; IPV. ī́ḷiṣva; PT. ī́ḷāna. PF. īḷé (3. s.). PP. īḷitá. GDV. ī́ḍya, īḷénya.

īr *set in motion*, II.: PR. ī́rte; ī́rate; SB. ī́rat; IPV. ī́rṣva; ī́rāthām; ī́rdhvam, ī́ratām; PT. ī́rāṇa. IPF. áiram, áir-a-t, du. 2. áir-a-tam; Ā. airata (3. pl.). PP. īrṇá (B.). CS. īráyati; SB. īráyāmahe; INJ. īráyanta; IPV. īráya, īráyatam; īráyasva; īráyadhvam; PT. īráyant. IPF. áirayat; áirayata; INF. īrayádhyai. PP. īritá.

īś *be master*, II. Ā.: PR. 1. ī́śe, 2. ī́kṣe and ī́śiṣe, 3. ī́ṣṭe, ī́śe and (once) ī́śate; ī́śāthe; ī́śmahe, ī́śidhve, ī́śate; INJ. ī́śata (3. s.); OP. ī́śīya, ī́śīta; PT. ī́śāna. PF. ī́śire; PT. īśāná.

īṣ *move*, I.: pr. íṣati, -te; éṣati; inj. éṣas; ipv. íṣatu, éṣatu; pt. éṣant; íṣamāṇa. pf. īṣé (1. 3.). pp. -īṣita.

1. **ukṣ** *sprinkle*, VI.: pr. ukṣáti, -te; ipv. ukṣátam, ukṣáta; ukṣéthām; pt. ukṣámāṇa. ao. iṣ: áukṣiṣam (B.). ft. ukṣiṣyáti (B.). ps. ukṣyáte (B.); pp. ukṣitá. gd. -úkṣya.

2. **ukṣ** (= vakṣ) *grow*, I. and VI.: pr. pt. úkṣant; ukṣámāṇa. ipf. áukṣat. ao. s: áukṣīs. pp. ukṣitá. cs. ukṣáyate.

uc *be pleased*, IV. P.: pr. ucyasi. pf. uvócitha, uvóca; ūciṣé, ūcé; pt. okiváṃs, ūcúṣ. pp. ucitá.

ud *wet*, VII.: pr. unátti; undánti; undáte (3. pl.). ipv. undhí (= unddhí); unátta; pt. undánt. VI. P.: pr. undáti (B.). ipf. áunat. pf. ūdúr. ps. udyáte; pp. uttá (B.). gd. -udya (B.).

ubj *force*, VI. P.: pr. ubjáti; ipv. ubjá, ubjátu; ubjátam; ubjántu; pt. ubjánt. ipf. 2. ubjas, 3. áubjat. pp. ubjitá. gd. -ubjya (B.).

ubh *confine*, VII. P.: ipf. unap (2. s.), áumbhan (TS.). VI. P.: ipv. umbhâta (2. pl.); ipf. áumbhat. IX. P.: ipf. ubhnā́s, áubhnāt. pp. ubdhá.

uṣ *burn*, I. P.: pr. óṣati; inj. óṣas; ipv. óṣa and óṣatāt, óṣatu; óṣatam; pt. óṣant. IX. P.: pt. uṣṇánt. ipf. uṣṇán. pf. uvóṣa (B.). ao. áuṣīt (B.). pp. uṣṭá (B.).

1. **ūh** *remove*, I.: pr. ū́hati; ipv. ū́ha. ipf. áuhat; áuhata, áuhan; Ā. áuhata (3. s.). ao. áuhīt (B.); op. uhyāt (B.). pp. ūḍhá (B.). gd. -ūhya and -úhya (B.). inf. -ūhitavái (B.).

2. **ūh** *consider*, I. Ā.: pr. óhate. II. Ā.: pr. óhate (3. pl.); pt. óhāna and ohāná. pf. ūhé; 2. du. ūhyā́the (= ūhā́the?). ao. áuhiṣṭa; pt. óhasāna.

ṛ *go*, VI. P.: pr. ṛcháti (-te, B.); sb. ṛchā́t; ipv. ṛchátu; ṛchántu. III. P.: pr. íyarmi, iyárṣi, íyarti; ipv. iyarta (2. pl.). V.: pr. ṛṇómi, ṛṇóti; ṛṇvánti; ṛṇvé; ṛṇviré; inj. ṛṇós; ṛṇván; Ā. ṛṇutá (3. s.); sb. ṛṇávas; ipv.: Ā. ṛṇvátām (3. pl.); pt. ṛṇvánt. ipf. ṛṇván. pf. ā́ritha, ā́ra; ārā́thur, ārúr; pt. āriváṃs; ārāṇá. ao.

root: **ā́rta**; **ā́rata**; INJ. **arta** (Ā. 3. s.); OP. **aryāt** (TS.); **arīta**; PT. **arāṇá**; a: **áram, ā́rat**; **ā́rata, ā́ran**; Ā. **ā́rata** (3. s.); **áranta**; SB. **arāma**; INJ. **aram**; **aran**; Ā. **arāmahi, aranta**; IPV. **aratam, aratām.** FT. **ariṣyáti** (B.). PP. **ṛtá.** GD. **ṛtvā́, -ṛ́tya.** CS. **arpáyati**; AO. red.: **arpipam**; PP. **arpitá** and **árpita.** GD. **-árpya, arpayitvā́** (AV.). INT. **álarṣi, álarti.**

ṛj *direct*, VI.: PR. **ṛñjáti, -te**; IPV. **ṛñjáta**; PT. **ṛñjánt.** VII. Ā.: PR. **ṛñjé**; **ṛñjáte** (3. pl.); IV.: PR. **ṛ́jyate**; PT. **ṛ́jyant.** I.: PR. **árjati** (B.). AO. PT. **ṛñjasāná.** INF. **ṛñjáse.**

ṛd *stir*, VI. P.: IPV. **ṛdántu.** IPF. **ā́rdan.** I.: PR. **árdati** (AV.). CS. **ardáyati**; SB. **ardáyāti.**

ṛdh *thrive*, V. P.: PR. **ṛdhnóti**; IPF. **ā́rdhnot.** IV.: PR. **ṛ́dhyati, -te**; IPV. **ṛ́dhyatām.** VII. P.: SB. **ṛṇádhat**; OP. **ṛndhyā́m**; PT. **ṛndhánt.** PF. **ānardha** (K.); **ānṛdhúr**; **ānṛdhé.** AO. root: **ā́rdhma** (B.); SB. **ṛdhát**; Ā. **ṛdhā́the** (2. du.); OP. **ṛdhyā́m, ṛdhyā́s, ṛdhyā́ma**; **ṛdhīmáhi**; PRC. **ṛdhyā́sam**; PT. **ṛdhánt**; a: OP. **ṛdhét, ṛdhéma**; iṣ: **ā́rdhiṣṭa** (B.). FT. **ardhiṣyáte** (B.); **ardhitā** (B.). PS. **ṛdhyáte**; IPV. **ṛdhyátām**; PP. **ṛddhá.** GDV. **árdhya.** CS. **ardháyati.** DS. **ī́rtsati**; PT. **ī́rtsant.**

ṛṣ *rush*, I.: PR. **árṣati, -te**; SB. **árṣāt**; INJ. **árṣat**; IPV. **árṣa, árṣatu**; **árṣata, árṣantu**; PT. **árṣant.** VI. P.: PR. **ṛṣáti**; PT. **ṛṣánt.** PP. **ṛṣṭá.**

ej *stir*, I. P.: PR. **éjati**; SB. **éjāti** and **éjāt**; IPV. **éjatu**; PT. **éjant.** IPF. **áijat.** CS. **ejáyati** (B.).

edh *thrive*, I. Ā.: PR. **édhate** (B.); IPV. **édhasva, édhatām** (B.). PER. PF. **edhā́m cakrire** (B.). AO. iṣ: OP. **edhiṣīyá.**

kan, kā *enjoy*, IV.: PR. PT. **kā́yamāna.** PF. **caké**; SB. **cākánas, cākánat**; **cākánāma**; INJ. **cākánanta**; OP. **cākanyāt**; IPV. **cākandhí, cākántu**; PT. **cakāná**; PPF. **cākán** (2. s.). AO. **ákāniṣam**; SB. **kā́niṣas.**

kam *love*: PF. PT. **cakamāná.** AO. red.: **ácīkamata** (B.). FT. **kamiṣyáte** (B.); **kamitā** (B.). CS. **kāmáyate**; SB. **kāmáyāse**; PT. **kāmáyamāna.**

kāś *appear*, I.: PR. **kā́śate** (B.). INT. **cā́kaśīmi, cā́kaśīti; cākaśyáte** (B.); SB. **cākaśān** (AV.); PT. **cā́kaśat.** IPF. **ácākaśam.** CS. **kāśáyati.**

kup *be angry*, IV.: PR. PT. **kúpyant.** PP. **kupitá.** CS. **kopáyati.**

1\. **kṛ** *make*, V.: PR. **kṛṇómi, kṛṇóṣi, kṛṇóti; kṛṇuthás, kṛṇutás; kṛṇmási, kṛṇuthá, kṛṇvánti;** Ā. **kṛṇvé, kṛṇuṣé, kṛṇuté; kṛṇmáhe, kṛṇváte;** INJ. **kṛṇváta** (3. pl.); SB. **kṛṇávā, kṛṇávas, kṛṇávat; kṛṇávāva; kṛṇávāma, kṛṇávātha** (VS.), **kṛṇávan;** Ā. **kṛṇávai, kṛṇávase, kṛṇávate; kṛṇávāvahai, kṛṇváite** (for **kṛṇávaite**); **kṛṇávāmahai, kṛṇávanta;** OP. **kṛṇvītá;** IPV. **kṛṇú, kṛṇuhí** and **kṛṇutā́t, kṛṇótu; kṛṇutám, kṛṇutā́m; kṛṇutá, kṛṇóta,** and **kṛṇótana, kṛṇvántu;** Ā. **kṛṇuṣvá, kṛṇutā́m; kṛṇvā́thām; kṛṇudhvám;** PT. **kṛṇvánt; kṛṇvāná.** IPF. **kṛṇavam, ákṛṇos, ákṛṇot; ákṛṇutam; ákṛṇuta, ákṛṇota** and **ákṛṇotana, ákṛṇvan;** Ā. **ákṛṇuta** (3. s.); **ákṛṇudhvam, ákṛṇvata.**
VIII.: **karómi, karóti; kurmás, kurvánti; kurvé, kuruté; kurváte;** SB. **karávas, karávāt;** IPV. **kurú, karótu;** Ā. **kurvátām.** PT. **kurvánt; kurvāṇá.** IPF. **ákaros, ákarot; ákurvan;** Ā. **kuruthā́s, ákuruta; ákurvata.**
II.: PR. **kárṣi; kṛthás; kṛthá;** Ā. **kṛṣé.**
PF. **cakára, cakártha, cakā́ra; cakráthur, cakrátur; cakṛmá, cakrá, cakrúr;** Ā. **cakré, cakṛṣé, cakré; cakrā́the, cakrā́te; cakriré;** OP. **cakriyā́s;** PT. **cakṛvā́ṃs; cakrāṇá.** PPF. **cakáram, ácakrat; ácakriran.** AO. root: **ákaram, ákar, ákar; kártam, ákartām; ákarma, ákarta, ákran;** Ā. **ákri, ákṛthās, ákṛta; ákrata;** INJ. **káram, kár;** SB. **kárāṇi, kárasi** and **káras, kárati** and **kárat; kárathas, káratas; kárāma, káranti** and **káran;** Ā. **kárase, kárate; kárāmahe;** OP. **kriyā́ma;** PRC. **kriyā́sma;** IPV. **kṛdhí; kṛtám** and **kártam; kṛtá** and **kártana;** Ā. **kṛṣvá; kṛdhvám;** PT. **kránt; krāṇá.** AO. a: **ákaras, ákarat;** IPV. **kara; karatam, karatām;** s: **ákārṣīt** (B.); Ā. **ákṛṣi** (B.). FT. **kariṣyáti; -te** (B.);

SB. kariṣyā́s. CO. ákariṣyat (B.). PS. kriyáte; PT. kriyámāṇa; AO. ákāri; PP. kṛtá. GDV. ká́rtva. GD. kṛtvā́, kṛtvī́, kṛtvā́ya. INF. kártave, kártavái; kártos; kártum. CS. kāráyati, kāráyate (B.). DS. cíkīrṣati. INT. PT. kárikrat and cárikrat.

2. kṛ *commemorate*: AO. s: ákārṣam; iṣ: ákāriṣam, ákārīt. INT. cárkarmi; SB. cárkiran; AO. cárkṛṣe (3. s.); GDV. carkṛ́tya.

kṛt *cut*, VI. P.: PR. kṛntáti; INJ. kṛntát; IPV. kṛntá; PT. kṛntánt. IPF. ákṛntat. PF. cakártitha, cakárta. AO. a: ákṛtas; PT. kṛtánt; red.: ácīkṛtas (B.). FT. kartsyā́mi. PS. kṛtyáte; PP. kṛttá. GD. -kṛ́tya.

kṛp *lament*, I. Ā.: PR. kṛ́pate; PT. kṛ́pamāṇa. IPF. ákṛpanta. PF. cakṛpe (K.). PPF. cakṛpánta. AO. root: ákṛpran; iṣ: ákrapiṣṭa. CS. PT. kṛpáyant; IPF. ákṛpayat.

kṛś *be lean*, IV. P.: PR. kṛ́śyati (B.). PF. cakárśa. PP. kṛśitá (B.). CS. karśáyati.

kṛṣ *plough*, I.: PR. kárṣati; -te (B.); INJ. kárṣat; IPV. kárṣa. VI.: PR. kṛṣáti; IPV. kṛṣátu; kṛṣántu; Ā. kṛṣásva; PT. kṛṣánt. PF. cakárṣa (B.). AO. red.: ácīkṛṣam; sa: ákṛkṣat (B.). FT. krakṣyé (B.). PS. kṛṣyáte; PP. kṛṣṭá. GD. kṛṣṭvā́ (B.). INT. 3. pl. cárkṛṣati; SB. cárkṛṣat; PT. cárkṛṣat; IPF. ácarkṛṣur.

kṝ *scatter*, VI. P.: PR. kiráti, -te; SB. kirā́si; IPV. kirá, kirátu. IPF. ákirat. AO. iṣ: SB. kāriṣat. PS. kīryáte (B.); PP. kīrṇá (B.).

kḷp *be adapted*, I.: PR. kálpate; IPV. kálpasva; PT. kálpamāna. IPF. ákalpata, ákalpanta. PF. cākḷpúr; cākḷpré. AO. red.: ácīkḷpat; SB. cīkḷpāti. FT. kalpsyáte (B.). PP. kḷptá. CS. kalpáyati; SB. kalpáyāti; kalpáyāvahai; IPV. kalpáya, kalpáyatu; kalpáyasva; PT. kalpáyant; IPF. ákalpayat. DS. cíkalpayiṣati (B.); GD. kalpayitvā́.

krand *cry out*, I. P.: PR. krándati; INJ. krándat; IPV. kránda, krándatu; PT. krándant. IPF. ákrandas, krándat. PF. cakradé. PPF. cakradas, cakradat.

AO. a: INJ. kradas; red.: ácikradas, ácikradat; ácikradan; INJ. cikradas; s: ákrān (2. 3. s.). CS. krandáyati. INT. kánikranti (3. s. = kánikrant-ti); PT. kánikradat.

kram *stride*, I. P.: PR. krā́mati; OP. krā́mema; IPV. krā́ma; PT. krā́mant; IPF. ákrāmat; Ā.: krámate; SB. krámāma; IPV. krámasva. PF. cakrā́ma, cakramúr; cakramé; cakramā́the; PT. cakramāṇá. PPF. cákramanta; AO. root: ákran; ákramur; INJ. kramur; a: ákramat, ákraman; s: Ā. ákraṃsta; ákraṃsata; SB. kráṃsate; iṣ: ákramiṣam and ákramīm, ákramīs, ákramīt; kramiṣṭa (3. s.); INJ. kramīs; IPV. kramiṣṭám. FT. kraṃsyáte; kramiṣyáti, -te (B.); PP. krāntá. GD. krāntvā́ (B.), -krámya. INF. -kráme; krámitum (B.); krámitos (B.). CS. krāmáyati (B.). INT. IPV. caṅkra-m-a-ta (2. pl.); caṅkramyáte (B.).

krī *buy*, IX.: PR. krīṇā́ti; krīṇīté; SB. krīṇā́vahai. IPF. ákrīṇan. FT. kreṣyáti, -te (B.). PS. krīyáte (B.); PP. krītá. GD. krītvā́, -krī́ya (B.).

krudh *be angry*, IV. P.: PR. krúdhyati. PF. cukródha (B.). AO. red.: ácukrudhat; SB. cukrudhāma; INJ. cukrudham; a: INJ. krudhas. PP. kruddhá. CS. krodháyati.

kruś *cry out*, I.: PR. króśati; IPV. króśatu; PT. króśant; króśamāna. AO. sa: ákrukṣat. PP. kruṣṭá (B.).

kṣad *divide*, I. Ā.: PR. kṣádāmahe. PF. cakṣadé; PT. cakṣadāná. INF. kṣádase.

kṣam *endure*, I. Ā.: OP. kṣámeta; IPV. kṣámadhvam. PT. kṣámamāṇa. PF. cakṣamé (B.); OP. cakṣamīthās.

kṣar *flow*, I. P.: PR. kṣárati; INJ. kṣárat; IPV. kṣára; kṣárantu; PT. kṣárant. IPF. ákṣarat; ákṣaran. AO. s: ákṣār. PP. kṣaritá (B.). INF. kṣáradhyai. CS. kṣāráyati (B.).

1. **kṣi** *possess*, II. P.: PR. kṣéṣi, kṣéti; kṣitás; kṣiyánti; SB. kṣáyas, kṣáyat; kṣáyāma; PT. kṣiyánt. I. P.: PR. kṣáyati; OP. kṣáyema (AV.); PT. kṣáyant. IV. P.:

PR. **kṣíyati**; OP. **kṣíyema**; IPV. **kṣíya**. AO. s: SB. **kṣéṣat**. FT. PT. **kṣeṣyánt**. CS. IPV. **kṣayáya**; INJ. **kṣepáyat**.

2. **kṣi** *destroy*, IX.: PR. **kṣiṇā́ti**; **kṣiṇánti**; INJ. **kṣiṇā́m**. IPF. **ákṣiṇās**. V.: PR. **kṣiṇómi**. IV. Ā.: PR. **kṣíyate**; **kṣíyante**. AO. s: INJ. **kṣeṣṭa** (AV.). PS. **kṣīyáte**; PT. **kṣīyámāṇa**; PP. **kṣitá**; **kṣīṇá** (AV.). GD. **-kṣíya** (B.). INF. **-kṣetos** (B.). DS. **cíkṣīṣati** (B.).

kṣip *throw*, VI. P.: PR. **kṣipáti**; INJ. **kṣipát**; IPV. **kṣipá**; PT. **kṣipánt**. AO. red.: INJ. **cikṣipas**; **cikṣipan**. PP. **kṣiptá**. INF. **-kṣeptos** (B.).

kṣṇu *whet*, II.: PR. **kṣṇáumi**; PT. **kṣṇuvāná**. PP. **kṣṇutá** (B.). GD. **-kṣṇutya** (B.).

khan, khā *dig*, I.: PR. **khánati**; SB. **khánāma**; OP. **khánema**; PT. **khánant**. IPF. **ákhanat**; **ákhananta**. PF. **cakhā́na**; **cakhnúr**. FP. PT. **khaniṣyánt**. PS. **khāyáte** (B.); PP. **khātá**. GD. **khātvā́** (B.); **khātvī́** (TS.), **-khāya** (B.). INF. **khánitum**.

khād *chew*, I. P.: PR. **khā́dati**; IPV. **khā́da**; PT. **khā́dant**. PF. **cakhā́da**. PP. **khāditá** (B.). GD. **khāditvā** (B.).

khid *tear*, VI.: PR. **khidáti**; INJ. **khidát**; OP. **khidét**. IPV. **khidá**; **khidánt**. IPF. **ákhidat**. PF. PT. **khidvā́ṃs**. GD. **-khidya** (B.).

khyā *see*: PF. **cakhyáthur**. AO. a: **ákhyat**; INJ. **khyát**; IPV. **khyátam**; **khyáta**. FT. **khyāsyáti** (B.). PS. **khyāyáte** (B.); PP. **khyātá**. GDV. **-khyeya**. GD. **-khyā́ya**. INF. **khyā́tum** (B.); **-khyái**. CS. **khyāpáyati**, **-te** (B.).

gam *go*, I.: PR. **gáchati**, **-te**; SB. **gáchāsi** and **gáchās**, **gáchāti** and **gáchāt**; **gáchātha**, **gáchān**; Ā. **gáchai**; OP. **gáchet**; **gáchema**; IPV. **gácha** and **gáchatāt**, **gáchatu** and **gáchatāt**; **gáchatam**, **gáchatām**; **gáchata**, **gáchantu**; Ā. **gáchasva** (AV.), **gáchatām**; **gáchadhvam**; PT. **gáchant**; **gáchamāna**. IPF. **ágachat**; **ágachanta**. PF. **jagáma**, **jagántha**, **jagā́ma**; **jagmáthur**, **jagmátur**; **jaganmá**, **jagmúr**; **jagmé**; OP. **jagamyā́m**, **jagamyā́t**; **jagamyā́tam**, **jagamyúr**; PT. **jaganvā́ṃs**, **jagmivā́ṃs**; **jagmāná**. Per. PF. **gamayā́ṃ cakāra** (AV.). PPF. **ájagan**

(2. s.); **ájaganta**; Ā. **ájagmiran**. AO. root: **ágamam, ágan** (2. 3. s.); **áganma, ágman; ágathās, ágata; gánvahi; áganmahi, ágmata**; SB. **gámāni, gámas, gámat; gámathas, gámatas; gámāma, gámanti**; INJ. **gán**; OP. **gamyā́s; gmīya** (B.); PRC. 3. s. **gamyā́s**; IPV. **gadhí** and **gahí, gántu; gatám** and **gantám, gantām; gatá, gánta** and **gántana, gámantu**; PT. **gmánt**; a: **ágamat, ágaman**; SB. **gamātas; gamātha**; INJ. **gáman; gaméyam, gamés, gamét; gaméma; gamémahi**; red.: **ájīgamam, ájīgamat**; s: **ágasmahi**; iṣ: **gamiṣṭam; gmiṣīya** (VS.). FT. **gamiṣyáti** (AV.); **gantā́** (B.). PS. **gamyáte**; AO. **ágāmi**; PP. **gatá**. GD. **gatvā́, gatvā́ya, gatvī́, -gátya**. INF. **gántave, gántavái, gámadhyai, gamádhye** (TS.); **gántos, -gámas**. CS. **gamáyati** and **gāmáyati**. DS. **jígāṃsati; jígamiṣati, -te** (B.). INT. **gánīganti**; PT. **gánigmat**.

1. **gā** *go*, III. P.: PR. **jígāsi, jígāti**; INJ. **jígāt**; IPV. **jígātam; jígāta**; PT. **jígat**. IPF. **ájigāt**. PF. OP. **jagāyā́t**. AO. root: **ágām, ágās, ágāt; ágātam, ágātām; ágāma, ágāta, águr**; SB. **gā́ni, gā́s, gā́t; gā́ma**; INJ. **gā́m; gā́ma, gúr**; IPV. **gātá** and **gātána**; s: INJ. **geṣam** (VS.); **geṣma** (AV.). DS. **jī́gāsa** (SV.). INF. **gā́tave**.

2. **gā** *sing*, IV.: PR. **gā́yasi, gā́yati; gā́yanti**; Ā. **gā́ye**; INJ. **gā́yat**; IPV. **gā́ya; gā́yata, gā́yantu**; PT. **gā́yant**. IPF. **ágāyat**. PF. **jagā́u** (B.). AO. s: INJ. **gāsi** (1. s.); siṣ: **ágāsiṣur**; SB. **gā́siṣat**. FT. **gāsyáti** (B.). PS. PT. **gīyámāna**; PP. **gītá**. GD. **gītvā́** (B.); **-gāya** (B.) and **-gīya** (B.). INF. **gā́tum** (B.). CS. **gāpáyati, -te** (B.). DS. **jígāsati** (B.).

gāh *plunge*, I. Ā.: PR. **gā́hase, gā́hate**; OP. **gā́hemahi**; IPV. **gā́hethām**; PT. **gā́hamāna**. IPF. **ágāhathās**. INT. **jáṅgahe**.

gur *greet*, VI.: PR. IPV. **gurásva**. PF. SB. **jugurat**; OP. **juguryā́s, juguryā́t**. AO. root: **gūrta** (3. s. Ā.). PP. **gūrtá**. GD. **-gū́rya**.

guh *hide*, I.: PR. **gū́hati, -te**; INJ. **gū́has; gū́hathās**;

IPV. gū́hata; PT. gū́hant; gū́hamāna. IPF. ágūhat. AO. a: guhás; INJ. guhás; PT. guhánt; guhámāna; sa: ághukṣat. PS. guhyáte; PT. guhyámāna; PP. gūḍhá; GDV. gúhya, -gohya. GD. gūḍhvī́. DS. júgukṣati.

1. gṛ *sing*, IX.: PR. gṛṇā́mi, gṛṇā́ti; gṛṇītás; gṛṇīmási, gṛṇánti; Ā. gṛṇé, gṛṇīṣé, gṛṇīté (and gṛṇé), gṛṇīmáhe; INJ. gṛṇītá (3. s. Ā.); IPV. gṛṇīhí, gṛṇā́tu; gṛṇītám, gṛṇītā́m; gṛṇītá, gṛṇántu; PT. gṛṇánt; gṛṇāná. GD. -gī́rya (B.). INF. gṛṇīṣáṇi.

2. gṛ *wake*: AO. red.: 2. 3. ájīgar; IPV. jigṛtám; jigṛtá. INT. jāgarti; jā́grati; SB. jā́garāsi (AV.), jā́garat; OP. jāgriyāma (VS.), jāgṛyā́ma (TS.); IPV. jāgṛhí and jāgṛtā́t; jāgṛtám, jāgṛtā́m; PT. jā́grat. IPF. ájāgar. PF. 1. s. jāgára. 3. jāgā́ra. PT. jāgṛvā́ṃs; FT. jāgariṣyā́ti, -te (B.); PP. jāgaritá (B.). CS. jāgaráyati (B.).

gṛdh *be greedy*, IV. P.: PR. PT. gṛ́dhyant. PF. jāgṛdhúr. AO. a: ágṛdhat; INJ. gṛdhás; gṛdhát.

gṝ *swallow*, VI. P.: PR. giráti. PF. jagā́ra. AO. root: SB. gárat, gáran; red.: ájīgar (2. s.); iṣ: INJ. gā́rīt. FT. gariṣyáti (B.). PP. gīrṇá. GD. -gī́rya (AV.). INT. SB. jálgulas; PT. jarguráṇá.

grabh *seize*, IX.: PR. gṛbhṇā́mi, gṛbhṇā́ti; gṛbhṇánti; gṛbhṇé; gṛbhṇáte; SB. gṛbhṇā́s; INJ. gṛbhṇītá (3. s.); IPV. gṛbhṇīhí. IPF. ágṛbhṇās, ágṛbhṇāt; ágṛbhṇan; ágṛbhṇata (3. pl. Ā.). PF. jagrábha (1. s.); jagṛbháthur; jagṛbhmá, jagṛbhúr; Ā. jagṛbhré and jagṛbhriré; OP. jagṛbhyā́t; PT. jagṛbhvā́ṃs; PPF. ájagrabham, ájagrabhīt. AO. root: ágrabham; ágṛbhran; PT. gṛbhāṇá; a: ágṛbham; red.: ájigrabhat; iṣ: ágrabhīm (TS.), ágrabhīt; ágrabhīṣma, ágrabhīṣur; ágṛbhīṣata (3. pl. Ā.). INJ. grabhīṣṭa (2. pl.). PP. gṛbhītá. GD. gṛbhītvā́, -gṛ́bhya. INF. -grabhé, -gṛbhé. CS. PT. gṛbháyant.

gras *devour*, I. Ā.: PR. grásate; OP. grásetām. PF. OP. jagrasītá; PT. jagrasāná. PP. grasitá.

grah *seize*, IX.: gṛhṇā́mi, gṛhṇā́ti; gṛhṇánti; gṛhṇé; gṛhṇīmáhe, gṛhṇáte; OP. gṛhṇīyā́t; IPV. gṛhṇāhi (AV.),

gṛhṇītā́t and **gṛhāṇá**; **gṛhṇā́tu**; **gṛhṇītám**; **gṛhṇántu**; PT. **gṛhṇánt**; **gṛhṇāná**. IPF. **ágṛhṇāt, ágṛhṇan**. PF. **jagráha, jagrā́ha**; **jagṛhmá, jagṛhúr**; **jagṛhé**. AO. **a**: INJ. **gṛhāmahi**; **iṣ**: **ágrahīt**; **ágrahīṣṭa**. FT. **grahīṣyáti** (B.); CO. **ágrahīṣyat** (B.), **ágrahaiṣyat** (B.). PS. **gṛhyáte**; PP. **gṛhītá**. GD. **gṛhītvā́, -gṛ́hya**. INF. **gráhītavái** (B.). **gráhītos** (B.). CS. **grāháyati** (B.). DS. **jíghṛkṣati, -te** (B.).

ghas *eat*: PF. **jaghása, jaghā́sa**; OP. **jakṣīyā́t**; PT. **jakṣivā́ṃs** (AV.). AO. root: **ághas** (2. 3. s.), **ághat** (3. s., B.); **ághastām** (3. du., B.); **ághasta** (2. pl., B.), **ákṣan**; SB. **ghásas, ghásat**; IPV. **ghástām** (3. du.); **s**: **ághās** (2. s.); red.: **ájīghasat**. PP. **-gdha** (TS.). DS. **jíghatsati**.

ghuṣ *sound*, I.: PR. **ghóṣati, ghóṣate**; SB. **ghóṣāt**; **ghóṣān**; PT. **ghóṣant**. PF. **jughóṣa** (B.). PS. AO. **ghóṣi**. GD. **-ghúṣya**. CS. **ghoṣáyati**.

cakṣ *see*, II.: PR. **cákṣe** (= **cákṣ-ṣe**), **cáṣṭe**; **cákṣāthe**; **cákṣate**; P. **cákṣi** (= **cákṣ-ṣi**); IPF. **cakṣur**. I. Ā.: PR. **cákṣate** (3. s.); IPF. **cákṣata** (3. s.). PF. **cacákṣa**; **cacakṣé** (B.). PPF. **ácacakṣam**. GDV. **cákṣya**. GD. **-cákṣya**. INF. **-cákṣe, cákṣase**; **-cákṣi**. CS. **cakṣáyati**.

car *move*, I. P.: PR. **cárati**; SB. **cárāṇi**; **cárāva, cárātas**; **cárān**; **cárātai** (AV.); INJ. **cárat**; OP. **cáret**; IPV. **cára, cáratu**; **cárata, cárantu**; PT. **cárant**. IPF. **ácarat**. PF. **cacā́ra**; **cerimá, cerúr**. AO. red.: **ácīcarat**; **s**: **ácārṣam** (B.); **iṣ**: **ácāriṣam**; INJ. **cā́rīt**. FT. **cariṣyā́mi**. PS. **caryáte** (B.); PP. **caritá**; GDV. **-caréṇya**. GD. **caritvā́** (B.); **-cárya** (B.). INF. **caráse, cáritave, carádhyai**; **cáritavái** (B.); **cáritum** (B.); **cáritos** (B.). CS. **cāráyati, -te** (B.). DS. **cícarṣati** (B.), **cícariṣati** (B.). INT. **cárcarīti**; PT. **carcūryámāṇa**.

cāy *note*, I.: PR. **cā́yati** (B.); PT. **cā́yamāna**. PER. PF. **-cāyāṃ cakrur** (B.). AO. **iṣ**: **ácāyiṣam**. PS. **cāyyáte**. GD. **cāyitvā́**; **-cā́yya**.

1. **ci** *gather*, V.: PR. **cinóti**; **cinvánti**; **cinuté**; SB. **cinávat**; OP. **cinuyā́ma**; IPV. **cinuhí, cinótu**; **cinvántu**;

cinuṣvá; PT. **cinvánt**; **cinvāná**. I.: PR. **cáyase, cáyate; cáyadhve**; INJ. **cáyat**; OP. **cáyema**. PF. **cikā́ya; cikyé; cikyiré**. AO. root: **ácet**; IPV. **citána, ciyántu**; s: **ácaiṣam** (B.); iṣ: **cáyiṣṭam**. FT. **ceṣyáti, -te** (B.). PS. **cīyáte** (B.); PP. **citá**. GD. **citvā́** (B.). INF. **cétum** (B.); **cétavái** (B.). DS. **cíkīṣate** (B.).

2. ci *note*, III.: PR. **cikéṣi** (AV.); IPV. **cikīhí** (AV.), **ciketu** (TS.); Ā. (3. s.) **cikitām** (AV.); PT. **cíkyat**. IPF. **áciket; ácikayur** (B.). PF. **cikā́ya; cikyátur; cikyúr**; Ā. 2. du. **cikéthe** (for **cikyā́the**). AO. root: **ácet**; Ā. **ácidhvam**. PP. **citá**. DS. **cíkīṣate**.

cit *perceive*, I.: PR. **cétati; cétathas; cétatha**; Ā. **cétate; cétante**; INJ. **cétat**; IPV. **cétatām**; PT. **cétant**; IPF. **ácetat**. II. Ā.: PR. **cité** (3. s.). PF. **cikéta; cikitúr**; Ā. **cikité; cikitré** and **cikitriré**; SB. **cikitas, cíketati** and **cíketat; cíketathas**; IPV. **cikiddhí**; PT. **cikitvā́ṃs; cikitāná**; PPF. **ciketam; áciketat**. AO. root: **ácet**; PT. **cítāna**; PS.: **áceti**; s: **ácait**. INF. **citáye**. CS. **cetáyati, -te** and **citáyati, -te**; SB. **cetáyāni, cetáyātai** (TS.); OP. **citáyema**. DS. INJ. **cíkitsat**. INT. **cékite** (3. s.); SB. **cékitat**; PT. **cékitat**.

cud *impel*, I.: PR. **códāmi; códate**; INJ. **códat**; IPV. **códa, códata; códasva, códethām**. CS. SB. **codáyāsi, codáyāt; codáyāse, codáyāte**; PP. **coditá**.

cyu *move*, I.: PR. **cyávate**; INJ. **cyávam; cyávanta**; IPV. **cyávasva; cyávethām; cyávadhvam**. PF. **cicyuṣé, cucyuvé** (3. s.); INJ. **cucyavat**; OP. **cucyuvīmáhi, cucyavīráta**. PPF. **ácucyavat, ácucyavīt; ácucyavītana, ácucyavur**. AO. s: **cyoṣṭhās**. FT. **cyoṣyate** (B.). PP. **cyutá**. CS. **cyāváyati, -te**.

chad or chand *seem*, II.: PR. **chántsi**. PF. **cachánda**; OP. **cachadyā́t**. AO. s: **áchān; áchānta** (=**áchānt-s-ta**), **áchāntsur**; SB. **chántsat**. CS. **chadáyati; chandáyase**; INJ. **chadáyat**; SB. **chadáyātha; chandáyāte**; IPF. **áchadayan**.

chid *cut off*, VII.: PR. **chinádmi, chinátti**; IPV. **chindhí**

(= chinddhí), chináttu; chintám (= chinttám). PF. cichéda; cichidé (B.). AO. root: chedma; a: áchidat; áchidan; s: áchaitsīt (B.); INJ. chitthā́s. FT. chetsyáti, -te (B.). PS. chidyáte; PT. chidyámāna; AO. áchedi; PP. chinná. GD. -chídya; chittvā́ (B.). INF. chéttavái (B.); chéttum (B.). DS. cíchitsati, -te (B.).

jan *generate*, I.: PR. jánati; SB. jánāt; INJ. jánat; IPV. jánatu; PT. jánant; jánamāna. IPF. ájanat; jánata (3. s.); ájananta. PF. jajā́na; jajñátur; jajñúr and jajanúr; Ā. jajñiṣé, jajñé; jajñiré; PT. jajñāná. AO. root: ájani (1. s.); red.: ájījanat, ájījanan; INJ. jījanam; jījananta; iṣ: jániṣṭām (3. du.); Ā. ájaniṣṭhās, ájaniṣṭa; OP. janiṣīyá, janiṣīṣṭá. FT. janiṣyáti, -te; janitā́ (B.); CO. ájaniṣyata (B.). PS.: AO. ájani; jáni, jā́ni. GDV. jántva and jánitva. GD. janitvī́. INF. jánitos. CS. janáyati, -te; SB. janáyās; OP. janáyes; IPV. janáya, janáyatu; janáyatam; janáyata. DS. jíjaniṣate (B.).

jambh *chew*: AO. red.: ájījabham; iṣ: SB. jámbhiṣat. PP. jabdhá. CS.: IPV. jambháya; jambháyatam; PT. jambháyant. INT. jañjabhyáte (B.); PT. jáñjabhāna.

jas *be exhausted*, I.: PR. PT. jásamāna; IV.: IPV. jásyata. PF. jajā́sa; IPV. jajastám. AO. red.: ájījasata (3. s., B.). CS. jāsáyati (B.).

jā *be born*, IV. Ā.: PR. jā́yate; INJ. jā́yata; OP. jā́yemahi; IPV. jā́yasva, jā́yatām; jā́yadhvam; PT. jā́yamāna. IPF. ájāyathās, ájāyata; ájāyanta. PP. jātá.

1. ji *conquer*, I.: jáyati, -te; SB. jáyāsi, jáyās, jáyāti; jáyāva, jáyātha; Ā. jáyātai (AV.); INJ. jáyat; OP. jáyema; IPV. jáyatu; Ā. jáyantām; PT. jáyant. IPF. ájayat. II. P.: PR. jéṣi. PF. jigétha, jigā́ya; jigyáthur; jigyúr; Ā. jigyé; PF. jigīvā́ṃs; jigivā́ṃs (B.); AO. root: INJ. jés; IPV. jitám; s: ájaiṣam, 3. ájais (= ájais-t); ájaiṣma; SB. jéṣas, jéṣat; jéṣāma; INJ. jéṣam (VS.), jés; jéṣma, jáiṣur (AV.). FT. jeṣyáti; PT. jeṣyánt. PP. jitá; GDV. jétva. GD. jitvā (B.); -jítya. INF. jiṣé; jétave (B.); jétum (B.). CS. jāpáyati (B.); ájījapata

(VS.) and ájījipata (TS.). DS. jígīṣati, -te; PT. jígīṣamāṇa.

2. ji *quicken*, V.: PR. jinóṣi; jinvé. IPF. ájinot (B.).

jinv *quicken* (=V. ji-nu + a), I.: PR. jínvasi, jínvati; jínvathas; jínvatha, jínvanti; Ā. jínvate; IPV. jínva, jínvatu; jínvatam; jínvata; PT. jínvant. IPF. ájinvat; ájinvatam. PF. jijinváthur. FT. jinviṣyáti (B.). PP. jinvitá.

jīv *live*, I. P.: PR. jī́vati; SB. jī́vāni, jī́vās, jī́vāti and jī́vāt; jī́vātha, jī́vān; OP. jī́vema; IPV. jī́va, jī́vatu; jī́vatām; jī́vata, jī́vantu; PT. jī́vant. PF. jijī́va (B.). AO. root: PRC. jīvyā́sam; iṣ: INJ. jī́vīt. FT. jīviṣyáti (B.). PS. jivyáte (B.); PP. jīvitá. GDV. jīvanī́ya. GD. jīvitvā́ (B.). INF. jīváse; jī́vitavái, jīvā́tave (TS. VS.); jī́vitum (B.). CS. jīváyati. DS. jíjīviṣati (B.); jújyūṣati (B.); PP. jijyūṣitá (B.).

juṣ *enjoy*, VI.: PR. juṣáte; OP. juṣéta; juṣérata; PT. juṣámāṇa; IPF. ájuṣat; ájuṣata. PF. jujóṣa; jujuṣé; SB. jújoṣati, jújoṣat; jújoṣatha, jújoṣan; Ā. jújoṣate; IPV. jujuṣṭana; PT. jujuṣvā́ṃs; jujuṣāṇá. PPF. ájujoṣam. AO. root: ájuṣran; SB. jóṣati, jóṣat; Ā. jóṣase; PT. juṣāṇá; iṣ: SB. jóṣiṣat. PP. juṣṭá *gladdened* and júṣṭa *welcome*. GD. juṣṭvī́. CS. joṣáyate; SB. joṣáyāse.

jū *speed*, IX. P.: PR. junā́ti; junánti; SB. junā́s. I. Ā.: PR. jávate. PF. jūjuvúr; SB. jūjuvat (= jūjavat); PT. jūjuvā́ṃs; jūjuvāná. PP. jūtá. INF. javáse.

jūrv *consume*, I. P.: PR. jū́rvati; SB. jū́rvās; IPV. jū́rva; PT. jū́rvant. AO. iṣ: jū́rvīt.

jṛ *sing*, I. Ā.: PR. járate; SB. járāte; OP. járeta; IPV. járasva, járatām; PT. járamāṇa. INF. jarádhyai.

jṝ, jur *waste away*, I. P.: PR. járati; IPV. járatam; PT. járant. VI. P.: PT. juránt. IV. P.: PR. jī́ryati, jū́ryati; PT. jū́ryant; IPF. ájūryan. PF. jajā́ra; PT. jujurvā́ṃs. AO. iṣ: jāriṣur. PP. jīrṇá, jūrṇá. CS. jaráyati, -te; PT. jaráyant and jāráyant.

jñā *know*, IX.: PR. jānā́ti; jānīmás, jānīthá, jānánti; jānīté; jānáte; SB. jānā́ma; jānā́mahai; OP. jānīthā́s;

IPV. jānīhí, jānītā́t, jānā́tu; jānītá, jānántu; jānīdhvám, jānátām; PT. jānánt; jānāná. IPF. ájānām, ájānāt; ájānan; Ā. 3. pl. ájānata. PF. jajñáu; jajñé; PT. jajñivā́ṃs and jānivā́ṃs. AO. root: OP. jñeyā́s (Gk. γνοίης); s: ájñāsam (B.); ájñāsthās; INJ. jñeṣam; siṣ: ájñāsiṣam. FT. jñāsyáti, -te (B.); jñātā́ (B.). PS. jñāyáte; AO. ájñāyi; PP. jñātá; GDV. jñeya (B.). GD. jñātvā́ (B.), -jñā́ya (B.). INF. jñā́tum (B.), jñā́tos (B.). CS. jñapáyati; AO. ájijñipat (TS.); PS. jñapyáte (B.); PP. jñaptá (B.); jñāpáyati (B.). DS. jíjñāsate.

jyā *overpower*, IX.: PR. jinā́ti; OP. jinīyā́t; PT. jinánt. IV. Ā.: PR. jī́yate. PF. jijyáu (B.). AO. siṣ: ájyāsiṣam (B.). FT. jyāsyáti, -te (B.). PS. jīyáte; PP. jītá. DS. jíjyāsati.

jval *flame*, I. P.: PR. jválati (B.). PF. jajvā́la (B.). AO. ájvālīt (B.). FT. jvaliṣyáti (B.). PP. jvalitá (B.). CS. jvaláyati (B.).

taṃs *shake*: PF. tatasré. PPF. átataṃsatam. AO. a: átasat. CS. taṃsáyati, -te; INF. taṃsayádhyai. INT. SB. tantasáite; GDV. -tantasā́yya.

takṣ *fashion*, I. P.: PR. tákṣati; SB. tákṣāma; INJ. tákṣat; IPV. tákṣatam; tákṣata, tákṣantu; PT. tákṣant. IPF. átakṣat. II. P.: PR. tāṣṭi (B.), tákṣati (3. pl.); IPV. tāḷhí. IPF. átakṣma, átaṣṭa. V. P.: PR. takṣṇuvanti (B.). PF. tatákṣa (takṣáthur, takṣúr); tatakṣé. AO. iṣ: átakṣiṣur. PP. taṣṭá.

tan *stretch*, VIII.: PR. tanóti; tanmási, tanvánti; tanuté; SB. tanávāvahai; INJ. tanuthā́s; IPV. tanú, tanuhí, tanótu; Ā. tanuṣvá; tanudhvám; PT. tanvánt; tanvāná. IPF. átanuta; átanvata. PF. tatántha, tatā́na and tātā́na; Ā. 1. tatané, 3. tatné and taté (√tā); tatniré and teniré; SB. tatánat; tatánāma, tatánan; INJ. tatánanta; OP. tatanyúr; PT. tatanvā́ṃs. AO. root: átan; Ā. 2. átathās, 3. átata; átnata (3. pl.); a: átanat; INJ. tanat; s: átān and átāṃsīt; átasi (B.); átaṃsmahi (B.); iṣ: átānīt. FT. taṃsyáte (B.). PS. tāyáte;

AO. átāyi (B.). PP. tatá. GD. tatvā́ (B.), tatvā́ya (VS.), -tátya (B.). INF. tántum (B.).

tap *heat*, I.: PR. tápati, -te; SB. tápāti; INJ. tápat; IPV. tápatu; PT. tápant. IPF. átapat. IV. P.: PR. tápyati (B.). PF. 1. tatápa. 3. tatā́pa; tepé; SB. tatápate; PT. tepāná. AO. root: PT. tapāná; red.: átītipe (3. s.); SB. tītipāsi; s: átāpsīt; átapthās; INJ. tāpsīt; tāptam. FT. tapsyáti (B.). PS. tapyáte; AO. átāpi; PP. taptá. GD. taptvā́ (B.), -tápya. INF. táptos (B.). CS. tāpáyati, -te (AV.); PS. tāpyáte (B.).

tam *faint*, IV. P.: PR. tā́myati (B.). PF. tatā́ma (B.). AO. a: INJ. tamát. PP. tāntá (B.). INF. támitos (B.). tamáyati (B.).

tij *be sharp*, I. Ā.: PR. téjate; PT. téjamāna. PF. IPV. titigdhí (B.). PP. tiktá. DS. títikṣate. INT. tétikte.

tu *be strong*, II. P.: PR. távīti. PF. tūtā́va. PPF. tūtos, tūtot. INT. PT. távītvat (= távītuat).

tuj *urge*, VII.: PR. tuñjánti; tuñjáte (3. pl.); PT. tuñjāná. VI.: PR. tujéte; PT. tujánt. PF. OP. tutujyā́t; PT. tūtujāná and tū́tujāna. PS. tujyáte. INF. tujáse, tujáye, -túje. CS. PT. tujáyant.

tud *thrust*, VI.: PR. tudáti; IPV. tudá; tudántu; PT. tudánt. IPF. tudát. PF. tutóda. PP. tunná.

tur (= tṝ) *pass*, VI.: PR. turáti, -te; IV. P.: IPV. tū́rya; II. P.: OP. turyā́ma. PF. OP. tuturyā́t; tuturyā́ma. PP. tūrtá (B.). GD. -tū́rya. INF. turváṇe. CS. turáyate. DS. tūtūrṣati.

tṛd *split*, VII.: PR. tṛṇádmi, tṛṇátti; tṛntte (B.); IPF. átṛṇat; átṛndan. PF. tatárditha, tatárda; PT. tatṛdāná. AO. root: SB. tárdas. PP. tṛṇṇá (VS.). GD. -tṛ́dya. INF. -tṛ́das.

tṛp *be pleased*, V. P.: PR. tṛpṇóti; SB. tṛpṇávas; IPV. tṛpṇuhí; tṛpṇutám; tṛpṇutá; VI. P.: PR. tṛmpáti; IPV. tṛmpá; IV.: PR. tṛ́pyati. PF. tātṛpúr; PT. tātṛpāṇá. AO. root: PRC. tṛpyā́sma; a: átṛpat; PT. tṛpánt; red.: átītṛpas; átītṛpāma. CO. átarpsyat (B.). PP. tṛptá. CS. tarpáyati, -te; DS. títarpayiṣati. DS. títṛpsati; SB. títṛpsāt.

tṛṣ *be thirsty*, IV.: PR. **tṛ́ṣyati, -te**; PT. **tṛ́ṣyant.** PF. **tātṛṣúr**; PT. **tātṛṣāṇá** and **tatṛṣāṇá.** AO. root: PT. **tṛṣāṇá**; a: **tṛṣát**; red.: **átītṛṣāma**; INJ. **tītṛṣas.** PP. **tṛṣitá.** CS. **tarṣáyati** (B.).

tṛh *crush*, VII. P.: PR. **tṛṇéḍhi**; **tṛṃhánti**; IPV. **tṛṇéḍhu**; SB. **tṛṇáhān** (AV.); PT. **tṛṃhánt.** PF. **tatárha.** AO. a: **átṛham.** PS. **tṛhyáte**; PP. **tṛḷhá, tṛḍhá.** GD. **tṛḍhvā́.**

tṝ *cross*, I.: PR. **tárati, -te**; SB. **tárāthas**; INJ. **tárat**; OP. **táret**; IPV. **tára**; PT. **tárant.** IPF. **átarat.** VI.: PR. **tiráti, -te**; SB. **tirā́ti**; INJ. **tiránta**; OP. **tiréta, -tana** (2. pl.); IPV. **tirá**; **tiráta, tirántu**; **tirádhvam**; PT. **tiránt.** IPF. **átirat.** III.: PT. **títrat.** VIII. Ā.: **tarute.** PF. **tatā́ra**; **titirúr**; PT. **tatarus-** (weak stem) and **titirvā́ṃs.** AO. red.: **átītaras**; iṣ: **átārīt**; **átāriṣma** and **átārima, átāriṣur**; SB. **tā́riṣas, tā́riṣat**; INJ. **tā́rīs, tā́rīt**; OP. **tāriṣīmahi.** PS. AO. **átāri**; PP. **tīrṇá.** GD. **tīrtvā́.** INF. **-tíram, -tíre**; **tarádhyai**; **tarīṣáṇi.** CS. **tāráyati.** DS. **títīrṣati** (B.). INT. **tártarīti**; **tartūryánte**; PT. **táritrat.**

tyaj *forsake*: PF. **tityā́ja**; IPV. **tityagdhí.** PP. **tyaktá** (B). GD. **-tyájya** (B.).

tras *be terrified*, I. P.: PR. **trásati.** AO. red.: **átitrasan**; iṣ: **trā́sīs** (B.). PP. **trastá** (B.). INF. **trasas.** CS. **trasáyati.** INT. **tātrasyáte** (B.).

trā *rescue*, IV. Ā.: PR. **trā́yase**; **trā́yadhve, trā́yante**; IPV. **trā́yasva, trā́yatām**; **trā́yethām, trā́yetām**; **trā́yadhvam, trā́yantām**; PT. **trā́yamāṇa.** II. Ā.: IPV. **trā́sva**; **trā́dhvam.** PF. **tatré.** AO. s.: **átrāsmahi** (B.). SB. **trā́sate**; **trā́sāthe**; OP. **trā́sīthām.** FT. **trāsyáte** (B.). PP. **trātá** (B.). INF. **trā́maṇe.** CS. GDV. **trayayā́yya.**

tviṣ *be stirred*, II. P.: IPF. **átviṣur.** VI. Ā.: **átviṣanta.** PF. **titviṣé**; PT. **titviṣāṇá.** PPF. **átitviṣanta.** PP. **tviṣitá.** INF. **tviṣé.**

tsar *approach stealthily*, I. P.: PR. **tsárati.** PF. **tatsā́ra.** AO. s.: **átsār**; iṣ: **átsāriṣam** (B.). GD. **-tsárya** (B.).

daṃś, daś *bite*, I. P.: PR. **dáśati**; IPV. **dáśa**; PT. **dáśant.** PF.

PT. dadaśvā́ṃs. PP. daṣṭá. GD. daṃṣṭvā́ (B.). INT. PT. dándaśāna.

dakṣ *be able*, I.: PR. dákṣati, -te; IPV. dákṣata; PT. dákṣamāṇa. PF. dadakṣé (B.). AO. red.: ádadakṣat (B.). FT. dakṣiṣyáte (B.). GDV. dakṣā́yya. CS. dakṣáyati (B.).

dagh *reach to*, V.: PR. OP. daghnuyā́t (B.). AO. root: INJ. dhak (2. 3. s.); daghma; PRC. daghyā́s (3. s.); IPV. dhaktám. FT. daghiṣyánte (B.). INF. -dághas (B.), -dághos (B.).

dabh, dambh *harm*, I. P.: PR. dábhati; SB. dábhāti; INJ. dábhat. V. P.: PR. dabhnuvánti; IPV. dabhnuhí. PF. dadā́bha, dadámbha; debhúr; INJ. dadabhanta. AO. root: dabhúr; INJ. dabhúr. PS. dabhyáte; PP. dabdhá. GDV. dábhya. INF. -dábhe; dábdhum (B.). CS. dambháyati. DS. dípsati; SB. dípsāt; PT. dípsant; PR. dhī́psati (B.).

das, dās *lay waste*, IV. P.: PR. dásyati; OP. dásyet. I. P.: PR. dā́sati; SB. dā́sāt; INJ. dā́sat; PT. dā́sant. PF. PT. dadasvā́ṃs. AO. a: INJ. dasat; PT. dásamāna; iṣ: dā́sīt. PP. dastá (B.). CS. dasáyate; dāsáyati.

dah *burn*, I. P.: PR. dáhati; SB. dáhāti. II. P.: PR. dhákṣi. PF. dadā́ha (B.). AO. s.: ádhākṣīt; ádhāk (3. s.); INJ. dhā́k (3. s.); PT. dhákṣant and dákṣant. FT. dhakṣyáti; PT. dhakṣyánt. PS. dahyáte; PP. dagdhá. GD. dagdhvā́ (B.); -dáhya (B.). INF. -dáhas (B.), dágdhos (B.), dágdhum (B.). DS. dhī́kṣate (B.).

1. dā *give*, III.: PR. dádāti; dátte; SB. dádas, dádat; dádan; dádātai (AV.), dádāmahe; INJ. dadās, dadāt; OP. dadyā́t; dadīmáhi, dadīrán; IPV. daddhí, dehí, dattā́t, dádātu; dattám, dattā́m; dattá and dádāta, dádātana, dádatu; Ā. datsvá; PT. dádat; dádāna; IPF. ádadām, ádadās, ádadāt; ádattam; ádadāta, ádattana, ádadur; Ā. ádatta. I.: dadati; dadate; INJ. dadat; IPV. dadatām (3. s.); IPF. ádadat; ádadanta. PF. dadā́tha, dadáu; dadáthur, dadátur; dadá, dadúr; Ā. dadé, dadā́the, dadriré; PT. dadvā́ṃs, dadivā́ṃs (AV.), dadā-

vā́ṃs (AV.); dadāná. ao. root: ádās, ádāt, dā́t; ádāma, ádur, dúr. Ā. ádi, ádithās (B.), ádita (B.); ádimahi (TS.) and ádīmahi (VS.); sb. dā́s, dā́ti, dā́t; inj. dúr; op. deyām; ipv. dā́tu; dātám, dātā́m; dātá; dīṣvá (VS.); a: ā́dat. s.: ádiṣi; sb. dā́sat, dā́sathas; inj. deṣma (VS.); iṣ: ádadiṣṭa (SV.). ft. dāsyáti; -te (B.); dadiṣyé (K.); dātā́ (B.). ps. dīyáte; pt. dadyámāna; ao. dā́yi; pp. -dāta, dattá, -tta. gdv. déya. gd. dattvā́, dattvā́ya; -dā́ya, -dadya (AV.). inf. -dái, dā́tave, dā́tavái, dā́mane, dāváne; -dā́m (B.), dā́tum; dā́tos. cs. dāpáyati. ds. pt. dítsant, dídāsant.

2. dā *divide*, II. P.: pr. dā́ti; dā́nti; ipv. dā́ntu. VI. P.: pr. dyā́mi, dyáti; dyā́masi; ipv. dyátu; dyátām; IV.: pr. dáyāmasi; ipv. dáyasva, dáyatām; pt. dáyamāna. ipf. dáyanta. pf. dadiré (B.). ao. root: ádimahi (B.), adīmahi (VS., K.); s: op. diṣīyá. ps. dīyáte; pp. diná; -tta (B.). gd. -dā́ya.

3. dā *bind*, VI. P.: pr. dyáti; ipf. ádyas. ps. ao. dā́yi; pp. ditá.

dāś *make offering*, I. P.: pr. dā́śati; sb. dā́śāt; op. dā́śema; ipf. ádāśat. II. P.: pr. dā́ṣṭi; pt. dā́śat. V. P.: pr. dāśnóti. pf. dadā́śa. sb. dadāśas, dádāśati and dádāśat; pt. dadāśvā́ṃs, dāśvā́ṃs, dāśivā́ṃs (SV.). cs. ádāśayat (B.).

diś *point*, VI.: pr. diśā́mi. ipv. diśátu; pt. diśánt; diśámāna. pf. didéśa; sb. dídeśati; ipv. didiḍḍhí, dídeṣṭu; didiṣṭána. ppf. didiṣṭa (3. s. Ā.). ao. root: ádiṣṭa; s.: ádikṣi; sa: ádikṣat (B.). pp. diṣṭá. gd. -díśya. inf. -díśe. int. dédiṣṭi; ipf. dediśam; ádediṣṭa; dediśyáte.

dih *smear*, II.: pr. dégdhi; dihánti; sb. déhat; pt. dihāná. ipf. ádihan. ao. s.: ádhikṣur (B.). pp. digdhá.

1. dī *fly*, IV.: pr. dī́yati; -te; inj. dī́yat; ipv. dī́ya. ipf. ádīyam. int. inf. dédīyitavái.

2. dī, dīdī *shine*: pr. dīdyati (3. pl.); sb. dī́dayat; ipv. didīhí and dīdihí; pt. dī́dyat; dī́dyāna. ipf.

ádīdes, ádīdet. PF. didéthe, dīdā́ya; dīdiyúr; SB. dīdáyasi and dīdáyas, dīdáyati and dīdáyat. PT. dīdivā́ṃs.

dīkṣ *be consecrated*, I. Ā.: PR. dī́kṣate (B.). PF. didīkṣé and didīkṣúr (B.). AO. red.: ádidīkṣas (B.); iṣ: ádīkṣiṣṭa (B.). FT. dīkṣiṣyáte (B.). PP. dīkṣitá. GD. dīkṣitvā́ (B.). CS. dīkṣáyati (B.). DS. dídīkṣiṣate (B.).

dīp *shine*, IV. Ā.: PR. dī́pyate. AO. red.: ádidīpat; ádīdipat (B.); INJ. didīpas. CS. dīpáyati.

dīv *play*, IV.: PR. dī́vyati; dīvyate (B.). PF. didéva. PP. dyūtá. GD. -dī́vya.

du, dū *burn*, V. P.: PR. dunóti; dunvánti; PT. dunvánt. AO. iṣ: SB. dáviṣāṇi (or from du *go*?). PP. dūná.

duṣ *spoil*, IV. P.: PR. dúṣyati (B.). AO. red.: ádūduṣat; a: duṣát (B.); iṣ: doṣiṣṭam (B.). CS. dūṣáyati; FT. dūṣayiṣyā́mi.

duh *milk*, II. P.: PR. dógdhi; duhánti; Ā. dugdhé; duhạ́te and duhaté, duhrate and duhré; SB. dóhat; dóhate; OP. duhīyát, duhīyán; IPV. 3. du. dugdhā́m; Ā. 3. s. duhā́m; 3. du. duhāthām; 3. pl. duhrā́m (AV.) and duhrátām (AV.); PT. duhánt; dúghāna, dúhāna, and duhāná; IPF. ádhok; duhúr; áduhan (B.) and áduhran (AV.). I. Ā.: PR. dóhate. VI.: IPF. áduhat (TS.). PF. dudóha, dudóhitha; duduhúr; Ā. duduhé; duduhré and duduhriré; PT. duduhāná. AO. s: ádhukṣata (3. pl.); INJ. dhukṣata (3. pl.); OP. dhukṣīmáhi; sa: ádhukṣas, ádukṣat and ádhukṣat; ádhukṣan, dukṣán and dhukṣán; Ā. ádhukṣata, dukṣata and dhukṣata; INJ. dukṣas; Ā. 3. dukṣata and dhúkṣata; pl. dhukṣánta; IPV. dhukṣásva. PS. duhyáte; PT. duhyámāna; PP. dugdhá. GD. dugdhvā́ (B.). INF. duhádhyai; dohási; dógdhos (B.). CS. doháyati (B.). DS. dúdukṣati.

1. dṛ *pierce*, II. P.: PR. dárṣi. IX. P.: OP. dṛṇīyā́t (B.). PF. dadā́ra; PT. dadṛvā́ṃs. AO. root: ádar; s: SB. dárṣasi, dárṣat; Ā. dárṣate; OP. darṣīṣṭá. PS. dīryáte (B.); PS. dīrṇá (B.). GD. -dīrya (B.). CS. daráyati; dārayati

(B.). INT. **dárdarīmi, dárdarīti**; SB. **dárdirat**; IPV. **dardṛhí** and **dādṛhí, dardartu**; PT. **dárdrat**; **dáridrat** (TS.); IPF. **ádardar, dardar** (2. 3. s.); **ádardṛtam**; **ádardirur.**

2. **dṛ** *heed*: AO. **ádṛthās** (B.); s: **dṛḍhvam** (B.). PS. **driyáte** (B.). GD. **-dṛ́tya.**

dṛp *rave*, IV. P.: PR. **dṛ́pyati.** AO. a: **ádṛpat** (B.). FT. **drapsyáti** (B.) and **drapiṣyáti** (B.). PP. **dṛptá** and **dṛpitá.**

dṛś *see*: PF. **dadárśa**; Ā. **dadṛkṣé, dádṛśe**; **dádṛśre, dadṛśrire** (TS.); IPV. (3. pl. Ā.) **dadṛśrām** (AV.); PT. **dadṛśvā́ṃs**; **dádṛśāna.** AO. root: **ádarśam** (B.); **ádarśma** (TS.), **ádṛśma** (B.), **ádarśur** (B.); Ā. 3. pl. **ádṛśran, ádṛśram**; SB. **dárśati, dárśathas, dárśan**; INJ. **dárśam**; PT. **dṛśāná** and **dṛ́śāna**; a: **ádṛśan**; INJ. **dṛśan**; OP. **dṛśéyam**; s: **ádrāk** (B.) and **ádrākṣīt** (B.); Ā. **ádṛkṣata** (3. pl.); SB. **dṛ́kṣase**; sa: **dṛkṣam** (K.); red. **ádīdṛśat** (B.). FT. **drakṣyáti** (B.). PS. **dṛśyáte**; AO. **ádarśi** and **dárśi**; PP. **dṛṣṭá**; GDV. **dṛśénya.** GD. **dṛṣṭvā́, dṛṣṭvā́ya, -dṛ́śya.** INF. **dṛśé, dṛśáye**; **dráṣṭum.** CS. **darśáyati.** DS. **dídṛkṣase.**

dṛh *make firm*, I. P.: IPV. **dṛ́ṃha**; **dṛ́ṃhata**; IPF. **ádṛṃhat.** VI. Ā.: PR. **dṛṃhéthe**; IPV. **dṛṃhántām**; PT. **dṛṃhánt.** IPF. **dṛṃháta** (3. s.). IV.: IPV. **dṛ́hya**; **dṛ́hyasva.** PF. PT. **dādṛhāṇá.** PPF. **ádadṛhanta.** AO. iṣ: **ádṛṃhīs, ádṛṃhīt.** PP. **dṛḍhá.** CS. **dṛṃháyati.**

dyut *shine*, I. Ā.: PR. **dyótate.** PF. **didyóta**; **didyutúr**; Ā. **didyuté**; PT. **didyutāná.** AO. root: PT. **dyutánt**; **dyútāna** and **dyutāná**; a: **ádyutat** (B.); red.: **ádidyutat**; INJ. **didyutas**; s.: **ádyaut.** FT. **dyotiṣyáti** (B.). PP. **dyuttá.** GD. **-dyutya** (B.). CS. **dyutáyati** (*shine*), **dyotáyati** (*illumine*). INT. **dávidyutati** (3. pl.); SB. **dávidyutat**; PT. **dávidyutat**; IPF. **dávidyot.**

1. **drā** *run*, II. P.: IPV. **drā́ntu.** PF. **dadrúr**; PT. **dadrāṇá.** AO. s: SB. **drāsat.** CS. **drāpáyati** (B.); DS. **dídrāpayiṣati** (B.). INT. PT. **dáridrat.**

2. drā *sleep*, II. P.: PR. drā́ti (B.). AO. siṣ: ádrāsīt (B.). FT. drāsyáti (B.). PP. drāṇá.

dru *run*, I. P.: drávati. PF. dudrā́va (B.); SB. dudrávat. PPF. ádudrot. AO. red.: ádudruvat (B.). FT. droṣyáti (B.). PP. drutá (B.). GD. drutvā́ (B.); -drútya (B.). CS. draváyati (*flows*); drāváyati. INT. PF. dodrāva.

druh *be hostile*, IV. P.: PR. drúhyati (B.). PF. 1. dudróha, 2. dudróhitha. AO. a: druhás; INJ. druhás; druhán; sa: ádrukṣas (B.). FT. dhrokṣyáti. PP. drugdhá. GD. -drúhya. INF. drógdhavái. DS. dúdrukṣat.

dviṣ *hate*, II.: PR. dvéṣṭi; dviṣmás; SB. dvéṣat; dvéṣāma; Ā. dvéṣate; IPV. dvéṣṭu; PT. dviṣánt. PF. didvéṣa (B.). AO. sa: INJ. dvikṣát; Ā. dvikṣata (3. s.). PP. dviṣṭá. GDV. dvéṣya, -dviṣeṇya. INF. dvéṣṭos (B.).

dhan *run*: PF. SB. dadhánat; OP. dadhanyúr; PT. dadhanvā́ṃs. CS. dhanáyan; Ā. dhanáyante; dhanáyanta.

dhanv *run*, I. P.: PR. dhánvati; SB. dhánvāti; IPV. dhánva. PF. dadhanvé; dadhanviré. AO. iṣ: adhanviṣur.

dham, dhmā, *blow*, I. P.: PR. dhámati; PT. dhámant. IPF. ádhamat. PS. dhamyáte; dhmāyáte (B.); PP. dhamitá and dhmātá. GD. dhmā́ya (B.).

1. dhā *put*, III.: PR. dádhāmi, dádhāsi, dádhāti; dhatthás; dadhmási and dadhmás, dhattá, dádhati; Ā. dadhé, dhatsé, dhatté; dadhā́the, dadhā́te; dádhate; SB. dádhāni, dádhas, dádhat; dádhathas; dádhāma, dádhan; Ā. dádhase, dádhate; dádhāvahai; OP. dádhīta and dadhītá; dadhīmáhi; IPV. dhehí and dhattā́t, dádhātu; dhattám, dhattā́m; dhattá and dhattána, dádhatu; Ā. dhatsvá; dádhatām. PT. dádhat; dádhāna. IPF. ádadhām, ádadhās, ádadhāt; ádhattam; ádhatta, ádadhur; Ā. ádhatthās, ádhatta. PF. dadhā́tha, dadháu; dadhátur; dadhimá, dadhúr; Ā. dadhiṣé, dadhé; dadhā́the, dadhā́te; dadhidhvé, dadhiré and dadhré; IPV. dadhiṣvá; dadhidhvám. AO. root: ádhām, dhā́s, ádhāt and dhā́t; dhātam, ádhātām;

ádhur; Ā. ádhithās, ádhita; ádhītām; ádhīmahi; SB. dhā́s, dhā́ti and dhā́t; dhā́ma; dhéthe, dháithe; dhā́mahe; INJ. dhā́m; dhúr; Ā. dhīmahi; OP. dheyā́m; dheyúr; IPV. dhā́tu; dhātam; dhā́ta, dhātana, and dhetana, dhā́ntu; Ā. dhiṣvá; a: ádhat (SV.), dhát; s: ádhiṣi (B.); ádhiṣata (B.); SB. dhā́sathas; dhā́satha; INJ. dhāsur; OP. dhiṣīyá (B.), dheṣīyá (MS.). FT. dhāsyati, -te (B.); dhātā́ (B.). PS. dhīyáte; AO. ádhāyi; PP. hitá, -dhita. GD. dhitvā́ (B.), -dhā́ya. INF. -dhe, dhā́tave, dhā́tavái, dhiyádhyai; -dhā́m; dhā́tum (B.); dhā́tos. CS. dhāpáyati; SB. dhāpáyāthas. DS. dídhiṣati, -te; INJ. dídhiṣanta; OP. dídhiṣema; dídhiṣeya; IPV. dídhiṣantu; PT. dídhiṣāṇa; dhítsati, -te; GDV. didhiṣā́yya.

2. dhā *suck*, IV. P.: PR. dháyati. AO. root: ádhāt. PP. dhītá. GD. dhītvā́ (B.), -dhī́ya (B.). INF. dhā́tave. CS. dhāpáyate; -ti (B.).

1. dhāv *run*, I.: PR. dhā́vati, -te. PPF. ádadhāvat. AO. iṣ: ádhāvīt (B.). CS. dhāváyati.

2. dhāv *wash*, I.: PR. dhā́vati, -te. AO. iṣ: ádhāviṣṭa. PP. dhautá. CS. dhāvayati, -te (B.).

dhī *think*, III.: PR. dī́dhye; dīdhyāthām and dīdhīthām (AV.); SB. dī́dhayas; dī́dhayan; PT. dī́dhyat; dī́dhyāna. IPF. ádīdhet, dīdhet; ádīdhayur; Ā. ádīdhīta. PF. dīdháya; dīdhimá, dīdhiyúr and dīdhyúr; dīdhiré. PF. dhītá. INT. dedhyat (TS.).

dhū *shake*, V.: PR. dhūnóti; dhūnuté; SB. dhūnávat; IPV. dhūnuhí and dhūnú; dhūnutá; Ā. dhūnuṣvá; PT. dhūnvant; dhūnvāná. IPF. ádhūnot; Ā. ádhūnuthās, ádhūnuta. VI. P.: PR. dhuváti; OP. dhūvét. PF. dudhuvé; OP. dudhuvītá. PPF. dūdhot. AO. root: PT. dhuvāná; s: Ā. ádhūṣata (3. pl.). FT. dhaviṣyáti, -te (B.). PS. dhūyáte; PP. dhūtá. GD. dhūtvā́ (B.), -dhū́ya. INT. dódhavīti; PT. dódhuvat and dávidhvat; PF. davidhāva.

dhṛ *hold*: PF. dādhártha, dādhā́ra; dadhré, dadhriré.

AO. root: INJ. **dhṛthā́s**; red.: **ádīdharat**; **dīdhār** (2. 3. s.); INJ. **dī́dharat**; IPV. **didhṛtám**; **didhṛtá**. FT. **dhariṣyáte**. PS. **dhriyáte**; PP. **dhṛtá**. GD. **dhṛtvā́** (B.), **-dhṛ́tya** (B.). INF. **dhármaṇe**; **dhartári**; **dhártavái** (B.). CS. **dhāráyati**, **-te**; FT. **dhārayiṣyáti**; PS. **dhāryáte** (B.). INT. **dárdharṣi**; IPF. **ádardhar**; **dādharti** (B.); 3. pl. **dādhrati** (B.); IPV. **dādhartu** (B.).

dhṛṣ *dare*, V.: PR. **dhṛṣṇóti**; IPV. **dhṛṣṇuhí**. PF. **dadhárṣa**; **dādhṛṣúr**. SB. **dadhárṣati** and **dadhárṣat**; Ā. **dadhṛṣate**; INJ. **dadharṣīt**; PT. **dadhṛṣvā́ṃs**; PPF. **dádhṛṣanta**. AO. a: INJ. **dhṛṣát**; PT. **dhṛṣánt**; **dhṛṣámāṇa**; **dhṛṣāṇá** (AV.); iṣ: **ádharṣiṣur** (B.). PP. **dhṛṣṭá** and **dhṛṣitá**. GDV. **-dhṛṣya**. GD. **-dhṛṣya** (B.). INF. **-dhṛ́ṣe**; **-dhṛ́ṣas**. CS. **dharṣáyati** (B.).

dhyā *think*, IV. P.: PR. **dhyā́yati**. PF. **dadhyáu** (B.). AO. siṣ: **ádhyāsiṣam** (B.). PER. FT. **dhyātā́** (B.). PP. **dhyātá** (B.). GD. **dhyātvā́**. DS. **dídhyāsate** (B.).

dhraj, **dhrāj** *sweep*, I.: PR. PT. **dhrájant**; **dhrā́jamāna**. IPF. **ádhrajan**. AO. iṣ: OP. **dhrājiṣīyá**.

dhvaṃs *scatter*, I. P.: PR. **dhváṃsati**, **-te** (B.). PF. **dadhvasé**. AO. a: **dhvasán**. PP. **dhvasta** (B.). CS. **dhvasáyati**; **dhvaṃsáyati**, **-te** (B.).

dhvan *sound*: AO. iṣ: **ádhvanīt**. PP. **dhvāntá**. CS. **ádhvānayat**; AO. INJ. **dhvanáyīt**.

dhvṛ *injure*, I. P.: PR. **dhvárati** (B.). AO. s: Ā. **ádhūrṣata** (3. pl.). INF. **dhū́rvaṇe**. DS. **dúdhūrṣati**.

nakṣ *attain*, I.: PR. **nákṣati**, **-te**; INJ. **nákṣat**; IPV. **nákṣasva**; PT. **nákṣant**; **nákṣamāṇa**. IPF. **ánakṣan**. PF. **nanakṣúr**; **nanakṣé**.

nad *sound*, I. P.: PR. **nádati**. CS. **nadáyati**. INT. **nā́nadati** (3. pl.); **nānadyáte** (B.); PT. **nā́nadat**.

nam *bend*, I.: PR. **námati**, **-te**. PF. **nānā́ma**; **nemé**. PPF. **nanámas**. AO. red.: INJ. **nīnamas**; s: **ánān** (K.); Ā. **ánaṃsata** (3. pl., B.). SB. **náṃsai**, **naṃsante**; PT. **namasāná**. FT. **naṃsyáti** (B.). PP. **natá**; GDV. **nántva**. GD. **-nátya** (B.). INF. **-námam**, **-náme**. CS. **namáyati**.

INT. nánnamīti; nánnate (3. s.); PT. nánnamat; nánnamāna; IPF. ánannata (3. s.).

1. naś *be lost*, IV. P.: PR. náśyati; I.: PR. náśati, -te. PF. nanā́śa; neśúr (B.). AO. red.: ánīnaśat; néśat; INJ. nī́naśas; néśat. FT. naśiṣyáti. PP. naṣṭá. CS. nāśáyati; INF. nāśayádhyai.

2. naś *attain*, I.: PR. náśati, -te. AO. root: ā́naṭ (2. 3. s.), náṭ (3. s.); ánaṣṭām; INJ. nák and náṭ (3. s.); Ā. náṃśi; OP. naśīmáhi; s: SB. nákṣat. INF. -náśe. DS. ínakṣasi; INJ. ínakṣat.

nas *unite*, I. Ā.: PR. násate; násāmahe; INJ. násanta. AO. root: OP. nasīmáhi.

nah *bind*, IV.: PR. náhyati; IPV. náhyatana (2. pl.); PT. náhyamāna. PF. nanā́ha. PS. PT. nahyámāna; PP. naddhá. GD. -náhya (B.).

nāth, nādh *seek aid*, I. Ā.: PR. nā́thate (B.); PT. nā́dhamāna. PP. nāthitá; nādhitá.

nij *wash*, II. Ā.: PT. nijāná. III.: IPV. niniktá (2. pl.). AO. a: ánijam; s: ánaikṣīt; INJ. nikṣi. PP. niktá. GD. niktvā́ (B.), -níjya (B.). INF. -níje. CS. nejáyati (B.). INT. nenikté; IPV. nenigdhí.

nind, *revile*, I. P.: PR. níndati; SB. níndāt; IPV. nindaṭa. PF. nindimá; ninidúr. AO. root: PT. nidāná; iṣ: ánindiṣur; SB. níndiṣat. PS. nindyáte; PP. ninditá. DS. SB. ninitsāt.

nī *lead*, I.: PR. náyati, -te; SB. náyāti, náyāt; Ā. náyāsai (AV.); INJ. náyat; náyanta; IPV. náyatu; Ā. náyasva; PT. náyant; náyamāna; IPF. ánayat. II.: PR. néṣi (= IPV.); nethá; IPF. ánītām (3. du.). PF. ninétha, ninā́ya; ninyáthur; ninye (B.); SB. ninīthás; OP. ninīyā́t; IPV. ninétu. AO. s: ánaiṣṭa (2. pl.); áneṣata (3. pl.); SB. néṣati, néṣat; néṣatha; INJ. naiṣṭa (2. pl.); Ā. neṣṭa (3. s.); iṣ: ánayīt (AV.). FT. neṣyáti; -te (B.); nayiṣyáti (B.). PS. nīyáte; PP. nītá. GD. nītvā́ (B.), -nī́ya. INF. neṣáṇi; nétavái (B.); nétum (B.), náyitum (B.); nétos (B.). DS. ninīṣati (B.). INT. nenīyáte.

nu *praise*, I.: PR. návati; návāmahe, návante; INJ. návanta; PT. návant; návamāna. IPF. ánavanta. II. P.: PT. nuvánt; IPF. ánāvan. PPF. ánūnot, nūnot; AO. s: Ā. ánūṣi; ánūṣātām; ánūṣata; INJ. nūṣata (3. pl.); iṣ: Ā. ánaviṣṭa. GDV. návya. INT. nónavīti; nonumás and nonumási; SB. nónuvanta; IPF. návīnot; ánonavur; PF. nónāva; nónuvur.

nud *push*, VI.: PR. nudáti, -te; PF. nunudé; nunudré. AO. root: INJ. nutthā́s; iṣ: INJ. nudiṣṭhā́s. FT. notsyáte (B.). PP. nuttá; nunná (SV.). INF. -núde; -nudas. INT. ánonudyanta (B.).

nṛt *dance*, IV. P.: PR. nṛ́tyati; IPV. nṛ́tya, nṛ́tyatu; PT. nṛ́tyant. AO. root: nṛtur (PF.?); a: PT. nṛtámāna; iṣ: ánartiṣur. PP. nṛttá. CS. nartáyati.

pac *cook*, I.: PR. pácati, -te; SB. pácāni, pácāti, pácāt; INJ. pácat; IPV. pácata, pácantu. IV. Ā.: PR. pácyate. PF. papā́ca; pecé. PPF. ápeciran. AO. s: SB. pákṣat. FT. pakṣyáti, -te (B.); paktā́ (B.). PS. pacyáte. GD. paktvā́. INF. páktave. CS. pācáyati, -te (B.).

pat *fly*, I. P.: PR. pátati; SB. pátāti, pátāt INJ. pátat; OP. pátet; IPV. pátatu; PT. pátant. IPF. ápatat. PF. papā́ta; petáthur, petátur; paptimá, paptúr; OP. papatyā́t; PT. paptivā́ṃs. AO. red.: ápaptat and ápīpatat; ápaptāma, ápaptan; INJ. paptas, paptat; paptan; IPV. paptata. FT. patiṣyáti; CO. ápatiṣyat (B.). PS. AO. ápāti (B.); PP. patitá. GD. patitvā́, -pátya (B.). INF. páttave; pátitum (B.). CS. patáyati, -te; pātáyati. DS. pípatiṣati. INT. pā́patīti; SB. pā́patan.

pad *go*, IV.: PR. pádyate; padyati (B.); IPV. pádyasva; PT. pádyamāna; IPF. ápadyanta. PF. papā́da; pedé (B.). AO. root: ápadmahi, ápadran; SB. padāti, padāt; PRC. padīṣṭá; red.: ápīpadāma; s: INJ. patsi (1. s.), patthā́s. FT. patsyati (B.). PS. AO. ápādi, pā́di; PP. panná. GD. -pádya. INF. -pádas; páttum (B.), páttos (B.). CS. pādáyati, -te; PS. pādyáte (B.); DS. pípādayiṣati (B.).

pan *admire*, I. Ā.: PR. INJ. **pánanta**. PF. **papána** (1. s.); **papné**. AO. iṣ: **paniṣṭa** (3. s.). PS. **panyáte**; PP. **panitá**. CS. **panáyati, -te**; GDV. **panayā́yya**. INT. PT. **pánipnat**.

paś *see*, IV.: PR. **páśyati, -te**; SB. **páśyāni, páśyāsi** and **páśyās, páśyāt; páśyāma, páśyān**; INJ. **páśyat**; OP. **páśyet; páśyeta**; IPV. **páśya; páśyasva**; PT. **páśyant; páśyamāna**; IPF. **ápaśyat; ápaśyanta**. Cp. **spáś**.

1. **pā** *drink*, I.: PR. **píbati, -te**; SB. **píbāsi, píbāti** and **píbāt; píbāva, píbāthas, píbātas**; INJ. **píbat**; IPV. **píbatu; píbasva; píbadhvam**; PT. **píbant**; IPF. **ápibat**. III.: PR. **pipīte** (B.), **pipate** (B.); OP. **pipīya** (B.); IPF. **ápipīta** (B.); IPV. **pipatu** (K.); PT. **pipāná** and **pípāna** (AV.). PF. **papā́tha, papáu; papáthur, papúr**; Ā. **papé; papiré**; OP. **papīyā́t**; PT. **papivā́ṃs; papāná**. AO. root: **ápām, ápās, ápāt; ápāma, ápur**; SB. **pā́s; pāthás; pā́nti**; PRC. **peyā́s** (3. s.); IPV. **pāhí, pātu; pātám, pātā́m; pātá** and **pātána, pā́ntu**; PT. **pā́nt**; S: INJ. **pāsta** (3. s.). FT. **pāsyáti, -te** (B.). PS. **pīyáte**; AO. **ápāyi**; PP. **pītá**. GD. **pītvā́, pītvī́; -pā́ya**. INF. **pītáye, pā́tave, pā́tavái; pā́tos** (B.); **píbadhyai**. CS. **pāyáyati**; DS. **pípāyayiṣet** (K.). DS. **pípāsati; pípīṣati**; PT. **pípīṣant**.

2. **pā** *protect*, II.: PR. **pā́mi, pā́si, pā́ti; pāthás, pātás; pāthá, pāthána, pā́nti**; SB. **pā́t; pā́tas**; IPV. **pāhí, pā́tu; pātám, pātā́m; pātá, pā́ntu**; PT. **pā́nt; pāná**; IPF. **ápām, ápās, ápāt; ápāma, ápur**. AO. S: SB. **pā́sati**.

pi, pī *swell*, I. Ā.: PR. **páyate**. II. Ā.: PT. **píyāna**. V.: PR. **pinvire**; PT. **pinvánt**, f. **pinvatī́; pinvāná**. PF. **pīpétha, pīpā́ya; pipyáthur; pipyúr; pipyé** (3. s.); SB. **pīpáyas, pīpáyat; pīpáyatas; pīpáyan; pīpáyata; pīpáyanta**; INJ. **pīpes**; IPV. **pīpihí, pīpaya; pipyatam, pipyatām; pipyata** PT. **pīpivā́ṃs; pípyāna** and **pīpyāná**. PPF. **ápipe; ápipema, ápīpyan; ápīpayat; ápīpayanta**. PP. **pīná** (AV.).

pinv *fatten*, I.: PR. **pínvati, -te**; INJ. **pínvat; pínvanta**;

ipv. pínva; pínvatam; pínvata; Ā. pínvasva, pínvatām; pínvadhvam; pt. pínvant; pínvamāna; ipf. ápinvam, ápinvas, ápinvat; ápinvatam; ápinvata, ápinvan; Ā. 3. s. ápinvata. pf. pipinváthur. pp. pinvitá (B.). cs. pinváyati (B.). Cp. pi *swell*.

piś *adorn*, VI.: pr. piṃśáti, -te. pf. pipéśa; pipiśúr; Ā. pipiśé; pipiśré. ao. root: pt. piśāná. ps. piśyáte; pp. piṣṭá; piśitá. int. pt. pépiśat; pépiśāna.

piṣ *crush*, VII. P.: pr. pináṣṭi; piṃṣánti; inj. piṇák (2. 3. s.); ipv. pináṣṭana; pt. piṃṣánt; ipf. piṇák. VI. P.: ipf. ápīṣan (AV.). pf. pipéṣa; pipiṣé. ao. sa: ápikṣan (B.). ps. piṣyáte (B.); pp. piṣṭá. gd. piṣṭvā́ (B.). inf. péṣṭavāi (B.); péṣṭum (B.).

pīḍ *press*: pf. pipīḍé. cs. pīḍáyati.

puṣ *thrive*, IV. P.: pr. púṣyati. pf. pupóṣa; op. pupuṣyā́s; pt. pupuṣvā́ṃs. ao. root: prc. puṣyā́sam (B.); puṣyā́sma (B.); a: op. puṣéyam; puṣéma. pp. puṣṭá. inf. puṣyáse. cs. poṣáyati.

pū *cleanse*, IX.: pr. punā́mi, punā́ti; punánti; punīté; punáte (AV.) and punaté; ipv. punīhí and punītā́t, punā́tu; punītām; punītá, punītána and punāta, punántu; pt. punánt; punāná; ipf. ápunan. I. Ā.: pr. pávate; sb. pávāte; ipv. pávasva, pávatām; pávadhvam, pávantām; pt. pávamāna; ipf. ápavathās. pf. pupuvúr (B.); pupuvé (B.). ppf. ápupot. ao. iṣ: ápāviṣur; inj. paviṣṭa (3. s.). ps. pūyáte; pp. pūtá. gd. pūtví; pūtvā́; -pūya (B.). inf. pavitum (B.). cs. paváyat, -te (B.), pāváyati (B.).

pṛ *pass*, III. P.: pr. píparṣi, píparti; pipṛthás; pipṛthá, píprati; ipv. pipṛhí and pipṛtā́t, pípartu; pipṛtám; pipṛtá and pípartana. ao. red.: ápīparam, ápīparas; ápīparan; inj. pī́paras, pī́parat and pīpárat; s: sb. párṣati, párṣat; ipv. parṣa; iṣ: sb. pā́riṣat. inf. parṣáṇi. cs. pāráyati; sb. pāráyāti; pt. pāráyant.

pṛc *mix*, VII.: pr. pṛṇákṣi; pṛñcánti; Ā. pṛñcé, pṛṅkté; pṛñcáte (3. pl.); inj. pṛṇák (3. s.); op. pṛñcītá; ipv.

pṛndhí (= pṛṅgdhí), pṛṇáktu; pṛṅktám; PT. pṛñcánt; pṛñcāná; IPF. ápṛṇak (3. s.). III. P.: IPV. pipṛgdhí; pipṛktá. PF. papṛcúr (B.); SB. papṛcāsi; OP. papṛcyā́m, papṛcyā́t; PT. papṛcāná. AO. root: SB. párcas; OP. pṛcīmáhi; PT. pṛcāná; s: áprāk; Ā. ápṛkṣi, ápṛkta. PS. pṛcyáte; PP. pṛktá; -pṛgṇa. INF. -pṛ́ce; pṛ́cas.

pṛṇ *fill*, VI.: PR. pṛṇáti; SB. pṛṇáithe (du. 2.); IPV. pṛṇá; pṛṇáta; pṛṇásva; pṛṇádhvam; IPF. ápṛṇat. INF. pṛṇádhyai. Cp. pṝ *fill*.

pṝ *fill*, IX.: PR. pṛṇā́mi, pṛṇā́si, pṛṇā́ti; pṛṇītás; pṛṇánti; SB. pṛṇā́ti, pṛṇāt; OP. pṛṇīyā́t; IPV. pṛṇīhí, pṛṇā́tu; pṛṇītám; pṛṇītá, pṛṇītána; Ā. pṛṇīṣvá; PT. pṛṇánt; IPF. ápṛṇās, ápṛṇāt. III.: PR. píparmi, píparti; píprati (3. pl.); IPV. pípartu; pipṛtā́m; pípartana; IPF. ápiprata (3. s. = ápipṛta). PF. OP. pupūryā́s; PT. papṛvā́ṃs. AO. root: IPV. pūrdhí; PRC. priyāsam (AV.); red.: ápūpuram (B.); INJ. pīparat; IPV. pūpurantu; iṣ: pūriṣṭhās (B.). PS. pūryáte (B.); PP. pūrṇá; pūrtá. INF. -puras (K.). CS. pūráyati; SB. pūráyāti.

pyā *fill up*, IV. Ā.: PR. pyā́yase; IPV. pyā́yasva, pyā́yatām; pyā́yantām; PT. pyā́yamāna. AO. siṣ: OP. pyāsiṣīmahi (AV.). PP. pyātá. CS. pyāyáyati; PS. pyāyyáte (B.).

prach *ask*, VI.: PR. pṛcháti, -te; SB. pṛchāt; pṛchā́n; Ā. pṛchái. PF. paprácha; paprachúr (B.). AO. s: áprākṣam, áprāṭ; áprākṣīt. FT. prakṣyáti (B.). PS. pṛchyáte; PP. pṛṣṭá; GDV. papṛkṣéṇya. INF. -pṛ́cham, -pṛ́che; práṣṭum.

prath *spread*, I. Ā.: PR. práthate. PF. 2. paprā́tha (= paprát-tha?); Ā. paprathé and páprathe (3. s.); SB. papráthas, papráthat; papráthan; INJ. paprathanta; PT. paprathāná. AO. root: PT. prathāná; iṣ: 3. s. Ā. áprathiṣṭa; práthiṣṭa. CS. pratháyati, -te.

prā *fill*, II. P.: PR. prā́si. PF. paprā́tha, paprá and papráu; papráthur, paprátur; paprúr; Ā. papṛṣé, papré; PT. papṛvā́ṃs. AO. root: áprāt; SB. prā́s; s: 3. s. áprās. PS. AO. áprāyi; PP. prātá.

prī *please*, IX.: PR. prīṇā́ti; prīṇīté; PT. prīṇánt; prīṇāná. IPF. áprīṇāt. PF. pipriyé; SB. pipráyas, pipráyat; IPV. piprīhí; pipráyasva; PT. pipriyāṇá. PPF. ápiprayam, ápipres (B.); ápiprayan. AO. s: ápraiṣīt (B.); SB. préṣat. PP. prītá. GD. prītvā́ (B.). DS. píprīṣati.

pruth *snort*, I.: PR. próthati; PT. prothánt; próthamāna. GD. -prúthya. INT. PT. pópruthat.

pruṣ *sprinkle*, V.: PR. pruṣṇuvánti; pruṣṇuté; SB. pruṣṇávat. VI. P.: IPV. pruṣá; PT. pruṣánt. IV. P.: IPF. ápruṣyat (B.). IX. P.: PT. pruṣṇánt (B.). FT. PT. proṣiṣyánt. PP. pruṣitá.

plu *float*, I.: PR. plávate; plávati (B.). PF. pupluvé (B.). AO. red.: ápiplavam (B.); s: áploṣṭa (B.). FT. ploṣyáti, -te (B.). PP. plutá. GD. -plūya (K.). CS. plāváyati (B.). INT. poplūyáte (B.).

psā *devour*, II. P.: PR. psā́ti. PS. ápsīyata (B.); PP. psātá. GD. -psā́ya (B.).

phaṇ *spring*: CS. phāṇáyati. INT. PT. pánīphaṇat.

bandh *bind*, IX.: PR. badhnā́mi; badhnīmás, badhnánti; Ā. badhnáte (3. pl.); IPV. badhāná, badhnā́tu; badhnántu; Ā. badhnītā́m (3. s.). IPF. ábadhnāt; ábadhnan; Ā. ábadhnīta (3. s.). PF. babándha; bedhúr. FT. bhantsyáti. PS. badhyáte; PP. baddhá. GD. baddhvā́; baddhvā́ya (B.); -bádhya (B.). INF. -bádhe. CS. bandháyati (B.).

bādh *oppress*, I. Ā.: PR. bā́dhate. PF. babādhé. AO. iṣ: INJ. bādhiṣṭa. PP. bādhitá. GD. -bā́dhya. INF. bā́dhe. CS. bādháyati. DS. bī́bhatsate; bíbādhiṣate (B.). INT. bābadhe (3. s.); badbadhé; PT. bā́badhāna; badbadhāná.

budh *wake*, I. P.: PR. bódhati; SB. bódhāti; INJ. bódhat; IPV. bódhatu. IV.: PR. búdhyate; OP. búdhyema; IPV. búdhyasva; búdhyadhvam; PT. búdhyamāna. PF. bubudhé; SB. bubodhas, búbodhati; bubodhatha; PT. bubudhāná. AO. root: Ā. 3. pl. ábudhran, ábudhram; IPV. bodhí (2. s.); PT. budhāná; a: INJ.

budhánta; red.: ábūbudhat; s: Ā. ábhutsi; ábhutsmahi, ábhutsata; iṣ: sb. bódhiṣat. ft. bhotsyáti (B.). ps. ao. ábodhi; pp. buddhá. gd. -budhya (B.). inf. -búdhe. cs. bodháyati; bodháyate (B.). int. bóbudhīti (B.).

bṛh *make big*, VI. P.: pr. bṛháti. I.: pr. bṛ́ṃhati, -te (B.). pf. babárha; pt. babṛhāṇá. ao. iṣ: inj. bárhīs, bárhīt. cs. barháya. int. sb. bárbṛhat; ipv. barbṛhi.

brū *say*, II.: pr. brávīmi, brávīṣi, brávīti; brūmás, bruvánti; Ā. bruvé, brūṣé, brūté and bruvé; bruvā́te; bruváte; sb. brávāṇi and brávā, brávasi and brávas, brávat; brávāma, brávātha (AV.), brávan; Ā. brávāvahai, brávaite; brávāmahai; op. brūyā́t; brūyā́tam; Ā. bruvītá; bruvīmáhi; ipv. brūhí and brūtā́t, brávītu; brūtám; brūtá and brávītana, bruvántu; pt. bruvánt; bruvāṇá. ipf. ábravam, ábravīs, ábravīt; ábrūtām; ábravīta, ábruvan.

bhakṣ *eat*: ao. red.: ábabhakṣat (B.); cs. bhakṣáyati; bhakṣáyate (B.); ps. bhakṣyáte (B.).

bhaj *divide*, I.: pr. bhájati, -te. II. P.: pr. bhákṣi (= ipv.). pf. 2. s. babháktha (B.), 3. s. babhā́ja; Ā. bhejé; bhejā́te; bhejiré; pt. bhejāná. ao. red.: ábībhajur (B.); s: ábhāk and ábhākṣīt; Ā. ábhakṣi, ábhakta; sb. bhákṣat; inj. bhā́k (2. 3. s.); op. bhakṣīyá, bhakṣītá; bhakṣīmáhi; prc. bhakṣīṣṭá. ft. bhakṣyáti, -te (B.). ps. bhajyáte; pp. bhaktá. gd. bhaktvā́; bhaktvā́ya; -bhajya (B.). cs. bhājáyati; ps. bhājyáte.

bhañj *break*, VII. P.: pr. bhanákti; ipv. bhandhí, bhanáktu; pt. bhañjánt. ipf. ábhanas (for ábhanak, AV.). pf. babháñja. ps. bhajyáte.

bhan *speak*, I.: pr. bhánati; bhánanti; inj. bhánanta. ipf. bhánanta.

bhas *devour*, III.: pr. bábhasti; bápsati; sb. bábhasat; bápsathas; pt. bápsat. VI. P.: pr. bhasáthas. I. P.: inj. bhásat.

bhā *shine*, II. P.: bhā́si, bhā́ti; bhā́nti; ipv. bhāhí; pt. f. bhā́tī. ft. bhāsyáti (B.).

bhikṣ *beg*, I. Ā.: PR. **bhíkṣate**; INJ. **bhíkṣanta**; OP. **bhíkṣeta**; PT. **bhíkṣamāṇa**. PF. **bibhikṣé** (B.).

bhid *split*, VII.: PR. **bhinádmi, bhinátsi, bhinátti**; **bhindánti**; SB. **bhinádas, bhinádat**; INJ. **bhinát** (2. 3. s.); OP. **bhindyā́t**; IPV. **bhindhí, bhináttu**; **bhinttá**; PT. **bhindánt**; **bhindāná**. IPF. **bhinát** (2. 3. s.); **ábhinat** (3. s.); **ábhindan**. PF. **bibhéda**; **bibhidúr**. AO. root: **ábhedam, bhét** (2. 3. s.), **ábhet** (3. s.); SB. **bhédati**; INJ. **bhét** (2. s.); PT. **bhidánt**; a: OP. **bhidéyam**; s: INJ. **bhitthā́s**. FT. **bhetsyáte** (B.). PS. **bhidyáte** (B.); AO. **ábhedi** (B.); PP. **bhinná**. GD. **bhittvā́**; **-bhídya**. INF. **bhéttavái** (B.); **bhéttum** (B.). DS. **bíbhitsati**.

bhī *fear*, III. P.: PR. **bibhéti**; **bíbhyati**; INJ. **bibhés**; OP. **bibhīyā́t**; IPV. **bibhītá, bibhītána**; PT. **bíbhyat**; IPF. **bibhés, ábibhet**. I. Ā.: PR. **bháyate**; SB. **bháyāte**; IPV. **bháyatām** (3. s.); IPF. **ábhayanta**; PT. **bháyamāna**. PF. **bibháya** (1. s.), **bibhā́ya** (B. also **bībhāya**); **bibhyátur**; **bibhyúr**; PT. **bibhīvā́ṃs**; PER. PF. **bibhayā́ṃ cakāra**. AO. root: INJ. **bhés** (TS.); **bhema**; PT. **bhiyāná**; red.: **bībhayat**; **ábībhayur** (Kh.); **ábībhayanta**; s: **bhaiṣīs** (AV.); **ábhaiṣma, ábhaiṣur**; PT. **bhiyásāna** (AV.). CO. **ábheṣyat** (B.). PP. **bhītá**. INF. **bhiyáse**. CS. **bhīṣáyate** (B.); AO. **bībhiṣas**; **bībhiṣathās**.

1. **bhuj** *enjoy*, VII. Ā.: PR. **bhuṅkté**; **bhuñjáte** and **bhuñjaté**; SB. **bhunájāmahai**; PT. f. **bhuñjatī́**. PF. **bubhujé**; **bubhujmáhe, bubhujriré**. AO. root: SB. **bhójate**; INJ. **bhójam**; a: OP. **bhujéma**; IPV. **bhujá** (TS.). PS. **bhujyáte** (B.). INF. **bhujé**; **bhójase**. CS. **bhojáyati**.

2. **bhuj** *bend*, VI. P.: INJ. **bhuját**; IPV. **bhujá** (VS.). PPF. **ábubhojīs**. GD. **-bhujya** (B.).

bhur *quiver*, VI.: INJ. **bhuránta**; IPV. **bhurántu**; PT. **bhurámāṇa**. INT. **járbhurīti**; PT. **járbhurat**; **járbhurāṇa**.

bhū *be*, I.: PR. **bhávati**; **bhávate** (B.). PF. **babhū́va**, **babhū́tha** and **babhū́vitha, babhū́va**; **babhūváthur**, **babhūvátur**; **babhūvimá, babhūvá, babhūvúr**; OP.

babhūyā́s, babhūyā́t; IPV. babhū́tu; PT. babhūvā́ṃs. AO. root: ábhuvam, ábhūs, ábhūt; ábhūtam, ábhūtām; ábhūma, ábhūta and ábhūtana, ábhūvan; SB. bhúvāni, bhúvas, bhúvat; bhūthás, bhūtas; bhúvan; INJ. bhúvam, bhū́s, bhū́t; bhūma; OP. bhūyā́s, bhūyāt; bhūyā́ma; PRC. bhūyā́sam, 3. bhūyā́s; bhūyā́sma, bhūyā́sta; IPV. bodhí (for bhūdhí), bhūtu; bhūtám; bhūtá and bhūtána; a: bhúvas, bhúvat; red.: ábūbhuvas. FT. bhaviṣyáti; bhavitā́ (B.). PP. bhūtá. GDV. bhávya and bhāvyá; bhávītva. GD. bhūtvī́, bhūtvā́; -bhū́ya. INF. bhuvé, -bhúve, -bhvè; bhūṣáṇi; bhávitum (B.); bhávitos (B.). CS. bhāváyati. DS. búbhūṣati. INT. bóbhavīti.

bhṛ *bear*, I.: PR. bhárati, -te. III.: PR. bíbharmi, bíbharṣi, bíbharti; bibhṛthás, bibhṛtás; bibhṛmási and bibhṛmás, bibhṛthá, bíbhrati; SB. bíbharāṇi, bíbharat; OP. bibhṛyā́t; IPV. bibhṛhí, bíbhartu; bibhṛtā́m; bibhṛtā́ (TS.); PT. bíbhrat; IPF. ábibhar. PF. jabhártha, jabhā́ra; jabhrúr; Ā. jabhṛṣé, jabhré; jabhriré; babhā́ra (B.); Ā. babhré; PT. babhrāṇá; SB. jabhárat. PPF. ájabhartana. AO. root: PRC. bhriyā́sam; IPV. bhṛtám; s: ábhārṣam, 3. ábhār; ábhārṣṭam; SB. bhárṣat; INJ. 3. s. bhā́r; iṣ: ábhāriṣam. FT. bhariṣyáti; bhartā́ (B.). CO. ábhariṣyat. PS. bhriyáte; SB. bhriyāte; AO. bhā́ri; PP. bhṛtá. GD. -bhṛtya. INF. bhártum; bhártave, bhártavái; bháradhyai; bhármaṇe. DS. búbhūrṣati (B.). INT. jarbhṛtás; bháribhrati (3. pl.); SB. bháribharat; PT. bháribhrat.

bhraṃś *fall*, I.: PR. INJ. bhráṃśat. AO. a: INJ. bhraśat. PP. -bhṛṣṭa; bhraṣṭá. CS. PT. bhrāśáyant.

bhrāj *shine*, I. Ā.: PR. bhrā́jate; PT. bhrā́jamāna. AO. root: ábhrāṭ; PRC. bhrājyā́sam. PS. AO. ábhrāji.

maṃh, mah *be great*, I.: PR. máṃhate; máhe (3. s.); OP. máhema, máheta; IPV. máṃhatam; PT. máṃhamāna. IPF. ámaṃhata. PF. māmahé (1. 3.); SB. māmáhas; INJ. māmahanta; IPV. māmahasva, māmahantām; PT.

māmahānā́. PP. **mahitā́** (B.). INF. **mahé, maháye.** CS. **maháyati, -te**; INJ. **maṃháyam**; PT. **maháyant**; **maháyamāna.**

majj *sink*, I. P.: **májjati.** AO. root: OP. **majjyā́t** (B.). FT. **maṅkṣyáti, -te** (B.). GD. **-májjya.** CS. **majjáyati** (B.).

math, manth *stir*, IX.: PR. **mathnā́mi**; **mathnīté** (B.); IPV. **mathnītá, mathnántu**; PT. **mathnánt**; IPF. **ámathnāt**; I. **mánthati, -te**; **máthati** (AV.). PF. **mamā́tha**; **methúr** (B.); Ā. **methiré** (B.). AO. root: SB. **máthat**; iṣ: **ámanthiṣṭām** (3. du.); **ámathiṣata** (B.); INJ. **máthīs, máthīt.** FT. **manthiṣyáti** (B.); **mathiṣyáti, -te** (B.). PS. **mathyáte**; PP. **mathitá.** GD. **mathitvā́** (B.); **-máthya** (B.). INF. **mánthitavái**; **máthitos** (B.).

mad *be exhilarated*, I.: PR. **mádati**; **-te.** III. P.: PR. **mamatsi.** II. P.: PR. **mátsi** (= IPV.). IV. P.: PR. **mā́dyati** (B.). PF. **mamā́da**; SB. **mamádas, mamádat**; **mamádan**; IPV. **mamaddhí, mamáttu**; **mamattána.** PPF. **amamadur.** AO. root: IPV. **mátsva**; red.: **ámīmadas**; Ā. **ámīmadanta**; s: **ámatsur**; Ā. **ámatta** (3. s.); **ámatsata** (3. pl.); SB. **mátsati** and **mátsat**; **mátsatha**; INJ. **matsata** (3. pl.); iṣ: **ámādiṣur.** PS. PT. **madyámāna**; PP. **mattá.** GDV. **-mā́dya.** INF. **máditos** (B.). CS. **madáyati**; **mādáyati, -te**; SB. **mādáyāse, mādáyāte**; **mādáyaite**; **mādáyādhve** and **mādáyādhvai**; INF. **mādayádhyai**; PP. **maditá.**

man *think*, IV. Ā.: PR. **mányate.** VIII. Ā.: PR. **manvé**; **manmáhe, manvaté**; SB. **manávai, manávate**; INJ. **manvata** (3. pl.); OP. **manvītá**; IPV. Ā.: **manutā́m** (3. s.); PT. **manvāná**; IPF. **ámanuta** (3. s.); **ámanvata** (3. pl.). PF. **mené** (B.); **mamnā́the, mamnā́te**; OP. **mamanyā́t**; IPV. **mamandhí.** PPF. **ámaman** (3. s.). AO. root: **ámata**; **ámanmahi**; SB. **mánāmahe, mánanta**; PT. **manāná**; s: Ā. **ámaṃsta**; **ámaṃsātām**; **ámaṃsata**; SB. **máṃsai, máṃsase, máṃsate** and **máṃsatai** (TS.); **máṃsante**; INJ. **máṃsthās, maṃsta** and **māṃsta** (AV.); OP. **masīyá, maṃsīṣṭhā́s, maṃsīṣṭá**; **maṃsīmáhi**;

maṃsīrata ; IPV. mandhvam (B.). FT. maniṣyé ; maṃsyáte (B.). PP. matá. GD. -matya (B.). INF. mántave, mántavái ; mántos (B.). CS. mānáyati ; OP. mānáyet. DS. mī́māṃsate (AV.), -ti (B.) ; AO. iṣ : ámīmāṃsiṣṭhās (B.). PP. mīmāṃsitá (AV.).

mand *exhilarate*, I. : PR. mándati, -te. PF. mamánda ; SB. mamandat ; PT. f. mamandúṣī. PPF. ámamandur. AO. root : mandúr ; PT. mandāná ; iṣ : ámandīt ; ámandiṣur ; mándiṣṭa (3. s. Ā.) ; ámandiṣātām (3. du. Ā.) ; OP. mandiṣīmáhi (VS.). INF. mandádhyai. CS. mandáyati ; INF. mandayádhyai.

1. mā *measure*, III. : PR. mime, mímīte ; mimāte ; mimīmahe, mimate ; OP. mimīyās, mímīyāt ; IPV. mimīhí, mímātu ; mimītám, mimītā́m ; Ā. mimīṣva ; mímāthām ; PT. mímāna. IPF. ámimīthās, ámimīta. PF. mamátur ; mamúr ; mamé (1. 3.) ; mamā́te ; mamiré ; AO. root : IPV. māhí ; māsvá ; PT. mā́na (TS.) ; s : ámāsi ; SB. mā́sātai (AV.). PS. AO. ámāyi ; PP. mitá ; GDV. méya (AV.). GD. mitvā́ ; -mā́ya. INF. -mé, -mái.

2. mā *bellow*, III. P. : PR. mímāti ; mimanti. PF. mimā́ya ; SB. mīmayat. PPF. ámīmet. INF. mā́tavái. INT. PT. mémyat.

mi *fix*, V. P. : PR. minómi, minóti ; SB. minávāma ; INJ. minván ; IPV. minótu. IPF. minván. PF. mimā́ya ; mimyúr. PS. mīyáte ; PT. mīyámāna ; PP. mitá. GD. -mitya (B.).

mikṣ *mix* : PF. mimikṣáthur, mimikṣátur ; mimikṣé ; mimikṣiré. IPV. mimikṣvá. CS. mekṣáyati (B.).

mith *alternate*, I. : PR. méthāmasi ; Ā. méthete. VI. P. : PT. mithánt. PF. mimétha. PP. mithitá.

miś *mix* : DS. mímikṣati ; IPV. mímikṣa ; mímikṣatam, mímikṣatām.

miṣ *wink*, VI. P. : PR. miṣáti ; miṣánti ; PT. miṣánt. INF. -míṣas.

mih *shed water*, I. : PR. méhati ; PT. méhant ; méghamāna.

AO. sa: **ámikṣat** (B.). FT. **mekṣyáti.** PP. **mīḍhá.** INF. **mihé.** CS. **meháyati.** INT. **mémihat** (B.).

mī *damage,* IX.: PR. **minā́mi, minā́ti; minīmási, minánti;** SB. **minat; minā́ma;** INJ. **minīt** (AV.); **minan;** PT. **minánt; minānā́.** IPF. **áminās, áminat; áminanta.** IV. Ā.: PR. **mī́yase, mī́yate;** OP. **mīyeta** (B.). PF. **mimā́ya; mīmaya** (AV.). AO. s: INJ. **meṣi, meṣṭhās, meṣṭa.** PS. **mīyáte;** AO. **ámāyi** (B.); PP. **mītá.** INF. **métos** (B.); **-míyam, -míye.** INT. PT. **mémyāna.**

mīv *push,* I. P.: PR. **mī́vati;** PT. **mī́vant.** PP. **-mūta; mīvitá** (B.). GD. **mī́vya** (B.).

muc *release,* VI.: PR. **muñcáti, -te;** SB. **muñcā́si, muñcā́t;** IPV. **muñcátu;** Ā. **muñcátām;** PT. **muñcánt; muñcámāna.** IPF. **ámuñcat;** Ā. **ámuñcata.** IV. Ā.: PR. **múcyase;** SB. **múcyātai** (AV.). PF. **mumucmáhe, mumucré;** SB. **mumucas; múmocati, múmocat, mumucat;** IPV. **mumugdhí, mumóktu;** 2. du. **mumuktám, mumócatam; mumócata;** PT. **mumucāná.** PPF. **ámumuktam.** AO. root: **ámok; ámuktam;** Ā. **ámugdhvam;** PRC. **mucīṣṭa;** a: **mucás, ámucat;** SB. **mucā́ti; mucā́te;** INJ. **mucás, mucát;** IPV. **mucá;** Ā. **mucádhvam;** s: **ámauk** (B.); Ā. **ámukṣi, ámukthās;** INJ. **mauk** (VS.); Ā. **mukṣata** (3. pl.); OP. **mukṣīya.** FT. **mokṣyáti, -te** (B.). PS. **mucyáte;** AO. **ámoci;** INJ. **móci;** PP. **muktá.** GD. **muktvā́** (B.); **-múcya.** INF. **moktum** (B.). DS. **múmukṣati, -te; mókṣate** (B.); PT. **múmukṣamāṇa.**

mud *be merry,* I. Ā.: PR. **módate.** PF. **mumóda.** AO. root: OP. **mudīmáhi;** iṣ: PRC. Ā. **modiṣīṣṭhās.** PS. AO. **ámodi.** INF. **mudé.** CS. **modáyati, -te** (B.); DS. **múmodayiṣati** (B.).

muṣ *steal,* IX. P.: PR. **muṣṇā́ti;** PT. **muṣṇánt;** IPF. **ámuṣṇās, ámuṣṇāt; ámuṣṇītam.** I. P.: PR. **móṣatha.** AO. iṣ: INJ. **móṣīs.** PP. **muṣitá.** GD. **-múṣya.** INF. **muṣé.**

muh *be dazed,* IV. P.: PR. **múhyati.** PF. **mumóha** (B.). AO. a: **ámuhat** (B.); red.: **ámūmuhat.** FT. **mohiṣyáti** (B.). PP. **mugdhá; mūḍhá** (AV.). INF. **muhé.** CS. **moháyati;** GD. **mohayitvā́.**

mūrch, mūr *thicken*, I. P.: IPF. **ámūrchat.** PP. **mūrtá** (B.). CS. **mūrcháyati** (B.).

1. **mṛ** *die*, I.: PR. **márati, márate; márāmahe;** SB. **márāti; márāma;** Ā. **márai.** PF. **mamā́ra; mamrúr;** PT. **mamṛvā́ṃs.** AO. root: **ámṛta;** INJ. **mṛthā́s;** OP. **murīyá;** red.: **ámīmarat** (B.). FT. **mariṣyáti** (AV.). PS. **mriyáte;** PP. **mṛtá.** GD. **mṛtvā́** (B.). CS. **māráyati.**

2. **mṛ** *crush*, IX. P.: IPV. **mṛṇīhí;** PT. **mṛṇánt.** PS. **mūryáte** (B.); PP. **mūrṇá** (AV.). INT. IPV. **marmartu.**

mṛc *injure*: AO. s: PRC. **mṛkṣīṣṭá.** PP. **mṛktá.** CS. **marcáyati;** SB. **marcáyāt.**

mṛj *wipe*, II.: PR. **mā́rṣṭi; mṛjánti; mṛjé; mṛjmáhe;** IPV. **mā́rṣṭu;** Ā. **mṛkṣvá; mṛḍḍhvám;** PT. **mṛjāná;** IPF. **mṛṣṭá** (3. s. Ā.); **ámṛjata.** VII.: OP. **mṛñjyā́t** (B.); IPV. **mṛṇájāni** (B.); IPF. **mṛñjáta** (3. pl.). PF. **mamā́rja; māmṛjúr; mamṛjé** and **māmṛjé;** OP. **māmṛjītá.** AO. sa: **ámṛkṣat; ámṛkṣāma;** Ā. **ámṛkṣanta;** IPV. **mṛkṣatam;** red.: **ámīmṛjanta** (B.); s: **ámārkṣīt** (B.); iṣ: **ámārjīt** (B.). FT. **mrakṣyáte** (B.), **mārkṣyáte** (B.); **mraṣṭā́** (B.). PS. **mṛjyáte;** PP. **mṛṣṭá;** GDV. **márjya.** GD. **mṛṣṭvā́; mārjitvā́** (B.); **-mṛ́jya.** INF. **-mṛ́jas** (B.). CS. **marjáyati, -te; mārjáyati, -te** (B.). INT. **marmṛjyáte; marīmṛjyáte** (B.); SB. **mármṛjat; mármṛjanta;** PT. **mármṛjat; mármṛjāna** and **marmṛjāná; marmṛjyámāna;** IPF. **marmṛjmá, marmṛjata.**

mṛḍ *be gracious*, VI.: PR. **mṛḍáti; mṛḍáte** (B.); SB. **mṛḷā́ti** and **mṛḷā́t;** IPV. **mṛḷá** and **mṛḍátāt** (AV.), **mṛḷátu.** PF. OP. **mamṛḍyúr.** CS. **mṛḍáyati.**

mṛṇ *crush*, VI. P.: PR. **mṛṇáti;** INJ. **mṛṇát;** IPV. **mṛṇá.** IPF. **ámṛṇat.** AO. root: **mṛṇyúr** (K.); red.: **ámīmṛṇan.**

mṛd *crush*: AO. PRC. **mṛdyā́sam** (B.); FT. **mardiṣyáte** (B.). PS. **mṛdyáte** (B.); PP. **mṛditá.** GD. **-mṛ́dya** (B.). INF. **márditos** (B.).

mṛdh *neglect*, I. P.: PR. **márdhati.** VI.: PR. SB. **mṛdhā́ti.** AO. root: OP. **mṛdhyā́s;** iṣ: SB. **márdhiṣat;** INJ. **márdhīs; mardhiṣṭam.** PP. **mṛddhá.**

mṛś *touch*, VI.: PR. **mṛśáti, -te.** PF. **māmṛśúr; mamṛśé** (B.). AO. sa: **ámṛkṣat;** INJ. **mṛkṣas; mṛkṣata** (2. pl.). PP. **mṛṣṭá.** GD. **-mṛ́śya.** INF. **-mṛ́śe.** CS. **marśáyati** (B.). INT. SB. **mármṛśat;** IND. **marīmṛśyáte** (B.).

mṛṣ *not heed*, IV.: PR. **mṛ́ṣyate.** PF. **mamárṣa.** AO. root: INJ. **mṛṣṭhā́s;** a: INJ. **mṛṣánta;** red.: INJ. **mīmṛṣas;** iṣ: INJ. **marṣiṣṭhās.** INF. **-mṛ́ṣe.**

med *be fat*, IV. P.: IPV. **médyantu.** VI. Ā.: IPV. **medátām** (3. s.). CS. **medáyati.**

myakṣ *be situated*, I. P.: IPV. **myákṣa.** PF. **mimyákṣa; mimikṣúr;** Ā. **mimikṣiré.** AO. root: **ámyak;** PS. **ámyakṣi.**

mrad *crush*, I.: PR. **mrádate;** IPV. **mráda.** FT. **mradiṣyáti, -te.** INF. **-mrade** (B.). CS. **mradáyati.**

mruc, mluc *set*, I. P.: PR. **mrócati; mlócati** (B.); PT. **mrócant.** PF. **mumlóca** (B.). AO. a: **ámrucat** (B.). PP. **mruktá** (B.); **mluktá.** INF. **mrúca.**

mlā *relax*, IV. P.: PR. **mlā́yati** (B.). PP. **mlātá; mlāná** (B.). CS. **mlāpáyati.**

yaj *sacrifice*, I.: PR. **yájati, -te;** SB. **yájāti, -te;** OP. **yájeta;** IPV. **yájatu; yájantām;** PT. **yájant; yájamāna.** IPF. **áyajat; áyajanta.** PF. **ījé** (1. 3. s.), **yejé** (3. s.); **ījā́the ījiré;** PT. **ījāná.** AO. root: IPV. **yákṣva;** red.: **áyīyajat** (B.); s: **áyās, áyāṭ;** s: **áyākṣīt;** Ā. **áyaṣṭa** (3. s.); SB. **yákṣat;** du. 2. **yákṣatas,** 3. **yákṣatām;** Ā. **yákṣate;** INJ. **yā́ṭ** (2. s.); Ā. **yákṣi** (1. s.); OP. **yakṣīyá;** sa: IPV. **yakṣatām** (3. du.). FT. **yakṣyáte; yakṣyáti** (B.); **yaṣṭā́** (B.). PP. **iṣṭá.** GD. **iṣṭvā́.** INF. **yájadhyai; yajádhyai** (TS.); **yáṣṭave; yáṣṭum.** CS. **yājáyati** (B.). DS. **íyakṣati, -te;** SB. **íyakṣān;** PT. **íyakṣant; íyakṣamāṇa.**

yat *stretch*, I.: PR. **yátati, -te;** SB. Ā. **yátaite** (3. du.); OP. **yátema; yátemahi;** IPV. **yátatam;** Ā. **yátasva; yátantām;** PT. **yátant; yátamāna.** PF. **yetiré.** AO. root: PT. **yatāná** and **yátāna;** iṣ: **áyatiṣṭa** (B.). FT. **yatiṣyáte** (B.). PP. **yattá.** GD. **-yátya** (B.). CS. **yātáyati, -te;** PS. **yātyáte** (B.).

yam *stretch out,* I.: PR. yáchati, -te; SB. yáchāt; OP. yáchet; IPV. yácha and yáchatāt, yáchatu. IPF. áyachat; Ā. áyachathās. PF. yayántha, yayā́ma; yemáthur, yemátur; yemimá, yemá, yemúr; Ā. yemé (3. s.); yemā́te; yemiré; PT. yemānā́. AO. root: yamam; áyamur; SB. yámas, yámati and yámat; yáman; Ā. yámase, yámate; OP. yamīmáhi; PRC. yamyā́s (3. s.); IPV. yandhí; yantam; yanta and yantana; a: OP. yamet; s: áyāṃsam, áyān (3. s.); Ā. áyāṃsi (B.), áyaṃsta; áyaṃsata; SB. yáṃsat; yáṃsatas; yáṃsan; Ā. yáṃsate; INJ. Ā. yaṃsi; PT. yamasānā́; iṣ: yámiṣṭa (3. s. Ā.). FT. yaṃsyáti (B.). PS. yamyáte; AO. áyāmi (B.); PP. yatá; GDV. yaṃsénya. GD. -yátya. INF. yámitavái, yántave; yámam; yántum (B.). CS. yāmáyati; yamáyati (B.). DS. yíyaṃsati (B.). INT. yáṃyamīti.

yas *be heated,* III. P.: IPV. yáyastu. IV. P.: PR. yásyati. PP. yastá; yasitá (B.).

yā *go,* II. P.: PR. yā́ti; yā́nti; OP. yāyā́m; IPV. yāhí, yā́tu; yātám; yātá and yātána, yā́ntu; PT. yā́nt. IPF. áyās, áyāt; áyātam; áyāma, áyātana, áyur (B.). PF. yayā́tha, yayáu; yayáthur; yayá, yayúr; PT. yayivā́ṃs. AO. s: áyāsam; áyāsur; SB. yā́sat; INJ. yeṣam; siṣ: áyāsiṣam, áyāsīt; áyāsiṣṭām; áyāsiṣṭa, áyāsiṣur; SB. yā́siṣat; PRC. Ā. yāsiṣīṣṭhās; IPV. yāsiṣṭam; yāsiṣṭa. FT. yāsyáti. PP. yātá. GD. yātvā́ (B.); -yā́ya (B.). INF. yā́tave, yā́tavái (B.); -yái. CS. yāpáyati (B.).

yāc *ask,* I.: PR. yā́cati, -te. PF. yayā́ce (B.). AO. iṣ: áyācīt; áyāciṣṭa (B.); SB. yā́ciṣat; Ā. yā́ciṣāmahe. FT. yāciṣyáte. PP. yācitá; yācitvā́ and yā́cya (B.). INF. yācitum. CS. yācáyati.

1. yu *unite,* VI.: PR. yuváti, -te. II. yáuti; Ā. yuté; SB. yávan; IPV. yutā́m (3. s. Ā.); PT. yuvānā́. PF. yuyuvé. PER. FT. yuvitā́ (B.). PP. yutá. GD. -yū́ya. DS. yúyūṣati. INT. yoyuvé; PT. yóyuvat (AV.); yóyuvāna.

2. yu *separate,* III.: PR. yuyóti; SB. yuyávat; INJ. yuyo-

thā́s, yuyota; OP. **yuyuyā́tām**; IPV. **yuyodhi, yuyótu**; **yuyutám** and **yuyótam**; **yuyóta** and **yuyótana**. I. P.: PR. **yúchati**; IPV. **yúchantu**; PT. **yúchant**. AO. root: SB. **yávanta**; OP. **yuyā́t** (B.); 3. du. **yūyā́tām** (B.); PRC. **yūyā́s** (3. s.); red.: INJ. **yūyot**; s: **yóṣati** and **yóṣat**; **yóṣatas**; INJ. **yūṣam** (AV.); **yáus** (2. s.); **yauṣṭam**; **yauṣma, yauṣṭa, yauṣur**; Ā. **yoṣṭhās** (B.); iṣ: INJ. **yā́vīs**. PS. AO. **áyāvi**; PP. **yutá**. INF. **yótave, yótavái**; **yótos**. CS. **yāváyati**; **yaváyati**. INT. PT. **yóyuvat**; IPF. **áyoyavīt**; PF. **yoyāva**.

yuj *join*, VII.: **yunákti**; **yuñjánti**; **yuṅkté**; **yuñjáte**; SB. **yunájat**; **yunájan**; Ā. **yunájate** (3. s.); INJ. **yuñjáta** (3. pl.); IPV. **yuṅdhí, yunáktu**; **yunákta, yuñjántu**; Ā. **yuṅkṣvá, yuṅtā́m**; 2. du. **yuñjā́thām**; **yuṅgdhvám**; PT. **yuñjánt**; **yuñjāná**; IPF. **áyunak** and **ā́yunak**; **ā́yuñjan**; Ā. **áyuñjata** (3. pl.). PF. **yuyója**; **yuyujmá**; Ā. **yuyujé**; **yuyujré**; SB. Ā. **yuyójate** (3. s.); PT. **yuyujāná**. AO. root: Ā. **áyuji, áyukthās, áyukta**; **áyujmahi, áyugdhvam, yújata** and **áyujran**; SB. **yójate**; INJ. **yójam**; Ā. **yukta** (3. s.); OP. **yujyāva, yujyā́tam**; IPV. **yukṣvá**; PT. **yujāná**; s.: **áyukṣi**; **áyukṣātām** (3. du.); **áyukṣata** (3. pl.). FT. **yokṣyáti** (B.); **yokṣyáte**; **yoktā́** (B.). PS. **yujyáte**; AO. **áyoji**; INJ. **yóji**; PP. **yuktá**. GD. **yuktvā́, yuktvā́ya**. INF. **yujé**; **yóktum** (B.).

yudh *fight*, IV.: PR. **yúdhyati, -te**; SB. **yúdhyai**. IV.: IPV. **yúdhya**; PT. **yúdhyant**; **yúdhyamāna**; IPF. **áyudhyas, áyudhyat**. I. P.: PR. **yódhanti** (AV.). II. P. **yótsi** (= IPV.). PF. **yuyódha**; **yuyudhúr**; Ā. **yuyudhā́te** (3. du.). AO. root: SB. **yódhat**; IPV. **yódhi**; PT. **yodhāná**; iṣ: **áyodhīt**; SB. **yódhiṣat**; INJ. **yódhīs**; IPV. **yodhiṣṭam**. FT. **yotsyáti, -te** (B.). PP. **yuddhá**. GDV. **yódhya, yudhénya**. GD. **-yuddhvī́**. INF. **yudhé, yudháye**; **yúdham**. CS. **yodháyati**. DS. **yúyutsati, -te**.

yup *obstruct*: PF. **yuyópa**; **yuyopimá**. AO. red.: **áyūyupan** (B.). PP. **yupitá**. CS. **yopáyati**. INT. **yoyupyáte** (B.).

yeṣ *be heated*, I. P.: PR. **yéṣati**; PT. **yéṣant.**

raṃh *hasten*, I.: PR. **ráṃhate**; PT. **ráṃhamāṇa.** IPF. **áraṃhas**; Ā. **áraṃhata** (3. s.). PF. PT. **rārahāṇá.** CS. **raṃháyati, -te.**

rakṣ *protect*, I.: PR. **rákṣati, -te.** PF. **rarákṣa**; PT. **rārakṣāṇá.** AO. iṣ: **árakṣīt**; **árākṣīt** (B.); SB. **rákṣiṣas, rákṣiṣat.** PP. **rakṣitá.** CS. **rakṣáyate** (B.).

raj *colour*, IV.: IPF. **árajyata.** PP. **raktá** (B.). CS. **rajáyati.** INT. **rárajīti.**

rad *dig*, I.: PR. **rádati, -te**; INJ. **rádat**; IPV. **ráda**; **rádantu**; Ā. **rádantām** (3. pl.); PT. **rádant.** IPF. **áradat, rádat.** II. P.: **rátsi** (= IPV.). PF. **raráda.** PP. **raditá.**

radh, randh *make subject*, IV. P.: IPV. **rádhya, rádhyatu.** PF. **rāradhúr.** AO. root: IPV. **randhí** (= **randdhí**); a: SB. **rádhāma**; INJ. **rádham**; red.: SB. **rīradhā**; INJ. **rīradhas, rīradhat**; **rīradhatam**; **rīradhata**; iṣ: INJ. **rándhīs.** PP. **raddhá.** CS. **randháyati**; SB. **randháyāsi.**

ran *rejoice*, I.: PR. **ráṇati**; INJ. **ráṇanta**; IPV. **ráṇa.** IV. P.: PR. **ráṇyasi, ráṇyati**; **ráṇyathas**; **ráṇyanti.** PF. **rāráṇa** (1. s.); SB. **rāráṇas, rāráṇat**; **raráṇatā** (2. pl.). INJ. **rārán** (3. s.); IPV. **rārandhí**; **rāranta** (2. pl.), **rārántu.** PPF. **árāraṇur.** AO. iṣ: **árāṇiṣur**; INJ. **ráṇiṣṭana.** CS. **raṇáyati.**

rap *chatter*, I. P.: PR. **rápati**; INJ. **rápat**; OP. **rápema.** IPF. **árapat.** INT. **rárapīti.**

rapś *be full*, I. Ā.: **rápśate**; **rápśante.** PF. **rarapśé.**

rabh, rambh *grasp*, I.: PR. **rábhate.** PF. **rarabhmá**; Ā. **rārabhé**; **rebhiré**; PT. **rebhāṇá.** AO. s: 3. s. Ā. **árabdha**; PT. **rabhasāná.** PP. **rabdhá.** GD. **-rábhya.** INF. **-rábham**; **-rábhe.** CS. **rambháyati, -te** (B.). DS. **rípsate** (B.).

ram *rejoice*, I. Ā.: PR. **rámate.** IX. P.: IPF. **áramṇās, áramṇāt.** AO. red.: **árīramat**; SB. **rīramāma**; INJ. **rīraman**; s: Ā. **áraṃsta** (3. s.); **áraṃsata** (3. pl.); INJ. **raṃsthā́s**; siṣ: INJ. **raṃsiṣam.** FT. **raṃsyáte**; **-ti** (B.). PP. **ratá** (B.). GD. **ratvā́** (B.). INF. **rántos** (B.). CS. **ramáyati** and **rāmáyati.**

1. **rā** *give*, III.: IPV. **rirīhi**; Ā. **rarāsva** (AV.); **rarāthām** (3. du.); **rarīdhvam**; SB. **rárate**; PT. **rárāṇa**. II.: PR. **rā́si** (=IPV.); **rāté** (B.); PF. **rarimá**; **raré** (1. s.), **rariṣé**; **rarā́the**; PT. **rarivā́ṃs**; **rarāṇá**. AO. root: **árādhvam**; IPV. **rā́sva**; s: **árāsma**; **árāsata** (3. pl.); SB. **rā́sat**; **rā́san**; Ā. **rā́sate** (3. s.); OP. **rāsīyá**; IPV. Ā. **rāsatām** (3. s.); **rāsāthām** (2. du.); **rāsantām** (3. pl.); PP. **rātá**.

2. **rā** *bark*, IV. P.: PR. **rā́yasi**; IPV. **rā́ya**; PT. **rā́yant**.

rāj *rule*, I. P.: PR. **rā́jati**. II. P.: PR. **rā́ṣṭi**; INJ. **rā́ṭ**. AO. iṣ: **árājiṣur**. INF. **rājáse**. CS. **rājáyati** (B.), **-te**.

rādh *succeed*, IV. Ā.: IPV. **rā́dhyatām**; PT. **rā́dhyamāna**. V. P.: PR. **rādhnóti** (B.). PF. **rarā́dha**. AO. root: **árādham** (B.); SB. **rādhat** and **rādhati**; **rādhāma**; PRC. **rādhyā́sam**; **rādhyā́sma**; red.: **árīradhat** (B.); s: **árātsīs**; iṣ: INJ. **rādhiṣi** (1. s.). FT. **rātsyáti**. PS. AO. **árādhi**; PP. **rāddhá**; GDV. **rā́dhya**. GD. **rāddhvā́** (B.). **-rādhya** (B.). INF. **irádhyai**. CS. **rādháyati**.

ri *flow*, IX.: PR. **riṇā́ti**; **riṇīthás**; **riṇánti**; Ā. **riṇīté**; **riṇáte**; INJ. **riṇā́s**; **riṇán**; PT. **riṇánt**; **riṇāná**. IPF. **riṇā́s**, **áriṇāt**; **áriṇītam**; **áriṇīta**. IV.: PR. **rī́yate**; **rī́yante**; PT. **rī́yamāṇa**.

ric *leave*, VII. P.: PR. **riṇákti**; SB. **riṇácāva**; INJ. **riṇák** (3. s.). IPF. **áriṇak** (2. s.); **riṇák** (3. s.). PF. **riréca**; **riricáthur**; Ā. **ririkṣé**, **riricé**; **riricā́the**; **riricré**; OP. **riricyā́m**, **riricyā́t**; PT. **ririkvā́ṃs**; **riricāná**. PPF. **árirecīt**. AO. root: INJ. Ā. **rikthā́s**; IPV. **riktám**; s: **ā́raik** (3. s.); Ā. **árikṣi**; red.: **árīricat** (B.). FT. **rekṣyáte** (B.). PS. **ricyáte**; IPF. **áricyata**; AO. **áreci**; PP. **riktá**. CS. **recáyati** (B.).

rip *smear*: PF. **riripúr**. PP. **riptá**. Cp. **lip**.

ribh *sing*, I. P.: PR. **rébhati**; **rébhanti**; PT. **rébhant**. IPF. **rébhat**. PF. **rirébha**. PS. **ribhyáte**.

riś *tear*, VI.: PR. **riśā́mahe**; IPV. **riśántām**; PT. **riśánt**. PP. **riṣṭá**.

riṣ *be hurt*, IV.: PR. **ríṣyati**; SB. **ríṣyās**, **ríṣyāti** and **ríṣyāt**; OP. **ríṣyet**; **ríṣyema**. I. P.: SB. **réṣāt**; INJ. **réṣat**. AO.

a : **áriṣan** ; SB. **riṣāma, riṣātha** and **riṣāthana** ; PT. **ríṣant** and **riṣánt** ; red. : INJ. **rīriṣas, rīriṣat** ; **rīriṣata** (2. pl.) ; OP. **rīriṣes** ; PRC. Ā. **rīriṣīṣṭa** and **ririṣīṣṭa** (3. s.). PP. **riṣṭá.** INF. **riṣé** ; **riṣás.** CS. **reṣáyati** ; INF. **riṣayádhyai.** DS. **ríriksati.**

rih *lick*, II. : PR. **réḍhi** ; **rihánti** ; 3. pl. **riháte** and **rihaté** ; PT. **rihánt** ; **ríhāṇa** (VS.) and **rihāṇá.** PF. PT. **ririhvā́ṃs.** PP. **rīḍhá.** INT. **rerihyáte** ; PT. **rérihat** ; **rérihāṇa.** Cp. **lih.**

1. ru *cry*, VI. P. : PR. **ruváti** ; INJ. **ruvát** ; IPV. **ruvá** ; PT. **ruvánt.** II. (B.) **ráuti** ; **ruvánti.** PF. **ruruviré** (B.). AO. iṣ : **árāvīt** ; **árāviṣur.** PP. **rutá.** INT. **róravīti** ; PT. **róruvat** ; **róruvāṇa** (B.) ; IPF. **ároravīt.**

2. ru *break* : AO. iṣ : **rā́viṣam.** PP. **rutá.** INT. PT. **róruvat.**

ruc *shine*, I. : PR. **rócate.** PF. **ruróca** ; **rurucúr** ; **rurucé** (3. s.) ; INJ. **rurucanta** ; OP. **rurucyā́s** ; PT. **rurukvā́ṃs** ; **rurucāná.** AO. root : PT. **rucāná** ; red. : **árūrucat** ; Ā. **árūrucata** (3. s., B.) ; iṣ : Ā. **árociṣṭa** (3. s.) ; OP. **ruciṣīyá** (AV.) and **rociṣīyá** (B.). PS. AO. **ároci.** PP. **rucitá** (B.). INF. **rucé.** CS. **rocáyati** ; **-te** (B.). INT. PT. **rórucāna.**

ruj *break*, I. P. : PR. **rujáti.** PF. **rurójitha, rurója.** AO. root : INJ. **rók** ; red. : **árūrujatam** (2. du.). PP. **rugṇá.** GD. **ruktvā́** (B.) ; **-rújya** (B.). INF. **-rúje.**

rud *weep*, II. P. : PR. **róditi** ; **rudánti** ; SB. **ródāt** (Kh.) ; PT. **rudánt.** IPF. **árodīt** (B.). AO. a : **árudat.** CS. **rodáyati.**

1. rudh *obstruct*, VII. : PR. **ruṇádhmi, ruṇáddhi** ; Ā. **rundhé** (= **runddhé**) ; **rundhate** (3. pl.) ; SB. Ā. **ruṇádhāmahai** ; IPV. **rundhí** (= **runddhí**) ; Ā. **rundhām** (= **runddhām,** 3. s.) ; PT. **rundhāná** ; IPF. Ā. **árundhata** (3. pl.). PF. **rurṓdhitha** ; Ā. **rurudhré.** AO. root : **árodham** ; **árudhma** ; a : **árudhat** ; **árudhan** ; INJ. **rudhát** ; PT. **rudhánt** ; s : **áraut** ; **árautsīt** (B.) ; Ā. **árutsi** (B.), **áruddha** (B.). FT. **rotsyáti, -te** (B.). PS. **rudhyáte** ; PP. **ruddhá.** GD. **-rúdhya.** INF. **-rúdham, rúndham** (B.), **-ródham** (B.) ; **róddhos** (B.). DS. **rúrutsate** (B.).

2. rudh *grow*, I. P.: PR. ródhati; INJ. ródhat.
rup *break*, IV. P.: PR. rúpyati (B.). AO. red.: árūrupat. PP. rupitá. CS. ropáyati (B.).
ruh *ascend*, I.: PR. róhati, -te. PF. ruróhitha, ruróha; ruruhúr. AO. root: PT. rúhāṇa; a: áruham, áruhas, áruhat; áruhāma, áruhan; SB. ruhā́va; INJ. ruham, rúhat; OP. ruhéma; IPV. ruhá; ruhátam; sa: rukṣás, árukṣat; árukṣāma. FT. rokṣyáti (B.). PP. rūḍhá. GD. rūḍhvā́, -rúhya. INF. -rúham; róhiṣyai (TS.); róḍhum (B.). CS. roháyati; -te (B.); ropáyati (B.). DS. rúrukṣati.
rej *tremble*, I.: PR. réjati, -te; INJ. réjat; réjanta (3. pl.); PT. réjamāna; IPF. árejetām (3. du.); árejanta. CS. rejáyati.
lap *prate*, I. P.: PR. lápati; PT. lápant. FT. lapiṣyáti (B.). PP. lapitá. CS. lāpáyati; -te (B.). INT. lā́lapīti.
labh *take*, I. Ā.: PR. lábhate. PF. lebhiré; PT. lebhāná. AO. s (B.): Ā. álabdha; álapsata. FT. lapsyáti, -te (B.). PS. labhyáte (B.); PP. labdhá. GD. labdhvā́; -lábhya (B.). CS. lambháyati, -te (B.). DS. lípsate; lī́psate (B.); PS. lipsyáte (B.).
likh *scratch*, VI.: PR. likháti; -te (B.). PF. lilékha (B.). AO. red.: álīlikhat (B.); iṣ: INJ. lékhīs. PP. likhitá. GD. -líkhya (B.).
lip *smear*, VI. P.: PR. limpáti. PF. lilépa, lilipúr (B.). AO. s: álipsata (3. pl.). PS. lipyáte (B.); PP. liptá. GD. -lípya (B.).
lih *lick*, II.: PR. léḍhi (B.). CS. leháyati. INT. PP. lelihitá (B.).
lī *cling*, I. Ā.: PR. láyate; IPV. láyantām. PF. lilyé (B.); lilyúr; -layāṃ cakre. AO. s: áleṣṭa (B.). PP. līná. CS. lāpáyati (B.). INT. lelā́yati; PF. lelā́ya.
lup *break*, VI. P.: PR. lumpáti; OP. lumpét. PS. lupyáte; PP. luptá. GD. -lúpya. CS. lopáyati, -te (B.).
lubh *desire*, IV. P.: PR. lúbhyati. AO. red.: álūlubhat (B.). PP. lubdhá (B.). CS. lobháyati; DS. lúlobhayiṣati (B.).

lū *cut* (B.), IX. P.: PR. lunā́ti. V. P.: PR. lunóti. PP. lūná.

vakṣ *increase* (= 2. ukṣ): PF. vavákṣitha, vavákṣa; vavakṣátur; vavakṣúr; Ā. vavakṣé; vavakṣiré. PPF. vavákṣat. CS. vakṣáyati.

vac *speak*, III. P.: PR. vívakmi, vívakti; IPV. vívaktana. PF. uváktha, uvā́ca and vavā́ca; ūcimá, ūcúr; Ā. ucişé; PT. ūcāná. AO. root: PRC. ucyā́sam (B.); red.: ávocat; SB. vócā, vócāsi, vócāti and vócati; vócāma; Ā. vócāvahai; INJ. vócam, vócas, vócat; vócan; Ā. vóce; vócanta; OP. vocéyam, vocés, vocét; vocétam; vocéma, vocéyur; Ā. vocéya; vocémahi; IPV. vocatāt, vocatu; vocatam; vocata. FT. vakṣyáti; CO. ávakṣyat (B.); vaktā́ (B.). PS. ucyáte; AO. ávāci; PP. uktá; GDV. vā́cya. GD. uktvā́ (B.); -úcya (B.). INF. váktave; -vā́ce; váktum (B.); váktos (B.). CS. vācáyati (B.). DS. vívakṣati, -te (B.). INT. IPF. ávāvacīt.

vaj *be strong*; CS. *strengthen*: PR. vājáyāmas, -masi; Ā. vājáyate; IPV. vājáya; PT. vājáyant.

vañc *move crookedly*, I. P.: PR. váñcati. PF. vāvakré. PS. vacyáte.

vat *apprehend*, I.: PR. OP. vátema; PT. vátant. AO. red.: ávīvatan. CS. vātáyati.

vad *speak*, I.: PR. vádati, -te; SB. vádāni, vádāsi and vádās, vádāti; vádāthas; vádāma, vádān; INJ. vádat; OP. vádet; Ā. vádeta; IPV. váda, vádatu; Ā. vádasva; vádadhvam; PT. vádant. IPF. ávadan; Ā. ávadanta. PF. ūdimá; ūdé (B.). AO. root: PRC. udyā́sam (B.); iṣ: ávādiṣam; ávādiṣur; Ā. ávādiran (AV.); SB. vā́diṣas; INJ. vā́diṣur. FT. vadiṣyáti; -te (B.). PS. udyáte; PP. uditá. GD. -udya (B.). INF. váditum (B.): váditos (B.). CS. vādáyati, -te (B.); PS. vādyáte (B.). DS. vívadiṣati (B.). INT. vā́vadīti; IPV. vāvadītu; PT. vā́vadat; Ā. vāvadyáte (B.).

vadh *slay*, I. P.: OP. vádheyam, vádhet; IPV. vádha. AO. root: PRC. vadhyā́sam; OP. vadhyā́t (B.); iṣ: á-

vadhiṣam and **vádhīm, ávadhīs, ávadhīt** and **vádhīt; ávadhiṣma**; SB. **vádhiṣas**; INJ. **vádhīs, vádhīt; vadhiṣṭa** and **vadhiṣṭana** (2. pl.), **vadhiṣur**; Ā. **vadhiṣṭhās**; IPV. **vadhiṣṭam** (2. du.).

van *win*, VIII.: PR. **vanósi, vanóti; vanuthás**; Ā. **vanvé, vanuté**; SB. **vanávat**; Ā. **vanávase**; INJ. **vanvan**; OP. **vanuyā́ma**; IPV. **vanvántu**; Ā. **vanuṣvá, vanutā́m; vanudhvám, vanvátām**; PT. **vanvánt; vanvāná**; IPF. **ávanos; ávanvan**; Ā. **ávanvata.** VI. and I.: PR. **vanáti** and **vánati**; Ā. **vanase, vánate**; SB. **vanā́ti; vánās; vánāva**; Ā. **vánāmahai**; INJ. **vanas**; Ā. **vanta** (= **vananta**); OP. **vanés; vanéma; vanémahi**; IPV. **vánatam; vanata**; Ā. **vanatām** (3. s.). PF. **vāvántha, vāvā́na; vavanmá**; Ā. **vavné**; SB. **vāvánat**; IPV. **vāvandhí**; PT. **vavanvā́ṃs.** AO. root: **váṃsva**; SB. **váṃsat; váṃsāma**; Ā. **váṃsate**; INJ. **váṃsi**; OP. **vaṃsīmáhi** and **vasīmáhi**; iṣ: SB. **vániṣat**; Ā. **vániṣanta.** PRC. **vaniṣīṣṭá**; siṣ: OP. **vaṃsiṣīyá.** PP. **-vāta.** INF. **-vantave.** CS. **vānáyantu.** DS. **vívāsati**; SB. **vívāsāt.**

vand *greet*, I. Ā.: PR. **vándate.** PF. **vavánda; vavandimá**; Ā. **vavandé; vavandiré.** AO. iṣ: OP. **vandiṣīmáhi.** PS. AO. **vándi**; PP. **vanditá**; GDV. **vándya.** INF. **vandádhyai.**

vap *strew*, I.: PR. **vápati, -te.** PF. **ūpáthur**; Ā. **ūpiṣé, ūpé** (3. s.). AO. s: **ávāpsīt** (B.). FT. **vapsyáti** (B.). PS. **upyáte**; AO. **vā́pi**; PP. **uptá.** GD. **-úpya.** CS. **vāpáyati** (B.).

vam *vomit*, II.: SB. **váman.** IPF. **ávamīt; ávamat** (B.). PF. **uvā́ma** (B.). AO. s: **ávān** (B.). PP. **vāntá** (B.).

valg *leap*, I. P.: PR. **válganti.** IPF. **ávalgata** (2. pl.). PT. **válgant.**

vaś *desire*, II.: PR. **váśmi, vákṣi, váṣṭi; uśmási** and **śmási, uśánti**; IPV. **váṣṭu**; PT. **uśánt; uśāná.** I. P.: PR. **váśanti**; SB. **váśāma**; INJ. **váśat**; IPF. **ávaśat.** III. P.: PR. **vavákṣi; vivaṣṭi**; IPV. **vivaṣṭu.** PF. **vāvaśúr**; Ā. **vāvaśé**; PT. **vāvaśāná.**

1. **vas** *shine*, VI. P.: PR. **ucháti**; SB. **uchā́t**; **uchā́n**; INJ. **uchát**; OP. **uchét**; IPV. **uchá, uchátu**; **ucháta, uchántu**; PT. **uchánt**; IPF. **áuchas áuchat.** PF. **uvā́sa**; **ūṣā́** (2. pl.), **ūṣúr**; PT. f. **ūṣúṣī** (TS.). AO. root: **ā́vas** (2. 3. s.); Ā. **ávasran**; s: **ávāt** (3. s.). CO. **ávatsyat** (B.). PP. **uṣṭá.** INF. **vástave.** CS. **vāsáyati.**

2. **vas** *wear*, II. Ā.: PR. **váste**; **vásāthe**; **vásate** (3. pl.); INJ. **vásta** (3. s.); **vásata** (3. pl.); OP. **vasīmahi**; IPV. **vásiṣva, vástām** (3. s.); **vásāthām** (TS.); PT. **vásāna**; IPF. **ávasthās**; **ávasta.** PF. **vāvasé**; PT. **vāvasāná.** AO. iṣ: **ávasiṣṭa** (3. s.). CS. **vāsáyati, -te**; FT. **vāsayiṣyáte.**

3. **vas** *dwell*, I.: PR. **vásati**; **vásate** (B.). PF. **ūṣátur**; **ūṣimá**; PT. **ūṣivā́ṃs**; **vāvasāná.** PER. **-vāsāṃ cakre** (B.). AO. root: **vásāna**; red.: **ávīvasat**; s: **ávātsīs.** FT. **vatsyáti** (B.). GD. **uṣitvā́** (B.); **-úṣya** (B.). DS. **vívatsati** (B.). CS. **vāsáyati, -te**; PS. **vāsyáte** (B.).

vah *carry*, I.: PR. **váhati, -te.** PF. **uvā́ha**; **ūháthur, ūhátur**; **ūhúr**; Ā. **ūhiṣé**; **ūhiré.** AO. root: OP. **uhītá**; IPV. **voḷhám** (2. du.), **voḷhā́m**; Ā. **voḍhvám**; PT. **úhāna**; s: **ávāṭ, vā́ṭ**; **ávākṣur**; SB. **vákṣas, vákṣati** and **vákṣat**; **vákṣathas, vákṣatas**; **vákṣan**; INJ. **vā́kṣīt.** FT. **vakṣyáti**; **voḍhā́** (B.). PS. **uhyáte**; PP. **ūḍhá.** GD. **ūḍhvā́** (B.); **-úhya.** INF. **vóḍhum**; **vóḍhave, vóḍhavái** (B.); **-vā́he**; **váhadhyai.** CS. **vāháyati** (B.); INT. **vanīvāhyáte** (B.).

1. **vā** *blow*, II. P.: PR. **vā́mi, vā́ti**; **vātás**; **vā́nti**; IPV. **vāhí, vā́tu**; PT. **vā́nt**; IPF. **ávāt.** IV. P.: PR. **vā́yati**; **vā́yatas**; **vā́yanti.** PF. **vaváu** (B.). AO. siṣ: **ávāsīt** (B.). CS. **vāpáyati.**

2. **vā** *weave*, IV.: PR. **váyati**; **váyate** (B.); IPV. **váya**; **váyata**; PT. **váyant**; IPF. **ávayat**; **ávayan.** PF. **ūvúr.** FT. **vayiṣyáti.** PS. **ūyáte** (B.); PP. **utá.** INF. **ótum**; **ótave, ótavái**; **vā́tave** (AV.).

vājayá *desire booty*, den.: PR. PT. **vājayánt.**

vāñch *desire*, I. P.: IPV. **vā́ñchantu.**

vāś *bellow*, I. P.: PR. **vā́śati.** IV. Ā.: PR. **vā́śyate.** PF. **vavāśiré** and **vāvaśré**; PT. **vāvaśāná.** PPF. **ávāvaśītām** (3. du.); **ávāvaśanta.** AO. red.: **ávīvaśat**; **ávīvaśan**; Ā. **ávīvaśanta**; iṣ: Ā. **ávāśiṣṭhās** (B.). INT. PT. **vā́vaśat.** CS. **vāśáyati.**

vic *sift*, VII. P.: PR. **viñcánti**; IPV. **vináktu**; PT. **viñcánt**; IPF. **ávinak.** III. P.: PR. **víveksi.** PF. PT. **vivikvā́ṃs.** PS. **vicyáte**; PP. **viktá** (B.).

vij *tremble*, VI.: PR. **vijánte**; IPV. **vijántām**; PT. **vijámāna**; IPF. **ávije.** PF. **vivijré.** AO. root: INJ. Ā. **vikthā́s, viktá**; red.: INJ. **vīvijas.** PS. **viktá.** CS. **vejáyati** (B.). INT. **vevijyáte**; PT. **vévijāna.**

1. **vid** *know*, II. P.: PR. **vidmás**; SB. **védas, védati** and **védat**; **védathas**; OP. **vidyā́m, vidyā́t**; **vidyā́tam**; **vidyā́ma, vidyúr**; IPV. **viddhí** and **vittā́t, véttu**; **vittám.** IPF. **ávedam, ávet** and **vét**; **ávidur** (B.). PF. **véda** (1. 3.), **véttha**; **vidáthur**; **vidmá, vidá, vidúr**; Ā. **vidmáhe** (B.), **vidré**; PER. **vidā́m cakāra** (B.); PT. **vidvā́ṃs.** AO. iṣ: **ávedīt** (B.); PER. **vidām akran** (B.). FT. **vediṣyáti, -te** (B.); **veditā́** (B.). PP. **viditá.** GD. **viditvā́.** INF. **vidmáne**; **véditum** (B.); **véditos** (B.). CS. **vedáyati, -te.** DS. **vívidiṣati** (B.).

2. **vid** *find*, VI.: PR. **vindáti, -te.** II. **vitsé, vidé** (3. s.); **vidré**; IPV. **viddhí**; Ā. 3. s. **vidām** (AV.); PT. **vídāna** and **vidāná.** PF. **vivéditha, vivéda**; **vividáthur**; **vividúr**; Ā. **vividé, vivitsé**; **vividré** and **vividriré**; SB. **vividat**; PT. **vividvā́ṃs.** AO. a: **ávidam, ávidas, ávidat**; **ávidāma, ávidan**; Ā. **ávidanta**; SB. **vidā́s, vidā́t**; **vidāthas**; **vidātha**; INJ. **vidám, vidás, vidát**; **vidán**; Ā. **vidáta** (3. s.); **vidánta**; OP. **vidéyam, vidét**; **vidéma**; Ā. **vidéya**; PRC. **videṣṭa** (AV.); IPV. **vidátam**; PT. **vidánt**; s: Ā. **ávitsi.** FT. **vetsyáti, -te** (B.). PS. **vidyáte**; AO. **ávedi, védi**; PP. **vittá**; **vinná.** GDV. **vidā́yya.** GD. **vittvā́, -vídya** (B.). INF. **vidé, véttave**; **véttos** (B.). DS. **vívitsati** (B.). INT. SB. **vévidāma.** PT. **vévidat**; **vévidāna.**

vidh *worship*, VI.: SB. **vidhā́ti**; INJ. **vidhát**; **vidhán**; Ā. **vidhánta**; OP. **vidhéma**; **vidhémahi**; PT. **vidhánt**; IPF. **ávidhat**.

vip *tremble*, I.: PR. **vépate**; PT. **vépamāna**; IPF. **ávepanta**. PF. **vivipré**. AO. root: PT. **vipāná**; red.: **ávīvipat**; iṣ: **ávepiṣṭa** (B.). CS. **vepáyati**, **vipáyati**.

viś *enter*, VI.: PR. **viśáti**, **-te**. PF. **vivéśa** (1. 3.), **vivéśitha**; **viviśúr** and (once) **viveśur**; Ā. **viviśré**; OP. **viviśyā́s**; PT. **viviśivā́ṃs** (TS.), **-viśivā́ṃs** (AV.). PPF. **áviveśīs**. AO. root: Ā. **áviśran**; s: **ávikṣmahi**, **ávikṣata** (3 pl.); iṣ: INJ. **véśīt**; sa: **ávikṣat** (B.). FT. **vekṣyáti** (B.). PP. **viṣṭá**. GD. **-víśya**. INF. **-víśam**; **véṣṭavái** (B.). CS. **veśáyati**, **-te**.

viṣ *be active*, III.: PR. **víveksi**, **víveṣṭi**; **viviṣṭás**; **viviṣmás**; SB. **víveṣas**; IPV. **viviḍḍhí**; IPF. **áviveś** and **vivés** (2. s.), **vivés** (3. s.). I. P.: PT. **véṣant**; IPF. **áveṣan**. PF. **vivéṣa**; **viviṣúr**. PPF. **áviveṣīs**. AO. iṣ: **véṣiṣas**. FT. **vekṣyáti**, **-te** (B.). PS. **viṣyáte** (B.); PP. **viṣṭá**. GD. **viṣṭvī́**; **-víṣya**. INF. **-víṣe**. INT. **véveṣmi**; **veviṣyáte** (B.); OP. **veviṣyāt**; PT. **véviṣat**; **véviṣāṇa**.

viṣṭ, **veṣṭ** *wrap*, I. P.: IPV. **véṣṭatām** (3. du.). PP. **viṣṭitá**. CS. **veṣṭáyati**, **-te** (B.).

vī *enjoy*, II.: **vémi**, **véṣi**, **véti**; **vīthás**; **vyánti**; SB. **váyati**; INJ. **vés**; IPV. **vīhí**, **vihí** and **vītā́t**, **vétu**; **vītám**; **vyántu**; PT. **vyánt**; **vyāná**. IPF. **ávyan**. PF. **vivā́ya**; **vivyé**. AO. s.: SB. **véṣat**. PS. **vīyáte**. PP. **vītá**. INF. **vītáye**. INT. **véveti**; **vevīyáte**.

vīḍ *make strong*: CS. SB. **vīḷáyāsi**; IPV. **vīḷáyasva**. PP. **vīḷitá**.

1. **vṛ** *cover*, V.: PR. **vṛṇóti**; Ā. **vṛṇvé**; **vṛṇváte** and **vṛṇvaté**; PT. **vṛṇvánt**; IPF. **ávṛṇos**, **ávṛṇot**; Ā. **ávṛṇvata** (3. pl.); PR. **ūrṇómi**, **ūrṇóti**; **ūrṇuthás**, **ūrṇutás**; Ā. **ūrṇuṣé**, **ūrṇuté**; INJ. **ū́rṇot**; IPV. **ūrṇuhí** and **ūrṇú**, **ūrṇótu**; **ūrṇutá**, **ūrṇuvántu**; Ā. **ūrṇuṣvá**; PT. **ūrṇuvánt**; **ūrṇvāná**; IPF. **áurṇos**, **áurṇot**. I.: PR. **várathas**; Ā. **várate**; **várethe**; **várante**; SB. **várāte**; INJ. **váranta**.

IX.: IPF. ávṛṇīdhvam (AV.). PF. vavártha, vavā́ra; vavrúr; Ā. vavré; PT. vavṛvā́ṃs. PPF. ávāvarīt. AO. root: vám (= váram), ā́var and vár (2. 3. s.); ávran; Ā. ávṛta; INJ. vár (2. 3. s.); vrán; IPV. vṛdhí; vartam; varta; vrāṇá; red.: ávīvaran; Ā. ávīvarata (3. s.); s: SB. várṣathas; iṣ: ávārīt (B.). PS. AO. ávāri; PP. vṛtá. GD. vṛtvā́, vṛtvī́; vṛtvā́ya; -vṛ́tya. INF. vártave. CS. vāráyati, -te; DS. vívārayiṣate (B.). INT. ávarīvar.

2. vṛ *choose*, IX. Ā.: PR. vṛṇé, vṛṇīsé, vṛṇīté; vṛṇīmáhe, vṛṇáte; INJ. vṛṇītá (3. s.); OP. vṛṇītá; IPV. vṛṇīṣvá; vṛṇīdhvám, vṛṇátām; PT. vṛṇāná; IPF. ávṛṇi, ávṛṇīta; ávṛṇīmahi. PF. vavṛṣé; vavṛmáhe. AO. root: ávri, ávṛta; SB. váras, várat; váranta; INJ. vṛtá (3. s.); OP. vurītá (3. s.); PT. urāṇá; s: ávṛṣi; ávṛḍhvam (B.), ávṛṣata. FT. variṣyáte (B.). PP. vṛtá. GDV. vā́rya; váreṇya.

vṛj *twist*, VII.: PR. vṛṇákṣi, vṛṇákti; vṛñjánti; Ā. vṛñjé, vṛṅkté; vṛñjā́te; vṛñjáte; SB. vṛṇájan; IPV. vṛṅdhí, vṛṇáktu; vṛṅktá, vṛñjántu; Ā. vṛṅkṣvá. IPF. ávṛṇak (2. 3. s.); ávṛñjan. PF. vavṛjúr; Ā. vāvṛjé; OP. vavṛjyúr; IPV. vavṛktám (2. du.); PT. f. vavarjúṣ-ī; (á-)varjuṣī (AV.). AO. root: várk (2. 3. s.), ávṛk (AV.); ávṛjan; Ā. ávṛkta; SB. várjati; várjate; INJ. várk; OP. vṛjyā́m; vṛjyā́ma; PRC. vṛjyā́s (3. s.); IPV. varktam (2. du.); s: ávārkṣīs (B.); Ā. ávṛkṣmahi; INJ. Ā. vṛkṣi; sa: ávṛkṣam. FT. varkṣyáti, -te (B.). PS. vṛjyáte; PP. vṛktá. GD. vṛktvī́; -vṛ́jya. INF. -vṛ́je; vṛjádhyai; vṛñjáse. CS. varjáyati. DS. vívṛkṣate (B.). INT. PT. várīvṛjat; CS. PT. varīvarjáyant (AV.).

vṛt *turn*, I. Ā.: vártate. PF. vavárta and vāvárta; vāvṛtúr; Ā. vāvṛté; SB. vavártati, vavártat and vavṛtat; OP. vavṛtyā́m, vavṛtyā́s, vavṛtyā́t; IPV. vavṛttána (2. pl.); PT. vavṛtvā́ṃs. PPF. ávavṛtran; Ā. ávavṛtranta. AO. root: ávart; Ā. ávṛtran; SB. vártat; IPV. varta (= vartta, 2. pl.); a: ávṛtat; red.: ávīvṛtat; s: Ā. ávṛtsata. FT. vartsyáti; vartitā (B.). CO. ávartsyat (B.). PP. vṛttá. GD. -vṛ́tya. INF. -vṛ́te; -vṛ́tas (B.). CS.

vartáyati, -te; PS. **vartyáte** (B.); INF. **vartayádhyai.** DS. **vívṛtsati**; **-te** (B.). INT. **várvarti** (= **várvartti**) and **varīvarti** (= **varīvartti**); **várvṛtati** (3. pl.); Ā. **varīvṛtyáte** (B.); IPF. **ávarīvar** (3. s.); **ávarīvur** (3. pl.).

vṛdh *grow*, I.: PR. **várdhati, -te.** PF. **vavárdha**; **vāvṛdhátur**; **vāvṛdhúr**; Ā. **vāvṛdhé**; **vāvṛdháte**; SB. **vāvṛdhāti**; Ā. **vāvṛdhate**; OP. **vāvṛdhīthā́s**; IPV. **vāvṛdhásva**; PT. **vāvṛdhvā́ṃs**; Ā. **vāvṛdhāná.** PPF. **vāvṛdhanta.** AO. **a**: **ávṛdham, ávṛdhat**; **vṛdhāma, ávṛdhan**; PT. **vṛdhánt**; **vṛdhāná**; red.: **ávīvṛdhat**; **ávīvṛdhan**; Ā. **ávīvṛdhadhvam, ávīvṛdhanta**; **s**: PT. **vṛdhasāná**; **iṣ**: OP. **vardhiṣīmáhi.** PP. **vṛddhá.** INF. **vṛdhé**; **vṛdháse**; **vāvṛdhádhyai** (PF.). CS. **vardháyati, -te.** INT. GDV. **vāvṛdhénya.**

vṛṣ *rain*, I. P.: PR. **várṣati**; IPV. **várṣantu**; PT. **várṣant.** VI. Ā.: **vṛṣásva**; **vṛṣéthām** (2. du.). PF. IPV. **vāvṛ́ṣasva**; PT. **vāvṛṣāṇá.** AO. **s**: **ávarṣīs, ávarṣīt.** FT. **varṣiṣyáti** (B.); **vraṣṭā́** (MS.). PP. **vṛṣṭá.** GD. **vṛṣṭvī́**; **vṛ́ṣṭvā́** (B.); **-várṣṭos** (B.). CS. **varṣáyati.**

vṛh *tear*, VI. P.: PR. **vṛháti**; INJ. **vṛhát**; OP. **vṛhéva**; IPV. **vṛhá** and **vṛhátāt**; **vṛhátam**; **vṛháta**; IPF. **ávṛhas.** PF. **vavárha.** AO. **sa**: **ávṛkṣat** (B.). PS. **vṛhyáte** (B.); AO. **várhi**; PP. **vṛḍhá** (B.). GD. **-vṛ́hya.** INF. **-vṛhas.**

ven *long*, I. P.: PR. **vénati**; INJ. **vénas**; IPV. **vénatam** (2. du.); PT. **vénant.** IPF. **ávenat.**

vyac *extend*, III. P.: PR. **viviktás** (3. du.); INJ. **vivyak** (3. s.). IPF. **ávivyak**; **áviviktām** (3. du.); **ávivyacur.** PF. **vivyáktha, vivyā́ca.** PPF. **vivyácat**; Ā. **vivyacanta.**

vyath *waver*, I.: PR. **vyáthate.** AO. red.: **vivyathas** (B.); **iṣ**: SB. **vyáthiṣat**; INJ. **vyáthiṣṭhās**; **vyáthiṣmahi.** PP. **vyathitá.** INF. **vyathiṣyai** (B.). CS. **vyatháyati**; AO. **vyathayīs** (AV.).

vyadh *pierce*, IV. P.: PR. **vídhyati.** PF. **vivyā́dha** (B.); PT. **vividhvā́ṃs.** AO. **s**: **vyā́tsīs** (B.). PP. **viddhá.** INF. **-vídhe.** CS. **vyādháyati** (B.). DS. **vívyatsati** (B.).

vyā *envelope*, IV.: PR. **vyáyati, -te**; OP. **vyáyeyam**; IPV.

vyáyasva; PT. **vyáyant**. IPF. **ávyayam, ávyayat**. PF. **vivyathúr**; Ā. **vivyé**; PT. **vivyāná**; PER. PF. **-vyayā́ṃ cakāra** (B.). AO. a: **ávyat**; **ávyata** (2. pl.); Ā. **ávyata** (3. s.) and **vyáta**. PS. **vīyáte** (B.); PP. **vītá**. GD. **-vī́ya** (B.).

vraj *proceed*, I. P.: IPV. **vrájata** (2. pl.); PT. **vrájant**. PF. **vavrā́ja**. AO. iṣ: **ávrājīt** (B.). FT. **vrajiṣyáti** (B.). PP. **vrajitá** (B.). GD. **-vrájya** (B.). CS. **vrājáyati** (B.).

vraśc *cut up*, VI. P.: PR. **vṛścáti**; SB. **vṛścā́t**; INJ. **vṛścás**; IV.: **vṛścá, vṛścátu**; PT. **vṛścánt**. IPF. **ávṛścat** and **vṛścát**. PS. **vṛścyáte**; PP. **vṛkṇá**. GD. **vṛṣṭvā́**; **vṛktvī́**.

śaṃs *praise*, I.: PR. **śáṃsati, -te**. PF. **śaśáṃsa** (B.); **śaśaṃsé** (B.). AO. root: IPV. **śastá** (2. pl.); iṣ: **áśaṃsiṣam, áśaṃsīt**; SB. **śáṃsiṣas, śáṃsiṣat**; INJ. **śáṃsiṣam**. FT. **śaṃsiṣyáti** (B.). PS. **śasyáte**; AO. **śáṃsi**; PP. **śastá**; GDV. **śáṃsya**; **śaṃstavya** (B.). GD. **śastvā́** (B.). INF. **-śáse**.

śak *be able*, V. P.: PR. **śaknómi, śaknóti**; **śaknuvánti**; SB. **śaknávāma**. IPF. **áśaknuvan**. PF. **śaśā́ka**; **śekimá, śeká, śekúr**. AO. root: SB. **śákas, śákat**; OP. **śakyā́m**; IPV. **śagdhí, śaktám**; a: **áśakam, áśakat**; **áśakan**; INJ. **śakan**; OP. **śakéyam**; **śakéma**. FT. **śakṣyáti, -te** (B.). INF. **śáktave**. DS. **śíkṣati, -te**.

1. **śad** *prevail*: PF. **śāśadúr**; Ā. **śāśadmáhe, śāśádré**; PT. **śā́śadāna**.

2. **śad** *fall*: PF. **śaśā́da** (B.); **śedúr** (B.). FT. **śatsyáti**.

śap *curse*, I.: PR. **śápati**; **śápate** (AV.); SB. **śápātas** (3. du.); PT. **śápant**. IPF. **áśapata** (2. pl.). PF. **śaśā́pa**; **śepé** (1. 3. s.), **śepiṣé**. AO. s: INJ. **śāpta** (2. pl.). PP. **śaptá** (B.). CS. **śāpáyati**.

1. **śam, śim** *labour*, IV. P.: **śámyati** (B.); **śímyati**; IPV. **śímyantu**; PT. **śímyant**. PF. **śaśamé**; SB. **śaśámate** (3. s.); PT. **śaśamāná**. AO. iṣ: Ā. **áśamiṣṭhās, áśamiṣṭa**. PP. **śamitá** (B.).

2. **śam**, *be quiet*, IV. (B.): PR. **śā́myati, -te**. PF. **śaśā́ma** (B.); **śemúr** (B.). AO. a: **áśamat** (B.); red.: **áśīśamat**. PP. **śāntá**. CS. **śamáyati**.

śā *sharpen*, III. : PR. **śíśāmi, śíśāti ; śiśīmási ;** Ā. **śíśīte ;** IPV. **śiśīhí, śíśātu ; śiśītám, śiśītā́m ; śiśītá** (2. pl.) ; PT. **śíśāna.** IPF. **śiśās, áśiśāt ;** Ā. **śiśīta** (3. s.). PF. PT. **-śaśāná.** PP. **śitá.** GD. **-śā́ya.**

śās *order*, II. : **śā́smi, śāssi ;** Ā. **śāsté ; śāsmáhe, śāsáte ;** SB. **śā́san ;** IPV. **śādhí ; śāstána, śāsátu ;** PT. **śā́sat ; śā́sāna.** IPF. **áśāsam ;** Ā. **áśāsata** (3. pl.). PF. **śaśā́sa ; śaśāsúr ;** INJ. **śaśā́s ;** IPV. **śaśādhí.** AO. root : SB. **śā́sas ;** a : Ā. **śiṣāmahi ;** INJ. **śíṣat ;** PT. **śiṣánt.** PP. **śiṣṭá ;** GD. **-śíṣya** (B.).

śikṣ (= DS. of **śak**) *be helpful* : PR. **śíkṣati, -te ;** SB. **śíkṣās, śíkṣāt ; śíkṣān ;** INJ. **śíkṣat ;** OP. **śíkṣeyam ; śíkṣema ;** IPV. **śíkṣa, śíkṣatu ; śíkṣatam ;** PT. **śíkṣant ;** Ā. **śíkṣamāṇa.** IPF. **áśikṣas ; áśikṣatam.**

śiṣ *leave*, VII. P. : PR. **śináṣṭi** (B.). PF. **śiśiṣé** (B.). AO. a : **śiṣas.** FT. **śekṣyáti, -te** (B.). PS. **śiṣyáte ;** AO. **śéṣi ;** PP. **śiṣṭá.** GD. **-śiṣya** (B.).

śī *lie*, II. Ā. : PR. **śéṣe, śáye** (3. s.) ; **śáyāte** (3. du.) ; **śémahe, śére** and **śérate ;** OP. **śáyīya, śáyīta** (3. s.) ; IPV. 3. s. **śétām** and **śáyām** (AV.) ; PT. **śáyāna ;** IPF. **áśeran.** I. : PR. **śáyate ; śáyadhve, śáyante ;** IPF. **áśayat ; áśāyatam ;** Ā. **áśāyata** (3. s.). PF. **śiśyé** (B.) ; **śiśyiré** (B.) ; PT. **śaśayāná.** AO. s : SB. **śéṣan ;** iṣ : Ā. **áśayiṣṭhās.** FT. **śayiṣyáti, -te** (B.) ; **śayitā́se** (B.). INF. **śayádhyai.**

śuc *gleam*, I. : PR. **śócati, -te.** PF. **śuśóca ;** OP. Ā. **śuśucītá** (3. s.) ; IPV. **śuśugdhí ;** PT. **śuśukvā́ṃs ; śuśucāná.** AO. a : **áśucat ;** PT. **śucánt ;** Ā. **śucámāna ;** red. : **śūśucas ;** INJ. **śūśucas ; śūśucan ;** iṣ : INJ. **śócīs ;** PS. **áśoci.** INF. **śucádhyai.** CS. **śocáyati ;** PT. **śucáyant.** INT. SB. **śóśucan ;** Ā. **śóśucanta ;** PT. **śóśucat ; śóśucāna.**

śudh, śundh *purify*, I. P. : PR. **śúndhati ;** IPV. **śúndhata** (2. pl.). IV. P. : PR. **śúdhyati** (B.). PP. **śuddhá.** CS. **śundháyati ; śodháyati** (B.).

śubh, śumbh *beautify*, I. Ā. : PR. **śóbhate ;** PT. **śóbhamāna ; śúmbhate ;** PT. **śúmbhamāna ;** VI. P. : PR. **śumbháti ;** SB. **śumbhā́ti ;** IPV. **śumbhá ; śumbháta, śumbhántu ;**

PT. **śumbhámāna.** AO. root: PT. **śubhāná; śúmbhāna;** red.: **áśūśubhan; áśūśubhanta** (B.). PP. **śumbhitá; śubhitá** (B.). INF. **śubhé; śobháse; śúbham.** CS. **śubháyati, -te; śobháyati.**

śuṣ *dry,* IV. P.: PR. **śúṣyati;** IPV. **śúṣya, śúṣyatu; śúṣyantu.** GD. **-śúṣya** (B.). CS. **śoṣáyati.**

śū, śvā *swell,* IV. P.: PR. PT. **śváyant.** PF. **śūśuvúr;** Ā. **śūśuvé;** SB. **śūśuvat; śūśávāma;** OP. **śūśuyā́ma;** PT. **śūśuvā́ṃs;** Ā. **śū́śuvāna.** AO. a: **áśvat** (B.); s: PT. **śavasāná.** INF. **śūṣáṇi; śváyitum** (B.).

śṛdh *be defiant,* I.: PR. **śárdhati; śárdhate** (B.); INJ. **śárdhat;** IPV. **śárdha;** PT. **śárdhant.** CS. **śardháyati.**

śṝ *crush,* IX.: PR. **śṛṇā́mi, śṛṇā́si, śṛṇā́ti; śṛṇīmási;** IPV. **śṛṇīhí, śṛṇā́tu; śṛṇītám; śṛṇántu;** PT. **śṛṇāná.** IPF. **áśṛṇāt.** PF. **śaśré.** AO. iṣ: **áśarīt.** FT. **śariṣyáte** (B.). PS. **śīryáte;** AO. **śā́ri;** PP. **śīrṇá; -śīrta.** GD. **-śī́rya** (B.). INF. **śárītos.**

śnath *pierce,* II. P.: SB. **śnáthat;** IPV. **śnathihi.** AO. red.: **śiśnatham, áśiśnat** and **śiśnáthat;** INJ. **śiśnathas;** iṣ: IPV. **śnathiṣṭam; śnathiṣṭana.** PP. **śnathitá.** INF. **-śnáthas.** CS. **śnatháyati, -te.**

śyā *coagulate,* IV.: PR. **śyā́yati** (B.). PS. **śīyáte** (B.); PP. **śītá; śīná.** CS. **śyāyáyati** (B.).

śrath *slacken,* IX.: PR. **śrathnīté;** PT. **śrathnāná.** IPF. **śrathnās; áśrathnan.** PF. **śaśrathé.** AO. red.: **śiśráthas, śiśráthat;** IPV. **śiśrathantu.** PP. **śṛthitá.** CS. **śratháyati, -te.**

śram *be weary,* IV. P.: PR. **śrā́myati.** PF. **śaśramúr;** PT. **śaśramāṇá.** AO. a: **áśramat;** INJ. **śramat;** iṣ: Ā. **áśramiṣṭhās;** INJ. **śramiṣma.** PP. **śrāntá.** GD. **-śrámya** (B.).

śrā (śrī, śṛ) *boil,* IX.: PR. **śrīṇánti; śrīṇīṣé;** IPV. **śrīṇīhí; śrīṇītá** and **śrīṇītána;** PT. **śrīṇánt;** Ā. **śrīṇāná.** IPF. Ā. **áśrīṇīta** (3. s.). PP. **śrātá; śṛtá.** CS. **śrapáyati;** PS. **śrapyáte** (B.); AO. **áśiśrapat** (B.).

śri *resort,* I.: PR. **śráyati; -te.** PF. 1. **śiśráya,** 3. **śiśrā́ya;**

Ā. **śiśriyé**; OP. **śiśrītá** (3. s.); PT. **śiśriyāṇá**. PPF. **áśiśret**; **áśiśrayur**. AO. root: **áśres, áśret**; **áśriyan**; red.: **áśiśriyat**; s: **áśrait** (AV.). FT. **śrayiṣyáti, -te** (B.). PS. **śrīyáte** (B.); PP. **śritá**; AO. **áśrāyi**. INF. **śráyitavái** (B.). CS. **śrāpáyati** (VS.).

śriṣ *clasp*, I.: SB. **śréṣāma**. AO. a: INJ. **śriṣát**. INF. **-śríṣas**.

śrī *mix*, IX.: PR. **śrīṇā́ti**; **śrīṇīté**. PP. **śrītá**. INF. **śriyáse**.

śru *hear*, V.: PR. **śṛṇómi, śṛṇóti**; **śṛṇvánti**; Ā. **śṛṇviṣé, śṛṇuté** and **śṛṇvé**; **śṛṇviré**; SB. **śṛṇávas, śṛṇávat**; **śṛṇávāma, śṛṇávan**; OP. **śṛṇuyā́t**; **śṛṇuyā́ma**; IPV. **śṛṇudhí, śṛṇuhí** and **śṛṇú, śṛṇótu**; **śṛṇutám**; **śṛṇutá** and **śṛṇóta, śṛṇótana, śṛṇvántu**; **śṛṇuṣvá**; PT. **śṛṇvánt**; IPF. **áśṛṇavam, áśṛṇos**; **áśṛṇvan**. PF. 1. **śuśráva**, 3. **śuśrā́va**; Ā. **śuśruvé** (3. s.); SB. **śuśravat**; OP. **śuśrūyā́s**; **śuśrūyā́tam**; PT. **śuśruvā́ṃs**. PPF. **áśuśravur**; Ā. **áśuśravi** (1. s.). AO. root: **áśravam, áśrot**; **áśravan** (AV.); SB. **śrávat**; **śrávathas, śrávatas**; PRC. **śrūyā́sam, śrūyā́s** (3. s.); IPV. **śrudhí, śrótu**; **śrutám**; **śrutá** and **śróta, śruvántu**; a: INJ. **śrúvat**; red.: **áśuśravat**; **áśuśruvat** (B.); s: **áśrauṣīt** (B.). FT. **śroṣyáti** (B.). PS. **śrūyáte**; AO. **áśrāvi, śrā́vi**; PP. **śrutá**; GDV. **śrútya**; **śravā́yya**. GD. **śrutvā́**; **-śrútya**. CS. **śraváyati, śrāváyati**. DS. **śúśrūṣate**.

śruṣ *hear*, I.: INJ. **śróṣan**; IPV. **śróṣantu**; PT. **śróṣamāṇa**.

śvañc *spread*, I. Ā.: IPV. **śváñcasva**; PT. **śváñcamāna**. PF. Ā. SB. **śaśvacái**. CS. **śvañcáyas**.

śvas *blow*, II.: PR. **śvásiti**; Ā. **śuṣé**; IPV. **śvasihí**; PT. **śvasánt** and **śuṣánt**; Ā. **śuṣāṇá**; IPF. **áśvasīt** (B.). I.: PR. **śvásati, -te** (AV.). PP. **śvasitá** (B.). INF. **-śvásas**. CS. **śvāsáyati**. INT. PT. **śā́śvasat**.

śvit *be bright*: AO. root: **áśvitan**; PT. **śvitāná**; red.: **áśiśvitat**; s: **áśvait**.

ṣṭhīv *spew*, I. P.: PR. **ṣṭhī́vati**. IPF. **áṣṭhīvan**. PF. **tiṣṭhéva** (B.). PP. **ṣṭhyūtá** (B.).

sagh *be equal to*, V. P.: IPF. **ásaghnos.** AO. root: SB. **sághat**; PRC. **saghyā́sam** (B.).

sac *accompany*, I. Ā.: PR. **sácate.** III.: PR. **síṣakṣi**; **síṣakti**; **sáścati** (3. pl.); INJ. Ā. **saścata** (3. pl.); IPV. **siṣaktu**; **siṣakta**; PT. **sáścat** and **saścát.** I.: PR. **sáścasi**; Ā. **sáśce** (1. s.); INJ. **sáścat**; IPV. **sáścata** (2. pl.); IPF. **ásaścatam** (2. du.). PF. **saścimá, saścúr**; Ā. **saściré**; **seciré** (AV.); PT. **saścivā́ṃs.** AO. root: IPV. **sákṣva**; PT. **sacānā́**; s: Ā. **ásakṣata** (3. pl.); SB. **sákṣat**; INJ. **sakṣata** (3. pl.); OP. **sakṣīmáhi.** INF. **sacádhyai**; **sakṣáṇi.**

saj, sañj, *hang*, I. P.: PR. **sájati.** IPF. **ásajat.** PF. **sasáñja** (B.); **sejúr** (B.). AO. s: Ā. **ásakta.** PS. **sajyáte** (B.); AO. **ásañji** (B.); PP. **saktá.** GD. **-sajya** (B.). INF. **sáṅktos** (B.). DS. **sísaṅkṣati** (B.).

sad *sit*, I. P.: PR. **sī́dati**; SB. **sī́dāti**; INJ. **sī́dan**; OP. **sī́dema**; IPV. **sī́datu**; PT. **sī́dant.** IPF. **ásīdat.** PF. **sasáttha, sasā́da**; **sedáthur, sedátur**; **sedimá, sedá, sedúr**; Ā. **sediré**; OP. **sasadyā́t**; PT. **sedúṣ-.** AO. a: **ásadat**; **ásadan**; INJ. **sádas, sádat**; OP. **sádema**; IPV **sáda, sádatu**; **sádatam, sádatām**; **sádata, sádantu**; Ā. **sádantām**; PT. **sádant**; red.: **ásīṣadan**; s: SB. **sátsat.** FT. **satsyáti** (B.). PS. **sadyáte** (B.); AO. **ásādi, sā́di**; PP. **sattá**; **sanná** (AV.); GDV. **sádya.** GD. **-sádya.** INF. **-sáde**; **-sádam**; **sáttum** (B.). CS. **sādáyati, -te**; PS. **sādyáte** (B.).

san *gain*, VIII. P.: PR. **sanóti**; SB. **sanávāni, sanávat**; **sanávatha**; OP. **sanuyā́m**; **sanuyā́ma**; IPV. **sanuhí, sanótu**; **sanvántu.** IPF. **ásanos, ásanot**; **ásanvan.** PF. **sasā́na**; PT. **sasavā́ṃs.** AO. a: **ásanam, ásanat**; **ásanāma, ásanan**; INJ. **sánam, sánat**; OP. **sanéyam, sanét**; IPV. **sána**; PT. **sánant**; iṣ: **ásāniṣam**; SB. **sániṣat**; Ā. **sániṣāmahe, sániṣanta**; IPV. **sániṣantu.** FT. **saniṣyáti.** PP. **sātá.** GDV. **sánitva.** INF. **sanáye**; **sātáye.** DS. **síṣāsati.** INT. Ā. **saniṣṇata** (3. pl.).

sap *serve*, I.: PR. **sápati, -te.** PF. **sepúr.** AO. red.: INJ. **sīṣapanta.**

saparyá *honour*, den.: PR. **saparyáti**; SB. **saparyā́t**; OP. **saparyéma**; IPV. **saparyá**; PT. **saparyánt.** IPF. **ásaparyan.** AO. **ásaparyait** (AV.). GDV. **saparyéṇya.**

sas *sleep*, II. P.: PR. **sásti**; **sastás**; IPV. **sástu**; **sastā́m**; **sasántu**; PT. **sasánt**; IPF. **ásastana.** III. P.: PR. **sásasti** and **sasásti.**

sah *prevail*, I.: PR. **sáhate**; PT. **sáhant** and **sā́hant**; Ā. **sáhamāna.** PF. **sāsā́ha**; Ā. **sasāhiṣé, sasāhé**; SB. **sāsáhas, sāsáhat**; OP. **sāsahyā́t**; **sāsahyā́ma**; PRC. Ā. **sāsahīṣṭhā́s**; PT. **sāsahvā́ṃs** and **sāhvā́ṃs**; Ā. **sāsahāná** and **sehāná.** AO. root: OP. **sahyā́s**; **sāhyā́ma**; PRC. **sahyās** (3. s.); PT. **sahāná**; s: **ásākṣi** and **sākṣi**; **sakṣmahi** (B.); SB. **sákṣati** and **sákṣat**; **sā́kṣāma**; Ā. **sā́kṣate**; OP. **sākṣīyá**; IPV. **sā́kṣva**; PT. **sákṣant**; Ā. **sahasāná**; iṣ: **ásahiṣṭa**; OP. **sahiṣīváhi**; **sahiṣīmáhi** and **sāhiṣīmáhi.** FT. **sakṣyáte** (B.). PP. **sāḍhá.** GD. **-sáhya.** INF. **sáhadhyai**; **-sáham** (B.). DS. **sī́kṣati, -te.**

sā *bind*, VI.: PR. **syáti, -te**; IPV. **syá, syátu**; **syátam, syátām**; Ā. **syásva**; **syádhvam.** IPF. **ásyat.** AO. root: **ásāt**; SB. **sā́t**; OP. **sīmáhi**; IPV. **sāhi**; a: OP. **sét** (VS.). PP. **sitá.** GD. **-sā́ya.** INF. **-sái**; **sā́tum** (B.).

sādh *succeed*, I.: PR. **sā́dhati, -te.** AO. red.: SB. **sīṣadhāti**; **sīṣadhāma**; INJ. **sīṣadhas.** CS. **sādháyati.**

si *bind*, IX. P.: PR. **sinā́ti**; **sinīthás**; IPV. **sinā́tu.** PF. **siṣā́ya**; INJ. **siṣet.** AO. root: IPV. **sitám.** INF. **sétave.**

sic *pour*, VI.: PR. **siñcáti, -te.** PF. **siṣéca**; **siṣicátur**; **sisicúr**; **sisicé.** AO. a: **ásicat**; **ásican**; SB. **sicāmahe.** FT. **sekṣyáti** (B.). PS. **sicyáte**; AO. **áseci** (B.); PP. **siktá.** GD. **siktvā́** (B.); **-sicya.** INF. **séktavái** (B.).

1. **sidh** *repel*, I. P.: PR. **sédhati.** PF. **siṣédha.** AO. iṣ: **ásedhīs.** PP. **siddhá** (B.). GD. **-sídhya.** INF. **séddhum** (B.). INT. PT. **séṣidhat.**

2. **sidh** *succeed*, IV. P.: PR. **sídhyati.** PP. **siddhá** (B.).

sīv *sew*, IV.: PR. IPV. **sī́vyatu**; Ā. **sī́vyadhvam**; PT. **sī́vyant.** PP. **syūtá.** GD. **-sī́vya.**

su *press*, V.: PR. **sunóti; sunutás; sunuthá, sunvánti;** Ā. **sunvé; sunviré;** SB. **sunávat; sunávāma;** Ā. **sunávai;** IPV. **sunú, sunótu; sunutá** and **sunóta, sunótana;** Ā. **sunudhvám;** PT. **sunvánt; sunvāná.** PF. **suṣā́va; suṣumá;** PT. **suṣuvā́ṃs; suṣvāṇá.** PPF. **ásuṣavur** and **ásuṣuvur** (B.). AO. root: IPV. **sótu; sutám; sóta, sótana;** PT. **suvāná, svāná.** FT. **saviṣyáti** (B.); **sotā́** (B.). PS. **sūyáte;** AO. **ásāvi;** PP. **sutá;** GDV. **sótva.** GD. **-sútya** (B.). INF. **sótave; sótos.**

sū *generate, impel*, VI. P.: PR. **suváti;** SB. **suvā́ti;** IPV. **suvá, suvátāt, suvátu; suvátām; suvántu;** PT. **suvánt;** IPF. **ásuvat.** II. Ā.: PR. **súve, sū́te; súvāte** (3. du.); **súvate** (3. pl.); INJ. **sū́ta** (3. s.); PT. **suvāná;** IPF. **ásūta.** PF. **sasū́va; suṣuvé.** PPF. **ásuṣot** (MS.); **ásuṣavur** (B.). AO. iṣ: **ásāvīt; ásāviṣur;** SB. **sā́viṣat;** INJ. **sā́vīs.** FT. **soṣyáti, -te** (B.); PT. **sū́ṣyant.** PS. **sūyáte;** PP. **sūtá.** GD. **sūtvā́** (B.); **-sútya** (B.). INF. **sū́tave, sū́tavái; sávitave.** INT. **sóṣavīti.**

sūd *put in order*: PF. **suṣūdimá;** SB. **súṣūdas, súṣūdat** and **súṣūdati; súṣūdatha;** IPV. **suṣūdáta** (2. pl.). AO. red.: **ásūṣudanta.** CS. **sūdáyati, -te;** SB. **sūdáyāti.**

sṛ *flow*, III.: PR. **sísarṣi, sísarti;** Ā. **sísrate** (3. pl.); IPV. **sisṛtám;** Ā. **sísratām** (3. pl.). PT. **sísrat.** PF. **sasā́ra; sasṛvá** (B.); **sasrúr;** Ā. **sasré; sasrā́the;** PT. **sasṛvā́ṃs; sasrāṇá.** AO. a: **ásaram, ásaras, ásarat; ásaran;** IPV. **sára;** s: SB. **sárṣat.** FT. **sariṣyáti.** PS. AO. **ăsāri** (B.); PP. **sṛtá** (B.). GD. **sṛtvā́** (B.); **sṛ́tya** (B.). INF. **sártave, sártavái.** CS. **sāráyati, -te.** DS. **sisīrṣati** (B.). INT. **sarsré** (3. s.); PT. **sársrāṇa.**

sṛj *emit*, VI.: PR. **sṛjáti, -te.** PF. **sasárja;** Ā. **sasṛjé; sasṛjmáhe, sasṛjriré;** OP. **sasṛjyā́t;** PT. **sasṛjāná.** PPF. **ásasṛgram** (3. pl.). AO. root: **ásṛgran, ásṛgram;** PT. **sṛjāná;** s: **srā́s** (2. s., AV.), **ásrāk** (3. s.), **ásrāṭ** (B.); **ásrāṣṭam** (2. du.); Ā. **ásṛkṣi, ásṛṣṭa; ásṛkṣmahi, ásṛkṣata;** SB. **srákṣat;** INJ. **srāṣṭam;** Ā. **sṛkṣāthām** (2. du.). FT. **srakṣyáti** (B.). PS. **sṛjyáte;** AO. **ásarji;** PP. **sṛṣṭá.**

GD. sṛṣṭvā; -sṛ́jya (B.). CS. sarjáyati, -te (B.). DS. sísṛkṣati, -te (B.).

sṛp *creep,* I. P.: PR. sárpati. PF. sasárpa (B.). AO. a: ásṛpat; INJ. sṛpat; s: Ā. ásṛpta (B.). FT. srapsyáti (B.) and sarpsyáti (B.). PP. sṛptá (B.). GD. sṛptvā́ (B.); -sṛ́pya. INF. sṛ́pas (B.). DS. sísṛpsati. INT. sarīsṛpyáte (B.).

sev *attend upon,* I. Ā.: PR. séve, sévate; IPV. sévasva.

skand *leap,* I. P.: PR. skándati; SB. skándāt; IPV. skánda; PT. skándant; IPF. áskandat. PF. caskánda. AO. root: skán (3. s.); s: áskān (B.) and áskāntsīt (B.). FT. skantsyáti (B.). PP. skanná. GD. -skándya (B.) and -skádya (B.). INF. -skáde, -skádas. CS. skandáyati. INT. SB. caniṣkadat; IPF. kániṣkan (3. s.).

skabh or skambh *prop,* IX.: PR. skabhnā́ti; PT. skabhnánt; Ā. skabhāna (B.). PF. cāskámbha; skambhátur; skambhúr; PT. caskabhāná. PP. skabhitá. GD. skabhitvī́. INF. -skábhe.

sku *tear,* II. P.: PR. skáuti (B.). V. P.: PR. skunóti. PS. skūyáte; PP. skutá. INT. coṣkūyáte.

stan *thunder,* II. P.: IPV. stanihi; INJ. stán (3. s.). I. P.: IPV. stána. AO. iṣ: ástānīt. CS. stanáyati. INT. IPV taṃstanīhi.

stabh or stambh *prop,* IX.: stabhnā́mi; IPV. stabhāná; IPF. ástabhnās, ástabhnāt. PF. tastámbha; tastabhúr; PT. tastabhvā́ṃs; tastabhāná. PPF. tastámbhat. AO. s: ástāmpsīt (B.); iṣ: ástambhīt, stámbhīt. PP. stabhitá; stabdhá (B.). GD. stabdhvā́, -stábhya (B.).

stu *praise,* II.: PR. stáumi (AV.); stóṣi, stáuti (AV.); stumási, stuvánti; Ā. stuṣé; SB. stávat; stávāma, stávatha; Ā. stávai; INJ. stáut; OP. Ā. stuvītá; stuvīmáhi; IPV. stuhí, stáutu; PT. stuvánt; stuvāná, stávāna and stavāná; IPF. ástaut. I. Ā.: stávate and stáve (3. s.); INJ. stávanta; OP. stáveta; PT. stávamāna. PF. tuṣṭā́va; tuṣṭuvúr; Ā. tuṣṭuvé; SB. tuṣṭávat; PT. tuṣṭuvā́ṃs; tuṣṭuvāná. PPF. átuṣṭavam. AO. s: ástauṣīt (B.); Ā. ástoṣi, ástoṣṭa; ástoḍhvam, ástoṣata; sb. stóṣāṇi, stóṣat; stóṣāma; inj. stóṣam; iṣ: ástāvīt (B.). ft. stoṣyáti, -te (B.); staviṣyáti, -te. co. ástoṣyat. ps. stūyáte; ao. ástāvi; pp. stutá; gdv. stuṣéyya. gd. stutvā́; -stútya (B.). inf. stavádhyai, stótave; stótum (B.). cs. stāváyati (B.).

stubh *praise*, I. P.: pr. stóbhati; ipv. stóbhata, stóbhantu; pt. stóbhant. II. Ā.: pt. stubhāná. pp. stubdhá (B.). cs. stobháyati.

stṝ *strew*, IX.: pr. stṛṇā́mi; stṛṇītháná, stṛṇánti; Ā. stṛṇīté; inj. stṛṇīmáhi; ipv. stṛṇīhí; stṛṇītám (2. du.); stṛṇītá; Ā. stṛṇītā́m (3. s.); pt. stṛṇánt; stṛṇāná; ipf. ástṛṇāt; ástṛṇan. V.: pr. stṛṇóṣi; stṛṇuté. pf. tastā́ra (B.); tastarúr (B.); Ā. tistiré (3. s.); tastriré; pt. tistirāṇá. ao. root: ástar; Ā. ástṛta (B.); sb. stárate; stárāmahe; inj. stár (2. s.); s: ástṛṣi (B.); op. stṛṣīyá; iṣ: ástarīs. ft. stariṣyáti, -te (B.). ps. striyáte (B.); ao. ástāri; pp. stṛtá; stīrṇá. gd. stīrtvā́ (B.); -stī́rya (B.). inf. -stíre, stṛṇīṣáṇi; stárītave (AV.); stártave (B.), stártavái (B.); stáritavái (B.), -starītavái (B.). ds. tístīrṣate (B.); tústūrṣate (B.).

sthā *stand*, I.: pr. tíṣṭhati, -te. pf. tastháu; tastháthur, tasthátur; tasthimá, tasthúr; Ā. tasthé, tasthiṣé, tasthé; tasthiré; pt. tasthivā́ṃs; tasthāná. ao. root: ásthām, ásthās, ásthāt; ásthāma, sthāta, ásthur; Ā. ásthithās, ásthita; ásthiran; sb. sthā́s, sthā́ti and sthā́t; sthā́tas; inj. sthā́m, sthā́t; sthúr; op. stheyā́ma; ipv. sthātam (2. du.); sthāta; pt. sthā́nt; a: ā́sthat (AV.); s: ásthiṣi (B.); ásthiṣata (3. pl.); inj. stheṣam (VS.). ft. sthāsyáti. ps. sthīyáte (B.); pp. sthitá. gd. -sthā́ya. inf. sthā́tum (B.); sthā́tos (B.). cs. sthāpáyati, -te; ao. átiṣṭhipam, átiṣṭhipas, átiṣṭhipat; inj. tiṣṭhipat. ds. tíṣṭhāsati (B.).

snā *bathe*, II. P.: pr. snā́ti; ipv. snāhi; pt. snā́nt. pp. snātá. gdv. snā́tva. gd. snātvā́; -snā́ya. inf. snā́tum (B.). cs. snāpáyati; -te (B.); snapáyati (AV.).

spaś *see*: PF. paspaśé; PT. paspaśāná. AO. root: áspaṣṭa (3. s.). PP. spaṣṭá. CS. spāśáyate.

spṛ *win*, V.: PR. spṛṇvaté; SB. spṛṇávāma; IPV. spṛṇuhí. PF. paspā́ra (B.). AO. root: áspar (2. s.); SB. spárat; INJ. spár (2. s.); IPV. spṛdhí; s: áspārṣam. PP. spṛtá. GD. spṛtvā́. INF. spárase.

spṛdh *contend*, I. Ā.: PR. spárdhate; PT. spárdhamāna. PF. Ā. paspṛdhā́te (3. du.); paspṛdhré; PT. paspṛdhāná. PPF. ápaspṛdhethām (2. du.). AO. root: Ā. áspṛdhran; PT. spṛdhāná. GD. -spṛ́dhya. INF. spárdhitum.

spṛś *touch*, VI.: PR. spṛśáti, -te. PF. SB. paspárśat. AO. red.: SB. pispṛśati; INJ. pispṛśas; s: áspr̄kṣam (B.); sa: áspṛkṣat. PP. spṛṣṭá. GD. spṛṣṭvā (B.); -spṛ́śya (B.). INF. -spṛ́śe; spṛ́śas (B.). CS. sparśáyati (B.), -te.

spṛh *be eager*: CS. spṛháyanti; OP. spṛháyet. IPF. áspṛhayam. GDV. spṛhayā́yya.

sphur *jerk*, VI.: PR. sphuráti; Ā. sphuráte (B.); SB. sphurā́n; INJ. sphurát; IPV. sphurá; sphurátam (2. du.); PT. sphuránt. IPF. ásphurat. AO. iṣ: spharīs (√sphṛ).

sphūrj *rumble*, I. P.: PR. sphū́rjati. CS. sphūrjáyati.

smi *smile*, I.: PR. smáyate; INJ. smáyanta; PT. smáyamāna. PF. siṣmiyé; PT. siṣmiyāṇá.

smṛ *remember*, I.: PR. smárati, -te. PS. smaryáte (B.); PP. smṛtá.

syand *move on*, I. Ā.: PR. syándate. PF. siṣyadúr; Ā. siṣyadé. AO. red.: ásiṣyadat; ásiṣyadanta; s: ásyān (3. s.). FT. syantsyáti (B.). PS. AO. syándi (B.); PP. syanná. GD. syanttvā́ (B.); syattvā́ (B.), -syadya (B.). INF. -syáde; syánttum (B.); CS. syandáyati (B.); INF. syandayádhyai. INT. PT. sániṣyadat.

sras, sraṃs *fall*, I. Ā.: PR. sráṃsate (B.). PF. sasraṃsúr (B.). AO. root: ásrat (VS.); a: OP. srasema; red.: ásisrasan; iṣ: ásraṃsiṣata (B.). PP. srastá. GD. -sraṃsya (B.). INF. -srásas. CS. sraṃsáyati.

sridh *blunder*, I. P.: PR. srédhati; IPV. srédhata; PT.

srédhant. IPF. **ásredhan.** AO. a: INJ. **sridhat**; PT. **sridhāná.**

sru *flow*, I.: PR. **srávati.** PF. **susrā́va**; **susruvúr**; INJ. **susrot.** PPF. **ásusrot.** AO. iṣ: **ásrāvīs** (B.). PP. **srutá.** INF. **srávitave**; **srávitavái.** CS. **srāváyati**; **-te** (B.).

svaj *embrace*, I.: PR. **svájate**; SB. **svájāte, svájātai** (AV.); INJ. **svájat**; IPV. **svájasva**; **svájadhvam.** PF. **sasvajé**; **sasvajā́te** (3. du.); PT. **sasvajāná.** PPF. **ásasvajat.** PP. **svaktá** (B.). INF. **-sváje.**

svad, svād *sweeten*, I.: PR. **svádati, -te**; Ā. **svā́date**; SB. **svádāti**; IPV. **sváda**; **svádantu**; Ā. **svádasva.** AO. red.: INJ. **siṣvadat.** PP. **svāttá.** INF. **-súde.** CS. **svadáyati, -te**; PP. **svaditá.**

svan *sound*: AO. iṣ: **ásvanīt**; INJ. **svanīt.** CS. **svanáyati**; PP. **svanitá.** INT. SB. **saniṣvaṇat.**

svap *sleep*, II. P.: PR. IPV. **sváptu**; PT. **svapánt.** I. P.: PR. **svápati.** PF. **suṣupúr**; INJ. **suṣupthās** (B.); PT. **suṣupvā́ṃs**; **suṣupāṇá.** AO. red.: **siṣvapas** and **siṣvap** (2. s.). FT. **svapsyáti** (B.); **svapiṣyā́mi.** PP. **suptá.** GD. **suptvā́.** INF. **sváptum** (B.). CS. **svāpáyati.**

svar *sound*, I. P.: PR. **svárati.** PF. INJ. **sasvár** (3. s.). AO. s: **ásvār** (3. s.); **ásvārṣṭām** (3. du.); iṣ: **ásvārīs** (B.). INF. **sváritos** (B.). CS. **svaráyati.**

svid *sweat*, I. Ā.: PR. **svédate.** PF. PT. **siṣvidāná.** PP. **svinná.** CS. **svedáyati** (B.).

han *strike*, II.: PR. **hánmi, háṃsi, hánti**; **hathás, hatás**; **hanmás, hathá, ghnánti**; SB. **hánas, hánati** and **hánat**; **hánāva**; **hánāma**; **hánātha** (AV.), **hánan**; INJ. **hán** (3. s.); OP. **hanyā́t, hanyā́ma**; IPV. **jahí, hántu**; **hatám, hatā́m**; **hatá** and **hantana, ghnántu**; PT. **ghnánt.** I.: PR. **jíghnate**; **-ti** (B.). PF. **jaghántha, jaghā́na**; **jaghnáthur**; **jaghnimá, jaghnúr**; Ā. **jaghné** (B.); SB. **jaghánat**; PT. **jaghanvā́ṃs**; **jaghnivā́ṃs** (B.). AO. iṣ: **áhānīt** (B.). FT. **haniṣyáti**; **-te** (B.). PS. **hanyáte**; PP. **hatá**; GDV. **hántva.** GD. **hatvā́, hatvī́**; **hatvā́ya**; **-hátya.** INF. **hántave, hántavái**; **hántum.** CS. **ghātáyati** (B.).

DS. jíghāṃsati; AO. ájighāṃsīs (B.). INT. jáṅghanti; SB. jaṅghánāni, jaṅghanas, jaṅghanat; jaṅghanāva; Ā. jaṅghananta; IPV. jaṅghanīhi; PT. jáṅghanat; ghánighnat.

har *be gratified*, IV.: PR. háryati; SB. háryāsi and háryās; IPV. hárya; PT. háryant. IPF. áharyat; Ā. áharyathās.

1. **hā** *leave*, III. P.: PR. jáhāmi, jáhāsi, jáhāti; jáhati; SB. jáhāni; jáhāma; OP. jahyā́t; jahyúr; IPV. jahītāt, jáhātu; jahītam; jahīta; PT. jáhat. IPF. ajahāt; ájahātana, ájahur. PF. jahā́; jahátur; jahúr. AO. root: áhāt (B.); s: ahās (3. s.); Ā. áhāsi, áhāsthās; INJ. hā́sīs; siṣ: INJ. hāsiṣṭam, hāsiṣṭām; hāsiṣṭa, hāsiṣur. FT. hāsyáti; hāsyáte (B.). PS. hīyáte; AO. áhāyi; PP. hīná; hāna (B.); jahitá. GD. hitvā́, hitvī́, hitvā́ya; -hā́ya (B.). INF. hā́tum (B.). CS. AO. jīhipas.

2. **hā** *go forth*, III. Ā.: PR. jíhīte; jíhāte; jíhate; INJ. jíhīta; IPV. jihīṣva, jihītām (3. s.); jihāthām (2. du.); jíhatām (3. pl.); PT. jíhāna. IPF. Ā. ájihīta; ájihata. PF. jahiré. AO. red.: jījananta; s: Ā. áhāsata (3. pl.); INJ. hāsthās. FT. hāsyáte (B.). PP. hāná (B.). GD. -hāya. INF. hā́tum. CS. hāpáyati. DS. jíhīṣate.

hi *impel*, V.: PR. hinómi, hinóṣi, hinóti; hinmás and hinmási, hinvánti; Ā. hinvé (1. 3.); hinváte and hinviré; SB. hinávā; INJ. hinván; IPV. hinuhí, hinutā́t, hinú; hinótam; hinutá, hinóta and hinótana, hinvántu; PT. hinvánt; hinvāná; IPF. áhinvan. PF. jighā́ya (B.); jighyúr (B.). AO. root: áhema, áhetana, áhyan; IPV. heta; PT. hiyāná; a: áhyam; s: áhait (3. s., AV.); áhaiṣīt (B.); Ā. áheṣata (3. pl.). PP. hitá. GDV. hétva. INF. -hyè.

hiṃs *injure*, VII.: hinásti; híṃsanti; Ā. híṃste (AV.); IPV. hinástu; OP. hiṃsyā́t (B.); PT. híṃsāna; IPF. áhinat (3. s., B.). I.: PR. híṃsati, -te (B.). PF. jihiṃsimá. PPF. jíhiṃsīs. AO. iṣ: INJ. hiṃsiṣam, hiṃsīs, hiṃsīt; hiṃsiṣṭam (2. du.); hiṃsiṣṭa, hiṃsiṣur. FT. hiṃsiṣyáti, -te (B.). PS. hiṃsyáte; PP. hiṃsitá; GDV.

himsitavyà. GD. **himsitvá.** INF. **hímsitum** (B.), **hímsitos** (B.). DS. **jíhimsisati** (B.).

hīḍ *be hostile,* I.: PT. **héḷant**; Ā. **héḷamāna**; **hīḍamāna** (B.). PF. **jihíḷa** (1. s.), **jīhīḍa** (AV.); Ā. **jihīḷé**; **jihīḷiré**; PT. **jihīḷāná.** AO. red.: **ájīhiḍat**; iṣ: Ā. **hīḍiṣātām** (TA.). PP. **hīḍitá.** CS. PT. **heḷáyant.**

hu *sacrifice,* III.: PR. **juhómi, juhóti**; **juhumás, júhvati**; Ā. **juhvé, juhuté**; **júhvate**; SB. **juhávāma**; OP. **juhuyát**; **juhuyáma**; **juhudhí** (B.), **juhótu**; **juhutá** and **juhóta, juhótana**; Ā. **juhudhvám**; PT. **júhvat**; **júhvāna**; IPF. **ájuhavur**; Ā. **ájuhvata.** PF. **juhvé**; **juhuré**; **juhviré** (B.); per. **juhavám cakāra** (B.). AO. s: **áhauṣīt** (B.). FT. **hoṣyáti.** PS. **hūyáte**; AO. **áhāvi**; PP. **hutá.** GD. **hutvá** (B.). INF. **hótavái**; **hótum** (B.), **hótos** (B.).

hū *call,* I. Ā.: PR. **hávate**; INJ. **hávanta**; PT. **hávamāna.** VI.: PR. **huvé** (1. 3.); **huvámahe**; INJ. **huvát**; OP. **huvéma**; Ā. **huvéya**; PT. **huvánt**; IPF. **áhuve**; **áhuvanta.** III.: PR. **juhūmási** and **juhūmás.** II.: PR. **hūté**; **hūmáhe.** PF. **juhāva**; Ā. **juhvé**; **juhūré**; **juhuviré** (B.). AO. root: Ā. **áhvi**; **áhūmahi**; INJ. **hóma**; a: **áhvam, áhvat**; **áhvāma**; Ā. **áhve**; **áhvanta**; s: Ā. **áhūṣata** (3. pl.). PS. **hūyáte**; PP. **hūtá**; GDV. **hávya.** GD. **-hūya** (B.). INF. **hávītave**; **huvádhyai.** DS. **júhūṣati** (B.). INT. **jóhavīmi, jóhavīti**; SB. Ā. **johuvanta**; IPV. **johavītu**; IPF. **ájohavīt**; **ájohavur.**

1. **hṛ** *take,* I.: PR. **hárati, -te**; SB. **hárāṇi, hárāt**; **hárāma, hárān**; OP. **háret**; **hárema**; IPV. **hára**; **hárata, hárantu**; PT. **hárant.** IPF. **áharat.** PF. **jahára, jahártha** (B.); **jahrúr**; Ā. **jahré** (B.). AO. root: **áhṛthās** (B.); s: **áhārṣam, áhār** (3. s.); Ā. **áhṛṣata** (3. pl.). FT. **hariṣyáti, -te** (B.); **hartá** (B.); CO. **áhariṣyat** (B.). PS. **hriyáte**; PP. **hṛtá.** GD. **hṛtvá** (B.); **-hṛtya.** INF. **haráse**; **hártavái** (B.); **hártos** (B.); **hártum** (B.). CS. **hāráyati, -te** (B.). DS. **jíhīrṣati.**

2. **hṛ** *be angry,* IX. Ā.: PR. **hṛṇīṣé, hṛṇīté**; INJ. **hṛṇīthás**; IPV. **hṛṇītám** (3. s.); PT. **hṛṇāná.**

hṛṣ *be excited*, I. : PR. hárṣate ; IPV. hárṣasva ; PT. hárṣant ; hárṣamāṇa. PF. PT. jāhṛṣāṇá. PP. hṛṣitá. CS. harṣáyati, -te. INT. SB. jarhṛṣanta ; PT. járhṛṣāṇa.

hnu *hide*, II. : PR. hnutás ; Ā. hnuvé. PP. hnutá. GDV. hnavā́yya.

hrī *be ashamed*, III. P. : PR. jíhreti. AO. root : PT. -hrayāṇa. PP. hrītá (B.).

hvā *call*, IV. : PR. hváyati ; hváye ; SB. hváyāmahai ; OP. hváyetām (3. du.) ; IPV. hváya, hváyatu ; hváyantu ; Ā. hváyasva ; hváyethām (2. du.) ; hváyantām ; PT. hváyamāna. IPF. áhvayat ; áhvayanta. AO. áhvāsīt (B.). FT. hvayiṣyáti, -te (B.). INF. hváyitavái (B.) ; hváyitum (B.).

hvṛ *be crooked*, I. Ā. : PR. hvárate. IX. P. : PR. hruṇā́ti. III. : SB. juhuras ; Ā. juhuranta ; INJ. juhūrthās ; PT. juhurāṇá. AO. red. : jihvaras ; INJ. jihvaras ; jihvaratam (2. du.) ; s : INJ. hvā́r (2. s.), hvārṣīt ; iṣ : hvāriṣur. PP. hvṛtá, hrutá. CS. hvāráyati.

APPENDIX II

VEDIC METRE.

1. The main principle governing Vedic metre [1] (the source of all later Indian versification) [2] is measurement by number of syllables.[3] The metrical unit here is not the *foot* in the sense of Greek prosody, but the *foot* (**pāda**) or *quarter* [4] in the sense of the verse or line which is a constituent of the stanza. Such verses consist of eight, eleven, twelve, or (much less commonly) five syllables. The verse is further more or less regulated by a quantitative rhythm (unaffected by the musical accent) in which short and long syllables alternate. Nearly all metres have a general iambic rhythm inasmuch as they show a preference for the even syllables (second, fourth, and so on) in a verse being long rather than short. In every metre the rhythm of the latter part of the verse (the last four or five syllables), called the cadence, is more rigidly regulated than that of the earlier part. Verses of eleven and twelve syllables are characterized not only by their cadence, but by a caesura after the fourth or the fifth syllable, while verses of five and eight syllables have no such metrical pause.

---

[1] Called **chándas** in the RV. itself.

[2] Except the two metres **Āryā** and **Vaitālīya** which are measured by *morae*.

[3] This seems to have been the only metrical principle in the Indo-Iranian period, because in the Avesta the character of a verse depends solely on the number of syllables it contains, there being no quantitative restriction in any part of it.

[4] A figurative sense (derived from *foot* = *quarter* of a quadruped) applicable because the typical stanza has four lines.

Verses combine to form a stanza or ṛc, the unit of the hymn, which generally consists of not less than three or more than fifteen such units. The stanzas of common occurrence in the RV. range, by increments of four syllables, from twenty syllables (4 × 5) to forty-eight (4 × 12) syllables in length.[1] A stanza may consist of a combination of metrically identical or of metrically different verses; and either two or three stanzas may further be combined to form a strophe.

a. The following general rules of prosody are to be noted. 1. The end of a verse regularly coincides with the end of a word[2] because each verse in a stanza is independent of the rest in structure. 2. The quantity of the first and last syllables of a verse is indifferent. 3. A vowel becomes long by position if followed by two consonants. One or both of these consonants may belong to the following word. The palatal aspirate **ch** and the cerebral aspirate **ḷh** (**ḍh**) count as double consonants. 4. One vowel is shortened before another;[3] **e** and **o** are also pronounced **ĕ** and **ŏ** before **ă**. 5. The semivowels **y** and **v**, both within a word and in Sandhi, have often to be pronounced as **i** and **u**; e.g. **siā́ma** for **syā́ma**; **súar** for **svàr**; **ví uṣā́ḥ** for **vy uṣā́ḥ**; **vidátheṣu añján** for **vidátheṣv añján**. 6. Contracted vowels (especially **ī** and **ū**) must often be restored; e.g. **ca agnáye** for **cāgnáye**; **ví índraḥ** for **vī̀ndraḥ**; **ávatu ūtáye** for **ávatūtáye**; **ā́ indra** for **éndra**. 7. Initial **a** when dropped after **e** and **o** must nearly always be restored. 8. The long vowel of the gen. pl. ending **ām**, and of such words as **dā́sa**, **śū́ra**, and **e** (as **jyá-iṣṭha** for **jyéṣṭha**) or **ai** (as **á-ichas** for **áichas**) must often be pronounced as equivalent to two short syllables. 9. The spelling of a few words regularly misrepresents their metrical value; thus **pāvaká** must always be pronounced as **pavāká**, **mṛḷaya** as **mṝḷaya**, and **suvāná** nearly always as **svāná**.

---

[1] There are also several longer stanzas formed by adding more verses and consisting of 52, 56, 60, 64, 68, and 72 syllables; but all these are rare: only two stanzas of 68 and one of 72 are found in the RV.

[2] No infringement of this rule occurs in any metre of the RV. but the comparatively rare **Dvipadā Virāj** (4 × 5), in which three exceptions are met with.

[3] The vowels **ī**, **ū**, **e** when **Pragṛhya** (25, 26), however, remain long before vowels. When a final long vowel is the result of Sandhi, it also remains long; **tásmā adāt** for **tásmai adāt**.

I. Simple Stanzas.

2. The Vedic hymns consist chiefly of simple stanzas, that is, of such as are formed of verses which are all metrically identical. Different stanzas are formed by combining three, four, five, or six identical verses. The following is an account of the various types of verse and of the different simple stanzas formed by them.

A. **Verse of eight syllables.** This is a dimeter verse consisting of two equal members of four syllables each, the opening and the cadence. In the opening the first and third syllable are indifferent, while the second and fourth are preferably long. When the second is short, the third is almost invariably long. In the cadence the rhythm is typically iambic, the first and third syllables being almost always short, while the second is usually long (though it is not infrequently short also). Thus the prevailing scheme of the whole verse is ⏒ – ⏒ – | ⏑ – ⏑ ⏒ |

a. Even after every admissible vowel restoration a good many verses of this type exhibit the anomaly (which cannot be removed without doing violence to the text) of having one syllable too few; e. g. **tám tuā vayám̐ pito.** There are also here a very few instances of one or even two syllables too many; e. g. **agním īḷe | bhujám̐ yávi | ṣṭham** and **vayám̐ tád as | ya sámbhṛtam̐ | vásu.**

3. *a.* The **Gāyatrī**[1] stanza consists of three[2] octosyllabic verses;[3] e. g.

---

[1] Next to the Triṣṭubh this is the commonest metre in the RV., nearly one-fourth of that Saṃhitā being composed in it; yet it has entirely disappeared in Classical Sanskrit. The Avesta has a parallel stanza of 3 × 8 syllables.

[2] The first two Pādas of the Gāyatrī are treated as a hemistich in the Saṃhitā text, probably in imitation of the hemistich of the Anuṣṭubh and the Triṣṭubh; but there is no reason to believe that in the original text the second verse was more sharply divided from the third than from the first.

[3] By far the commonest variation from the normal type is that in which the second syllable of the cadence is short (⏑ ⏑ ⏑ ⏒). This occurs about as often in the first verse of Gāyatrīs as in the second and third combined.

agním īḷe | puróhitam | – ᴗ – – | ᴗ – ᴗ ᴗ |
yajñásya de | vám ṛtvíjam | – – ᴗ – | ᴗ – ᴗ ᴗ |
hótāraṃ ra | tnadhā́tamam || – – – – | ᴗ – ᴗ ᴗ ||

a. A comparatively rare but sufficiently definite variety of Gāyatrī[1] differs from the normal type by having a decided trochaic rhythm in the cadence,[2] while the iambic rhythm of the opening is more pronounced than usual; e. g.

tuáṃ no ag | ne máhobhiḥ | ᴗ – ᴗ – – ᴗ – ᴗ |
pāhí víśva | syā árāteḥ | – ᴗ – – | – ᴗ – – |
utá dviṣó | mártiasya || ᴗ – ᴗ – | – ᴗ – ᴗ ||

b. The **Anuṣṭubh**[3] stanza consists of four octosyllabic verses, divided into two hemistichs; e. g.

ā́ yás te sar | pirāsute | – – – – | ᴗ – ᴗ – |
ágne śám ás | ti dhā́yase || – – ᴗ – | ᴗ – ᴗ – ||
áiṣu dyumnám | utá śrávaḥ | – – – ᴗ | ᴗ – ᴗ ᴗ |
ā́ cittáṃ már | tieṣu dhāḥ || – – – – | ᴗ – ᴗ – ||

a. In the latest hymns of the RV. there begins a tendency to differentiate the first from the second verse of an Anuṣṭubh hemistich by making the end of the former trochaic, while the cadence of the latter becomes more strictly iambic. Although in these hymns the iambic cadence of the first verse is still the most frequent (25 per cent.) of all varieties, it is already very nearly equalled by the next commonest (23 per cent.), which is identical with the normal and characteristic cadence of the first verse in the epic Anuṣṭubh[4] (śloka). The scheme of the whole hemistich according to this innovation[5] then is: ⏓ – ⏓ – | ᴗ – – ⏓ || ⏓ – ⏓ – | ᴗ – ᴗ ⏓ || e.g. **keśī́ viṣá | sya pā́treṇa || yád rudréṇā́ | pibat sahá ||**

---

[1] The only long series of such trochaic Gāyatrīs occurs in RV. viii. 2, 1–39.

[2] The trochaic Gāyatrī is commonest in Maṇḍalas i and viii, which taken together contain about two-thirds of the total number of examples in the RV.

[3] The frequency of this metre is about one-third that of Gāyatrī in the RV., but in the post-Vedic period it has become the predominant metre. The Avesta has a parallel stanza of 4 × 8 syllables.

[4] Where the iambic cadence in the first verse has entirely disappeared.

[5] This is the regular type of the Anuṣṭubh in the AV.

c. The **Paṅkti** stanza consists of five octosyllabic verses[1] divided into two hemistichs of two and of three verses respectively. In origin it seems to be an extension of the Anuṣṭubh by the addition of a fifth verse. This is indicated by the fact that in hymns consisting entirely of Paṅktis the fifth verse of every stanza is (except in i. 81) regularly a refrain (e. g. in i. 80). The following is an example of a Paṅkti stanza:—

itthā́ hí sóma ín máde | brahmā́ cakā́ra várdhanam ||
śáviṣṭha vajrinn ójasā | pṛthivyā́ níḥ śaśā áhim | árcann ánu svarā́jiam ||

d. In about fifty stanzas of the RV. the number of octosyllabic verses is increased to six and in about twenty others to seven, generally by adding a refrain of two verses to an Anuṣṭubh (e.g. viii. 47) or to a Paṅkti (e.g. x. 133, 1–3). The former is called **Mahāpaṅkti** (48), the latter **Śakvarī** (56).

4. B. **Verses of eleven syllables** differ from those of eight in consisting of three members (the opening, the break, and the cadence). They also contrast with the latter in two other respects: their cadence is trochaic[2] (– ⏑ – ⏓) and they have a caesura, which follows either the fourth[3] or the fifth syllable. The rhythm of the syllables preceding the caesura is prevailingly iambic, being ⏓ – ⏓ –[4] or ⏓ – ⏓ – ⏓.[5] The rhythm of the break between the caesura and the cadence is regularly ⏑ ⏑ – or ⏑ ⏑[6] |. Thus the scheme of

---

[1] The Avesta has a parallel stanza of 5 × 8 syllables.

[2] The only irregularity here is that the first syllable of the cadence may be short when it coincides with the end of a word.

[3] This appears to have been the original position of the caesura because the parallel verse of the Avesta has it there and never after the fifth syllable.

[4] Identical with the opening of the octosyllabic verse.

[5] The fourth syllable here is sometimes short: the fifth is then always long.

[6] The first of these two syllables is sometimes, but rarely, long in the old hymns of the RV., still more rarely in the later hymns, and hardly ever in B.

the whole normal verse of eleven syllables is:

(*a*) ⏓ – ⏓ –, ⏑ ⏑ – | – ⏑ – ⏓ | or
(*b*) ⏓ – ⏓ – ⏓, ⏑ ⏑ | – ⏑ – ⏓ |

a. Apart from corruptions or only seeming irregularities (removable by restoration of vowels) several verses of this type have one syllable too many or too few;[1] e.g. **tā́ no vidvā́ṃsā, mánma vo | cetam adyá**[2] (12); **tám īṃ gíro, jána | yo ná pátnīḥ**[3] (10). Occasionally two syllables are wanting after the caesura or the verse is too long by a trochee added at the end; e.g. **tá ū ṣú ṇo, [. .] ma | hó yajatrāḥ** (9); **ayáṃ sá hótā, [⏑ ⏑] yó dvijánmā** (9); **ráthebhir yāta, ṛṣṭi | mádbhir áśva | parṇaiḥ** (13).

5. The **Triṣṭubh** stanza, the commonest in the RV.,[4] consists of four verses of eleven syllables[5] divided into two hemistichs. The following are hemistichs of each type:

(*a*) **anāgāstvé, aditi | tvé turā́saḥ | imáṃ yajñáṃ, dadhatu | śróṣamāṇāḥ ||**
(*b*) **asmā́kaṃ santu, bhúva | nasya gópāḥ | píbantu sómam, áva | se nŏ adyá ||**

a. A few Triṣṭubh stanzas of only two verses (**dvipadā**) occur (e.g. vii. 17). Much commoner are those of three verses (**virāj**), the first two of which (as in the Gāyatrī stanza) are treated in the Saṃhitā text as a hemistich; the whole of some hymns is composed in this three-line metre (e.g. iii. 25). Fairly frequent are also Triṣṭubh stanzas of five verses[6] divided into two hemistichs of two and three verses respectively. They are always of isolated occurrence, appearing generally at the end of (Triṣṭubh) hymns, but never forming an entire hymn.

---

[1] This anomaly also appears in the metre of later Vedic texts and of Pāli poetry.

[2] The extra syllable in such cases is perhaps due to the verse being inadvertently continued after a fifth syllable caesura as if it were a fourth syllable caesura.

[3] The deficiency of a syllable in such cases may have been partly due to the similarity of the decasyllabic Dvipadā Virāj (8) with which Triṣṭubh verses not infrequently interchange.

[4] About two-fifths of the RV. are composed in this metre.

[5] The Avesta has a parallel stanza of 4 × 11 syllables with caesura after the fourth syllable.

[6] These are accounted Atijagatī (52) or Śakvarī stanzas by the ancient metricians when the fifth verse is a repetition of the fourth. If it is not a repetition it is treated in the Saṃhitā text as a separate verse (as v. 41, 20; vi. 63, 11) and is called an **ekapadā** by the metricians.

6. C. **The verse of twelve syllables** is probably an extension[1] of the Triṣṭubh verse by one syllable which gives the trochaic cadence of the latter an iambic character.[2] The rhythm of the last five syllables is therefore – ⏑ – ⏑ ⏓. The added syllable being the only point of difference, the scheme of the whole verse is:

(a) ⏓ – ⏓ –, ⏑ ⏑ – | – ⏑ – ⏑ ⏓ | or
(b) ⏓ – ⏓ – ⏓, ⏑ ⏑ | – ⏑ – ⏑ ⏓ |

a. Several examples occur of this type of verse (like the Triṣṭubh) having one, and occasionally two, syllables too many or too few; e.g. **mā́ no mártāya, ripáve vājinīvasū** (13); **ródasī ā́, vada | tā gaṇaśri-yaḥ** (11); **sá dṛḷhé cit, abhí tṛ | ṇatti vā́jam ár | vatā** (14); **píbā sómam, [⏑ ⏑] e | nā́ śatakrato** (10).

7. The **Jagatī** stanza, the third in order of frequency in the RV., consists of four verses of twelve syllables divided into two hemistichs. The following hemistich gives an example of each of the two types of verse:

anānudó, vṛṣabhó | dódhato vadháḥ |
gambhīrá ṛṣvó, ásam | aṣṭakāviaḥ ||

a. There is an eleven syllable variety of the Jagatī verse which is sufficiently definite in type to form entire stanzas in two hymns of the RV. (x. 77, 78). It has a caesura after both the fifth and the seventh syllable, its scheme being ⏓ – ⏓ – ⏑, – –, ⏑ – ⏑ ⏓ | The following hemistich is an example:

abhraprúṣo ná, vācā́, pruṣā vásu |
havíṣmanto ná, yajñā́, vijānúṣaḥ ||

8. D. The **verse of five syllables** resembles the last five syllables of the Triṣṭubh verse in rhythm, its commonest form being ⏑ – ⏑ – ⏓, and the one next to it in frequency – – ⏑ – ⏓ |[3]

---

[1] It is probably not Indo-Iranian, because though a verse of 12 syllables occurs in the Avesta, it is there differently divided (7+5).

[2] As the Gāyatrī verse is never normally found in combination with the Triṣṭubh, but often with the Jagatī verse, it seems likely that the iambic influence of the Gāyatrī led to the creation of the Jagatī, with which it could form a homogeneous combination.

[3] That is, its first syllable is less often long than short

The **Dvipadā Virāj stanza**[1] consists of four such verses divided into two hemistichs;[2] e. g.

pári prá dhanva | índrāya soma |
svādúr mitrā́ya | pūṣṇé bhágāya ||

a. Owing to the identity of the cadence a Dvipadā hemistich[3] not infrequently interchanges in the same stanza with a Triṣṭubh verse;[4] e. g.

priyā́ vo nā́ma | huve[5] turā́ṇām |
ā́ yát tṛpán, maruto | vāvasānā́ḥ ||

b. The mixture of Dvipadā hemistichs with Triṣṭubh verses led to an entire hymn (iv. 10) being composed in a peculiar metre consisting of three pentasyllabic verses[6] followed by a Triṣṭubh; e. g.

ágne tám adyá | áśvaṃ ná stómaiḥ | krátuṃ ná bhadrám |
hṛdispṛ́śam, ṛdhiā́ | mā[7] ta óhaiḥ ||

II. Mixed Stanzas.

9. The only different verses normally used in combination to form a stanza are the Gāyatrī and the Jagatī. The principal metres thus formed are the following:

a. Stanzas of **28 syllables** consisting of three verses, the first two of which are treated as a hemistich:

---

[1] This stanza is somewhat rare, occurring in the RV. not much more than a hundred times.

[2] The otherwise universal rule that the end of a verse must coincide with the end of a word is three times ignored in this metre (at the end of the first and third verses).

[3] With this metre compare the defective Triṣṭubh verse of ten syllables (4 *a*).

[4] This interchange occurs especially in RV. vii. 34 and 56.

[5] Here the verb, though the first word of the verse (App. III, 19 *b*), is unaccented. This is because the end of the first and the third verse in this metre has a tendency to be treated like a caesura rather than a division of the stanza. Cp. note 2.

[6] These three verses are treated as a hemistich in the Saṃhitā text.

[7] The verb is accented because in the Saṃhitā text it is treated as the first word of a separate verse.

1. **Uṣṇih**: 8 8 12; e. g.

> **ágne vā́ja | sya gómataḥ |**
> **ī́śānaḥ sa | haso yaho ||**
> **asmé dhehi, jātave | do máhi śrávaḥ ||**

2. **Purauṣṇih**: 12 8 8; e. g.

> **apsú antár, amṛ́tam | apsú bheṣajám |**
> **apā́m utá | práśastaye ||**
> **dévā bhava | ta vājínaḥ ||**

3. **Kakubh**: 8 12 8; e. g.

> **ádhā hí in | dra girvaṇaḥ |**
> **úpa tvā kā́mān, maháḥ | sasṛjmáhe ||**
> **udéva yán | ta udábhiḥ ||**

b. Stanzas of **36 syllables** consisting of four verses divided into two hemistichs: **Bṛhatī** 8 8 12 8; e. g.

> **śácībhir naḥ | śacīvasū |**
> **dévā náktaṃ | daśasyatam ||**
> **mā́ vāṃ rātír, úpa da | sat kádā caná |**
> **asmád rātíḥ | kádā caná ||**

c. Stanzas of **40 syllables** consisting of four verses divided into two hemistichs: **Satobṛhatī** 12 8 12 8; e. g.

> **jánāso agníṃ, dadhi | re sahovṛ́dham |**
> **havíṣmanto | vidhema te ||**
> **sá tváṃ no adyá, sumá | nā ihā́vitā́ |**
> **bhávā vā́je | ṣu santia ||**

10. There are besides two much longer mixed stanzas of seven verses,[1] each of which is split up into three divisions of three, two, and two verses respectively in the Saṃhitā text.

a. Stanzas of **60 syllables** consisting of six Gāyatrī verses and one Jagatī: **Atiśakvarī** 8 8 8, 8 8, 12 8;[2] e. g.

---

[1] These are the composition of a very few individual poets.
[2] Only about ten examples of this metre occur in the RV.

**suṣumā́ yā | tam ádribhiḥ |
góśrītā mat | sarā́ imé |
sómāso mat | sarā́ imé ||
ā́ rājānā | divispṛśā |
asmatrā́ gan | tam úpa naḥ ||
imé vāṃ mitrā, -varu | ṇā gávāśiraḥ |
sómāḥ śukrā́ | gávāśiraḥ ||**

b. Stanzas of 68 syllables consisting of four Gāyatrī and three Jagatī verses: **Atyaṣṭi**[1] 12 12 8, 8 8, 12 8; e. g.

**sá no nédiṣṭhaṃ, dádṛś | āna ā́ bhara |
ágne devébhiḥ, sáca | nāḥ sucetúnā |
mahó rāyáḥ | sucetúnā ||
máhi śavi | ṣṭha nas kṛdhi |
saṃcákṣe bhu | jé asiái ||
máhi stotṛ́bhyo, magha | van suvī́riam |
máthīr ugró | ná śávasā ||**

a. Besides the above mixed metres various other but isolated combinations of Gāyatrī and Jagatī verses occur in the RV., chiefly in single hymns. There are stanzas of this kind containing 20 syllables (12 8);[2] 32 syllables (12 8, 12);[3] 40 syllables (12 12, 8 8);[4] 44 syllables (12 12, 12 8)[5]; 52 syllables (12 12, 12 8 8).[6]

β. 1. Triṣṭubh verses are quite often interspersed in Jagatī stanzas, but never in such a way as to form a fixed type of stanza or to make it doubtful whether a hymn is a Jagatī one.[7] This practice probably arose from the interchange of entire Triṣṭubh and Jagatī stanzas in the same hymn bringing about a similar mixture within a single stanza. 2. An occasional licence is the combination of a Triṣṭubh with a Gāyatrī verse in the same stanza. This combination appears as a regular mixed stanza (11 8, 8 8) in one entire hymn (RV. x. 22).[8] 3. The combination of a Triṣṭubh verse with a Dvipadā Virāj hemistich has already been noted (8 *a*).

---

[1] This is the only comparatively common long metre (of more than 48 syllables) in the RV., where more than 80 Atyaṣṭi stanzas occur.

[2] RV. viii. 29. [3] RV. ix. 110. [4] RV. x. 93.

[5] RV. viii. 35. [6] RV. v. 87.

[7] But the intrusion of Jagatī verses in a Triṣṭubh hymn is exceptional in the RV., though very common in the AV. and later.

[8] Except stanzas 7 and 15, which are pure Anuṣṭubh and Triṣṭubh respectively.

III. Strophic Stanzas.

11. Two or three stanzas are often found strophically combined in the RV., forming couplets or triplets.

A. Three simple stanzas (called **tṛca**) in the same metre are often thus connected. Gāyatrī triplets are the commonest; less usual are Uṣṇih, Bṛhatī, or Paṅkti triplets; while Triṣṭubh triplets are rare. A hymn consisting of several triplets often concludes with an additional stanza in a different metre.

a. It is a typical practice to conclude a hymn composed in one metre with a stanza in another. A Triṣṭubh stanza at the end of a Jagatī hymn is the commonest; a final Anuṣṭubh stanza in Gāyatrī hymns is much less usual; but all the commoner metres are to some extent thus employed except the Gāyatrī, which is never used in this way.

B. Two mixed stanzas in different metres are often combined, the RV. containing about 250 such strophes. This doubly mixed strophic metre, called **Pragātha,** is of two main types:

1. The **Kākubha Pragātha** is much the less common kind of strophe, occurring only slightly more than fifty times in the RV. It is formed by the combination of a Kakubh with a Satobṛhatī stanza: 8 12, 8+12 8, 12 8; e.g.

ā́ no áśvā | vad aśvinā |
vartír yāsiṣṭam, madhu | pātamā narā ||
gómad dasrā | híraṇyavat ||
suprāvargám, suvī́ryam | suṣṭhú vā́riam |
ánādhṛṣṭam | rakṣasvínā ||
asmínn ā́ vām, āyā́ne | vājinīvasū |
víśvā vāmā́ | ni dhīmahi ||

2. The **Bārhata Pragātha** is a common strophe, occurring nearly two hundred times in the RV. It is formed by the combination of a Bṛhatī with a Satobṛhatī stanza: 8 8, 12 8+12 8, 12 8; e.g.

dyumní vāṃ | stómo aśvinā |
krívir ná sé | ka ā́ gatam ||
mádhvaḥ sutásya, sá di | ví priyó nárā |
pātáṃ gaurā́v | ivériṇe ||
píbataṃ gharmáṃ, mádhu | mantam aśvinā |
ā́ barhíḥ sī | dataṃ narā ||
tā́ mandasānā́, mánu | ṣo duroṇá ā́ |
ní pātaṃ vé | dasā váyaḥ ||

a. Of these two types there are many variations occurring in individual hymns, chiefly by the addition of one (8), two (12 8), three (12 8 8), or once (vii. 96, 1–3) even four verses (12 12 8 8).

APPENDIX III

THE VEDIC ACCENT.

1. The accent is marked in all the texts of the four Vedas as well as in two Brāhmaṇas, the Taittirīya (including its Āraṇyaka) and the Śatapatha (including the Bṛhadāraṇyaka Upaniṣad).

The Vedic, like the ancient Greek, accent was a musical one, depending mainly on pitch, as is indicated both by its not affecting the rhythm of metre and by the name of the chief tone, **udātta** *raised*. That such was its nature is, moreover, shown by the account given of it by the ancient native phoneticians. Three degrees of pitch are to be distinguished, the high, properly represented by the **udātta**, the middle by the **svarita** (*sounded*), and the low by the **anudātta** (*not raised*). But in the Rigveda the Udātta, the rising accent, has secondarily acquired a middle pitch, lower than the initial pitch of the Svarita. The Svarita is a falling accent representing the descent from the Udātta pitch to tonelessness. In the Rigveda it rises slightly above Udātta pitch before descending: here therefore it has something of the nature of a circumflex. It is in reality always an enclitic accent following an Udātta, though it assumes the appearance of an independent accent when the preceding Udātta is lost by the euphonic change of a vowel into the corresponding semivowel (as in **kvà** = **kúà**). In the latter case it is called the independent Svarita. The Anudātta is the low tone of the syllables preceding an Udātta.

2. There are four different methods of marking the accent in Vedic texts. The system of the Rigveda, which is

followed by the Atharvaveda, the Vājasaneyi Saṃhitā, the Taittirīya Saṃhitā and Brāhmaṇa, is peculiar in not marking the principal accent at all. This seems to be due to the fact that in the RV. the pitch of the Udātta is intermediate between the other two tones. Hence the preceding Anudātta, as having a low pitch, is indicated below the syllable bearing it by a horizontal stroke, while the following Svarita, which at first rises to a slightly higher pitch and then falls, is indicated above the syllable bearing it by a vertical stroke; e. g. **a̱gninā̍ = agnínā; vīryà̍m = vīryàm** (for **vīríàm**). Successive Udāttas at the beginning of a hemistich are indicated by the absence of all marks till the enclitic Svarita which follows the last of them or till the Anudātta which (ousting the enclitic Svarita) follows the last of them as a preparation for another Udātta (or for an independent Svarita); e. g. **tāv ā yā̍tam = tā́v ā́ yātam; tavet tat sa̱tyam**[1] **= távét tát satyám.** On the other hand, all successive unaccented syllables at the beginning of a hemistich are marked with the Anudātta; e. g. **va̱i̱śvā̱na̱ram =vaiśvānarám.** But all the unaccented syllables following a Svarita remain unmarked till that which immediately precedes an Udātta (or independent Svarita); e. g. **i̱mam me̍ gaṅge yamune sarasvati̱ śutu̍dri = imám me gaṅge yamune sarasvati | śútudri.**

a. Since a hemistich of two or more Pādas is treated as a unit that consists of an unbroken chain of accented and unaccented syllables, and ignores the division into Pādas, the marking of the preceding Anudātta and the following Svarita is not limited to the word in which the Udātta occurs, but extends to the contiguous words not only of the same, but of the succeeding Pāda; e. g. **a̱gninā̍ ra̱yim a̍śnava̱t poṣa̍m e̱va di̱ve-dive = agnínā rayím aśnavat |**

[1] Here the enclitic Svarita, which would rest on the syllable sa if the following syllable were unaccented, is ousted by the Anudātta, which is required to indicate that the following syllable tyam has the Udātta.

pόṣam evá divé-dive; sa náḥ pitevá sūnave gné sūpāyano bhava = sá naḥ pitéva sūnávé 'gne sūpāyanó bhava.[1]

b. When an independent Svarita[2] immediately precedes an Udātta, it is accompanied by the sign of the numeral 1 if the vowel is short and by 3 if it is long, the figure being marked with both the Svarita and the Anudātta; e.g. **apsv1antaḥ = apsù antáḥ; rāyo 3 vaniḥ = rāyò 'vániḥ** (cp. 17, 3).

3. Both the Maitrāyaṇī and the Kāṭhaka Saṃhitās agree in marking the Udātta with a vertical stroke above (like the Svarita in the RV.), thereby seeming to indicate that here the Udātta rose to the highest pitch; e.g. **agninā**. But they differ in their method of marking the Svarita. The Maitrāyaṇī indicates the independent Svarita by a curve below; e.g. **vīryam = vīryàm**; but the dependent Svarita by a horizontal stroke crossing the middle of the syllable or by three vertical strokes above it; while the Kāṭhaka marks the independent Svarita by a curve below only if an unaccented syllable follows, but by a hook below if the following syllable is accented; e.g. **vīryaṃ = vīryàṃ badhnāti; vīryaṃ = vīryàṃ vyácaṣṭe**; the dependent Svarita has a dot below the accented syllable.[3] The Anudātta is marked in both these Saṃhitās with a horizontal stroke below (as in the RV.).[4]

4. In the Sāmaveda the figures 1, 2, 3 are written above the accented syllable to mark the Udātta, the Svarita, and

---

[1] In the Pada text on the other hand, each word has its own accent only, unaffected by contiguous words. The two above hemistichs there read as follows: **agninā rayim aśnavat poṣam eva dive dive; saḥ naḥ pitā iva sūnavé agné su upāyanaḥ bhava.**

[2] As in **kvà = kúa, vīryàm = vīriàm.**

[3] In L. v. Schroeder's editions of these two Saṃhitās the Udātta and the independent Svarita only are marked.

[4] When the text of any of the Saṃhitās is transliterated in Roman characters, the Anudātta and the enclitic Svarita are omitted as unnecessary because the Udātta itself is marked with the sign of the acute; thus **agninā** becomes **agnínā.**

the Anudātta respectively as representing three degrees of pitch; e.g. **$\overset{3}{\text{ba}}\overset{1}{\text{rhi}}\overset{2}{\text{ṣi}}$** = **b$\underline{\text{a}}$rhiṣi** (**barhíṣi**). The figure 2 is, however, also used to indicate the Udātta when there is no following Svarita; e.g. **$\overset{3}{\text{gi}}\overset{2}{\text{rā}}$** = **g$\underline{\text{i}}$rā** (**girá**). When there are two successive Udāttas, the second is not marked, but the following Svarita has 2r written above; e.g. **$\overset{3}{\text{d}}\overset{1}{\text{viṣo}}$ $\overset{2r}{\text{martyasya}}$** (**dviṣó mártyasya**). The independent Svarita is also marked with 2r, the preceding Anudātta being indicated by 3k; e.g. **$\overset{3k}{\text{ta}}\overset{2r}{\text{nvā}}$** = **tanvà**.

5. The Śatapatha Brāhmaṇa marks the Udātta only. It does so by means of a horizontal stroke below (like the Anudātta of the RV.); e.g. **p$\underline{\text{u}}$ruṣaḥ** = **púruṣaḥ**. Of two or more successive Udāttas only the last is marked; e.g. **agnir hi vai dhūr $\underline{\text{a}}$tha** = **agnír hí vái dhúr átha**. An independent Svarita is thrown back on the preceding syllable in the form of an Udātta; e.g. **man$\underline{\text{u}}$ṣyeṣu** = **manúṣyeṣu** for **manuṣyèṣu**. The Svarita produced by change to a semivowel, by contraction, or the elision of initial a is similarly treated; e.g. **$\underline{\text{e}}$vaita$\underline{\text{d}}$** = **évaitád** for **evaìtád** (= **evá etád**).

6. **Accent of single words.** Every Vedic word is, as a rule, accented and has one main accent only. In the original text of the RV. the only main accent was the Udātta which, as Comparative Philology shows, generally rests on the same syllable as it did in the Indo-European period; e.g. **ta-tá-s** *stretched*, Gk. τα-τό-ς; **jā́nu** n. *knee*, Gk. γόνυ; **á-dṛś-at**, Gk. ἔ-δρακ-ε; **bhára-ta**, Gk. φέρε-τε.[1] But in the written text of the RV. the Svarita appears to be the main accent in some words. It then always follows a **y** or **v** which represents original i or u with Udātta; e.g. **rathyàm**

---

[1] But φερόμενο-ς (**bháramāṇas**) by the secondary Greek law of accentuation which prevents the acute from going back farther than the third syllable from the end of a word.

= **rathíàm**[1]; **svàr**[2] = **súàr** n. *light*; **tanvàm** = **tanúàm**.[3] Here the original vowel with its Udātta must be restored in pronunciation except in a very few late passages.

7. **Double Accent.** One form of dative infinitive and two types of syntactical compounds have a double accent. The infinitive in **tavai**, of which numerous examples occur both in the Saṃhitās and the Brāhmaṇas, accents both the first and the last syllable; e.g. **é-tavái** *to go*; **ápa-bhar-tavái** *to take away*. Compounds both members of which are duals in form (186 A 1), or in which the first member has a genitive ending (187 A 6 *a*), accent bothmembers; e.g. **mitrā́-váruṇā** *Mitra and Varuṇa*; **bṛ́has-páti** *lord of prayer*. In B. a double accent also appears in the particle **vā́vá**.

8. **Lack of Accent.** Some words never have an accent; others lose it under certain conditions.

A. Always enclitic are:

a. all cases of the pronouns **ena** *he, she, it*, **tva** *another*, **sama** *some*; and the following forms of the personal pronouns of the first and second persons: **mā, tvā; me, te; nau, vām; nas, vas** (109 *a*), and of the demonstrative stems **i** and **sa**: **īm** (111 n. 3) and **sīm** (180).

b. The particles **ca** *and*, **u** *also*, **vā** *or*, **iva** *like*, **gha, ha** *just*, **cid** *at all*, **bhala** *indeed*, **samaha** *somehow*, **sma** *just, indeed*, **svid** *probably*.

B. Liable to loss of accent according to syntactical position are:

a. vocatives, unless beginning the sentence or Pāda.

b. finite verbs in principal clauses, unless beginning the sentence or Pāda.

c. oblique cases of the pronoun **a**, if unemphatic (replacing a preceding substantive) and not beginning the sentence or Pāda; e.g. **asya jánimāni** *his* (Agni's) *births* (but **asyá uṣásaḥ** *of that dawn*).

---

[1] Acc. of **rathī́** *charioteer*.
[2] In the TS. always written **súvar**.
[3] Acc. of **tanū́** *body*.

d. **yáthā** *as* almost invariably when, in the sense of **iva** *like*, it occurs at the end of a Pāda; e. g. **tāyávo yathā** *like thieves*; **kám** *indeed* always when following **nú, sú, hí.**

1. Accentuation of Nominal Stems.

9. The most important points to be noted here are the following:—

A. **Primary Suffixes:**

a. Stems in **-as** accent the root if neut. action nouns, but the suffix if masc. agent nouns; e. g. **áp-as** n. *work*, but **ap-ás** *active*. The same substantive here, without change of meaning, sometimes varies the accent with the gender; e. g. **rákṣ-as** n., **rakṣ-ás** m. *demon*.

b. Stems formed with the superlative suffix **iṣṭha** accent the root; e. g. **yájiṣṭha** *sacrificing best*. The only exceptions are **jyeṣṭhá** *eldest* (but **jyéṣṭha** *greatest*) and **kaniṣṭhá** *youngest* (but **kániṣṭha** *smallest*).[1] When the stem is compounded with a preposition, the latter is accented; e. g. **ā́-gamiṣṭha** *coming best*.

c. Stems formed with the comparative suffix **īyāṃs** invariably accent the root; e. g. **jáv-īyāṃs** *swifter*. When the stem is compounded with a preposition, the latter is accented; e. g. **práti-cyavīyāṃs** *pressing closer against*.

d. Stems formed with **tar** generally accent the root when the meaning is participial, but the suffix when it is purely nominal; e. g. **dā́-tar** *giving* (with acc.), but **dā-tár** *giver*.

e. Stems in **man** when (neut.) action nouns, accent the root, but when (masc.) agent nouns the suffix; e. g. **kár-man** n. *action*, but **dar-mán**, m. *breaker*. The same substantive here varies, in several instances, in accent with the meaning and gender (cp. above, 9 A *a*); e. g. **bráhman** n. *prayer*, **brahmán** m. *one who prays*; **sád-man**, n. *seat*, **sad-mán**, m. *sitter*. When these stems are compounded with prepositions,

[1] These two exceptions arise simply from the desire to distinguish the two meanings of each of them. See below (16, footnote 2).

the latter are nearly always accented; e. g. **prá-bharman**, n. *presentation.*

B. **Secondary Suffixes**:

a. Stems in **-in** always accent the suffix; e. g. **aśv-ín** *possessing horses.*

b. Stems in **tama**, if superlatives, hardly ever accent the suffix (except **puru-táma** *very many*, **ut-tamá** *highest*, **śaśvat-tamá** *most frequent*), but if ordinals, the final syllable of the suffix; e. g. **śata-tamá** *hundredth.*

c. Stems in **ma**, whether superlatives or ordinals, regularly accent the suffix; e. g. **adha-má** *lowest*; **aṣṭa-má** *eighth*: except **ánta-ma** *next* (but twice **anta-má**).

2. Accentuation of Compounds.

10. Stated generally, the rule is that iteratives, possessives, and governing compounds accent the first member, while determinatives (Karmadhārayas and Tatpuruṣas), and regularly formed co-ordinatives accent the last member (usually on its final syllable). Simple words on becoming members of compounds generally retain their original accent. Some, however, always change it: thus **víśva** regularly becomes **viśvá**; others do so in certain combinations only: thus **pū́rva** *prior* becomes **pūrvá** in **pūrvá-citti** f. *first thought*, **pūrvá-pīti** f. *first draught*, **pūrvá-hūti** *first invocation*; **médha** *sacrifice* shifts its accent in **medhá-pati** *lord of sacrifice* and **medhá-sāti** f. *reception of the sacrifice*, and **vīrá** *hero* in **puru-vī́ra** *possessed of many men* and **su-vī́ra** *heroic.* An adjective compound may shift its accent from one member to another on becoming a substantive or a proper name; e. g. **sú-kṛta** *well done*, but **su-kṛtá**, n. *good deed*; **á-rāya** *niggardly*, but **a-rā́ya** m. name of a demon.

a. Iteratives accent the first member only, the two words being separated by Avagraha in the Pada text, like the members of other compounds; e.g. **áhar-ahar** *day after day*; **yád-yad** *whatever*; **yáthā-yathā** *as in each case*; **adyá-adya**, **śváḥ-śvaḥ** *on each to-day, on each to-morrow*; **prá-pra** *forth and again*; **píba-piba** *drink again and again.*

b. In governing compounds the first member, when it is a verbal noun (except **śikṣā-nará** *helping men*) is invariably accented; e.g. **trasá-dasyu** *terrifying foes*, name of a man; present or aorist participles place the accent, wherever it may have been originally, on their final syllable; e.g. **tarád-dveṣas** *overcoming* (**tárat**) *foes*. When the first member is a preposition, either that word is accented, or the final syllable of the compound if it ends in **a**; e.g. **abhí-dyu** *directed to heaven*, but **adhas-pad-á** *under the feet*; **anu-kāmá** *according to wish* (**kā́ma**).

c. Bahuvrīhis normally accent their first member; e.g. **rā́ja-putra** *having kings as sons* (but **rāja-putrá** *son of a king*); **viśváto-mukha** *facing in all directions*; **sahá-vatsa** *accompanied by her calf.*

a. But about one-eighth of all Bahuvrīhis accent the second member (chiefly on the final syllable). This is commonly the case when the first member is a dissyllabic adjective ending in **i** or **u**, invariably in the RV. when it is **purú** or **bahú** *much*; e.g. **tuvi-dyumná** *having great glory*; **vibhu-krátu** *having great strength*; **puru-putrá** *having many sons*; **bahv-anná** *having much food.*[1] This also is the regular accentuation when the first member is **dvi** *two*, **tri** *three*, **dus** *ill*, **su** *well*, or the privative particle **a** or **an**;[2] e.g. **dvi-pád** *two-footed*, **tri-nā́bhi** *having three naves*, **dur-mánman** *ill-disposed*, **su-bhága** *well-endowed*, **a-dánt** *toothless*, **a-phalá** *lacking fruit* (**phála**).

d. Determinatives accent the final member (chiefly on the final syllable).

1. Ordinary Karmadhārayas accent the final syllable; e.g. **prathama-jā́** *first-born*, **prātar-yúj** *early yoked*, **mahā-dhaná** *great spoil*. But when the second member ends in **i**, **man**, **van**, or is a gerundive (used as a n. substantive), the penultimate syllable is accented; e.g. **dur-gṛ́bhi** *hard to hold*; **su-tárman** *crossing well*; **raghu-pátvan** *swift-flying*; **pūrva-péya**, n. *precedence in drinking*.

---

[1] The later Saṃhitās tend to follow the general rule; e.g. **purú-nāman** (SV.) *many-named*.

[2] Bahuvrīhis formed with **a** or **an** are almost invariably accented on the final syllable as a distinction from Karmadhārayas (which normally accent the first syllable, as **á-manuṣa** *inhuman*); e.g. **a-mātrá** *measureless*.

a. The first member is, however, accented under the following conditions. It is generally accented when it is an adverbial word qualifying a past participle in **ta** or **na** or a verbal noun in **ti**; e.g. **dúr-hita** *faring ill*; **sadhá-stuti** *joint praise*. It is almost invariably accented when it is the privitive particle **a** or **an**[1] compounded with a participle, adjective, or substantive; e.g. **án-adant** *not eating*, **á-vidvāṃs** *not knowing*, **á-kṛta** *not done*, **á-tandra** *unwearied*, **á-kumāra** *not a child*. The privative particle is also regularly accented, when it negatives a compound; e.g. **án-aśva-dā** *not giving a horse*, **án-agni-dagdha** *not burnt with fire*.

2. Ordinary Tatpuruṣas accent the final syllable; e.g. **gotra-bhíd** *opening the cow-pens*, **agnim-indhá** *fire-kindling*, **bhadra-vādín** *uttering auspicious cries*; **uda-meghá** *shower of water*. But when the second member is an agent noun in **ana**, an action noun in **ya**, or an adjective in **i**, or **van**, the radical syllable of that member is accented; e.g. **deva-mā́dana** *exhilarating the gods*; **ahi-hátya** n. *slaughter of the dragon*; **pathi-rákṣi** *protecting the road*; **soma-pā́van** *Soma-drinking*.

a. The first member is, however, accented when it is dependent on past passive participles in **ta** and **na** or on action nouns in **ti**; e.g. **devá-hita** *ordained by the gods*, **dhána-sāti** *acquisition of wealth*. It is usually also accented, if dependent on **páti** *lord*; e.g. **gṛhá-pati** *lord of the house*. Some of these compounds with **páti** accent the second member with its original accent; some others in the later Saṃhitās, conforming to the general rule, accent it on the final syllable; thus **apsarā-patí** (AV.) *lord of the Apsarases*, **ahar-patí** (MS.) *lord of day*, **nadī-patí** (VS.) *lord of rivers*.

β. A certain number of Tatpuruṣas of syntactical origin, having a genitive case-ending in the first member nearly always followed by **páti**, are doubly accented; e.g. **bṛ́has-páti** *lord of prayer*. Other are **apā́ṃ-nápāt** *son of waters*, **nárā-śáṃsa** (for **nárāṃ-śáṃsa**) *praise of men*, **śúnaḥ-śépa** *Dog's tail*, name of a man. The analogy of these is followed by some Tatpuruṣas without case-ending in the first member: **śácī-páti** *lord of might*; **tánū-nápāt** *son of himself* (**tanū́**); **nṛ́-śáṃsa** *praise of men*.

---

[1] Sometimes, however, the first syllable of the second member is accented; e.g. **a-jára** *unaging*; **a-mítra** m. *enemy* (*non-friend*: **mitrá**); **a-mṛ́ta** *immortal* (from **mṛtá**).

e. Regularly formed Dvandvas (186 A 2. 3) accent the final syllable of the stem irrespective of the original accent of the last member; e. g. **ajāváyaḥ** m. pl. *goats and sheep*; **aho-rātrā́ṇi** *days and nights*; **iṣṭā-pūrtám** n. *what is sacrificed and presented.*

a. The very rare adverbial Dvandvas accent the first member: **áhar-divi**[1] *day by day*, **sāyám-prātar** *evening and morning.*

β. Co-ordinatives consisting of the names of two deities, each dual in form (Devatā-dvandvas), accent both members; e. g. **índrā-váruṇā** *Indra and Varuṇa*; **sū́ryā-mā́sā** *Sun and Moon.* A few others, formed of words that are not the names of deities, are similarly accented; e. g. **turvā́śā-yádū** *Turvaśa and Yadu*; **mātárā-pitárā** *mother and father.*[2]

3. Accent in Declension.

11. *a.* The vocative, when accented at all (18), invariably has the acute on the first syllable; e. g. **pítar** (N. **pitā́**), **déva** (N. **devá-s**). The regular vocative of **dyú** (**dyáv**) is **dyàus**, i. e. **díaus** (which irregularly retains the **s** of the nom.: cp. Gk. Ζεῦ), but the accent of the N., **dyáus**, usually appears instead.

b. In the **a** and **ā** declensions the accent remains on the same syllable throughout (except the vocative); e. g. **devá-s**, **devá-sya**, **devā́-nām**. This rule includes monosyllabic stems, pronouns, the numeral **dvá**, and radical **ā** stems; e. g. from **má**: **máyā**, **má-hyam**, **máy-i**; from **tá**: **tá-sya**, **té-ṣām**, **tā́-bhis**; from **dvá**: **dvā́-bhyām**, **dváyos**; from **jā́** m. f. *offspring*: **jā́-bhyām**, **jā́-bhis**, **jā́-bhyas**, **jā́-su**.

a. The cardinal stems in **a**, **páñca**, **náva**, **dáśa** (and its compounds) shift the accent to the vowel before the endings **bhis**, **bhyas**, **su**, and to the gen. ending **nām**; **aṣṭá** shifts it to all the endings and **saptá** to the gen. ending; e. g. **pañcá-bhis**, **pañcā-nā́m**; **saptá-bhis**, **saptā-nā́m**; **aṣṭā-bhís**, **aṣṭā-bhyás**, **aṣṭā-nā́m**.

---

[1] This is perhaps rather an irregular iterative in which the first member is repeated by a synonym.

[2] Occasionally these compounds become assimilated to the normal type by losing the accent and even the inflexion of the first member; e. g. **indrāgnī́** *Indra and Agni*, **indra-vāyū́** *Indra and Vāyu.*

β. The pronoun **a** *this*, though sometimes conforming to this rule (e. g. **á-smai, á-sya, á-bhis**), is usually treated like monosyllables not ending in **a**; e. g. **a-syá, e-ṣā́m, ā-sā́m.**

c. When the final syllable of the stem is accented, the acute is liable to shift (except in the **a** declension) to the endings in the weak cases.

1. In monosyllabic stems (except those ending in **a**) this is the rule;[1] e. g. **dhī́** f. *thought*: **dhiy-ā́, dhī-bhís, dhī-nā́m**; **bhū́** f. *earth*: **bhuv-ás, bhuv-ós**; **náu** f. *ship*: **nāv-ā́, nau-bhís, nau-ṣú** (Gk. *ναυ-σί*); **dánt**, m. *tooth*: **dat-ā́, dad-bhís.**[1]

There are about a dozen exceptions to this rule: **gó** *cow*, **dyó** *sky*; **nṛ́** *man*, **stṛ́** *star*; **kṣā́m** *earth*; **tán** *succession*, **rán** *joy*, **ván** *wood*; **ví** m. *bird*; **víp** *rod*; **svàr** *light*; e. g. **gáv-ā, gáv-ām, gó-bhis; dyáv-i, dyú-bhis; nár-e, nṛ́-bhis, nṛ́-ṣu** (but **nar-ā́m** and **nṛ-ṇā́m**); **stṛ́-bhis; kṣám-i; tán-ā** (also **tan-ā́**); **ráṇ-e, ráṃ-su; váṃ-su** (but **van-ā́m**); **ví-bhis, ví-bhyas** (but **vī-nā́m**); G. **víp-as; sū́r-as** (but **sūr-é**); also the dative infinitives **bā́dh-e** *to press* and **vā́h-e** *to convey*. The irregular accentuation of a few other monosyllabic stems is due to their being reduced forms of dissyllables; these are **drú** *wood* (**dā́ru**), **snú** *summit* (**sā́nu**), **śván** *dog* (Gk. *κύων*), **yūn** (weak stem of **yúvan** *young*); e. g. **drú-ṇā; snú-ṣu; śúnā, śvá-bhis; yū́n-ā.**

2. When the final accented syllable loses its vowel either by syncope or change to a semivowel, the acute is thrown forward on a vowel ending; e. g. from **mahimán** *greatness*: **mahimnā́; agní** *fire*: **agny-ós; dhenú** *cow*: **dhenv-ā́; vadhū́** *bride*: **vadhv-ái** (AV.); **pitṛ́** *father*: **pitr-ā́.**

a. Polysyllabic stems in **í, ú, ṛ́** and, in the RV., usually those in **ī́**, throw the acute on the ending of the gen. pl. also, even though the final vowel of the stem here retains its syllabic character; e. g. **agnī-nā́m, dhenū-nā́m, dātṛ-ṇā́m, bahvī-nā́m** (cp. 11 *b a*).

3. Present participles in **át** and **ánt** throw the acute forward on vowel endings in the weak cases; e. g. **tud-ánt** *striking*: **tudat-ā́** (but **tudád-bhis**). This rule is also

---

[1] At the end of a compound a monosyllabic stem loses this accentuation; e. g. **su-dhī́** *wise*, **sudhī́-nām.**

followed by the old participles **mahā́nt** *great* and **bṛhánt** *lofty*; e. g. **mahat-ā́** (but **mahád-bhis**).

4. In the RV. derivatives formed with accented **-añc** throw the acute forward on vowel endings in the weak cases when the final syllable contracts to **īc** or **ūc**; e. g. **praty-áñc** *turned towards*: **pratīc-ā́** (but **pratyák-ṣu**); **anv-áñc** *following*: **anūc-ás**; but **prā́ñc** *forward*: **prā́c-i.**[1]

4. Verbal Accent.

12. *a.* The **augment** invariably bears the acute, if the verb is accented at all (19); e. g. impf. **á-bhavat**; aor. **á-bhūt**; plup. **á-jagan**; cond. **á-bhariṣyat.** The accentuation of the forms in which the augment is dropped (used also as injunctives) is as follows. The imperfect accents the same syllable as the present; e. g. **bhárat**: **bhárati**; **bhinát**: **bhinátti.** The pluperfect accents the root; e. g. **cākán** (3. s.); **namámas, tastámbhat**; **tatánanta**; but in the 3. pl. also occur **cakṛpánta, dádhṛṣanta.**

The aorist is variously treated. The **s** and the **iṣ** forms accent the root; e. g. **váṃ-s-i** (**van** *win*); **śáṃs-iṣ-am.** The root aorist (including the passive form) accents the radical vowel in the sing. active, but the endings elsewhere; e. g. 3. s. **várk** (√**vṛj**); pass. **véd-i**; 2. s. mid. **nut-thā́s.** The aorists formed with **-a**[2] or **-sa** accent those syllables; e. g. **ruhám, vidát**; **budhánta**; **dhuk-ṣá-nta.** The reduplicated aorist accents either the reduplicated syllable; e. g. **nī́naśas, pī́parat, jī́janan**; or the root, as **pīpárat, śiśnáthat.**

b. **Present System.** The accent in the **a** conjugation (as in the **a** declension) remains on the same syllable throughout: on the radical syllable in verbs of the first and fourth classes, on the affix in the sixth (125); e. g. **bhávati**; **náhyati**; **tudáti.**

---

[1] In the other Saṃhitās, however, the accent is generally retained on the stem; thus the AV. forms the f. stem **pratī́c-ī** (RV. **pratīc-ī́**).

[2] In the **a** aorist several forms are found accenting the root; e. g. **áranta, sádatam, sánat.**

The graded conjugation accents the stem in the strong forms (126), but the endings in the weak forms. In the strong forms the radical syllable is accented in the second[1] and the reduplicative syllable in the third class;[2] and the stem affix in the fifth, eighth, seventh, and ninth classes; e. g. **ás-ti, ás-a-t, ás-tu**; **bíbhar-ti**; **kṛ-ṇó-ti, kṛ-ṇáv-a-t**; **man-áv-a-te**; **yu-ná-j-mi, yu-náj-a-t**; **gṛh-ṇā́-ti, gṛbh-ṇā́-s** (2. s. sub.); but **ad-dhí, ad-yúr**; **bi-bhṛ-mási**;[3] **kṛ-ṇv-é, kṛ-ṇu-hí**; **van-u-yā́ma, van-v-ántu**;[4] **yuṅk-té, yuṅk-ṣvá**; **gṛ-ṇī-mási, gṛ-ṇī-hí.**

c. **Perfect.** The strong forms (the sing. 1. 2. 3. ind. and 3. impv. act. and the whole subjunctive) accent the radical syllable, the weak forms (cp. 140) the endings; e. g. **cakā́ra**; **jabhár-a-t, vavárt-a-ti**; **mumók-tu**; but **cakr-úr, cakṛ-máhe**; **vavṛt-yā́m**; **mu-mug-dhí.** The participle accents the suffix; e. g. **cakṛ-vā́ṃs, cakr-āṇá.**

d. **Aorist.** The injunctive is identical in accentuation (as well as form) with the unaugmented indicative (see above, 12).

a. The root aor. accents the radical syllable in the subjunctive; e. g. **kár-a-t, śráv-a-tas, gám-a-nti, bháj-a-te**; but the endings in the opt. and impv. (except the 3. s. act.),[5] and the suffix in the participle;[6] e. g. **aś-yā́m, aś-ī-máhi**; **kṛ-dhí, ga-tám, bhū-tá** (but 3. s. **śró-tu**), **kṛ-ṣvá**; **bhid-ánt, budh-āná.**

---

[1] Eleven verbs of this class accent the root throughout: **ās** *sit*, **īḍ** *praise*, **īr** *set in motion*, **īś** *rule*, **cakṣ** *see*, **takṣ** *fashion*, **trā** *protect*, **niṃs** *kiss*, **vas** *wear*, **śī** *lie*, **sū** *bring forth*; e. g. **śáye**, &c.

Occasionally the 2. s. impv. mid. accents the root in other verbs also; e. g. **yák-ṣva** (√**yaj**).

[2] Four verbs, **ci** *note*, **mad** *exhilarate*, **yu** *separate*, **hu** *sacrifice*, accent the radical syllable; e. g. **juhó-ti.** A few other verbs do so in isolated forms; e. g. **bibhár-ti** (usually **bíbhar-ti**).

[3] In the third class the reduplicative syllable is accented in the weak forms also if the ending begins with a vowel; e.g. **bí-bhr-ati.**

[4] In the second, fifth, seventh, eighth, and ninth classes the final syllable of the 3. pl. mid. is irregularly accented in **rihaté** (beside **riháte**); **kṛṇv-até, vṛṇv-até, spṛṇv-até, tanv-até, manv-até**; **bhuñj-até** (beside **bhuñj-áte**); **pun-até, riṇ-até.**

[5] The radical syllable (in its strong form) is also in several instances accented in the 2. pl. act.; e. g. **kár-ta** beside **kṛ-tá**; **gán-ta, gán-tana** beside **ga-tá**, &c.

[6] In the mid. part. the root is, in several instances, accented; e. g. **dyút-āna.**

β. The s and iṣ aor. accent the root in the subjunctive but the endings in the opt. and impv.; e. g. **yák-ṣ-a-t** (√**yaj**), **bódh-iṣ-a-t**; but **bhak-ṣ-īyá** (√**bhaj**), **dhuk-ṣ-ī-máhi** (√**duh**), **edh-iṣ-ī-yá** (AV.); **aviḍ-ḍhi, aviṣ-ṭám**.[1] The s aor. accents the root in the act. part., but nearly always the suffix in the irregularly formed middle;[2] e. g. **dák-ṣ-ant** (√**dah**), **arca-s-āná**.

γ. The a aorist accents the thematic vowel throughout the moods (as in the unaugmented indicative) and the part.; e. g. **vidát**; **vidéyam**; **ruhá-tam**; **tṛpánt, guhá-māna**.[3]

δ. The sa aor. accents the suffix in the impv.: **dhak-ṣá-sva** (√**dah**). The same accentuation would no doubt appear in the subjunctive and optative, but no examples of those moods (nor of the part.) occur.

ε. In the reduplicated aor. the treatment of the subj. and opt. is uncertain because no normally formed accented example occurs; but in the impv. the ending is accented; e. g. **jigṛ-tám, didhṛ-tá**.[4]

e. **Future.** The accent in all forms of this tense remains on the suffix **syá** or **i-ṣyá**; e. g. **e-ṣyā́mi**; **kar-i-ṣyáti**; **kariṣyánt**.

f. **Secondary conjugations.** As all these (except the primary intensive) belong to the a conjugation, they accent the same syllable throughout. The causative (168) accents the penultimate syllable of the stem, as **krodh-áya-ti** *enrages*; the passive, the secondary intensive (172), and the denominative (175), accent the suffix **yá**; e. g. **pan-yá-te** *is admired*; **rerih-yá-te** *licks repeatedly*; **gopā-yá-nti** *they protect*.[5] The desiderative (169) accents the reduplicative syllable; e. g. **pí-prī-ṣa-ti** *desires to please*. The primary intensive agrees with the third conjugational class in accenting the reduplicative syllable in the strong forms, but the endings with initial consonant in the weak forms of the indic. act.; e. g. **jó-havī-ti, jar-bhṛ-tás**, but 3. pl. **várvṛt-ati**; in the mid. ind. the reduplicative syllable is more frequently accented

---

[1] No accented impv. forms occur in the s. aor. In the siṣ aor. the only accented modal form occurring is the impv.: **yā-siṣ-ṭám**.

[2] Neither the iṣ nor the siṣ aor. forms participles.

[3] But the root is accented, in several imperatives and participles, e. g. **sána, sádatam, khyáta**; **sádant, dásamāna**.

[4] No participial form occurs in this aor.

[5] A certain number of unmistakable denominatives, however, have the causative accent; e. g. **mantrá-yati** *takes counsel* (**mántra**).

than not; e. g. **té-tik-te**, less often **ne-nik-té**. In the subj. and part. the reduplicative syllable is regularly accented; e. g. **jáṅ-ghan-a-t, jáṅ-ghan-a-nta; cékit-at, cékit-āna.** The accentuation of the imperative[1] was probably the same as that of the present reduplicating class (12 *b*); but the only accented forms occurring are in the 2. s. act., as **jāgṛ-hí, carkṛ-tā́t.**

5. Accent of Nominal Verb Forms.

13. *a.* **Tense Participles** when compounded with one or more prepositions retain their original accent (while the prepositions lose theirs); e. g. **apa-gáchant** *going away*, **vi-pra-yántaḥ** *advancing*, **pary-ā-vívṛtsan** *wishing to turn round*; **apa-gácha-māna; apa-jaganvā́ṃs, apa-jagm-āná.**

a. A single preposition, or the first of two, not infrequently becomes separated by the interposition of one or more words or by being placed after the participle. It is then treated as independent and recovers its accent; e. g. **ápa dṛḷhā́ni dárdrat** *bursting strongholds asunder*; **ā́ ca párā ca pathíbhiś cárantam** *wandering hither and thither on his paths*; **mádhu bíbhrata úpa** *bringing sweetness near*; **prá vayā́m uj-jíhānāḥ** *flying up to a branch*; **avasṛjánn úpa** *bestowing*. Occasionally an immediately preceding preposition is not compounded with the participle and is then also accented; e. g. **abhí dákṣat** *burning around*; **ví vidvā́n**[2] *discriminating*; **abhí ā-cárantaḥ** *approaching*.

b. On the other hand, the **past passive participle**,[3] when compounded with one or more prepositions, generally loses its accent; e. g. **ní-hita** *deposited*.[4] When there are two prepositions the first remains unaccented; e. g. **sam-ā́-kṛtam** *accumulated*; or the first may be separated and independently accented; e. g. **prá yát samudrá ā́hitaḥ** *when dispatched forth to the ocean*.

---

[1] No accented form of the optative occurs.

[2] Probably in distinction from **vividvā́n** simple reduplicated participle of **vid** *find*.

[3] Which itself is always accented on the final syllable; e. g. **ga-tá, pati-tá, chin-ná.**

[4] In several instances, however, it retains its accent; e. g. **niṣ-kṛtá** *prepared*. This is the case with prepositions that are not used independently.

c. **Gerundives in ya** (or **tya**) and **tva** accent the root; e. g. **cákṣ-ya** *to be seen*, **śrú-t-ya** *to be heard*, **carkṛ́-tya** *to be praised*, **vák-tva** *to be said*; those in **āyya, enya, anīya** accent the penultimate of the suffix; e. g. **pan-ā́yya** *to be admired*, **ī́kṣ-eṇya** *worthy to be seen*, **upa-jīv-anī́ya** (AV.) *to be subsisted on*; while those in **tavya** accent the final syllable: **jan-i-tavyà** (AV.) *to be born*. When compounded with prepositions (here always inseparable) gerundives nearly always retain the accent of the simple form; e. g. **pari-cákṣ-ya** *to be despised*; **abhy-ā-yaṃsénya** *to be drawn near*; **ā-mantraṇī́ya** (AV.) *to be addressed*.

14. **Infinitives** are as a rule accented like ordinary cases that would be formed from the same stem.

a. Dative infinitives from stems in **i, ti, as, van** accent the suffix; those in **dhyai**, the preceding thematic **a**; and those formed from the root, the ending; e. g. **dṛśáy-e** *to see*, **pītáy-e** *to drink*, **carás-e**[1] *to move*, **dā-ván-e**[2] *to give*, **tur-váṇ-e**[3] *to overcome*; **iy-á-dhyai**[4] *to go*; **dṛś-é** *to see*.

a. When radical infinitives are compounded with prepositions the root is accented; e.g. **sam-ídh-e** *to kindle*, **abhi-pra-cákṣ-e**[5] *to see*.

b. The dative infinitive from stems in **man**, the accusative and the abl. gen. from roots, and all from stems in **tu** accent the root; e. g. **dā́-man-e** *to give*;[6] **śúbh-am** *to shine*, **ā-sád-am** *to sit down*; **ava-pád-as** *to fall down*; **dā́-tum** *to give*, **gán-tos** *to go*, **bhár-tav-e** *to bear*, **gán-tav-ái**[7] *to go*.

a. When compounded, infinitives from **tu** stems accent the preposition;[8] e. g. **sáṃ-kar-tum** *to collect*; **ní-dhā-tos** *to put down*; **ápi-dhā-**

---

[1] In these the root is sometimes accented, as **cákṣ-as-e** *to see*.

[2] This infinitive also appears with independently accented prepositions; **prá dāváne** and **abhí prá dāváne**.

[3] The root is once accented in **dhū́r-vane** *to injure*.

[4] In these the root is sometimes accented; e. g. **gáma-dhyai**.

[5] The regular accentuation of monosyllabic stems when compounded: cp. 11 *c*, 1.

[6] But **vid-mán-e** *to know*.

[7] With a secondary accent on the final syllable: cp. above, 7.

[8] But when the preposition is detached the infinitive retains its accent; e. g. **prá dāśúṣe dā́tave** *to present to the worshipper*.

tav-e *to cover up*; **ápa-bhar-tavái** [1] *to be taken away*. When there are two prepositions the first may be separate and independently accented; e.g. **ánu prá-voḷhum** *to advance along*, **ví prá-sartave** *to spread*.

15. **Gerunds** formed with **tvī, tvā, tvāya** accent the suffix, but when they are compounded with prepositions (here always inseparable) and formed with **yā́** or **tyā́**, they accent the root; e.g. **bhū-tvā́** *having become*, **ga-tvī́** and **ga-tvā́ya** *having gone*; **saṃ-gṛ́bh-yā** *having gathered*, **upa-śrú-tya** (AV.) *having overcome*.

16. **Case forms used as adverbs** frequently shift their accent to indicate clearly a change of meaning.[2] The accusative neuter form is here the commonest; e.g. **dravát** *quickly*, but **drávat** *running*; **aparám** *later*, but **áparam** as n. adj.; **uttarám** *higher*, but **úttaram** as n. adj.; adverbs in **vát** e.g. **pratna-vát** *as of old*, but the acc. n. of adjectives in **vant** do not accent the suffix. Examples of other cases are: **dív-ā** *by day*, but **div-ā́** *through heaven*; **aparā́ya** *for the future*, but **áparāya** *to the later*; **sanā́t** *from of old*, but **sánāt** *from the old*.

6. Sandhi Accent.

17. 1. When two vowels combine so as to form a long vowel or diphthong, the latter receives the Udātta, if either or both the original vowels had it; e.g. **ā́gāt = ā́ agāt**; **nudasvā́tha = nudasva átha**; **kvét = kvà it**;[3] **nā́ntaraḥ = ná ántaraḥ**.

a. But the contraction of í i is accented as ì,[4] the enclitic Svarita (í ì) having here ousted the preceding Udātta; e.g. **divìva** [5] = **diví iva**.[6]

---

[1] Retaining the secondary accent on the final syllable.

[2] Such a shift is found in nouns to indicate either a simple change of meaning, e.g. **jyéṣṭha** *greatest*, but **jyeṣṭhá** *eldest*; or a change of category also, e.g. **gómatī** *rich in cows*, but **gomatī́** name of a river; **rājaputrá** *son of a king*, but **rā́japutra** *having sons as kings*.

[3] But when a Svarita on a final vowel is followed by an unaccented initial vowel, it of course remains, e.g. **kvèyatha = kvà iyatha**.

[4] In the RV. and AV., but not in the Taittirīya texts, which follow the general rule.

[5] RV. and AV., but **divī́va** in the Taittirīya texts.

[6] This is the **praśliṣṭa** or contracted Svarita of the Prātiśākhyas.

2. When ĭ and ŭ with Udātta are changed to **y** and **v**, a following unaccented vowel receives the Svarita;[1] e.g. **vy ȁnaṭ = ví ānaṭ**. Here the Svarita assumes the appearance of an independent accent; but the uncontracted form with the Udātta must almost invariably be pronounced in the RV.

3. When accented **á** is elided it throws back its Udātta on unaccented **e** or **o**; e.g. **sūnávé ʼgne = sūnáve ágne**; **vó ʼvasaḥ = vo ávasaḥ**. But when unaccented **a** is elided, it changes a preceding Udātta to Svarita;[2] e.g. **sò ʼdhamáḥ = só adhamáḥ**.[3]

7. Sentence Accent.

18. The **vocative,** whether it be a single word or a compound expression, can be accented on its first syllable only.

a. It retains its accent only at the beginning of a sentence or Pāda,[4] that is, when having the full force of the case it occupies the most emphatic position; e.g. **ágne, sūpāyanó bhava** *O Agni, be easy of access*; **ū́rjo napāt sahasāvan**[5] *O mighty son of strength.* This rule also applies to doubly accented dual compounds; e.g. **mítrā-varuṇā**[6] *O Mitra and Varuṇa.* Two or more vocatives at the beginning of a sentence are all accented; e.g. **ádite, mítra, váruṇa** *O Aditi, O Mitra, O Varuṇa.* Two accented vocatives are sometimes applicable to the same person; e.g. **ū́rjo napād,**

---

[1] This is the **kṣaipra** or *quickly pronounced* Svarita of the Prātiśākhyas.

[2] This is the **abhinihita** Svarita of the Prātiśākhyas.

[3] Here the Svarita (**ó à**) has ousted the preceding Udātta.

[4] This applies to the second as well as the first Pāda of a hemistich, indicating that both originally had a mutually independent character, which is obscured by the strict application of Sandhi and the absence of any break in marking the accent, at the internal junction of the Pādas of a hemistich.

[5] The corresponding nom. would be **ūrjó nápāt sáhasāvā**.

[6] The nom. is **mitrā́-váruṇā**.

bhádraśocise *O son of strength, O propitiously bright one* (both addressed to Agni).[1]

b. When it does not begin the sentence or Pāda, the vocative, being unemphatic, loses its accent; e. g. **úpa tvā agne divé-dive | dóṣāvastar**[2] **dhiyā́ vayám | námo bháranta émasi** *to thee, O Agni, day by day, O illuminer of darkness, bringing homage with prayer we come*; **ā́ rājānā maha ṛtasya gopā**[3] *hither* (come), *O ye two sovereign guardians of great order*; **ṛténa mitrā-varuṇāv | ṛtāvṛdhāv ṛtaspṛśā |** *through Law, O law-loving, law-cherishing Mitra and Varuṇa*;[4] **yád indra brahmaṇaspate**[5] **| abhidrohám cárāmasi |** *if, O Indra, O Brahmaṇaspati, we commit an offence.*

19. The verb is differently accented according to the nature of the sentence.

A. The finite verb in a **principal sentence** is unaccented; e. g. **agním īḷe puróhitam** *I praise Agni the domestic priest.*

This general rule is subject to the following restrictions:

a. A sentence being regarded as capable of having only one verb, all other verbs syntactically connected with the subject of the first are accented as beginning new sentences;[6] e. g. **téṣām pāhi, śrudhí hávam** *drink of them, hear our call*; **taráṇir íj jayati, kṣéti, púṣyati** *the energetic man conquers, rules, thrives*; **jahí prajā́m náyasva ca** *slay the progeny and bring* (it) *hither.*

b. The verb is accented if it begins the sentence or if,

---

[1] Here the second voc. is accented as in apposition, whereas if it were used attributively it would be unaccented as in **hótar yaviṣṭha sukrato** *O youngest wise priest.*

[2] Accented because the first word of the Pāda.

[3] This might represent two vocatives addressed to the same persons; their accented form would then be: **rā́jānā, máha ṛtasya gopā.**

[4] Here the rule that the whole of the compound voc. must be unaccented overrides the rule that the first word of the Pāda must be accented, i. e. here **ṛ́tāvṛdhāv.**

[5] An example of two independent unaccented vocatives.

[6] A subject or object coming between two such verbs is generally counted to the first.

though not beginning the sentence, it coincides with the beginning of a Pāda ; e. g. **śáye vavríś, cárati jihváyādán** | **rerihyáte yuvatím viśpátiḥ sán** *the covering lies* (there); *he* (Agni) *moves eating with his tongue*; *he kisses the maiden, being the lord of the house*; **áthā te ántamānām** | **vidyā́ma sumatīnā́m** *then may we experience thy highest favours.*

c. Vocatives being treated as extraneous to a sentence, a verb immediately following an initial one, becomes the first word of the sentence and is accordingly accented ; e. g. **ágne, juṣásva no havíḥ** *O Agni, enjoy our sacrifice.* Thus the sentence **índra, jíva ; sū́rya, jíva ; dévā, jívata** *O Indra, live; O Sūrya, live; O gods, live* contains three accented verbs as beginning three sentences, while the three preceding vocatives are accented as being at the head of those sentences, though syntactically outside them.

d. Sometimes the verb when emphatic, though not beginning the sentence, is accented if followed by the particles **íd** or **caná** ; e. g. **ádha smā no maghavañ carkṛtā́d ít** *then be mindful of us, bountiful one*; **ná devā bhasáthaś caná** (him) *O gods, ye two never consume.*

B. The verb of a **subordinate clause** (introduced by the relative **yá** and its derivatives, or containing the particles **ca** and **céd** *if*; **néd** *lest*, **hí** *for*, **kuvíd** *whether*) is always accented ; e. g. **yám yajñám paribhū́r ási** *what offering thou protectest*; **gṛhā́n gacha gṛhapátnī yáthā‿ásaḥ** *go to the house that thou mayest be the lady of the house*; **índraś ca mṛḷáyāti no, ná naḥ paścā́d aghám naśat** *if Indra be gracious to us, no evil will hereafter reach us*; **tvám hí baladā́ ási** *for thou art a giver of strength.* The relative may govern two verbs ; e. g. **yénā sūrya jyótiṣā bā́dhase támo, jágac ca víśvam udiyárṣi bhānúnā** *the light with which thou, O Sun, drivest away the darkness and arousest all the world with thy beam.*

The rule is subject to the extension that principal clauses in form may be accented as subordinate in sense under the following conditions :

a. The first of two clauses, if equivalent to one introduced by 'if' or 'when' is occasionally accented; e. g. **sám áśvaparṇāś cáranti no náro, asmā́kam indra rathíno jayantu** *when our men winged with steeds come together, may our car-fighters, Indra, win victory.*

β. The first of two antithetical clauses is frequently accented,[1] especially when the antithesis is clearly indicated by corresponding words like **anyá-anyá, éka-éka, ca-ca, vā-vā**; e.g. **prá-pra͜anyé yánti, páry anyá āsate** *while some go on, others sit down*; **sám ca͜idhásva agne, prá ca bodhaya͜enam** *both be kindled, Agni, and waken this man's knowledge.* When the verb of two such clauses is the same, it usually appears (accented) in the first only; e. g. **dvipác ca sárvaṃ no rákṣa, cátuṣpād yác ca naḥ svám** *protect both every biped of ours and whatever quadruped is our own.*

γ. The verb of the second clause is accented if it is a 1. pers. subjunctive or 2. pers. imperative[2] with a final meaning, and the verb of the first clause is a 2. pers. impv. of **ā́+i, gam,** or **yā** *go*; e. g. **éta, dhíyaṃ kṛṇávāma** *come, we will offer prayer*; **tū́yam ā́ gahi, káṇveṣu sú sácā píba** *come quickly, beside the Kaṇvas drink thy fill.* In B. the verb of the first clause is an impv. of either **ā́-i** or **prá-i**; e.g. **éhi͜idáṃ pátāva** (ŚB.) *come, we will now fly thither*; **préta tád eṣyā́mo yátra͜imā́m ásurā vibhájante** *come, we will go thither where the Asuras are dividing this* earth (ŚB.). The second verb is, however, in similar passages not infrequently left unaccented in B.

Verbal Prepositions.

20. A. In principal clauses the preposition, which is detached and usually precedes but sometimes follows the verb, is accented; e.g. **ā́ gamat** *may he come*; **gávām ápa vrajáṃ vṛdhi** *unclose the stable of the kine*; **jáyema sáṃ yudhí spṛ́dhaḥ** *we would conquer our adversaries in fight*; **gámad vā́jebhir ā́ sá naḥ** *may he come to us with booty.*

a. When there are two prepositions, both are independent and accented; e.g. **úpa prá yāhi** *come forth*; **pári spáśo ní ṣedire** *the spies have sat down around*; **ágne ví paśya bṛhatā́ abhí rāyā́** *O Agni, look forth towards* (us) *with ample wealth.*

---

[1] This accentuation is more strictly applied in B. than in V., and among the Saṃhitās least strictly in the RV.

[2] In B. the accented verb is either a subjunctive or a future.

a. When **á** is immediately preceded by another preposition (not ending in i) it alone is accented, both prepositions being compounded with the verb; e. g. **sam-á-kṛṇoṣi jīváse** *thou fittest* (them) *to live*; but **práty á tanuṣva** *draw* (thy bow) *against* (them).

B. In subordinate clauses the exact reverse takes place, the preposition being generally compounded and unaccented; e. g. **yád . . niṣídathaḥ** *when ye two sit down.* It is, however, often separated by other words from the verb, when it commonly commences the Pāda, or much less frequently follows the verb; e. g. **ví yó mamé rájasī** *who measured out the two expanses*; **yás tastámbha sáhasā ví jmó ántān** *who with might propped earth's ends asunder.* Occasionally the preposition is detached and accented even immediately before the verb; e. g. **yá áhutim pári véda námobhiḥ** *who fully knows the offering with devotion.*

a. When there are two prepositions, either both are compounded and unaccented or the first only is detached and accented; e. g. **yūyám hí devīḥ pari-pra-yāthá** *for ye, O goddesses, proceed around*; **yátra‿abhí saṃ-návāmahe** *where we to* (him) *together shout*; **sáṃ yám ā-yánti dhenávaḥ** *to whom the cows come together.*

a. Very rarely both prepositions are detached and accented; e. g. **prá yát stotá . . úpa gīrbhír ī́ṭṭe** *when the praiser lauds him with songs.*

VEDIC INDEX

This index contains all Sanskrit words and affixes occurring in the grammar, except the verbs in Appendix I, which can be found at once owing to their alphabetical order. Indifferent words occurring in examples of Sandhi, of nominal derivation (Chapter VI), or of Syntax, as well as in Appendixes II and III, are excluded.

The figures refer to paragraphs unless pages are specified.

ABBREVIATIONS

A. = adjective. act., active. adv., adverb, adverbial. ao., aorist. Bv., Bahuvrīhi. cd., compound. cj., conjunction. cond., conditional. conj., conjugation, -al. corr., correlative. cpv., comparative. cs., causative. dec., declension. dem., demonstrative. den., denominative. der., derivative, derivation. ds., desiderative. encl., enclitic. Dv., Dvandva. f.n. foot-note. ft., future. gd., gerund. ij., interjection. indec., indeclinable. inf., infinitive. inj., injunctive. int., intensive. inter., interrogative. ipv., imperative. irr., irregularities. itv., iterative. mid., middle. N., nominative. n., neuter. neg., negative. nm., numeral. nom., nominal. ord., ordinal. par., paradigm. pcl., particle. per., periphrastic. pf., perfect. ppf., pluperfect. poss., possessive. pp., past passive participle. pr., present. pri., primary. prn., pronoun, pronominal. prp., preposition, prepositional. prs., person, personal. ps., passive. pt., participle. red., reduplication, reduplicated. ref., reflexive. rel., relative. rt., root. sb., subjunctive. sec., secondary. sf., suffix. spv., superlative. synt., syntactical. Tp., Tatpuruṣa. v., vocative. vb., verb, verbal. w., with.

GENERAL INDEX

The abbreviations occurring in this index have been explained at the beginning of Appendix I and of the Vedic Index.

The figures refer to paragraphs unless pages are specified.

Printed in England at the Oxford University Press